UPGRADING AND REPAIRING PCs:

A+ Certification Study Guide,
Second Edition

Scott Mueller
Mark Edward Soper

201 West 103rd Street,
Indianapolis, Indiana 46290

Contents at a Glance

Upgrading and Repairing PCs: A+ Certification Study Guide, Second Edition

International Standard Book Number: 0-7897-2453-7

Library of Congress Catalog Card Number: 00-104011

Printed in the United States of America

First Printing: March, 2001

04   03   02   01   4   3   2   1

Trademarks

Warning and Disclaimer

Associate Publisher
Greg Wiegand

Executive Editor
Jill Hayden

Development Editor
Mark Reddin

Managing Editor
Thomas Hayes

Project Editor
Tonya Simpson

Copy Editor
Julie McNamee

Indexer
Erika Millen

Proofreader
Harvey Stanbrough

Technical Editor
Mark Reddin

Team Coordinator
Sharry Gregory

Media Developer
Jay Payne

Interior Designer
Ann Jones

Cover Designer
Ann Jones

Page Layout
Timothy Osborn

Contents

About the Authors

Scott Mueller has sold more than two million copies of his bestseller *Upgrading and Repairing PCs* since it became an instant classic in 1988. Scott's industry-defining hardware book has been translated into 11 languages and has received accolades from PC technicians, enthusiasts, and students worldwide.

Scott is president of Mueller Technical Research, an international research and corporate training firm. Since 1982, MTR has specialized in the industry's longest-running, most in-depth, accurate, and effective corporate PC hardware and technical training seminars, maintaining a client list that includes Fortune 500 companies, the U.S. and foreign governments, and major software and hardware corporations, as well as PC enthusiasts and entrepreneurs. His seminars have been presented to thousands of PC-support professionals throughout the world.

Scott has developed and presented training courses in all areas of PC hardware and software. He is an expert in PC hardware, operating systems, and data-recovery techniques. For more information about a custom PC hardware or data-recovery training seminar for your organization, contact Lynn at

Mueller Technical Research
21 Spring Lane
Barrington Hills, IL 60010-9009
Phone: (847) 854-6794
Fax: (847) 854-6795
Web: www.upgradingandrepairingpcs.com
    www.m-tr.com

If you have questions about PC hardware, suggestions for the next version of the book, or any comments in general, send them to Scott via email at scottmueller@compuserve.com.

When he is not working on PC-related books or teaching seminars, Scott can usually be found in the garage working on performance projects. This year a Harley Road King with a Twin-Cam 95ci Stage III engine continues as the main project (it's amazing how something with only two wheels can consume so much time and money <g>), along with a modified 5.7L '94 Impala SS and a 5.9L Grand Cherokee (hotrod SUV).

Mark Edward Soper is president of Select Systems and Associates, Inc., a technical writing and training organization located in Evansville, Indiana. Get more information at the Select Systems Web site at www.selectsystems.com.

Mark has taught computer troubleshooting and other technical subjects to thousands of students from Maine to Hawaii since 1992. He is an A+ Certified hardware technician and a Microsoft Certified Professional. He's been writing technical documents since the mid-1980s and is the author of the *Complete Idiot's Guide to High-Speed Internet Connections*. Mark has written and contributed to several other Que books, including *Upgrading and Repairing PCs, 11th* and *12th Editions*; *Upgrading and Repairing Networks, Second Edition*; *Special Edition Using Windows Millennium*; and *Upgrading and Repairing PCs, 12th Edition, Academic Edition*. Mark also co-authored both the first and second editions of *Upgrading and Repairing PCs, Technician's Portable Reference*. Watch for details about these and other book projects at the Que Web site at www.mcp.com.

Mark also has been writing for major computer magazines since 1990, with more than 130 articles in publications such as *PCNovice/SmartComputing Guides*, *PCNovice*, *SmartComputing*, and the *PCNovice/SmartComputing Learning Series*. His early work was published in *WordPerfect Magazine*, *The WordPerfectionist*, and *PCToday*. Mark welcomes comments at mesoper@selectsystems.com.

Dedication

To Donald E. Christmas
My father-in-law:
His skilled hands
His sharp mind
His willingness to wrestle with a problem to its solution instructs and inspires those who value good work.
—Mark E. Soper

Acknowledgments

The author of the book is just one of the many people who contribute to its success.

I want to thank

Almighty God—who created and sustains the world in an orderly way and thus makes computers possible.

Cheryl—who always told me I could write, and whose love and support keep me going through long hours of writing and rewriting.

Kate—whose enthusiasm for using computers is leading her to success in college and in love.

Hugh—my future son-in-law—whose quiet appreciation of my work encourages me.

Jeremy—who is discovering the joy of making broken computers whole again.

Ed—whose A+ Certification makes his worklife better even while his lovely wife Erin makes going home and doing college homework more than bearable.

Ian—whose agile mind and fingers have redesigned my Web site and whose profound outlook on life and eternity remind me of the ultimate realities.

Greg Wiegand—who made sure the promise of the book was kept alive while we waited...and waited...and waited for the new A+ Certification standards.

Jill Hayden—who kept the book (and me) on track with her laser-beam focus on your needs.

Mark Reddin—whose devotion to quality helped stomp out errors.

Sharry Gregory—who kept everything organized and kept those checks coming!

Tom and Tonya—who kept chapters flowing in the right directions.

Julie—who made sure that what I wanted to write came out clearly.

Erika—whose indexes help you find what you're looking for.

Jay and Emmett—who make the CD a valuable addition to the book.

And everybody else at Que who work together to make sure you get the best computer books on the market.

Finally, to Scott Mueller, whose work has been a constant inspiration to me since 1988.

—Mark E. Soper

Tell Us What You Think!

As the reader of this book, *you* are our most important critic and commentator. We value your opinion and want to know what we're doing right, what we could do better, what areas you'd like to see us publish in, and any other words of wisdom you're willing to pass our way.

As an Associate Publisher for Que, I welcome your comments. You can fax, email, or write me directly to let me know what you did or didn't like about this book—as well as what we can do to make our books stronger.

Please note that I cannot help you with technical problems related to the topic of this book, and that due to the high volume of mail I receive, I might not be able to reply to every message.

When you write, please be sure to include this book's title and author as well as your name and phone or fax number. I will carefully review your comments and share them with the authors and editors who worked on the book.

Fax: 317-581-4666

Email: feedback@quepublishing.com

Mail: Greg Wiegand
          Que
          201 West 103rd Street
          Indianapolis, IN 46290 USA

Introduction

Welcome to Scott Mueller's *Upgrading and Repairing PCs: A+ Certification Study Guide* from Que! We are pleased that you chose this book as your A+ Certification study aid. Co-author Mark Edward Soper has more than 15 years' experience with PCs, has trained thousands of students in computer troubleshooting, and is also the co-author of Scott Mueller's *Upgrading and Repairing PCs: Technician's Portable Reference*, also available from Que.

About the Exam

To help you understand more about the A+ Certification exam process, here's some history and some background about the current version of the A+ Certification tests.

History of A+ Certification

The history of A+ Certification goes back to 1993, when CompTIA (the Computer Industry Training Association) recognized the need for a vendor-neutral, wide-ranging, standardized test to measure the capabilities of computer technicians worldwide. CompTIA's membership of 7,500 computer hardware and software manufacturers, distributors, retailers, resellers, VARs, system integrators, and training, service, telecommunications, and Internet companies provided expert help in designing the requirements for A+ Certification. The original version of the A+ Certification test included a Macintosh module, but the July 31, 1998 revision dropped that module and introduced two new tests: a revised Core hardware test and a DOS/Windows test, which tested knowledge of Windows 3.1, Windows 95, and MS-DOS. The January 31, 2001 revision made significant changes to the Core hardware test to reflect new technologies and changed the name (and focus) of the other test to Operating Systems (see "Current Tests" later in this introduction).

What A+ Certification Means

A+ Certification is designed to measure the skills and knowledge that an entry-level computer technician with at least six months of hands-on experience will have. However, there is no requirement that you work as a computer technician before you take either module of the current A+ Certification test. Because more and more companies of all types either require or prefer A+ Certification for both experienced and new-hire computer technicians, you've made a wise choice to use this text to prepare for the certification exams.

Current Tests

The 1998 revisions of the A+ Certification tests were replaced at the end of January 2001 by a completely revised duo of tests known as the A+ Core Hardware and the A+ Operating Systems tests. Anyone seeking to be A+ Certified after January 31, 2001 must pass both tests. However, the former 90-day limit to pass both exams was dropped in 2000; as long as you pass both exams before they are revised again, you can take as much time as you need between exams to prepare.

Existing A+ Certification holders are certified for life and need not retake either module. The tests are administered by Prometric and VUE (Virtual University Enterprises). Both companies have made arrangements with computer organizations around the country to administer the self-guided tests using computer workstations. The testing programs found on the CD-ROM included with this book accurately simulate the testing process, which consists of selecting one or more correct answers from a total of four possible answers to a series of questions.

A+ Core

The A+ Core test represents the hardware side of A+ Certification. It tests your knowledge of basic computer hardware, troubleshooting techniques, and networking hardware.

A+ Operating Systems

The A+ Operating Systems test verifies the technician's ability to use the Windows 9x and Windows 2000 operating systems in a troubleshooting and equipment-configuration environment. It tests your knowledge of essential Windows GUI and command-prompt commands and programs, hard-disk and other hardware configuration, and network-software configuration.

See the CompTIA Web site (www.comptia.com) for information about the number of questions on the test, the time limit, and the scores you need to achieve to pass both parts of the exam.

After you complete both tests with a passing grade, you will receive your A+ Certification information in the mail.

How to Use This Book

Because failing either module of the A+ Certification test means that you must retake that module and pay again for the test, it is important that you know how to use this study guide to get the most out of it. This section will help you use your *Upgrading and Repairing PCs: A+ Certification Study Guide* for maximum benefit.

Book Methodology

The *Upgrading and Repairing PCs: A+ Certification Study Guide* is organized in two ways. First, it is organized by major topic. Chapters 1 through 11 cover material that is found primarily on the A+ Core exam. Chapters 12 through 16 cover material that is found primarily on the A+ Operating Systems exam. Chapter 17, "Networking," and Chapter 18, "Troubleshooting Principles," contain material that will be found on both exams.

Second, each chapter is cross-referenced to the A+ outline for the test or tests it will help prepare you for. (See Appendix D, "Objectives Index," to review the outline of objectives for the A+ Core and A+ Operating Systems exams.)

How This Book Is Organized

We chose an integrated design for this book to make it easier for you to understand how each objective relates to another without the repetition that would be required if we used an objective-by-objective approach. This book provides another benefit: You get a "big picture" view of the major hardware and software components in your computer. And, because hardware and software issues are deeply interrelated (you can't run hardware without software drivers, and software doesn't run well on inadequate hardware), covering both tests in the same book makes it easier for you to see how hardware and software work together.

Because this A+ Certification Guide is designed to be your main source of information for the A+ Certification exams, we have organized the book to help you master the material as quickly, easily, and completely as possible. Each chapter has the same multi-section organization that you'll see listed here to break down the learning of each major topic in an organized fashion.

- Each chapter opens with a list of several "While You Read" practice questions. These questions *cannot* be answered with a simple true/false or yes/no answer, but will require that you apply the knowledge you gain in each chapter to determine the best response. The more difficult questions that you'll find on both A+ exams use this method, so this is a good way to prepare for these exams, as well as to prepare for the real-life challenges that will follow in your technical career.

- Almost every chapter in this book contains several figures and diagrams. The figures are designed to give you an up-close view of hardware that you might not have seen or might not be fully familiar with. The charts are designed to provide you with a visual method of learning appropriate concepts.

- The "Summary" section in each chapter provides a short review of the major topics in the chapter.
- At the end of each chapter, the answers to the "While You Read" practice questions are provided. To reinforce the material in each chapter, you should then take the chapter practice test on the CD. This test will help you retain the information found in each chapter.

Effectively Using the CD-ROM Resources

The CD-ROM included with this book provides several major resources:

- An Adobe Acrobat-based version of this text, enabling you to read and review the book while using your computer.
- CD-ROM testing software that simulates the actual A+ exams and cross-references each question to the appropriate portions of the text for help in answering the question. The tests use three different structures to help you master the material and prepare for the A+ exams.
- Electronic versions of *Upgrading and Repairing PCs: Technician's Portable Reference, 2nd Edition,* the Upgrading Help File and General Technical Reference files from *Upgrading and Repairing PCs, 12th Edition, Academic Edition* to provide you with additional study and reference resources.
- Three videos from *Upgrading and Repairing PCs, 12th Edition.*
- Sample beep codes from several popular BIOSes.

For more information about this exciting CD-ROM content, see Appendix C, "CD-ROM Instructions."

Basic Concepts

1. What does RAM need on a regular basis to preserve its contents?
2. How many nibbles are in 32 bits? How many bytes?
3. How is firmware related to hardware and software?
4. Of IRQ, DMA, I/O port addresses, and memory addresses, which two are used for data transfer?
5. Is there a difference between 1MB and 1 million bytes? Explain.
6. Which is likely to be thicker, a printer cable or a modem cable? Why?

Introduction

To understand the operation of personal computers, you need to understand some of the basic terms and concepts you will encounter. In this chapter, you'll learn about data measurements, the differences between permanent and temporary memory, what hardware, software, and firmware are, how data is transferred through the computer, and the four methods used to regulate data movement and access to different devices attached to the computer.

The Essential Parts of Any Computer

All computers need a CPU (central processing unit) to create and modify information. All computers need instructions that tell the CPU what to do. All computers need a place to store the instructions and the output they produce (data), and all computers need a workspace where the CPU can work with instructions and data.

These essential parts can be broken down into three categories: hardware, software, and firmware.

As a computer technician, you will be dealing on a day-to-day basis with the three major parts of any computing environment. Whether you're working on a computer, printer, or component such as a video card, you must determine whether the problem involves hardware, software, firmware, or a combination of these three.

Hardware Overview

Hardware is the physical part of computing. From disk drives to printer cables, from speakers to printers, hardware is the part of computing you can pick up, move around, open, and close. Although hardware might represent the glamorous side of computing (whose computer is faster, has a larger hard disk, more memory, and so on), it can do nothing without software and firmware to provide instructions.

Hardware failures can take place because of loose connections, electrical or physical damage, or incompatible devices.

For more about troubleshooting hardware failures, see *Upgrading and Repairing PCs, 12th Edition*, Chapter 25, "PC Diagnostics, Testing, and Maintenance."

Software Overview

Software provides the instructions that tell hardware what to do. The same computer system can be used for word processing, gaming, accounting, or Web surfing by installing and using new software. Software comes in various types, including operating systems, application programs, and utility programs.

Operating systems provide standard methods for saving, retrieving, changing, printing, and transmitting information. The most common operating systems today are various versions of Microsoft Windows. The 2001 version of A+ Certification focuses on Windows 9x and Windows 2000 Professional, but much of what you learn can also apply in various amounts to Windows Me and Windows NT 4.0, as well as MS-DOS.

Because operating systems provide the "glue" that connects hardware devices and applications, they are written to work on specified combinations of CPUs and hardware.

Operating system commands come in two major types: internal and external. *Internal* commands are those built into the operating system when it starts the computer. *External* commands require that you run a particular program that is included with the operating system.

Application programs are used to create, store, and modify information you create, also called *data*. Because an operating system provides standard methods for using storage, printing, and network devices to work with information, applications must be written to comply with the requirements of an operating system and its associated CPUs. A+ Certification does not require any knowledge of application programs, but to provide the best technical support, you should learn the basics of the major applications your company supports, such as Microsoft Office, Corel WordPerfect Office, Adobe Photoshop, and many others.

Utility programs are used to keep a computer in good working condition or to set up new devices. In the operating system chapters, you'll learn how to use the major utilities that are included with Windows 9x and Windows 2000 Professional.

Because these utilities have limited capabilities, you might also want to invest in other utility programs, such as Symantec's Norton System Works, in your day-to-day work; however, only standard Windows utilities, such as ScanDisk and Defrag, are covered on the A+ Certification Exam.

Firmware Overview

Firmware represents a middle ground between hardware and software. Like hardware, firmware is physical: a chip or chips attached to devices such as motherboards, video cards, network cards, modems, and printers. However, firmware is also software: Firmware chips (such as the motherboard BIOS) contain instructions for hardware testing, hardware configuration, and input/output routines. In essence, firmware is "software on a chip," and the task of that software is to control the device to which the chip is connected.

Because firmware works with both hardware and software, changes in either one can cause firmware to become outdated. Outdated firmware can lead to device or system failure or even data loss.

Traditionally, the only way to change firmware was to remove the chip and replace it with one containing new instructions. Most firmware today is "flashable," meaning that its contents can be changed through software. You'll learn more about the most common type of firmware, the motherboard's BIOS, in Chapter 3, "BIOS and CMOS Configuration."

Memory: RAM and ROM

There are two types of memory in a computer: RAM and ROM. In the early days of personal computing, some vendors made their systems sound more impressive by adding these two totals. However, their function in computer systems is very different.

The contents of RAM (Random Access Memory) can be accessed in any order and can change instantly. The contents of RAM are in constant flux as you start a computer; load its operating system and drivers for particular devices; load an application; create, store, change, and copy data; and shut down the computer.

Programs are loaded into RAM; until data is stored, it exists only in RAM (that's why you should save your work so often!). The "enemies" of data stored in RAM include

- System crashes
- User error (forgetting to save before you close a program)
- Power failures

Because RAM must receive a steady dose of electricity to keep its contents around, even momentary power failures can destroy its contents. Because all data must be created or changed in RAM before it's stored, you must make sure that RAM is working correctly. In Chapter 4, "RAM," you'll learn more about adding, configuring, and using RAM.

ROM stands for Read-Only Memory, meaning that its contents can't be changed by normal computer operations. Because ROM's contents don't change when a system is powered down or restarted, it's the perfect storage place for firmware. As we saw earlier, firmware is the "software on a chip" used to control various devices in the computer. ROM isn't suitable for software storage, however, because its capacity is too limited for today's large programs. And, of course, ROM can't be used to store data files that are constantly changing.

The way that ROM chips have been made has changed several times over the years. Originally, ROMs contained a permanently etched pattern; later, ROMs were made of reprogrammable materials that could be changed through controlled ultraviolet light or electricity. Because the chip had to be removed from the motherboard for replacement or reprogramming, changing the contents of ROMs was difficult and inconvenient.

Current ROMs can be reprogrammed with software. This process is called *flashing* the ROM and is performed with the BIOS firmware found on motherboards and in modems, among other devices. The reasons for upgrading ROMs are covered in Chapter 3.

Measurement: Bits, Bytes, and Beyond

The basic unit of measurement for all parts of the computer that involve the storage or management of information (RAM, storage, ROM) is the byte. Software stored on a floppy disk occupies a finite number of bytes; a modem can transmit so many bytes per second; RAM is measured in megabytes. Understanding bytes and the other measurements derived from bytes is essential to choosing the correct sizes for RAM configurations, storage media, and much more. Some of the A+ Certification test questions typically deal with RAM and hard disk size measurements, as will your day-to-day work.

If you are storing text-only information in the computer, each character of that text (including spaces and punctuation marks) equals a byte. Thus, to calculate the number of bytes in the following sentence, count the letters, numbers, spaces, and punctuation marks:

```
"This book is written by Mark Edward Soper."
12345678901234567890123456789012345678901234
       |        |         |         |
       10       20        30        40
```

From this scale, you can see that the sentence uses 44 bytes. You can prove this to yourself by starting up Windows Notepad (or using MS-DOS's EDIT) and entering the text just as you see it printed here. Save the text as EXAMPLE.TXT and view the directory information (MS-DOS) or the File properties. You'll see that the text is exactly 44 bytes.

Do most computer programs store just the text when you write something? To find out, start up a word-processing program, such as Windows' WordPad. Enter the same sentence again, and save it as EXAMPLE (WordPad will name it EXAMPLE.DOC). As before, view the directory information or File properties. When saved in WordPad, the same text takes up 4,608 bytes! What happened?

File Overhead and Other Features

When data you create is stored in a computer, it must be stored in a particular arrangement suitable for the program that created the information. This arrangement of information is called the *file format.*

A few programs, such as MS-DOS Edit and Windows Notepad, store only the text you create. You might notice that if you had wanted to boldface any part of the sentence that these programs lack the capability to do so. All that Edit and Notepad can store is text. As you have seen, in text-only storage, a character equals a byte.

In computer storage, however, pure text is seldom stored alone. WordPad and other word-processing programs allow you to **boldface**, <u>underline</u>, *italicize,* and make text larger or smaller. Most modern programs also allow you to insert tables, create columns of text, and insert pictures into the text.

To keep all this non-text information arranged correctly with the text, WordPad and other programs must store references to these additional features along with the text, making even a sentence or two into a relatively large file, even if none of the extra features is actually used in that particular file. Thus, for most programs, the bytes used by the data they create is the total of the bytes used by the text or other information created by the program and the additional bytes needed to store the file in a particular file format.

Because different programs store data in different ways, it's possible to have an apparent software failure take place because a user tries to open a file made with program "A" with program "B." Unless program "B" contains a converter that can understand and translate how program "A" stores data, program "B" can't read the file, and might even crash. To help avoid problems, Windows associates particular types of data files with matching programs, allowing you to open the file with the correct program by double-clicking the file in Explorer or File Manager.

Although a byte represents the basic "building block" of storage and RAM calculation, certain measurements are better performed with multiples of a byte. All calculations of the capacity of RAM and storage are done in bits and bytes. Eight bits is equal to one byte.

Table 1.1 provides the most typical values and their relationship to the byte.

Table 1.1 Measurements		
Measurement	Number of Bytes/Bits	Calculations
Byte	1 byte	
Bit	1/8 of a byte	Byte/8
Nibble	1/2 of a byte (4 bits)	Byte/4
Kilobit (Kb)	Digital: 1,000 bits Binary: 1,024 bits (128 bytes)	
Kilobyte (KB)	Digital: 1,000 bytes Binary: 1,024 bytes	
Megabit (Mb)	Digital: 1,000,000 bits Binary: 1,048,576 bits (131,072 bytes)	1 kilobit^2
Megabyte (MB)	Digital: 1,000,000 bytes Binary: 1,048,576 bytes (1,024KB)	1 kilobyte^2
Gigabit (Gb)	Digital: 1,000,000,000 bits Binary: 1,073,741,824 bits	1 kilobit^3
Gigabyte (GB)	Digital: 1,000,000,000 bytes Binary: 1,073,741,824 bytes	1 kilobyte^3

Numbering Systems Used in Computers

Three numbering systems are used in computers: decimal, binary, and hexadecimal. Decimal is also known as base 10. Binary is also known as base 2, and hexadecimal is also known as base 16. Here's an illustration to help you remember the basic differences between them.

You already are familiar with the decimal system: Look at your hands. Now, imagine your fingers are numbered from 0–9, for a total of 10 places.

The binary system doesn't use your fingers; instead, you count your hands: one hand represents 0, and the other 1, for a total of two places.

The hexadecimal system could be used by a pair of spiders who want to count: One spider's legs would be numbered 0–7, and the other spider's legs would be labeled 8, 9, A–F to reach a total of 16 places.

As a technician, you will work most often with decimal measurements ("64MB of RAM"), but occasionally you will also work with hexadecimal measurements ("memory conflict at C800 in upper memory"). The typical rule of thumb is use the system that produces the smallest *meaningful* number. If you need to convert between these systems, you can use any scientific calculator, including the Windows 98 Calculator program (select View, Scientific from the menu).

Decimal Numbering System

We use the decimal or base 10 system for everyday math. A variation on straight decimal numbering is to use "powers of 2" as a shortcut for large values. For example, drive storage sizes often are defined in terms of decimal bytes, but the number of colors that a video card can display can be referred to as "24-bit" (or 2^{24}), which is the same as 16,777,216 colors.

Binary Numbering System

All data is stored in computers in a stream of 1s (on) and 0s (off). Because only two characters (0 and 1) are used to represent data, this is called a "binary" numbering system. Text is converted into its numerical equivalents before it is stored, so binary coding can be used to store all computer data and programs.

Table 1.2 shows how you would count from 1 to 10 (decimal) in binary.

Table 1.2 Decimal Numbers 1–10 and Binary Equivalents									
Decimal	1	2	3	4	5	6	7	8	9	10
Binary	1	10	11	100	101	110	111	1000	1001	1010

Because even a small decimal number occupies many places if expressed in binary, binary numbers are usually converted into hexadecimal or decimal numbers for calculations or measurements.

There are several ways to convert a decimal number into binary:

- Use a scientific calculator with conversion
- Use the division method

To use the division method:

1. Divide the number you want to convert by 2.
2. Record the remainder: either 0 or 1.
3. Divide the resulting answer by 2 again.

4. Repeat the process, recording the remainder each time.

5. When the last answer is divided, the binary is recorded from Least Significant Bit (LSB) to Most Significant Bit (MSB). Reverse the order of bit numbers so that MSB is recorded first and the conversion is complete.

Table 1.3 demonstrates how to use this conversion process to convert the decimal number of 10 to its binary equivalent.

Table 1.3   Converting a Decimal Number to Binary

Bit Order LSB Least Significant Bit to MSB Most Significant Bit	LSB						MSB
Number to Divide	10	5	2	1	7	3	1
Divisor (always 2)	2	2	2	2	2	2	2
Quotient	5	2	1	0	3	1	1
Remainder	0	1	0	1	1	1	1
Reverse Bit Order	MSB						LSB
Answer	1	1	1	1	0	1	0

Hexadecimal Numbering System

A third numbering system used in computers is hexadecimal. Hexadecimal numbering is also referred to as base 16, a convenient way to work with data because 16 is also the number of bits in 2 bytes or 4 nibbles. Hexadecimal numbers use the digits 0–9 and letters A–F to represent the 16 places (0–15 decimal). Hexadecimal numbers are used to represent locations in data storage, data access, and RAM. Table 1.4 shows how decimal numbers are represented in hex.

Table 1.4   Decimal and Hexadecimal Equivalents

Decimal	0	1	2	3	4	5	6	7	8	9	10	11	12	13	14	15
Hexadecimal	0	1	2	3	4	5	6	7	8	9	A	B	C	D	E	F

To convert decimal to hexadecimal, use the same division method listed previously, but use 16 rather than 2 as the divisor.

Table 1.5 demonstrates how to use this conversion process to convert the decimal number of 65,536 (the start of upper memory) to its hexadecimal equivalent.

Table 1.5   Converting a Decimal Number to Hexadecimal

Bit Order	LSB				MSB
Number to Divide	65536	4096	256	16	1
Divisor (always 16)	16	16	16	16	16
Quotient	4096	256	16	1	0
Remainder	0	0	0	0	16
Hex Equivalent	0	0	0	0	A

Table 1.5 continued					
Bit Order	*LSB*			*MSB*	
Change Bit Order	MSB			LSB	
Answer (record as MSB to LSB)	A	0	0	0	0

The most typical uses for hexadecimal numbering are

- Upper memory addresses for add-on cards and for memory-management use
- I/O port addresses for use with an add-on card

Binary Versus Decimal MB/GB

In Table 1.1 earlier, you read entries for decimal and binary kilobit/byte, megabit/byte, and gigabit/byte measurements. A great deal of confusion in the industry has been caused by the indiscriminate use of both types of measurements for hard disk storage.

Hard disk manufacturers almost always rate their drives in decimal megabytes (multiples of 1 million bytes) or decimal gigabytes (multiples of 1 billion bytes), which is also the standard used by disk utilities, such as CHKDSK, ScanDisk, and FORMAT. However, most BIOSes and the MS-DOS/Windows FDISK utility list drive sizes in binary megabytes or binary gigabytes. Although the actual number of bytes is identical, the differences in numbering are confusing.

Take a hard disk rated by its maker as 8.4GB. This is 8,400,000,000 bytes (decimal). However, when the drive is detected and configured by the BIOS and partitioned with FDISK, its size is listed as only 7.82GB (binary). At first glance, you might believe you've lost some capacity (see Figure 1.1).

However, as you've already seen, there is a substantial difference between the number of bytes in a binary gigabyte and one billion bytes. This different numbering system, not any loss of bytes, accounts for the seeming discrepancy. Use this information to help explain to a customer that the "missing" capacity of the hard disk isn't really missing (see Figure 1.2).

Quick Estimations from Digital to Binary and Back

As you've seen from the tables listed earlier, digital and binary MB, GB, and so on, are simply two different number scales for the same number of bytes. However, because different routines in the computer use different calculations, here's a quick method you can use to approximate the differences between the two systems.

To calculate the approximate FDISK (binary) size of a drive of at least 1 billion bytes from its decimal size, multiply the listed size (the size listed on the drive faceplate or box) by .93. For smaller drives, use .95.

To calculate the approximate decimal size of a drive of at least 1GB from its binary equivalent, multiply the binary equivalent by 1.07. For smaller drives, use 1.05.

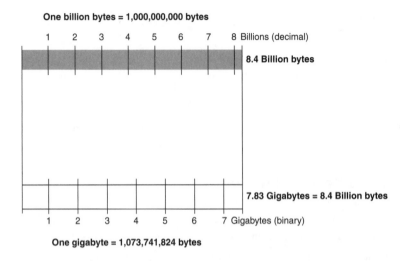

One billion bytes = 1,000,000,000 bytes

One gigabyte = 1,073,741,824 bytes

Figure 1.1
The capacity of the popular 8.4GB hard disk size is 8.4 billion bytes (top bar), but most BIOSes and Windows 98's FDISK measure drives in binary gigabytes (bottom bar).

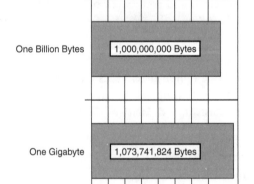

Billions Versus Gigabytes

Figure 1.2
A binary gigabyte (or "true" gigabyte) has over 73 million more bytes than a decimal gigabyte (one billion bytes).

Serial Versus Parallel Information Transfer

Information flows through the computer in many ways. The CPU is the central point for most information. When you start a program, the CPU instructs the storage device to load the program into RAM. When you create data and print it, the CPU instructs the printer to output the data.

Because of the different types of devices that send and receive information, two major types of data transfers take place within a computer: parallel and serial. The main difference between parallel and serial data transfers is illustrated in Figure 1.3.

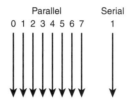

Figure 1.3
Parallel data transfers move data 8 bits at a time, whereas serial data transfers move 1 bit at a time.

Parallel Information Transfers

Parallel transfers use multiple "lanes" for data and programs, and in keeping with the 8 bits = 1 byte nature of computer information, most parallel transfers use multiples of 8. Parallel transfers take place between the following devices:

- CPU and RAM
- CPU and interface cards
- LPT (printer) port and parallel printer
- SCSI port and SCSI devices
- RAM and interface cards (either via the CPU or directly with DMA)

As you can see from the preceding list, parallel transfers are the rule within the computer. What are the benefits of parallel transfers?

- Multiple bits of information are sent at the same time.
- At identical clock speeds, parallel transfers are faster than serial transfers because more data is being transferred.

At first glance, it looks as if there's no reason at all to use any type of information transfer other than parallel, but parallel transfers also have problems:

- Many wires or traces (wire-like connections on the motherboard or expansion cards) are needed, leading to interference concerns and thick, expensive cables.

■ Excessively long parallel cables or traces can cause data to arrive at different times. This is referred to as "signal skew" (see Figure 1.4).

■ Differences in voltage between wires or traces can cause "jitter."

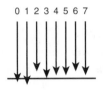

Figure 1.4
Parallel cables that are too long can cause signal skew, allowing the parallel signals to become "out of step" with each other.

The result of these limitations is that a number of compromises have had to be included in computer and system design:

■ Short maximum lengths for parallel and SCSI cables

■ Dual-speed motherboards (running the CPU internally at much faster speeds than the motherboard)

Fortunately, there is a second way to transmit information: serial transfers.

Serial Transfers

A *serial* transfer uses a single "lane" in the computer for information transfers.

The following devices in the computer use serial transfers:

■ Serial ports (also called RS-232 or COM ports)

■ Modems (which can be internal devices or can connect to serial ports)

■ USB (Universal Serial Bus) ports

■ IEEE-1394 (FireWire, i.Link) ports

For more information on RS-232, USB, and IEEE-1394 devices, see *Upgrading and Repairing PCs, 12th Edition,* Chapter 16, "Serial, Parallel, and Other I/O Devices." For more information about modems, see *Upgrading and Repairing PCs, 12th Edition,* Chapter 18, "Internet Connectivity."

Serial transfers have the following characteristics:

■ One bit at a time is transferred to the device.

■ Transmission speeds can vary greatly, depending on the sender and receiver.

■ Very few connections are needed in the cable and ports (one transmit, one receive, and a few control wires).

■ Very long cables work as well as short cables.

Some users would add another point: Serial transfers are slow. Although this was certainly true with RS-232 serial ports, the new USB and IEEE-1394/i.Link ports are not only much faster than RS-232 ports, but they are as fast (USB) or much faster (IEEE-1394) than the fastest EPP-type parallel port (see "USB Ports," page 139, and "IEEE-1394," page 165, for more information).

The extra speed is possible because serial transfers don't have to worry about interference or other problems caused by running so many data lines together.

IRQs, DMAs, I/O Port Addresses, and Memory Addresses

As we saw in the previous section, the computer transfers information between many different types of devices. How does the CPU "know" when a device is ready? How does a device with data to send "tell" the CPU when it needs to send information? How does the CPU "know" which memory location contains the information it needs? To help you understand the answers to these questions, you need to learn about four major resources that are used by most devices that talk to the CPU.

IRQs

IRQs, or *Interrupt Requests*, are a series of 8 or 16 lines that run between the CPU and both built-in and expansion card devices. Most devices use at least one IRQ. As the name implies, IRQs allow devices to interrupt the CPU to signal for attention when they need to send or receive data. Without IRQs, the CPU would run in isolation, never pausing to take care of any devices. The IRQ can be compared to a telephone's ringer. When the telephone rings, you pick it up. If the ringer is broken, you would never know if you were getting a telephone call. The different IRQs can be compared to a multiline phone in which each line is set aside for a different department.

Because IRQs are used to handle different hardware devices, there's a simple rule of thumb: Generally, no two ISA devices should have the same IRQ assignment. There are exceptions, as you'll see in "Standard IRQ and I/O Port Addresses," page 131. PCI devices may support IRQ sharing with Windows 98 and Windows 2000 Professional, depending on the motherboard's configuration.

The number of total IRQs available to you depends on the types of cards and expansion slots you use. 8-bit ISA expansion slots, such as those used in the original IBM PC and PC/XT, could use IRQs up to 7 only. The ISA 16-bit and wider expansion slots can use up to IRQ 15. The typical and default IRQ usage appears in Table 1.6.

Table 1.6	Default and Typical IRQ Assignments		
IRQ	Use	User Accessible	Notes
0	System Timer	No	Reserved for system use.
1	Keyboard	No	Reserved for system use.

Table 1.6   continued

IRQ	Use	User Accessible	Notes
2/9		Yes	Referred to as IRQ 9 on systems with IRQs 0–15; IRQ 2 and 9 are really the same IRQ under two different numbers.
3	COM 2/COM 4	Yes	
4	COM 1/COM 3	Yes	
5	LPT 2 *Sound card*	Yes	Sound card might also use an additional IRQ.
6	Floppy drive interface	No	Reserved for system use.
7	LPT 1	Yes	
8	Real-time clock	No	Reserved for system use.
10		Yes	
11		Yes	
12	PS/2 Mouse	Yes	Can be used if system doesn't have PS/2 mouse port.
13	Math coprocessor	No	Reserved for system use.
14	Primary IDE drive interface	Yes	
15	Secondary IDE drive interface	Yes	

IRQs are used by the system in the following way: You issue a command DIR C:>LPT1 on the keyboard (IRQ 1). The IRQ is routed to the CPU, which "looks" at the keyboard and interprets the command. It uses IRQ 14 (IDE hard disk interface) to pass the command to the hard disk. Because the user has asked to print the command (>LPT1), the CPU uses IRQ 7 to "wake up" the parallel port and print the directory listing. Meantime, the system timer (IRQ 0) has kept everything working. As you look at the printout, you see the date- and timestamps next to the file listings, letting you know that the real-time clock (IRQ 8) is also on the job. Thus, even a simple operation uses several interrupt requests on several different lines.

I/O Port Addresses

The system resource used even more often than IRQs, but one that causes fewer problems, is the I/O port address. The I/O port address is used to pass information between a given device and a system. Even simple devices that don't require an IRQ to function need one or more I/O port addresses. If you compare the IRQ to a telephone ringer, the I/O port address can be compared to the telephone transmitter and receiver, which do the actual work of sending and receiving your voice after you pick up the ringing telephone.

Your computer has 65,535 I/O port addresses (numbered hexadecimally), but uses only a relative few of them. Addresses might be followed by an "h", indicating hexadecimal.

Each device uses an exclusive range of I/O port addresses for the actual transmission of data to and from the device. For situations in which two devices (such as COM 1 and COM 2) share a single IRQ, the I/O port addresses are still unique to each device. Often, information about an add-on card will list only the starting address, but you should know both the first and last I/O port address used by the device to keep from overlapping addresses, which will cause the devices to fail.

As you can see from Figure 1.5, different types of devices use different amounts of I/O address space. Some devices use a continuous "block" of addresses, such as the LPT1 (parallel) port, which uses eight addresses (0378-037Fhex). Others use only one or two addresses, or sometimes just a (literal) bit of a single address. For example, most systems don't have a secondary floppy controller, so the addresses reserved for it (0370–0375, bit 7 of 0377) will be available for another device.

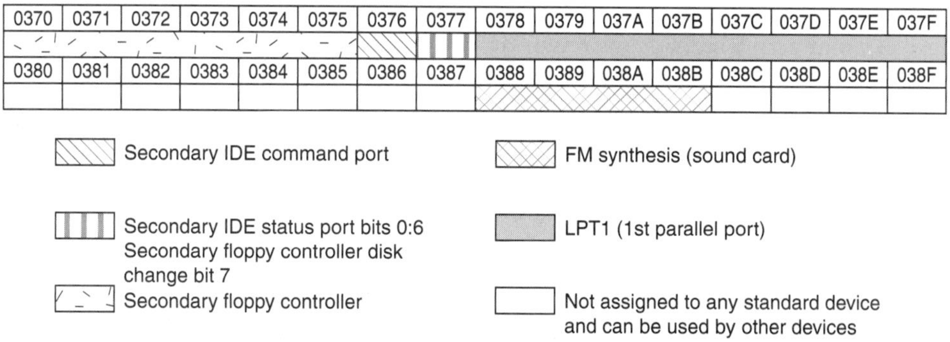

0370	0371	0372	0373	0374	0375	0376	0377	0378	0379	037A	037B	037C	037D	037E	037F
0380	0381	0382	0383	0384	0385	0386	0387	0388	0389	038A	038B	038C	038D	038E	038F

Secondary IDE command port

FM synthesis (sound card)

Secondary IDE status port bits 0:6
Secondary floppy controller disk change bit 7

LPT1 (1st parallel port)

Secondary floppy controller

Not assigned to any standard device and can be used by other devices

Figure 1.5
A section of the I/O port address map appears here. Devices listed use the port addresses listed if they are present.

I/O port addresses are used by the system in the following way: You issue a command DIR C:>LPT1 on the keyboard. The keystrokes pass through the keyboard interface's I/O addresses 0060h, 0064h. When the hard disk receives the command to read the directory listing, the command is given through I/O port 03F6, and the status is monitored through bits 0:6 of I/O port 03F7. When the directory listing is redirected to the printer, the output is routed through LPT1's I/O port addresses 0378–037F.

I/O port addresses are used to transfer data between most devices and the CPU. Both add-on card and motherboard devices use I/O port addresses, and there are many to choose from.

Memory Addresses

The physical memory (RAM) installed into the computer is divided into memory addresses; each address equals a byte of RAM. For normal operations, the system automatically determines which memory address to use for retrieving existing information or for temporary location of new memory addresses. These addresses are also given in hexadecimal notation.

However, the graphics card and a few other add-on cards also use memory, and in these cases, you must make sure that no two cards use the same memory addresses and that no card uses a memory location already used by the system. Video cards contain both RAM and ROM, and both types of memory require memory addresses. Memory managers such as EMM386.EXE that can be used to support MS-DOS software running under Windows 9x can also use memory addresses that are not in use by cards.

You'll learn more about how memory addresses are used in Chapter 4, "RAM."

DMA—Direct Memory Access

As you saw earlier in this chapter, the CPU is responsible for many tasks, including that of being a sort of "traffic cop" overseeing the transfer of information between itself, memory, and various devices. Although a police officer on the corner of a busy intersection helps keep bumper-to-bumper rush-hour drivers on their best behavior, this manual stop-go-stop process isn't the fastest way to get around town—or around the motherboard.

The expressway, beltway, or freeway that bypasses surface streets, traffic lights, and hand-signaling police officers is a faster way to travel when conditions are favorable. Similarly, bypassing the CPU for memory to add-on board transfers (either direction) is also a faster way to travel.

This process of bypassing the CPU is called *Direct Memory Access (DMA)*. DMA transfers can be done in two ways; some DMA transfers (such as those done by tape backup drives or by PCI cards using bus-mastering) do not require a particular DMA channel; however, some devices, such as popular ISA sound cards and the ECP mode of the parallel port, require that we select an unused DMA channel. Table 1.7 lists the standard DMA channel uses. In Table 1.7, standard uses appear in **bold** type, and typical uses (which can change) are shown in *italic* type.

Table 1.7   Standard and Typical DMA Channel Uses

DMA Channel #	Use	Notes
0	*Some sound cards*	Requires 16-bit or wider card
1	*Sound card*	SoundBlaster standard; also used by "clones"
2	**Floppy drive**	
3	*LPT port in ECP mode*	
4	**System Reserved**	
5	*Sound card*	Requires 16-bit or wider card; some sound cards use only DMA 1 or use DMA 0 instead of 5
6		Requires 16-bit or wider card
7		Requires 16-bit or wider card

Because DMA is used for high-speed data transfer, and because there are relatively few DMA channels, some users are tempted to "share" them between devices. *Never do this.* If two devices using DMA are used at the same time, a catastrophic loss of data could result. Because the CPU is not involved in DMA transfers, there's no "traffic cop" in case of disaster!

One of my favorite "disaster" stories was related by long-time *Byte* magazine columnist Jerry Pournelle in July, 1994. He installed a sound card on a system that already had an unusual hard disk interface that used DMA; both devices were set to DMA 5. When he tried to record sound samples with the sound card, the flow of hard disk data and the flow of sampled sound "collided" on DMA 5, wiping out the entire contents of his hard disk! DMA conflicts are rare, but they're never funny.

You'll learn more about DMA and the devices that use it in Chapter 5, "Input/Output Devices and Cables."

Summary

The basic parts of a computer include the CPU, storage, RAM, and software/firmware to make it operate. Programs are loaded into RAM, which is volatile. Firmware used to control basic system operations is ROM, which is not volatile.

All calculations of the capacity of RAM and storage are done in bits and bytes. 8 bits = 1 byte. Storage devices are rated by their manufacturer in decimal megabytes and gigabytes, but the seemingly "smaller" binary megabytes and gigabytes are used by most BIOS chips and by programs such as FDISK. There is no difference in byte capacity between decimal and binary systems, just the number of bytes per measurement unit. Decimal measurements for drive capacity and modem data transfer are based on multiples of 1,000; binary measurements for drive capacity and memory are based on multiples of 1,024 (as in Mb, MB, Gb, GB, and so on).

Data flows through the computer in two ways: serial and parallel. Parallel data transfers are more popular and are used by RAM, the CPU, and parallel ports. Serial data transfers use simpler, less expensive cabling and can run at speeds much slower and much faster than parallel data transfers. Serial transfers are used by serial (COM), USB, and i.Link ports.

IRQs are used to notify the CPU of devices that need attention; the system has 16 IRQs, although many are used by the system and can't be accessed for use by add-on cards. Data is transferred between most devices through I/O port addresses; 65,535 I/O ports are available. Memory addresses are used by devices (such as video cards) that use memory. DMA transfers speed up data flow between RAM and add-on cards.

QUESTIONS AND ANSWERS:

1. What does RAM need on a regular basis to preserve its contents?
    A: Electricity. RAM's contents are lost unless it is "recharged" many times a second by the system.

2. How many nibbles are in 32 bits? How many bytes?
    A: There are four bits in a nibble. 32/4 = 8 nibbles.

    There are eight bits in a byte. 32/8 = 4 bytes.

3. How is firmware related to hardware and software?
    A: Firmware has characteristics of both hardware and software. It's a physical device (a chip), so it's like hardware. It contains programs, so it's like software.

4. Of IRQ, DMA, I/O port addresses, and memory addresses, which two are used for data transfer?
    A: DMA and I/O port addresses are used for data transfer, IRQ is used to signal the CPU or device, and memory addresses are used for devices containing memory

5. Is there a difference between 1MB and 1 million bytes? Explain.
    A: 1MB can equal 1 million bytes, or it might be more than 1 million bytes because some devices use "MB" for the so-called "Decimal MB," which equals exactly 1 million bytes. Other devices use "binary MB," in which 1MB = 1,024×1,024, which is well over 1 million bytes.

6. Which is likely to be thicker, a parallel printer cable or an RS-232 modem cable? Why?
    A: A parallel printer cable is almost always thicker because it contains eight data lines; the RS-232 (serial) modem cable contains only one.

The Motherboard and CPU

WHILE YOU READ

1. What are two differences between ATX and Baby-AT motherboards?
2. Define the difference between motherboards and expansion boards.
3. Which of the following CPUs is a better choice for a memory-intensive application, a Pentium II 233MHz or a Celeron 300MHz? Why?
4. What type of connector is used for both mouse and keyboard?
5. If a motherboard has four PCI slots and four ISA slots but there is virtually no clearance between one of the ISA and one of the PCI slots, how many usable slots does it have? Why?

Introduction

For several years, I taught computer-troubleshooting classes around the country using one or more computers that were never enclosed in a case. To allow students to see the essentials of the computer (and save space), we assembled all the essential parts of each computer on anti-static mats on each group's table. They worked! This proves that the computer is the sum of the components inside the case and, as you will see in this chapter, the motherboard is the central connector among all the components that make up the computer.

The Motherboard

The motherboard represents the logical foundation of the computer. In other words, everything that makes a computer a computer must be attached to the motherboard. From the CPU to storage devices, from RAM to printer ports, the motherboard provides the connections that help them work together.

If you examine a motherboard carefully, you'll see fine copper-colored wire traces on the top and bottom that run between different parts of the motherboard. These wire traces are portions of the motherboard's bus structure. In a city, a bus takes passengers from one point to another; in a computer, a bus carries signals from one component to another.

The motherboard is essential to computer operation in large part because of the two major buses it contains: the *system bus* and the *I/O bus*. Together, these buses carry all the information between the different parts of the computer.

The System Bus

The system bus carries four different types of signals throughout the computer:

- Data
- Power
- Control
- Address

To help you understand this concept, compare the motherboard to a large city, such as Chicago.

If you were on the Sears Tower observation deck overlooking downtown Chicago one evening, you would first notice the endless stream of cars, trucks, and trains carrying people and goods from everywhere to everywhere else along well-defined surface routes (the expressways and tollways, commuter railroads, Amtrak, and airports). You can compare these routes to the *data bus* portion of the system bus, which carries information between RAM and the CPU. If you've ever listened to a station such as Chicago's WBBM, you've heard how traffic slows down when expressway lanes are blocked by construction or stalled traffic. In your computer, wider data buses that allow more "lanes" of data to flow at the same time promote faster system performance.

Now, imagine that you've descended to street level, and you've met with a local utility worker for a tour of "underground Chicago." On your tour, you will find an elaborate network of electric and gas lines beneath the street carrying the energy needed to power the city. You can compare these to the *power lines* in the system bus, which transfer power from the motherboard's connection to the power supply to the integrated circuits (ICs or "chips") and expansion boards connected to the motherboard.

Go back to street level, and notice the traffic lights used both on city streets and on the entrance ramps to busy expressways, such as the Eisenhower and the Dan Ryan. Traffic stops and starts in response to the signals. Look at the elevated trains or at the Metra commuter trains; they also move as directed by signal lights. These signals, which control the movement of road and rail traffic, can be compared to the *control lines* in the system bus, which control the transmission and movement of information between devices connected to the motherboard.

Finally, as you look around downtown, take a close look at the men and women toting blue bags around their shoulders or driving electric vans and Jeeps around the city. As these mail carriers deliver parcels and letters, they must verify the correct street and suite addresses for the mail they deliver. They correspond to the *address bus*, which is used to "pick up" information from the correct memory location among the megabytes of RAM in computer systems and "deliver" new programs and changes back to the correct memory locations.

The *I/O bus* connects storage devices to the system bus and can be compared to the daily flow of commuters and travelers into the city in the morning, and out again in the evening.

Between them, the system and I/O buses carry every signal throughout the motherboard and to every component connected to the motherboard.

Essential System Components Found on the Motherboard

Because the motherboard contains the system and I/O buses, it isn't surprising that the most central components to computing are found attached to the motherboard, as listed in Table 2.1.

Table 2.1   Components Located on All Motherboards

Component	Use	How Attached to Motherboard	Notes
CPU	Computational "brains" of computer	Dedicated socket or slot*	A few CPUs are soldered in place
RAM (random-access memory)	Programs are loaded into this for operation; data resides here until saved to storage device	Dedicated sockets and/or soldered	RAM can be upgraded to limits determined by CPU type, motherboard design
ROM (read-only memory)	Firmware containing drivers for standard devices; power-on self test	Dedicated socket	Most common ROM is the ROM BIOS

| | | How Attached to | |
Component	Use	Motherboard	Notes
Keyboard connector	Attach keyboard	Soldered	Can be damaged by careless insertion/removal of keyboard cable
CMOS/RTC chip**	Records BIOS settings; keeps date and time	Soldered	Some contain their own battery
Battery**	Maintains contents of CMOS/RTC chip	Soldered, socketed, or cabled	Many different types on older systems
Cache RAM	Holds a copy of last memory locations read for faster performance	Dedicated socket or surface-mounted	Introduced with 386-based systems; common with 486 and Pentium
Expansion slots	Allow expansion of computer's capabilities with new ports and so on	Soldered in place	ISA, VL-BUS, EISA, MCA, PCI, and AGP types

Table 2.1 continued

*"Dedicated" means that the socket or slot can only be used for the device listed.
**This component is found in all PCs using an Intel 286-class or faster CPU but is rarely found in PCs using an 8088 or 8086 CPU. Most of these computers used switches to set configuration options and didn't have built-in RTC (real-time clocks).

Figure 2.1 shows a typical Baby-AT motherboard with its components labeled. It includes connectors for a wide variety of internal and external ports, including hard disk, floppy disk, and serial and parallel ports.

All standard motherboards contain expansion slots, sockets for ROM BIOS, RAM, CPU, and keyboard connectors. All 286-class and faster motherboards also have a battery to maintain setup ("CMOS") information.

For more information about these components, see *Upgrading and Repairing PCs, 12th Edition*, Chapter 4, "Motherboards and Buses."

To learn more about RAM, see Chapter 4 "RAM." For more about the BIOS, see Chapter 3, "BIOS and CMOS Configuration."

Integrated Motherboard Ports

Although all motherboards contain the components listed in Table 2.1 previously, since the mid-1990s, more and more components formerly found on expansion cards have been added to the motherboard, as indicated in Table 2.2. Ports added to the motherboard are often referred to as *integrated* ports.

Integrated ports provide clear benefits to both users and technicians setting up a system. For users, integrated ports provide lower system purchase prices, faster component performance, centralized control of components through the ROM BIOS and CMOS, and an interior less crowded with add-on cards.

For technicians, the major benefits of integrated components are during initial setup; fewer components need to be installed to bring a system to meet standard requirements.

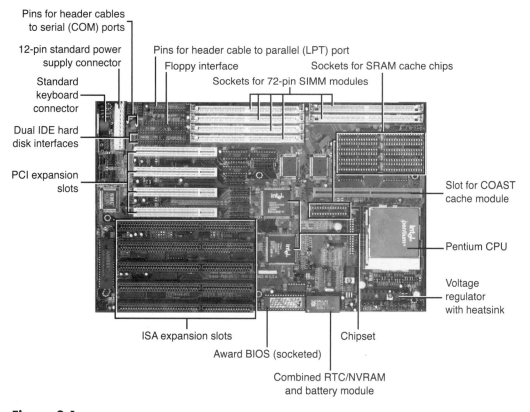

Pins for header cables to serial (COM) ports

12-pin standard power supply connector

Standard keyboard connector

Dual IDE hard disk interfaces

PCI expansion slots

Pins for header cable to parallel (LPT) port

Floppy interface

Sockets for 72-pin SIMM modules

Sockets for SRAM cache chips

Slot for COAST cache module

Pentium CPU

Voltage regulator with heatsink

ISA expansion slots

Award BIOS (socketed)

Chipset

Combined RTC/NVRAM and battery module

CH
2

Figure 2.1
A typical Baby-AT motherboard with built-in ports.

However, when systems must be repaired or upgraded, integrated components can be troublesome. If an integrated component fails, you must either replace the motherboard or disable the component in question (if possible) and replace it with an add-on card.

Table 2.2 Components Found on Recent and Current Motherboards

Component	Use	Form Factor	Notes
IDE interface	Runs IDE and ATAPI storage devices	40-pin connector (two rows of 20)	Most recent systems feature two
Floppy interface	Runs floppy-interface storage devices	34-pin connector (two rows of 17)	
PS/2 mouse port	Connector for PS/2 mouse	Mini-DIN 6-pin connector	
COM (serial) port	Connector for serial devices	DB-9 male or DB-25 male	Most systems feature two
LPT (parallel) port	Connector for parallel devices	DB-25 female	

Table 2.2 continued			
Component	Use	Form Factor	Notes
USB (Universal Serial Bus) port	Connector for USB devices and hubs	USB proprietary connector	
XVGA video	Connector for VGA-class monitors	DB-15 female	Found primarily on notebooks and low-cost desktop systems
Audio	Speaker and microphone connection for WAV and MIDI playback and WAV recording	Mini-jacks (check type!) for microphone and speakers	Found primarily on notebooks and low-cost desktop systems

Figure 2.2 shows how ATX motherboards, the current standard, integrate external ports into the rear of the motherboard instead of using cables to the motherboard, as seen in Figure 2.1.

Most recent systems include serial, parallel, floppy disk drive, and IDE hard disk interfaces on the motherboard, and the newest ones also include USB ports.

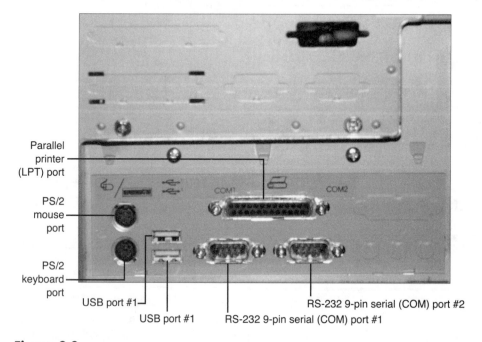

Figure 2.2

A typical ATX motherboard back panel shows marked ports for easy device connection.

See Chapter 5, "Input/Output Devices and Cables," for more about serial, parallel, USB, mouse, and keyboard ports.

Motherboard Types

There are several basic motherboard designs:

- Baby-AT
- LPX
- ATX
- NLX

As you maintain, troubleshoot, and upgrade systems, you must be able to recognize each of these motherboard types. Recognizing different motherboard types will enable you to determine whether

- The computer uses a standard motherboard and can be upgraded by changing its motherboard
- The computer uses a proprietary motherboard that cannot be interchanged

The following tables and accompanying illustrations indicate the major differences between the different motherboard types.

Baby-AT and ATX Motherboards

Baby-AT and ATX motherboards are found in the most popular types of computers: mid-size and large-size desktop and tower systems. The Baby-AT motherboard is a reduced-size version of the motherboard found in the IBM AT computer, introduced in 1984. Although Baby-AT motherboards can still be found in some systems, most computers using standard motherboard designs since mid-1996 have used the ATX motherboard instead. Table 2.3 compares these two industry standards.

Table 2.3   Characteristics of Baby-AT Versus ATX

Features	Baby-AT	ATX
Expansion slots run parallel with long edge	Yes	No
Expansion slots run parallel with short edge	No	Yes
CPU might block some expansion slots	Yes	No
CPU separated from expansion slots	No	Yes
Built-in I/O* ports	Varies	Yes
I/O ports require cables between connector and motherboard	Yes	No
I/O ports attach directly to motherboard on a two-row horizontal plate at rear of motherboard	No	Yes
Floppy disk drive and hard disk connectors near drive bays	No	Yes

Serial, parallel, USB, and PS/2 mouse ports

Essentially, ATX motherboards provide a clean, uncluttered interior layout that's easier to service than Baby-AT–based systems. Because ATX motherboards are wider than Baby-

AT motherboards, ATX motherboards must be used in ATX cases because ATX motherboards are turned 90 degrees relative to Baby-AT motherboards. If you need to upgrade a system with a Baby-AT case, you must find a Baby-AT motherboard with the performance and features needed. Because the Baby-AT form factor is becoming obsolete, there are far fewer choices available than if you are upgrading a system based on the ATX form factor.

Also, ATX motherboards use different power connectors than most Baby-AT motherboards do. Baby-AT motherboards (see Figure 2.3) use a 12-pin power connector; ATX motherboards (see Figure 2.4) use a 20-pin power connector (see Chapter 8, "Power Supplies and Circuit Testing," for details about the differences in power supplies).

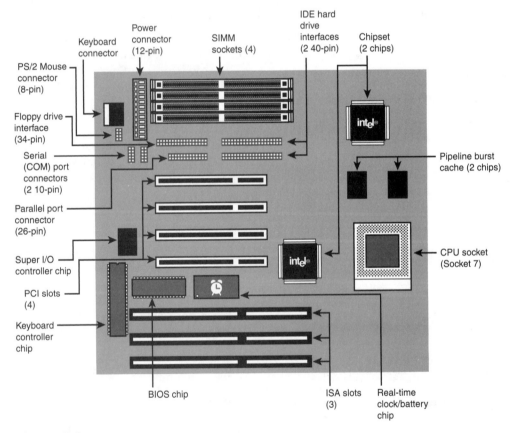

Figure 2.3
On a typical Baby-AT motherboard, the expansion slots run parallel to the long side of the motherboard.

Several different variations of the standard ATX design have been introduced, including the mini-ATX, micro-ATX, and Flex-ATX versions. These all have the major ATX features listed in the previous table but are smaller and have fewer expansion slots. The

Flex-ATX motherboards, in particular, cannot use slot-based processors, such as the Intel Pentium II, Pentium III, or some Celerons, but only socketed processors (see "The CPU" later in this chapter).

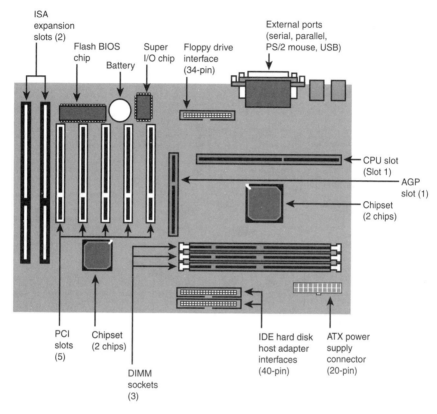

Figure 2.4
In a typical ATX motherboard, the expansion slots run parallel to the short side of the motherboard, and the built-in ports are at the back side of the motherboard.

LPX and NLX Motherboards

Many low-cost computers, especially desktop models, don't use either Baby-AT or an ATX-family motherboard. Instead, they use one of the following motherboard types: LPX or NLX. The LPX design was introduced in 1987 and is still used today. The NLX design was introduced in late 1996 and, unlike LPX, is a true standard.

Both of these motherboard designs use a special card called a riser card (or "Christmas Tree") instead of regular expansion slots. The riser card contains multiple expansion slots. However, there are several differences between LPX and NLX designs, and they are not interchangeable. Table 2.4 compares the characteristics of LPX and NLX motherboards.

The NLX riser card, shown in Figure 2.5, contains the expansion slots and power connector, whereas the motherboard contains the CPU socket or slot and RAM sockets.

Unlike LPX designs, NLX motherboards are standard designs that can be interchanged. The NLX motherboard attaches to the riser card and can be removed from the system without removing the riser card.

As with NLX, the LPX riser card contains the expansion slots, but LPX motherboards are not interchangeable between systems. The riser card must also be removed before the motherboard can be removed (see Figure 2.6).

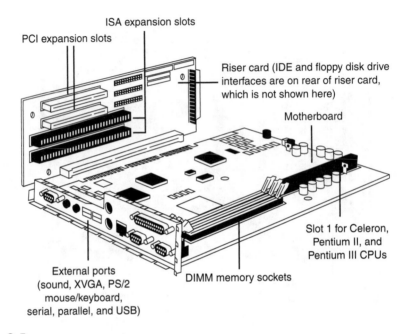

Figure 2.5
An NLX riser card with motherboard attached.

The following components appear in Figure 2.6:

1. Riser card
2. ISA expansion slots
3. Power supply connector (12-pin)
4. Connector to motherboard
5. Floppy interface
6. IDE interface
7. Battery
8. Video RAM

9. Built-in ports
10. Riser card connector
11. Chipset
12. Level 2 cache
13. ROM BIOS
14. CPU in socket
15. SIMM socket

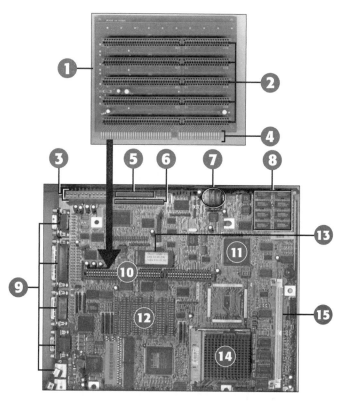

Figure 2.6
A typical LPX motherboard (bottom) with riser card (top).

As you can see from Table 2.4, NLX motherboards represent a true industry standard, compared with the older LPX motherboards. In fact, because different vendors who make LPX-based systems make significant changes to the basic design, it is really a misnomer to refer to LPX as a true industry standard. NLX-based systems are popular in corporations that need systems which can repaired quickly.

Table 2.4   LPX Versus NLX Motherboards

Feature	LPX	NLX
Riser card contains expansion slots	Yes	Yes
Expansion slots are parallel to the motherboard	Varies*	Yes
Built-in I/O and drive ports	Yes	Yes
Built-in VGA or better video	Yes	Yes
Single row of I/O ports on rear of system	Yes	No
Two rows of I/O ports on rear of system	No	Yes
Riser card located in middle of motherboard	Yes	No
Riser card located on inside edge of motherboard	No	Yes
Riser card attaches to motherboard slot	Yes	No
Motherboard attaches to slot on riser card	No	Yes

CH
2

Table 2.4 continued		
Feature	LPX	NLX
Riser card contains IDE hard disk and floppy disk drive ports	No	Yes
Industry-standard design interchangeable with newer models	No	Yes
Motherboard can be removed without removing riser card	No	Yes

See the next section, "Double-Deck Variations on LPX."

"Double-Deck" Variations on LPX

Some systems that use LPX-type motherboards actually use a double-deck design: The riser card that attaches to the motherboard looks like a T and has its expansion slots on top, running parallel to the motherboard, as shown in Figure 2.7. These systems keep the expansion slots at right angles to the motherboard. The riser card might need to be removed for certain upgrades or system adjustments. This is a common feature found on IBM Aptiva, Acer Aspire, and some Hewlett-Packard computers. This variation is also proprietary. Systems that use any type of an LPX-style motherboard can be upgraded only by exchanging components that attach to the motherboard, but not by replacing the motherboard.

The following components are listed in Figure 2.7:

1. Power switch connector
2. Power supply connector three-wire
3. Speaker power connector
4. Power supply connectors for P1 and P2
5. IDE hard disk interface #1
6. IDE hard disk interface #2
7. Floppy disk interface
8. Power supply connector to riser card
9. CPU regulator
10. CPU socket for Pentium
11. Pentium-class CPU
12. Heat sink on CPU
13. L2 Cache memory socket
14. DIMM memory module socket
15. Battery (CR-2032 model)
16. VESA feature connector for built-in video
17. Riser card connector (riser card has PCI and ISA slots)
18. Wake Up on Ring jumper (for modems on serial ports)
19. Wake Up on Ring connector

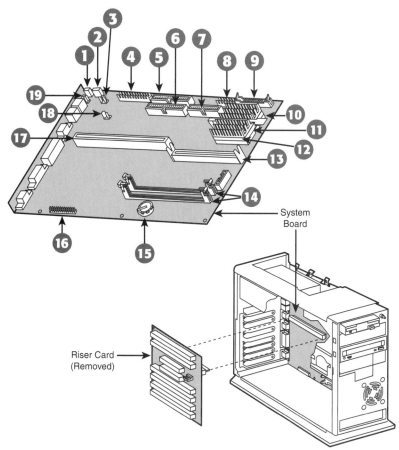

Riser Card
(Removed)

System
Board

Figure 2.7
A typical "double-deck" LPX motherboard and "T"-shaped riser card.

Motherboard Installation and Removal

Most Baby-AT motherboards are held in place by a combination of plastic stand-off spacers and brass spacers; most ATX-family motherboards use brass spacers only. If you look at an unmounted motherboard from the top, you can see that motherboards have several holes around the edges and one or two holes toward the middle of the motherboard. When a Baby-AT motherboard is installed in a computer, you'll see that one or two of the holes have a screw in them that attaches to a brass spacer, which itself is attached to the bottom or side of the case. The remainder of the holes have the top of a plastic spacer inserted in them; the bottom of the spaces fits into a teardrop-shaped mounting hole on the bottom or side of the computer case. ATX-family motherboards, on the other hand, usually are attached to brass spacers either built into the case or a removable motherboard tray.

Before you start working with motherboards or other static-sensitive parts, see "Electro Static Discharge (ESD)," page 327 for ESD and other precautions you should follow.

CH
2

Step-by-Step Motherboard Removal

Removing the motherboard is an important task for the computer technician. Understanding this procedure can help you both in your day-to-day work and in the A+ Certification Core hardware exam.

To remove ATX or Baby-AT motherboards from standard cases, follow these steps:

1. Disconnect all external and internal cables attached to add-on cards after labeling them for easy reconnection.

2. Disconnect all ribbon cables attached to built-in ports (I/O, storage, and so on) after labeling them for easy reconnection.

3. Disconnect all cables leading to internal speakers, keylocks, speed switches, and so on after labeling them for easy reconnection.

   All these cables must be removed before the motherboard can be removed. Marking them enables you to properly attach them to the new motherboard.

4. Remove all add-on cards and place them on an anti-static mat or in anti-static bags (see "Electrostatic Discharge (ESD)," page 327, for details about ESD precautions).

5. Disconnect the power-supply leads from the motherboard. The new motherboard must use the same power-supply connections as the current motherboard.

6. Unscrew the motherboard mounting screws and store for reuse; verify that all screws have been removed.

7. If the motherboard uses plastic spacers, gently push the motherboard toward the front of the case (for desktop units) or toward the bottom of the case (for tower units) to release the plastic stand-off spacers from the mounting grooves, as shown in Figure 2.8. To release the motherboard from the case, remove the screws, and then push the motherboard to release the plastic stand-off spacers from the teardrop-shaped mounting holes.

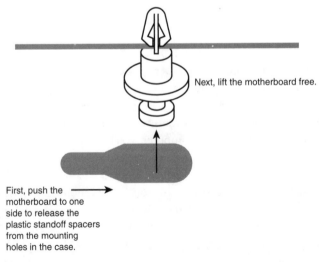

Next, lift the motherboard free.

First, push the motherboard to one side to release the plastic standoff spacers from the mounting holes in the case.

Figure 2.8
Most Baby-AT motherboards are held in place by plastic stand-off spacers.

8. Lift the motherboard and plastic stand-off spacers out of the case and place on an anti-static mat. If the motherboard is an ATX-type, remove the I/O shield and store it with the old motherboard. If the motherboard is a Baby-AT type, remove the external connectors for serial, parallel, and other ports from the case and store with the old motherboard. Sometimes they will be attached to punch-outs in the case; more often, they are attached to slot covers. Use the appropriate-sized hex driver or screwdriver to remove them.

9. If you are planning to install a replacement motherboard, use a pair of pliers to squeeze together the tops of the plastic spacers in the old motherboard. Then, push them from the top until they fall out of the motherboard. They can be inserted into the new motherboard. These spacers come in different heights for use with different types of cases.

CH
2

Step-by-Step Motherboard Installation

Before you install the new motherboard into the computer, be sure you have added memory and configured the CPU speed, multiplier, type, and voltage settings on the motherboard.

To learn more about adding memory, see "Specifying Memory for a Given System," page 99, "Installing SIMMs," page 102, and "Installing DIMMs," page 103.

To learn more about configuring the motherboard for a particular CPU, see "The CPU" later in this chapter.

Making these changes after the motherboard is installed in the computer is normally very difficult. To install the motherboard, follow these steps:

1. Place the new motherboard over the old motherboard to determine which mounting holes should be used for standoffs (if needed) and which should be used for brass spacers. Matching the motherboards helps you determine that the new motherboard will fit correctly in the system.

2. Take any plastic stand-off spacers you removed from the old motherboard and push them through the bottom of the appropriate holes on the new motherboard. The spacers prevent the motherboard from shorting out on the bottom of the case.

3. Place the new motherboard into the case, and make sure the plastic stand-off spacers (if used) are lined up in the correct teardrop-shaped mounting grooves at the bottom or sides of the case. If the motherboard is ATX-type, place the I/O shield and connector at the back of the case. Some systems use only brass spacers; line up the mounting holes on these motherboards with the spacers.

4. Gently push the new motherboard into place until the plastic stand-off spacers snap into the mounting grooves (if present). Make sure the board is level and parallel with the side or bottom of the case. Avoid flexing the motherboard; excessive flex can damage the system or I/O bus wires and destroy the motherboard. If the motherboard is ATX-type, make sure the I/O shield is correctly positioned at the rear of the case. The I/O shield is marked to help you determine the port types on the rear of the motherboard.

5. Determine which holes in the motherboard have brass stand-off spacers beneath them, and secure the motherboard using the screws removed from the old motherboard.

6. Reattach the wires to the speaker, reset switch, IDE host adapter, and power lights.

7. Attach the new ribbon cables supplied with the motherboard's I/O ports if present. These are normally attached to slot covers, but if your case has punchouts for these ports, knock out the holes, remove the ports from the slot covers, and attach them to the case. This will prevent the loss of usable slots. These are not required with ATX or NLX motherboards.

8. Reattach the ribbon cables from the drives to the motherboard's IDE and floppy disk drive interfaces. Match the ribbon cable's colored side to pin 1 on the interfaces.

9. Reattach the power supply connectors to the motherboard.

10. Insert the add-on cards you removed from the old motherboard; make sure your existing cards don't duplicate any features found on the new motherboard (such as sound, IDE, and so on). If they do, and you want to continue to use the card, you must disable the corresponding feature on the motherboard.

The CPU

One of the most important components found on any motherboard is the *CPU*, or *Central Processing Unit*. The CPU is the brains of the computer, requesting information from devices, modifying and creating information, and then sending information to devices. Recognizing different CPU types is very important in determining

- Which computers are capable of performing certain tasks
- Which computers are obsolete
- Which computers can be updated through a CPU change

The following tables provide an overview of CPU types, including their speed, voltage, and socket type. Use Table 2.5 along with the illustrations to help you recognize the major CPUs. The 2001 version of the A+ Certification exam covers Pentium, Pentium-equivalent, and newer processors.

For information about older CPUs, see *Upgrading and Repairing PCs, 12th Edition,* Chapter 3, "Microprocessor Types and Specifications."

For any given CPU to work with any given motherboard, the voltage, socket type, and clock speeds must match. Although adapters can be used to adjust voltage and clock speeds, adapters cannot change a CPU's pinout to allow a Pentium to fit in place of a 486-class CPU, for example.

Starting with 486DX2 CPUs, CPUs began to have two clock speeds: a core speed (the speed at which operations took place inside the CPU) and a slower bus speed (the speed at which RAM memory was accessed). When comparing systems with similar clock speeds, the one with the faster bus speed is preferred because it can access RAM faster.

Table 2.5 lists the physical characteristics of major CPU types, starting with the Intel Pentium. Use this table to verify compatibility with motherboards and to make sure that the system is correctly configured. Table 2.5 lists chips in order by socket or slot type used. Most chips on these charts were produced by Intel. Use the footnotes to determine additional manufacturing sources and other notes. The chip types are defined later, in Table 2.6.

Table 2.5   Physical Characteristics of Major CPU Types; Intel Pentium and Newer

CPU Type	Clock Speeds (MHz)	Motherboard (Bus) Speeds Supported	Core Voltage	Socket Type
Pentium	60–66	Same	5	Socket 4
Pentium	75–233	50, 60, 66MHz	3.3	Sockets 5, 7
Pentium MMX	200–233	66MHz	2.8	Socket 7
AMD K5	100–166	66MHz	3.3	Sockets 5, 7
AMD K6	166–300	66MHz	2.9–3.2	Socket 7, Super 7
AMD K6-2	266–500	66MHz	2.2	Socket 7, Super 7
AMD K6-III	400–450	66MHz	2.4	Socket 7, Super 7
Cyrix 6x86	100	66MHZ	2.8	Socket 7, Super 7
Cyrix MII	300–433PR*	60–100MHz	2.9	Socket 7, Super 7
Pentium Pro	150–200MHz	60–66MHz	3.1–3.3	Socket 8
Pentium II	233–333MHz	66MHz	Regulated by CPU	Slot 1
Pentium II	350–450MHz	100MHz	Regulated by CPU	Slot 1
Celeron	266–433MHz	66MHz	Regulated by CPU	Slot 1
Celeron	300MHz up	66MHz	Regulated by CPU	Socket 370
Pentium III	450MHz up	100MHz up	Regulated by CPU	Slot 1, Socket 370
VIA Cyrix III	433PR up	100MHz up	Regulated by CPU	Socket 370
AMD Athlon	500MHz up	200MHz up	Regulated by CPU	Slot A, Socket A
AMD Duron	700MHz up	200MHz	Regulated by CPU	Socket A
Pentium 4	1.4GHz up	400MHz	Regulated by CPU	Socket 423

*PR = Performance Rating; Cyrix and VIA Cyrix CPUs are rated by estimated performance compared to a comparable Intel CPU, rather than by actual clock speeds.

The Intel Celeron, Pentium III, Pentium 4, AMD Athlon and Duron, and VIA Cyrix III CPUs are currently being produced, so maximum speeds are subject to change and are not listed.

Voltage

Most Socket 5, Socket 7, and Super Socket 7–compatible CPUs use different voltage settings, depending on clock speed and design revisions. Motherboards that use these CPUs must be used with voltage regulators set to the correct voltage to avoid CPU damage. Voltage regulators are built into many motherboards, or they can be "sandwiched" between the CPU socket and the CPU. Voltage regulators must be set to the correct voltage for the particular CPU model installed, or the CPU can be damaged.

CH
2

CPUs that use Socket 370, Slot 1, Slot A, or Socket A feature automatic voltage regulation, enabling the CPU to set the correct operating voltage. Some motherboards using these CPUs might allow the user to vary the voltage from the default settings for special purposes.

CPUs such as the Pentium, Pentium II, Celeron, AMD K6, and others actually represent a "family" of models that can use different voltage levels and even CPU sockets. You should physically examine any system, before replacing or upgrading the CPU, to verify the exact CPU type and socket in use.

Physical CPU Packaging Types

CPUs have been packaged in many different forms since the first IBM PC was produced in 1981. During the lifespan of any given CPU, more than one physical packaging type can be used. Thus, you always should physically examine a system that you want to upgrade with a new CPU. Make sure you determine which slot or socket type it has so you know which packaging type to ask for. Some desktop computers have soldered CPUs that cannot be removed for replacement or upgrading.

Table 2.6 defines the packaging types used for both older and current processors, as seen in the preceding Table 2.5.

For the A+ Certification exam, you should know the major acronyms and their meanings.

Table 2.6 Physical Chip Packaging Types		
Physical Packaging Acronym	Sample CPU and Other Chips	Meaning and Notes
DIP	8088, 8086 Early 80287 Math coprocessors	Dual Inline Pin. A rectangular, ceramic chip with easily bent thin metal legs down the long sides of the chip. A recessed "dimple" at one end corresponds with a similar cutout at one end of the socket for keying. This packaging type is no longer used for CPUs but is still used for BIOS (firmware) chips used on motherboards, video cards, SCSI host adapters, and network cards. BIOS DIPs have fewer pins than CPU DIPs, and often have a sticker indicating the manufacturer over the top of the chip.
PGA	80486DX 80386DX Pentium 60 and 66	Pin Grid Array. A square, ceramic chip with several rows of pins on the underside, leaving the middle open. Introduced with some 80286 models, this is the basis for the most popular CPU packaging types used today.
LCC	80286	Leadless Chip Carrier. A square, ceramic chip with flush contacts on all four sides. With no way to lock into place, these CPUs were actually held in place by a snap-on cover. These are the rarest of the three physical chip types used for 80286 CPUs.

Table 2.6 continued		
Physical Packaging Acronym	Sample CPU and Other Chips	Meaning and Notes
PLCC	80286 80387SX Math coprocessor	Plastic Leaded Chip Carrier. A square, ceramic chip with protruding contacts on all four sides. These slightly springy metal contacts held the chip in place but didn't provide a reliable keying method; a special PLCC chip puller is recommended if you work on systems using this type of chip.
PQFP	80386SX	Plastic Quad Flat Pack. A square, ceramic chip that resembles the PLCC but is surface-mounted to the motherboard.
SPGA	Pentium MMX AMD Athlon, Duron	Staggered Pin Grid Array. A variation on PGA, which staggers the pins in each row for greater pin density in the same space.
SECC	Early Pentium II	Single Edge Contact Cartridge. The first slot-mounted CPU in the Intel family, the cartridge is a shell that encloses an SEC (Single Edge Contact) module with the Pentium II CPU and Level 2 cache. A similar package (although with different electrical contacts) is used on the original AMD Athlon CPU.
SECC2	Pentium II Pentium III	Single Edge Contact Cartridge version 2. A simplified, less-expensive form of SECC that covers only one side of the Pentium II SEC and allows for better cooling.
SEPP	Celeron (slot 1)	Single Edge Processor Package. A version of the SECC without any plastic cover. Adapters using this design are available to allow PPGA-based Celerons to attach to Slot 1 motherboards.
PPGA	Celeron (Socket 370)	Plastic Pin Grid Array. A low-cost version of PGA used by the newest Celeron CPUs.

Socket and Slot Types

Most 486 and Pentium-class CPUs fit into square sockets of various types. These sockets have different pinouts and electrical characteristics, making it important that you match the CPU you want to use to the sockets designed to handle it. You should note the most popular CPUs that use each socket type for the test (see Table 2.7).

CH

2

Table 2.7   CPU Socket Types

Socket Type	For CPU Types	Number of Pins	Notes
Socket 1	486 SX, DX, SX2, DX2, DX2 and DX4 OverDrive	169	17×17 PGA; 5 volts
Socket 2	486 SX, DX, SX2, DX2, DX2 and DX4 OverDrive, Pentium OverDrive	238	19×19 PGA; 5 volts
Socket 3	486 SX, DX, SX2, DX2, DX2 and DX4 OverDrive, Pentium OverDrive	237	19×19 PGA; 5 volts or 3.3 volts
Socket 4	Pentium 60/66	273	21×21 PGA; 5 volts
Socket 5	Pentium 75-133, OverDrive	320	37×37 SPGA; 3.3/3.5 volts
Socket 7	Pentium 75-233, MMX, AMD K5, K6, Cyrix 6x86, M1, MII	321	37×37 SPGA; uses voltage regulator on motherboard
Socket 8	Pentium Pro	387	Dual SPGA; automatic voltage regulation
PGA 370	Celeron	370	37×37 SPGA; automatic voltage regulation
PGA 423	Pentium 4	423	SPGA; automatic voltage regulation
Socket A	AMD Athlon, Duron	462	SPGA; automatic voltage regulation

Table 2.8 lists the major CPU slot types. Both AMD and Intel have moved away from slot-mounted CPUs for most applications, although the Intel Pentium III Xeon continues to use Slot 2.

Table 2.8   CPU Slot Types

Slot Type	For CPU Types
Slot 1	Intel Pentium II, Celeron
Slot A	AMD Athlon
Slot 2	Intel Pentium II Xeon, Pentium III Xeon

Starting with Socket 3 (used for 486 CPUs), CPU sockets typically feature a so-called Zero Insertion Force (ZIF) socket design, with a handle that you raise to release the CPU and lower to clamp the CPU in place. All except the Pentium Pro are square sockets. Most CPU sockets, starting with Socket 3, have the socket name molded into the top of the socket for easy identification. The Pentium Pro Socket 8 is distinctive because of its rectangular design. See Figure 2.9 for a comparison of these sockets.

Figure 2.10 shows how the 386DX and 486DX/2 OverDrive CPUs compare with the Pentium. All these chips use square sockets, but their pinouts and sizes are different; they cannot be interchanged.

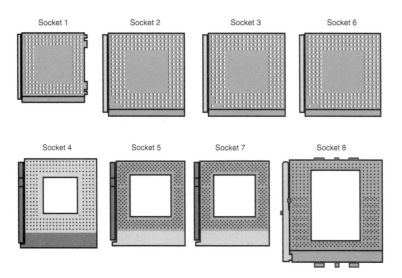

Figure 2.9
486 (top row) and Pentium/Pentium Pro sockets (bottom row). The most common 486 socket was Socket 3, while the most common Pentium socket is Socket 7.

Figure 2.10
Three popular generations of socketed CPUs: the 386DX top and bottom views (left); the 486DX top and bottom views (center), and the Pentium top and bottom views (right). Pin 1 of each CPU is indicated by the beveled corner of the CPU.

After developing a line of slot-mounted Pentium II, Celeron, and early Pentium III CPUs, Intel returned to sockets with the Socket 370 for current Celeron and Pentium III processors, as seen in Figure 2.11. Note the differences in pin layout between the Pentium and Celeron CPUs; these CPUs are not interchangeable.

Figure 2.11
A Celeron in PPGA Socket 370 form (right) and a Pentium (left), with the SEPP adapter for inserting a SPGA Celeron into a Slot 1 motherboard at rear.

Internal CPU Characteristics Affecting Performance

Besides core and bus clock speeds, several other factors influence the true speed of a CPU:

- The register size and data bus.

  These refer to the width of data that can be accessed in each CPU operation; the register size refers to data management inside the CPU, whereas the data bus refers to data transfer between the CPU and RAM. Some CPUs have a bottleneck created by having a data bus narrower than the register size; having a data bus wider than the register size increases speed by allowing the CPU to perform two data-transfer operations at the same time.

- Presence or absence of a math coprocessor circuit to perform faster floating-point math (used by CAD and spreadsheet programs). Although most CPUs prior to the Pentium used a separate math coprocessor, the Pentium and all newer CPUs covered on the A+ Certification exam have a built-in math coprocessor.

- The amount of RAM the CPU can access.

  Larger amounts are better, although the actual motherboard design limits most systems to far less RAM than the CPU can use.

- The presence or absence of cache RAM (RAM that holds a copy of main memory for faster access by the CPU).

  Level 1 cache is part of the CPU itself; Level 2 cache might be on the CPU assembly or chip (but not inside the CPU) or might be on the motherboard. Small CPU cache sizes or no CPU cache slows down the system.

- The amount and speed of cache RAM.

  Larger and faster cache RAM improves system speed, especially for operations that take place entirely or primarily in RAM.

Table 2.9 reviews these internal characteristics of the same CPUs listed in the previous table. Use this table to determine the best optimization methods for a given CPU and when looking for CPUs for servers and other tasks requiring large amounts of memory. Note that CPUs used in notebook computers might have different specifications.

For the A+ Certification exam, you should know which processors include both Level 1 and Level 2 cache, and you should also review "CPU Optimization Scenarios," later in this chapter.

For more information on how cache memory works, see "Cache RAM and Main Memory," page 104.

Table 2.9 Internal Characteristics of Major CPUs—Pentium and Newer

CPU	Internal Data Bus (Register)	Data Bus	Max Memory	Math Co-Processor	Level 1 and Level 2 Cache	Level 2 Cache Speed
Pentium	32-bit	64-bit	4GB	Integrated	16KB - L1	N/A
Pentium MMX	32-bit	64-bit	4GB	Integrated	32KB - L1	N/A
AMD K5	32-bit	64-bit	4GB	Integrated	16KB - L1	N/A
AMD K6	32-bit	64-bit	4GB	Integrated	64KB - L1	N/A
AMD K6-2	32-bit	64-bit	4GB	Integrated	64KB - L1	N/A
Pentium Pro	32-bit	64-bit	64GB	Integrated	16KB - L1 256KB, 512KB, 1GB - L2	CPU speed
Pentium II	32-bit	64-bit	64GB	Integrated	32KB - L1 512KB - L2	Half CPU speed
Pentium III	32-bit	64-bit	64GB	Integrated	32KB - L1 512KB - L2	Half CPU speed
"Coppermine" version as above except					32KB - L1 256KB - L2	Full CPU speed
Celeron (266–300MHz)	32-bit	64-bit	64GB	Integrated	32KB - L1	N/A
Celeron (300A up)	32-bit	64-bit	64GB	Integrated	32KB - L1 128KB - L2	Full CPU speed

CH
2

Table 2.9   continued

CPU	Internal Data Bus (Register)	Data Bus	Max Memory	Math Co-Processor	Level 1 and Level 2 Cache	Level 2 Cache Speed
AMD Athlon Slot A	32-bit	64-bit	8TB	Integrated	128KB - L1 512KB - L2	Half CPU speed (models 1 and 2) Full CPU speed (model 4)
AMD Athlon Socket A	32-bit	64-bit	8TB	Integrated	128KB - L1 512KB - L2	Full CPU speed
AMD Duron	32-bit	64-bit	8TB	Integrated	128KB - L1 64KB - L2	Full CPU speed

Level 1 cache RAM has been present in all Pentium-class and newer CPUs. Level 2 cache RAM can be on the CPU or the motherboard, and systems that lack Level 2 cache of any kind, such as the original Celeron 266 and 300, run very slowly. A small amount of full-speed cache RAM performs better than a larger amount of cache RAM running at a lower speed.

Although a given CPU might be able to access 4GB or more of RAM, the actual factor determining how much RAM a system can use is the motherboard design.

CPU Installation and Removal

CPUs are one of the most expensive components found in any computer. Because a CPU can fail, or more likely, need to be replaced with a faster model, knowing how to install and remove CPUs is important. On the A+ Certification Exam, you should be prepared to answer questions related to the safe removal and replacement of Pentium-class or higher CPUs.

The methods used for CPU removal vary according to two factors: the CPU type and the socket type.

As you saw in Table 2.7, almost all CPUs are socketed. Traditional sockets hold the CPU in place by tension on the chip's legs, pins, or leads. Thus, to remove these chips, you must pull the chip out of the socket. Because the chip's legs, pins, or leads are fragile, special tools are strongly recommended for removing chips that are not mounted in ZIF sockets.

See Table 2.6 for a definition of each of the following physical chip packaging types; Table 2.7 cross-references chip types to the recent CPU types that use them.

PGA-Type CPU (Pentium, Pentium Pro, and Similar Models)—No ZIF Socket

Pentium-class socketed processors (refer to Table 2.7) use some version of the PGA (Pin-Grid Array) design (refer to Table 2.6) and are installed in ZIF sockets; these sockets have a handle that can be lifted to release the processor. However, you might encounter a few Pentium-class processors that are not installed in ZIF sockets. A chip extractor must be used to remove these processors from their sockets.

If the CPU has a removable heat sink or fan that is attached to the motherboard, remove the heat sink before removing the CPU. These heat sinks have a horizontal bar that attaches to the motherboard on two sides of the CPU. Squeeze the clip at one end to release the bar and work it loose from the other side of the CPU. Then, disconnect the CPU fan (if included) from its power source and lift the assembly away. Then use one or two PGA chip extractors to remove the PGA chip; this tool resembles a small rake. These extractors are often supplied with 486 or Pentium-class chip upgrades.

1. Slide the chip extractor's "fingers" under any side of the CPU (see Figure 2.12). If you have two chip extractors, place the second one on the opposite side of the CPU.

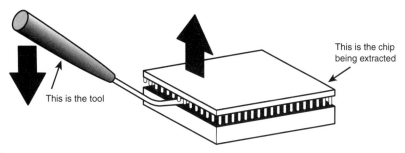

This is the chip
being extracted

This is the tool

Figure 2.12
Insert the PGA chip extractor under the side of the CPU and gently push down on the handle to loosen the CPU; move the extractor to the opposite side and repeat until the chip can be removed.

2. Push gently down on the handle of the chip extractor to pry up the CPU. If you have only one extractor, move the extractor to the opposite side and repeat; do *not* try to remove the chip with a single application of the extractor because the uneven force will bend the CPU's pins and might damage the socket.

3. Repeat until the chip is free; place it in anti-static packaging.

To insert a PGA-type CPU (no ZIF Socket), find the corner of the chip that is cut off (beveled) and might also be marked with a dot; this indicates Pin 1. The underside of some chips might be marked with a line pointing toward Pin 1. Then follow these steps:

1. Line up the Pin 1 corner with the corner of the socket also indicated as Pin 1 (look for an arrow or other marking on the motherboard). If you put the chip in with Pin 1 aligned with the wrong corner and apply the power, you will destroy the chip.

2. Gently press the chip into the socket. Make sure you are pressing evenly on all sides of the chip because uneven force will cause pins to bend. Stop when the chip is firmly in the socket. See Figure 2.13.

3. Attach the heat sink or fan if required at this time.

Beveled corner of 486SX CPU indicating Pin 1

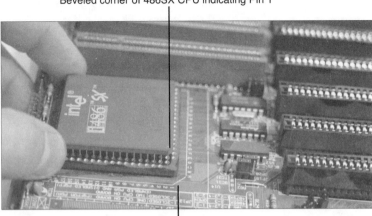

Pin 1 marking on motherboard

Figure 2.13
Line up the beveled corner (also marked with a dot) of a socketed CPU with Pin 1 on the socket.

4. Gently press the chip into the socket to squeeze the socket leads against the chip; continue until the chip top is flush with the edges of the socket.

For more information on installing socketed processors in your system, see "Prepare the New Motherboard" in Chapter 12 of *Upgrading and Repairing PCs, 12th Edition.*

PGA-Type CPU in a ZIF Socket

ZIF sockets are used on Socket 3 486-based systems and on almost all desktop systems using Pentium, Pentium Pro, or similar Socket 5, Socket 6, Socket 7, Socket 8, or Socket 370 CPUs. They allow easy installation and removal of the CPU.

ZIF sockets have a lever which, when released, loosens a clamp that holds the CPU in place.

If the CPU has a removable heat sink or fan that is attached to the motherboard, remove the heat sink before removing the CPU. These heat sinks have a horizontal bar that attaches to the motherboard on two sides of the CPU. Squeeze the clip at one end to release the bar and work it loose from the other side of the CPU. Then, disconnect the CPU fan (if included) from its power source and lift the assembly away. Then remove the CPU this way:

1. Push the lever on the ZIF socket slightly to the outside of the socket to release it.

2. Lift the end of the lever until it is vertical (see Figure 2.14). This releases the clamping mechanism on the CPU.

3. Grasp the CPU on opposite sides, making sure not to touch the pins, and remove it from the socket. Put it into anti-static packaging.

To insert a PGA-type CPU into a ZIF Socket, find the corner of the chip that is cut off (beveled) and might also be marked with a dot; this indicates Pin 1. The underside of some chips might be marked with a line pointing toward Pin 1. Then follow these steps:

1. Line up the Pin 1 corner with the corner of the socket also indicated as Pin 1 (look for an arrow or other marking on the motherboard). If you put the chip in with Pin 1 aligned with the wrong corner and apply the power, you will destroy the chip.

2. Make sure the lever on the ZIF socket is vertical; insert the CPU into the socket and verify that the pins are fitting into the correct socket holes. On 486 chips with Socket 3, it's normal for a row of holes to be visible on all four sides of the chip.

3. Lower the lever to the horizontal position and snap it into place to secure the CPU.

4. Attach the heat sink or fan if required at this time.

Figure 2.14
The lever on a ZIF socket clamps the chip into place when lowered and releases it when raised.

Slot-Type CPU (SECC, SECC2, SEPP, or AMD Athlon Slot A)

Slot-based CPUs require a retention mechanism be attached to the motherboard to hold the CPU. To remove a slot-type CPU

1. Push down on the retainers at each end of the CPU to release the CPU from the retention mechanism.

2. Disconnect the power lead to the CPU fan (if present).

3. Remove the CPU and fan/heatsink from the retention mechanism.

Figure 2.15 shows the retention mechanism after the CPU is removed.

Retention mechanism

Figure 2.15
The retention mechanism for a Slot 1 motherboard used by Pentium II and Celeron CPUs.

To attach a slot-type CPU:

1. Attach the CPU retention mechanism to the motherboard. Leave the foam backing on the bottom of the motherboard while pushing the supports into place. Lift up the motherboard and secure the retention mechanism with the screws supplied.

   Some motherboards are shipped with the retention mechanism already installed, so this step might not apply to you.

2. Attach the fan and heatsink to the CPU if not already attached; some CPUs have a factory-attached heatsink/fan, while others require you to add it in the field.

3. Match the pinouts on the bottom of the CPU to the motherboard's slot; note that the slot has two sides of unequal length, making it easy to match the slot with the CPU.

4. Insert the CPU into the retention mechanism; push down until the retaining clips lock the CPU into place. Figure 2.16 shows the CPU in place.

5. Connect the power lead from the fan (if present) to the motherboard or drive power connector as directed.

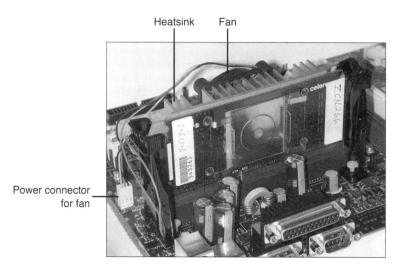

Heatsink   Fan

Power connector
for fan

Figure 2.16
A Slot 1–based Celeron CPU after installation. The heatsink and fan are attached to the
rear of the CPU.

CPU Optimization

Because the CPU is the "brains" of the computer, and because faster data flow to and
from the CPU is a critical factor in overall performance, you need to know how to optimize the CPU's performance. This can be done by making changes in the motherboard's
CPU configuration and in the configuration of devices that communicate directly with
the CPU.

Adjusting Speed and Multiplier Settings

As you saw earlier in this chapter, most recent CPUs have two clock speeds; an internal or
"core" clock speed, and an external or "bus" clock speed. The CPU's core clock speed is a
multiple of the bus speed. Pentium-class CPUs have four major external clock speed
options, including 50MHz, 60MHz, 66MHz, and 100MHz. The bus speed is multiplied
by a multiplier factor to determine the CPU's core, or internal, clock speed.

A motherboard's capability to use a given CPU depends in part on its support for the CPU's
bus speed and clock multiplier. Some motherboards provide you with a single speed/multi-
plier setting that makes the correct adjustments for you. Many motherboards have a chart of
correct jumper settings silk-screened to the top surface. Jumpers are small pins that are used
on many motherboards to configure these settings; you must place a jumper block (a small
plastic device with a metal insert) over two pins to choose a setting (see Figure 2.17).

If you don't set the speed jumpers correctly, your system will not run properly.

Silkscreened
jumper settings

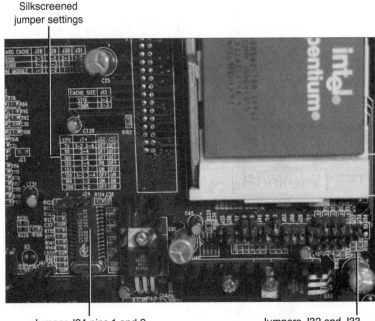

Jumper J24 pins 1 and 2   Jumpers J32 and J33

Figure 2.17
This motherboard has a jumper across J24's pins 1 and 2 and no jumpers on J32 or
J33 to configure it correctly for the Pentium 100 CPU on board.

Other motherboards require you to set the CPU bus speed and multiplier to the correct
options. These settings can be made on the motherboard with jumper blocks, through the
CMOS setup program, or automatically by the CPU. Your motherboard or system manual will have a listing of the correct jumper or CMOS setup options to select for all CPUs
supported by your motherboard.

For more information on setting the jumper blocks for your CPU, see *Upgrading and
Repairing PCs, 12th Edition,* Chapter 24, "Building or Upgrading Systems."

Whenever you replace an old CPU with a new, faster CPU, you must set these options
correctly. Otherwise, you are running the chip at the wrong speed, which is called *overclocking* or *underclocking.*

Note that some motherboards do *not* allow bus speed or multiplier changes, meaning that
specially designed upgrade CPUs with the capability to override the motherboards' limitations must be used. Also, note that motherboards made for older Pentium, Pentium II,
and Celeron CPUs often do not permit bus speeds of 100MHz or higher, limiting the
speed of new CPUs you purchase for these boards.

You also will need to change the voltage setting on many motherboards if you change to a
faster CPU on a Socket 7 or Super Socket 7 motherboard. These motherboards, unlike
Slot 1, Socket 370, Slot A, or Socket A-based motherboards, require you to select the

correct voltage for the CPU you install. If you don't select the correct voltage setting, you might damage the CPU.

Overclocking and Underclocking

If you replace a Pentium-type CPU with a 50MHz or 60MHz clock speed with a faster model with a 66MHz bus speed, but you don't change the multiplier, you run the CPU lower than its design speed. This is called underclocking. For example, if you replace a Pentium 90 with a Pentium 233 and adjust the multiplier (from 1.5 to 3.5) but you don't adjust the bus speed from 60 to 66MHz, the new CPU can't run above 210MHz (60×3.5).

Similarly, overclocking is running a CPU at a faster bus speed, such as running a Pentium 150 (60×2.5) at 166 MHz (66×2.5), a higher multiplier, or both. Although some "hot rodders" like to overclock to increase performance, it isn't recommended in routine use because too fast a speed can cause overheating and void system or CPU warranties.

Correct Bus Speeds and Multiplier Settings for Popular CPUs

The tables that follow show you the correct bus speed and multiplier settings for a wide range of CPUs. For the A+ Certification exam, you should understand the basic concept of how the bus speed and multiplier are used to set the CPU's core clock speed.

Table 2.10 lists the correct bus speed and multiplier settings for some typical Intel and AMD CPUs, such as the Pentium, Pentium-MMX, AMD K5, AMD K6, and earlier Pentium II and Celeron models.

Table 2.10   Clock Speed and Multiplier Settings for Pentium-Class CPUs 75–333MHz

CPU	Core Clock Speed (MHz)	Bus Speed (MHz) X	Multiplier
Pentium 75	75	50	1.5
Pentium 90	90	60	1.5
Pentium 100	100	66	1.5
Pentium 120	120	60	2
AMD K5 120			
Pentium OverDrive 125	125	50	2.5
Pentium 133	133	66	2
Pentium 150	150	60	2.5
Pentium 166	166	66	2.5
AMD K5			
Pentium Pro 180	180	60	3
Pentium 200	200	66	3
Pentium II-233	233	66	3.5
AMD K6/233			
AMD K6/266	266	66	4
Pentium II/266			
AMD K6/300	300	66	4.5
AMD K6-2/300	300	100	3
Pentium II/300			
Pentium II/333	333	66	5

Most CPUs with core (internal) speeds between 60MHz and 333MHz run at bus (motherboard) speeds up to 66MHz.

Table 2.11 shows the correct core and clock-multiplier speeds used on CPUs running at 350MHz and above, such as newer Celeron, Pentium II, Pentium III, and AMD K6-series CPUs.

Table 2.11   Clock Speed and Multiplier Settings for Pentium-Class CPUs 350MHz and Higher

CPU Model	Core Clock Speed (MHz)	Bus Speed (MHz) X	Multiplier
Pentium II/350	350	100	3.5
AMD K6-2/350			
Celeron/366	366	66	5.5
AMD K6-2/366			
AMD K6-2/380	380	95	4
Pentium II/400	400	100	4
AMD K6III/400			
Celeron/433	433	66	6.5
Pentium II/450	450	100	4.5
AMD K6III/450			
Celeron/466	466	66	7
AMD K6-2/475	475	95	5
Pentium II/500	500	100	5
AMD K6-2/500			
Pentium II/550	550	100	5.5
Pentium II/600	600	100	6
Pentium II/650	650	100	6.5
Pentium III/700	700	100	7.0

Some Pentium III and Athlon-based systems with core speeds above 700MHz now use a 133MHz bus speed.

Adding Main and Cache RAM

Because the fastest access the CPU has to data is to access it directly from RAM, there are two ways to optimize CPU performance through making adjustments to RAM:

- Increasing RAM memory in the system optimizes CPU performance by providing a larger "pool" from which to draw program code and data. Inadequate RAM forces the CPU to request the correct information from storage devices, which are much slower than RAM.

- Increasing cache memory in the system provides an even faster "shortcut" for the CPU's access to information. You can compare cache memory to an ATM; it's usually faster to go to the ATM for money than it is to go inside the bank and stand in line. However, you can't use the ATM for all transactions; sooner or later you'll need to go inside the bank. Similarly, cache memory is like an ATM for information; it's faster to retrieve the information from cache memory than from main memory *if* the information is available there. Cache memory retains a copy of the last information read from main memory, so for repeated reads of the same memory locations, cache memory is used rather than main memory. However, if cache memory doesn't have the correct information, your system will retrieve the information you need from main memory (the "bank" in this comparison).

The fastest cache memory is located directly inside the CPU and is known as Level 1 cache. Level 1 cache was very small on the 486 and original Pentium CPUs that pioneered its use. Today, most CPUs feature 32KB or more of this high-speed RAM.

Level 2 cache refers to cache one level outside the CPU core. On 486 and most Pentium-class CPUs, Level 2 cache is found on the motherboard, although many "economy" systems leave it off. The original Celeron 266MHz and 300MHz models also lacked Level 2 cache, making them very slow.

The Pentium Pro, Pentium II, Pentium III, Celeron 300A and faster models, AMD K6III, and Athlon and Duron CPUs all feature built-in Level 2 cache. This cache, ranging in size from 128KB to 1MB, is built into the CPU module or chip but is not inside the CPU core. Level 2 cache on the motherboard is accessed at bus (motherboard) speed, but Level 2 cache on the CPU can be accessed at half the CPU speed (for example, Pentium II, and early Pentium III and Slot A AMD Athlons) or at full CPU speed (for example, Celeron 300A and above, newer Pentium IIIs, Socket A AMD Athlons, and Durons).

Level 3 cache refers to motherboard-based cache on systems whose CPUs have both Level 1 and Level 2 cache memory. Many systems that use the AMD K6III CPU feature Level 3 cache.

Depending on the system, therefore, you can increase cache size and speed by

- **Upgrading the CPU**—If you have an original (non-MMX) Pentium, you can replace it with a K6-2, K6III, or Pentium MMX and increase your 16KB Level 1 cache up to 32KB (Pentium MMX) or 64KB (K6-2, K6III). If you have the original 266MHz or 300MHz Celerons, which lack Level 2 cache, replace these processors with either Pentium II or Celerons (300A or faster), which have Level 2 cache on board.

  Because of limitations in some motherboards' voltage levels, multipliers, or clock-speed settings, you might need to purchase special upgrade versions of these CPUs. Upgrade-ready CPUs made to adapt to the limitations of older systems are sold by Intel (OverDrive products), Evergreen Technologies, Kingston Technologies, PowerLeap, and others.

- **Upgrading the motherboard**—Add Level 2 cache to your motherboard if it has provision for it (see "Upgrading Cache RAM," page 107). Some economy motherboards for Pentium CPUs don't have Level 2 cache, or have a fixed amount. Consider replacing those motherboards with a model containing more Level 2 cache (512KB or more). Motherboards made for Pentium II/III/Celeron CPUs usually don't feature Level 2 cache because the CPUs already include it.

To learn more about how cache memory works and how to upgrade it, see "Cache RAM and Main Memory," page 104.

CPU Optimization Scenarios

The A+ Certification exam typically includes questions about CPU optimization, and you will also encounter customers in your day-to-day work who need your help to upgrade their systems to higher performance. Use the scenarios here to help you learn how to select upgrades that will boost performance.

To help you use these scenarios to prepare for the examination, make sure you understand the following topics covered earlier in this chapter:

- CPU socket types and compatible CPUs
- CPU cache memory types and sizes

These topics will prepare you to choose the best CPU type to use for an upgrade to a given system.

- Your system has a Pentium 75MHz CPU on board with no Level 2 cache. The motherboard has no sockets to add Level 2 cache. To boost performance to the greatest extent through a CPU cache, you must select a CPU that has a large memory cache on-board.

  Which of the following CPUs will provide the biggest performance lift?

  > OverDrive 125
  > Pentium MMX 233
  > AMD K6III-400

  AMD K6III is the best choice because of its higher clock speed, its large Level 1 cache (64KB), and its 256KB of Level 2 cache.

The following are potential drawbacks you should be aware of:

- A BIOS upgrade might be necessary, and an upgrade version of the chip should be used if the motherboard lacks direct support for this CPU. The upgrade version of the chip will provide correct voltage and clock-multiplier support for older motherboards. Upgrade versions are not made by AMD, but are made by third-party vendors.
- You have two older PCs you can use for a memory-intensive operation, a system with a Pentium II 233MHz and a Celeron 300. Which is a better choice?

  To answer this question correctly, look at the cache size of both processors, not just the clock speed.

  The Pentium II 233MHz is a better choice because it has both Level 1 and Level 2 cache (512KB). The Celeron 300, although slightly faster, lacks any Level 2 cache. If a Pentium II 233MHz is compared to a Celeron 300A or faster, the faster Celeron would be a better choice because the 300A and faster models have 128KB of Level 2 cache.

Recognizing Expansion Slot Types

In order of speed, the CPU accesses cache memory at the fastest speed, followed by main memory, and then cards mounted in expansion slots.

The A+ Certification exam, as well as your day-to-day work, tests your ability to recognize the different expansion slot types and be able to choose the most appropriate slot for a given type of card. Most systems have mixtures of two or more of the slot types discussed in the following sections.

Table 2.12 compares expansion slot designs by speed, data bus width, and suggested uses; you must know the speed and bus width of these slots for the exam. Most systems today primarily have PCI expansion slots, but one or two ISA slots are found on many recent systems.

Table 2.12   Technical Information About Expansion Slot Types

Slot Type	Bus Width	Slot Speed	Status	Suggested Uses
ISA	8-bit, 16-bit	Approx. 8MHz	Obsolete	Modems, serial and parallel ports
EISA	32-bit	Approx. 8MHz	Obsolete	Server-optimized network interface cards, all ISA cards
VL-Bus	32-bit	25–33MHz[1]	Obsolete	Video, IDE hard disk, all ISA cards
PCI	32-bit, 64-bit[2]	25–33MHz[3]	Current	Video, network, SCSI, sound card
AGP	32-bit	66MHz[4]	Current	Video

[1] *Runs at full speed of 486SX/DX processor 25–33MHz; runs at bus speed of 486DX2/SX2/DX4 processors (25–33MHz).*
[2] *64-bit versions found mostly on network servers and high-performance workstations.*
[3] *Runs at half bus speed on Pentium motherboards running at 50–66MHz; runs at one-third bus speed on motherboards running at 100MHz.*
[4] *AGP 1x runs a single transfer per cycle; AGP 2x makes two transfers per cycle, doubling its effective speed; AGP 4x makes four transfers per cycle, quadrupling its effective speed.*

ISA

The oldest slot type is ISA (Industry Standard Architecture). ISA slots come in two forms: a slot with a single long connector, which could send or receive 8 bits of data, and a 16-bit or AT-style slot. This 8-bit slot was developed for the IBM PC in 1981; the 16-bit or AT style slot adds a shorter connector to the first one. It sends or receives 16 bits of data per operation and was developed for the IBM AT in 1984.

Although many systems still contain at least one ISA slot, the ISA slot is now considered obsolete; many of the newest systems now have no ISA slots. Many systems that contain ISA slots have at least one that's called a "shared" slot, a pair of tightly spaced slots that share or a single slot cover at the back in the case. One slot or the other, but not both, can be used. Figure 2.18 shows ISA slots compared to EISA slots.

EISA

A short-lived variation on ISA was the EISA slot (Enhanced Industry Standard Architecture) introduced in 1989. It is a deeper version of the ISA slot, designed to use both 32-bit EISA cards and ISA cards. This expansion slot is found today primarily in older 386-based and 486-based network servers and was never popular for desktop computers. Notice in

Figure 2.18 that the extra contacts are visible, allowing the EISA slot to use both EISA and ISA cards. 30-pin SIMM sockets with SIMMs attached are at the left side of the slots; they are slanted to allow cards to fit over them.

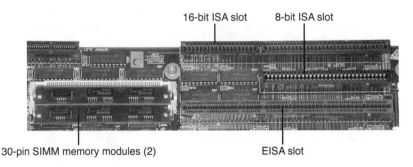

16-bit ISA slot   8-bit ISA slot

30-pin SIMM memory modules (2)   EISA slot

Figure 2.18
A 386-based server with a 16-bit ISA slot (top), an 8-bit ISA PC-style slot (middle), and an EISA slot (bottom).

VL-Bus
A= second variation on ISA was introduced in late 1992. The VESA local-bus (or VL-Bus) added a 32-bit connector to the standard ISA slot (some EISA motherboards also have the VL-Bus slot extensions). When 486-based machines were popular, this slot was the leading high-speed interface, and a few of the early Pentium-based systems also feature these slots. After Pentium computers replaced 486s, this slot faded from view and has not been used since the early Pentium-based systems sold in 1994-95. Figure 2.19 shows a typical VL-Bus multi-I/O card. You should be able to distinguish VL-Bus cards and slots from ISA cards/slots for the A+ Certification Exam.

PCI
Starting in 1993-94, the PCI (Peripheral Component Interconnect) slot rapidly replaced VL-Bus slots in both late-model 486-based machines and in most Pentium-class computers. Most computers today have at least half their slots in the PCI format, and many low-cost computers have only PCI slots on board.

Most recent systems that have at least one ISA slot often place the ISA slot so close to a PCI slot that only one slot cover at the rear of the system is available (see Figure 2.20). This "combo" or "shared" slot feature allows you to choose whether you want to use the slower ISA slot or the faster PCI slot.

AGP
The Accelerated Graphics Port, or AGP slot, was introduced in 1996 strictly for high-speed video; it is typically found on systems using Pentium II, Pentium III, Celeron, or AMD Athlon and Duron CPUs, and on some systems using the AMD K6-2 or K6-III CPUs. Shown alongside a PCI slot in Figure 2.21, the AGP slot is faster than PCI slots and has the capability to "borrow" main memory when creating 3D textures, making it popular for advanced gaming and for advanced business graphics. Many low-cost computers have built-in AGP video that cannot be upgraded. Better computers feature an AGP slot.

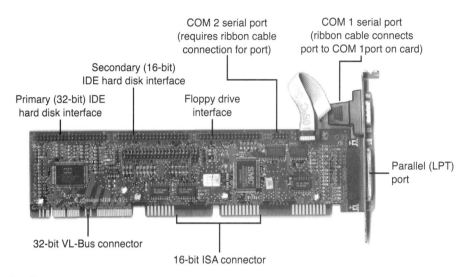

COM 2 serial port
(requires ribbon cable
connection for port)

COM 1 serial port
(ribbon cable connects
port to COM 1port on card)

Secondary (16-bit)
IDE hard disk interface

Primary (32-bit) IDE
hard disk interface

Floppy drive
interface

Parallel (LPT)
port

32-bit VL-Bus connector

16-bit ISA connector

Figure 2.19
A typical VL-Bus Multi-I/O card with IDE hard disk, floppy disk, and dual serial and single parallel ports. Although VL-Bus was originally designed for faster video cards, hard drive interface cards like this one were equally popular.

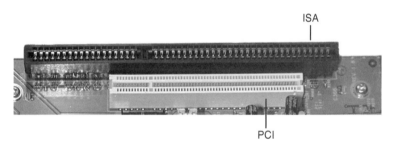

ISA

PCI

Figure 2.20
Note the narrow space between these slots of a typical ISA/PCI combo (shared) slot.

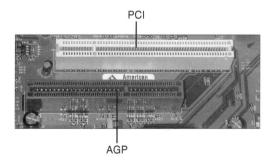

PCI

AGP

Figure 2.21
An AGP video slot (bottom) compared to a PCI slot (top); the AGP slot typically is a dark-brown plastic and is offset toward the middle of the motherboard compared to the PCI or ISA slots.

Figure 2.22 shows how typical AGP, PCI, and ISA cards compare to each other. Note that the components of AGP and PCI cards are on the opposite side from the components on ISA cards.

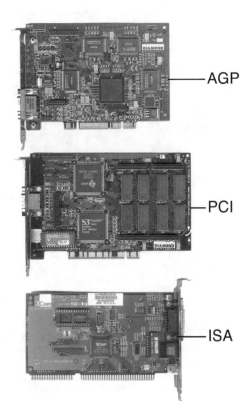

Figure 2.22
A typical AGP video card (top) compared to a typical PCI video card (middle) and a typical ISA network card (bottom).

Troubleshooting

Because the motherboard is the "home" for the most essential system resources, it's often the source of many different problems. Here are some typical problems associated with the motherboard that cause the system to lock up, and solutions for them. This section focuses on some common causes of problems that are likely to be covered on the A+ Certification exam.

For more information about troubleshooting CPUs, see *Upgrading and Repairing PCs, 12th Edition*, Chapter 3, "Microprocessor Types and Specifications." For more information about troubleshooting motherboards and expansion buses, such as ISA, PCI, and AGP, see *Upgrading and Repairing PCs, 12th Edition*, Chapter 4, "Motherboards and Buses."

Overheating of CPU or System

A system that overheats will stop operating, but not before serious damage can result. Most CPUs today are fitted with "active" heat sinks that contain a fan. If the fan stops working, an overheated CPU follows.

Fan failures can be caused by dirt in the fan, worn-out bearings, or a bad connection to the motherboard or drive-cable power. In most cases, it's better to replace the CPU fan than to try to clean it. If you must clean it

1. Remove the fan/heatsink from the CPU.
2. Place it on a surface covered with old newspapers or waste paper.
3. Blow it out with compressed air.

If you opt for a replacement, improve reliability and life by specifying a ball-bearing fan rather than the typical (and cheap) sleeve-bearing units.

Overheating can also be caused by a dirty power supply or case fan, or by missing slot covers. Clean or replace the fans, and replace the slot covers.

Don't overlook cleaning out the inside of the case, because a dirty case interior will eventually clog other components due to the system's airflow.

Corrosion on Memory Contacts

Memory contacts can become unreliable for various reasons (see "Troubleshooting," page 110 for details). If your system locks up

1. Remove the memory modules and gently wipe them off to remove any built-up film or corrosion. An Artgum eraser (but not the conventional rubber or highly abrasive ink eraser) can be used for stubborn cases.
2. Reinsert the modules and lock them in place.

Loose CPU and BIOS Chips

Some CPUs and all BIOS chips are installed in sockets without locking mechanisms. The cycle of heating (during operation) and cooling (after the power is shut down) leads to "chip creep," in which the chips gradually loosen in the sockets.

To cure chip creep, push the chips back into their sockets. Use even force or alternately push on each end of DIPs.

For more about cleaning the system, see "Dirt and Dust," page 239, and "Cleaning Equipment Safely," page 324.

Missing Slot Covers

Missing slot covers can cause your system to overheat and can cause components in your system to radiate radio-frequency interference (RFI) to other devices in your home or office.

Whenever you remove a card from a system, you should insert a slot cover in place of that card. Unlike some other components, slot covers can be interchanged freely among systems and should be kept for reuse when cards are installed in systems.

CH
2

Expansion Slot Blocked by CPU

Because of the location of the CPU socket on most Baby-AT motherboards, you might not be able to use 3/4-length or full-length cards in some slots on Baby-AT systems that use Pentium-class CPUs. Pentium-class CPUs must use large passive or active heatsinks to dissipate the heat produced during operation, and these heatsinks will cause the CPU assembly to block the slot.

The solution is to move the long card to another slot or to swap cards in slots until you find a combination that works properly.

Dead Short in System

A dead short in your system will prevent a computer from showing any signs of life when you turn it on. Leaving a loose screw inside the system and failing to fasten a slot cover or card in place are two common causes for dead shorts, because these problems can cause metal parts to touch live components on the motherboard.

The solution is to open the case and remove or secure any loose metal parts inside the system. Dead shorts can also be caused by power supply-related problems. For more about the power supply and dead shorts, see "Troubleshooting Power Problems" in Chapter 8.

Compatibility Guidelines

Before you purchase memory, card, or CPU upgrades for a system, check BIOS configuration and physical issues inside the case to be sure the upgrade will fit and work correctly. It might be necessary to "shuffle" cards or remove a card in a "combo" slot to free up the slot for its other use.

To determine compatibility with your system, you must do two things: Check the version of the standard supported by the card and motherboard, and check the physical dimensions of the card versus the actual clearances in the case.

Standards such as VL-Bus, PCI, and AGP have been available in multiple versions. Mismatching the versions supported by the card and the motherboard can result in problems. Some motherboards enable you to adjust the version support (such as PCI 2.0 versus PCI 2.1) in the BIOS setup program to solve problems. Some of the original AGP 1x cards will not work in Super 7 motherboards, but only in Pentium II or Celeron motherboards. Consult the card and motherboard vendors for specific requirements.

Three factors can prevent installation of a given card in a system: The card is too long for the slot due to obstructions, the slot is not available because it's a "shared" or "combo" slot and the other part of the combo slot is already in use, or the slot is blocked by a ribbon cable for an I/O port in another slot or on the motherboard.

Baby-AT is particularly vulnerable to blocked ISA or PCI expansion slots because of the location of the CPU (between the slots and the front of the case). Modern CPUs, with their heatsinks and cooling fans, can partially block up to three slots.

Most systems today often offer a mixture of ISA and PCI slots. A typical mixture is one AGP, five PCI, and one ISA, making seven physical slots, but only six slot covers are available on the back of the computer. The ISA and one of the PCI slots share a single slot cover, meaning that you can use either the ISA slot or the PCI slot. Many systems route extra ports on I/O cards or the built-in I/O ports on the motherboard to connectors on slot brackets.

To overcome these obstacles, try these suggestions:

- Open the system and check the usable length of these slots before you order or install the card. Move cards to different slots to free up space if necessary.

- Check the ratio of ISA to PCI card slots carefully before you order cards. PCI cards are available for almost any need (including modem and extra I/O devices) and PCI slots predominate on recent and current systems, so PCI cards should be your first choice. Use ISA cards only when you run out of PCI slots, and try to use "salvage" ISA cards from systems you have in storage or are about to scrap.

- Unscrew I/O ports from slot brackets and relocate to punchouts in the back of most cases.

Summary

The motherboard is the heart of the computer because it contains connectors for the CPU, main and cache RAM, I/O ports, and expansion slots. Motherboards can be categorized by their shape, the presence of I/O ports, their processor, and the type(s) of expansion slots they use.

The most important part of the motherboard is the CPU. CPUs can be classified by their internal and external clock speed, internal and external data bus, memory address size, and amounts of Level 1 and Level 2 cache.

Choosing the correct expansion cards for a particular task will improve system performance and allow for the best use of the system interior.

To prepare for the A+ Certification exam, review the major motherboard and CPU types by both their logical and physical characteristics. Make sure you can recognize the major CPU socket/slot types and the major expansion bus types. Review the CPU optimization methods and the CPUs that have both Level 1 and Level 2 cache on board, as well as those with only Level 1 cache on board.

QUESTIONS AND ANSWERS:

1. What are two differences between ATX and Baby-AT motherboards?
    A: (Any two of the following are acceptable.) Baby-AT motherboards are long, whereas ATX boards are wide. Baby-AT motherboards place the CPU in line with some expansion slots; ATX motherboards place the CPU in a separate area of the motherboard. Baby-AT motherboards don't always have built-in serial, parallel, and other ports, and must use ribbon cables between the motherboard and the connector; ATX motherboards connect built-in ports directly to the motherboard. ATX motherboards use a 20-pin power connector; Baby-AT motherboards use a 12-pin power connector. ATX systems use wider cases than Baby-AT systems.

2. Define the difference between motherboards and expansion boards.
    A: Motherboards contain system and expansion bus; expansion boards connect to the expansion bus. Motherboards connect with all parts of the system; expansion cards connect with the expansion bus and with the I/O devices they service.

3. Which of the following CPUs is a better choice for a memory-intensive application, a Pentium II 233MHz or a Celeron 300MHz? Why?
    A: The Pentium II 233MHz is a better choice because of its combination of Level 1 (32KB) and Level 2 (512KB) cache. The Celeron 300MHz lacks Level 2 cache, but the 300A has 128KB of Level 2 cache.

4. What type of connector is used for both mouse and keyboard?
    A: The mini-DIN or PS/2 connector can be used for both, but each connector is dedicated to one device or the other.

5. If a motherboard has four PCI slots and four ISA slots but there is virtually no clearance between one of the ISA and one of the PCI slots, how many usable slots does it have? Why?
    A: This system has only seven usable slots; the slots closer to each other than normal are "combo" slots. You can use either the PCI or the ISA slot, not both.

BIOS and CMOS Configuration

1. Explain the difference between BIOS and CMOS.
2. If you want the computer to test the memory, which type of boot process (warm or cold) will you want the customer to perform? Why?
3. If you have computers with a Phoenix BIOS and an AMI BIOS, will they have the same beep codes? Why or why not?
4. What type of device is needed to display BIOS error codes? What do you also need to understand the codes?
5. Which CMOS setup screen might need to be adjusted when using Windows 95, 98, or 2000?
6. If you have a bootable CD-ROM containing the original system setup, what BIOS option do you adjust if you need to restore the system with its original software? What should be listed first and second?

Introduction

Next to the CPU, the BIOS is the most important chip found on the motherboard. A firmware device, the BIOS provides vital services at bootup, hardware standards for your system and, through its configuration utility, many ways to customize your system. To understand the differences between hardware, software, and firmware, see "The Essential Parts of Any Computer," page 6.

The BIOS (Basic Input Output System) chip performs a variety of important tasks during system operation. On systems that use 32-bit versions of Microsoft Windows (Windows 95 or newer), the BIOS has relatively little to do with system operation after the boot process has been completed. However, during the boot process, the BIOS is an extremely critical component. Tasks that the BIOS chip performs include

- Configuration and control of standard devices
- The power-on self test (POST)
- The location of an operating system, to which it turns over control of the system by using the Bootstrap loader

The CMOS (Complementary Metal-Oxide Semiconductor) chip stores the settings that you make with the BIOS configuration program. The BIOS offers you many different options for most system components controlled by the BIOS, but until the settings are stored in the CMOS, the system is unable to run.

The BIOS and Standard Devices

The BIOS is a complex piece of firmware ("software on a chip") that provides support for the following devices and features of your system:

- Selection and configuration of storage devices, such as hard drives, floppy drives, and CD-ROM drives
- Configuration of main and cache memory
- Configuration of built-in ports, such as IDE hard disk, floppy disk, serial, parallel, PS/2 mouse, and USB
- Selection and configuration of special motherboard features, such as memory error correction, antivirus protection, and fast memory access
- Support for different CPU types, speeds, and special features
- Support for advanced operating systems, including networks, Windows 9x, and Windows 2000 (Plug and Play)
- Power management

Storing System Settings

To enable the BIOS to perform these tasks, two other components on the motherboard work with the BIOS: the CMOS chip, also known as the RTC/NVRAM

(Real-Time-Clock/Non-Volatile RAM), and the battery. The CMOS stores the settings that you make with the BIOS configuration program and contains the system's Real-Time-Clock circuit. Power from a battery attached to the motherboard is used by the CMOS to keep its settings. Figure 3.1 shows a typical socketed BIOS and battery. The A+ Certification test might ask you to identify these devices on a motherboard and to explain their operation.

Battery

BIOS

Figure 3.1
The CR2032 battery has become the most common removable battery on Pentium-class systems. The Award BIOS label lists support for "586" (Pentium-class) CPUs, PnP (Plug and Play for Windows 95), and PCI slots.

Most recent systems use various models of lithium batteries, which can last from two to five years. Figure 3.2 shows three of the many battery types used on motherboards over the years.

The most common batteries you will see in Pentium-class and newer systems are the DS12887A-type clock/battery chip seen in Figure 3.2 (left) and the CR-2032 lithium battery seen in both Figure 3.1 and Figure 3.2 (center). The AA-size Eternacell in Figure 3.2 on the right was used in many early 286- and 386-based systems made by Zenith Data Systems and others. Knowing that battery types can vary is not as important for the A+ Certification test as it will be for your day-to-day work.

Figure 3.2
The Dallas Semiconductor DS12887A (left) clock/battery chip, CR-2032 lithium battery (center), and the AA-size 3.6 volt Eternacell (right) have all been used in computers for maintaining CMOS settings.

When the battery starts to fail, the clock will start to lose time. Complete battery failure causes the loss of all CMOS configuration information. When this takes place, the system cannot be used until you install a new battery and re-enter all CMOS configuration information by using the CMOS configuration program.

Because the battery maintaining settings can fail at any time, and viruses and power surges can also affect the CMOS configuration, you should record important information before it is lost. See "Saving and Recording BIOS/CMOS Settings," later in this chapter, for details.

POST

The POST (power-on self test) portion of the BIOS allows the BIOS to find and report errors in the computer's hardware. For the POST to work correctly, the system must be configured correctly, as you will see in "System Configuration," later in this chapter.

The POST checks the following parts of the computer:

- The CPU and the POST ROM portion of the BIOS
- The system timer
- Video display card
- Memory
- The keyboard
- The disk drives

The system will stop the boot process if it encounters a serious or fatal error (see the following "Beep Codes" section). During the POST process, the BIOS uses any one of several methods to report problems:

- Beep codes
- Onscreen error messages
- POST error codes

Beep Codes

Beep codes are used by most BIOS versions to indicate either a fatal error or a very serious error. A *fatal error* is an error that is so serious that the computer cannot continue the boot process. A fatal error would include a problem with the CPU, the POST ROM, the system timer, or memory. The *serious error* that beep codes report is a problem with your video display card or circuit. Although systems can boot without video, seldom would you want to because you can't see what the system is doing.

Beep codes vary by the BIOS maker. Some companies, such as IBM, Acer, and Compaq, create their own BIOS chips and firmware. However, most other major brands of computers and virtually all "clones" use a BIOS made by one of the "Big Three" BIOS vendors: American Megatrends (AMI), Phoenix Technologies, and Award Software (now owned by Phoenix Technologies).

As you might expect, the beep codes and philosophies used by these three companies vary a great deal. AMI, for example, uses beep codes for over 10 "fatal" errors. It also uses eight beeps to indicate a defective or missing video card. Phoenix uses beep codes for both defects and normal procedures (but has no beep code for a video problem), and the Award BIOS has only a single beep code (one long, two short), indicating a problem with video.

Because beep codes do not report all possible problems during the startup process, you should not rely exclusively on beep codes to solve system problems.

You can hear some typical beep codes by using the CD-ROM included with this book.

Onscreen Error Messages

Most BIOS versions do an excellent job of giving you onscreen error messages indicating what the problem is with the system. These messages can indicate problems with memory, keyboards, hard disk drives, and other components. Some systems document these messages in their manuals, or you can go to the BIOS vendors' Web site for more information. Keep in mind that the system almost always stops after the first error, so a serious problem early in the boot process will stop the system before the video card has been initialized to display error messages.

POST Codes and POST Cards

In Chapter 1, "Basic Concepts," you learned about the different ways data passes through the system. One method, used by virtually all devices, is to send data through one of

65,535 I/O port addresses. The POST also uses an I/O port address (usually 80h), send-ing a series of codes indicating the progress of testing and booting. The hexadecimal codes output by the BIOS change rapidly during a normal startup process as different milestones in the boot process are reached. These codes provide vital clues about what has gone wrong when your system won't boot and you don't have a beep code or onscreen messages to help you.

To monitor these codes, you need a POST card such as the one shown in Figure 3.3, available from a variety of vendors, including JDR Microdevices (www.jdr.com) or Jensen Tools (www.jensentools.com). These cards are available in versions that plug into either ISA or PCI expansion slots. The simplest ones have a two-digit LED area that displays the hex codes, whereas more complicated (and expensive) models also have additional built-in tests.

The same hex code has different meanings to different BIOSes. For example, POST code 31h means "display (video) memory read/write test" on an AMI BIOS, but it means "test base and extended memory" on the Award BIOS, and it is not used on Phoenix BIOS. As with other types of error messages, check your manual or the BIOS maker's Web site for the meaning of any given code.

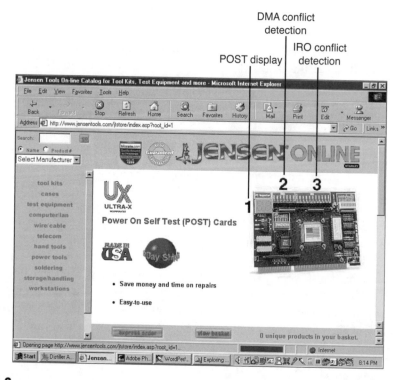

Figure 3.3
The Ultra-X PC Inspector card features POST display (1), DMA conflict detection (2), and IRQ conflict detection (3) among its many features.

The best way to learn to use a POST card is to plug it into a healthy system and watch the codes change during a normal system startup. Typically, the codes change very quickly until the final code (often "FF") is reached and the system starts. On a defective system, the codes will pause or stop when a defective item on the system is tested. The cards remove easily and need not be left in systems routinely.

To prepare yourself for the A+ Certification exam, make sure you can identify the three different methods computers use for identifying errors (beep codes, onscreen codes, and POST codes) and when each method is most appropriate for discovering why a computer cannot boot.

Transferring Control to the Operating System with the Bootstrap Loader

During the POST, drives and other standard devices have been detected. Frequently, information about the CPU, hard disk, floppy disk drive, memory size and type, and ports are displayed onscreen at the end of the POST (see Figure 3.4).

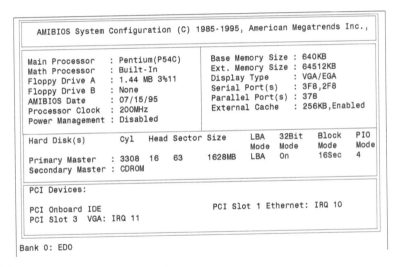

Figure 3.4
A typical Pentium-based system configuration screen displayed on system startup. Use this information for a quick view of the system's features, including CPU type and speed, RAM size and type, drive configuration, and more.

Next, the BIOS searches for an operating system on the drives listed in the BIOS configuration as bootable drives. The first drive containing an operating system will be used to start the computer, and at that point the BIOS transfers control of most of the computer to the operating system. The portion of the BIOS responsible for starting the system is called the *bootstrap loader* (from the old expression "pulling yourself up by your bootstraps").

For a more detailed look at how the startup process works after the BIOS locates the operating system, see *Upgrading and Repairing PCs, 12th Edition*, Chapter 25, "The Hardware Boot Process."

Warm and Cold Booting

A *cold boot* or *hard boot* refers to starting the computer with the power or reset switch, which runs the entire POST and bootstrap process. A warm boot or soft boot skips the POST and refers to restarting the computer with the MS-DOS Ctrl+Alt+Del key sequence or the Windows 9x/2000 Start, Shutdown, Restart menu. Figure 3.5 shows a typical screen displayed during a cold boot.

```
         American
         Megatrends      AMIBIOS (C)1996 American Megatrends Inc.,
AP53/AX53 R3.60    Aug.28.1996
65152KB OK
WAIT...
Pri Master: POIRA71A IBM-DJAA-31700
Pri Slave : Not Detected
Sec Master: 4.14     NEC                  CDROM DRIVE:251
Sec Slave : Not Detected




(C)  American Megatrends Inc.,
51-0411-001771-00111111-071595-82439HX-F
```

Figure 3.5
The screen during a cold boot. Note the memory test at the upper-left side.

On an MS-DOS–based system whose hard disk and floppy disk drives are connected to the motherboard, the BIOS is used to operate the drives. However, for systems using Windows 95 and newer, device drivers are loaded by the operating system to replace the BIOS. Still, without the BIOS, the system would not know what hardware was onboard or whether it was working.

System Configuration

For the BIOS to be able to start the computer, you've seen that it must find an operating system on a hard disk or floppy disk drive. But how does the BIOS know where the drives are located or what types they are?

Floppy disk drives and hard disk drives are two of the most important items that must be configured in the BIOS. If the drive types are not correctly identified in the BIOS, the BIOS will not be able to start the system. Whenever you build a system or change major components, you need to run the BIOS setup program to check or change settings.

Starting the Setup Program

On most systems built since the late 1980s, the BIOS configuration program is stored in the BIOS chip itself. On a few current systems, as with the original IBM AT, the setup program must be run from a floppy disk drive or the hard drive. The original IBM PC and PC/XT had only a few settings, and these were made by manipulating a series of small rocker or slide switches called *DIP switches*.

ROM-based setup programs are normally started by pressing one or more keys in combination within the first few seconds after turning on the computer. Although these keystrokes vary from system to system, the most popular keys on current systems include the escape (Esc) key, the Delete key, the F1 key, and various combinations of Ctrl+Alt+ another specified key. Most computers display the correct key(s) to press during the initial startup screen. Check with your system vendor for the appropriate keystrokes or to see if you need to run a program from MS-DOS or Windows to configure your system.

Because the settings you make in the BIOS setup program are stored in the nonvolatile RAM of the CMOS chip, the settings are often called *CMOS settings*.

In the following section, we will review the typical setup process, looking at each screen of a typical Pentium-class system.

Step-by-Step CMOS/BIOS Configuration

The A+ Certification exam will test your knowledge of basic CMOS/BIOS configuration. To help you prepare for the exam, this section covers the most important portions of the CMOS/BIOS setup process.

To start the CMOS setup process, press the correct key(s) during the bootstrap process or run the setup program from hard disk or floppy disk after the computer has started. On virtually all systems built since the early 1990s, you'll start with a menu screen, as shown in Figure 3.6. This menu, as well as the contents of the screens listed, will vary according to your BIOS brand, version, and motherboard type.

Select Standard CMOS Setup to begin.

Other systems will immediately display the Standard CMOS Setup screen, which is typically used to configure drive, date, and time settings.

Standard CMOS Configuration

The standard CMOS configuration screen (see Figure 3.7) includes settings for items such as

- Date
- Time
- Floppy disk drive types for drives A: (first floppy disk drive) and B: (second floppy disk drive)
- Hard drives connected to the IDE interface

To make selections here, you normally press keys to cycle through the different options, including date and time.

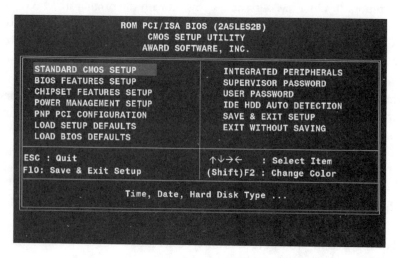

Figure 3.6
Select the menu item from this CMOS Setup menu to examine or change settings.

The time must be entered in the 24-hour format (1:00PM = 13:00, and so on). Enable daylight savings unless your state or area (Arizona, Hawaii, and parts of Indiana) doesn't switch to DST in the spring and summer.

Change the default floppy drive types to match your current configuration if necessary. See "Floppy Disk Drives," page 191, for details on selecting the correct floppy disk drive type.

To select the correct hard drive type, you can use one of three methods:

- Manually enter the correct settings.
- Use an auto-detection feature located here or from the main menu.
- Allow the system to detect the hard drives during every system boot.

Some systems also display the amount of memory onboard on this screen, but only extremely old systems based on 386 or older processors require that you manually enter the amount of RAM in the system. On virtually all systems using a 286 processor or better, the standard CMOS configuration screens are extremely similar, varying mainly in the number and types of drives that can be used.

The standard setup screen is the single most important screen in the entire BIOS/CMOS setup process. If the drives are not defined correctly, the system cannot boot.

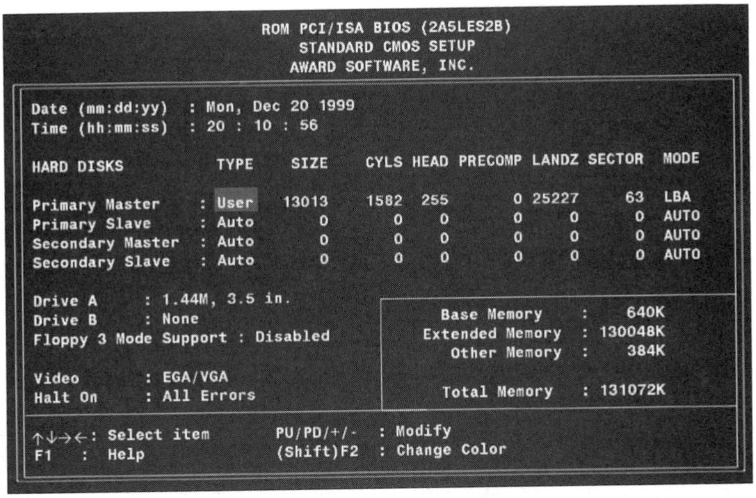

```
            ROM PCI/ISA BIOS (2A5LES2B)
                 STANDARD CMOS SETUP
               AWARD SOFTWARE, INC.

  Date (mm:dd:yy)  : Mon, Dec 20 1999
  Time (hh:mm:ss)  : 20 : 10 : 56

  HARD DISKS       TYPE    SIZE    CYLS HEAD PRECOMP LANDZ SECTOR  MODE

  Primary Master   : User   13013  1582  255      0 25227     63   LBA
  Primary Slave    : Auto       0     0    0      0     0      0   AUTO
  Secondary Master : Auto       0     0    0      0     0      0   AUTO
  Secondary Slave  : Auto       0     0    0      0     0      0   AUTO

  Drive A   : 1.44M, 3.5 in.
  Drive B   : None
  Floppy 3 Mode Support : Disabled      Base Memory     :    640K
                                    Extended Memory : 130048K
                                       Other Memory   :    384K
  Video     : EGA/VGA
  Halt On   : All Errors             Total Memory    : 131072K

  ↑↓→←: Select item    PU/PD/+/-  : Modify
  F1   : Help          (Shift)F2  : Change Color
```

Figure 3.7
A typical standard setup screen. On this system, hard drives can be detected during the
boot process ("Auto" setting), but they can also be user-defined, as shown here.

Automatic Configuration of BIOS/CMOS Settings

Many versions of the AMI and Award BIOS allow you to automatically configure all
screens except the Standard setup screen with a choice of these options from the main
menu:

- BIOS Defaults (also referred to as Original/Fail-Safe on some systems)
- Setup Defaults (also referred to as Optimal on some systems)
- Turbo

Use BIOS defaults to troubleshoot the system because these settings are very conservative
in memory timings and other options. Normally, the Setup defaults provide better performance. Turbo, if present, speeds up the memory refresh rate used by the system. As you
view the setup screens in this chapter, you'll note these options are listed. If you use
either automatic setup after you make manual changes, all your manual changes will be
overridden!

Appropriately, the graphical AMI WinBIOS uses a tortoise, a hare, and an eagle for these
three options.

With many recent systems, you can select Optimal or Setup Defaults, save your changes,
and exit, and the system will work acceptably. However, you might want more control
over your system. In that case, look at the following screens and make the changes
necessary.

CH
3

Advanced CMOS Configuration

The advanced CMOS configuration screen, shown in Figure 3.8, allows you to adjust optional details about the computer. In this screen, you can adjust the NumLock setting, type of video, keyboard repeats speed, settings for cache memory, and other special features. Most systems built since the early 1990s include this screen.

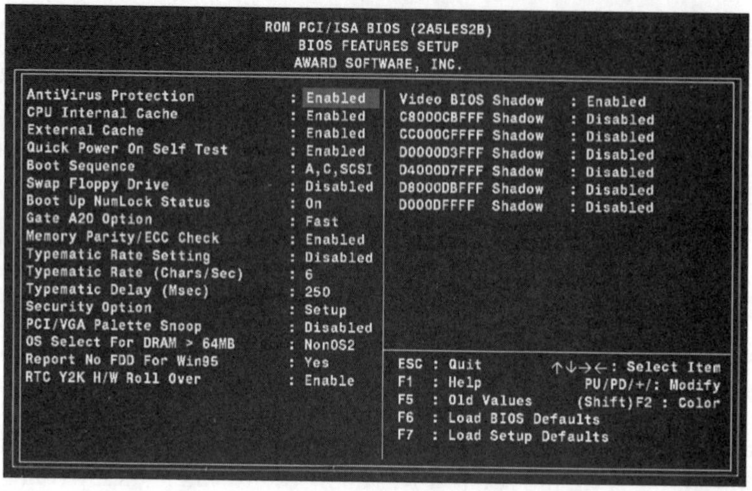

```
                    ROM PCI/ISA BIOS (2A5LES2B)
                        BIOS FEATURES SETUP
                        AWARD SOFTWARE, INC.

 AntiVirus Protection        : Enabled    Video BIOS Shadow    : Enabled
 CPU Internal Cache          : Enabled    C8000CBFFF Shadow    : Disabled
 External Cache              : Enabled    CC000CFFFF Shadow    : Disabled
 Quick Power On Self Test    : Enabled    D0000D3FFF Shadow    : Disabled
 Boot Sequence               : A,C,SCSI   D4000D7FFF Shadow    : Disabled
 Swap Floppy Drive           : Disabled   D8000DBFFF Shadow    : Disabled
 Boot Up NumLock Status      : On         DC000DFFFF Shadow    : Disabled
 Gate A20 Option             : Fast
 Memory Parity/ECC Check     : Enabled
 Typematic Rate Setting      : Disabled
 Typematic Rate (Chars/Sec)  : 6
 Typematic Delay (Msec)      : 250
 Security Option             : Setup
 PCI/VGA Palette Snoop       : Disabled
 OS Select For DRAM > 64MB   : NonOS2
 Report No FDD For Win95     : Yes        ESC : Quit         ↑↓→←: Select Item
 RTC Y2K H/W Roll Over       : Enable     F1  : Help         PU/PD/+/: Modify
                                          F5  : Old Values   (Shift)F2 : Color
                                          F6  : Load BIOS Defaults
                                          F7  : Load Setup Defaults
```

Figure 3.8

A typical Advanced CMOS Configuration screen, also known as the BIOS Features screen—use this screen to enable or disable anti-virus hardware features, adjust boot sequence, and adjust memory options such as cache and parity checking.

Table 3.1 lists the most important options and my recommendations.

Table 3.1   Recommended Advanced CMOS Settings

Option	Setting	Reason
Write-Protect Boot Sector, Virus Warning, or Antivirus Protection	Enable for normal system use	This doesn't really stop viruses, but it will help prevent users from accidentally FORMATting or FDISKing the hard disk.
Cache Internal and External	Enabled	Cache memory makes system faster (see "Adding Main and Cache RAM," page 54.
Boot Sequence	C: (first hard disk), A: (floppy disk drive), CD-ROM, C:, A:	Prevents users from booting with floppy floppy disk left in A: won't spread disks; boot sector viruses to the system; system won't stop if floppy disk is left in A:.
Shadowing	Enable for memory addresses containing firmware (BIOS) chips	Copies firmware contents such as system BIOS, video BIOS, and add-on card BIOS to RAM. Located between 640KB-1MB (upper memory blocks).

Table 3.1 continued		
Option	Setting	Reason
LBA mode	See "Overcoming Hard Disk Capacity Limitations with LBA Mode," page 211	

Depending on the system, you might be able to boot from CD-ROM, ZIP, or LS-120 drives in addition to the floppy disk drives and hard drives traditionally available as boot devices, as shown in Figure 3.9.

Depending on the BIOS version, you might need to press the ESC key, as in Figure 3.9, to return to the main menu, or use cursor keys to move directly to another menu screen.

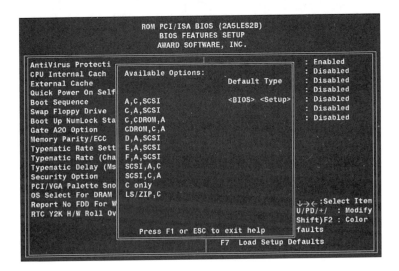

Figure 3.9
This recent Pentium-class system offers a variety of boot options. To view the settings for any CMOS configuration option, either use the help key (F1) as shown here, or press the correct key to step through the options for the setting.

Advanced Chipset/Chipset Features Configuration

The Advanced Chipset/Chipset Features Configuration screen, like the one shown in Figure 3.10, offers many advanced options that vary by the system. The following are some typical features of this menu:

- **Memory types, speed and timing**—Adjust the values here to match the memory installed in the system (such as parity, non-parity, SDRAM, EDO, and so on).

- **Cache adjustments**—Some Cyrix CPUs require the user to disable pipelining for proper operation.

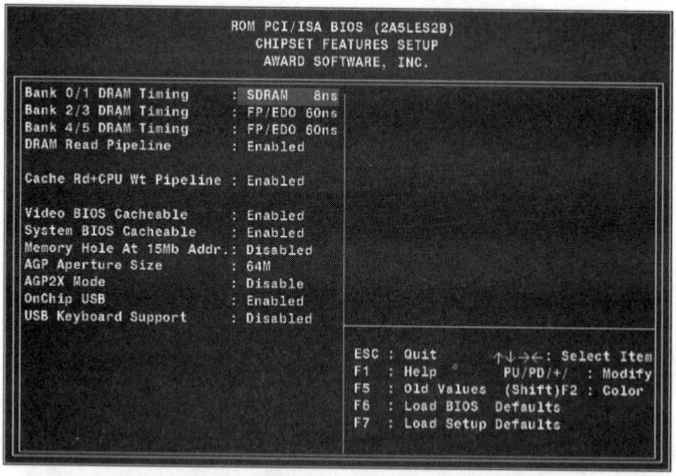

```
                    ROM PCI/ISA BIOS (2A5LES2B)
                       CHIPSET FEATURES SETUP
                        AWARD SOFTWARE, INC.

   Bank 0/1 DRAM Timing     : SDRAM   8ns
   Bank 2/3 DRAM Timing     : FP/EDO 60ns
   Bank 4/5 DRAM Timing     : FP/EDO 60ns
   DRAM Read Pipeline       : Enabled

   Cache Rd+CPU Wt Pipeline : Enabled

   Video BIOS Cacheable     : Enabled
   System BIOS Cacheable    : Enabled
   Memory Hole At 15Mb Addr.: Disabled
   AGP Aperture Size        : 64M
   AGP2X Mode               : Disable
   OnChip USB               : Enabled
   USB Keyboard Support     : Disabled

                                   ESC : Quit       ↑↓→←: Select Item
                                   F1  : Help        PU/PD/+/  : Modify
                                   F5  : Old Values  (Shift)F2 : Color
                                   F6  : Load BIOS  Defaults
                                   F7  : Load Setup Defaults
```

Figure 3.10
This recent system's USB (Universal Serial Bus) and AGP (Advanced Graphics Port) options are located on the Chipset Features configuration screen, along with the usual system and memory-timing options.

- **Configuration of USB ports**—If you upgrade a system to Windows 98 or Windows 2000, you might need to enable the USB ports; systems with older versions of Windows (which didn't support USB) might not have the USB ports enabled. The USB Keyboard Support feature must be enabled if a USB keyboard is installed to allow the keyboard to operate outside of Windows.

- **Configuration of the AGP slot**—Depending on the specific AGP video card installed (if any), you might need to set the size of the memory aperture used to transfer data between the system and the AGP port and select the AGP mode (1x, 2x, and 4x).

Power Management Configuration

Virtually all systems built since the mid-1990s are designed to allow power management; watch for the EPA "Energy Star" logo when you start the computer.

Power management works like this: After a user-defined period of inactivity, devices such as the monitor, the hard drive, or even the CPU will go into different low-power modes:

- **Standby mode**—Shuts off the hard drive and blanks monitor screens that use Display Power Management Signaling. Move the mouse or press a key to "wake up" the system.

- **Suspend mode**—Turns off the CPU clock to save even more power. Systems that fully support suspend mode allow you to choose a special shutdown option that "remembers" what programs and files were open, and can bring the system back to that state when the power is restored.

Early power-management systems require that you, the user, keep working with the mouse or keyboard to prevent the system from going into power-saving modes, which can cause modem or network transfers to be interrupted, losing data.

On most newer systems, such as the one featured in Figure 3.11, you can prevent the system from going into power-saving modes, or to wake up when activity takes place, by setting these options by either the device name (modem, hard drive, floppy disk drive, parallel port, serial port) or by the device's IRQ (see "IRQs, DMAs, I/O Port Addresses, and Memory Addresses," page 17).

I have always regarded power management as being a great idea that does not always work well in practice.

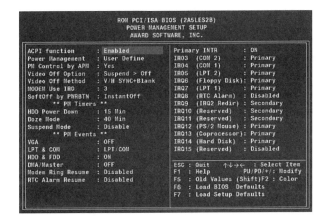

Figure 3.11
This recent system has support for both ACPI power management (used by Windows 98) and APM (used by earlier versions of Windows).

To make power management work, you need to make sure that

- Devices such as hard drives and monitors can be powered down and powered back up without loss of information.

- Power management is set to monitor network and Internet devices, such as modems and network cards, for activity to prevent the connection from being dropped.

- All devices installed in a system are monitored for activity to prevent data loss. For example, Figure 3.11 does not list IRQ 15 (used by the secondary IDE host adapter in most systems) as a PM (power management) event. Activity on IRQ 15 will not wake up the system, although the computer could be reading data from devices on IRQ 15 or saving data to devices on IRQ 15.

- Users understand how power management works.

Normal signs of power management in use include

- Monitors with blinking power lights, or power lights a different color than normal, while the screen remains blank
- Keyboards that seem "dead" for a few seconds after you start typing (because the hard drive must spin up)

Users who are unfamiliar with power management might panic and reboot the computers (losing their data!) or demand that you "fix" their systems. Sometimes, the best fix is to disable power management completely or to use Windows to configure power management settings through its Power icon in Control Panel. For systems that have ACPI-compatible BIOS chips that also run Windows 98 or Windows 2000, Windows should be used to manage power.

Adjust the system to the user's requirements, and continue.

PnP (Plug-and-Play) Configuration Screen

Plug-and-Play (PnP) configuration allows either the operating system or the system BIOS to select hardware settings for PnP-compatible cards when first installed and to change those settings when new cards are installed. PnP BIOS support has been part of virtually all systems shipped with Windows 95 or newer versions of Windows, and virtually all add-on cards and other devices (such as printers, monitors, modems, and so on) also support PnP configuration.

Early versions of the Plug-and-Play Configuration screen (see Figure 3.12) were introduced with the first Pentium-based systems with PCI slots, because PCI cards could configure themselves. PnP can be used with PnP-compatible ISA cards as well as with PCI and AGP cards. If you are using Windows 95, 98, or 2000, set Plug and Play Operating System to Yes. Unless you have problems with installing cards, that is normally all you need to set. If you are having problems adding cards, you can set IRQs to be available to PnP devices (add-on cards that are set by Windows) or to ISA/Legacy devices (ports built into the motherboard or ISA cards you must set manually).

Some systems, as in this example, also allow you to enable or disable IRQ use for USB, VGA video, and ACPI power management. You can disable IRQ usage for any or all of these devices, but some devices might not work if no IRQ is assigned.

Built-In Ports/Peripherals Setup

You can enable or disable most ports built into recent systems with the Built-in Ports/Peripherals Setup screen, shown in Figure 3.13. (Some systems with PS/2 mouse ports require that you adjust a jumper block on the motherboard.) On some systems, this screen also lets you adjust advanced hard disk options, such as PIO mode and block mode.

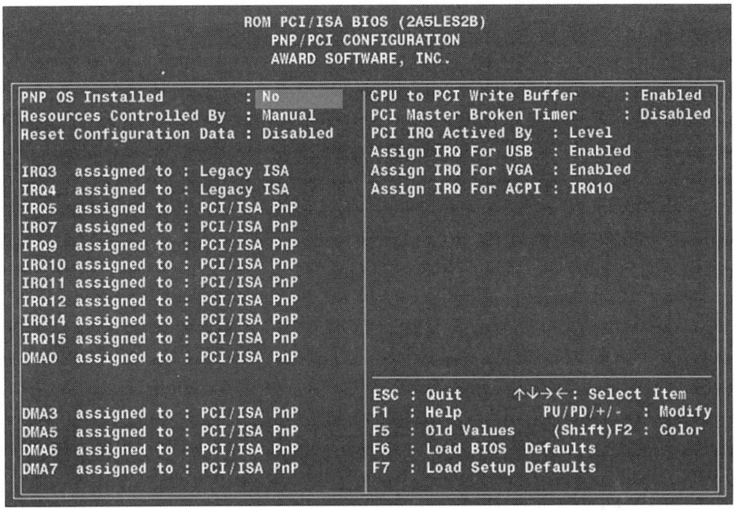

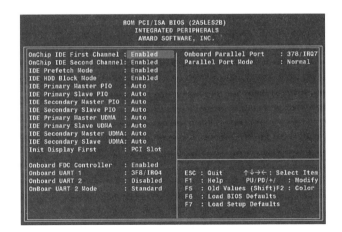

Figure 3.12
A typical Plug-and-Play configuration screen. By changing PnP options for IRQs and DMA channels to Legacy, you can reserve selected IRQs and DMAs for non-PnP cards.

Figure 3.13
This system's COM 2 port (UART 2) is disabled to allow an internal modem to be installed as COM 2.

Generally, you disable a built-in port if you add a card containing a port that will conflict with it. For example, you can disable COM 2 (serial port 2) to allow you to install an internal modem. You can also adjust the IRQ and I/O port addresses used by the built-in parallel and serial ports. On some systems, the LBA mode setting for hard disks and USB configuration options are also found on this screen. After observing or changing the settings, return to the main menu and continue.

See "IDE Performance Optimization," page 212, for information about hard disk options PIO mode and block mode.

Security/Passwords

You can enable two types of passwords on many systems: a power-on password that must be entered to allow any use of the system, and a setup password that must be entered to allow access to the BIOS/CMOS setup. If you don't have all the settings recorded (with screen printouts or by writing them down), this can be dangerous to enable.

Why? If the passwords are lost, users are locked out of the system, and you would need to remove the battery or use the "clear CMOS" jumper on the motherboard to erase the CMOS record of the passwords—and all other settings. This would require reconfiguring the system BIOS from scratch!

Because passwords are useful to prevent tampering with system settings, record the system information first, before you enable this feature.

Saving and Recording BIOS/CMOS Settings

Most BIOSes allow you to save your changes, or discard changes you might have made accidentally, when you exit the main menu and restart the system.

A few old BIOSes automatically save any changes, even bad ones. In either case, be sure to review the standard CMOS setup screen and any others you viewed to make sure the settings are acceptable before you save and exit. You should record critical BIOS settings, such as drive type information and any other changes from a system's default settings. Many technicians find it useful to add a sticker with drive type and other information to the rear of a system or to the inside of the system cover.

Getting Support for Your BIOS

Although BIOSes are developed by just a handful of companies (IBM, Compaq, and Acer develop for their own systems, and Phoenix, AMI, and Award for others and for "clone" motherboards), each BIOS is unique to the motherboard it's matched with. Therefore, for specific help with your BIOS (errors, configuring, troubleshooting), your best bet is to go back to the system or motherboard maker.

The relationship of BIOS makers and motherboard makers is similar to the difference between standard and custom vans.

A standard van is sold by a dealer who is associated with the van maker. This is similar to the situation with Compaq, IBM, or Acer PCs: The same company makes both the PC and its BIOS.

A custom van has been modified from a "bare-bones" cargo van and sold by a third-party company. If you're having problems with the van, it's no longer the van that Ford or Daimler/Chrysler produced. You must go back to the custom van maker for help. This is the situation with Phoenix, AMI, and Award BIOSes; they have been modified by the system and motherboard makers. The BIOS makers' Web sites can provide general help, but not the specifics of your system, because the BIOS is no longer their product after it goes on a motherboard.

BIOS Upgrades

During the lifetime of any computer, its BIOS might need to be upgraded. Upgrading the BIOS means to change its contents with software (if it is a flash BIOS) or to replace the physical chip (if it isn't a flash BIOS). Most systems sold since 1995 have flash BIOS chips that can be upgraded with software.

Because the BIOS chip bridges hardware to the operating system, you will need to upgrade the BIOS whenever your current BIOS version is unable to properly support

- New hardware, such as large IDE hard drives and ZIP/LS-120 removable-storage drives
- Faster CPUs
- New operating systems and features, such as Windows 98 and 2000, which feature ACPI power management
- New BIOS options, such as PnP support and Y2K compatibility

Although software drivers can be used as workarounds for hard drive and Y2K compliance, BIOS is best.

BIOS upgrades must be performed very carefully because an incomplete or incorrect BIOS upgrade will prevent your system from being accessed. Regardless of the method, for maximum safety I recommend the following initial steps:

- Back up important data.
- Record the current BIOS configuration, especially hard disk settings (see Chapter 7, "BIOS Configuration").

BIOS configuration information might need to be re-entered after a BIOS upgrade, especially if you must install a different chip.

Flash BIOS Upgrade

Before beginning a Flash BIOS upgrade, you must determine where to get your BIOS upgrade. The BIOS manufacturers (Phoenix, AMI, and Award/Phoenix) do not sell BIOS upgrades because their basic products are modified by motherboard and system vendors (see "Getting Support for Your BIOS" earlier in this chapter).

For major brands of computers, go to the vendor's Web site and look for "downloads" or "tech support" links. The BIOS upgrades are listed by system model.

If your system is a generic system (that is, it came with a "mainboard" or "motherboard" manual and other component manuals rather than a full system manual), you need to contact the motherboard maker. Some systems indicate the maker during bootup. Others display only a mysterious series of numbers. You can decode these numbers to get the motherboard's maker. See the following Web sites for details:

- Wim's BIOS page (www.ping.be/bios/)
- Phoenix Technologies' Award Software Manufacturers' Page (www.phoenix.com/pcuser/bios_award_vendors.html)
- American Megatrend's BIOS Support page (www.ami.com/support/bios.html)

Download the correct BIOS upgrade for your system or motherboard. For generic motherboards, Wim's BIOS page (www.ping.be/bios/) also has links to the motherboard vendors' Web sites.

You might also need to download a separate loader program, or the download might contain both the loader and the BIOS image. If the Web site has instructions posted, print or save them to a floppy disk for reference.

Next, install the BIOS upgrade loader and BIOS image to a floppy disk. Follow the vendor's instructions.

After installation is complete, restart your system with the floppy disk containing the upgrade. Press a key if necessary to start the upgrade process.

Some upgrades run automatically; others require that you choose the image from a menu, and prompt you to save your current BIOS image to a floppy disk. Choose this option if possible so you have a copy of your current BIOS in case there's a problem.

After the update process starts, it takes about three minutes to rewrite the contents of the BIOS chip with the updated information. *Don't turn off the power!* Wait for a message indicating the BIOS upgrade has been completed.

Remove the floppy disk and restart the system to use your new BIOS features.

Physical BIOS Chip Replacement/Update

On motherboards whose BIOSes can't be upgraded with software, you might be able to purchase a replacement BIOS from vendors, such as Micro Firmware (for Phoenix BIOS upgrades at www.firmware.com) or Unicore (for Award, AMI, and Phoenix BIOS upgrades at www.unicore.com).

Before you order a BIOS chip replacement, consider the following issues:

- BIOS chip upgrades cost about $60–$80 each.
- Although the BIOS will be updated, the rest of the system might still be out of date.
- For not much more than the cost of the BIOS chip itself, you might be able to purchase a new motherboard (without RAM or CPU) that will give you similar BIOS features as well as advanced features (PCI and AGP slots, built-in sound, and so on) that might be missing from your existing motherboard.

If you still need to update the BIOS chip itself, first verify that the vendor has the correct BIOS chip replacement. It might be a different brand of BIOS than your current BIOS. If so, make sure that you have recorded your hard drive information. You will need to re-enter this and other manually configured options into the new BIOS's setup program.

The vendor will identify the BIOS chip you need by the motherboard ID information displayed at bootup. Unicore Software offers a free download utility to display this information for you. To replace the chip, follow these steps:

1. Locate the BIOS chip on your motherboard after you open the case to perform the upgrade. It usually has a sticker listing the BIOS maker and model number.

2. The BIOS is a DIP-type chip. The vendor typically supplies a chip extraction tool to perform the removal.

To remove a DIP (used primarily for BIOS today), use the appropriately sized DIP puller tool if you have one. This tool resembles an inverted "U" with small flat hooks on each point. If a DIP puller is not available, you can use a pair of flat-bladed screwdrivers. Follow these steps:

1. Place one end of the tool between the end of the chip and the end of the socket; repeat for the other side.

2. If you are using the DIP puller, gently tighten the tool around the ends of the chip and pull upward to loosen; if you are using the screwdrivers, gently lift upward on both handles to loosen. Pushing down on the screwdriver handles could damage the motherboard.

3. Gently rock the ends of the chip to free it, and straighten any bent pins when you finish removing it.

4. Remove the existing BIOS chip carefully and put it on anti-static material in case you need to re-use it in that system.

5. Align the new BIOS chip's dimple with the matching cutout on one end of the socket.

6. Adjust the legs on the new BIOS chip so it fits into the sockets, and press it down until the legs on both sides are inserted fully.

7. Double-check the alignment and leg positions on the BIOS chip before you start the system; if the chip is aligned with the wrong end of the socket, you'll destroy it when the power comes on.

8. Turn on the system, and use the new BIOS's keystroke(s) to start the setup program to re-enter any information. You might get a "CMOS" error at startup, which is normal with a new BIOS chip. After you re-enter the BIOS data from your printout and save the changes, the system will run without error messages.

CH

3

BIOS Troubleshooting

Because the BIOS is the essential "glue" that joins hardware to the operating system, you need to know how to deal with errors. Follow these steps to solve BIOS problems.

Incorrect CMOS Configuration

If the system can't start after a BIOS upgrade or a battery replacement, the CMOS might be corrupted. Re-enter the correct settings, save changes, and restart. An onscreen error message will usually indicate a CMOS problem. Otherwise, the settings might have been adjusted by a user. Try using the BIOS Setup auto-configure options, double-check drive configurations, save changes, and restart.

Incorrect Flash BIOS or Failed Update

If you use the wrong flash BIOS file to update your BIOS, or if the update process doesn't finish, your system can't start. You might need to contact the system or motherboard maker for service. Some BIOSes contain a "mini-BIOS" that can be reinstalled from a reserved part of the chip. Systems with this feature have a jumper on the motherboard called the "flash recovery" jumper. Micro Firmware's Web site lists popular motherboards using Phoenix BIOSes that have this feature.

To use this feature, download the correct flash BIOS, make the floppy disk, and take it to the computer with the defective BIOS. Set the jumper to Recovery, insert the floppy disk, and rerun the setup process. Listen for beeps and watch for the drive light to run during this process, because the video won't work. Turn off the computer, reset the jumper to Normal, and restart the computer.

If the update can't be installed, your motherboard might have a jumper that write-protects the flash BIOS. Check the manual to see if your system has this feature. To update a BIOS on a system with a write protected jumper, you must

1. Disable the write-protection.
2. Perform the update.
3. Re-enable the write-protection to keep unauthorized people from changing the BIOS.

Summary

The BIOS contains a POST (power on self test) routine that tests memory, video, hard drives, floppy disk drives, and other important system components.

The BIOS also contains a bootstrap program that locates the operating system after the POST and transfers control to it.

The BIOS uses three methods to report errors: beep codes, onscreen error messages, and BIOS POST codes.

The BIOS contains tables of supported devices and options; the CMOS chip is used to store the options chosen with the BIOS setup program.

The CMOS chip is battery-backed.

You must verify correct floppy disk drive and hard drive configurations before a system can be started. These settings are found in the standard CMOS setup screen.

By making adjustments to other BIOS screens, you can adjust the performance of the system, configure the system for compatibility with Windows PnP-compatible boards, adjust or disable built-in ports, and control power management.

A BIOS needs to be upgraded when you want to use new hardware, new software, or new features not included in the current BIOS.

BIOS upgrades can be performed with software (flash BIOS) or by replacing the chip.

QUESTIONS AND ANSWERS:

1. Explain the difference between BIOS and CMOS.
   A: The BIOS contains options you select from; the CMOS stores the options you choose.

2. If you want the computer to test the memory, which type of boot process (warm or cold) will you want the customer to perform? Why?
   A: Have the customer perform a cold boot by shutting off the system and restarting it, or by using the reset button. Cold boots run the entire POST, including the RAM test, and warm boots don't.

3. If you have computers with a Phoenix BIOS and an AMI BIOS, will they have the same beep codes? Why or why not?
   A: They will not have the same beep codes because the BIOSes are designed to produce different beep codes.

4. What type of device is needed to display BIOS error codes? What do you also need to understand the codes?
   A: You need a POST card to display the codes and a list of codes specific to that computer, motherboard, or BIOS version to understand them.

5. Which CMOS setup screen might need to be adjusted when using Windows 95, 98, or 2000?
   A: The Plug and Play setup might need to be adjusted.

6. If you have a bootable CD-ROM containing the original system setup, what BIOS option do you adjust if you need to restore the system with its original software? What should be listed first and second?
   A: Change the boot order or boot sequence option in the Advanced Setup/CMOS Features screen. List the CD-ROM first, followed by C: (first) hard drive.

CH
3

RAM

1. Explain the difference between a SIMM and a DIMM.
2. Why is SDRAM faster than EDO RAM?
3. To add RAM to a system, you must know what two facts?
4. Where is Level 1 cache located?
5. List two places Level 2 cache can be located.
6. Where is Level 3 cache located?
7. What is a cache hit?
8. What is a memory bank?
9. How can caching be disabled?

Introduction

When it's time for the CPU to process something, RAM is the workspace it uses. Ever-increasing amounts of RAM are needed as operating systems and applications get more powerful and add more features. Because RAM is one of the most popular upgrades to add to any system during its lifespan, you need to understand how RAM works, what types of RAM exist, and how to add it to provide the biggest performance boost to the systems you maintain.

RAM is used for programs and data, and by the operating system for disk caching (using RAM to hold recently accessed disk sectors). Thus, a RAM increase improves transfers between the CPU and both RAM and disk drives.

Memory Types and Forms

Physical forms of RAM have changed greatly over the years since the first IBM PC was introduced. Throughout the 1980s, most systems used individual memory chips in capacities ranging from 64KB to 1MB. In the late 1980s, memory modules (multiple memory chips on a miniature board) became popular, and this type of memory is still the standard today, although specific forms and capacities are changing rapidly.

The same physical form (chip or module) can be used for RAM with different speeds, types, and sizes. Memory can also be purchased in forms that allow the system to detect or even correct memory errors.

To specify the correct memory for any given system, you must choose the correct options for that system, including the following:

- **Form factor**—Whether DIMM, SIMM, or another standard or proprietary type, the memory must be designed to fit into the memory upgrade sockets in the system.

- **Memory type**—You must install memory modules that contain memory chips of the types specified by the system. Normally, all memory in the system should use the same types of chips (EDO, SDRAM, DDR, RAMBUS RIMM, and so forth).

- **Memory speed**—Memory chips (and the modules created with those chips) have different speed ratings; you must choose modules that meet the speed requirements of the system you are upgrading. For best results, all memory should be the same speed.

- **Memory capacity (KB or MB)**—You must choose modules that meet the capacity requirements of the system you are upgrading.

- **Socket and module metals**—Whereas the latest RIMM and DIMM modules and sockets are all gold-plated, earlier SIMM modules and sockets could be either tin-plated or gold-plated. Mixing metals can cause long-term corrosion, leading to memory failures.

All of these factors must be specified correctly to get the correct memory for any given system.

Memory Banks

All memory must be added in "banks." A *bank of memory* is the amount of memory (in bits) equal to the data bus of the CPU. Therefore, a bank isn't a fixed amount of memory but varies with the data bus of the CPU. In other words, for a CPU with a 64-bit data bus (Pentium, PII, PIII, Celeron, K6, Athlon, and so on), a bank of memory is the total of one or more identical modules (same type, size, speed, and so on) that add up to 64 bits in width.

If your system needs multiple modules and you don't add the full number, the system ignores partial banks.

See the "Using a RAM Calculator" section later in this chapter to see how to use this information to determine how many modules to add to a system.

Memory Chips and Modules

The first fact you need to know when you order memory for a system is whether it uses memory in individual chips or in modules. The original form of memory used in the IBM PC, XT, and AT models and other computers of the time (early to mid-1980s) was individual RAM chips, ranging in size from 16KB to 1MB. Because memory chips are sized in bits, not bytes, it took multiple chips to reach a given capacity. Starting in the late 1980s, memory modules became popular and still are the most common type of memory used today.

Although chips are long superseded for current use, it's still helpful to see how memory chips were used in older systems because memory modules are multiple memory chips on small, easy-to-replace circuit boards.

Calculating Memory Sizes with Chips

In Chapter 1, "Basic Concepts," you learned that 8 bits make a byte. Most individual memory chips are 1-bit devices, although some were 4 bits (1 nibble) wide. If an old 386-based system uses 256Kb × 1 chips and it contains 1MB of memory, how many chips will the system require? Step-by-step, here's the math:

1MB = 1,024KB

1,024KB = 4 × 256KB

256KB = 8 chips × 256Kb per chip

1,024KB = 32 chips × 256Kb per chip

If the system had used 256Kb × 4 chips, the chip count would have been far lower:

256KB = 2 chips × (256Kb × 4) per chip

1,024KB = 8 chips × (256Kb × 4) per chip

Therefore, the system used either thirty-two 256Kb × 1 or eight 256Kb × 4 chips to achieve 1MB of RAM. However, when you actually open the system and look at the motherboard, you would probably find 36 or 12 chips rather than 32 or 8. The extra 4 chips aren't "spares"; instead, they provide a crude form of error-detection called *parity checking* that works with 9 bits of memory rather than 8.

Parity Versus Non-Parity Memory

Parity-checking works like this: Whenever memory is accessed, each data bit has a value of 0 or 1. When these values are added to the value in the parity bit, the result should be an odd number. This is called *odd parity*. A memory problem will typically cause the data bit values plus parity bit value to total an even number. This triggers a parity error, and your system halts with a parity-error message.

To fix this type of error, you must open the system, push all memory chips back into place, and test the memory thoroughly if you have no spares, or replace the memory if you have spare memory chips. Some systems' error message tells you the logical location of the error, so you could take the system documentation and determine which chip or group of chips to replace.

Parity-checking has always cost more because of the extra chips involved, and it fell out of fashion starting in the mid-1990s. Systems that lack parity checking freeze up when a memory problem occurs without any message onscreen.

Beyond Parity—ECC

For critical applications, network servers have long used a special type of memory called *ECC*, which stands for *Error Correcting Code* memory. This memory allows the system to correct single-bit errors and notify you of larger errors. More expensive systems today have optional ECC support that can require special ECC-compatible memory or use parity-checked memory along with special motherboard features to enable ECC. ECC memory actually corrects errors, unlike parity checking, which only warns you of memory errors.

This is recommended for maximum data safety, although parity and ECC do provide a small slowdown in performance in return for the extra safety. ECC memory modules use the same types of memory chips used by standard modules, but they use more chips and might have a different internal design to allow ECC operation.

Single and Multi-Bit Chips

With systems that used memory chips, there were two ways of installing memory to achieve parity. For systems that used 1-bit–wide chips, each group of memory sockets was a group of nine rather than eight, and each socket used an identical memory chip. For systems that used 4-bit–wide chips for data, memory was added in threes, with two sockets for the larger 4-bit–wide chips, and the third socket using a 1-bit–wide chip.

Multi-bit chips are still used today, no longer as chips, but in memory modules. Figure 4.1 compares a parity-checking module to a non-parity module.

Memory Module Types

All systems built since the early 1990s have used some form of memory modules, and most of these systems have used standard versions of these modules.

These modules come in these major types:

- **Single Inline Pin Package (SIPP)**—A short-lived variation on the 30-pin SIMM, which substituted pins for the edge connector used by SIMM modules.

- **Single Inline Memory Module (SIMM)**—Has a single row of 30 or 72 edge connectors on the bottom of the module. "Single" comes from the fact that both sides of the module have the same pinout.

- **Dual Inline Memory Module (DIMM)**—The most common form has 168 edge connectors on the bottom of the module. "Dual" comes from the fact that each side of the module has a different pinout.

- **Small Outline DIMM (SODIMM)**—A compact version of the standard DIMM module, available in both a 72-pin version and a 144-pin version for use in recent-model notebook computers.

- **Rambus Inline Memory Module (RIMM)**—A memory module using Direct Rambus memory (RDRAM) chips.

- **Small Outline RIMM (SORIMM)**—A compact version of the standard RIMM module.

CH

4

Figure 4.1

A parity-checked 30-pin SIMM module (top) and a non-parity 30-pin SIMM (bottom). Each SIMM uses two 4-bit chips for data, but the SIMM on top adds a 1-bit chip (at right) for parity checking.

All modules except for certain versions of the 30-pin SIMM and its sibling, the SIPP, use multi-bit chips to achieve their high capacities. IBM helped pioneer 30-pin SIMMs with its IBM XT/286 system introduced in 1986. Although some signals were different, these SIMMs looked the same as "generic" 30-pin SIMMs used by other computer makers. IBM also helped pioneer the 72-pin SIMM with its PS/2 line of computers introduced in 1987. The 286-based and 386-based systems in this line (Model 50 and above) were among the first to use the 72-pin SIMM, although it was several years before other systems adopted it.

SIMM modules containing 9 bits or multiples of 9 bits (36 bits) support either parity or ECC, depending on the system. DIMM modules with 72 bits support ECC error-correction.

SIMMs and DIMMs can have memory chips (often very thin) on one or both sides of their circuit boards. The difference is in the connectors: SIMMs have either 30-pin or 72-pin connectors and require two or more SIMMs to make the full data width of the Pentium class processor; DIMMs have 168-pin connectors, and each DIMM supplies the full data width for today's Pentium class processors. 72-pin SODIMM modules are 32-bit devices, and 144-pin SODIMM modules are 64-bit devices.

On Pentium-class systems, you need two 32-bit SIMMs to create the 64-bit memory bank needed. DIMM contain 64 bits of RAM (the equal of two 32-bit SIMMs) in one device.

Unlike the other memory module types listed here, RIMM and SORIMM modules use only Direct Rambus memory chips. Some systems require that RIMM and SORIMM modules be added in identical pairs, and others allow single RIMMs to be installed.

For more details about SIMMs, DIMMs, and RIMMs, see "Memory Module Form Factors" later in this chapter.

Memory Speeds

Memory chips, and the modules built from them, have become faster over the years. Memory speeds are rated in nanoseconds (ns). When you add memory to a system, you should follow two guidelines to ensure that the system will work properly after the memory upgrade is complete:

- New memory added to a system must be at least as fast as the existing memory.
- A smaller nanosecond (ns) rating equals faster memory. For example, memory rated at 8ns access time is faster than memory rated at 10ns access time.

Memory speeds are affected by the type of memory chips used in the module.

Memory Chip Types

Several different types of memory chips have been used in memory modules and as chips. Table 4.1 compares the features, uses, and speeds of the most popular chip types. Don't mix different types of memory in a system! Differences in timing will usually cause system crashes.

For the A+ Certification exam, you need to know the meaning of the major chip type names and their features. Most current systems use SDRAM DIMMs, and many older Pentium-class systems use EDO SIMMs.

Table 4.1 Major Types of Memory Chips

Memory Chip Type	Features	How Used	Typical Speeds
DRAM (Dynamic RAM)	"Dynamic" refers to the contents; this type of RAM requires frequent recharges of electricity to keep its contents valid	Memory chips in old systems; variations include FPM and EDO	100ns or slower
Fast-Page Mode DRAM ("standard SIMM memory")	Faster access than regular DRAM by using paging and burst-mode techniques	30-pin and 72-pin SIMM	70ns, 80ns, 100ns
Extended Data Out (EDO) DRAM	Faster access than FPM by overlapping accesses to different memory addresses	72-pin SIMM, some 168-pin DIMMs	60ns
SRAM (Static RAM)	Many times bulkier and more expensive than same quantity of DRAM; requires electricity much less often than any type of DRAM because it's made from transistors	Used for main memory in some early 386-based systems from PC's Limited (now Dell), Wyse, and others; used for memory cache in newer systems	10ns, 15ns, 20ns, and slower
SDRAM (Synchronous DRAM)	Much faster than older DRAM types by running in synch with the motherboard bus speed	Most 168-pin DIMMs	SDRAM is usually rated by motherboard speed, not by module speed. Motherboard speeds of 66MHz, 100MHz (PC-100), and 133MHz (PC-133) use different DIMMs
Double Data Rate SDRAM	Similar to regular SDRAM but makes two transfers per clock cycle	184-pin DIMMs	DDR-SDRAM is usually rated by motherboard speed; PC-200 (100 × 2) and PC-266 (133 × 2) are current types

CH

4

| Table 4.1 continued | | | |
Memory Chip Type	Features	How Used	Typical Speeds
RDRAM	16-bit memory chips make two 800MHz transfers over the Direct Rambus channel per cycle	168-pin RIMM	Empty RIMM module sockets must be occupied by a continuity module (which resembles a RIMM, but without RDRAM chips); memory is rated by 2x motherboard speed; common are PC-600, PC-700, and PC-800

Memory Module Form Factors

Each of these module types uses a different motherboard connector. Table 4.2 compares the bit widths, sizes, types, and speeds of popular memory modules.

The first major use of 30-pin SIMMs was in the IBM XT/286, a lower-cost version of the IBM AT introduced in 1986. The 30-pin SIMMs used by IBM had different signals on five pins than the so-called "generic" SIMMs used by systems such as the Compaq 386s and many others. This type of memory fell out of favor in the early 1990s because four of these SIMMs were required to make a single bank of memory with a 486-class CPU.

The first major use of 72-pin SIMMs was in the IBM PS/2 Model 50 and above, introduced in 1987. Figure 4.2 shows a side-by-side comparison of a 72-pin SIMM and 30-pin SIMMs. 72-pin SIMMs became the standard in later-model 486s and most Pentiums. The rise of the Pentium II in the late 1990s has caused this type of memory to also begin to go out of fashion. See Figure 4.3 for examples of 30-pin and 72-pin SIMMs.

The 168-pin DIMM was introduced with the first Pentium II-based systems, and it is also standard on the Pentium III, Celeron, AMD Athlon, and most Super Socket 7 systems. See Figure 4.4 for an example of a 168-pin DIMM, the most common module in use since 1998.

Some recent systems use 168-pin RIMM modules or 184-pin DDR SDRAM DIMMs. See Figures 4.5 and 4.6 for examples of these memory modules. For the A+ Certification exam you should be able to distinguish these modules from each other by appearance, data bus width, and speed.

Figure 4.2
A typical single-sided 72-pin SIMM (top) compared to 30-pin SIMMs (middle and bottom). Note the cutout on the left side of each SIMM; this is a keying feature to prevent improper insertion of the SIMM into its socket.

Figure 4.3
A typical 168-pin SDRAM DIMM module. The three different-sized contacts on the bottom assure reliable keying during installation.

Table 4.2   Major Types of Memory Modules

Memory Module Type	Bit Widths	Common Sizes (KB/MB)	Common Type	Common Speeds
SIPP (Single Inline Pin Package)	8-bit, 9-bit*	256KB, 1MB	FPM	100ns, 80ns
SIMM (Single Inline Memory Module)—30 pin	8-bit, 9-bit*	256KB, 1MB, 4MB	FPM	100ns, 80ns, 70ns
SIMM—72 pin	32-bit, 36-bit*	512KB, 2MB, 4MB, 8MB, 16MB, 32MB	FPM, EDO	100ns, 70ns, 60ns

Table 4.2   continued

Memory Module Type	Bit Widths	Common Sizes (KB/MB)	Common Type	Common Speeds
DIMM (Dual Inline Memory Module)—168 pin	64-bit, 72-bit*	32MB, 64MB, 128MB, 256MB	EDO, SDRAM	60ns (EDO) 15ns and faster (SDRAM)
RIMM (Rambus Inline Memory Module)—168 pin	128Mbit, 144Mbit*	32MB, 64MB, 128MB, 256MB, 512MB	RDRAM only	PC-600 PC-700 PC-800

Allows parity checking or ECC error-correction if supported by motherboard.

Figure 4.4
A typical 168-pin RIMM RDRAM module. (Photo courtesy Micron Technologies.)

SODIMMs are small versions of DIMMs used mainly in notebook computers. SIPPs resemble 30-pin SIMMs but had projecting pins on the bottom of the module in place of edge contacts; they were seldom used.

Figure 4.5
A typical 184-pin DDR SDRAM module. (Photo courtesy Micron Technologies.)

Specifying Memory for a Given System

When you must specify memory for a given system, there are several variables you need to know:

- Memory module type (72-pin SIMM, EDO, SDRAM, and so on)
- Onboard memory type (FPM, EDO, SDRAM, and so on)
- Memory module speed (70ns, 60ns, PC-100, and so on)
- Error-checking (parity, non-parity, ECC)
- Allowable module sizes and combinations (see motherboard documentation)
- The number of modules needed per bank of memory
- The total number of modules that can be installed

Using a RAM Calculator

If you know two variables about a system, you can determine how many memory modules that system needs. You need to know the following:

- The system's data bus width (in bits)
- The data bits in each memory module your system uses (ignore parity or ECC bits if any)

To calculate the amount or number of memory modules that your system needs, divide the data bus width (D) by the number of bits per memory module (M) that your system uses. The result will be the number of modules needed (N). Table 4.3 shows sample calculations.

Table 4.3   Calculation of Memory Modules Needed

CPU's Data Bus Width (D)	Bits per Module (Module Type) (M)	Calculation D/M	Number of Modules Needed = N
64-bit Pentium, PII, PIII, others	64-bit (DIMM module)	64/64	1
64-bit Pentium, PII, PIII, others	32-bit (72-pin SIMM)	64/32	2
32-bit 486, 386DX	32-bit (72-pin SIMM)	32/32	1
32-bit	8-bit (30-pin SIMM or SIPP)	32/8	4

Figure 4.6 illustrates how a 64-bit CPU (such as a Pentium) accesses RAM. Only 32 bits of data can flow to a 72-pin SIMM, so a pair must be used to form a bank of RAM (represented by illustration A as shown in Figure 4.6).

This formula also works for systems using memory chips, but keep in mind that many of those old systems use mixtures of 4-bit and 1-bit chips.

Buy the largest-capacity modules you can that will work with the system. For example, it's better to use a single 128MB DIMM module than to use two 64MB modules if you need to add 128MB of RAM to a system. This allows you to use fewer modules, which reduces heat and can leave room for additional memory upgrades in the future. However, many older systems can't use the full capacity of newer, larger modules of the same connector type; check the system manual to verify which sizes will work in a given system.

On systems that use RIMM RDRAM modules, you will need to consult the system manual for the details of adding memory. Although each RIMM can function as a bank, some systems use a memory access technique called interleaved memory, which requires that a pair of identical RIMMs be installed in the system.

Specifying Memory Modules

To specify 30-pin SIMM memory modules, provide the following information:

- Size (KB or MB)
- Parity or non-parity
- Number of chips (3-chip and 9-chip are both parity-checked; 2-chip and 8-chip are non-parity; don't mix 2/3 chip and 8/9 chip modules due to timing differences)

■ Speed (ns)

■ Connector metal type (tin or gold; should match motherboard socket)

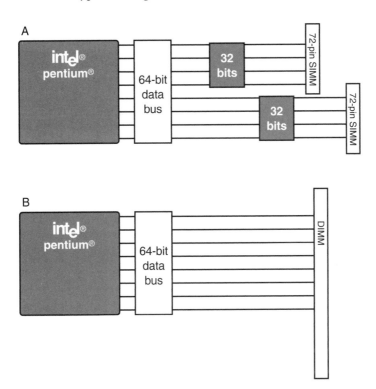

Figure 4.6
A 64-bit CPU (such as a Pentium) accesses RAM by using a pair of 72-pin SIMMS to form a bank of RAM (illustration A). Compare that to a single DIMM, in which the DIMM has the same width (64 bits) as the CPU (illustration B).

Table 4.4 shows some examples of 30-pin SIMM specifications. These modules are very expensive to purchase new. Try to obtain them by salvage or from other computer users; many of these are lying around computer shops or repair centers today because they are obsolete.

Table 4.4	Specifying 30-Pin SIMMs (Examples)				
Size	Parity/ Non-Parity	Chip Count	Speed	Connector Type	Standard Designation
4MB	parity	3 chip	70ns	tin	4Mx9-70x3 tin
256KB	non-parity	8 chip	80ns	gold	256Kx8-80x8 gold

To specify a 72-pin SIMM, the information needed is similar, but you don't need to specify the chip count. Instead, you specify the memory type. Multiply the first number listed in the standard designation by 4 to get the actual size of the module. 32 is the number of data bits; 36 is the number of data plus parity bits. Table 4.5 shows some examples of 72-pin SIMM specifications.

Table 4.5 Specifying 72-Pin SIMMs (Examples)					
Size	*Parity/ Non-Parity*	*Memory Type*	*Speed*	*Connector Type*	*Standard Designation*
4MB	non-parity	FPM	70ns	tin	1Mx32-70 tin
16MB	parity	EDO	60ns	gold	4Mx36EDO-60 gold

To learn more about the problems that can result from mixing tin and gold connectors, see "Avoid Mixing Metals in RAM and Sockets" later in this chapter.

To specify SDRAMs, you must specify the following:

- Size (MB)
- Non-parity (64-bit), ECC (72-bit)
- Motherboard speed (66MHZ, 100MHz, 133MHz)
- Voltage (3.3 volts for PCs)
- Buffered, unbuffered, registered
- Standard (168-pin) or DDR (184-pin)
- CAS Latency (CL2 is faster than CL3)

CAS Latency refers to how quickly a memory module can prepare data for use by the PC. Most systems are designed to use CL3 memory, but CL2 memory is somewhat faster. Check the system documentation to determine the specific SDRAM memory modules needed for a given system.

SDRAM DIMMs made for 66MHz-bus CPUs, such as Celerons or Pentium IIs running at 333MHz or less, are often referred to as PC-66 DIMMs. SDRAM DIMMs made for 100MHz-bus CPUs, such as Pentium IIs running at 350MHz or faster, are referred to as PC-100 DIMMs. SDRAM DIMMs made for 133MHz-bus CPUs, such as the 733MHz and faster Pentium III "Coppermine" CPUs, are referred to as PC-133 DIMMs.

Because of the many options you specify, these modules are normally ordered by indicating the motherboard or system rather than by specifying a standard module type, as with SIMMs (earlier in this section). Although it's easy to interchange SIMMs, the many differences in DIMMs make "harvesting" them from older systems for newer systems risky.

Installing SIMMs

As with any device, correct orientation of memory modules with their sockets is critical both for your real-world work and for the A+ Certification test.

SIMM modules have one end with a cut off lower corner, corresponding to a projection, or "bump," at the matching end of the SIMM socket. This provides a keying mechanism designed to keep you from installing the SIMM backward.

To install the SIMM

1. Line up the cutout end of the SIMM with the correct end of the socket.

2. Insert the SIMM at a 35-degree angle, ensuring that the connector is solidly in the socket, as shown in Figure 4.7. Do not touch the tin or gold-plated connectors on the bottom of the module; this can cause corrosion or ESD.

3. Push the top of the SIMM until the SIMM is aligned with the socket and is locked in place. If the SIMM slips out of the socket, double-check the orientation. The "bump" on the keyed end of the SIMM will force an incorrectly aligned SIMM out of the socket.

Figure 4.7
With either a 30-pin or 72-pin SIMM (shown here), insert the SIMM at an angle into the SIMM socket.

Some SIMM sockets are at a 90-degree angle to the motherboard, but many 30-pin SIMM sockets on motherboards or on expansion cards are at a 30-degree angle to the motherboard or expansion card. Determine the approximate insertion angle from the socket, not the board.

If you need to install two or more SIMMs, make sure you install the SIMMs that will be blocked by other SIMMs first so you don't need to remove any modules to complete the installation.

Installing DIMMs

DIMM sockets have an improved keying mechanism and a better locking mechanism compared to SIMMs.

To install the DIMM

1. Line up the DIMM's connectors with the DIMM socket. Note that the DIMM and its connector have three sections: short, medium, and long (see Figure 4.8).

2. After verifying that the DIMM and its socket match, push the DIMM straight down into the socket until the swivel locks on each end of the socket snap into place at the top corners of the DIMM module. Do not touch the gold-plated connectors on the bottom of the module; this can cause corrosion or ESD.

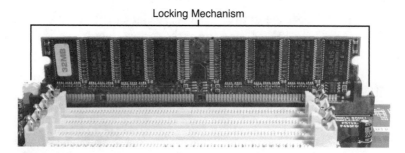

Locking Mechanism

Figure 4.8
A typical SDRAM DIMM is shown partway down in its socket. Note the position of the swivel lock on the left side of the socket.

Cache RAM and Main Memory

As you learned in Chapter 2, "The Motherboard and CPU," CPUs with Level 1 and/or Level 2 cache RAM perform RAM-bound operations much more quickly than CPUs that lack cache.

The order in which the CPU accesses memory is Level 1 cache, then Level 2 cache (if necessary), and finally, main memory (if necessary). This process is detailed here:

1. Level 1 cache is checked. If the desired memory location is here, this is a cache "hit" and the CPU uses it.

2. If the desired memory location is not found here, this is a cache "miss" and the CPU then checks Level 2 cache.

   If the desired memory location is here, this is a cache "hit" and the CPU uses it.

3. If the desired memory location is not found here, this is a cache "miss" and the CPU then retrieves the location from main memory.

4. Both caches are refreshed with the latest information when the CPU fetches information from main memory, enabling the CPU to use cache memory successfully on future memory accesses (see Figure 4.9).

Locations for Level 2 Cache

As you learned in Chapter 2, Level 2 cache refers to high-speed memory outside the CPU core.

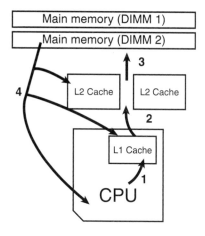

Figure 4.9
The CPU accesses Level 1 cache (1), then Level 2 cache (2), and then main memory (3) in search of required information. If the CPU must access main memory, it refreshes both caches when it retrieves the information (4).

Although the Intel Pentium Pro, Pentium II, Pentium III, most Celerons, AMD K6III, Athlon, and Duron CPUs contain their own Level 2 cache, Level 2 cache can also be present on Pentium-class and older systems. In these cases, the Level 2 cache, if present, is found on the motherboard. Therefore, to improve system performance, you should add Level 2 cache to the motherboards of systems whose CPUs don't provide it.

256KB Level 2 cache is adequate to cache up to 64MB of RAM; for higher amounts of RAM, upgrade to 512KB or 1MB of Level 2 cache (on motherboard) if possible.

Table 4.6 lists the types of Level 2 cache and the systems on which they can be found. To prepare for the A+ Certification exam, you should be prepared to identify the different types of Level 2 cache memory visually.

Table 4.6   Level 2 Cache Types and Uses

Cache Type	Details	Sizes	Typical Systems
SRAM chips (Figure 4.10)	4 or 8 data chips, 1 TAGRAM chip usually socketed	64KB, 256KB	486 and early Pentium
COAST module (Figures 4.11, 4.12)	Dedicated slot	256KB	Late-model 486 and some Pentium
Pipeline-burst chips (Figure 4.13)	Rectangular surface-mount chips on motherboard	256KB, 512KB, 1MB	Late-model Pentium, K6

CH
4

Empty SRAM cache sockets (4)   SRAM chips installed as cache RAM (4)

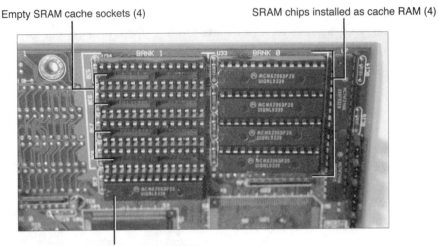

SRAM chip installed as TAG RAM (1)

Figure 4.10
A bank of SRAM cache chips. SRAM cache requires a TAG RAM chip (lower left) and four or eight SRAM chips for data caching (right).

COAST cache module

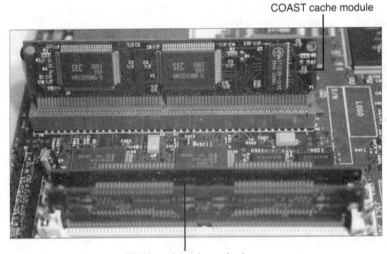

SIMM modules (rear view)

Figure 4.11
A COAST cache module is shown inserted into its socket. A COAST module resembles a SIMM but is taller and has a different connector.

Some systems offer both SRAM sockets and a COAST module socket. The COAST module is recommended for reliability and speed because it normally uses pipeline-burst cache, which is significantly faster than SRAM cache.

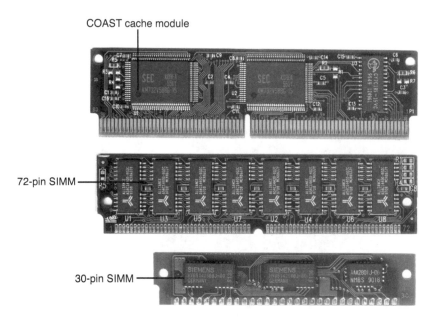

COAST cache module

72-pin SIMM

30-pin SIMM

Figure 4.12
A COAST cache module (top) is compared to a 72-pin SIMM (middle) and a 30-pin
SIMM module (bottom).

The most recent Socket 7 and Super Socket 7 motherboards have fixed amounts of Level
2 cache provided by pipeline-burst cache chips surface-mounted to the motherboard, as
seen in Figure 4.13. Unless the motherboard also features a slot for a COAST cache module, you cannot add cache memory to these motherboards. A motherboard replacement
will be necessary to upgrade the Level 2 cache.

Upgrading Cache RAM

Three methods can be used to upgrade cache RAM:

- Add SRAM cache chips or a COAST cache module to the motherboard.
- Replace the motherboard.
- Replace the CPU.

The best option depends on the exact hardware the system has. Look at the scenarios in
Table 4.7 for guidelines you can use.

CH

4

Socket 7 Pentium MMX CPU (without heatsink) Voltage regulator for Socket 7

Pipeline-burst
cache memory chips

Figure 4.13
A typical Socket 7 motherboard with 256KB of pipeline-burst cache built in.

Table 4.7   Cache Upgrade Scenarios

CPU	Current Level 2 Cache	Cache Options on Motherboard	Best Cache Upgrade
Pentium 100	128KB	COAST socket (occupied)	Replace COAST module with 256KB or 512KB module (check documentation); replace CPU with K6III CPU (has 256KB Level 2 cache onboard) in upgrade module
486-DX2 66MHz	None	Sockets for 256KB SRAM chips	Install 256KB SRAM chips
Celeron 300MHz	None	None	Replace CPU with Celeron 300A or faster (128KB Level 2 cache onboard) or Pentium II (512KB cache onboard)
Pentium 233MHz	256KB	None (cache is surface-mounted)	Replace motherboard with new motherboard containing 512KB or 1MB cache

In some cases, the only way to increase Level 2 cache is to replace either the motherboard or CPU.

See "Internal CPU Characteristics Affecting Performance," page 44 for more information on CPUs that contain Level 2 cache.

Installing SRAM Chips

SRAM chips, such as those seen in Figure 4.10, are used for cache memory in many older Pentium-based systems. To install these chips, follow this procedure:

1. Match the semicircular dimple at one end of the chip to the small semicircular cutout at one end of the socket.

2. Align the legs of the chip with the socket's connectors.

3. Gently press the chip into place by pressing with your thumb alternately at one end then the other end of the chip.

4. Stop and withdraw the chip if any pins are bent; straighten the pins and continue.

5. Press the chip all the way into the socket.

6. Repeat as needed to populate all sockets needed for the amount of cache memory you are installing.

CH
4

7. Adjust jumpers on the motherboard to indicate the amount of cache memory present.

8. Start the system BIOS setup program and verify that external (Level 2) cache is enabled.

Installing a COAST Module

COAST modules, such as those seen in Figures 4.10 and 4.11, are used to provide cache memory on many Pentium-based systems. To install a COAST module, follow this procedure:

1. Align the long and short sides of the COAST module with the corresponding motherboard connector. Do not touch the gold-plated connectors on the bottom of the module; this can cause corrosion or ESD.

2. Push the COAST module straight down into the connector.

3. Adjust jumpers on the motherboard to indicate the amount of cache memory present.

4. Start the system BIOS setup program and verify that external (Level 2) cache is enabled.

Troubleshooting

Because all information you create with a computer starts out in RAM, keeping RAM working properly is very important. The A+ Certification exam covers troubleshooting of all major system modules, including memory. Study the problems and solutions in this section to help prepare for memory troubleshooting questions that might be on the exam.

Avoid Mixing Metals in RAM and Sockets

Two types of metal are used for contacts on SIMMs: gold and tin. Putting gold-tipped SIMMs in tin sockets or tin-tipped SIMMs in gold sockets is asking for corrosion and eventual system lockups. Match the metal to avoid problems. If you have systems that have mixed metals and you can't change them, periodically remove the memory modules, wipe off the contacts carefully, and reinstall them.

Avoid Mismatching RAM Speeds

Motherboards are designed to use particular speeds of memory modules, and all memory modules installed in a computer should meet or exceed the memory speed required by the system. Depending on the system, memory might be rated in nanoseconds (ns) or by the bus speed of the CPU (such as PC-100 or PC-133).

If memory is installed that is slower than the system is designed to handle, some systems might slow down automatically to adjust to the slower access time, but others might crash as soon as the slower memory is accessed. Some systems allow you to adjust the speed of each memory bank, and others assume all memory is the same speed. Figure 4.14 shows some common memory-chip speed markings.

Memory speeds are listed on the memory chips themselves, either individual chips or those found on modules.

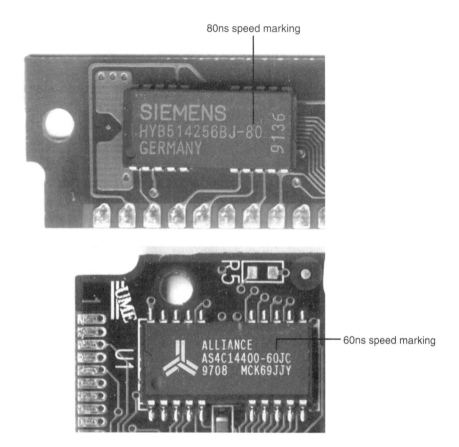

Figure 4.14
Read the chip speeds on SIMMs or DIMMs to determine their speed. The 30-pin SIMM at the top is an 80ns unit. The 72-pin SIMM at the bottom has faster RAM, running at 60ns.

Although the listing varies, most often it's the last two numbers (often following a dash) on the memory module: xxxxx - 15 (15ns) yyyyyyyy - 60 (60ns). Some old memory used an abbreviated marking: xxxxx-7 (70ns) yyyyy - 10 (100ns).

To verify speeds, you can use a RAM tester. For more information about testing RAM with both diagnostics software and hardware testing devices, see "Other Methods for RAM Testing," later in this chapter.

EDO Compatibility with Other RAM Types

Although DIMM modules are available in both SDRAM and EDO types, and many motherboards can use one or the other, don't mix them. Their timings aren't compatible; EDO RAM has an access speed of 60ns, while SDRAM has access speeds of 15ns or less, depending on whether it is PC-66, PC-100, or PC-133 compatible.

EDO memory can be used with FPM memory if the memory is in separate banks. EDO will be forced to slow down to match FPM's slower access. Some systems require that you enable EDO support in the BIOS setup.

"Parity Error—System Halted"

Parity errors halt your system and require you to restart your computer. To use parity checking, you must be using parity-checked RAM (x9 or x36 module types). Parity error can result from

- Mixing parity and non-parity RAM on parity-checked systems
- Mixing slow and fast RAM in the same bank or on the same motherboard
- Loose or corroded chip and module connectors

If you enable parity checking in the BIOS setup and don't have parity modules, you'll have immediate errors. You can use parity memory along with non-parity memory by disabling parity checking.

RAM Sizing Errors at Bootup

Most systems test memory, and many will alert you to a change in the memory size detected compared to the BIOS value. To determine which module is affected

- Note the memory count reached onscreen when the memory error is detected.
- Check the motherboard documentation to see which modules must be installed first.
- Change one module at a time, starting with the one you think is defective, until the error goes away.
- Disable cache RAM in the BIOS setup when testing memory.

A memory-sizing error that won't go away after all memory is changed might indicate a defective motherboard or defective cache memory.

Determining Whether Cache RAM Is the Source of a Memory Problem

Because cache RAM holds a copy of the information in main memory, errors in cache RAM can appear to be errors in system RAM. Use the following procedure to determine whether cache RAM is the cause of a memory problem:

1. Disable the external cache first.

2. If the memory problem goes away, replace the cache chips, module, or motherboard, and retest.

3. If the problem persists after replacing cache, repair or replace the motherboard.

4. Next, disable internal (CPU cache), if necessary.

5. If the memory problem goes away, replace the CPU and retest.

6. If the problem returns after you replace the CPU, repair or replace the motherboard.

Other Methods for RAM Testing

Many utility programs, including CheckIt, AMIDiag, QAPlus, and others, feature powerful memory-testing programs that can run continuously and use many more testing options than the fast POST test performed by the computer at startup.

Most versions of Himem.sys driver used by MS-DOS and Windows can also be used for memory testing at bootup.

If you install or replace a large number of memory modules, a dedicated RAM tester provides the most accurate and complete method for finding RAM problems. RAM testers can be used to

- Determine memory type, size, and true speed.

- Separate good from bad RAM when all RAM is removed from a system.

- Heat-test and stress-test RAM independently of the motherboard or operating system.

Summary

Adding RAM to systems improves performance by minimizing disk accesses and by providing a larger workspace. Adding cache RAM to systems improves performance for memory-bound operations. To add RAM to a system, you must know both the CPU type and the type(s) of modules the system needs to determine the number of memory modules needed. SDRAM DIMMs are the most common modules used on 1998 and newer systems and can be added one at a time. Some advanced systems use RIMM or DDR SDRAM modules. 72-pin EDO SIMMs are popular with older 486s. Cache RAM can be added to older motherboards, but most new and recent motherboards must be replaced to increase RAM. Replacing the CPU is an alternative way to add or increase Level 2 cache.

CH

4

QUESTIONS AND ANSWERS:

1. Explain the difference between a SIMM and a DIMM.
   A: SIMMs come in 30-pin or 72-pin types and must be used in multiples to make a bank. DIMMs come in 168-pin type only and can be used alone to make a bank.

2. Why is SDRAM faster than EDO RAM?
   A: Faster access time and synchronized to the motherboard

3. To add RAM to a system, you must know what two facts?
   A: The CPU type (to determine the data bus) and the RAM type (to determine the number of modules to use)

4. Where is Level 1 cache located?
   A: Always in the CPU core

5. List two places Level 2 cache can be located.
   A: Motherboard or on CPU (outside core)

6. Where is Level 3 cache located?
   A: On motherboard if a system has a CPU with both L1 and L2 caches (AMD K6III)

7. What is a cache hit?
   A: When cache RAM has the desired memory location

8. What is a memory bank?
   A: The amount of RAM (in bits) = data bus of CPU, using identical, matched modules

9. How can caching be disabled?
   A: Use BIOS setup program

Input/Output Devices and Cables

WHILE YOU READ

1. What is daisy-chaining, and which I/O port types allow it? Which I/O port type uses hubs to facilitate daisy-chaining?
2. What popular type of input device can be attached to a dedicated or standard port? What are those ports?
3. What is the difference between parallel and IEEE-1284 interfacing?
4. What device can be attached to a serial port or can contain one?
5. Why should a sound card be installed before other devices?
6. Which I/O port types require Windows 98 or newer versions to operate? Do these ports support hot-swap devices?

Introduction

This chapter covers the configuration, setup, and uses of the fundamental input/output devices most computers have in common:

- Parallel port
- Serial port
- Modem
- Keyboard
- Mouse
- Sound card
- USB
- IEEE-1394

If the system you are maintaining uses Windows 9x or Windows 2000, the Control Panel, shown in Figure 5.1, contains several important icons you'll use to control these ports: System, Mouse, and Modem. See the appropriate following sections for details.

Figure 5.1
The Windows 9x Control Panel can be accessed from the Windows Explorer or by choosing Start, Settings, Control Panel.

This contrasts with MS-DOS, which used individual device drivers or applications to control hardware devices. Windows 3.1 and Windows NT 4.0 use less sophisticated versions of the Control Panel.

Parallel Port

The parallel port, also known as the LPT (for Line Printer) port, was originally designed for use with parallel printers. The parallel port is among the most versatile of I/O ports in the system because it is also used by a variety of devices, including tape backups, external CD-ROM and optical drives, scanners, and removable-media drives such as ZIP drives.

The parallel (LPT) port is unusual because it uses two completely different connector types: All IBM and compatible computers since the first IBM PC of 1981 have used the DB25F port shown in Figure 5.2, with pins 1–13 on the left and pins 14–25 on the right. This is also referred to as the type IEEE-1284A connector (IEEE-1284 is an international standard for parallel port connectors, cabling, and signaling).

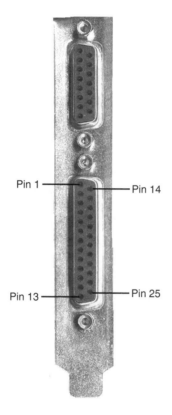

Figure 5.2
The LPT (parallel) port (bottom) is often found on the same multi-I/O card bracket as the game port (top).

The port used by parallel printers of all types, however, is the same Centronics port used since the days of the Apple II and other early microcomputers of the late 1970s, as seen in Figure 5.3. This port is also referred to as the IEEE 1284-B port. It is an edge connector with 36 connectors; 18 per side. Some recent Hewlett-Packard LaserJet printers also use a miniature version of the Centronics connector known as the IEEE 1284-C, which is also a 36-pin edge connector.

Figure 5.3
The LPT (parallel) port on a typical inkjet printer. The curved wires on each side of the Centronics port hold the printer cable in place for a more secure connection.

Thus, a parallel printer cable also has different connectors at each end, as seen in Figure 5.4.

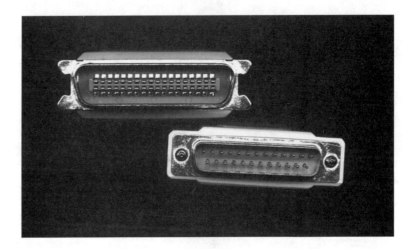

Figure 5.4
The ends of a typical IBM-style parallel cable. The Centronics 36-pin connector (upper left) connects to the printer; the DB-25M connector (lower right) connects to the computer's DB-25F parallel port.

Parallel cables have the pinout described in Table 5.1. As you prepare for the A+ Certification test, you should note that the parallel designation for the LPT port comes from its use of eight data lines (pins 2–9) and that the port has provisions for printer status messages (pins 10–12).

Table 5.1	Parallel Port Pinout (DB-25F Connector)					
Pin #	Description	I/O	Pin #	Description	I/O
1	-Strobe	Out	14	-Auto Feed	Out
2	+Data bit 0	Out	15	-Error	In
3	+Data bit 1	Out	16	-Initialize Printer	Out
4	+Data bit 2	Out	17	-Select Input	Out
5	+Data bit 3	Out	18	-Ground (Data bit 0 Return)	In
6	+Data bit 4	Out	19	-Ground (Data bit 1 Return)	In
7	+Data bit 5	Out	20	-Ground (Data bit 2 Return)	In
8	+Data bit 6	Out	21	-Ground (Data bit 3 Return)	In
9	+Data bit 7	Out	22	-Ground (Data bit 4 Return)	In
10	-Acknowledge	In	23	-Ground (Data bit 5 Return)	In
11	+Busy	In	24	-Ground (Data bit 6 Return)	In
12	+Paper End	In	25	-Ground (Data bit 7 Return)	In
13	+Select	In			

Parallel Port Configuration

The configuration of the LPT port consists of

- Selecting the port's operating mode
- Selecting the IRQ, I/O port address, and DMA channel (for certain modes)

For an overview of how IRQ, I/O port address, and DMA channels are used, see "IRQs, DMAs, I/O Port Addresses, and Memory Addresses," page 17.

LPT Port Operating Modes

The LPT port can be configured for a variety of operating modes. The options available for a particular port depend on the capabilities of the system.

Standard Mode

The standard mode of the LPT port is the configuration first used on PCs, and it is the only mode available on many 386-based and earlier systems. On some systems, this is also known as compatible mode. Although configuration for this mode typically includes both the IRQ and I/O port address, only the I/O port address is actually used for printing. If the parallel port is used in standard/compatible mode, IRQ 7 can be used for another device. The standard mode is the slowest mode (150KBps output/50KBps input), but it is the most suitable mode for older printers. In this mode, eight lines are used for output, but only four lines are used for input. The port can send or receive, but only in one direction at a time.

This mode will work with any parallel cable.

PS/2—Bidirectional

The next mode available on most systems is the PS/2 or bidirectional mode. This mode was pioneered by the old IBM PS/2 computers and is the simplest mode available on some computer models.

Bidirectional mode is more suitable for use with devices other than printers because eight lines are used for both input and output. This mode also uses only I/O port addresses. This mode is no faster than compatible mode for printing but accepts incoming data at a faster rate than compatible mode; the port sends and transmits data at 150KBps.

This mode requires a bidirectional printer cable or IEEE-1284 printer cable.

IEEE-1284 High-Speed Bidirectional Modes

Three modes that are fully bidirectional (able to send and receive data 8 bits at a time) and are also much faster than the original PS/2-style bidirectional port, include

- **EPP (Enhanced Parallel Port)**—Uses both an IRQ and an I/O port address. This is the mode supported by most high-speed printers and drives attached to the parallel port.
- **ECP (Enhanced Capabilities Port)**—Designed for the daisy-chaining of different devices (such as printers and scanners) to a single port. It uses an IRQ, an I/O port address, and a DMA channel, making it the most resource-hungry of all the different parallel port modes.
- **EPP/ECP**—Require an IEEE-1284-compatible parallel cable. Many recent systems support a combined EPP/ECP mode, making it possible to run devices preferring either mode on a single port.

These modes, which transmit data at up to 2MBps and receive data at 500KBps, have all been incorporated into the IEEE-1284 parallel-port standard. Most Pentium-based and newer systems have ports that comply with at least one of these standards.

These modes are suitable for use with

- High-speed laser and inkjet printers
- External tape-backup drives, optical drives, and ZIP drives
- Scanners
- Direct Cable Connection, LapLink, Interlink, and other data-transfer programs

Comparing IEEE-1284 and Standard Centronics Parallel Cables

IEEE-1284 cables feature several types of shielding in both the cable and at the printer end of the cable. This shielding is designed to minimize interference from outside sources.

IEEE-1284 cables use a twisted wire-pair construction internally, running 18 wire pairs to the printer. The wire pairs help minimize crosstalk (interference between different wires in the cable). As a result, IEEE-1284 cables are both a good deal thicker and more expensive than ordinary or bidirectional printer cables. They are available for both direct connection and switchbox use with appropriate switchboxes (see Figure 5.5).

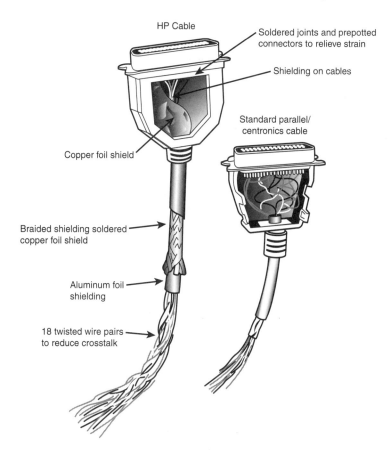

Figure 5.5
This comparison of an IEEE-1284 parallel cable (left) and a standard parallel cable (right) shows clearly the extra shielding and other features added to the IEEE-1284 cable to permit faster and more reliable printing.

Standard and Optional Parallel Port Settings

Parallel ports can be configured as LPT1, LPT2, and LPT3. When a single parallel port is found in the system, regardless of its configuration, it is always designated as LPT1. The configurations for LPT2 and LPT3, shown in Table 5.2, apply when there are multiple parallel ports in the system.

CH
5

Table 5.2 Typical Parallel Port Hardware Configuration Settings

LPT Port #	IRQ	I/O Port Address Range
LPT1	7	3BC-38Fh or 378-37Fh
LPT2	5	378-37Fh or 278-27Fh
LPT3	5	278-27Fh

If one of the ports is an ECP or EPP/ECP port, DMA 3 is normally used on most systems along with the IRQ and I/O port address ranges listed here. Some computers default to DMA 1, but this will conflict with most sound cards (see "Sound Cards," page 158).

Some 16-bit ISA or PCI-based multi-I/O cards can place the parallel port at any available IRQ up to 15.

How to Configure or Disable Parallel Ports

Depending on the location of the parallel port, there are several ways to configure the port settings. These include

- BIOS setup program for built-in ports
- Jumper blocks or DIP switch configuration for I/O cards in expansion slots
- Plug and Play (PnP) mode for use with Windows 9x and Windows 2000

Follow these steps to adjust the configuration of a parallel port built into the system's motherboard:

1. Start the BIOS setup program.
2. Change to the peripherals configuration screen (see Figure 5.6).

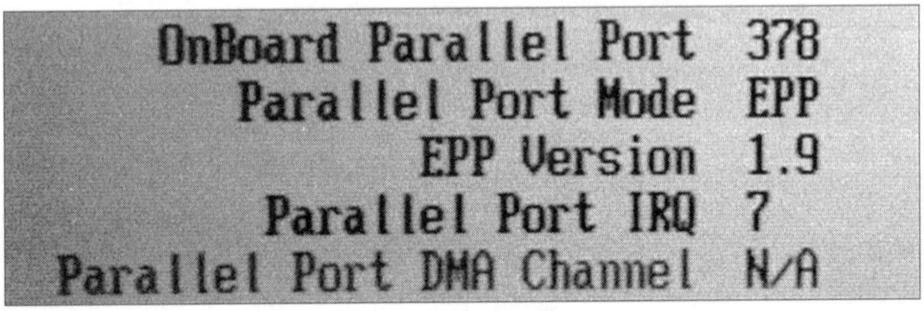

```
OnBoard Parallel Port    378
    Parallel Port Mode    EPP
         EPP Version    1.9
      Parallel Port IRQ    7
Parallel Port DMA Channel   N/A
```

Figure 5.6
A typical BIOS/CMOS setup screen showing a parallel port set for the IEEE-1284 EPP mode (also known as EPP version 1.9). This system also supports the IEEE-1284 ECP mode, as shown by the Parallel Port DMA Channel option at the bottom of the screen.

3. Select the mode, IRQ, I/O port address, and DMA channel if required.
4. Save changes and exit; the system reboots.

Follow these steps to adjust the configuration of a parallel port using jumper blocks or DIP switches attached to an expansion card:

1. Turn off the system's power.
2. Remove the parallel port or multi I/O card (see Figure 5.7).
3. Adjust the jumper blocks or DIP switches to select the mode, IRQ, I/O port address, and DMA channel if required. Check the card's documentation for details.
4. Reinsert the card into the expansion slot.
5. Restart the system.

Many recent systems will display the new port or new configuration during the initial boot up process (see "Transferring Control to the Operating System with the Bootstrap Loader," page 71).

To adjust the configuration of a parallel port using a configuration program, start the configuration program, select the mode, IRQ, I/O port address, and DMA channel if required, save the changes, and exit.

Jumper blocks for port configuration

CH
5

Figure 5.7
A typical multi I/O card using jumper blocks for configuration of the parallel, serial, and game ports on the card (upper left). Although some of these cards have clearly marked settings, most require that you have the documentation available to make sense of the jumper block options.

Follow these steps to adjust the configuration of a Plug and Play Windows 9x parallel port:

1. Open the Windows 9x Control Panel.

2. Open the System icon.

3. Select the Device Manager tab.

4. Select the Ports (COM and LPT) icon.

5. Select the LPT port you want to change.

6. Click the Properties button.

7. Click the Resources tab (see Figure 5.8).

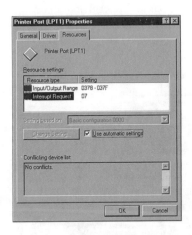

Figure 5.8
The LPT port's standard settings can be changed by turning off the Use Automatic Settings option and selecting an alternate configuration, or by manually adjusting the IRQ and I/O port address

8. Deselect the Use Automatic Settings option if enabled.

9. Select a different Basic Configuration until you find the settings you want, or manually select from available IRQ, I/O port address, and DMA channels, selecting options that don't cause conflicts (two devices using the same setting).

10. Click OK if asked whether you want to make manual changes.

11. Close the Device Manager.

If you adjust the configuration of a Windows 9x PnP parallel port to ECP or ECP/EPP, the port will be detected as a new device and a different port driver will be installed.

Troubleshooting Parallel Ports

Parallel port problems usually result from the following causes:

- IRQ conflicts between devices
- Incorrect selection of parallel port mode for devices attached to a parallel port
- Incorrect order of devices when daisy-chaining multiple devices
- Cabling problems, including inadequate cabling for the parallel port mode selected, cabling too long for reliable printing, damage to port or cable, and incorrect cabling of parallel port header cable on Baby-AT systems
- Inadequate printer sharing device for mode selected.

Solutions to these problems are covered in the following sections. For printer-specific troubleshooting, see the appropriate sections of Chapter 9, "Printers."

IRQ Conflicts

If the parallel port and another device are both set to the same IRQ, neither device is likely to work. To avoid IRQ conflicts, make sure no other device is using the same IRQ as the parallel port. Normally, this requires that the conflicting device be moved to a different IRQ.

The most likely causes of an IRQ conflict include ISA sound cards, which normally use either IRQ 5 (conflicts with LPT 2) or IRQ 7 (conflicts with LPT 1).

Incorrect LPT Port Mode for Attached Devices

If a parallel device designed to use an IEEE-1284 mode, such as EPP, ECP, or EPP/ECP, is attached to a parallel port that has the wrong mode selected or is set to slower modes, such as PS/2 bidirectional or standard/compatible, the device will work very slowly, or it might not work at all. Use the correct parallel port mode for the devices you need to attach to the port, and use an IEEE-1284–compatible cable to provide support for all parallel port modes.

Problems with Daisy-Chained Devices

Many computer users take advantage of the ability to attach multiple devices to a parallel port to attach devices such as tape backups, removable-media drives, and scanners to the same port as their printer. In many cases, the printer and any other single device can share the printer port. However, trying to use two or more devices along with the printer can cause slow performance or device failure.

To achieve success in using multiple parallel devices

- Check the device documentation for suggestions on which devices can be installed and in what order—in many cases, a printer and scanner or printer and removable-media drive will work, but other combinations might not work.

CH

5

- Use the correct parallel port mode for the devices.
- Consider adding a second parallel port for some devices, or switch to USB devices that can be connected to a USB hub.

Cabling and Port Problems

Parallel cables can cause several problems with printers and other devices. Low-quality cables that are longer than 10 feet can cause garbled printing, and cables that don't support the port mode will prevent the port from reaching its maximum speed.

To avoid cabling problems, use a high-quality printer cable; cables that meet the IEEE-1284 standard are recommended and will work well with any parallel port mode. IEEE-1284 cables provide the shielding necessary to assure reliable printing beyond the 10-foot distance limitation of low-quality cables.

If you need to print at very long distances away from your computer, consider attaching the printer to a network or use a line converter (which changes parallel to serial signals).

Damaged cables will cause printing problems. If the printer will not print at all or prints garbage output, replace the cable with a known-working cable and retry the print job. Damaged ports will cause problems with any cable.

Parallel ports on Baby-AT motherboards are not built into the motherboard; instead, a ribbon cable brings the parallel signals from the motherboard to the external parallel connector. If the port fails on a brand-new system with a Baby-AT motherboard, make sure the cable is correctly attached to the motherboard. Verify that pin 1 on the header pins is attached to the red-striped wire used for pin 1 on the cable. Header cables are matched to the motherboard type; if you change motherboards, be sure to replace the old parallel-port header cable with the cable for the new motherboard (see Figure 5.9).

If the parallel port fails on a Baby-AT machine after an internal card or drive has been installed, the header cable might have been bumped loose from the motherboard. Check for proper positioning and reattach if necessary.

To determine whether a parallel port is damaged, first make sure there are no IRQ conflicts and that the header cable (if any) is properly attached to the motherboard. Then, use a diagnostic program such as AMIDIAG, Norton Utilities, or others and attach the appropriate loopback plug to the port. If the port is unable to pass a loopback test, the port is damaged and should be replaced.

Switchbox Problems

Switchboxes are a popular way to help two or more printers or other parallel devices share a single port. However, inexpensive switchboxes that use a rotary switch can damage the sensitive parallel ports on laser printers. Also, non-IEEE-1284–compliant switchboxes will prevent bidirectional operation of printers. Without a bidirectional connection to the printer, some printers can't be configured or send status reports back to the computer. To determine whether the switchbox is the problem, connect the printer or other device directly to the computer. If the device functions properly when connected directly but has problems when connected through a switchbox, the switchbox is not properly transmitting all the signals.

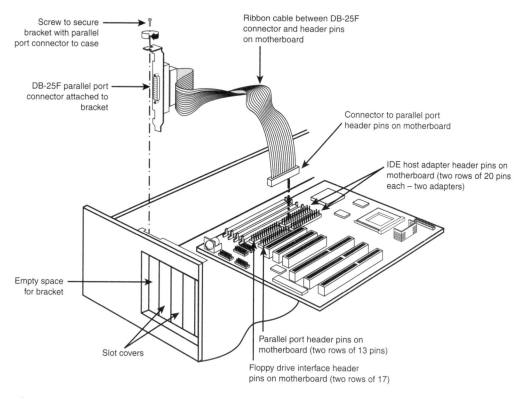

Figure 5.9
Installing a parallel port header cable. The cable provides an external DB-25F parallel port connector for a typical Baby-AT motherboard.

With any combination of parallel devices (printers, drives, scanners, and so on), use IEEE-1284–compatible switchboxes that can be switched electronically and IEEE-1284–compatible switchboxes.

Serial Ports

Serial ports, also known as RS-232 or COM (communication) ports (see Figure 5.10), rival parallel ports in versatility. Serial ports are used to connect

- External modems
- Serial mice
- Plotters
- Label printers

- Serial printers
- File transfer programs such as Direct Cable Connection, LapLink, and Interlink

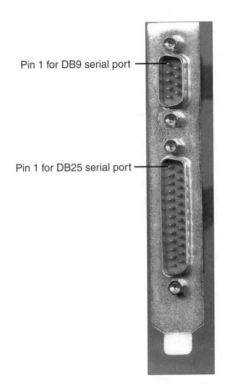

Pin 1 for DB9 serial port

Pin 1 for DB25 serial port

Figure 5.10
A 9-pin serial port or DB9M (top) and a 25-pin serial port or DB25M (bottom) on a typical extension bracket from a multi I/O card. The ribbon cables used to connect the ports to the card can be seen in the background.

Serial ports transmit data one bit at a time, and their maximum speeds are far lower than parallel ports. However, serial cables can carry data reliably at far greater distances than parallel cables.

Serial ports, unlike parallel ports, have no provision for daisy-chaining; only one device can be connected to a serial port.

Serial ports come in two forms:

- DB-9 male
- DB-25 male

Either type can be adapted to the other connector type. The difference is possible because serial communications need only a few wires. Unlike parallel printers, which use a standard cable, each type of serial device uses a specially wired cable.

Serial Port Pinouts

At a minimum, a serial cable must use at least three wires, plus ground:

- A transmit data wire
- A receive data wire
- A signal wire

Tables 5.3 and 5.4 can be used to determine the correct pinout for any specified serial cable configuration. Unlike parallel devices, which all use the same standard cable, serial devices use differently wired cables. A modem cable, for example, will be wired much differently than a serial printer cable. And different serial printers might each use a unique pinout.

The DB-9 (9-pin male) connector is the more common of the two serial port connector types.

Table 5.3   9-Pin Serial Port Pinout

Use	Pin	Direction
Carrier Detect	1	In
Receive Data	2	In
Transmit Data	3	Out
Data Terminal Ready	4	Out
Signal Ground	5	—
Data Set Ready	6	In
Request to Send	7	Out
Clear to Send	8	In
Ring Indicator	9	In

The 25-pin serial port has many additional pins but is seldom used today. The major difference between it and the 9-pin serial interface is support for current loop data, a type of serial communications primarily used for data collection. Table 5.4 lists the pinouts for the 25-pin connector; unused pins are omitted.

Table 5.4   25-Pin Serial Port Pinout

Use	Pin	Direction
Transmit Data	2	Out
Receive Data	3	In
Request to Send	4	Out
Clear to Send	5	In
Data Set Ready	6	In
Signal Ground	7	—
Received Line Signal Indicator	8	In
+ Transmit Current Loop Data	9	Out
- Transmit Current Loop Data	11	Out
+ Receive Current Loop Data	18	In
Data Terminal Ready	20	Out

CH

5

Table 5.4   continued

Use	Pin	Direction
Ring Indicator	22	In
- Receive Current Loop Return	25	In

When a 9-pin to 25-pin serial port adapter is used (see Figure 5.11), the pins are converted (see Table 5.5).

Table 5.5   9-Pin to 25-Pin Serial Port Converter Pinout

Use	Pin # (9-Pin)	Pin # (25-Pin)
Carrier Detect (CD)	1	8
Receive Data (RD)	2	3
Transmit Data (TD)	3	2
Data Terminal Ready (DTR)	4	20
Signal Ground (SG)	5	7
Data Set Ready (DSR)	6	6
Request to Send (RTS)	7	4
Clear to Send (CTS)	8	5
Ring Indicator (RI)	9	22

Serial ports assume that one end transmits and the other end receives.

Figure 5.11
A typical DB-25 to DB-9 serial port converter, which allows a 25-pin serial port (left) to connect to 9-pin serial devices (right).

Null-Modem Cables

A null-modem cable allows two computers to communicate directly with each other by crossing the receive and transmit wires. The best-known of these programs is LapLink, but the Microsoft MS-DOS Interlink and Windows 9x Direct Cable Connection can also use this type of cable. Although these programs support serial-cable transfers, parallel-port transfers are much faster and are recommended with MS-DOS and Windows 95.

However, Windows NT 4.0 and earlier do *not* support using the parallel port for file transfers, so to use LapLink or similar products, you must use the serial null-modem cable, as shown in Figure 5.12.

Standard IRQ and I/O Port Addresses

Serial ports require two settings: IRQ and I/O port address. Table 5.6 lists the standard IRQ and I/O port addresses used for COM ports 1–4. Some systems and add-on cards allow alternative IRQs to be used.

Table 5.6 Standard Settings for COM (Serial) Ports 1–4		
COM Port #	IRQ	I/O Port Address
1	4	3F8-3FFh
2	3	2F8-2FFh
3	4	3E8-3EFh
4	3	2E8-2EFh

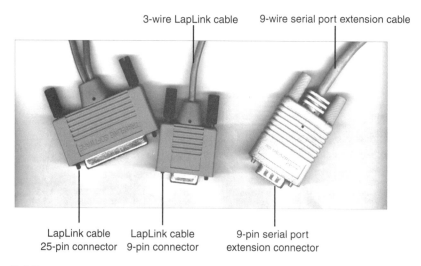

3-wire LapLink cable   9-wire serial port extension cable

LapLink cable   LapLink cable   9-pin serial port
25-pin connector   9-pin connector   extension connector

Figure 5.12
A LapLink serial cable with connectors for either 25-pin or 9-pin serial ports. Only three wires are needed, allowing the cable to be much thinner than the 9-pin serial extension cable also shown.

IRQ 4 is shared by default between COM 1 and COM 3; IRQ 3 is shared by default between COM 2 and COM 4. If a device on COM 1 and a device on COM 3 that share the same IRQ are used at the same time, both devices will stop working and they might shut down the system.

The most common situation that causes such a conflict is the use of a mouse connected to COM 1 and a modem connected to COM 3. Use the modem, and the mouse quits working (and so does Windows).

CH
5

As you saw in Chapter 1, "Basic Concepts," this happens because computers are "interrupt-driven"; they use IRQs to determine which device needs to be listened to. When one device (the mouse) is already using the IRQ, the other device (the modem) gets a "busy signal."

Just as the only solution to busy signals is a second phone line, the preferred solution to IRQ conflicts is to move the second device using an IRQ to a different IRQ. Your ability to do this depends on the serial port.

How to Configure or Disable Serial Ports

Depending on the location of the serial port, there are several ways to configure the port settings to select different IRQ and I/O port addresses for a serial port, or to disable the serial port. These include

- BIOS setup program for built-in ports
- Mechanical (jumper blocks or DIP switch) or software configuration for I/O cards in expansion slots
- Plug and Play (PnP) mode for use with Windows 95

To adjust the configuration of a serial port built into the system's motherboard

1. Start the BIOS setup program.
2. Change to the peripherals configuration screen.
3. Select the serial port you want to adjust.
4. To change the port's configuration, choose the IRQ and I/O port address you want to use, or select Disabled to prevent the system from detecting and using the serial port.
5. Save changes and exit; the system reboots.

To adjust the configuration of a serial port on an I/O card that uses jumper blocks or DIP switches

1. Turn off the system's power.
2. Remove the serial port or multi-I/O card.
3. Locate the jumper blocks or DIP switches for the serial port you want to adjust.
4. Move the jumper blocks or DIP switches to select the IRQ and I/O port address you want to use, or adjust the jumper blocks or DIP switches to disable the port.
5. Reinsert the card into the expansion slot.
6. Restart the system.

Many recent systems will display the new port or new configuration during the initial bootup process (see "Transferring Control to the Operating System with the Bootstrap Loader," page 71).

To adjust the configuration of a serial port using a configuration program, start the configuration program, select the serial port, select the IRQ and I/O port address desired or select the disable port option, save the changes, and exit.

To adjust the configuration of a Plug and Play Windows 9x serial port

1. Open the Windows 9x Control Panel.
2. Open the System icon.
3. Select the Device Manager tab.
4. Select the Ports (COM and LPT) icon.
5. Select the COM port you want to change.
6. Click the Properties button.
7. Select the Resources tab (see Figure 5.13).

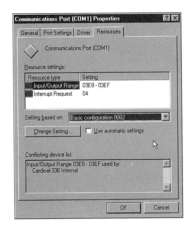

Figure 5.13
Windows 9x detects conflicts between settings for your COM port and other devices.

8. Deselect the Use Automatic Settings option if enabled.
9. Select a different Basic Configuration until you find the settings you want, or manually select from available IRQ and I/O port addresses, selecting options that don't cause conflicts (two devices using the same setting). You also can click the Disable in This Hardware Profile box to disable the port.
10. Click OK if asked whether you want to make manual changes.
11. Close the Device Manager.

Serial Cabling

There is no such thing as a "universal RS-232 cable" that can connect your PC to any and every serial device. A serial cable that connects your PC to a modem has a different pinout than a serial cable that connects your PC to a specified serial printer. If you can purchase a premade cable for a serial application (to connect an external modem, for example), do so, and save yourself the trouble of building a cable. Otherwise, you must obtain the correct pinouts if you want to build the cable yourself or order a correctly wired one from a custom cable shop.

Serial Port Software Configuration

Unlike parallel ports, serial ports have many different configuration options. Through software settings at the computer end, and by hardware or software settings at the device end, serial devices can use

- A wide variety of transmission speeds, from as low as 300bps (bits per second) to as high as 115,200 bps
- Different word lengths (7 bit or 8 bit)
- Different methods of flow control (XON/XOFF or DTR/DSR)
- Different methods of ensuring reliable data transmission (even parity, odd parity, no parity, 1-bit or 2-bit parity length)

Although simple devices such as mice and label printers don't require that these settings be made manually (the software drivers do it), serial printers used with PCs running terminal-emulation software, PCs communicating with mainframe computers, serial pen plotters, serial printers, and PCs using modems often do require that these options be set correctly. Both ends of a serial connection must have these configurations set to identical values, or the communications between your computer and the other device will fail. Figure 5.14 shows how to use the Windows 9x properties sheet to set the stop bits, word length, and parity for a serial modem.

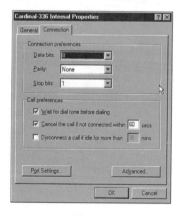

Figure 5.14
You can adjust the word length and parity options for a serial modem in its Connection properties. Use the General tab to set speed.

Serial Port UARTs

All serial ports must contain a UART (Universal Asynchronous Receive Transmit) chip. The UART chip is the "heart" of the serial port, because it does the actual transmitting and receiving of data. Problems with serial ports that cannot run fast enough to reliably receive and transmit to a particular device, or are unable to run in a multitasking environment such as Windows, can often be traced back to an obsolete UART chip. There are several major types of UART chips:

- **8250 series**—The 8250 series of UARTs are not fast enough to support modems running faster than 9600bps. They have no means to buffer received data, and will drop characters if used with Windows. This chip was used primarily in IBM PC and PC/XT-type computers. The 8250B is the best chip of this series.

- **16450**—The 16450 UART will run reliably at speeds up to 19,200bps. It was introduced with the IBM AT.

- **16550A**—This series of UARTs have a 16-byte FIFO (First In, First Out) buffer for reliable multitasking without data loss and can run at speeds of up to 115,200bps. This is the standard UART used in the serial ports included on virtually all Pentium-class or better motherboards.

- **16650 and above**—These UARTs have 32-byte or larger FIFO buffers and support speeds of 230,400bps or above; special serial port and multi-I/O cards often include one or more of these UARTs.

Determining Which UART a Serial Port Uses

You can use the Windows 9x or 2000 Device Manager to determine the UARTs installed in a system. Follow this procedure:

1. Open the Control Panel icon.
2. Open the Modems icon.
3. Click the Diagnostics tab (see Figure 5.15).
4. Select a serial port or modem.
5. Click the More Info button.
6. The port or modem's IRQ, starting I/O port address, and UART type will be displayed. Additional information will be displayed if you selected a modem.

Upgrading the UART Chip

If a system or I/O card uses a socketed 16450 chip, you can replace it with a 16550A or better chip to upgrade the UART. Most recent computers and I/O cards use a Super I/O chip that contains a UART equivalent and LPT port inside a custom chip, rather than using a standard UART chip.

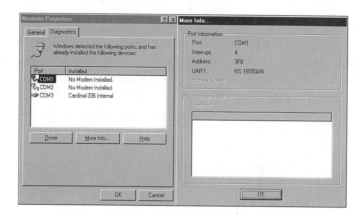

Figure 5.15
You can determine the IRQ, I/O port address, and UART type for any COM port or modem in your Windows 9x or 2000 system with the Diagnostics tab for modems.

In such cases, you can replace obsolete UARTs by disabling the existing serial ports (see "How to Configure or Disable Serial Ports," earlier in this chapter), and then add a faster serial-port card containing a fast UART.

Serial Port Troubleshooting

The A+ Certification exam tests your knowledge of both normal operations and troubleshooting procedures for major system components. Use this section to prepare for troubleshooting questions involving serial ports and modems (because most internal modems contain UARTs, the same troubleshooting tips apply to internal modems as to serial ports).

COM 4 I/O Port Conflicts

Some ATI and other brands of video cards use an I/O port range that conflicts with the default I/O port range used by COM 4 (2E8-2EF). To prevent conflicts, you will need to choose one of the following solutions:

- Change the I/O port address used by COM 4
- Disable COM 4
- Change the video card's I/O port address range to a non-conflicting option with the Windows Device Manager

Serial Port Drops Characters when Multitasking

The FIFO (first-in, first-out) buffers used in the 16550AF and higher series of UART chips allow a computer to reliably multitask while receiving or sending data through a serial port or internal modem. If characters are being dropped when data is sent or received through the serial ports, check the UART type present in the system. If the UART is an 8250 series or 16450 series device (which lack FIFO buffers), the internal modem or serial port should be replaced with a device containing a 16550AF or better UART.

If characters are being dropped on a system with the correct UART, you can use the Modem properties sheet in Windows 9x or 2000 to adjust the connection. To adjust the connection

1. Open the Control Panel folder.

2. Open the Modems icon.

3. Select the modem.

4. Click Properties.

5. Click Connection.

6. Click Port Settings.

7. To solve problems with receiving data, adjust the Receive buffer toward Low. To solve problems with sending data, adjust the Transmit buffer toward High.

8. Make sure that Use FIFO Buffers is checked if your modem or serial port has a 16550AF or faster UART.

9. Click OK until all modem dialogs are closed.

Can't Connect Serial Devices to Port Because of Mismatched Connectors

The original IBM PC's RS-232 serial ports used a 25-pin connector, but the IBM AT and most subsequent PC-compatible computers use a 9-pin connector; some systems use a 9-pin connector for COM 1 and a 25-pin connector for COM 2. Occasionally, some serial devices using one type of connector must be connected to serial ports that use the other type of connector. Use the appropriate 9-pin to 25-pin adapter to allow a 9-pin port to use a 25-pin device, or vice versa.

Cabling and Port Problems

Damaged or incorrectly wired serial cables can cause several problems with any serial device. To avoid cabling problems, verify that you are using the correct serial cable with any given device. For serial-port external modems, purchase a modem cable; for serial printers, buy a cable made especially for that printer, and so forth.

Damaged cables will cause device problems. If an external serial device will not work at all or produces garbage input or output, first check the communications parameters for the port and the devices. If these are correct, replace the cable with a known-working cable and retry the device. Damaged ports will cause problems with any cable.

Serial ports on Baby-AT motherboards are not built into the motherboard. Instead, a ribbon cable brings the RS-232 serial port signals from the motherboard to the external serial port connectors. If one or both serial ports fail on a brand-new system with a Baby-AT motherboard, make sure the cables are correctly attached to the motherboard—verify that pin 1 on the header pins is attached to the red-striped wire used for pin 1 on the cable.

CH
5

Header cables are matched to the motherboard type; if you change motherboards, be sure to replace the old serial-port header cable with the cable for the new motherboard (see Figure 5.16).

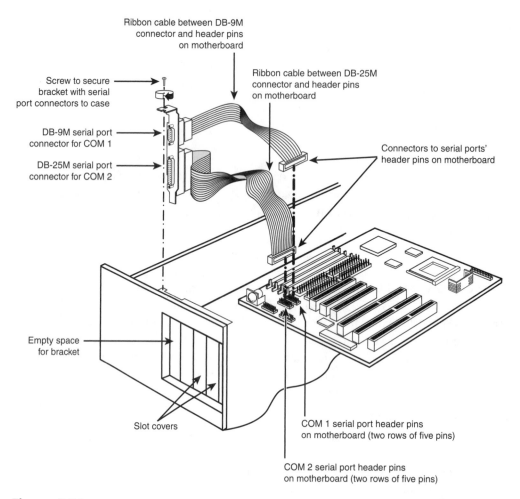

Ribbon cable between DB-9M connector and header pins on motherboard

Ribbon cable between DB-25M connector and header pins on motherboard

Screw to secure bracket with serial port connectors to case

DB-9M serial port connector for COM 1

DB-25M serial port connector for COM 2

Connectors to serial ports' header pins on motherboard

Empty space for bracket

Slot covers

COM 1 serial port header pins on motherboard (two rows of five pins)

COM 2 serial port header pins on motherboard (two rows of five pins)

Figure 5.16

Installing a serial port header cable. The cable provides two external serial port connections (a DB-9M and a DB-25M) for a typical Baby-AT motherboard.

If one or both serial ports fail on a Baby-AT machine after an internal card or drive has been installed, the header cables might have been bumped loose from the motherboard. Check for proper positioning and reattach if necessary.

To determine whether a serial port is damaged, first make sure there are no IRQ conflicts (see "Standard IRQ and I/O Port Addresses," earlier in this chapter) and that the header cable (if any) is properly attached to the motherboard. Then, use a diagnostic program, such as AMIDIAG, Norton Utilities, or others, and attach the appropriate loopback plug to the port. If the port is unable to pass a loopback test, the port is damaged and should be replaced.

Adding Serial and Parallel Ports to an Existing System

You can add ports by installing a single-port or multi-port card or by using a switchbox to share a single port among two or more devices. If you choose to install a single-port or multi-port (multi-I/O card), you must

1. Determine the remaining IRQ and I/O port addresses available in the computer.

2. Configure the ports on the card to use available settings.

3. Insert the card into the correct slot.

4. Run any software driver or configuration software after you restart the computer. Plug and Play–compatible cards are usually configured automatically by systems with Plug and Play system BIOSes and Windows 9x or 2000.

Serial-, parallel-, and multi-port cards are available in both ISA and PCI forms. PCI cards are recommended for their greater speed, their capability to safely share IRQs, and their capability to be used in both current and future systems.

Adding ports to an existing system is usually preferable to using a switchbox. A switchbox is an acceptable alternative when

- Each device can be used independently of the other devices connected to the switchbox.

- The switchbox can reliably transmit all the signals from the computer to the device.

- The switchbox will not damage any computer or device attached to it.

Automatic-sensing switchboxes with IEEE-1284 support work well for sharing a single printer among two computers or running two printers off a single LPT port.

Switchboxes can also be used with serial devices that don't use resident software drivers. They can be used with a modem or a label printer, for example, but not with a mouse.

USB Ports

The Universal Serial Bus port, which began to show up in computers starting in 1997, is now beginning to fulfill its destiny as an eventual replacement for both RS-232 serial and LPT parallel ports. USB versions of printers, scanners, mice, keyboards, home and small-office networks, modems, external drives, and other devices are now available.

Most recent systems have two USB ports, as shown in Figure 5.17.

CH

5

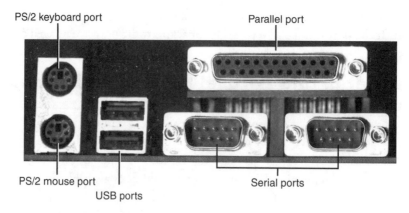

PS/2 keyboard port

Parallel port

PS/2 mouse port

USB ports

Serial ports

Figure 5.17
A typical ATX motherboard's I/O port panel before installation into a case. The PS/2 mouse and keyboard ports, twin USB ports, parallel port, and twin RS-232 serial ports are all visible. Each USB port will be able to host as many as 127 USB devices.

Speeds and Technical Details

USB ports run at a top speed of 12Mbps, with low-speed devices running at 1.5Mbps, and a single USB port is designed to handle up to 127 devices through the use of multi-port hubs and daisy-chaining of hubs.

USB devices can be hot-swapped (connected and disconnected without turning off the system). The USB ports in the computer use a single IRQ and a single I/O port address, regardless of the number of physical USB ports or devices attached to those ports.

The maximum length for a cable attached to high-speed (12Mbps) USB devices is five meters, whereas the maximum length for low-speed (1.5Mbps) devices is three meters. USB cables use two different types of connectors: Series A and Series B. Series A connectors are used on USB root hubs (the USB connectors in the computer) and USB external hubs. Series B connectors are used for devices that use a removable USB cable, such as a USB printer. Generally, you need a Series A-to-Series B cable to attach most devices to a USB root or external hub. Cables that are Type A-to-Type A or Type B-to-Type B are used to extend standard cables, and can cause problems if the combined length of the cables exceeds recommended distances. Figure 5.18 shows the two different types of USB connectors.

When a USB hub is enabled in a computer running Windows 98 or Windows 2000, two devices will be visible in the Windows Device Manager: a USB root hub and a PCI-to-USB universal host controller, which uses the single IRQ and I/O port address required by USB hardware. If an external USB hub is attached to the computer, a USB hub also will be listed in the Windows Device Manager (see Figure 5.19).

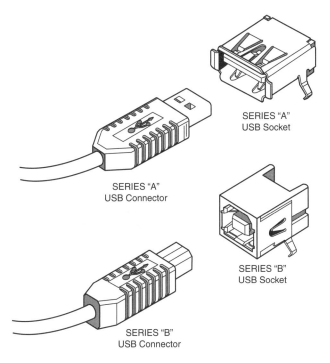

Figure 5.18
USB Series A and Series B cables and receptacles. Note the fork-shaped USB logo on the top of the cable plugs.

Requirements for USB Operation

Because USB ports were not part of the original IBM PC architecture, they are not supported by the traditional IBM compatible BIOS as are COM and LPT ports. Instead, you need a recent-model computer with USB ports built-in, USB support provided in the system BIOS, and the USB ports enabled in the system BIOS or an add-on card with USB ports plus drivers in your operating system.

Windows 95B OSR 2.1 and above feature a USB driver, but this will not work with all USB devices. For best results, use Windows 98, Windows Me, or Windows 2000, all of which feature integrated USB support.

Troubleshooting USB Ports

Many of today's most popular add-ons connect to USB ports only, and an increasing number of low-cost "legacy-free" systems no longer offer any ports other than USB ports for attaching external peripherals. Your ability to troubleshoot USB devices is important both for the A+ Certification test and for your day-to-day work with modern and forthcoming PCs.

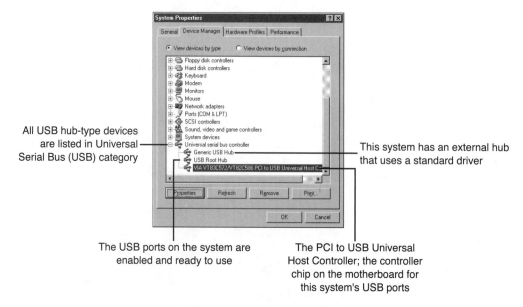

All USB hub-type devices are listed in Universal Serial Bus (USB) category

This system has an external hub that uses a standard driver

The USB ports on the system are enabled and ready to use

The PCI to USB Universal Host Controller; the controller chip on the motherboard for this system's USB ports

Figure 5.19
USB devices as shown by the Windows 98 Device Manager; note the fork-shaped USB logo for the USB category and devices.

USB Devices Not Recognized

The following are several reasons why a USB device won't be recognized when it is installed:

- **USB port not enabled in system BIOS**—If a system is upgraded from Windows 95 to Windows 98 or Windows 2000, its USB ports might not be enabled because most releases of Windows 95 don't have USB support. To enable USB support

  1. Restart the system.
  2. Start the BIOS setup program.
  3. Locate the correct menu for the USB ports (might be Advanced Chipset, Peripherals, or Other, depending on the system).
  4. Enable the port.
  5. Save the changes.
  6. Exit the system and reboot.
  7. Insert the Windows CD-ROM if required to complete installing drivers for the USB ports.

- **USB port not properly designed on older systems**—Some of the early USB ports do not conform to current USB standards and will not work with some or all USB peripherals, even using Windows 98 or Windows 2000. Disable these ports and replace them with an add-on card containing USB ports.

■ **No operating system support**—Windows 98, Windows Me, and Windows 2000 support most USB devices, but older versions of Windows do not. Some late releases of Windows 95 OSR 2.x (also known as Windows 95B or Windows 95C) are supplied with a USB driver supplement, but many devices will not work with Windows 95 at all even when the supplement is installed. Windows 2000 uses different drivers than Windows 98 or Windows Me, so some USB devices supported by Windows 98 and Windows Me might not work with Windows 2000.

USB Port Problems

Problems with the USB port after operating system and driver issued have been resolved might be caused by the following issues:

■ **USB device support not installed**—Some USB devices install their drivers automatically when the device is first plugged into the system; others require the user to install the drivers first and then connect the device. Check the device's instructions for details.

■ **USB device attached through an external hub**—Some external USB hubs are unpowered, and if too many devices requiring USB power are attached, some devices will not receive enough power from the computer and will stop working. Use a powered hub instead. To verify that the hub is the problem, disconnect the device from the hub and connect it directly to a USB port on the computer. If the USB device is detected, the hub should be replaced with a powered version.

■ **USB controller displays yellow ! sign in Windows Device Manager**—The USB PCI to USB controller (which runs the USB ports in the computer) requires an IRQ and an I/O port address range that are unique, unless IRQ sharing has been enabled in the system BIOS. Select nonconflicting IRQ and I/O port address ranges in the properties sheet (Resources tab) for the USB controller, and restart the system if necessary.

■ **Too many high-speed USB devices attached to a single port**—If the speed of existing devices drops after attaching a new device to the same USB hub, connect the new device to another USB port. Use a new hub if needed to separate high-speed from low-speed USB devices.

CH
5

Modems

Modems derive their name from the process they perform. A modem sending data modulates digital computer data into analog data suitable for transmission over telephone lines to the receiving modem, which demodulates the analog data back into computer form. Modems share two characteristics with serial ports:

■ Both use serial communication to send and receive information.

■ Both often require adjustment of transmission speed and other options.

In fact, most external modems require a serial port to connect them to the computer; some external modems use the USB port instead.

Most modems in use today run at speeds of 28.8Kpbs, 33.6Kbps, or 56Kbps. So-called 56Kbps modems are subject to two limitations, however: FCC regulations prevent their use at speeds above 53Kbps, and speeds above 33.6Kbps apply only to downloads from ISPs (Internet service providers) and their special modems. If you make a direct connection between two PCs, the fastest speed you can have in either direction is just 33.6Kbps (if both modems can run at least that fast).

Modems come in four types: internal, external, PCMCIA (PC Card), and USB. Internal modems, such as the one shown in Figure 5.20, fit into an ISA or PCI expansion slot (see "Recognizing Expansion Slot Types," page 57, and contain either their own serial port (UART chip) or require a particular operating system to run (called Winmodems).

External modems, such as the one shown in Figure 5.21, must be connected to an I/O port, usually a serial port. They require an external power source, but their portability and front-panel status lights make them better for business use in the minds of many users.

PCMCIA (PC Card) modems, like normal internal modems, contain their own UART chips. A typical PC Card modem (see "PC Cards (PCMCIA Cards)," page 314, for more information) appears in Figure 5.22.

Modem Configuration and Setup

The following steps are required before you can use a modem:

1. The modem must be physically installed in your system or connected to your system.

2. The modem must be turned on and detected by the system.

3. The correct software drivers must be installed for the modem and operating system in use.

When a modem is in use, parameters such as connection speed, word length, and others must be set to match the remote computer's requirements (see "Serial Port Software Configuration" earlier in this chapter for details). The default settings for the modem or the serial port attached to an external modem can be overridden by communications software.

Modem Installation with Windows 9x (Me) and Windows 2000

When a modem is installed with Windows 9x, Windows Me, or Windows 2000, the operating system, not the communications program, controls the modem. The physical modem installation varies by modem type:

■ Install an external modem by attaching a serial modem cable between the RS-232 connector on the modem to the serial (COM) port on the computer and plugging the modem into a power source. With a USB modem, plug the modem into the USB port; most USB modems require no external power source.

■ Install an internal modem by inserting it into the correct type of expansion slot.

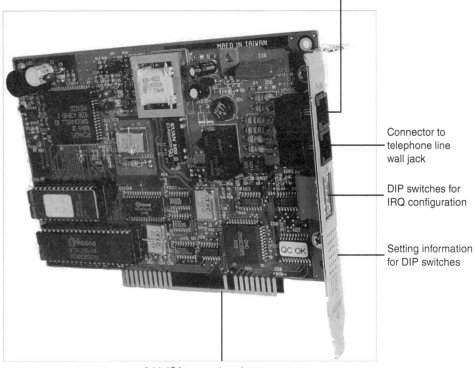

Connector to
telephone allows
modem and phone
to share a line

Connector to
telephone line
wall jack

DIP switches for
IRQ configuration

Setting information
for DIP switches

8-bit ISA expansion slot connector

Figure 5.20

A typical internal modem with an 8-bit ISA connector. Modems with an 8-bit expansion slot connector cannot use IRQs above 9, making conflicts with other devices more likely than with 16-bit ISA or PCI modems.

After you physically install the modem, follow these additional steps:

1. If the modem is external, connect it to the computer and turn it on.

   The modem might be detected and have its software installed during the system startup. If so, skip to step 4.

2. Open the Modems icon in the Control Panel (see Figure 5.23).

3. Click Add. Windows will offer to look for the new modem. If you select this option, Windows will check each serial port for a new modem. If you do not have Windows look for your modem, you must choose the modem from the list of known modems, or use Have Disk to have Windows use the setup files you received with the modem.

Figure 5.21
A typical external modem. Watch the signal lights on the front of the unit for connection speed and dialing activity.

Figure 5.22
A typical PC Card (PCMCIA) modem. Most modems of this type require a dongle (a special connector) to attach them to the telephone line, but a few models are thick enough to accept a standard RJ-11 telephone jack.

4. After the new modem has been detected, Windows will prompt you for the location of driver software (.inf files) to configure the modem.

5. Use the Browse button to indicate the location, which can be any local or network drive.

6. After the software driver is installed, click Finish and the modem can be used.

Standard AT Commands

After you have installed a modem with Windows, you can use either communications software programs included with Windows, such as HyperTerminal, or third-party programs to operate the modem. Communications software uses AT commands to operate modems and change their default configuration.

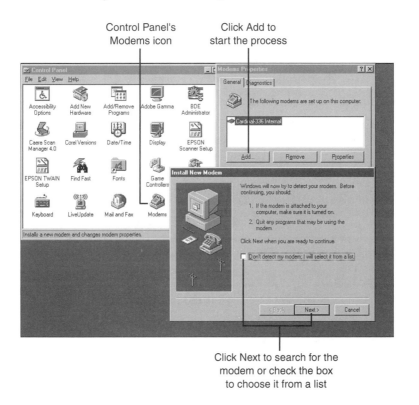

Control Panel's
Modems icon

Click Add to
start the process

Click Next to search for the
modem or check the box
to choose it from a list

Figure 5.23
When installing a modem with Windows 9x, you can choose to have Windows search for the modem or choose it yourself from the list of known modems.

AT stands for "attention," and the options that follow AT instruct the modem to perform particular operations. These commands were originally created for use with Hayes modems; because most modems use the standard Hayes command set, most of these commands will work with most modems. Check your modem's documentation for additions and exceptions to this list.

Table 5.7 lists the most important AT commands.

By using a communication program (such as Windows Terminal or HyperTerminal) that allows you to send these commands to the modem, you can learn more about the modem's condition, and be able to troubleshooting problems. The same commands are used by communication software to control the operation of modems.

Table 5.7   Standard AT Commands Used for Modem Control

AT Command	Meaning	Example
ATDT	Tone-dial the telephone number that follows	ATDT5551212
ATDP	Pulse-dial the telephone number that follows	ATDP5551212
+++	Escape sequence: Allows you to send the modem a command after you're connected to another modem	+++
ATH	Hangs up modem	ATH
ATZ	Resets modem to configuration referred to by the following number	ATZ0

AT commands can also be used to set the modem's volume, adjust additional dialing options, and perform various diagnostic tests.

S-Registers

AT commands can also be used to view or set S-registers, which are used to store or adjust timing and other technical details.

To see the current settings for S-registers and other settings stored in your modem, use this command within your terminal program:

```
AT&V
```

The information displayed by the AT&V command (see Figure 5.24) will vary from modem to modem. You can alter the values that your modem displays for S-registers and other settings by sending your modem the appropriate AT commands if needed.

Initialization Strings

An initialization string is a series of AT& modem commands sent to the modem by the communications program before dialing the number and connecting with the remote computer. AT& commands are used to set special modem options. Normally, you will not need to edit this directly; instead, by selecting the modem and the desired options in the communications program, the program will build the initialization string for you. A typical initialization string for a US Robotics modem is

```
AT&F&C1&D2X7&H1&R2&K3&B1&A3^M
```

You can manually edit the initialization string within most communications programs if the settings are incorrect for your modem. See the modem's documentation for the specific AT& commands that apply to that model.

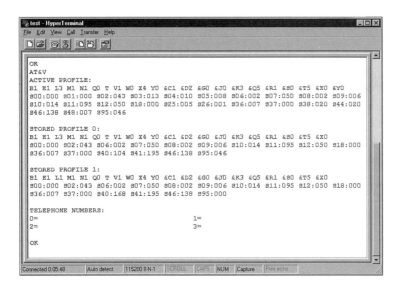

Figure 5.24
Using HyperTerminal to view the current settings for the author's Cardinal modem with the AT&V command.

Cabling

Two types of cabling are needed for an external modem; only one is needed for an internal modem. RJ-11 telephone cable is the "silver satin" cable included with most modems. Run the cable from the "Line" jack on the back of the modem to the telephone wall jack.

The "phone" jack on the back of both internal and external modems allows you to plug in your normal telephone and still use it, whether the computer is on or off. The modem will take over the telephone line when it actually is in use.

The RJ-11 connector is keyed to plug in only one way. Use the plastic lever on the connector to release it when you need to remove the cable from either the modem or the wall jack.

The RS-232 modem cable is also required by external modems; this cable is a standard item.

Replacement

If you must replace a modem for Windows 9x, Windows Me, and Windows 2000, you will need to perform the following steps:

1. Open the Modems icon in the Control Panel.

2. Select the modem you are replacing.

3. Select Remove.

4. After the modem is removed from the list, follow the appropriate steps (refer to the previous set of steps) to physically remove the old modem from the system, install the new modem, and configure the new modem.

Modem Troubleshooting

With so much technical support, program and firmware upgrades distributed through the Internet, and research that must be done over the Internet, modems are critical to many users. The sections that follow describe typical modem problems and solutions that you might encounter on the A+ Certification test and in your day-to-day work.

No Dial Tone

Because modems use telephone lines to connect with remote computers, you normally will hear a dial tone when the modem begins to make a connection. Unless your modem is configured to ignore the dial tone, a lack of a dial tone will prevent your modem from dialing. No dial tone can be caused by

- **Bad or loose RJ-11 "silver satin" telephone cable**—Check connections at the modem and the wall jack, replace defective, worn, brittle, or broken cables, and retry the call.

- **Active connection to another computer**—Hang up the modem. Use the ATH command in your terminal program if necessary, or turn off an external modem for a few seconds to break the connection.

Slow Connection

Normally, modems should make connections at or near their rated speeds. A dialog box appears during the modem connection process to indicate the connection speed. If the modem connects much slower than its rated speed, check the following issues:

- **Incorrect modem driver**—Windows can use standard modem drivers at various speeds up to 56Kbps, but in most cases, these drivers will not provide connections as fast as drivers made for the particular modem model. Download and install the correct driver for your modem.

- **Incorrect initialization string**—The initialization string configures the modem, and incorrect values can affect modem speed. If you cannot download a replacement driver, manually edit the initialization string to the values recommended for the modem by the modem vendor.

- **Poor line conditions**—Because modems convert digital to analog data and analog data back to digital, good line quality is essential to modem operation. Most modems auto-negotiate during the initial connection process to find a speed at which both can communicate reliably. If the connection speed is significantly less than normal and the weather is good, hang up the connection and try again. Rainy weather tends to make many older telephone systems less reliable, creating audible noise on the line that also interferes with modem use.

Problems with 56Kbps Connections

The inability to reach connections beyond 33.6Kbps with 56Kbps modems can be caused by temporary or permanent line problems or by incorrect matching of the 56Kbps protocol used by the computer's modem with those used by the ISP. Check these issues for solutions:

- **Inability to connect above 33.6Kbps**—So-called 56Kbps modems reach speeds above the normal 33.6Kbps for downloading data only if an all-digital connection can be made between the modem and the telephone company's central switch. A high-quality line should achieve these faster than normal connections most of the time; a line that is affected by weather frequently will not be able to allow connections above 33.6Kbps. Some lines cannot achieve results above 33.6Kbps regardless of weather because of built-in limitations in the telephone line itself. As with weather-related conditions, hang up a slow connection and try the connection again, particularly if you do achieve results higher than 33.6Kbps at least some of the time.

- **Incorrect 56Kbps dial-up number**—Three different protocols are used by 56Kbps modems: the X2 and K56flex were developed by different companies using incompatible technologies, and both have been replaced by the international V.90 standard. Most ISPs have converted their equipment to support V.90, so modems that support only the older X2 or K56flex standards might not be able to connect at speeds above 33.6Kbps. Older modems should be upgraded to V.90 through firmware upgrades or physical replacement. If the ISP still supports X2 or K56flex for 56Kbps connections, use the correct phone numbers provided by the ISP to connect with the correct modem type. If you call a V.90-only number with an X2 or K56flex modem, you will not be able to connect at speeds higher than 33.6Kbps.

CH
5

Gibberish Onscreen During Connection

Modems are serial devices, and whenever serial devices connect, both the sending and receiving devices must use matching connection speeds, word length, stop bits, parity, and flow control. Most ISPs use standard settings for these options (8-bit word length, no parity, one stop bit), but some mainframe computers might use 7-bit word length, even parity, and other differences. If you see gibberish when you connect with another computer instead of the normal login screen, there is a mismatch in serial port settings. Contact the help desk managing the remote computer for the correct settings and try your connection again after resetting the correct connection values.

Modem Not Detected During Installation

Most modems used with Windows 9x, Windows Me, or Windows 2000 are Plug and Play modems; the system BIOS and operating system detect the modem, install its software, and select the correct IRQ and I/O port address for internal models. If the modem is not detected, check the following:

- For external serial-port modems, make sure the modem is connected to a power source and turned on.

- For external USB modems, make sure the USB ports are enabled in the system, that Windows 98, Windows Me, or Windows 2000 are in use to support the USB port, and that the modem is connected to either a built-in USB port or a powered external hub.

- For internal modems, check to see whether the modem has an IRQ conflict with existing devices. An ISA modem must have its own IRQ; no sharing is permitted. For example, if you want to use COM 2 for the internal modem, you must disable the computer's existing COM 2; use the system BIOS to disable COM 2 before installing the modem. You might need to set the IRQ for the expansion slot or reserve an IRQ for use by an ISA device in the System Properties sheet. Some ISA modems can be set for manual IRQ configuration. If you choose this option, use the Device Manager to determine which IRQs are available for use by the modem and select an IRQ that is not in use.

Keyboard

The keyboard remains the primary method used to send commands to the computer and enter data.

There are two major keyboard connectors, shown in Figure 5.25:

- 5-pin DIN (originating with the IBM PC)
- 6-pin mini-DIN (originating with the IBM PS/2)

Figure 5.25
Typical 6-pin mini-DIN (left) and 5-pin DIN (right) keyboard connectors.

Both types of keyboards can be interchanged if they are built for IBM AT-type computers or newer by using adapters to change the pinouts and connector.

Installation and Replacement

To install the keyboard, turn off the power and insert the connector end of the keyboard cable into the keyboard connector (usually on the back of the computer). No special drivers are required unless the keyboard has special keys, a programmable feature, or is a wireless model that uses a receiver.

To remove the keyboard, turn off the power before removing the connector end of the keyboard cable from the keyboard connector.

Troubleshooting

Keyboard problems usually result from a few simple causes:

- A damaged keyboard connector on the computer
- A damaged keyboard cable
- Dirt, dust, or gunk in the keyboard

The following are some ways to avoid these problems:

- Don't plug a keyboard into a system that's powered up. This is an "excellent" way to destroy the motherboard!
- Don't plug a keyboard into a system at an angle. This tends to break the solder joints that attach the keyboard connector to the motherboard.
- Don't use sprays to clean a keyboard; use a cloth dampened with an antistatic surface cleaner (such as Endust for Electronics) to wipe off grime while the system is turned off.
- Use compressed air to remove dirt and dust under the keys, or remove the keys if possible for cleaning.

Mouse

Next to the keyboard, the mouse is the most important device used to send commands to the computer. For Windows users who don't perform data entry, the mouse is even more important than the keyboard. Mouse alternatives, such as trackballs or touchpads, are considered mice because they install and are configured the same way.

Four major interface types are used for mice:

- Serial
- Bus
- 6-pin mini-DIN (PS/2)
- USB

The bus mouse, which uses an 8-pin round connector, is seldom seen today. Most mice supplied with systems use the PS/2 connector. Most mice purchased at retail stores come with a serial connector, along with an adapter that allows them to be used on a PS/2 mouse port, as in Figure 5.26.

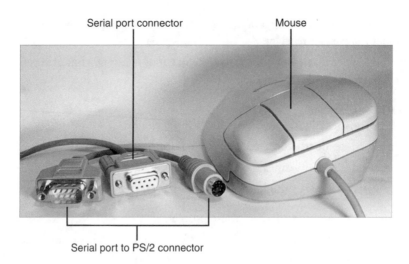

Serial port connector   Mouse

Serial port to PS/2 connector

Figure 5.26
A typical serial mouse supplied with a PS/2 mouse port adapter.

The newest type of mouse interface is the USB port, which can be used for a wide variety of devices.

Installation and Replacement

The physical installation of a mouse is extremely simple. Turn off the computer and plug the mouse into the appropriate connector.

Unlike keyboards, mice require software drivers. Although many mice today emulate or act like the Microsoft mouse, some mice require different software drivers. Mice with wheels or toggles for screen scrolling should be installed with the drivers included with the mice, because standard drivers might not support the scrolling feature.

Mouse Configuration

A serial mouse uses the IRQ and I/O port address of the serial port it is connected to.

A PS/2 mouse uses IRQ 12; if IRQ 12 is not available, the device using that IRQ must be moved to another IRQ to allow IRQ 12 to be used by the mouse.

A bus mouse uses a special interface board that plugs into an 8-bit or 16-bit ISA slot. It might use DIP switches, jumper blocks, or a software configuration program to allow the user to select an unused IRQ and I/O port address range. If the bus mouse port is part of another card (such as some old ATI VGA cards), it still requires separate settings.

A USB mouse uses the IRQ and I/O port address of the USB port to which it is connected. Because a single USB port can support up to 127 devices through the use of hubs, a USB mouse doesn't tie up hardware resources the way other mouse types do.

Mouse Software Installation

The MS-DOS mouse drivers need to be used only if mouse-compatible utility or recreational software that cannot run under Windows will be used on a system. To install MS-DOS drivers:

1. Copy the Mouse.com or Mouse.sys driver from the mouse setup software disk to a folder called \Mouse on the hard drive (C:).

2. Edit the autoexec.bat file and add an entry C:\Mouse\Mouse.com to start the mouse driver during the boot process.

   or

   If the mouse does not have a Mouse.com driver, you can add an entry to the Config.sys file instead to start the mouse during the boot process:

   ```
   DEVICE=C:\Mouse\Mouse.sys
   ```

For Windows 9x, Windows Me, or Windows 2000:

1. Open the Control Panel icon.

2. Open the Mouse icon.

3. Select the General tab.

4. Click the Change button.

5. Select the new mouse from the list, or click Have Disk if your mouse isn't listed.

6. Insert the Windows CD-ROM or vendor-supplied driver disk or CD-ROM, or use Browse to indicate its location.

7. Click Finish when the process is completed.

Mouse Configuration

Most mice are configured by software. The most common hardware option is a sliding switch on the bottom of some three-button mice that can be used to select either native mode or Microsoft Mouse emulation mode, which disables the middle button.

Software configuration allows more options, including

- Switching of left and right mouse buttons
- Speed of mouse pointer movement
- Acceleration factors
- Double-click speed

With Windows 9x and above, these options are configured through the Mouse icon in the Control Panel (see Figure 5.27).

Mouse Maintenance

Most mice contain a ball that moves against rollers (some mice use optical sensors instead). The motion of the mouse ball against a mouse pad, desk, or tabletop can pick

CH

5

up dust and dirt that can cause erratic mouse-pointer movement. The ball and the rollers should be cleaned periodically. Clean the mouse with a specially designed mouse cleaning kit or use a non-abrasive damp cloth to remove gunk from the rollers and the ball.

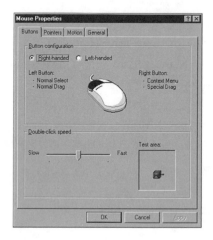

Figure 5.27
Windows 9x and newer versions allow you to change the mouse button assignment and double-click speed through the Mouse icon in the Control Panel.

To remove the mouse ball for access to the rollers:

1. Turn over the mouse; an access cover on the bottom of the mouse holds the ball in place.

2. Follow the arrows on the access cover to turn or slide the cover to one side; lift the plate out of the way to release the ball (see Figure 5.28).

3. Turn the rollers until you see dirt or grit; wipe them clean and clean the ball.

4. Shake loose dust and gunk out of the mouse.

5. When the cleaning process is finished, replace the ball and access panel.

Mice that lack a ball normally have optical sensors that pick up movement. Keep the sensors clear of dust and debris and the mouse will work properly; no disassembly is required.

Trackballs can also become dirty. Remove the trackball and clean the rollers to keep the trackball working properly.

Touchpads should be periodically wiped with a dampened cloth to remove skin oils that can prevent proper sensing of finger movements.

Mouse rollers

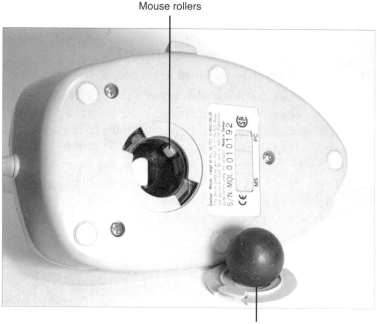

Mouse ball sitting on top of
its retaining ring after removal

Figure 5.28
Remove the retaining ring and mouse ball to clean the mouse ball, rollers, and other
internal parts of a mouse.

Mouse Troubleshooting

Although Windows supports keyboard shortcuts for some operations, a mouse is required
for maximum utility. Use this section to prepare for troubleshooting questions on the A+
Certification exam and day-to-day mouse problems.

Mouse Pointer Won't Move

If the mouse pointer won't move when the mouse is moved, check the following:

- **Check the mouse software driver**—Use the Mouse icon in the Control Panel to
  verify that the correct mouse driver has been selected under Windows. Using the
  wrong mouse driver can cause the mouse pointer to freeze.

- **Check the mouse connection to the system**—If a PS/2 or bus mouse isn't
  plugged in tightly, the system must be shut down, the mouse reconnected to the
  PS/2 mouse or bus mouse port, and the system restarted to enable the mouse to
  work. USB mice can be hot-swapped at any time. If a serial mouse is used on the
  system and it is not detected during Windows startup, Windows normally will display a message instructing you to plug in the mouse.

CH
5

■ **Check for hardware conflicts**—Serial, bus, and PS/2 mice must have exclusive access to the IRQ used by the port to which the mouse is connected. If you use another device that uses the same IRQ, the mouse pointer will freeze onscreen and the system can lock up. Use the Windows Device Manager to verify that there are no IRQ conflicts between the port used by the mouse and other devices.

■ **Make sure the mouse can work with a port adapter**—Many mice sold at retail can be used with either a serial port or PS/2 port, or with either a USB port or PS/2 mouse port. The mouse has one port type built-in and uses an adapter supplied with the mouse to attach to the other port type with which it is compatible. These mice also contain special circuitry to enable the mouse to work with either port type. Don't mix up the adapters used by different brands and models of mice; mismatches might not work. Mice bundled with systems typically don't have the extra circuitry needed to work with an adapter; they're built to attach to one port type only.

Jerky Mouse Pointer Movement

The most common cause of jerky mouse pointer movement is dirt or dust on the mouse or trackball rollers (which are used to transmit movement signals to the computer). See "Mouse Maintenance," earlier in this chapter, for details on mouse cleaning.

The speed of the mouse pointer can also be adjusted with the Mouse icon in the Windows Control Panel. Select the Movement tab and adjust the Cursor Speed and Acceleration tab to make the mouse pointer move faster or slower across the screen.

User Can't Double-Click Icons

Damaged mouse buttons can prevent a user from double-clicking on icons in Windows. Turn off the system if necessary, substitute an identical mouse, and restart the system to see if the mouse is the problem. If changing mice doesn't solve the problem, check the double-click speed. Use the Mouse icon in the Windows Control Panel to adjust the double-click speed to the user's preference.

Sound Cards

With the increase of multimedia applications for PCs, sound cards have become popular peripherals for educational, gaming, and business systems. Sound cards can be used for the following tasks:

■ Digital conversion of prerecorded audio

■ Playback of CD-ROM or Web-based audio content

■ Recording of sounds or speech

■ Voice control and dictation

■ Text-to-speech (computer "reads" text)

Sound cards have distinctive internal and external features, as you will see in the following figures.

External Features

All sound cards feature at least one speaker jack and a microphone jack that uses a mini stereo plug. Most sound cards also feature a 15-pin game port/MIDI port jack, and some have a line-in jack, a second speaker jack for 3D sound, and/or an external volume control thumbwheel (see Figure 5.29).

Combo sound/modem cards also feature a telephone-line jack for the modem feature.

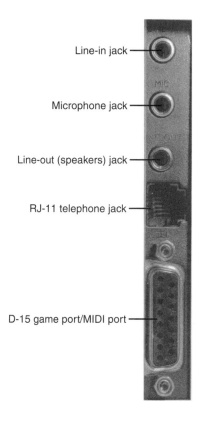

Line-in jack

Microphone jack

Line-out (speakers) jack

RJ-11 telephone jack

D-15 game port/MIDI port

Figure 5.29
Typical external jacks on a combined modem/sound card. This type of card can be found on many IBM and Packard-Bell computers and has also been sold as an add-on by some vendors.

Internal Features

All sound cards have an internal jack to allow music CDs to be played through the sound card's speakers. Sound cards that feature FM synthesis for MIDI files might also have a connector for a wavetable daughtercard. Many older sound cards also feature proprietary or IDE CD-ROM data cable connectors, particularly those sold with 486-based systems or as part of a multimedia kit.

Figure 5.30 illustrates all these features as shown on a typical sound card.

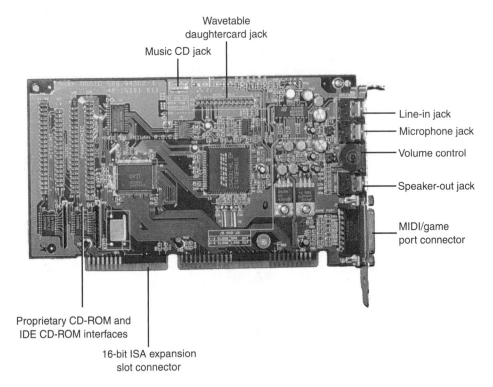

Figure 5.30
Typical internal and external features on a typical sound card with CD-ROM and IDE ports.

Types of Sound Cards

Sound cards can be installed into the expansion slots of a computer (ISA or PCI), or the equivalent sound circuits can be integrated into the motherboard. Both slot-mounted and integrated sound circuits will be referred to as "sound cards" in this section, except as noted.

Sound cards differ in their capability to handle different forms of audio content. All sound cards can play back digitized sound, but they differ in the quality of sound they can record and play back and in how they play MIDI musical scores:

- 8-bit sound cards cannot record or play back high-quality sound, but are long obsolete and rare. These old sound cards use only a single-edge connector for the 8-bit portion of the ISA slot.

- 16-bit or better sound cards can record and play back high-quality sound (44KHz or higher sampling rate). These cards are 16-bit ISA or PCI (32-bit).

- FM synthesis cards must create artificial versions of musical instruments to play MIDI scores. MIDI scores played on this type of sound card have poor musical quality.

- Wavetable cards use actual samples from real musical instruments to play MIDI scores. Less-expensive wavetable cards use system RAM or an optional daughter-card to store their samples, and can only work with a limited number of voices (musical instruments) such as 32 or 64. More expensive wavetable cards can store a larger number of voices, up to 512, either onboard the card, in system RAM, on an add-on memory module, or a combination of these.

Most recent sound cards use wavetable synthesis.

Physical Installation and Replacement

Sound cards that use jumper blocks for configuration should be set before installation into the system; most recent sound cards are configured with software or by Windows 95/98/2000's Plug and Play technology.

Because the sound quality of sound cards can be affected by interference, the best results are obtained if you can install the sound card into a slot that is one slot away from other cards and as far away from the power supply as possible.

Default Hardware Configuration

The default configuration of sound cards differs depending on whether the sound card will be used for MS-DOS programs or for Windows programs. Many sound cards use different settings to support DOS and Windows sound programs. The configuration listed in Table 5.8 is based on the defaults used by the Creative Labs SoundBlaster AWE64 Gold card, which represents a *de facto* standard for sound cards. Most other brands of sound cards use similar settings.

CH
5

Table 5.8 Standard and Optional Hardware Settings for Creative Labs SoundBlaster AWE64 Gold (Options for Some Settings in Parentheses)				
Feature	IRQ	DMA 8-Bit	DMA 16-Bit	Starting I/O Port Address
Audio	5 (2,7,10)	1 (0,3)	5 (6,7)	220h (240h, 260h, 280h)
FM Synthesis				388h
Joystick port				200h
MPU-401 (MIDI)				330h (300h)
Standard				
Wave synthesis				6x0, Ax0, Ex0
(select one)				(x=0-9,a-f)

This card uses one IRQ, two DMA, and up to five different I/O port addresses. Windows 9x and above enable you to select some "stripped-down" configurations with the Windows Device Manager that omit certain features.

Because sound cards are resource-hungry, the sound card should be the first add-on card installed in any system.

As Table 5.8 indicates, sound cards have multiple hardware devices on board. Figure 5.31 shows that the Windows Device Manager displays each hardware component in a sound card as a separate device.

Figure 5.31
A sound card's resources might be listed under multiple headings, as seen here: The Ensoniq AudioPCI, Ensoniq AudioPCI Legacy Device (for SoundBlaster emulation), and Gameport Joystick are all part of a single sound card.

Sound cards used with MS-DOS need

- The appropriate sound card driver to be installed in Config.sys.
- A SET statement in Autoexec.bat indicating card type and settings. In Figure 5.32, an actual SET statement used with a wavetable SoundBlaster card is listed, along with a color-coded key.

A card that emulates the Creative Labs SoundBlaster can have two different SET statements; one for SB emulation (as shown here), and one for its native mode, as in the Aztech 16AZCard used on some Gateway computers (see Figure 5.33).

Sound Card Troubleshooting

Sound cards can be difficult to troubleshoot because of their complex hardware requirements, software driver requirements, need to use add-on speakers for output, and potential for conflicts. Use this section to prepare for sound card troubleshooting questions that might appear on the A+ Certification exam or in your day-to-day work.

```
SET BLASTER=A220 I5 D1 H5 P330 T6 E620

audio I/O
IRQ
DMA
16-bit DMA
MIDI I/O
16 or 32-bit sound card
wavetable I/O
```

Figure 5.32
A SET BLASTER statement used with a typical wavetable-equipped SoundBlaster sound card. The color-coded legend is listed below the SET BLASTER statement.

The Card Plays Sounds but Can't Record CD-Quality Sound

Most ISA sound cards use two different DMA channels, typically DMA 1 for 8-bit sounds and DMA 5 for 16-bit sounds. If your sound card plays Windows startup and event sounds but you can't record sounds in CD quality (44KHz, stereo), check for conflicts between the sound card's DMA channels and another device that uses DMA. Verify that a 16-bit DMA (5, 6, or 7) is being used by the card's configuration by checking the sound card's configuration with the Windows Device Manager. Move any conflicting device to a different DMA channel.

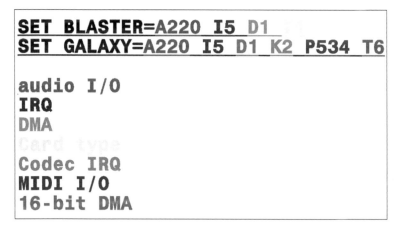

```
SET BLASTER=A220 I5 D1
SET GALAXY=A220 I5 D1 K2 P534 T6

audio I/O
IRQ
DMA
Card type
Codec IRQ
MIDI I/O
16-bit DMA
```

Figure 5.33
A SET BLASTER and SET GALAXY statement used by an Aztech 16AZ sound card. This card, like most cards that emulate the Sound Blaster, uses different resources and even different option names for the SB emulation and native (Aztech) modes. The color-coded legend is listed below the SET GALAXY statement.

Sound Card Won't Work in Some Systems but Works Okay in Others

An increasing number of low-cost computers have built-in sound circuits on the motherboard. Motherboards with this feature will conflict with add-on sound cards unless the motherboard-based sound is disabled before the sound card is installed.

Sound Playback Is Distorted or Choppy

Out-of-date drivers are the most common cause for distorted or choppy sound. Using ISA sound cards on fast systems also can cause choppy sound because the slow ISA bus can't keep up with the rest of the computer. Download and install the latest drivers for the sound card, and use PCI sound cards on recent and current systems for better sound quality.

No Sound at All from Sound Card

A sound card that doesn't play sound might not be defective; instead, the cause could be volume controls or speaker problems. Check the following:

- **On-card volume controls**—Some sound cards use an external volume control; make sure this is set to at least the midway point.

- **Windows mixer controls**—When a sound card is installed on a Windows system, a volume control for playback and recording features is normally installed in the system tray. Double-click the speaker icon to view the volume controls. If the play control is muted or set to minimum volume, you will not hear anything from the sound card. If individual features are muted or set to minimum volume, the sound card will play some types of sounds but not others.

- **Incorrect jack used for speakers**—As seen in Figure 5.29, the mini-jacks used for speaker, microphone, and line-in are identical. If the speakers are plugged into the wrong jack, you will hear nothing from the sound card. Verify you are using the correct jack for the speakers.

- **No power to speakers**—Most speakers used for computers can be powered by either DC batteries or by an AC adapter. Many low-cost speakers can play sounds at a low volume without power, but the speakers' built-in amplification is turned off if the speaker is turned on but no power is present. Leave the speaker power off if no external power is present, and use the Windows volume control to control the speaker volume.

- **Windows Device Manager**—If the sound card is not visible in the Windows Device Manager, install it with the Add/Remove Hardware icon in Control Panel. If one or more components are listed with the yellow ! sign indicating a problem, view the component properties and make sure that the proper drivers are installed and that there are no conflicts with other devices. Install new drivers or correct conflicts as needed, and restart the system if prompted to restore proper sound card operation.

Sound Card Works in Windows but Not for MS-DOS Programs

As seen in Figures 5.32 and 5.33 earlier in this chapter, MS-DOS uses SET statements to specify sound card resources for use with MS-DOS programs. Some sound cards automatically add the correct SET statements to the AUTOEXEC.BAT file or the AUTOEXEC.BAT parameters used with Windows 9x's MS-DOS mode, but others require you to run a special MS-DOS executable file to set the card for use with MS-DOS programs. Consult the card documentation for details.

Sound Card Can't Play MIDI Files

MIDI files are special types of sound files that store an instrumental music score that is played by the sound card using either FM-based simulation of different musical instruments or stored samples of different musical instruments. If the sound card can't play MIDI files, check the following:

- **MIDI port (also called the MPU-401 port) might be disabled in the sound card configuration or have a conflict with another device**—Use the Windows Device Manager to choose a configuration that enables the MIDI port or prevents a conflict with another device.

- **MIDI samples might not be loaded into RAM or have been corrupted**—MIDI instrumentation is built into some sound cards, but many use a so-called "soft wavetable" feature that stores the samples on disk and loads them into RAM. Reload the samples from the original sound card driver disks or CD-ROM and verify that they are being loaded into RAM.

Many sound cards come with a diagnostic routine that will

- Play digitized sounds through each speaker (left and right) and both (stereo)
- Play MIDI tracks

Use the sound card's diagnostics to check proper operation.

IEEE-1394

The IEEE-1394 port, a development of the FireWire port developed by Apple for the Macintosh, is also referred to as the i.LINK port by Sony. At 400Mbps, IEEE-1394 is the fastest and among the most flexible ports used on personal computers. IEEE-1394 can be implemented either as a built-in port on the motherboard or as part of an add-on card. Most systems don't have IEEE-1394 ports built in, so an add-on card must be added, as shown in Figure 5.34.

Some IEEE-1394 add-on cards also provide an internal port for the growing number of internal IEEE-1394 devices.

Standard IEEE-1394 ports and cables use a six-pin interface, but some digital camcorders use the alternative four-pin interface, which supplies data and signals but no power to the device (see Figure 5.35).

CH
5

IEEE-1394–Compatible Devices and Technical Requirements

IEEE-1394–compatible devices include internal and external hard drives, digital camcorders (also referred to as DV camcorders), Web cameras, and high-performance scanners and printers, as well as hubs, repeaters, and SCSI to IEEE-1394 converters. IEEE-1394 ports support hot-swapping, enabling you to add or remove a device from an IEEE-1394 port without shutting down the system.

Figure 5.34
A typical IEEE-1394 add-on card providing three six-pin ports. A standard six-pin cable is attached to the bottom port.

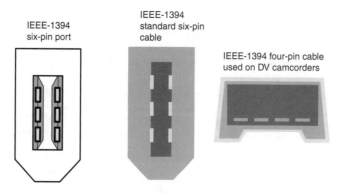

IEEE-1394
six-pin port

IEEE-1394
standard six-pin
cable

IEEE-1394 four-pin cable
used on DV camcorders

Figure 5.35
The IEEE-1394 port, six-pin cable, and four-pin cable.

Up to 16 IEEE-1394 devices can be connected to a single IEEE-1394 port through daisy-chaining, and the current speed supported by IEEE-1394 is 400Mbps; higher rates are possible.

Windows 98, Windows Me, and Windows 2000 all include IEEE-1394 support; Windows 95 and Windows NT 4.0 and earlier NT versions do not. IEEE-1394 cards are PCI-based and require the following hardware resources:

- One IRQ (it can be shared on systems that support IRQ sharing by PCI devices)
- One memory address range (must be unique)

The exact IRQ and memory address range used by a particular IEEE-1394 card can be determined by using the Windows Device Manager. When an IEEE-1394 card is installed, a device category called 1394 Bus Controller is added to the Device Manager, and the particular card installed is listed beneath that category.

Installing an IEEE-1394 Card

To install and configure the card, follow this procedure:

1. Turn off the computer and remove the case cover.
2. Locate an available PCI expansion slot.
3. Remove the slot cover and insert the card into the slot. Secure the card in the slot.
4. Some IEEE-1394 cards are powered by the PCI expansion slot, while others require the same 4-pin connector used by hard drives for power. Connect a power lead if the card requires it; you can use a Y-splitter to free up a power lead if necessary.
5. Restart the system and provide the driver disk or CD-ROM when requested by the system.
6. The IRQ and memory address required by the card will be assigned automatically.

Troubleshooting IEEE-1394 Cards and Devices

Because IEEE-1394 cards and devices are not supported by the system BIOS but require software drivers, many problems with these devices can be traced to loading incorrect drivers for the card or devices, or initial installation problems. Use this list of problems and solutions to prepare for the A+ Certification test and for day-to-day troubleshooting of these devices.

System Can't Detect the IEEE-1394 Card

If the IEEE-1394 card can't be detected after it is physically installed in the system, check the following:

- **The card's position in the slot**—If the card is not properly seated in the expansion slot, reseat it.
- **Power lead on cards that require an external power source**—Some IEEE-1394 cards require additional power from a four-pin power connector. If the power

CH

5

connector isn't connected to the card, the card will not work when the system is turned on. Connect the power to the card and restart the system.

■ **IRQ conflict**—Most systems that came with Windows 98, Windows Me, or Windows 2000 preinstalled are designed to allow IRQ sharing. Older systems that have been upgraded to one of these versions of Windows might not be equipped for IRQ sharing. You might need to restart the system and use the system BIOS setup program to select an unused IRQ for a particular PCI expansion slot or use the Windows Device Manager to reset either the IEEE-1394 card or the conflicting device to a different IRQ.

Incorrect Driver for IEEE-1394 Card or Device

Several different chipsets are used on IEEE-1394 cards and devices. If drivers for the wrong chipset are installed, the card or device will not function. If an IEEE-1394 card or device displays the yellow ! sign in the Windows Device Manager, check the properties for the card or device. If an IRQ or memory address conflict is not present, use the Driver tab to manually update to the correct driver.

Summary

The major I/O devices used in computers include the serial and parallel ports, USB and IEEE-1394 ports, mice, modems, keyboards, and sound cards. Most I/O devices offer many configuration options, including choices of IRQ, I/O port address, DMA channel, and other options.

Parallel ports generally are used for printers, but they also can be used for high-capacity removable storage and scanners. Serial ports generally are used for mice and external modems. Both parallel and serial ports can be used for direct-connect data transfer, and USB ports can be used for a wide variety of devices. All three types of ports are generally built into the motherboards of recent systems and can be retrofitted to older systems. Keyboard ports can be either 5-pin DIN or the same 6-pin DIN connector used for PS/2 mice, although keyboard and mouse ports cannot be interchanged. Sound chipsets are included on some motherboards, but sound cards in both ISA and PCI formats are used on more expensive systems. IEEE-1394 ports are almost always added to systems through PCI cards.

Serial, parallel, and keyboard ports are supported by the system BIOS; other ports and devices require software drivers specific to the device and operating system to function. USB and IEEE-1394 ports require Windows 98, Windows Me, or Windows 2000 to operate. Some USB devices supported by Windows 98 and Me are not supported by Windows 2000 due to differences in the operating systems' drivers.

Plug and Play ports and I/O devices generally request device driver and configuration software when the system is turned on for the first time after the device is installed.

QUESTIONS AND ANSWERS: ─────────

1. What is daisy-chaining, and which I/O port types allow it? Which I/O port type uses hubs to facilitate daisy-chaining?
    A: Daisy-chaining refers to attaching multiple devices to a single port. Each device in the daisy-chain has two connectors to "pass-through" signals. Parallel, USB, and IEEE-1394 ports allow multiple devices to be attached.

2. What popular type of input device can be attached to a dedicated or standard port? What are those ports?
    A: A mouse can be connected to the serial port (which is a standard port used for many items), a PS/2 port (used only for keyboards and mice), a bus mouse port (used only for bus mice), or a USB port.

3. What is the difference between parallel and IEEE-1284 interfacing?
    A: IEEE-1284 refers to several types of advanced, high-speed, bidirectional parallel interfacing. Not all parallel interfaces are IEEE-1284 compliant.

4. What device can be attached to a serial port or can contain one?
    A: A modem. External modems are attached to serial ports; most internal modems use a UART chip, which means they contain a serial port.

5. Why should a sound card be installed before other devices?
    A: It uses more hardware resources (IRQ, DMA, I/O port addresses) than any other common I/O card.

6. Which I/O port types require Windows 98 or newer versions to operate? Do these port support hot-swap devices?
    A: USB and IEEE-1394 ports require Windows 98, Windows Me, or Windows 2000; earlier versions of Windows do not support these ports. Both port types allow devices to be hot-swapped.

CH
5

Video

──── WHILE YOU READ ────

1. Which type of monitor can display millions of colors, digital or analog? Why?
2. How many colors are in 16-bit color?
3. If you switch from an ATI to a Matrox video card, do you need to adjust the CMOS display type? Why or why not?
4. What do you need to change when changing video cards?

Introduction

The monitor and video card work together to provide real-time notification to the user of the computer's activities. Because computer users spend all day (and sometimes all night) gazing into the display, keeping it working to full efficiency is important. This chapter helps you prepare for the A+ Certification exam by enhancing your understanding of the major types of displays and showing you how to configure and troubleshoot them.

The Video Card

The video card (also known as the graphics card or graphics accelerator) is an add-on card (or circuit on the motherboard of portable computers and some desktop computers) that creates the image you see on the monitor.

Video cards have been built using all the major expansion card types covered in Chapter 2, "The Motherboard and CPU," including

- ISA (16-bit and 8-bit)
- EISA
- VL-Bus
- PCI
- AGP

Pentium-class and newer systems almost always use either the PCI bus or the AGP bus for add-on cards, although low-cost computers often include built-in PCI-equivalent or AGP-equivalent video instead of video cards.

For more information about these expansion slot standards, see "Recognizing Expansion Slot Types," page 57.

From 1994 to 1997, the most common type of expansion slot used for video cards on late-model, 486-based systems and on most Pentium-based systems was PCI. Although PCI is still the leading general-purpose expansion slot type, the advent of the Pentium II CPU led to the development of the AGP expansion slot, which, unlike PCI or the obsolete VL-Bus, is dedicated solely to high-speed video. The AGP expansion slot is also used with other current CPUs, such as the Pentium III-, Celeron-, AMD Athlon- and Celeron-, and Super Socket 7-based systems. Figures 6.1 and 6.2 show the features of these current video card standards.

Note that some PCI video cards, such as the one shown in Figure 6.1, offer options for expanding memory, but AGP cards (and the newest PCI video cards) almost always use surface-mounted non-expandable memory. AGP video cards often have more RAM on board, and the AGP expansion slot connector is offset away from the rear card bracket, unlike the PCI card's connector, which starts next to the rear card bracket.

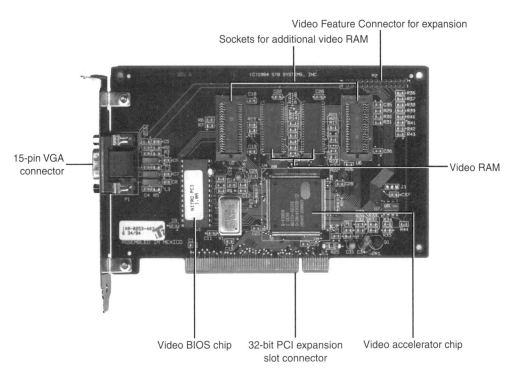

Figure 6.1
A typical PCI VGA video card with expandable memory.

Understanding the Video Card Accelerator Chip and Video BIOS Chip

All video cards except for the original IBM MDA have used a video BIOS chip, which occupies a portion of the upper memory addresses between 640KB and 1MB. See *Upgrading and Repairing PCs, 12th Edition*, Chapter 6, "Upper Memory Area (UMA)," for more detailed information. The video BIOS chip on VGA systems provides the basic VGA features used when your system starts up in text mode and in Windows 9x Safe Mode and Windows 2000 VGA Mode.

The video accelerator chip provides support for higher resolutions and color depths along with special acceleration and 3D features. This part of the video card must be enabled by software drivers written for that particular video chipset.

Video Card Display Types

Regardless of bus type, video cards are primarily distinguished from each other by the type of signal they produce and the type of monitor that must be used with each type of signal. Video cards and monitors come in three major categories:

- Digital
- Analog
- LCD displays

Figure 6.2
A typical high-end AGP VGA video card features video in and out, supports AGP 2x and 4x speeds, and has 64MB of RAM onboard. Photo courtesy ATI Technologies, Inc.

Digital Display Types

The original IBM PC, IBM AT, and compatible computers used several now-obsolete digital displays, all of which featured relatively low resolutions and either monochrome or limited color output.

All the digital video cards listed in Table 6.1 use a DB-9 female connector, but the pinouts for each type are completely different and are not interchangeable. To prepare for the A+ Certification exam, you should know the meanings of the acronyms and which standards support monochrome and which support color. Resolutions for all displays are given in pixels (onscreen dots); the first number is the horizontal size in pixels; the second is the vertical size in pixels.

Table 6.1   Digital Display Types

Display Card Type	Resolution	How to Recognize	Monitor Type	Notes
MDA (Monochrome Display Adapter)	720×348	Usually has DB-25 female (LPT) port on rear; pins 3–5 not used and usually are not present	TTL Monochrome (green or amber)	Text only; no bitmapped graphics
HGC (Hercules Graphics Card	720×348	Same as MDA	Same as MDA	Text plus Hercules bitmapped graphics; card widely cloned; most monochrome cards are "Herc clones"; some required software driver
CGA (Color Graphics Adapter)	320×200 4-color graphics 640×200 2-color text	Usually has one round (RCA) jack on rear; might have 4-pin and 6-pin jacks on side of card	TTL CGA color	Limited color palettes made for terrible "color"
EGA (Enhanced Graphics Adapter)	640×350 16-color graphics and supports CGA graphics; 640×350 monochrome text and graphics	No additional jacks on rear or side	TTL EGA color; TTL monochrome for monochrome mode	Highest resolution and color quality of any digital display

CH 6

VGA and Analog Displays

Virtually all systems built from 1989 on have used analog displays based on the VGA (Video Graphics Array) standard developed by IBM in 1987 for its then new PS/2 line of computers. An analog display is capable of displaying an unlimited number of colors by varying the levels of red, green, or blue per dot (pixel) onscreen. Practical color limits are based on the video card's memory and the desired screen resolution.

Most analog displays are CRT (cathode-ray tube)-based, using a picture tube that is similar to a TV's picture tube. Some LCD flat-panel displays also accept analog signals but must convert the analog signal to a digital signal before displaying the image onscreen.

All VGA cards made for use with standard analog monitors use a DB-15 15-pin female connector. This connector is the same size as the DB-9 connector used for the older digital video standards and serial ports, but it has three rows of pins (see Figure 6.3).

Figure 6.3
A typical early VGA card (top connector) also supported digital standards, such as EGA/CGA (bottom connector).

Some early VGA video cards could also support EGA and CGA displays and had both 9-pin and 15-pin output jacks.

The picture tubes used in CRT displays typically use one of three technologies to form the image:

- A phosphor triad (a group of three phosphors, red, green and blue). The distance between each triad is called the "dot pitch."

- An aperture grill, which uses vertical red, green, and blue phosphor strips. The distance between each group is called the "stripe pitch."

- A slotted mask, which uses small blocks of red, green, and blue phosphor strips. The distance between each horizontal group is also called "stripe pitch."

Generally, the smaller the dot or stripe pitch, the clearer and sharper the onscreen image will be. Typical standards for CRT monitors call for a dot pitch of .28mm or smaller.

LCD Digital Display Standards

With the increasing popularity of LCD displays for desktop computers, new digital display technologies have become popular on some high-end VGA cards. Two major digital display standards support LCD displays with digital interfaces:

- **Digital Flat Panel (DFP)**—This was adopted as a standard in February 1999 but has been largely superseded by DVI. DFP-compatible panels can be adapted to DVI.

- **Digital Visual Interface (DVI)**—DVI-D versions of this standard support digital-only displays, whereas DVI-I supports both digital and analog displays.

See Figure 6.4 for a comparison of analog VGA, DFP, and DVI connectors. Details about DFP and DVI are listed in Table 6.2.

Both DFP and DVI standards support VGA resolutions and color depth and are treated as VGA displays by software. An increasing number of high-end video cards have a DVI-I port and use a dual-head cable to connect to either digital LCD displays or analog VGA monitors. As you prepare for the A+ Certification exam, you should note the differences in appearance among these connections and the major features of the different display standards.

Table 6.2 LCD Digital Display Standards

Standard	Maximum Resolution	Analog Display Support	Pinout
Digital Flat Panel (DFP)	1280×1024	No	2 rows of 10 pins
Digital Visual Interface (DVI-D)	Single-link: 1280×1024 Dual-link: Supports resolutions above 1280×1024	No	3 rows of 8 pins (dual-link); single link omits pins 4, 5, 12, 13, 20, 21
Digital Visual Interface (DVI-I)	1280×1024 for digital displays	Yes	3 rows of 8 pins and 5-pin Micro/Cross analog output

CH
6

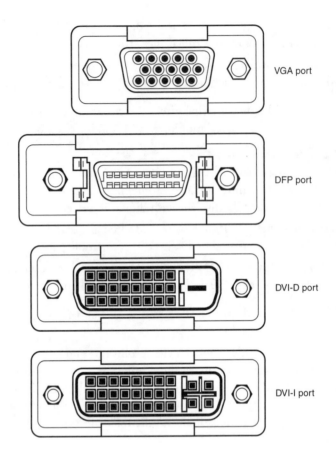

Figure 6.4
A comparison of VGA, DFP, DVI-D, and DVI-I ports.

VGA Color Depths and Memory Requirements

Table 6.3 lists the most common levels of VGA and the video card memory requirements needed to achieve resolutions and color depths. Standard VGA is equal to 16 colors at 640×480 resolution.

Video card colors can be referred to both by the number of colors and by the number of the factor of 2 needed to calculate that number of colors. "24-bit color" = 2^{24} = 16,777,216 colors. In preparing for the A+ Certification exam, note in particular the meaning of 8-bit, 16-bit, and 24-bit color and that the amount of video memory on the card needed to achieve 24-bit color at a given resolution is twice what is required to achieve 16-bit color.

Table 6.3	VGA Resolutions and Color Depth		
Resolution	Number of Colors	Color Depth Bit Rating	Video Card Memory Requirements
640×480	16	4-bit	256KB
640×480	256	8-bit	512KB
640×480	65,536	16-bit	1MB
640×480	16,777,216	24-bit	1MB
800×600	16	4-bit	256KB
800×600	256	8-bit	512KB
800×600	65,536	16-bit	1MB
800×600	16,777,216	24-bit	2MB
1024×768	16	4-bit	512KB
1024×768	256	8-bit	1MB
1024×768	65,536	16-bit	2MB
1024×768	16,777,216	24-bit	4MB

800×600 resolution is often referred to as Super VGA, and 1,024×768 resolution is sometimes referred to as Ultra VGA. Super VGA is often considered to be any color depth and resolution beyond standard VGA.

Achieving Higher Resolutions and Color Depths

All color depths 8-bit or higher and all resolutions 800×600 or higher require the following:

- Video card memory as required for the color depth and resolution desired
- Video driver customized to the video card and able to set color depth and resolution
- Monitor able to display resolution desired

This last option is important for users who want to "salvage" an older VGA-class monitor for use with a new system or new video card. Both video card and monitor must be set to the same resolution.

Both monitor and video card must also be set to run at the same vertical refresh rate. *Vertical refresh* refers to how quickly the monitor redraws the screen, and is measured in hertz (Hz), or times per second. Typical refresh rates for 14-inch diagonal to 17-inch diagonal measure monitors vary from 56Hz to 85Hz, with refresh rates over 72Hz causing less flicker onscreen. Flicker-free (72Hz or higher) refresh rates are better for the user, producing less eyestrain and more comfort during long computing sessions.

The vertical refresh in Windows 9x and 2000 can be adjusted through the Advanced portion of the Display properties sheet.

CH
6

I/O Port, Memory, and IRQ Usage

Video cards use at least two, and sometimes three of the standard hardware resources you first learned about in Chapter 1, "Basic Concepts." All video cards must use one or more

I/O port address ranges, and all video cards use a section of the system memory map called "upper memory." Some video cards also use an IRQ.

Table 6.4 lists typical settings by card type. Note that some newer VGA cards might use different I/O port and IRQ settings.

Table 6.4 I/O Port, Memory, and IRQ Usage by Card Type			
Card Type	I/O Port Address Range	Memory Range	IRQ
Monochrome display adapter and Hercules Graphics card	3B0–3BB	B0000–B0FFF (RAM)	None
CGA graphics card	3D0–3DF	B8000–BBFFF (RAM)	None
EGA graphics card	3C0–3CF or 2B0–2DF	A0000–BFFFF (RAM) C0000–C3FFF (Video BIOS ROM)	9 (on some models)
VGA graphics card	3C0–3CF Some ATI models also use 2E8–2EF, which conflicts with the default for COM 4	A0000–BFFFF (RAM) and C0000–C7FFF (Video BIOS ROM) Many 3D accelerator cards also use additional memory areas that vary by card	Varies; not used on some cards; 9 or other available IRQ on newer PCI and all AGP cards

The memory usage in this table refers to memory space allocated for the card, and isn't affected by the type of memory used on the video card.

Video Memory

Just as the CPU uses memory on the motherboard as a workspace to create information, the video card uses its own video memory as a place to create visual information that is displayed by the monitor. Just as different types of RAM affect the speed of the computer, different types of video RAM affect the speed of the video card.

Video memory comes in almost as many different types as motherboard memory. The following types of memory were reviewed in Chapter 4, "RAM," and their performance on video cards is comparable to their performance on the motherboard:

- **DRAM**—Dynamic RAM
- **EDO RAM**—Extended Data Out RAM

- **SDRAM**—Synchronous DRAM
- **DDR SDRAM**—Double Data Rate SDRAM

Of these four memory types, DDR SDRAM is the fastest and is extremely common on new high-performance video cards; because it is a variation on standard SDRAM, video card makers can easily adapt their designs to use it. DRAM and EDO RAM are often found on low-cost video cards.

Special types of video memory have also been created for the special needs of video display:

- **VRAM**—Video RAM allows data to be read from it and written to it at the same time; this type of operation is referred to as "dual-ported." Video RAM is very fast when compared to DRAM but has not proven to be very popular.
- **WRAM**—Window RAM is a modified version of VRAM. WRAM is also very fast when compared to DRAM but also is not very popular.
- **SGRAM**—Synchronous Graphics RAM is a faster version of SGRAM with additional circuitry designed especially for video cards. It is very popular on many current high-performance video cards.

At one time, video cards could be expanded with additional memory, just as motherboards have been for many years. However, rapid changes in video card technology and lower-cost production have virtually eliminated upgradeable video cards. If a video card needs more memory, you might need to replace it instead of adding memory to it. Use a model that has more memory plus other advanced features as a replacement.

Common Video Card Bus Types

The video card normally plugs into the same type of expansion slots that other cards do. Systems built before the mid-1990s used one of the following obsolete bus standards:

- ISA
- VL-Bus (VESA Local-Bus)
- EISA (Enhanced ISA)

EISA video cards are almost impossible to find, and ISA and VL-Bus video cards, although still available, are based on older designs that lack performance and the large amounts of video RAM common today.

Current systems feature one of these video card types:

- PCI slot-mounted
- PCI built-in
- AGP slot-mounted
- AGP built-in

CH
6

Built-in video uses two different types of memory:

- Dedicated memory chips on the motherboard
- Shared main memory (also known as Unified Memory Architecture)

Built-in video that uses shared main memory normally is slower than video that uses separate memory because main memory and video memory have different characteristics and speeds. If your system shares main memory for video, you normally can adjust how much memory is set aside for video by making adjustments in the system BIOS setup program. As much as 11MB of the 64MB of RAM found in some machines is set aside for built-in video by default.

You can normally replace built-in video with a video card, but if the built-in video is AGP-based and the system has no AGP slots, you'll need to use the slower PCI slots for upgrades (see the next section for details).

Installing a Video Card or Monitor

If you are replacing any EGA or VGA video card and monitor with an improved model, you don't need to make any adjustments in the BIOS setup program for the computer. From the BIOS's standpoint, all types of EGA and VGA are the same.

Although all video cards since the beginning of the 1990s are based on VGA, virtually every one uses a unique chipset that requires special software drivers to control acceleration features (faster onscreen video), color depth, and resolution. So, whenever you change video cards, you must change video driver software as well.

Windows 9x, Me, and 2000 also require that you change the monitor driver when you change monitors. Some monitors use a standard plug-and-play driver, but most have a specific driver that sets up the monitor's resolutions, refresh rates, power management, and other options.

Changing Video Cards in Windows 9x and Above

As you prepare for the A+ Certification test, you might want to practice these steps on a working PC to help you prepare for installation questions on the exam. Changing to standard VGA before changing video cards is recommended to avoid system crashes and error messages because all VGA-class video cards will use a standard VGA driver.

To change to Standard VGA before changing video cards, follow these steps:

1. Open the Display property sheet in the Control Panel.
2. Select the Advanced Properties button to display the Advanced Properties sheet (see Figure 6.5).
3. Select the Adapter tab.
4. Select the Change button.
5. Select Show All Devices.

Figure 6.5
You can set the adapter refresh rate and change to a different display adapter in the Windows 95 Advanced Display Properties sheet.

   6. Select (Standard Display Types) and choose Standard Display Adapter (VGA), as shown in Figure 6.6.

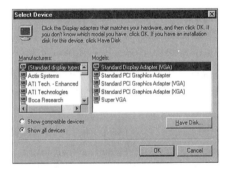

Figure 6.6
Select Standard Display Adapter (VGA), because all video cards are now VGA-compatible, and shut down the system before you change your video card.

   7. When prompted to reboot after accepting the change, shut down the system instead.

   8. Turn off the monitor.

   9. Disconnect the data cable attached to the video card.

   10. Remove the old video card.

CH
6

11. Insert the new video card; use an AGP-based card for best performance if possible; otherwise, use a PCI-based card.

12. To continue with the changeover to the new video card, reattach the data cable to the new video card.

13. Turn on the monitor.

14. Turn on the computer.

15. If the computer supports plug and play, the new video card will be detected during the startup process.

16. Provide video drivers as requested.

17. If the computer doesn't support plug and play, use the Add New Hardware Wizard in the Control Panel to install the card.

After the card is installed, choose the color depth, resolution, and refresh rate desired and restart the system.

The same procedure is used when changing monitors, except that you change the monitor type to VGA and switch out monitors instead of video cards. Changing the monitor type to VGA prevents damage to a new monitor because the refresh rate for VGA is low enough that all monitors (even inexpensive ones) will work correctly with it.

Adjusting Video Displays

Most video adjustments are made by adjusting monitor properties. Depending on the monitor, it might be necessary to make changes whenever the picture type changes or the monitor itself can memorize the settings and recall them on demand.

Picture Size Settings

If you change from graphics mode to text mode (for DOS commands) with any type of VGA card, you might need to adjust the vertical or horizontal picture size. This is because the text mode for VGA actually uses a different number of dots than the graphics mode does. Text-mode VGA resolution is 720×400, compared with 640×480 or higher in graphics mode. Figure 6.7 illustrates the differences in screen resolutions for common graphics and text-based VGA modes.

Typical picture adjustments available on virtually all monitors include

- Horizontal picture size
- Horizontal picture centering
- Vertical picture size
- Vertical picture centering

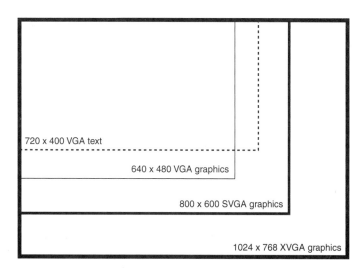

Figure 6.7
Visual comparison of screen resolutions in different VGA display modes.

Older monitors use a series of rotating knobs, usually on the front of the monitor, to adjust these settings. Generally, users want the picture to fill the screen and leave little or no black border around the actual picture area. On some older monitors, a special plastic tool that resembles a thin screwdriver must be used to adjust the picture size from the rear of the monitor.

Most monitors built since the mid-1990s have digital controls that can be adjusted for different resolutions and refresh rates. This allows the monitor to "remember" the picture size needed. Typically, you press a button on the front of the monitor to activate the digital controls. Then, you use other pushbuttons to adjust the picture. Monitors with digital controls also allow you to adjust for barrel (outward curving image sides) and pincushion (inward curving image sides) distortion. Some monitors require you to select the mode desired, but most will use the settings you made automatically as you switch from one resolution or mode to another. Figure 6.8 displays some of the image problems you might need to adjust with picture controls. Some digital picture controls also provide for degaussing the monitor.

CH
6

Figure 6.8
Typical geometry errors in monitors that can be corrected with digital picture controls available on most recent monitors.

Troubleshooting

Use Table 6.5 to help you prepare for video-related troubleshooting questions on the A+ Certification exam and your day to day work.

Table 6.5   Troubleshooting Monitors and Video Cards

Symptom	Problem	Solution
Color fringes around text and graphics on monitor screen	Magnetic distortion is affecting image quality	Use degaussing option (look for button, turn monitor off and on, or check diagnostics menu on some monitors)
Colors flicker onscreen	Loose video cable	Turn off monitor and system; tighten cable and restart
Picture changes size	Power supply not putting out consistent signals	Repair or replace monitor
Picture occasionally displays wavy lines	Interference caused by poorly shielded devices in the area	Look for source of interference (such as microwave oven); move interference away from computer

Symptom	Problem	Solution
Picture quality garbled while changing video mode in Windows 95	Wrong resolution or refresh rate selected	Press Enter key to cancel change; check video card and monitor documentation for resolutions and refresh rates supported by both; select from these
Can't select desired color depth at a given resolution	Video card does not have enough memory onboard for desired color depth/resolution combination	Upgrade video card memory, reduce color depth or resolution, or replace video card
Can't select desired color depth at a given resolution	Incorrect video card driver might be in use	Double-check video card driver selected; replace with correct video driver if necessary
Can't select resolution or refresh rate desired	Wrong monitor might be selected	Double-check monitor type; replace with correct monitor driver if necessary; MS-DOS and Windows 3.1 often require separate utility program for selecting resolution or refresh rates
No picture when replacing built-in video with a replacement video card	Old and new video circuits have a conflict	Move new video card to a different slot; check for a motherboard setting to disable onboard video; try a different video card model

High-Voltage Precautions

If you must service the monitor internally, take the following precautions:

- Use only plastic tools to adjust monitor settings on the back of the monitor.
- Discharge the coil on the CRT, which contains potentially lethal high voltage levels, before servicing the interior of the monitor.

For more details on this process, see "Discharging CRTs," page 331.

Using Known-Working Replacement Monitors for Troubleshooting

Because replacement monitors you might want to use will probably not be the same model, make sure you run the system in Windows 9x Safe Mode or Windows 2000 VGA

CH
6

Mode. Either way, you will use only standard VGA signals. Using the previous monitor's default modes can use resolutions or refresh rates that are not compatible with the monitor and might damage it.

Disposal of CRT

If you need to dispose of an obsolete monitor, contact your local solid waste management or landfill office for special instructions. As an alternative, you might be able to find a trade school repair shop that will use your monitor for classroom practice or as a source of repair parts.

Summary

The video subsystem contains two parts, the monitor and video card. To achieve the best results, these components should be matched to each other and should use the correct drivers for the operating system. Although most monitors and video cards are based on the VGA standard, using a generic driver will prevent you from achieving the maximum performance, resolution, and color depth that the equipment can achieve.

┌ QUESTIONS AND ANSWERS: ──────────

1. Which type of monitor can display millions of colors, digital or analog? Why?
   A: An analog monitor can display unlimited numbers of colors because it can vary the amounts of red, green, or blue at any amount.

2. How many colors are in 16-bit color?
   A: 2 to the 16th power (2^{16}) = 65,536 colors.

3. If you switch from an ATI to a Matrox video card, do you need to adjust the CMOS display type? Why or why not?
   A: No, you don't need to change the CMOS/BIOS display type because both are VGA cards.

4. What do you need to change when changing video cards?
   A: You need to change the video card drivers.

Storage

WHILE YOU READ

1. What hardware features allow two devices to connect to a single IDE channel?
2. What feature allows multiple SCSI devices to connect to a single host adapter?
3. What is the difference between an IDE and a SCSI cable?
4. Are IDE cables foolproof?
5. Can any SCSI adapter be used with any SCSI device?
6. What's the most likely reason the screen is blank after you add a new IDE hard drive and restart the system?

Floppy disk and hard disk storage devices are standard with virtually every PC. However, upgrades and additions to storage are frequently made during the life of a computer. Reliable storage of programs and data is a critical factor to customer satisfaction and computer use. In this chapter, you'll learn how to configure and troubleshoot major storage devices.

Common Characteristics of Magnetic Storage Devices

All magnetic storage devices have the following characteristics in common:

- Read/write heads use controlled electrical pulses to affect the magnetic structure of the media. Each disk surface has one read/write head, whereas double-sided media use two read/write heads—one per side.

- The media is double-sided on all but the earliest floppy disk drives.

- Hard drives use one or more double-sided platters formed from rigid materials such as aluminum or glass that are coated with a durable magnetic surface.

- All magnetic media is divided up into 512-byte areas called *sectors*.

- Sectors are organized in concentric circles from the edge of the media inward toward the middle of the platter. These concentric circles are called *tracks*.

- Hard drives have the following disk structures on their first track: a partition table, which identifies what parts of the hard disk are in use by different operating systems and stores the actual disk geometry in use; a master boot record; and two copies of the File Allocation Table (see the following bullet). Defects in track 0 will render the drive unusable.

- All magnetic media use a special area near the outer edge of the first side of the media to store a record of where files are located; this is called the *File Allocation Table (FAT)*. Two copies of the FAT are updated whenever a file is created, changed, or deleted.

- All magnetic storage devices require that media be formatted before it can be used. *Formatting* means that a logical magnetic pattern must be placed on the disk to enable data to be organized and located.

- Most floppy disks you purchase today have been preformatted at the factory and are ready to use.

- Hard drives using the IDE or SCSI interface must go through a preparation step called *FDISK* and must then be formatted before they can be used.

- Hard drives using the obsolete ST-412/506 and ESDI interfaces require a step called *low-level* formatting to be performed before FDISK can be run.

- A storage device that emulates magnetic storage, such as CD-ROM drives, requires software drivers that will make it appear as an ordinary drive to the system.

Floppy Disk Drives

Although most users today do not depend on floppy disk drives to the extent that they did in the early- to mid-1980s, floppy disk drives are still important as a source for emergency startup of computers and for backups of all files.

Floppy Disk Drive Types

Table 7.1 lists the standard floppy disk drive types that have been used and are still in use on IBM-compatible computers. A few early models of the IBM PC use single-sided 5.25-inch drives, which are not listed. These drives can use the same media as a 360KB (double-sided) drive.

Table 7.1   Standard Floppy Disk Drive Types

Form Factor in Inches	Capacity	Disk Type(s) Used (Inches)	Power Connector	Data Connector	Status
5.25	360KB	5.25 DSDD*	4-wire Molex	34-contact edge connector	Obsolete
5.25	1.2MB	5.25 DSHD,* 5.25 DSDD	4-wire Molex	34-contact edge connector	Obsolete
3.5	720KB	3.5 DSDD	4-wire miniature	34-pin connector	Obsolete
3.5	1.44MB	3.5 DSHD	4-wire miniature	34-pin connector	Current
3.5	2.88MB	3.5 DSED*	4-wire miniature	34-pin connector	Current

DSDD = Double-Sided Double Density

DSHD = Double-Sided High Density

DSED = Double-Sided Extra-high Density (used primarily by IBM computers and not very popular)

Figure 7.1 illustrates the differences between the power and data connectors for a typical 3.5-inch floppy disk drive (top) and the older 5.25-inch floppy disk drive (bottom).

Figure 7.2 illustrates the differences between the Molex power connector and the miniature power connector used on different types of floppy disk drives. The miniature 4-wire connector is commonly used with 3.5-inch floppy disk drives and some internal tape backups, whereas the larger Molex connector is used with 5.25-inch floppy disk drives, CD-ROM drives, and hard drives.

Distinguishing Marks of Different Disk Types

The reliability of data stored on a floppy disk can be affected by many factors, including the disks themselves. Table 7.2 and Figures 7.3 and 7.4 will help you distinguish between different disk types.

CH

7

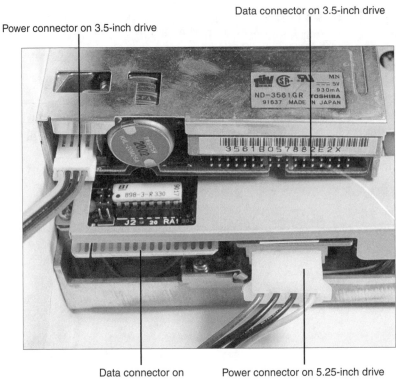

Power connector on 3.5-inch drive

Data connector on 3.5-inch drive

Data connector on 5.25-inch drive

Power connector on 5.25-inch drive

Figure 7.1
3.5-inch and 5.25-inch drives (rear view). The 3.5-inch power connector and the 5.25-inch power connector use the same power signals but are different sizes.

Table 7.2   Physical Characteristics of 5.25-Inch and 3.5-Inch Disks

Disk Type	Capacity	Jacket	Reinforced Hub	Write Protect	Media Sensor
5.25-inch DSDD	360KB	Flexible	Yes	Cover notch	N/A
5.25-inch DSHD	1.2MB	Flexible	No	Cover notch	N/A
3.5-inch DSDD	720KB	Rigid with metal shutter	N/A	Open hole in corner	No hole opposite write-protect
3.5-inch DSHD	1.44MB	Rigid with metal shutter	N/A	Open hole in corner	Hole opposite write-protect

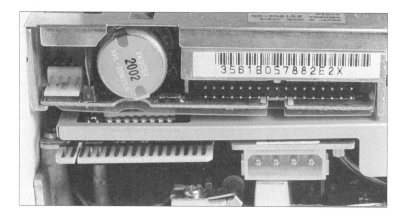

Figure 7.2
Details of the miniature 4-wire (top left) and Molex 4-wire (bottom right) power connectors; converters can be used to change a Molex power lead to operate with a drive using the smaller power connector.

Figure 7.3 illustrates the visible differences between double-density and high-density 5.25-inch floppy disks. In addition to the lack of a reinforcing ring on high-density disks, high-density media is dark gray in color, as opposed to the brown media used in DSDD disks.

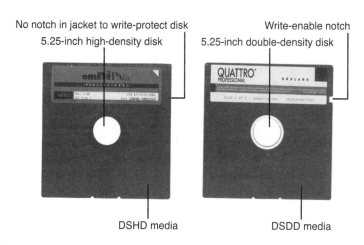

Figure 7.3
5.25-inch floppy disks. Most disks have a write-enable notch, but preprogrammed disks have a covered notch or a disk jacket without a notch.

Figure 7.4 illustrates the differences between 3.5-inch disks. Of the disks pictured in Figures 7.3 and 7.4, only the 3.5-inch DSHD disk is commonly used today. 1.44MB disks are often marked "HD" on their front and always have a media-sensing hole in the opposite corner from the write enable/protect slider.

Factors Required for Floppy Disk Drive Support

All 286-based and higher systems built since the late 1980s can support all the preceding drives through ROM BIOS configuration and the use of MS-DOS 3.3 or higher. Older systems require ROM BIOS updates or device drivers to use 3.5-inch drives, and IBM PC, PC/XT, and other systems based on 8088 or 8086 CPUs can't use DSHD drives.

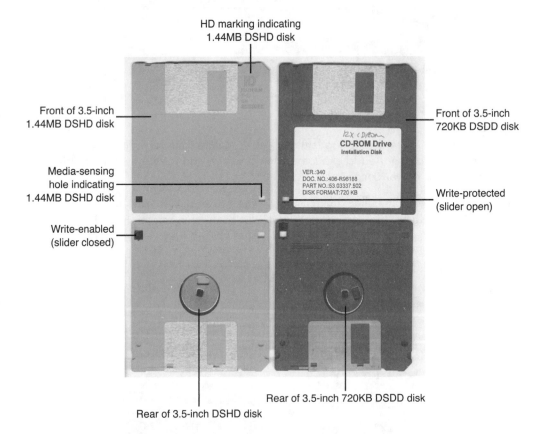

Figure 7.4
The 1.44MB disk has a slider set for write-enable; the 720KB disk has a slider set for write-protect.

Floppy Disk Drive Hardware Configuration

Floppy disk drive hardware configuration depends on several factors, including the following:

- **Correct CMOS configuration**—The system's BIOS configuration screen must have the correct drive selected for A: and B:.

- **Correct cable positioning and attachment**—The position of the drive(s) on the cable determine which is A: and which is B:. If the cable is not oriented properly, the drive will spin continuously.

The standard floppy disk drive interface uses a single IRQ and single I/O port address range, whether the interface is built in or on an expansion card:

- Floppy Drive IRQ: 6
- Floppy Drive I/O Port Address: 3F0-3F7h

The standard floppy disk drive interface can support two drives: Drive A: and Drive B:.

Unlike hard drives, floppy disk drives do not use jumpers to indicate which drive is which. Instead, the 34-pin floppy disk drive data cable has wires numbered 10 to 16 twisted in reverse between the connectors for Drive A: and Drive B:. Be sure to note the position of the twist in the cable; the 34-pin signal cable used for the obsolete ST0412/506 and ESDI hard drives might have a twist, but the twist in that cable type is away from pin 1.

The standard floppy disk drive cable has five connectors, as seen in Figure 7.5. The use for each connector is noted in Table 7.3.

Table 7.3   Standard Floppy Disk Drive Cable Connectors

Item	Position	Use
34-pin connector	End of cable	Connect to floppy disk drive interface
34-pin connector	Middle of cable	Connect to B: drive (3.5-inch)
34-connector (tongue and groove; edge connector)	Middle of cable	Connect to B: drive (5.25-inch)
Twist-in wires 10-16	Between B: drive connectors and A: drive connectors	Interface uses twist to determine drive letter: drive B: is before twist; A: is after twist
34-pin	Far end of cable	Connect to A: drive (3.5-inch)
34-connector (tongue and groove; edge connector)	Far end of cable	Connect to A: drive (5.25-inch)

In addition to the twist in the cable being nearer to pin 1, floppy disk drive data cables, like other internal ribbon cables, have a colored marking along the edge of the cable to indicate pin 1. The most typical marking used is a series of red dots, but sometimes the first wire is marked with a solid red or solid blue line, as shown in Figure 7.6.

Floppy Disk Drive Physical Installation and Removal

To install a 3.5-inch 1.44MB floppy disk drive as drive A:, follow these steps:

1. Select an empty 3.5-inch external drive bay; an *external* drive bay is a drive bay with a corresponding opening in the case.
2. Remove the dummy face plate from the case front.
3. For a tower system, remove the left side panel (as seen from the front). For a desktop system, remove the top.

CH
7

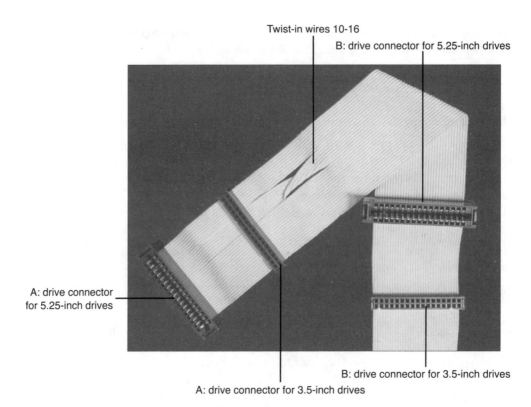

Twist-in wires 10-16

B: drive connector for 5.25-inch drives

A: drive connector
for 5.25-inch drives

B: drive connector for 3.5-inch drives

A: drive connector for 3.5-inch drives

Figure 7.5
Note the use of both edge and pin connectors, allowing both 5.25-inch and 3.5-inch drives to be used in any combination of A: and B:. Also note the twist in the typical floppy disk drive cable; this alone determines which drive is A: and which is B:.

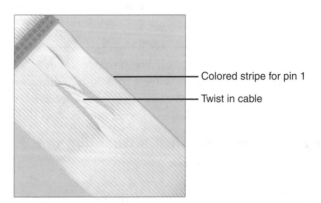

Colored stripe for pin 1

Twist in cable

Figure 7.6
Both the twist (nearer pin 1) and the colored stripe (upper-right side of the cable) indicate the correct alignment of the floppy disk drive cable with pin 1 on the floppy disk drive itself and pin 1 of the floppy disk drive interface connector.

4. If the 3.5-inch drive bay is a removable "cage," remove it from the system. This might involve pushing on a spring-loaded tab, as in Figure 7.7. Some drive bays pull straight out (as here), whereas others swing to one side.

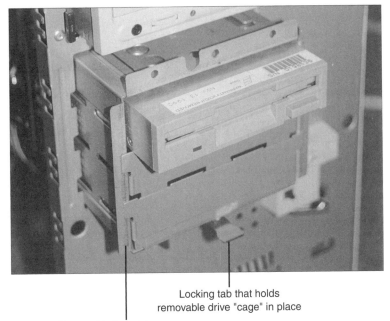

Locking tab that holds
removable drive "cage" in place

Removable faceplate on cage

Figure 7.7
A typical cage used by many tower cases for 3.5-inch drives.

5. Remove the floppy disk drive from its protective packaging. Test the screws you intend to use to secure the drive and ensure they're properly threaded and the correct length.

6. Check the bottom or rear panel of the drive for markings indicating pin 1; if no markings are found, assume pin 1 is the pin closest to the power supply connector.

7. Attach the 34-pin connector at the end of the floppy disk drive data cable with the twist to the data connector on the drive.

8. Run the other end of the floppy disk drive data cable through the drive bay into the interior of the computer. Then, connect it to the floppy disk drive interface on the motherboard or add-on card.

9. Attach the correct type of 4-wire power cable to the drive. You might need to slide the drive partway into the drive bay to make the connection.

CH
7

10. Secure the drive to the drive bay with the screws supplied with the drive or with the computer.

11. Replace the drive bay into the computer if present (see Figure 7.8).

Floppy drive attachment screw

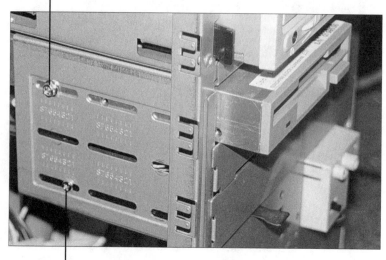

Hard drive attachment screw

Figure 7.8
A removable drive cage with the attachment screws for the floppy disk drive and hard drive. The opposite corner of each drive is also secured with screws (not shown).

12. Double-check power and data cable keying before starting the computer.

13. Follow these steps in reverse to remove the drive from the system.

Figure 7.9 shows how 3.5- and 5.25-inch floppy drives are cabled together.

BIOS Configuration

Floppy disk drives cannot be detected by the system; you must manually configure the floppy disk drive or floppy disk drives you add to the system.

To configure the floppy disk drive in the ROM BIOS, follow these steps:

1. Verify the correct physical installation as listed previously.

2. Turn on the monitor and then the computer.

3. Press the appropriate key(s) to start the BIOS configuration program.

4. Open the standard configuration menu.

5. Select Drive A: or the first floppy disk drive.

Figure 7.9
A 3.5-inch floppy disk drive connected as A: (left) and a 5.25-inch floppy disk drive connected as B: (right).

6. Use the appropriate keys to scroll through the choices; 3.5-inch 1.44MB is the correct choice for most recent and current systems (see Figure 7.10).

7. No other changes are necessary, so save your changes and exit to reboot the system.

For more information about the CMOS/BIOS setup process, see Chapter 3, "BIOS and CMOS Configuration."

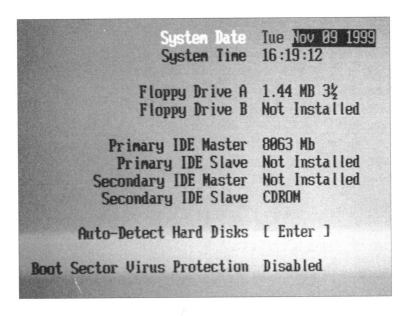

Figure 7.10
The standard setup menu of a typical system after selecting a 1.44MB 3.5-inch floppy disk drive as A:.

CH
7

The Care of Floppy Disks, Data, and Drives

You can protect the data on your floppy disks by following these recommendations; most of these suggestions also apply to higher-capacity removable media such as Zip, Jaz, LS-120, and tape backups:

- Do not open the protective metal shutter on 3.5-inch disks.
- Use Tyvek or paper sleeves to protect 5.25-inch disks.
- Store disks away from sources of magnetism or heat.
- Open the sliding write-protect cover on 3.5-inch disks, or cover the write-protect notch on 5.25-inch disks.

Floppy disk drives are a type of magnetic storage in which the read/write heads make direct contact with the media. This is similar to the way that tape drives work, and just like cassette or VCR heads, a floppy disk drive's read/write heads can become contaminated by dust, dirt, smoke, or magnetic particles flaking off the disk's media surfaces. For this reason, periodic maintenance of floppy disk drives will help to avoid the need to troubleshoot drives that cannot reliably read or write data.

The following are some guidelines for cleaning a floppy disk drive:

- Approximately every six months, or more often in dirty or smoke-filled conditions, use a wet-type head-cleaning disk on the drive.

  These cleaning kits use a special cleaning floppy disk that contains cleaning media in place of magnetic media, along with an alcohol-based cleaner. Add a few drops to the media inside the cleaning disk, slide it into the drive, and activate the drive with a command such as DIR or by using the Windows Explorer to clean the heads. Allow the heads to dry for about 30 minutes before using the drive.

- Whenever you open a system for any type of maintenance or checkup, review the condition of the floppy disk drive(s). Use compressed air to remove fuzz or hair from the drive heads and check the mechanism for smooth operation.

Troubleshooting Floppy Disk Drives

Floppy drives are relatively complex devices despite their small storage capacity. Problems can result from incorrect cabling, mechanical drive or media failures, incorrect BIOS configuration, dirt or dust, and interface failures. Use this section to prepare for troubleshooting questions on the A+ Certification exam as well as your day-to-day work with floppy drives.

Cabling Problems

Floppy drive data cables that are reversed (pin 1 to pin 33) at either the floppy drive interface on the motherboard/floppy controller card or at the drive itself will cause the drive light to come on and stay on. To correct this, turn off the system, remove and reattach the data cable, and restart the system.

Floppy drive data or power cables that are not attached to the drive will cause the system to display a floppy drive error when the drive is checked at system startup. Turn off the system, attach the missing cables, and restart the system to correct this problem.

BIOS Configuration Problems

Users must properly configure floppy drives in the BIOS setup program—there is not autodetect feature as there is for IDE hard drives. If the system produces a floppy drive error at startup or is unable to format, read, or write disks at the proper capacities, the drive type set in the system BIOS setup program might be inaccurate. Restart the system, start the BIOS setup program, and verify that the correct drive types are set for drive A: and drive B:. If a floppy-interface tape backup is connected to the system, it should not be configured in the BIOS setup program. Tape backups are detected and configured by the backup program, not by the system BIOS.

Drive Reliability and Compatibility Problems

Problems with drives reading and writing media can stem from

- **Dirty read/write heads**—Dirty read/write heads can result from the constant pressure of the drive's read/write heads on the relatively fragile magnetic surface of the disk and from the constant flow of air being pulled through the system by cooling fans located in the power supply and elsewhere. Dirty heads can cause read and write errors. To clean the drive heads, use a wet-technology head cleaner, which uses a blank disk containing a fabric cleaning disk instead of media and an alcohol-based head cleaner. Insert the disk and spin the drive with a program such as Explorer or Scandisk to clean the heads. Allow them to dry for a few minutes, and try the operation again.

- **Defective drive mechanisms**—Several parts of the floppy drive (see Figure 7.11, later in this chapter) are subject to failures, including the drive motor, the read/write heads, the head-positioning mechanism, and the shutter-retraction mechanism (3.5-inch drives only).

A floppy drive with a motor that runs too fast or too slow or has misaligned read/write heads will cause a drive to write data that can be read only by that drive. Media from other drives can't be read on a drive with these defects, and drives with these defects can't write data that can be read by other drives. Floppy drives with misaligned heads or off-spec drive motors can't be fixed and must be replaced.

If the head-positioning mechanism fails, data can't be read or written and the drive will not perform a seek at system startup. The head-positioning mechanism frequently uses a worm-drive mechanism (see Figure 7.11) that can be replaced or freed up if stuck.

If the shutter-retraction mechanism is jammed, you cannot insert a disk into a 3.5-inch drive. Remove the drive's top cover so that the drive mechanism is visible, as in Figure 7.11, and you should be able to insert the disk. The usual cause is a bent top cover; adjust the cover and replace it.

CH

7

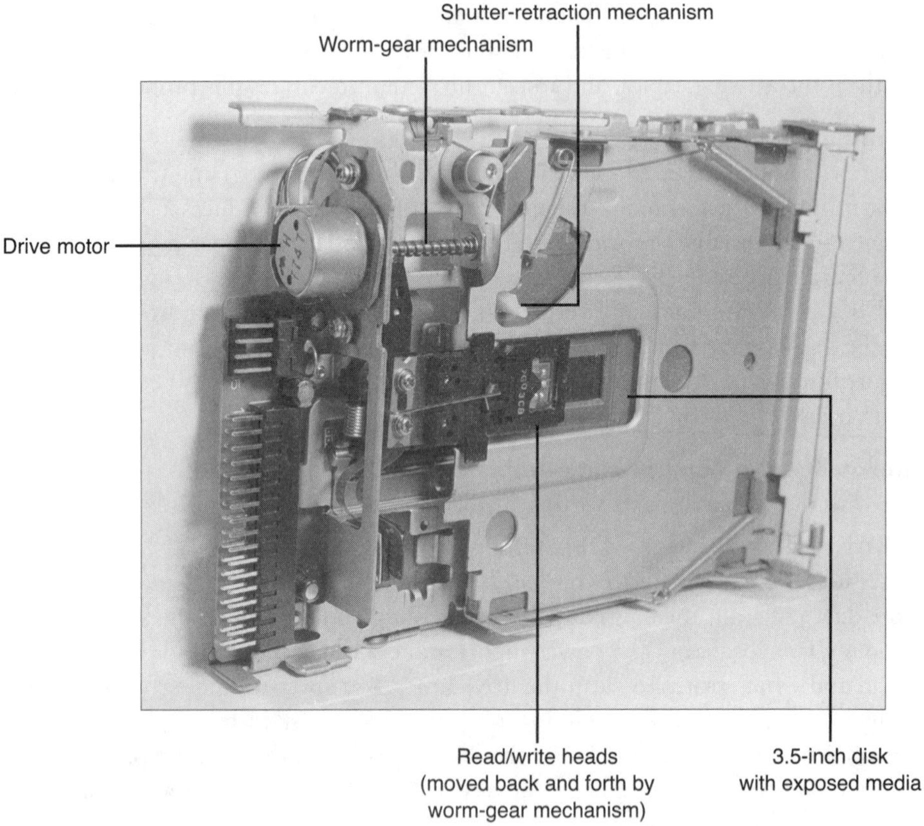

Figure 7.11
A typical 3.5-inch 1.44MB floppy disk drive with its top cover removed.

Changeline Problems

On AT-compatible floppy drives (1.2MB 5.25-inch and all 3.5-inch drives), pin 34 of the floppy interface senses disk changes and forces the system to reread the disk's file allocation table and display the content of the new disk when the disk is changed and viewed from a command prompt. This feature is referred to as *changeline support*.

If the DIR (directory) command displays the same contents for a different disk as for the first disk, changeline support has failed; this problem is also called the *phantom directory*. Because pin 34 uses the last connector on the floppy cable, check to see whether the cable is loose or damaged. See the next section for further troubleshooting steps.

Isolating Floppy Subsystem Problems

The floppy disk drive subsystem consists of three parts: the drive, the interface cable and the host adapter (built into the motherboard on most recent systems), along with the BIOS configuration for the drive. The troubleshooting options listed earlier dealt with the most likely causes of particular floppy disk drive problems. However, any part of the sub-system could cause a floppy disk drive problem. If you suspect a hardware failure, follow this procedure:

1. With most floppy disk drive problems, you should exchange the floppy disk drive cable first for a known working spare. This solves many problems because the cable is inexpensive and easily damaged.

2. Replace the drive. Floppy disk drives are also inexpensive and easily damaged; their design no longer permits major repairs.

3. If the problem persists, check the cable and drive on another system. If they check out OK, the floppy disk controller on the motherboard or host adapter card is probably defective. Replace the motherboard or host adapter with a new one.

Figure 7.11 shows the major components of a typical 3.5-inch disk drive. Components include a drive motor; a worm-gear mechanism, which moves read/write heads; and a shutter-retraction mechanism. The drive shown in Figure 7.11 has a 3.5-inch disk inserted; the shutter-retraction mechanism has pushed the shutter to one side so that the media is visible.

Hard Drives

Hard drives have used four different interface types since the first IBM PC/XT computer with a 10MB hard drive was introduced in 1982. Early hard drive interfaces, the ST-412/506 and ESDI, have been obsolete since the end of the 1980s and are no longer part of the A+ Certification exam. The current hard drive interfaces are IDE and SCSI.

Table 7.4 provides an overview of the hard drive interfaces; more complete information is in the sections following this table.

Table 7.4   Overview of Hard Drive Interface Types

Interface Type	Cable(s)	Typical Capacity Range	Controlled By	Number of Devices Per Interface	Preparation Required
ST-412/506	20-pin data 34-pin signal (might have twist away from pin 1 or no twist)	10MB–80MB	System BIOS or add-on card BIOS	2	Low-level format, FDISK, DOS format
ESDI	Same as ST-506	80–170MB	Add-on card BIOS	2	Low-level format, FDISK, DOS format

Table 7.4   Overview of Hard Drive Interface Types

Interface Type	Cable(s)	Typical Capacity Range	Controlled By	Number of Devices Per Interface	Preparation Required
IDE	40-pin cable; UDMA-66 uses a 40-pin cable with 80 wires	40MB and up	System BIOS or add-on card BIOS	2	FDISK, DOS format
SCSI	50-pin or 68-pin cable; can be internal or external	40MB and up	Add-on card BIOS	7 or 15	(Interface-specific prep), FDISK, DOS format

For more information about ST412/506 and ESDI drives and interfaces, see the companion CD-ROM to *Upgrading and Repairing PCs, 12th Edition,* ISBN 0-7897-2303-4. This CD contains the Sixth Edition of *Upgrading and Repairing PCs*; see Chapter 15, "Hard Disk Interfaces."

The following configuration information applies to all types of hard drives. For drives controlled by any system BIOS, the following information must be provided:

- Hard drive geometry
- Primary (also known as *Master*) drive or secondary (also known as *Slave*) drive

Hard drive geometry refers to several factors used to calculate the capacity of a hard drive. These factors include the following:

- The number of sectors per track
- The number of read/write heads
- The number of cylinders (all the tracks on all the platters)

Figure 7.12 will help you visualize how magnetic sectors are arranged on magnetic storage drives. The different colored blocks on the hard disk platter symbolize disk sectors; they are arranged in concentric circles (tracks), which are read by the read/write head that moves across the tracks. The three factors listed previously are used to calculate the size of the hard drive. Two hard drives can have the same capacity (in MB or GB) but have different geometries.

Hard drives have had increasingly smaller form factors, even as capacity has increased by astronomical amounts. The first hard drives used in PCs in the early- to mid-1980s were 5.25-inch wide and required a drive bay twice the height of today's 5.25-inch drives.

Current 5.25-inch drives (such as CD-ROM drives) are called "half-height" drives because the original hard drives used a single full-height drive bay.

The late 1980s saw full-height hard drives being replaced by half-height; most 5.25-inch drive bays and drives used in systems since the late 1980s have been half-height.

A few hard drives in the late 1980s were 3.5 inches wide but used a half-height bay. By about 1993, the current 3.5-inch wide, 1-inch high hard drive form factor had become common.

Figure 7.12
A typical 3.5-inch hard disk with its top removed.

If you must install a small form-factor drive into a larger drive bay, use the frame kit supplied with many drives sold in retail packaging, or purchase one separately. Many systems require that drives installed in 5.25-inch bays use drive rails, but 3.5-inch drives are usually screwed directly to the sides of the smaller drive bays.

IDE Hard Drive

Integrated Drive Electronics (IDE) began to replace the older drive interfaces starting in the late 1980s and continues to be, by far, the most popular drive interface used today. IDE drives were originally used in systems designed for ST-412/506 hard drives, and some of their characteristics date back to the need to be compatible with old BIOSes.

Some vendors prefer to use the term *AT attachment (ATA)* instead of IDE for their hard drives. Expect either term to be used on the exam.

IDE was originally designed for hard drives, but several other types of storage devices can also be attached to it:

CH

7

- CD-ROM drives (including CD-R, CD-RW, and DVD drives)
- Removable-media drives, such as ZIP and LS-120
- Tape backup drives

The previously listed drives are referred to as *AT Attachment Packet Interface (ATAPI)* drives, and they use the same master/slave jumpers and 40-pin data cable as standard IDE drives do. Depending on the system, these devices might be supported in the system ROM BIOS, but most often software drivers are used to control them. These devices should be installed on the secondary IDE channel, and hard drives should be installed on the primary IDE channel.

IDE Hardware Resources

The IDE hard disk interface, whether found on the motherboard on newer systems or as an add-on card on older systems, uses the same resources that were set aside for older drive interfaces. These resources are listed in Table 7.5.

Table 7.5 Standard Hardware Resource Use for IDE Hard Drive Interfaces			
IRQ	I/O Port	Address Range	Notes
Primary Interface	14	1F0–1FFh (newer systems might use additional ranges)	Same as used for ST-506 or ESDI
Secondary Interface	15	170–177h (newer systems might use additional ranges)	Not present on older systems

Each IDE hard drive interface, also known as an IDE *channel*, can operate two IDE drives. Therefore, systems with two IDE interfaces can operate up to four IDE drives.

Master and Slave Jumpers

With two drives possible per IDE cable, the IDE interface uses a simple method for determining which drive is which: master and slave jumper blocks, as seen in Figure 7.13.

Four different jumper positions are available on the bottom or rear of an IDE hard drive:

- No pins jumpered is used when only one drive is attached to the cable.
- Master pins jumpered is used when the drive is set as the master drive. This can be used when two drives are attached to the IDE cable on some systems or when only one drive is attached. It varies by model.
- Slave pins jumpered is used when the drive is set as a slave drive. Normally, it is used only when two drives are attached to the IDE cable.

■ Cable select pins jumpered is used when an IDE cable supporting cable select (cable sets master/slave) is used. Both drives must be set to cable select. This option is encountered primarily on systems that support UDMA-66 and faster versions of IDE/ATA. The 80-wire (40-pin) cable used for these versions of IDE/ATA supports cable select.

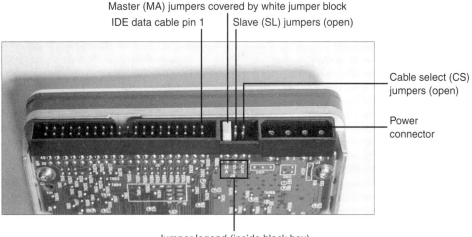

Master (MA) jumpers covered by white jumper block
IDE data cable pin 1   Slave (SL) jumpers (open)

Cable select (CS) jumpers (open)

Power connector

Jumper legend (inside black box)

Figure 7.13
A view from the rear of a typical IDE hard disk with the drive-select jumper set to "MA" (Master). On some drives, the drive-select jumpers are on the underside.

IDE Hard Drive Physical Installation

The following steps apply to typical IDE drive installations. If you are installing a CD-ROM or DVD drive using IDE, you will use a 5.25-inch bay, but the other steps will be the same.

1. Open the system and check for an existing 3.5-inch drive bay; use an internal bay if possible.

2. If a 3.5-inch drive bay is not available but a 5.25-inch drive bay is, attach the appropriate frame kit and rails as needed, as shown in Figure 7.14.

3. Jumper the drive according to its position on the cable: master, slave, or single drive.

4. Attach either the middle connector or end connector of the IDE data cable to the drive, matching the colored stripe on the cable to the end of the drive connector with pin #1. Then, detach the cable from the host adapter and other IDE drive if needed for slack and check the rear or bottom of the drive for pin #1 markings.

5. Slide the drive into the appropriate bay and attach as needed with screws or by snapping the ends of the rails into place.

CH
7

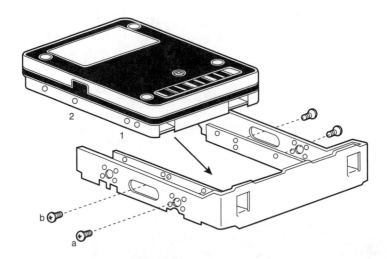

Figure 7.14
A typical frame kit for a 3.5-inch drive. Screw a attaches the frame at hole #1; screw b attaches the frame at hole #2, with corresponding attachments on the opposite side of the drive and frame.

6. Attach the power connector; most IDE hard drives use the larger 4-wire (Molex) power connector originally used on 5.25-inch floppy disk drives. Use a Y-splitter to create two power connectors from one if necessary.

7. Reattach the data cable to another IDE drive and host adapter if necessary.

8. Change the jumper on another IDE drive if necessary. For example, if you are adding a slave drive to a cable with one drive already attached, you might need to adjust the jumper on the existing drive from single to master.

9. Verify correct data and power connections to IDE drives and host adapters.

10. Turn on the system and start the BIOS configuration program.

IDE Data Cable Keying Standards

The following are the three different types of IDE cable and connector standards:

■ Some IDE cables have a raised projection in the middle of the cable connector, which is designed to correspond to a cutout on the IDE drive or host adapter shield around the connector pins.

■ Some IDE cable connectors plug the hole for pin 20 and are designed to be used with IDE drives or host adapters that omit pin 20. See Figure 7.15 for these keying methods.

■ Some IDE cable connectors don't use either method, making it easy to attach the cable incorrectly. This is the most popular type of cable because manufacturers can't agree on which of the positive keying methods listed previously should be standard.

Cutout for cables with raised projection keying method

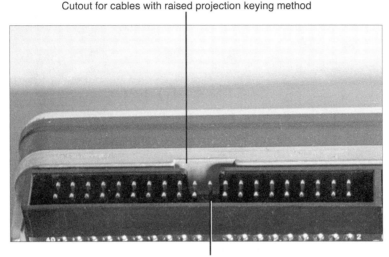

Missing pin 20 for cables with plugged pin 20 keying method

Figure 7.15
Many IDE hard drives, such as this one, support both the cutout and missing-pin positive keying methods.

BIOS Configuration of IDE Devices

Depending on the age of the system and the size of the IDE hard drive, several different methods for configuring the drive in the system BIOS are available:

- Manual selection of the IDE hard drive type
- Manual entry of IDE parameters
- Auto detection of the IDE hard drive type

Manual Selection of the IDE Hard Drive Type

This method of configuring the IDE hard drive in the BIOS is used only on very old systems with early IDE drives. Because the original IDE drives were used in systems designed for ST-506 interface drives, almost all IDE drives have a feature called *sector translation*, which enables the drive to operate with a BIOS configuration different from its designed configuration.

In other words, if you want to install a 200MB IDE drive in a system, and the system has a 200MB drive type, regardless of its geometry, that drive type will work and the drive can operate at its full capacity. However, the manufacturers' geometry is no longer valid for that drive. If you need to move the drive to another system, you should place a sticker on the drive and write down the geometry used to set up the drive so you can access the data on the drive. Whatever geometry was used when the drive was originally prepared with FDISK and DOS FORMAT must be entered when the drive is used in another system.

CH
7

Although the need for this feature has diminished as more advanced methods for setting up IDE hard drives have been developed, it is still possible to install brand new hard drives with an incorrect geometry.

Manual Entry of IDE Parameters

This feature started to become common in the BIOS configuration program around 1990, and virtually all systems still allow this today. Systems with this feature have a user-defined drive type that enables you to enter the correct cylinders, heads, sectors per track, and special configuration information. Unlike standard drive types, however, this information is not stored in the BIOS itself, but rather in the CMOS memory, which can be lost due to battery failure or other problems.

Auto Detection of the IDE Hard Drive Type

Auto detection is a variation on the user-defined drive type. Auto detection was developed in the early 1990s, enabling the BIOS to query the drive for the correct configuration information. This information also is placed in the user-defined drive type and stored in the CMOS memory (see Figure 7.16).

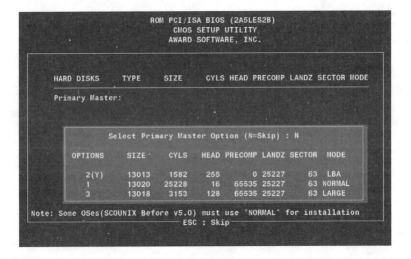

Figure 7.16
A typical CMOS/BIOS auto-detection screen. The Award BIOS (shown here) supports both LBA and LARGE translations as well as the drive's native (nontranslated) geometry.

Some BIOSes perform the automatic detection of the drive type every time you start the system by default. Although this enables you to skip configuring the hard drive, it also takes longer to start the system and prevents the use of nonstandard configurations for compatibility reasons.

To save time during the boot process and to allow you to see the actual values used for the drive in the system BIOS, you can use these methods:

- Detect the drive with the BIOS setup program.

- Configure the drive's geometry values manually by entering the manufacturer-supplied values into a user-defined drive type. Then, record the values on a sticker attached to the outside of the drive or the system unit in case the CMOS memory is corrupted and the data must be re-entered.

Depending on the system, ATAPI drives, such as Zip and LS-120, should be configured as Not Present or Auto in the system BIOS setup. These drives do not have geometry values to enter in the system. The CD-ROM setting should be used for ATAPI CD-ROM and similar optical drives, such as CD-R, CD-RW, and DVD. Using the correct BIOS configuration for ATAPI drives will enable them to be used to boot the system on drives and systems that support booting from ATAPI devices.

Overcoming Hard Disk Capacity Limitations with LBA Mode

When the IDE interface was developed, several limitations on the total capacity of an IDE hard disk existed:

- MS-DOS limitation of 1,024 cylinders per drive

- IDE limitation of 63 sectors per track

- BIOS limitation of 16 heads

These limitations resulted in a total capacity of 504MB, or approximately 528 million bytes. By 1994, these limitations were no longer theoretical; users were able to purchase drives that exceeded this size. They began to want a BIOS-based way to use the entire capacity of the drive.

Previously, systems that were incapable of using the entire capacity of a drive would use a software driver such as OnTrack's Disk Manager, but this approach could be risky to data.

The most common method for enabling larger IDE hard drives to be used is called *Logical Block Addressing (LBA)*.

LBA mode alters how the drive is accessed internally. It increases the BIOS limit to 255 heads and works around the MS-DOS limitation of 1,024 cylinders per drive by dividing the cylinders and multiplying the heads by the same factor. Thus, an LBA mode drive has the same capacity as a non-LBA mode drive, but its configuration is different.

For example, assume an IDE hard drive has a factory-defined configuration of 1,400 cylinders, 16 heads, and 63 sectors per track. To determine the drive capacity, multiply the cylinders by the heads by the sectors per track. Divide the result by 2,048, and the capacity is 689MB. However, because of the 1,024 cylinder limitation, the entire capacity of the drive is not available.

If LBA configuration is enabled in the system BIOS, the configuration reported to the operating system is altered to the following: 700 cylinders (1,400 divided by 2), 32 heads (16 multiplied by 2), and 63 sectors per track. The capacity remains the same—all 689MB are available to the system.

CH
7

MS-DOS and Windows are incapable of using more than 504MB of any IDE hard drive unless LBA mode is enabled. The Award BIOS (refer to Figure 7.16) also supports a different translation method called *LARGE*, but this method is not used by other BIOS makers and should be avoided. LBA mode is supported by all major BIOS and system makers.

If LBA mode is disabled after a drive has been prepared using LBA mode, the drive will not work properly.

With MS-DOS, the system at some point might try to write to data stored on areas past the barrier of 1,024 cylinders that LBA mode overcomes. Without LBA mode to translate the drive's full capacity, the system will loop back to the beginning of the drive and overwrite the partition table and file allocation table, destroying the drive's contents.

Systems running Windows 9x, Me, or 2000 will be incapable of booting, but no data loss will occur.

To learn how to use FDISK to see whether LBA mode is working, see Chapter 12, "Preparing Hard Drives with Windows."

Additional Drive-Size Limitations

Early versions of LBA-mode BIOS could not handle drives of more than 4,095 cylinders (approximately 2.1GB); many more recent systems cannot handle drives with more than 16,384 cylinders (approximately 8.4GB). Support for drives with more than 16,384 cylinders, referred to as *extended INT 13h* support, requires support in the operating system (Windows 95 or later).

Whenever possible, you should install a system BIOS upgrade to handle limitations of these types. If a BIOS upgrade is not available, you can install a special add-on card with an auxiliary BIOS onboard. The BIOS on the card can override your existing BIOS to provide the additional support necessary to operate the hard drive at full capacity.

IDE Performance Optimization

Most systems built since about 1994 offer several different ways to optimize the performance of IDE drives and devices. These include the following:

- Selecting the correct PIO or DMA transfer mode in the BIOS
- Selecting the correct block mode in the BIOS
- Installing busmastering Windows drivers
- Enabling DMA mode in Windows
- Adjusting disk cache software settings

PIO and DMA Transfer Modes

IDE hard drives are capable of operating at a wide variety of transfer speeds. Depending on when the drive was built, IDE hard drives are designed to run in one of two modes:

- PIO (Programmed Input/Output) mode
- Ultra DMA mode

These modes refer to different peak transfer rates the hard drive can achieve. Some systems automatically determine the correct transfer rate, whereas others require you to select the correct speed from a list of options. Selecting transfer rates too fast for the drive can cause data corruption, and selecting rates that are too low can slow down the system.

To achieve a given transfer rate, both the hard disk and the host adapter (card or built-in) must be capable of that rate. In addition, the host adapter must be configured to run at that rate.

Tables 7.6 and 7.7 list the most common transfer rates. Check the drive documentation or with the drive vendor for the correct rating for a given drive. Where PCI is listed as a required interface in either table, this refers either to the built-in IDE host adapter on systems with PCI slots (mostly Pentium-class and newer motherboards) or to add-on PCI host adapters.

Table 7.6   PIO Peak Transfer Rates

Mode	Peak Transfer Rate	Interface Type Required
PIO 0	3.33MBps	16-bit
PIO 1	5.22MBps	16-bit
PIO 2	8.33MBps	16-bit
PIO 3	11.11MBps	32-bit VL-Bus or PCI
PIO 4	16.67MBps	32-bit VL-Bus or PCI

Although PIO modes 3 and 4 require a fast 32-bit IDE interface, not every VL-Bus card is capable of such transfer rates; some require software drivers to achieve mode 3/mode 4 speeds. Check the documentation for the host adapter card or the BIOS configuration screen for systems using a built-in IDE interface to find out which speeds are supported.

Table 7.7   UDMA Peak Transfer Rates

Mode	Peak Transfer Rate	Interface Type Required
UDMA 2	33.33MBps	32-bit PCI
UDMA 4	66.66MBps	32-bit PCI
UDMA-100	100MBps	32-bit PCI

These modes are backward-compatible, enabling you to select the fastest available mode if your system lacks the correct mode for your drive. IDE drives are backward-compatible; you can select a slower DMA mode than the drive supports if your system doesn't support the correct DMA mode, or you can use PIO modes if your system has no UDMA options in the BIOS. Performance will be slower, but the drive will still work.

Drives that support UDMA mode 4 (also called Ultra ATA/66) or faster modes require (and usually are shipped with) a special cable. The cable has a 40-pin connector like normal IDE cables, but it has 80 wires—40 for data and signals, with each wire alternating with a ground wire. One end of the cable is made of blue plastic. This blue connector must be attached to the host adapter on the motherboard or PCI host adapter card. The Ultra ATA/66 cable uses cable select. The master drive must be attached to the end of the cable opposite the blue connector, the slave drive must be attached to the connector near the middle of the cable, and both drives must be jumpered to use cable select.

IDE Block Mode

IDE block mode refers to an improved method of data handling. Originally, a hard drive was allowed to read only a single 512-byte sector before the drive sent an IRQ to the CPU. Early in their history, some IDE hard drives began to use a different method called *block mode*, which enabled the drive to read multiple sectors, or blocks, of data before an IRQ was sent. Drives that support block mode run more quickly when block mode is enabled in the BIOS. Even though software drivers for block mode such as OnTrack's DriveRocket also can be used, all recent systems have block mode included in the BIOS.

Some systems automatically determine block mode capability when they auto-detect the drive. Others require that you enable or disable block mode manually, and still others allow you to select the number of blocks the drive can read. Some very old IDE drives do not support block mode and run more slowly when it is enabled. If you must set block mode manually, check with the drive vendor to see whether the drive supports block mode and what options to select if it does.

Figure 7.17 shows a typical system's BIOS Peripherals configuration screen, which enables the user to manually or automatically select PIO or UDMA modes and block mode.

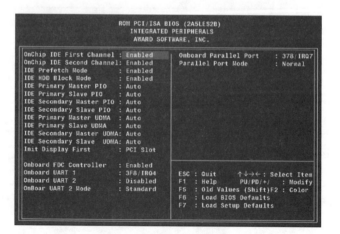

Figure 7.17

A typical peripheral configuration screen with automatic configuration of PIO, UDMA, and block modes for IDE drives. These options also can be set manually if necessary.

IDE Busmastering Drivers

A third way to improve IDE hard disk performance is to install busmastering drivers for the IDE host interface. A *busmaster* bypasses the CPU for data transfers between memory and the hard disk interface. This option is both operating system–specific and system-specific.

Only systems running Windows 9x and newer versions—but not MS-DOS or Windows NT—can use busmastering drivers, and only systems with certain Intel or other chipsets have busmastering drivers available. Check with the motherboard or system vendor for busmastering information.

Busmastering drivers require special support from the motherboard's chipset. The original retail version of Windows 95 doesn't include busmastering drivers, but Windows 95 OSR 2.x (also called Windows 95B), Windows 98, and newer versions come with busmastering support for motherboards with the correct Intel chipsets. Motherboards using other chipsets might require that you download the correct driver from the motherboard vendor if you are using Windows 95 OSR 2.x; Windows 98 and newer versions come with busmastering drivers for major non-Intel chipsets. In most cases, you must manually install the correct driver.

Because busmastering bypasses the CPU, be sure you are installing the correct drivers. Carefully read the motherboard or system vendor's instructions. You might not be able to use busmastering drivers if you use a CD-R or CD-RW drive connected to the IDE interface. In such cases, use the regular IDE host adapter driver supplied with Windows.

Enabling DMA Transfers for IDE Devices in Windows

Windows 9x and above allow the user to enable DMA transfers between IDE devices and the system. DMA transfers bypass the CPU for faster performance and are particularly useful for optimizing the performance of both hard drives and optical drives, such as high-speed CD-ROM drives and DVD drives.

Follow this procedure to enable DMA transfers for a particular IDE device in Windows 98:

1. Open the System properties sheet. Right-click My Computer and select Properties, or open the Control Panel and select System.

2. Click Device Manager.

3. Click the plus sign next to the Disk Drives category (for hard drives) or CDROM (for CD-ROM, CD-R/CD-RW, or DVD drives).

4. Click the drive for which you want to enable DMA transfers, and click Properties. Standard IDE hard drives are listed as Generic; other devices and CD-ROM/optical drives are listed by name.

5. Click Settings.

6. Click the DMA box to put a check mark next to DMA.

CH

7

7. Click OK.

8. Restart the computer as prompted.

Repeat this procedure for each IDE device.

If DMA is not available, you might need to install the correct busmastering driver for your system.

Adjusting Disk Caching Settings in Windows

Disk caches use a portion of memory to hold information flowing to and from disk drives. The system accesses the cache memory before accessing the main memory. If the information on disk is already in the cache memory, it is accessed far more quickly than if it were read from disk.

Disk cache software is incorporated into Windows 9x and newer Windows versions (MS-DOS and Windows 9x also include the Smartdrv.exe disk cache program for use at a command prompt).

The disk cache in Windows 9x and newer versions automatically adjusts to increases in physical RAM—as more RAM is added, the amount of RAM used for disk caching increases. The disk cache also varies in size—the amount of RAM used for disk caching varies with system activity. Windows uses two types of disk caching:

- **Write-behind caching**—This uses the disk cache for both disk reads and disk writes. This frees up an application saving data to disk to proceed to the next task.

- **Read-only caching**—This uses the disk cache for disk reads only. Disk writes go to the drive and cause delays with some applications.

By default, Windows uses write-behind caching for hard drives and read-only caching for floppy, removable-media, and CD-ROM/optical drives.

You can alter Windows 9x and new versions' disk caching settings by following this procedure:

1. Open the System properties sheet. Right-click My Computer and select Properties, or open the Control Panel and select System.

2. Click Performance.

3. Click File System.

4. Select options as directed next.

To enable Windows to use disk caching for hard drives most effectively, perform the following steps:

1. Select Hard Disk.

2. Select Network Server from the Typical role of this computer menu.

3. Drag the Read-ahead optimization selector to Full.

To enable write-behind caching for floppy and other removable disk drives, follow this procedure:

1. Click Removable Disk.
2. Click Enable Write-Behind Caching.

You must make sure all data has been saved to the disk before removing it.

To maximize caching for CD-ROM drives, follow this procedure:

1. Click CD-ROM.
2. Drag the Supplemental Cache Size selector to Large.
3. Select Quad-Speed or Higher from the Optimize Access Pattern menu.

You can disable write-behind disk caching by following this procedure (recommended for troubleshooting only because it slows down the system significantly):

1. Click Troubleshooting.
2. Click Disable Write-Behind Caching.

To complete the changes, click OK and restart the system when prompted.

EIDE and ATA Standards

Because the original IDE drives were developed as proprietary drive interfaces for use with brands such as Compaq and Zenith, the first IDE drives had major problems with compatibility and could not be auto-configured by the BIOS.

Although it can still be difficult to "mix and match" some IDE drives from different vendors, a series of standards for IDE drives are referred to as the *ATA* specifications (AT Attachment). Table 7.8 provides an overview of the differences in the various ATA/IDE specifications.

Table 7.8   ATA/IDE Specifications and Features

ATA Specification	Major Features
ATA-1 (original)	Standardized master/slave jumpers
	IDE Identify command for automatic configuration and detection of parameters
	PIO modes 0–2
	CHS (standard) and LBA (sector-translated) parameters
ATA-2	PIO modes 3–4
	Power management
	LBA translation for drives up to 8.4GB
	Primary and secondary IDE channels
	IDE block mode
ATA-3	S.M.A.R.T. self-diagnostics feature for use with monitoring software
	Password protection
	Improved reliability of PIO mode 4

CH

7

Table 7.8 continued	
ATA Specification	*Major Features*
ATA-4	UDMA/33
	ATAPI support
	80-wire/40-pin cable
ATA-5	UDMA/66
	Required use of 80-wire/40-pin cable with UDMA/66

Enhanced IDE is a marketing term used by some vendors to refer to the enhancements listed as ATA-2 in Table 7.8.

Troubleshooting IDE Drives

Problems with IDE drives can result from cabling, detection, geometry, physical damage, and jumpering issues. Use this section to prepare for IDE troubleshooting questions on the A+ Certification exam and in your day-to-day work.

Incompatible IDE Cables

IDE cables that use one keying method (plugged pin 20 or raised projection) cannot be plugged into drives or motherboards that use the other keying method. To correct the problem, replace the cable with a cable that either is not keyed or supports the same keying method as the motherboard and drive.

No Power to Drive

If the power cable is not plugged into an IDE drive during installation, it will not spin up when the system is turned on—you will not be able to hear the drive running and the system will not detect it. To correct the problem, turn off the system and reattach the power cable.

Cables Attached Incorrectly to IDE Interface or Drive

User errors in attaching cabling to IDE interfaces can cause detection problems. Many IDE cables do not use either keying method that is supported by IDE drives, making it easy to reverse either end of the IDE cable or to install the cable over only one row of connectors. If an IDE cable is reversed when it is attached to either the drive or the IDE host adapter, one of two symptoms are typical:

- Many systems will not display any information onscreen when restarted. These systems send a query to the drive and wait to complete the boot process until the drive responds. The drive never gets the message because the cable is attached incorrectly.

- Other systems will display a drive error because the drive cannot be detected during startup.

In both cases, if the power cable is attached to the drive, you will be able to hear the drive spinning as soon as the system is turned on.

The solution in either case is to make sure that the IDE cable's pin 1 (normally marked by a colored stripe) is attached to pin 1 on both the IDE host adapter (card or mother-board) and the IDE drive and that the cable attaches to both rows of pins on the drive and interface.

Drive Capacity Reported Incorrectly by BIOS

Drives with capacities higher than 8.4GB have geometries of 16 heads, 63 sectors per track, and more than 16,384 cylinders, but many system BIOSes will report only 16,384 cylinders and list a drive capacity of only 8.4 billion bytes (7.8 binary GB).

Some systems will support the full capacity of the drive, even if the BIOS reports only 8.4 billion bytes. These systems enable Enhanced Int 13h support when LBA mode is enabled. Other systems do not have Enhanced Int 13h support.

To determine whether the BIOS is supporting the full capacity of the drive, use FDISK with Windows 9x or Windows 2000 System Management to view the drive to determine whether the full capacity is available. If the drive reports only 8.4 billion bytes, upgrade the system BIOS or add an IDE host adapter card featuring LBA mode plus Enhanced Int 13h support to access the entire capacity of the drive.

Physical Damage to Drive

IDE drives can be damaged by shock and impact. If the BIOS cannot detect a drive and you already have checked BIOS configuration and cabling, the drive itself might be damaged. IDE drives should operate very quietly. A drive that makes scraping or banging noises when the system is turned on has sustained head or actuator damage and must be repaired or replaced.

Jumpering Issues

In most cases, if two IDE drives are attached to a single IDE cable, one drive must be jumpered as master and the other as slave. If both drives are jumpered as master or both as slave, neither drive can be autodetected by the BIOS or accessed by the system. If the original drive on the cable was working properly until a new drive was installed, check the jumpering on both the original (it should be set to master) and new drive (it should be set to slave).

If an 80-pin UDMA/66 cable is being used, both drives must be set to Cable Select and the cable sets master and slave (see "Master and Slave Jumpers," earlier in this chapter).

Some combinations of different brands of drives cannot be used on a single cable even if the jumpering is correct. If you are unable to detect one or both drives when two drives are connected to a single IDE cable and you have verified the jumpering is correct, the drives might not be fully compatible with ATA standards. Change the master to slave and the slave to master, move the slave drive to the other IDE cable and rejumper both drives, or use an UDMA/66 cable with Cable Select settings to enable both drives to work.

Drive Not Ready Error

Some IDE hard drives report "not ready" errors during initial system power-on, but if the system is restarted with a warm boot, the drive runs normally and starts the system. This is caused by a hard drive that has not spun up when the system tries to boot from the drive. To solve this problem, allow the system more time during the boot process to make sure the drive is ready before attempting to boot from it. This can be accomplished by

- Adjusting a delay timer option available in some BIOSes; this pauses the boot process a few seconds to allow the drive to start
- Disabling the quick boot option available in some BIOSes
- Allowing the system to perform a full memory count and test before booting

High-speed IDE CD-ROM and similar drives normally take several seconds to detect a new disk. Allow about five seconds before trying to read the contents of the media.

SCSI Interface

SCSI (Small Computer Systems Interface) is a more flexible drive interface than IDE because it can accommodate many devices that are not hard disk drives. The following are common uses for SCSI:

- High-performance and high-capacity hard drives
- Image scanners
- Removable-media drives such as ZIP, Jaz, and Castlewood Orb
- High-performance laser printers
- High-performance optical drives, including CD-ROM, CD-R, CD-RW, DVD-ROM, and other

So-called *narrow* SCSI host adapters (which use an 8-bit data channel) can accommodate up to seven devices of different varieties on a single connector. *Wide* SCSI host adapters use a 16-bit data channel and accommodate up to 15 devices on a single connector.

Multiple Device Support with SCSI Host Adapters

All true SCSI host adapters are designed to support multiple devices, although some low-cost SCSI host adapters made especially for scanners and ZIP drives might not support multiple devices (also known as daisy-chaining). Several SCSI features permit this:

- External SCSI peripherals have two SCSI ports, enabling daisy-chaining of multiple devices.
- Internal SCSI ribbon cables resemble IDE data cables, only wider.
- Both internal and external SCSI peripherals enable the user to choose a unique device ID number for each device to distinguish one peripheral from another in the daisy-chain (see Figure 7.18).

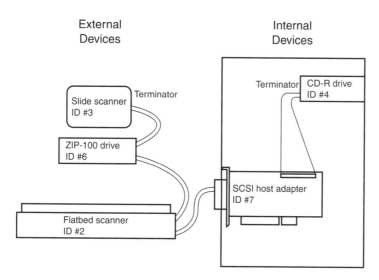

Figure 7.18

When a SCSI host adapter card with internal and external connectors is used, the SCSI daisy-chain can extend through the card. Note that the devices on each end of the chain are terminated, and each device (including the host adapter) has a unique device ID number.

Multiple device support enables the different types of devices listed previously to work on a single SCSI host adapter. For example, my office computer features a CD-R drive, flatbed scanner, slide scanner, and ZIP drive connected to the same card, with room for three additional miscellaneous SCSI devices on that card. Adaptec's SCSI Interrogator utility (see Figure 7.19), supplied as part of its EZ-SCSI Lite software, shows used and available SCSI device IDs.

SCSI Host Adapter Locations and Hardware Resources

Some system boards contain a SCSI host adapter, but most SCSI host adapters are add-on cards.

SCSI host adapters do not have standard IRQ or I/O port address settings because they are add-on devices rather than a standard part of the system architecture. Some high-performance ISA SCSI host adapters also use a DMA channel. In addition, SCSI host adapters designed to support bootable SCSI hard drives use a memory address for the ROM BIOS chip on the card.

The configuration options for three typical ISA-based SCSI host adapters are listed in Table 7.9. Most PCI-based SCSI cards use Windows Plug and Play technologies and have their IRQ and other settings assigned by the computer or operating system.

CH

7

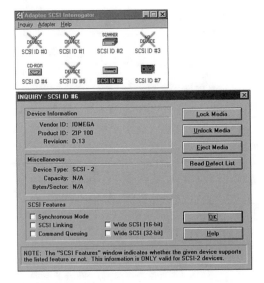

Figure 7.19

Adaptec's SCSI Interrogator displays the details of each SCSI device attached to your system as well as the used and available SCSI ID numbers. The configuration shown allows SCSI IDs 0, 1, 3, and 5 to be used for new devices.

Use this table to help you understand the need to select an appropriate SCSI host adapter for the devices you need to attach to it. In Table 7.9, only one IRQ and one I/O port address (and one DMA channel on some models) would be required for the SCSI card, regardless of the number of devices attached to the card.

Table 7.9 Typical SCSI Hardware Resource Usage Examples

Resources	Adaptec AVA-1505A	Adaptec AHA-1535A	Adaptec AHA-1540CF
IRQ	9	10	10
	10	11	11
	11	12	12
	12	14	14
		15	15
I/O Port Address	340–35Fh	130–133h	130–133h
	140–15Fh	334–337h	334–337h
		234–237h	234–237h
		230–233h	230–233h
		134–137h	134–137h
		330–333h	330–333h
DMA Channel	None	5	5
		6	6
		7	7

Table 7.9 continued			
Resources	*Adaptec AVA-1505A*	*Adaptec AHA-1535A*	*Adaptec AHA-1540CF*
Memory Address (for SCSI BIOS)	None	None	D8000h DC000h D4000h D0000h CC000h C8000h Disabled
Suitable for devices including	Scanner ZIP drive CD-ROM	Scanner ZIP drive CD-ROM CD-R/CD-RW	Scanner ZIP drive CD-ROM CD-R/CD-RW Bootable hard drives

Different SCSI cards have different settings for two reasons. More powerful SCSI cards offer additional configuration options to enable multiple SCSI cards to coexist in the same system without conflicts. Also, SCSI cards are not one-size-fits-all solutions, but are available with different features to suit the needs of different types of peripherals.

SCSI Standards

SCSI actually is the family name for a wide range of standards, which differ from each other in the speed of devices, number of devices, and other technical details. The major SCSI standards are listed in Table 7.10. SCSI host adapters are generally backward-compatible, enabling older and newer SCSI standards to be mixed on the same host adapter. However, mixing slower and faster devices can cause the faster devices to slow down unless you use a host adapter with dual buses that can run at different speeds. Table 7.10 lists the speeds and other characteristics of popular SCSI standards.

Table 7.10 Popular SCSI Standards				
Popular Name	*Speed*	*Number of Devices*	*Data Bus*	*Signal Type*
Fast	10MBps	7	8-bit	SE[1]
Fast-Wide	10MBps	15	16-bit	SE
Ultra	20MBps	7	8-bit	SE
Ultra-Wide	20MBps	15	16-bit	SE
Ultra2	40MBps	7	8-bit	LVD[2]
Ultra2Wide	80MBps	15	16-bit	LVD
Ultra3	160MBps	15	16-bit	LVD

1 Single-ended

2 Low-voltage differential

CH

7

8-bit versions of SCSI use a 50-pin cable or a 25-pin cable; wide (16-bit) versions use a 68-pin cable. 10MBps is the fastest speed supported by ISA cards, which are becoming obsolete. The faster speeds require a PCI bus card.

SCSI Signaling Types

In Table 7.10, SE stands for single-ended, a SCSI signaling type that runs at speeds of up to 20MBps only. SE signaling allows relatively inexpensive SCSI devices and host adapters to be developed, but it reduces the length of cables and the top speed possible.

Ultra2, Ultra2Wide, and Ultra3 devices all use a signaling standard called low voltage differential (LVD), which allows longer cable runs and faster, more reliable operation than the single-ended (SE) standard allows. Some LVD devices can also be used on the same bus with SE devices, but these multimode, or LVD/SE devices, will be forced to slow down to the SE maximum of 20MBps when mixed with SE devices on the same bus. Some advanced SCSI host adapters feature both an SE and an LVD bus to allow the same adapter to control both types of devices at the correct speeds.

SCSI Cables

Just as no single SCSI standard exists, no single SCSI cabling standard exists. In addition to the 50-pin versus 68-pin difference between standard and wide devices, differences also appear in the narrow SCSI external cables (see Figure 7.20).

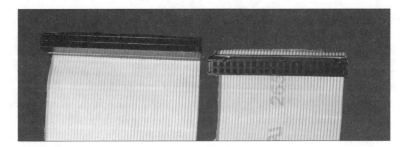

Figure 7.20
A narrow (50-pin) SCSI ribbon cable (left) compared to a 40-pin IDE cable (right).

SCSI 50-pin ribbon cables resemble IDE cables but are wider. However, three different types of narrow SCSI external connectors are available (see Figure 7.21):

- **50-pin Centronics**—Similar to, but wider than, the 36-pin Centronics port used for parallel printers.
- **50-pin high-density connector**—The Wide SCSI 68-pin connector uses the same design, but with 34 pins per row instead of 25 pins per row.
- **25-pin DB-25F**—Physically, but not electronically, similar to the DB-25F parallel printer port.

Figure 7.21
Three common SCSI external cables: high-density 50-pin (lower left), DB25M (upper left), and the Centronics 50-pin (right).

Most external 8-bit (narrow) SCSI devices support only one type of 50-pin connector. However, a few low-cost devices such as the Iomega ZIP-100 drive use only the 25-pin connector, which lacks much of the grounding found on the 50-pin cable. Some SCSI devices provide two different types of SCSI connectors. My slide scanner, for example, has a single Centronics 50-pin connector and a single DB25F connector.

Daisy-Chaining SCSI Devices

When you create a SCSI daisy-chain, you must keep all these factors in mind:

- Each device must have a unique SCSI device ID.
- Each end of the daisy-chain must be terminated. Some devices have an integral switch or jumper block for termination (see Figure 7.22), whereas some external devices require that you attach a terminator (which resembles the end of a SCSI cable) to the unused SCSI connector.

Figure 7.22
A SCSI-based internal CD-R drive with (left to right) well-marked jumpers for termination and device ID, power connector, data cable pin 1, and CD-audio cable.

CH
7

■ When daisy-chaining external devices, double-check the cable connector type and purchase appropriate cables. You will often need SCSI cables that have different connectors at each end because of the different connector types used (see Figure 7.23).

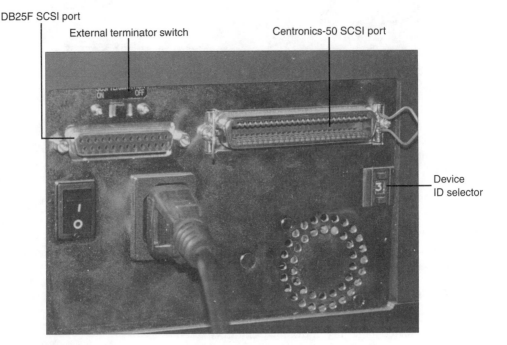

DB25F SCSI port

External terminator switch

Centronics-50 SCSI port

Device ID selector

Figure 7.23
External termination and device ID selector switches on a SCSI-based scanner. This scanner has both DB25F and Centronics-50 (also called LD50) SCSI ports.

SCSI Host Adapter Card Installation

For Windows 9x, Me, and 2000, follow these steps to install a Plug and Play SCSI host adapter card:

1. Check the card's documentation and make any required adjustments in the Plug and Play configuration in the BIOS before installing the card. You might need to change the type of IRQ setting used or reserve a particular IRQ for the card.

2. Install the card into the appropriate ISA or PCI expansion slot.

3. Turn on the system.

4. When the card is detected by the system, you'll be prompted for installation software. Insert the appropriate disk or CD-ROM and follow the prompt to complete the installation.

5. Reboot the system and use the Windows Device Manager to view the card's configuration.

Choosing an Appropriate SCSI Card for Your Devices

Before you can install a SCSI device, an appropriate SCSI card must be installed in the system. As you have previously seen, SCSI has several standards, and a wide range of cards has been designed for each standard.

Use Table 7.11 to help you choose a SCSI card that is adequate for the devices you want to use with the card. If you plan to buy more advanced devices later, buy a card that exceeds your devices' current requirements, because SCSI is backward compatible. If a customer has an existing SCSI card and wants to add a new SCSI device to it, be sure it meets the minimum requirements for that device.

Table 7.11 SCSI Card Selection Criteria	
Devices You Plan to Use	Minimum Features Required
Scanner, ZIP drive, CD-ROM	Any SCSI card
CD-R, CD-RW drive	Card with busmastering
Bootable hard drive	Card that matches drive's transfer rate and data bus and has an onboard BIOS

You should choose PCI-based cards for most uses, because ISA cards are becoming obsolete.

Installation of a SCSI Device

For Windows 9x, Me, and 2000, follow these steps to install a SCSI device:

1. Check the existing SCSI daisy-chain and note unused SCSI device IDs.
2. Set the SCSI device to an unused ID.
3. Turn off the system and attach the device to the appropriate SCSI cable.
4. If this device will be at the end of the daisy-chain, terminate it and disable termination for the previous end of the daisy-chain.
5. Turn on the computer; Windows should detect the new device. Install any required drivers as directed.
6. Reboot if required and test your new device.

Installing a SCSI Hard Drive

Many SCSI hard drives and some other devices support a feature called *SCAM* (SCSI Configuration AutoMagically), which automatically assigns SCSI device IDs. Use this option only if all devices on the SCSI host adapter, and the adapter itself, support SCAM.

Most SCSI hard drives will require preparation with a host-adapter–specific utility program. If you change host adapters after preparing a SCSI hard drive, its contents might not be readable.

Adjust the system BIOS setting for drive boot order to enable a SCSI drive connected to a bootable host adapter to be bootable. On systems that don't list SCSI as a boot option in the system BIOS, disable the IDE host adapter to enable the SCSI drive to boot.

CH

7

SCSI hard drives have many additional configuration options not used by other SCSI devices, including the following:

- Negotiation (of speed, bus width, and data transfer type)
- Enable/disable unit attention
- Parity checking for data
- Auto-start delay
- Remote start

Check the drive and host adapter documentation to resolve any conflicts.

Troubleshooting SCSI Devices

SCSI problems can usually be traced to incorrect device ID, termination, or cabling. Use this section to prepare for troubleshooting questions on the A+ Certification exam and your day-to-day work with SCSI devices.

External SCSI Device Isn't Available

External SCSI devices might not be available for any of the following reasons:

- Device not powered on when the system was turned on
- Incorrect termination
- Excess cable length

If an external SCSI device isn't turned on a few seconds before the system is turned on, it might not initialize properly. If an external SCSI device is not turned on and the system has booted, it might be possible to use the Device Manager to activate the device by following this procedure:

1. Turn on the device.
2. Open the Windows Device Manager.
3. Click Refresh and wait for the system to recheck all connected devices.
4. If the SCSI device now appears in the Device Manager, you should be able to use it normally.
5. If the device doesn't appear, restart the system.

SCSI is a daisy-chained interface; both ends of the daisy-chain must be terminated. Make sure that the terminator switch or external terminator is located at the end of the external daisy-chain. If a new device has been added to the end of the daisy-chain, you must disable termination of the old device and add termination to the new device.

Faster SCSI standards support shorter maximum cable lengths than slower standards. Check the overall length of the daisy-chain if some external devices are unavailable and use the shortest cable lengths possible to avoid exceeding standards.

External or Internal SCSI Device Isn't Available

If a new external or internal SCSI device is not available, two common reasons include

- Duplicate device ID numbers
- Failure to install drivers for device

If multiple SCSI devices have the same device ID number, the devices will interfere with each other. To solve this problem, power down all SCSI devices and the system and make sure each device has a unique device ID number before restarting.

Both the SCSI host adapter card and the SCSI devices attached to the card need operating system–compatible drivers to operate. With Windows 9x and newer Windows versions, such as Windows Me and Windows 2000, SCSI devices are typically Plug and Play, prompting you to install the driver the first time the device is found in the system. If the drivers are not loaded, use the Device Manager's properties sheet for each device to install a new driver.

If you need to install multiple SCSI devices, you should install one device and its device drivers before installing another device.

CD-ROM, CD-RW, and DVD-ROM Drives

CD-ROM, CD-RW, and DVD-ROM drives are the most popular types of optical drives in use. All three can read CD-ROM and CD music media. CD-RW drives can also read and write CD-Recordable and CD-Rewriteable media; most DVD-ROM drives can read CD-R and CD-RW media as well as their own native DVD-ROM media. The A+ Certification test normally refers to DVD-ROM drives as DVD drives; although there are many different standards for DVD recordable and rewriteable drives, these additional DVD standards are not major factors in the market today and are not on the test.

For more information about CD-ROM, CD-RW, and DVD drives, see *Upgrading and Repairing PCs, 12th Edition*, Chapter 13, "Optical Storage."

How CD-ROM and DVD Drives Store Data

The data are stored in a continuous spiral of indentations called *pits* and *lands* on the nonlabel side of the media from the middle of the media outward to the edge. All drives use a laser to read data; DVD stores more data because it uses a laser on a shorter wavelength than CD-ROM and CD-RW drives do, allowing for smaller pits and lands and more data in the same space. CD-R and CD-RW drives use special media types and a more powerful laser to write data to the media. CD-R media, which can appear gold, green, or blue on the nonlabel side, is a write-once media—the media can be written to during multiple sessions, but older data cannot be deleted. CD-RW media, which is silver on the nonlabel side, can be rewritten up to 1,000 times.

CH
7

Capacities and Technical Details

The standard capacity of older CD-ROM drives is 650MB—74 minutes of music. Newer drives and CD-R/CD-RW media support 700MB—80 minutes of music. Standard DVD drives support the DVD-5 standard, which stores 4.7GB on a single-sided, single-layer disk that is the same size as a CD-ROM but holds much more data and must be read by a different type of laser.

These drives are most commonly connected through the ATA/IDE interface, where they are referred to as ATAPI devices, but some high-performance models also connect through SCSI interfaces. Portable drives can use parallel, USB, or PC Card interfaces—USB is the most common interface on recent models. The term *CD-ROM* will be used in the rest of this section to refer to all of these drive types except where noted.

Drive speeds are measured by an X-rating: 1X equals 150KBps, the data transfer rate used for reading music CDs. Multiply the X-rating by 150 to determine the drive's data rate. Most drives run at variable speeds to hold down costs, so a so-called 52x drive produces its maximum 7,500KBps transfer rate only when it is reading the outer edges of the media on a full CD. For drives that work with different types of media, each media type is listed for the drive. For example, a drive that reads CD-ROMs at 32X (maximum), writes CD-R media at 12X, and rewrites CD-RW media at 10X would be said to have a speed rating of 12X/10X/32X; the usual speed order is CD-R/CD-RW/CD-ROM. A DVD drive that can read DVD media at 10X and CD-ROMs at 40X would be referred to as a 10X DVD (40X CD-ROM) drive.

Installing CD-ROM and DVD Drives

The installation of these drives follows the standard procedure used for each interface type. For example, ATAPI/IDE CD-ROM drives are set as master or slave, SCSI CD-ROM drives must be set to a unique device ID, and so on. If you want to play music CDs through your sound card's speakers, make sure you run the CD audio patch cable supplied with the drive to the CD audio jack on the sound card.

Windows installs driver software that makes all these types of drives appear like standard drives for reading data. You must use special programs to write data to CD-RW and CD-R media.

IDE/ATAPI Installation Issues

Generally, because data frequently is copied from a CD-ROM drive to the hard drive or from a hard drive to a CD-RW drive, ATAPI CD-ROM drives should be connected to the secondary IDE interface, and hard drives should be connected to the primary IDE interface.

On newer systems with a CD-ROM drive type in the system BIOS setup, be sure to set the BIOS drive type as CD-ROM. If you want to use the CD-ROM as a bootable device for use with Windows 2000 or vendor-supplied system recovery CDs, be sure that the CD-ROM is specified as the first device in the boot order.

Troubleshooting CD-ROM and DVD Drives

The same problems can occur with CD-ROM and DVD drives as with other drives or devices that use the same interface, but additional problems can occur because these drives use removable optical media. The following are some typical problems:

- Read delays after new media is inserted
- Can't read some media types in CD-ROM or DVD drives
- Damage to media prevents drive from reading media
- Can't play music through sound card's speakers

Read Delays After New Media Is Inserted

Read delays of several seconds are normal when you insert media into a CD-ROM drive; the drive must spin up the media to read it, and delays are sometimes longer with faster drives. A delay of more than about 10 seconds can indicate drive or media problems; clean the drive with a cleaning CD, which uses small brushes to wipe debris and dust away from the laser, and try the CD again.

Can't Read Some Media Types in CD-ROM or DVD Drives

Older CD-ROM drives (generally those under 24x speed) and first-generation DVD drives are unable to read CD-RW media, which has a lower reflectivity than CD-ROM or CD-R media. Newer DVD drives and virtually all CD-ROM drives at 24X or faster speeds use a modified laser to enable them to read CD-RW media.

CD-ROM drives that can read CD-RW media are called *MultiRead* drives. DVD drives that can read CD-RW and different types of DVD media are called *MultiRead2* drives. Look for these terms on the faceplate of compatible drives. Older drives that lack CD-RW compatibility cannot be upgraded—they must be replaced.

Damage to Media Prevents Drive from Reading Media

Because all types of CD-ROM drives are optical and read data recorded in a single spiral track, fingerprints or surface damage to the clear protective layer over the media surface will prevent data beneath the dirty or damaged surface from being read. A cracked or severely scratched CD-ROM cannot be read at all.

Dirty CD-ROMs can be cleaned with the same cleaners used for music CDs. Some surface scratches can be polished away with special repair kits available from computer and music stores, and special protective shields can be attached to the nonlabel (data) side of frequently used CD-ROMs to protect the media. Media should be stored in a protective sleeve or jewel case when not in use.

Can't Play Music Through Sound Card's Speakers

Many users like to use their computers as stereo systems, taking advantage of their CD-ROM drives and sound card hardware to play music in their homes or offices. If the user

CH

7

is unable to hear CDs being played through the CD player software supplied on most systems, check the following:

- **CD audio cable**—This cable must be run from the CD-ROM drive that will be used for CD music to the correct jack on the sound card. No music will be audible if the cable is not plugged in, is attached to the wrong drive, or is plugged into the wrong jack on the sound card.

- **Windows sound mixer controls**—In most cases, a speaker icon will be visible in the Windows system tray when sound hardware is installed. Click the speaker icon to display the mixer control. If the volume for CD audio is turned down to minimum or is muted, or if all audio is muted, no sound will be audible. Enable the sound and adjust the volume to hear music.

- **Volume control in CD player application**—The volume control in the player program might be set too low if the sound is not audible after checking the first two items. Adjust it as required.

Summary

All magnetic storage devices use 512-byte sectors to store data and have a FAT (File Allocation Table) structure to store pointers to file locations on the media.

All modern floppy disk drives use double-sided media. High-density media can store two or more times the capacity of double-density media because of its more advanced magnetic media. 3.5-inch disks use a rigid jacket and metal shutter to protect the media, whereas 5.25-inch disks must use an external sleeve to protect their flexible jacket and open read/write area. BIOS and operating system issues determine which systems can handle different types of floppy disk drives. The floppy disk drive interface uses IRQ 6 and I/O port address 3F0-3F7h. The floppy disk drive at the end of the cable beyond the twist is A:, and the drive in the middle of the cable is B:. Only systems with a "swap floppy disk drives" option in the BIOS can override this default. Floppy disk drives cannot be detected by the BIOS; you must select the correct drive types for A: and B: and cable the drives correctly to get them to work properly.

The magnetic media inside floppy disks can be damaged by touch, heat, or magnetism. Floppy disk drives should be cleaned with a wet-type cleaner about once every six months to ensure reliable read/write operation.

Floppy disk drive failures can be caused by incorrect cabling, incorrect BIOS configuration, defective drive mechanisms, or bad media.

Master and slave jumper settings on IDE drives are used to select the order of drives rather than their position on the data cable, unless cable-select is used. IDE drives and data cables do not always use positive keying, so be sure to match pin 1 (colored stripe) on the cable to pin 1 on the host adapter or drive.

IDE drives' sector translation feature enables them to use nonstandard geometries, but this feature should not be used unless a user-defined drive type is absent. You should record the geometry used for any IDE drive installation on the drive's cover as well as on the outside of the system because the same settings must be used if the drive is moved to another system or must be reinstalled. Automatic detection of the drive enables the drive to tell the system its correct geometry and translation scheme (such as LBA mode). For the best results, use this feature within the BIOS configuration and store the settings as a user-defined drive type.

Without LBA translation, a hard disk's geometry can't exceed 1,024 cylinders, 16 heads, and 63 sectors per track when used with MS-DOS or MS-DOS–based operating systems, such as Windows 9x, Windows NT, or Windows 2000. LBA mode overcomes this 504MB/528 million-byte barrier. Although LBA limitations can be overcome with software drivers supplied with IDE drives, a BIOS upgrade or add-on card with auxiliary BIOS is the best way to enable a system to use a big IDE hard drive.

Use the fastest PIO or UDMA mode supported by your drive and host adapter (or motherboard) for optimal IDE hard drive performance. Block mode enables IDE drives to read multiple sectors before an IRQ is issued. Enable block mode to improve drive performance in most circumstances. Use the BIOS's drive configuration or peripheral configuration screens to enable or disable block mode. Contact the motherboard or host adapter manufacturer for busmastering drivers and correct installation procedures.

ATA standards define common features shared by different brands of IDE drives but do not guarantee that you can put two different brands of IDE drives on the same data cable. The latest standard is ATA-5, providing support for UDMA/66 transfer rates.

IDE drive problems can be caused by bad or incompatible cables, BIOS configuration problems, and master/slave compatibility issues as well as physical damage and failures.

SCSI (Small Computer System Interface) is a multi-device standard often used with scanners and other devices as well as with hard drives. It enables daisy-chaining of multiple devices on a single host adapter. SCSI cards are among the most flexible cards in hardware configuration because they are an add-on, rather than being a standard part of a system. All wide SCSI devices use a 16-bit data bus. Wide interface cards can use 15 devices on the daisy-chain. Narrow SCSI devices and cards use an 8-bit data bus, with a maximum of only 7 devices on the daisy-chain. Be sure you know the cable connector types your SCSI devices use before you purchase SCSI cables or construct a daisy-chain of multiple SCSI devices.

Successful SCSI interface card installations depend on using nonconflicting settings for the card's IRQ and other hardware resources and installing the correct drivers for the card. If you want to mix high-speed and low-speed SCSI devices on a single interface card, choose a card with dual interfaces that can each run at a separate speed. Installing a SCSI device requires you to use a unique device ID and correct termination with any operating system. SCSI problems can result from device ID conflicts, incorrect termination, or not detecting all SCSI devices at system startup.

CH
7

QUESTIONS AND ANSWERS: —————————

1. What hardware features allow two devices to connect to a single IDE channel?
   A: Master and slave jumpers

2. What feature allows multiple SCSI devices to connect to a single host adapter?
   A: Device ID numbers

3. What is the difference between an IDE and SCSI cable?
   A: IDE cables are 40-pin, whereas SCSI ribbon cables can be 50-pin or 68-pin.

4. Are IDE cables foolproof?
   A: No. Some are keyed, but most aren't to enable them to be used with any combination of drives and host adapters.

5. Can any SCSI adapter be used with any SCSI device?
   A: No. Devices that use different SCSI standards require different SCSI host adapter cards. Cards that lack a BIOS can't be used for bootable SCSI hard drives, and cards that don't perform busmastering can't be used to make CD-Rs.

6. What's the most likely reason the screen is blank after you add a new IDE hard drive and restart the system?
   A: You've reversed one end of the data cable.

Power Supplies and Circuit Testing

WHILE YOU READ

1. What are the voltage levels on a baby-AT motherboard?
2. What are the voltage levels on an ATX motherboard?
3. List two uses for a multimeter besides testing DC current.
4. What system components should have no resistance when tested?
5. Where is the only fan located in some systems?
6. What information must you have about an RS-232 cable to test the leads for continuity?
7. Does a "dead" power supply always mean the power supply has failed?
8. What is the UL standard for surge suppression?
9. The volt-amp (VA) rating of a UPS unit should exceed the actual VA requirements of your system by a factor of at least how much for extended run time?

Power issues are largely ignored by most computer users, but a properly working power supply is the foundation to correct operation of the system. The power supply is vital to the health of the computer and should be tested when computer problems result to see if the power supply is at fault. To keep the power supply working properly, surge suppression and battery backup (UPS) units are highly recommended.

When the power supply stops working, the computer stops working. The power *supply* is really misnamed: It is actually a power *converter* that changes high-voltage alternating current (AC) to low-voltage direct current (DC).

During the conversion process, a great deal of heat is produced. A fan in the power supply dissipates the heat created by operating. That same fan is also used to cool the rest of the computer. In many older systems, the *only* cooling fan in the entire computer is the one built into the power supply. Newer systems, starting with advanced 486-type processors and almost all Pentium-class systems, use auxiliary fans on the CPU and the case to cool the faster, hotter CPUs now in use. Figure 8.1 shows a typical desktop computer's power supply. You can use the label attached to the top of the power supply to determine its wattage rating and see important safety reminders.

Figure 8.1
A typical power supply installed in a desktop computer provides the rating and safety information on top of the unit.

Power Supply Ratings

Power supplies are rated in watts; typically, power supplies in tower-case (upright case) machines use 300-watt or larger power supplies, reflecting the greater number of drives and cards that can be installed in these computers. Power supplies used in smaller desktop computers can be as low as 150 watts. The power supply rating is found on the top of the power supply, along with safety rating information and amperage levels produced by the power supply's different DC outputs.

An overloaded power supply has two major symptoms:

- Overheating.
- Spontaneous rebooting (cold boot with memory test) due to incorrect voltage on the Power Good line running from the power supply to the motherboard. See Figures 8.6 and 8.7, later in this chapter, for details.

Overheating can have multiple causes; follow the steps listed in the section "Causes and Cures of Power Supply Overheating," later in this chapter, before replacing an overheated power supply.

To determine whether Power Good or other motherboard voltage levels are within limits, perform the measurements listed in the section "Determining Power Supply DC Voltage Levels" later in this chapter.

Multivoltage Power Supplies

Most power supplies are designed to handle two different voltage ranges:

- 110–120 volt/60 cycle
- 220–240 volt/50 cycle

Standard North American power is now 115–120 volt/60 cycle AC (the previous standard was 110 volt). The power used in European and Asian countries is typically 230–240 volt/50 cycle AC (previously 220 volt). Power supplies typically have a slider switch with two markings: 115 (for North American 110–120 volt/60 cycle AC) and 230 (for European and Asian 220–240 volt/50 cycle AC). Figure 8.2 shows a slider switch set for correct North American voltage. If a power supply is set to the wrong input voltage, the system will not work. Setting a power supply for 230 volt with 110–120-volt current is harmless; however, feeding 220–240 volts into a power supply set for 115 volts will destroy the power supply.

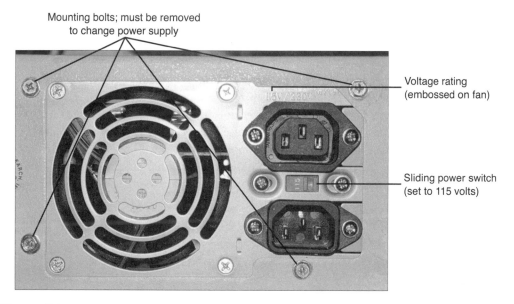

Figure 8.2
A typical power supply's sliding voltage switch set for correct North American voltage. Slide it to 230 volts for use in Europe and Asia. The drive's mounting screws are also visible.

Causes and Cures of Power Supply Overheating

Power supplies can overheat, causing system failure and possible component damage, due to any of the following causes:

- Overloading
- Fan failure
- Inadequate air flow outside the system
- Inadequate air flow inside the system
- Dirt and dust

Overloading

An overloaded power supply is caused by connecting devices that draw more power than the power supply is designed to handle. As you add more card-based devices to expansion slots and install more internal drives in a system, the odds of having an overloaded power supply increase.

If a power supply fails or overheats, check the causes listed in the following sections before determining whether you should replace the power supply. If you determine that you should replace the power supply, purchase a unit that has a higher wattage rating.

For more information about how to select an appropriately sized power supply, see "Power Supply Ratings" in *Upgrading and Repairing PCs, 12th Edition*, Chapter 21.

Fan Failure

The fan inside the power supply cools it and is partly responsible for cooling the rest of the computer. If the fan fails, the power supply and the entire computer are at risk of damage. The fan also might stop turning as a symptom of other power problems.

If the fan stops immediately after the power comes on, this usually indicates incorrect input voltage or a short circuit. If you turn off the system and turn it back on again under these conditions, the fan will stop each time. To determine whether the fan has failed, listen to the unit; it should make less noise if the fan has failed. You can also see the fan blades spinning rapidly on a power supply fan that is working correctly. If the blades aren't turning, the fan has failed. Note that if the fan has failed because of a short circuit or incorrect input voltage, you will not see any picture onscreen because the system cannot operate.

If the system starts normally but the fan stops turning later, this indicates a true fan failure instead of a power problem.

Should you try to replace a standard power supply fan? No. Because the power supply is a sealed unit, you would need to remove the cover from most power supplies to gain access to the fan. The wire coils inside a power supply retain potentially lethal electrical charges. Instead, scrap the power supply and replace it with a higher-rated unit. See "Removal and Replacement of the Power Supply" later in this chapter.

Inadequate Air Flow Outside the System

The power supply's capability to cool the system depends in part on free airflow space outside the system. If the computer is kept in a confined area (such as a closet or security cabinet) without adequate ventilation, power supply failures due to overheating are likely.

Even systems in ordinary office environments can have airflow problems; make sure that several inches of free air space exist behind the fan output for any computer.

Inadequate Air Flow Inside the System

As you have seen in previous chapters, the interior of the typical computer is a messy place. Wide ribbon cables, drive power cables, and expansion cards create small *air dams* that block air flow between the heat sources, such as the motherboard, CPU, drives, and memory modules, and the fan in the power supply.

You can do the following to improve air flow inside the computer:

- Use cable ties to secure excess ribbon cable and power connectors out of the way of the fans and the power supply.
- Replace any missing slot covers.
- Make sure that auxiliary case fans and CPU fans are working correctly.

Dirt and Dust

Most power supplies, except for a few of the early ATX power supplies, use a cooling technique called *negative pressure*; in other words, the power supply fan works like a weak vacuum cleaner, pulling air through vents in the case, past the components, and out through the fan.

Vacuum cleaners are used to remove dust, dirt, cat hairs, and so on from living rooms and offices, and even the power supply's weak impression of a vacuum cleaner works the same way.

When you open a system for any kind of maintenance, look for the following:

- Dirt, dust, hair, and gunk clogging the case vents
- A thin layer of dust on the motherboard and expansion slots
- Dirt and dust on the power supply vent and fans

You can use either a vacuum cleaner especially designed for computer use or compressed air to remove dirt and dust from inside the system. If you use compressed air, be sure to spread newspapers around the system to catch the dirt and dust. See Chapter 11 for more information.

Auxiliary Fans

Auxiliary fans can be attached to the following:

- The CPU's heatsink
- The case
- A card mounted in an expansion slot
- An empty drive bay

Some of these fans are designed to use a small power connector found on many recent motherboards (see Figure 8.3). Others borrow power from a Molex-type drive power connector (the type of power connector used by hard drives). A pass-through connection enables the same connector to power a drive (see Figure 8.4). A few upgrade-type CPUs have been built with an integrated fan that can draw its power directly from the CPU socket. Each of these fans should be checked for good working order and be kept clean.

Figure 8.3
A typical cooling fan and heatsink for a Pentium II-class CPU. This model uses a small three-wire pigtail (right) to connect directly to a special power connector on the motherboard.

Figure 8.4
A typical cooling fan and heatsink for a Pentium-class CPU. This model uses a Molex pass-through connector (left) that takes power from a standard disk drive power cable.

Replacement Power Supply Form Factors and Connectors

There are two major types of power connectors on motherboards:

- 12-pin, modeled after the original IBM PC power connector and used on baby-AT and LPX motherboards (see Figure 8.5)
- 20-pin, introduced with the first ATX motherboard and also used on Micro ATX and NLX motherboards (see Figure 8.6)

Most systems using the 12-pin power supply connector use a type of power supply referred to as LPX, whereas systems using the ATX power supply connector use the ATX power supply.

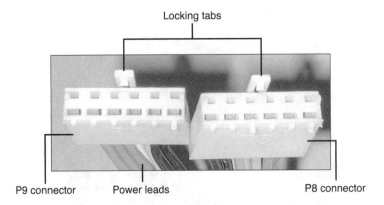

Figure 8.5
Twin 6-pin power connectors are used on LPX and other power supply types that attach to motherboards with a 12-pin connector.

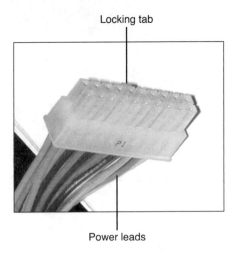

Figure 8.6
The ATX power supply has a single 20-pin power connector. The extra connectors (compared to the LPX design in Figure 8.5) provide support for 3.3 volts and for software- or keyboard-controlled power down. Many of these power supplies don't have an external power switch for that reason.

Figure 8.7 lists the pinouts for these connectors. Note that only 5-volt and 12-volt DC power levels are supported by 12-pin (LPX) power supplies, whereas ATX power supplies also support 3.3-volt DC power levels. Another difference between ATX and LPX connectors is that the ATX connector uses specially shaped holes and a locking clip for positive keying, while the LPX 12-pin connector requires the user to properly align the black wires of connectors P8 and P9 to make a correct connection.

ATX Power Connector Pinout

+3.3v	Orange	11		1	Orange	+3.3v
−12v	Blue	12		2	Orange	+3.3v
Ground	Black	13		3	Black	Ground
PS-On	Green	14		4	Red	+5v
Ground	Black	15		5	Black	Ground
Ground	Black	16		6	Red	+5v
Ground	Black	17		7	Black	Ground
−5v	White	18		8	Gray	Power Good
+5v	Red	19		9	Purple	+5v Standby
+5v	Red	20		10	Yellow	+12v

XT/AT/LPX Power Connector

	1	Orange	+5v (Power Good)	
	2	Red	+5v	
	3	Yellow	+12v	
	4	Blue	−12v	P8
	5	Black	Ground	
	6	Black	Ground	
	1	Black	Ground	
	2	Black	Ground	
	3	White	−5v	
	4	Red	+5v	P9
	5	Red	+5v	
	6	Red	+5v	

Figure 8.7
An ATX power connector (left) and baby-AT (LPX) power connector (right). The color coding in the figure represents the standard wire colors used.

Figure 8.8 shows a motherboard with both ATX and LPX power connectors. Most Baby-AT motherboards use the LPX power connector, and most ATX motherboards use the ATX power connector.

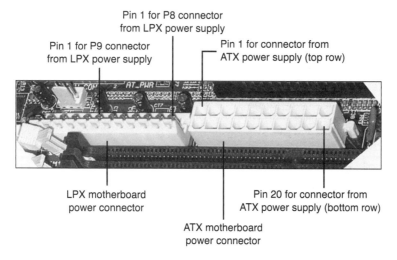

Figure 8.8
LPX (left) and ATX (right) power connectors on an early ATX motherboard.

ATX power supplies can have a rear power switch as well as the case power switch. Or, they might use only the case's power switch, which is usually attached to the motherboard instead of to the power supply. This is the most common situation with LPX power supplies.

An LPX power supply is the most popular of several types that use the 12-pin connector shown previously in Figure 8.7; the ATX-style power connector can also be used by the SFX power supply.

Each time you need to replace a power supply, the replacement must

- Have the same power supply connectors as the original
- Be the same form factor (shape, size, and switch location)
- Have the same or higher wattage rating

To ensure reliability, a power supply should have a UL (Underwriters Laboratory) or CSA (CSA International, formerly Canadian Standards Association) rating; these are the leading international standards associations for powered devices. Many very low-cost power supplies lack either rating and can produce erratic voltage levels or be unsafe.

Removal and Replacement of the Power Supply

Typical power supplies are held in place by several screws that attach the power supply to the rear panel of the computer. The power supply also is supported by a shelf inside the case, and screws can secure the power supply to that shelf.

To remove a power supply, follow these steps:

1. Turn off the computer using both front and rear power switches if present.
2. Disconnect the AC power cord from the computer.
3. Open the case to expose the power supply.
4. Disconnect the power supply from the motherboard.
5. Disconnect the power supply from all drives.
6. Disconnect the power supply from the case and CPU fans.
7. Remove the power-supply screws from the rear of the computer case.
8. Remove any screws holding the power supply in place inside the case.
9. Disconnect the power supply switch from the case front.
10. Lift the power supply from the case.

Before installing the replacement power supply, compare it to the original, making sure the form factor, motherboard power connectors, and switch position match the original.

To install the replacement power supply, follow these steps:

1. Lower the power supply into the case.
2. Connect the power supply switch to the case front.
3. Attach the power supply to the shelf with screws if required.
4. Attach the power supply to the rear of the computer case; line up the holes in the unit carefully with the holes in the outside of the case.

5. Connect the power supply to the case, CPU fans, drives, and motherboard.

6. Attach the AC power cord to the new power supply.

7. Turn on the computer. On systems with both a front and rear power switch, turn on the rear one first.

8. Boot the system normally to verify correct operation, and then run the normal shutdown procedure for the operating systems. If necessary, turn off the system with the front power switch only.

9. Close the case and secure it.

Testing Power Supplies with a Multimeter

One of the most flexible diagnostic tools is the *multimeter*. It is covered in this chapter because of its usefulness in testing power supplies, but it also can be used to test coaxial, UTP, serial, and parallel cables, as well as fuses, resistors, and batteries.

Multimeters are designed to perform many different types of electrical tests, including

- DC voltage and polarity
- AC voltage and polarity
- Resistance (Ohms)
- Diodes
- Continuity
- Amperage

All multimeters are equipped with red and black test leads. When used for voltage tests, the red is attached to the power source to be measured, and the black is attached to ground.

Multimeters use two different readout styles: digital and analog. *Digital* meters are usually auto-ranging, which means they automatically adjust to the correct range for the test selected and the voltage present. *Analog* meters, or non–auto-ranging digital meters, must be set manually to the correct range and can be damaged more easily by overvoltage.

Multimeters are designed to perform tests in two ways: in series and in parallel. Most tests are performed in *parallel* mode, in which the multimeter is not part of the circuit but runs parallel to it. On the other hand, amperage tests require that the multimeter be part of the circuit, so these tests are performed in *series* mode. Many low-cost multimeters do not include the ammeter feature for testing amperage (current), but you might be able to add it as an option.

Figure 8.9 shows a typical parallel mode test (DC voltage for a motherboard CMOS battery) and the current (amperage) test, which is a serial-mode test.

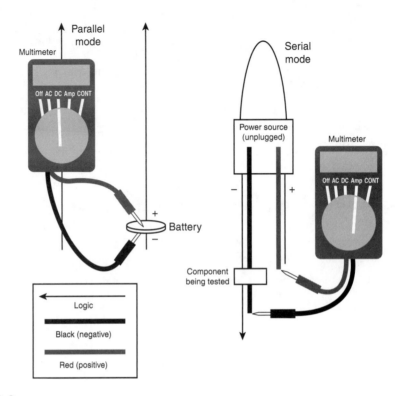

Figure 8.9
A parallel-mode (DC current) test setup (left) and an amperage (current) serial-mode test setup (right).

Table 8.1 covers testing procedures for common computer components.;

Table 8.1	Using a Multimeter		
Test to Perform	Multimeter Setting	Probe Positions	Procedure
AC voltage (wall outlet)	AC	Red to hot, black to ground.	Read voltage from meter; should be near 115V in North America.
DC voltage (power supply outputs to motherboard, drives, batteries)	DC	Red to hot, black to ground.	Read voltage from meter; compare to default values.

CH 8

Table 8.1 continued

Test to Perform	Multimeter Setting	Probe Positions	Procedure
Continuity (cables, fuses)	CONT	Red to lead at one end of cable; black to corresponding lead at other end. For a straight-through cable, check the same pin at each end. For other types of cables, consult a cable pinout to select the correct leads.	No CONT signal indicates a bad cable. Double-check leads and retest to be sure.
Resistance (Ohms)	Ohms	Connect one lead to each end of resistor.	Check reading; compare to rating for resistor. A fuse should have no resistance.
Amperage (Ammeter)	Ammeter	Red probe to positive lead of circuit; black lead to negative lead running through component to be tested.	Check reading; compare to rating for component (power tested disconnected!)

The following section discusses the procedure for using a multimeter to diagnose a defective power supply.

Troubleshooting Power Problems

A dead system that gives no signs of life when turned on can be caused by the following:

- Defects in AC power to the system
- Power supply failure or misconfiguration
- Temporary short circuits in internal or external components
- Power supply or other component failure

The following procedure will help you determine the actual cause of a dead system. If one of the test procedures in the following list corrects the problem, the item that was changed is the cause of the problem. Power supplies have a built-in safety feature that shuts down the unit immediately in case of short circuit. The following steps are designed to determine whether the power problem is caused by a short circuit or another problem:

1. Check the AC power to the system; a loose or disconnected power cord, a disconnected surge protector, or a surge protector that has been turned off will prevent a system from receiving power.

2. Check the AC voltage switch on the power supply; it should be set to 115 volts for North America. Turn off the power, reset the switch, and restart the system if the switch was set to 230 volts.

3. Check the keyboard connector; a loose keyboard connector could cause a short circuit.

4. Open the system and check for loose screws or other components such as loose slot covers, modem speakers, or other metal items that can cause a short circuit. Correct them and retest.

5. Check for fuses on the motherboard. Turn off the power, replace any blown fuse on the motherboard with a fuse of the correct rating, and retest.

6. Remove all expansion cards and disconnect power to all drives; restart the system and use a multimeter to test power to the motherboard and expansion slots per Table 8.2, later in this chapter.

7. If the power tests within accepted limits with all peripherals disconnected, reinstall one card at a time and check the power. If the power tests within accepted limits, reattach one drive at a time and check the power.

8. If a defective card or drive has a dead short, reattaching the defective card or drive should stop the system immediately upon power-up. Replace the card or drive and retest.

9. Test the Power Good line at the power supply motherboard connector with a multimeter.

Determining Power Supply DC Voltage Levels

A power supply, as you learned previously in this chapter, is designed to convert AC to DC power. By measuring the DC power at the motherboard and expansion slots, you can determine whether the power supply is performing this vital function correctly. A power supply that does not meet the measurement standards listed in Table 8.2 should be replaced.

Voltage measurements should be taken by checking an ISA expansion slot with the power on. The side of the ISA slot away from the power supply is called the "B" side. Four connectors (B3, B5, B7, and B9) carry power from the motherboard to the expansion cards.

Figure 8.10 shows where to make the measurements. Insert the red probe tightly into the space between the gold-colored "tooth" for each bus lead and the expansion slot. Press the black probe tightly against the *outside* of the power supply as a ground. Use the multimeter set for DC voltage to check the voltage at the ISA bus connections B3, B5, B7, and B9 as shown in Figure 8.9. The B-side is the side of the slot *away* from the power supply. The multimeter also can be used to check the Power Good or Power OK line by pushing the red lead through the open top of the power connector. If the motherboard has no ISA slots, you can check the 5-volt and 12-volt levels through the open top of the power connector using the pinout listed in Figure 8.7. See Table 8.2 for the acceptable voltage levels for each item.

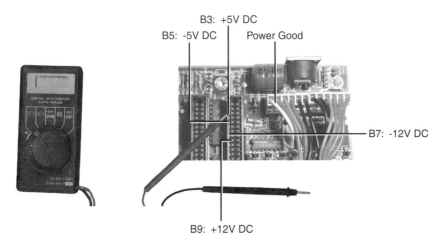

Figure 8.10
The red tip of the multimeter is being inserted into the B3 connector to test motherboard DC voltage. Some power supplies use colors different from the standard for Power Good, -5v, and -12v lines. This one uses a white wire for the Power Good line.

Table 8.2   Voltage Levels for ISA Bus Slots and Power Good/Power OK

Bus Lead #	Rated DC Volts	Minimum Acceptable	Maximum Acceptable
B3	+5.0	+4.8	+5.2
B5	-5.0	-4.5	-5.4
B7	-12.0	-10.8	-12.9
B9	+12.0	+11.5	+12.5
Power Good (pin 1 on P8) (pin 8 Power OK on ATX)	+5.0	+3.0	+6.0

If a power supply fails any of these measurements, replace it and retest the new unit.

Power Protection Types

Because computers and many popular computer peripherals run on DC power that has been converted from AC power, it's essential to make sure that proper levels of AC power flow to the computer and its peripherals. Extremely high levels of transient or sustained overvoltages can damage the power supply of the computer and peripherals, and voltage that is significantly lower than required will cause the computer and peripherals to shut down. A third problem with power is interference; "noisy" electrical power can cause subtle damage, and all three types of problems put the most valuable property of any computer, the data stored on the computer, at risk. Protect your computer's power supply and other components with appropriate devices:

- Surge suppressors, which are also referred to as surge protectors
- Battery backup systems, which are also referred to as UPS or SPS systems
- Power conditioning devices

Surge Suppressor

Properly designed surge suppressors can prevent power surges (chronic overvoltage) and spikes (brief extremely high voltage) from damaging your computer. Surge suppressors range in price from under $10 to close to $100 per unit, and the low-cost ones are often useless because they lack sufficient components to absorb dangerous surges.

Both spikes and surges are overvoltages: voltage levels higher than the normal voltage levels that come out of the wall socket. *Spikes* are momentary overvoltages, whereas *surges* last longer. Both can damage or destroy equipment and can come through data lines (such as RJ-11 phone or RJ-45 network cables) as well as through power lines. A surge suppressor must have a UL-1449 rating to be considered a "true" surge protector. Many low-cost units labeled "surge suppressors" actually have a different UL rating (UL 1363) for a multi-outlet strip ("transient voltage tap"). Although UL 1363 units can provide a minimal level of protection against modest overvoltages, UL 1449-rated units are recommended for significant protection. An alternative rating to look for is the IEEE-587 Category A rating; high-quality surge suppressors will normally have both UL-1449 and IEEE-587 Category A ratings (IEEE-587 Category B applies to major feeders and local branch circuits, and Category A applies to outlets and long branch circuits).

Beyond the UL-1449 rating, look for the following features to be useful in preventing power problems:

- A low UL-1449 let-through voltage level (400V AC or less). This might seem high compared to the 115 Volt standard, but power supplies have been tested to handle up to 800 V AC themselves without damage.
- IEEE 587A let-through voltage rating of under 100V.
- A covered-equipment warranty that includes lightning strikes (one of the biggest causes of surges and spikes).

- A high joule rating. Joules measure electrical energy, and surge suppressors with higher joule ratings can dissipate greater levels of surges or spikes.

- Fusing that will prevent fatal surges from getting through.

- Telephone, fax, and modem protection if your system has a modem or is connected to a telephone or fax.

- EMI/RFI noise filtration (a form of line conditioning).

- Site fault wiring indicator (no ground, reversed polarity warnings).

- Fast response time.

- Protection against surges on hot, neutral, and ground lines.

If you use surge protectors with these features, you will minimize power problems. The site-fault wiring indicator will alert you to wiring problems that can negate ground and can cause serious damage in ordinary use.

In preparing for the A+ Certification exam, you should pay particular attention to the UL and IEEE standards for surge suppressors and the major protection features just listed.

UPS and SPS

A *UPS (Uninterruptible Power Supply)* is another name for a battery backup unit. A UPS provides emergency power when a power failure strikes (a *blackout*) or when power falls below minimum levels (a *brownout*).

There are two different types of UPS systems: true UPS and SPS systems. A *true* UPS runs your computer from its battery at all times, isolating the computer and monitor from AC power. There is no switchover time with a true UPS when AC power fails because the battery is already running the computer. A true UPS inherently provides power conditioning (preventing spikes, surges, and brownouts from reaching the computer) because the computer receives only battery power, not the AC power coming from the wall outlet. True UPS units are sometimes referred to as *Line Interactive* battery backup units because the battery backup unit interacts with the AC line, rather than the AC line going directly to the computer and other components.

An *SPS (Standby Power Supply)* is also referred to as a UPS, but its design is quite different. Its battery is used only when AC power fails. A momentary gap in power (about 1ms or less) occurs between the loss of AC power and the start of standby battery power; however, this switchover time is far faster than is required to avoid system shutdown because computers can *coast* for several milliseconds before shutting down. SPS-type battery backup units are far less expensive than true UPSs, but work just as well as true UPSs when properly equipped with power-conditioning features.

In the rest of this section, the term *UPS* refers to both true UPS or SPS units except as noted, because most backup units on the market technically are SPS but are called UPS units by their vendors.

Battery backup units can be distinguished from each other by differences in

- **Run times**—The amount of time a computer will keep running on power from the UPS. A longer run-time unit uses a bigger battery and usually will cost more than a unit with a shorter run time. Fifteen minutes is a minimum recommendation for a UPS for an individual workstation; much larger systems are recommended for servers that might need to complete a lengthy shutdown procedure.

- **Network support**—Battery backup units made for use on networks are shipped with software that broadcasts a message to users about a server shutdown and shuts down the server automatically before the battery runs down.

- **Automatic shutdown**—Some low-cost UPS units lack this feature, but it is essential for servers or other unattended units. The automatic shutdown feature requires an open RS-232 serial port or USB port and appropriate software from the UPS maker. If you change operating systems, you will need to update the software for your UPS to be supported by the new operating system.

- **Surge suppression features**—Virtually all UPS units today have integrated surge suppression, but the efficiency of integrated surge suppression can vary as much as separate units. Look for UL-1449 and IEEE 587 Category A ratings to find reliable surge suppression in UPS units.

Buying the Correct-Sized Battery Backup System

UPS units are rated in VA (volt-Amps), and their manufacturers have interactive buying guides you can use online or download to help you select a model with adequate capacity. If you use a UPS with an inadequate VA rating for your equipment, your runtime will be substantially shorter than it should be.

You can calculate the correct VA rating for your equipment by adding up the wattage ratings of your computer and monitor and multiplying the result by 1.4. If your equipment is rated in amperage (amps), multiply the amp rating by 120 (volts) to get the VA rating.

For example, my computer has a 300-watt power supply, which would require a 420VA-rated UPS (300×1.4) and a 17-inch monitor that is rated in amps, not watts. The monitor draws 0.9 amps, which would require a 108VA-rated UPS (0.9×120). Add the VA ratings together, and my computer needs a 528VA-rated battery backup unit or larger. Specifying a UPS with a VA rating at least twice what is required by the equipment attached to the UPS will greatly improve the run time of the battery.

You should *not* attach laser printers to a UPS because their high current draw will cause the run time of the battery to be very short. In most cases, only the computer and monitor need to be attached to the UPS. However, inkjet printers and external modems have low current draw and can be attached to the UPS with little reduction in run time. In the previous example, a typical 600VA battery backup unit would provide about seven minutes of run time when used with my equipment. However, if I used a 1050VA battery backup, I could increase my run time to more than 20 minutes because my equipment would use only about half the rated capacity of the UPS unit.

Power Conditioning Devices

While power supplies are designed to work with voltages that do not exactly meet the 120-volt or 240-volt standards, power that is substantially higher or lower than what the computer is designed for can damage the system. Electrical noise on the power line, even with power at the correct voltage, also causes problems because it disrupts the correct sine-wave alternating-current pattern the computer, monitor, and other devices are designed to use.

Better-quality surge protectors often provide power filtration to handle EMI/RFI noise problems from laser printers and other devices that generate a lot of electrical interference. However, to deal with voltage that is too high or too low, you need a true power conditioner.

These units take substandard or overstandard power levels and adjust them to the correct range needed by your equipment. Some units also include high-quality surge protection features.

To determine whether you need a power-conditioning unit, you can contact your local electric utility to see if they loan or rent power-monitoring devices. Alternatively, you can rent them from power consultants. These units track power level and quality over a set period of time (such as over night or longer) and provide reports to help you see the overall quality of power on a given line.

Moving surge- and interference-causing devices such as microwaves, vacuum cleaners, refrigerators, freezers, and furnaces to circuits away from the computer circuits will help minimize power problems. However, in older buildings, or during times of peak demand, power conditioning might still be necessary. A true (line-interactive) UPS provides built-in power conditioning by its very nature (see the previous discussion).

Summary

Proper power supply operation and connection is essential to proper system performance. A multimeter is one of the most important testing devices you can own because of its versatility.

Power protection will help you guard your system against spikes, surges, brownouts, and blackouts. A complete power-management solution includes surge protection and a UPS battery backup unit. Systems attached to poor-quality power might also need power conditioning units.

QUESTIONS AND ANSWERS:

1. What are the voltage levels on a baby-AT motherboard?
   A: +5 and -5 volt and +12 and -12 volt

2. What are the voltage levels on an ATX motherboard?
   A: +5 and -5 volt, +12 and -12 volt, and +3.3 volts

3. List two uses for a multimeter besides testing DC voltage.
   A: Testing cables and testing ohms (resistance)

4. What system components should have no resistance when tested?
   A: Fuses

5. Where is the only fan located in some systems?
   A: The power supply

6. What information must you have about an RS-232 cable to test the leads for continuity?
   A: The pinout

7. Does a "dead" power supply always mean the power supply has failed?
   A: No. The system could have a correctable short, or the power supply could be set for the wrong voltage.

8. What is the UL standard for surge suppression?
   A: UL-1449

9. The volt-amp (VA) rating of a UPS unit should exceed the actual VA requirements of your system by a factor of at least how much?
   A: 2

Printers

WHILE YOU READ

1. Which current printer technology is impact based?
2. Why do inkjet printers need smooth paper for best results?
3. Which printer type produces warm printouts? Why?
4. Which printer technology is suitable for multipart forms? Why?
5. How does the laser in a laser printer help produce the image on the page?
6. Should you use the surge protector on/off switch to turn off an inkjet printer?

All printers have the following characteristics in common:

- A method of transferring characters (and often graphics) to paper. Except for a tiny number of specialized printers that use heat-sensitive paper stock, this involves some sort of ink or toner as well as a mechanism to transfer the ink or toner to the paper.
- One or more methods of feeding paper stock.
- An interface that connects the printer with the computer.
- A "language" used by software to send commands to the computer.
- Fonts and typefaces.

The details of these features are what separate the various types of printers from each other. You can expect 10% of the entire exam to cover printers. To do well on the printers portion of the A+ Certification exam, be sure to pay careful attention to the following issues:

- How printers create a page—note in particular the steps used by a laser printer to create a page
- Major components of dot-matrix, inkjet, and laser printers
- Typical printer operation and output problems and their solutions
- How printers are interfaced to the computer

The Printing Process

The specifics of the printing process vary with the printer type, but all printers have the same goal: to turn pages created with software into hard copy. The printing process is detailed in the following steps:

1. An application program in the computer sends a print request to the printer. Unlike MS-DOS applications, which send commands directly to the printer, Windows-based applications send the command to the Windows operating system, which relays the command to the printer.

2. Windows uses a print queue to manage print jobs, storing one or more print jobs in the default temporary directory until the printer is ready.

3. After the printer is ready, it receives a stream of data from the computer through its interface. The data stream contains commands that begin the printing process, select a page orientation and margins, and select built-in fonts and typefaces, or it contains instructions to create fonts and typefaces especially for this print job, depending on the printer and the typefaces and fonts in the document.

   If the data stream is appropriate for the printer, printing works correctly; if the data stream contains commands the printer doesn't recognize, garbage will be printed, with much paper wasting.

4. The printer feeds a page and prepares to print the document from the top of the page.

5. Character/line printers (dot-matrix and inkjet printers) immediately move the print head to the top-left page margin and use ink to begin to print characters and dot patterns line by line to print the page; the printhead moves back and forth while the paper advance mechanism moves the paper through the printer.

Character/line printers might pause periodically to receive data from the computer or for mechanical reasons.

Page printers (laser and LED printers) wait until the entire page is received before transferring the page to the print mechanism, which pulls the paper through the printer as the page is transferred from the printer to the paper; most page printers use toner, but some color models might use solid ink or special ribbons.

6. When the page is complete, both types of printers eject the page into a paper tray and immediately repeat the process with the next page of a multipage document.

Line Versus Page Printers

Printers that place a line at a time of characters are called *line printers* or *character printers*. Inkjet and dot-matrix printers print this way; these printers start printing a document as soon as the first line of information is received. Although both types of printers have memory buffers that can sometimes hold an entire page of information, these printers are not usually considered page printers.

Laser and LED printers, on the other hand, create a page at a time and are called *page printers*. These printers must receive the entire page before they can print the page; if multiple copies of a page are needed, these printers can hold the page in memory and print all the copies at once before starting on the next page. This feature is called *collating* and is controlled by software.

Printer Controls for Text and Graphics

Besides the imaging technology (dot-matrix, inkjet, laser, or LED) used by a printer, the two biggest influences on what page output looks like from a given printer are its typeface and font options and its printer language. The typeface and font options affect how text appears, and the printer language affects how the printer changes fonts and how it creates graphics on the printed page.

Fonts and Typefaces

All printers have a limited number of fonts built in. Depending on the printer, the fonts can have the following characteristics:

■ Scalable fonts can be printed at any size.

■ Fixed-size fonts can be printed only at certain sizes.

- Proportional fonts use different amounts of space for each letter. Their sizes are given in *points*; 72 points = 1 vertical inch. Most built-in and add-on fonts used today are proportional.

- Fixed-pitch fonts use the same amount of space for each letter. Pitch describes the horizontal space occupied by each letter; a 10-pitch font, for example, can put 10 characters into a horizontal inch.

Printer fonts are stored in the printer's firmware. Some laser and inkjet printers have a provision for font cartridges, enabling them to print more fonts with additional firmware.

The rise of scalable-font technologies such as TrueType has caused many recent printer models to omit font cartridge support.

The sample in Figure 9.1 lists the word "hamburgerfons" in Arial, Times New Roman, and Courier New 24-point fonts. The first two are proportional, and the last is fixed-pitch.

hamburgerfons
hamburgerfons
`hamburgerfons`

Figure 9.1
"Hamburgerfons" in Times New Roman (top), Arial (middle), and Courier New (bottom) fonts. Although each sample is the same size in points, the differences in font design cause each font to appear to be a different size.

Users of MS-DOS–based applications often can use only the printer's built-in fonts, but users of Windows 3.1 and above normally use scalable TrueType fonts that are sent to the printer as an outline that can be scaled as necessary for the document.

The default font for the printer can be set on the printer, as in Figure 9.2, but software settings for fonts in a document override it.

Some printers can print more fonts in portrait mode than landscape mode. *Portrait* mode uses the paper in its normal vertical orientation, whereas *landscape* mode prints as if the paper were inserted horizontally by rotating the fonts and graphics. A dot-matrix printer can print in portrait mode only when using built-in fonts; it must use scalable fonts and print very slowly to produce landscape printouts. Laser printers often feature both types of fonts, and both inkjet and laser printers can print scalable fonts quickly and are better suited to producing landscape documents than dot-matrix.

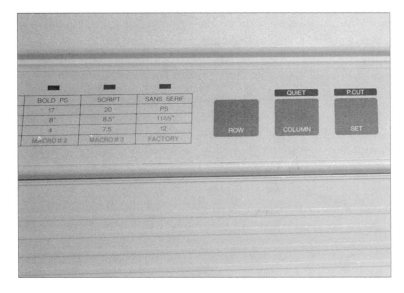

CH
9

Figure 9.2
A typical dot-matrix printer's font-control panel. A wide range of printer fonts and other settings can be selected from the grid at left by using the control buttons at right.

Printer Languages

Virtually any printer used on a computer is designed to print more than plain text. A printer's capability to work with scalable fonts, select fonts, and create graphics all depend on the features of the *printer language* in the printer.

The following are common methods of controlling the printer:

- Escape sequences
- Printer Control Language
- PostScript
- Host-based

Dot-matrix and inkjet printers generally use a simple language based on escape sequences—commands sent to the printer preceded by the ESC character (ASCII code 27). Epson printers pioneered this method of controlling the printer, and most dot-matrix printers either emulate the Epson ESC-P or ESC-P2 sequences or have their own sequence of commands.

Laser printers generally use either the Printer Control Language (PCL) developed by Hewlett-Packard or Adobe's PostScript. PCL is an enhanced version of the escape-sequence–based printer control used on dot-matrix printers. Various versions of PCL have been introduced over the years, with more and more features enabling PCL printers to print better graphics.

PostScript laser and inkjet printers use the Adobe PostScript language to send commands to the printer. PostScript provides printers with graphics power that is still unrivaled, even by the latest version of PCL (PCL6), and are preferred for graphic arts and advertising uses. Originally, PostScript was used strictly by laser printers, but many high-end inkjet printers—especially large-format models—are also PostScript-compatible.

A PostScript printer without a PCL language option cannot be used from an MS-DOS prompt for Print-Screen or other utility tasks, but can be controlled only by an application sending PostScript printer commands. PostScript can be retrofitted to a non-PostScript printer in two ways:

- By adding firmware (in the form of a cartridge or a special SIMM); this method is possible with many HP laser printers

- By using a software PostScript driver (also called a raster image processor—RIP) that enables non-PostScript printers to print PostScript

The first method produces faster printing, but the second method works with many additional printers.

The latest type of printer control is host-based. A host-based printer lacks a built-in interpreter for any of the previously mentioned printer control methods. Instead, it is controlled by the operating system (usually Microsoft Windows). These printers are inexpensive but cannot be used outside Windows, and normally cannot be used on a network.

When you are asked on the exam to troubleshoot printer problems, keep these differences in mind. Sending incorrect commands to the printer is a sure cause of garbage printing.

Paper Feed Types

Three major types of paper are used with printers:

- Single sheets
- Continuous tractor-fed
- Roll paper

Depending on the paper-feed type in the printer, a printer can use one or more of these paper types.

Single-Sheet Feed

The most common type of paper used today is *single sheets*. These are used by both laser and inkjet printers and by some impact dot-matrix printers. Most printers that use single sheets have paper trays that hold many sheets for easy printing of multipage documents. A few portable printers, however, require you to feed one sheet at a time.

Impact dot-matrix printers that can handle single sheets use a rubber roller called a *platen*, which is similar to the platen found in typewriters. It rolls the paper through and absorbs the impact of the printhead wires.

Because inkjet and laser printers are non-impact, they use small rollers instead of a platen to pull the paper through the printer.

Common problems with single-sheet paper feeds include

- Wrinkled or damaged sheets that will not feed properly
- Damp paper that sticks together

Single-sheet paper feeding is affected by paper quality. However, it is the major form of paper feed used today because it makes the production of high-quality printouts easier with laser and inkjet printers.

Tractor-Fed Paper

Tractor-fed paper can be easily recognized by its perforated edges. It is most often sold in folded, continuous sheets, with folding on the perforations that enables the pages to be separated after printing. Tractor-fed paper is used by most impact dot-matrix printers.

Two major types of tractor feeds exist on impact dot-matrix printers:

- Push tractor
- Pull tractor

Both types of tractor feeds use sprockets that fit through the perforations on the edge of tractor-fed paper. The feeders hold the paper in place with retainers that snap over the edges of the paper.

The *push* tractor is located before the printhead in the paper path (see Figure 9.3). Because of this, the push tractor has the advantage of allowing a printed sheet to be removed immediately after printing; this so-called *zero tear-off* feature avoids waste of forms. However, adjustment of the tractor mechanism is critical to avoid jams. This type of tractor feed is best used for printing just a few pages at a time on demand, as in point-of-sale billing and receipts.

The *pull* tractor is an older, simpler mechanism (see Figure 9.4). It is located after the printhead in the paper path, and therefore a sheet must be wasted whenever a print job is removed from the printer. The pull tractor tends to be more reliable for long print jobs and is best used for printing reports of many pages in length, such as those used for accounting or payroll.

Most tractor feeds can be adjusted horizontally to handle various widths of paper or to adjust the left margin. A few inexpensive dot-matrix printers use a simplified variation on the pull-tractor called *pinfeed*, which uses non-adjustable sprockets at either end of a platen.

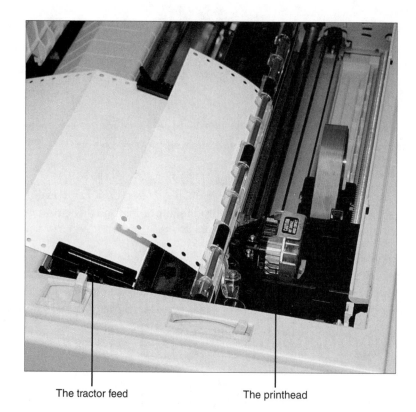

The tractor feed   The printhead

Figure 9.3
A typical dot-matrix printer with a push tractor feed, showing how the sheet can be removed without removing the paper from the tractor feed.

Misaligned tractors cause the paper to tear at the page perforations before the page is printed. In addition, with the widespread use of attractive but relatively weak microperforated paper that has nearly invisible perforations, the tractor perforations are likely to pull off as well.

Continuous roll paper can be sold either in a tractor-feed–compatible form (for use with dot-matrix printers) or as a plain roll (for use with inkjet printers).

Paper Paths and Paper Problems
Most printers use one or both of the following paper paths for printing:

- C-shaped or S-shaped
- Straight-through

The more turns the paper must pass through during the printing process, the greater the chances of paper jams.

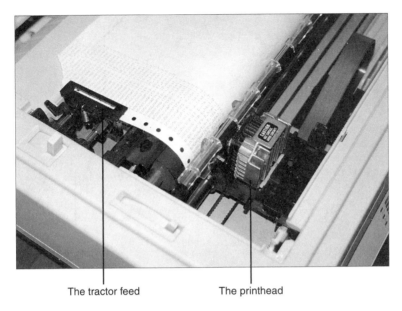

The tractor feed   The printhead

Figure 9.4
A typical dot-matrix printer with a pull tractor feed. The paper is pulled past the print-head by the tractor feed, and the paper must be rolled past the tractor feed before it can be torn off.

C-shaped paper paths are typical of some inkjet and many laser printers: The paper is pulled from the front of the printer, pulled through a series of rollers inside the printer during the print process, and then ejected through the front or top of the printer onto a paper tray (see Figure 9.5).

Some printers, especially those with bottom-mounted paper trays, have more complex paper paths that resembles an S.

A *straight-through* paper path is a typical option on laser printers with a C-shaped or even more complex paper path. Printers with this option have a rear paper output tray that can be lowered for use and that overrides the normal top paper output tray. Some also have a front paper tray. Use both front and rear trays for a true straight-through path. Inkjet printers with input paper trays at the rear of the printer and an output tray at the front also use this method.

Straight-through paper paths are recommended for printing envelopes and labels. On laser printers, the straight-through option works best if the software used for printing has an option to print multiple pages in reverse order, because a straight-through tray stacks printed pages face up rather than face down. Using a reverse-order printing command stacks the pages in their normal order in a straight-through paper tray.

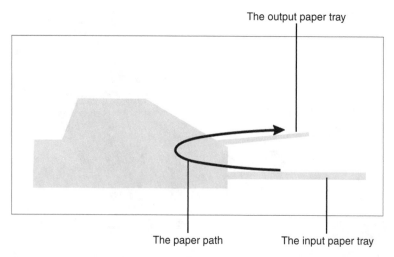

Figure 9.5
A C-shaped paper path on a typical inkjet printer. The paper is pulled face-down from the input paper tray and ejected face-up into the output tray. The C-curve makes feeding envelopes and thick stock difficult.

Major Printer Technologies and Interfaces

The following are the three major printer technologies in use today on personal computers:

■ Impact dot-matrix

■ Inkjet

■ Laser

A fourth technology, daisywheel printers, is long obsolete and virtually extinct. A fifth technology, thermal dot-matrix, is used in a few portable printers that use a ribbon, and in some point-of-sale credit-card terminals, cash registers, and receipt printers. To prepare for the A+ Certification exam, make sure you know the details of laser printer technology, and have a basic grasp of dot-matrix and inkjet technologies. Each of these printer types has distinct features making it most suitable for different tasks, and providing distinct servicing challenges.

Most printers in use today are connected through the parallel (LPT) interface, with some late-model laser and inkjet printers using the USB port as either an optional or standard interface. Some older dot-matrix and laser printers use serial interfaces as either an optional or standard interface. A few high-end inkjet and laser printers can be attached directly to an Ethernet network, but most are networked through a print server or a client PC with file and printer sharing software installed.

The oldest of the three technologies used today, impact dot-matrix, is discussed first because it is the basis for many features found in other printers.

Dot-Matrix

The dot-matrix printer is so named because it creates the appearance of fully formed characters from dots placed on the page.

The print mechanism of the dot-matrix printer is almost always an impact mechanism: a printhead containing 9–24 fine wires (called *pins*) arranged in one, two, or three columns is used along with a fabric ribbon, similar to typewriter technology. The wires are moved by an electromagnet at high speed against the ribbon to form dot patterns that form words, special characters, or graphics.

Dot-Matrix Printhead Types

The two major types of dot-matrix printheads are

- 9-pin
- 24-pin

A third type of dot-matrix printhead uses 18 pins and basically acts like a faster version of a 9-pin printhead.

To create a character, a dot-matrix printer uses a predefined series of columns called a *matrix*, in which each character is formed. As the printhead moves across the paper, commands from the computer rapidly move the 9, 18, or 24 pins in special sequences to form characters or graphics.

Figure 9.6 shows actual print samples from a typical 9-pin printer's draft mode, a typical 24-pin printer's draft mode, and the Near Letter Quality (NLQ) mode of the same 24-pin printer.

Figure 9.7 shows how small the printhead is in relation to the rest of the printer. Size is misleading, though, because a damaged printhead will render the rest of the printer useless.

Although 24-pin printheads produce much better-looking text in NLQ mode, their capability to print on multipart forms is limited because of their narrow wires. The smaller diameter causes a lighter impact on the top page, and subsequently even lighter impact on all the remaining pages. Typical form limits for a 24-pin printer are the original plus 3 non-carbon copies. 9-pin and 18-pin printheads use wider wires, and high-end printers with these printheads can handle up to 4 or more non-carbon copies as well as the original.

Durability in the field is also better with 9-pin/18-pin printheads; a broken pin in the printhead is more likely to result with the narrower wires used in the 24-pin printhead.

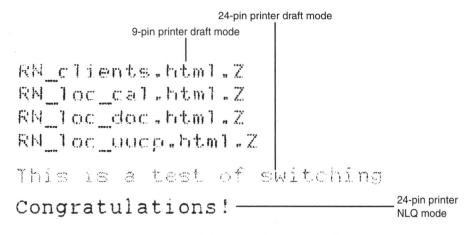

Figure 9.6
Actual print samples illustrating the differences in 24-pin and 9-pin printers. The narrower pins of the 24-pin printhead produce a reasonably good NLQ printout but hard-to-read results in draft mode.

Parts of a Dot-Matrix Printer

The components of a typical dot-matrix printer are identified in Figure 9.7.

Impact dot-matrix printers have the following parts moving in coordination with each other during the printing process:

- The paper is moved past the printhead vertically by pull or push tractors or by a platen.

- The printhead moves across the paper horizontally, propelled along the printhead carriage by a drive belt and printing as it moves from left to right. Bi-directional printing prints in both directions but is often disabled for high-quality printing because it can be difficult to align the printing precisely.

- The pins in the printhead are moving in and out against an inked ribbon as the printhead travels across the paper to form the text or create graphics.

- The ribbon is also moving to reduce wear during the printing process.

Impact dot-matrix printers thus have a lot of moving parts and traditionally high noise levels. This, along with their incapability to create truly high-quality, letter-quality text except at low speeds and high noise levels, have made them far less popular in recent years.

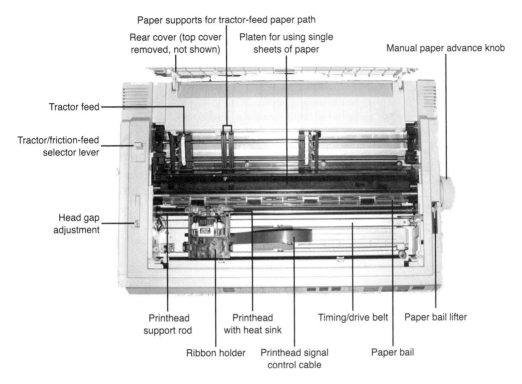

Paper supports for tractor-feed paper path

Rear cover (top cover removed, not shown)

Platen for using single sheets of paper

Manual paper advance knob

Tractor feed

Tractor/friction-feed selector lever

Head gap adjustment

Printhead support rod

Printhead with heat sink

Ribbon holder

Printhead signal control cable

Timing/drive belt

Paper bail

Paper bail lifter

CH 9

Figure 9.7

Components of a typical dot-matrix printer. The model pictured is a wide-carriage version, but its features are typical of models using either standard or wide-carriage paper.

However, impact dot-matrix printers will remain popular for tasks requiring multipart forms. Because impact dot-matrix printers use inexpensive ribbons designed to print millions of characters and can use fan-fold or single-sheet papers of all types, dot-matrix printers are the lowest cost-per-page of all printers.

Standard-Carriage Versus Wide-Carriage Models

Many printer manufacturers produce both standard-carriage (8.5×11-inch paper) and wide-carriage models (15.5 inches wide) of some of their dot-matrix printers. The wide-carriage models are preferred for accounting or other occupations requiring very wide printouts. Wide-carriage printers can fit about 80% more text on a line with the same-sized typeface.

Wide-carriage models can be adjusted to use standard paper, but often feature options such as a bottom paper feed for running high volumes of printing.

Maintenance for Impact Dot-Matrix Printers

To keep an impact dot-matrix printer in top condition, do the following:

- Change ribbons when the ribbon begins to dry out; the ink in the ribbon also helps lubricate the printhead; discard frayed ribbons because the fraying can snag a printhead's pins and break them.

- Use platen conditioner to keep the rubber platen supple; a platen that becomes hard can break printheads.

- Adjust the head gap whenever you change from ordinary paper to multipart forms, envelopes, labels, or other thicker-than-normal items, and when you return to normal paper; failure to set the head gap properly can result in smudged printing and broken pins in the printhead.

- Periodically clean out hair, dust, and paper shreds from the printer.

Dot-Matrix Printer Troubleshooting

The following problems are typical of dot-matrix printers; use this information to prepare for troubleshooting questions on the A+ Certification exam and day-to-day printer troubleshooting.

Typical dot-matrix printer problems include gaps in printed letters, paper jams and torn perforations, and faded printing.

Gaps in Printed Letters

Because of how dot-matrix printers work, a slight amount of space between the dots that make up a dot-matrix letter is normal, especially in draft mode (refer to Figure 9.7). However, if gaps are noticed in NLQ mode, this usually indicates that the printer has a bent or broken pin (see Figure 9.8). The first and third lines in Figure 9.8 show the effect of the broken wire, while the other lines are normal printing with an undamaged head.

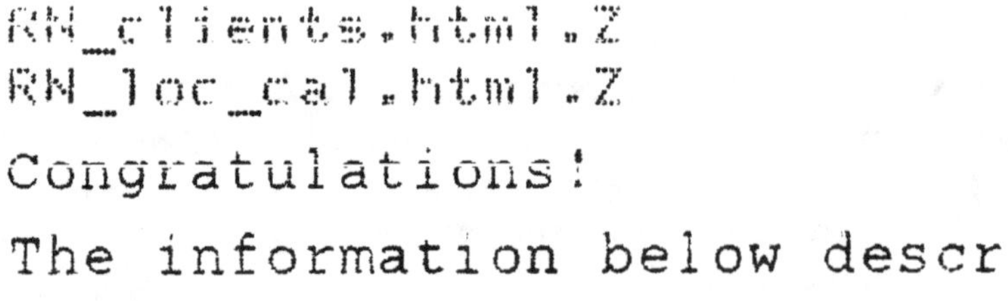

```
RN_clients.html.Z
RN_loc_cal.html.Z

Congratulations!
The information below descr
```

Figure 9.8
A broken wire in a printhead leaves a gap in printed text that is very noticeable, whether the printer is a 9-pin model (first two lines) or a 24-pin model printing in NLQ mode (third and fourth lines).

When a pin in the printhead has become bent or broken, the printhead must be repaired or replaced. Incorrect head gap settings are a typical cause of bent or broken pins; the head gap must be adjusted to match the thickness of the paper, forms, or label stock inserted in the printer. Another typical cause is the use of a dried-out or damaged printer ribbon; replace the ribbon when print quality fades to protect the printhead and produce sharper, easier-to-read printing.

Paper Jams and Tears at Perforations

Incorrect tractor-feed width and position settings are the typical causes of paper jams and torn sheets. Make sure the tractor feed is adjusted to the correct width, which will make the paper lay flat without putting undue stress on the tear-off perforations. Printers with push and pull tractors must have the tractor-feed and paper-feed options selected correctly to avoid jams and torn sheets.

Faded Printing

If the print is evenly faded, the ribbon is dried out. Replace the ribbon to achieve better print quality and protect the printhead. If the print appears more faded on the top of each line than on the bottom, the head gap is set too wide for the paper type in use. Adjust the head gap to the correct width to improve printing and protect the print head from damage.

Printhead Won't Move

The printhead should move back and forth during printing; if it won't move, check the drive belt and the gear mechanism. Jammed gears in the printer or a broken drive belt will prevent the drive belt from moving the printhead. Check the drive belt first to see if it is broken, and then check the gears that move the printhead. You might need to disassemble the printer to check the gears.

Paper Won't Advance

The paper advance, whether single-sheet or tractor feed, is also gear-driven. Jammed gears will prevent the paper advance from working. You might need to disassemble the printer to check the gears.

Some printers require special tools to remove the plastic shell; contact the printer's manufacturer for detailed disassembly instructions and recommended tools.

Most impact dot-matrix printers have a self-test feature onboard. Use this to determine the following:

- Which firmware the printer is using
- Which fonts and typefaces the printer includes

Normally, the self-test is activated by holding down a button, usually the LF (line feed) button, while the printer is turned on. If the printer is wide-carriage, make sure the paper in place is also wide-carriage; if you don't use wide-carriage paper, the printer will try to print on the platen, which could damage the printhead.

Inkjet Printers

Inkjet printers represent the most popular type of printer in small-office/home-office (SOHO) use today and are also popular in large offices. Their print quality can rival laser printers, and virtually all inkjet printers in use today are color capable.

From a tightly spaced group of nozzles, inkjet printers spray controlled dots of ink onto the paper to form characters and graphics. On a typical 1440×720dpi printer, the number of nozzles can be as high as 64 (32 in two columns) for black ink. The tiny ink droplet size and high nozzle density enables inkjet printers to perform the seemingly impossible at resolutions as high as 1,200dpi or above: fully formed characters from what is actually a high-resolution, non-impact, dot-matrix technology.

The printer's maximum resolution is determined from the number, spacing, and size of these nozzles. The printer's print quality, on the other hand, is determined by a combination of resolution, ink droplet size, and paper quality. Two major methods are used to create the ink dots. Most inkjet printers heat the ink to boiling, creating a tiny bubble of ink that is allowed to escape through the printhead onto the paper. This is the origin of the name BubbleJet for the Canon line of inkjet printers.

Another popular method uses a piezo-electric crystal to distribute the ink through the printhead. This method makes achieving high resolutions easier; the Epson printers using this method were the first to achieve 1,440×720dpi resolutions. This method also provides a longer printhead life because the ink is not heated and cooled. Both types of inkjet printers are sometimes referred to as *drop on demand* printers.

Inkjet printers are character/line printers. They print one line at a time of single characters or graphics up to the limit of the printhead matrix.

Larger characters are created by printing a portion of the characters across the page, advancing the page to allow the printhead to print another portion of the characters, and so on until the entire line of characters is printed. Thus, an inkjet printer is both a character and a line printer because it must connect lines of printing to build large characters.

The printing process for inkjet printers is similar to that for impact dot-matrix printers, except for the differences in printhead and the lack of a tractor mechanism on inkjet printers.

Figure 9.9 shows some of the typical components of an inkjet printer.

Inkjet printers are functionally fully formed character printers because their inkjet matrix is so finely formed that individual dots are not visible. Small droplets form the image.

Inkjet Printers and Ink Cartridges

Most models use a large single-reservoir tank of liquid ink for black and a separate tank with compartments for colors (typically cyan, magenta, and yellow). Some low-cost models require the user to interchange the black and color cartridges. This results in the use of so-called "process black" mixed from the three colors in situations in which black must be printed while the color cartridge is in the printer. The best models, however, use separate cartridges for each color. Inkjet printers are sometimes referred to as *CMYK* devices because of the four ink colors used on most models: **c**yan, **m**agenta, **y**ellow, and blac**k**. When the ink in a tank or compartment is exhausted, the cartridge needs to be replaced.

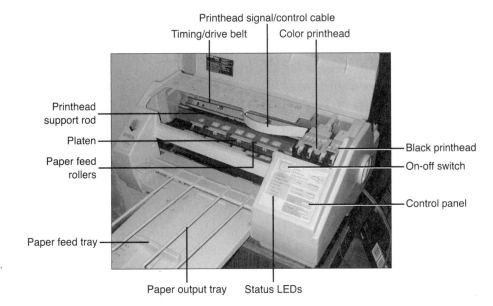

Printhead signal/control cable
Timing/drive belt
Color printhead
Printhead support rod
Platen
Paper feed rollers
Black printhead
On-off switch
Control panel
Paper feed tray
Paper output tray   Status LEDs

Figure 9.9
A typical inkjet printer with its cover open; note the similarity in design to the dot-matrix printer in Figure 9.7.

Inkjet printers produce very attractive pages, but the high cost of inkjet cartridges and the small numbers of pages per cartridge—as well as the higher cost of paper made for inkjet printing—makes inkjets the most expensive printer technology on a per-page basis.

How Inkjet Printheads and Ink Cartridges Relate
Depending on the printer, the printhead might be incorporated into the ink tank; be a separate, user-replaceable item; or be built into the printer.

Some inkjet printers feature an extra-wide (more nozzles) printhead or a dual printhead for very speedy black printing. Some models enable the user to replace either the ink cartridge only or an assembly comprising the printhead and a replaceable ink cartridge.

An inkjet printer is only as good as its printhead and ink cartridges. Clogged or damaged printheads or ink cartridges render the printer useless. If an inkjet printer fails after its warranty expires, you should check service costs carefully before repairing the unit. Failed inkjet printers are often "throwaway" models and can be replaced, rather than repaired, even during the warranty period.

Inkjet printers should never be turned off with a surge protector; doing so prevents the printer from self-capping its ink cartridges, which is a major cause of service calls and printer failures. Cleaning the printhead, either with the printer's own cleaning feature, a cleaning utility built into the printer driver, or with a moistened cleaning sheet, will restore most printers to service.

Always use the printer's own power switch, which enables the printer to protect the ink cartridges and perform other periodic tasks (such as self-cleaning) properly.

Inkjet Printer Paper-Feed Mechanisms

Most inkjet printers use single sheets of paper, but a few can use continuous paper rolls to create banners. In either case, the inkjet printer uses a series of rollers to pull the paper through the printer. Inkjet printers typically use either a C-shaped paper path (pulling the paper through the front and curving the paper past the printhead and out to the front-mounted tray), as in Figure 9.9, or a straight-through paper path.

Because the rollers usually touch all four edges of the paper, almost all inkjet printers have an unprintable border area of one-quarter to one-half inch; the largest area is often on the bottom of the sheet.

A few inkjet printers designed for graphic arts or advanced uses can use so-called "B" size paper (11×17-inch), but most use letter-size or smaller paper sizes only.

For more information about inkjet printer paper selection criteria, see the section titled "Inkjet Printers" in Chapter 22, "Printers and Scanners," in *Upgrading and Repairing PCs, 12th Edition.*

Periodic Maintenance for Inkjet Printers

Most inkjet printers have built-in or software-controlled routines for cleaning the ink cartridges and checking the alignment of two-pass characters. An example appears in Figure 9.10. Use these options when you notice poor-quality printouts.

Some models with dual printheads require you to adjust alignment whenever you use dual black-ink cartridges.

Inkjet printer cleaning kits come in two forms:

- A special sheet and cleaning spray
- A cleaning pad and liquid cleaner

The sheet and spray is used to clean the paper paths in the printer and to remove ink buildup on the printheads. Spray the cleaner onto the sheet, insert it into the printer as directed, and print a few lines of text to clean the printer.

The cleaning pad is designed for models with removable printheads (part of the ink cartridge on thermal-inkjet printer models). Soak the pad with the supplied fluid and rub the printhead over it to remove built-up ink.

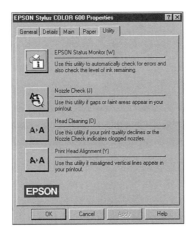

Figure 9.10
A typical inkjet printer's utility menu. Printers can also use printer Control Panel options to clean printheads, test printing, or align text.

Because both cleaning liquids and plain water can be used to clean up excess ink, inkjet printers should *not* be used when water resistance is of paramount concern. Inkjet inks are more water-resistant today than previously, but a careless spill can still destroy a digital masterpiece printed on an inkjet printer.

Troubleshooting Inkjet Printers

The following are typical problems and solutions for inkjet printers. Use this list to help you prepare for printer troubleshooting questions you might encounter on the A+ Certification exam and in your day-to-day work.

Smudged Printing

Smudged print output from an inkjet printer can be caused by dirty printheads or paper rollers and by incorrect resolution and media settings. Clean the printhead by using the printer's built-in cleaning routine; if this doesn't result in acceptable results, remove the printhead and clean it. If the printhead is built into the printer or if the paper feed rollers or platen have ink smudges, use a cleaning sheet to clean the paper feed rollers, platen, and printhead.

Check the printer properties setting in the operating system to ensure that the correct resolution and paper options are set for the paper in use. Incorrect settings can lead to excessive ink being used for a particular print job, leading to smudged output.

Unlike laser output, which can be handled as soon as the page is ejected, inkjet output requires time to dry. For best results, use paper specially designed for inkjet printers. Paper should be stored in a cool, dry environment; damp paper also will result in smudged printing. Make sure that the correct side of the paper is being used; many special inkjet papers (including photo papers) are designed for single-sided printing only.

Gaps in Printed Output or Uneven Characters

If uneven characters occur after the ink cartridge has been replaced, you might need to realign the printhead with the printer's utility program or printer properties sheet. This process prints out a series of long bars, after which the user selects which bar is properly aligned.

Gaps in printed output usually indicate a partially clogged printhead. See "Smudged Printing" (previous section) for instructions. Replacing the ink cartridge replaces the printhead on some printers, but on other printers the printhead is a separate removable device or is fixed in position.

No Output at All

Use the printer's self-test (activated by pressing a button or button combination on most printers when turned on; it varies by printer) to see if the printer can print any output. If the head moves and the paper advances but there is no output on the page, clean the printheads and retry. Replace ink cartridges if there is still no output.

If the self-test fails, check the drive belt; if it is broken or if the drive gears are jammed, the printer must be repaired or replaced (low-cost printers usually are not worth repairing). Try using the paper advance button; if the paper won't advance, and check for obstructions, such as stuck labels or torn sheets, in the paper path.

If the self-test works correctly, make sure the printer cable is attached correctly to the printer and computer, and retry the print job. If you get no results, make sure the proper port and driver are selected in Windows. If Windows sends print jobs to the wrong port, the printer won't receive the data and can't print. USB printers require a printer-specific driver as well as working USB ports and USB support in the operating system.

Garbage Printing

This can be caused by partially attached cables or by using the incorrect printer driver. Turn off the printer and computer if you use parallel or serial port cables before tightening the cable. Restart the printer and system, and retry.

If the printer is attached to the serial port, check the baud rate, word length, parity bits, and flow-control settings for the printer's serial port and the computer's serial port. Both printer and computer must use the same settings to produce correct printing. Adjust the printer's configuration or the computer's serial port settings (using the operating system's serial port Control Panel settings) as needed.

Check the operating system's printer driver. If the driver appears correct, replace the cable and retry. If the results are still garbage, reinstall the printer driver and retry.

If these steps don't solve the problem, the printer might have a damaged logic board or a damaged printhead data/signal cable. Repair or replace the printer.

Using the Self-Test on Inkjet Printers

The self-test on inkjet printers can be used to

- Check the condition of the nozzles in the printhead.
- Check the firmware (ROM) onboard the printer.

Depending on the model, the test might be brief, or more than one page might be printed.

As with dot-matrix printers, you hold down a specified key (often the paper-feed key) while starting the printer to activate the self-test feature.

Laser Printers

Laser printers combine the low noise of an inkjet printer with the waterproof printing of a dot-matrix printer and have a very low cost per page.

Laser printers are similar in many ways to photocopiers:

- Both use an electrostatically-charged drum to receive the image to be transferred to paper.
- Both use a fine-grained powdered toner that is heated to adhere to the paper.
- Both must feed the paper through elaborate paper paths for printing.

However, significant differences exist between the photocopier and its computer-savvy sibling:

- Laser printers produce images digitally, turning individual dots on and off; most copiers, however, are still analog devices.
- Laser printers work under the control of a computer; copiers have a dedicated scanner as an image source.
- Laser printers are optimized for both text and graphics, including continuous-tone photos; copiers must choose text or photo modes, with mediocre results at best on anything other than scanned text.
- Laser printers use much higher temperatures than copiers to bond printing to the paper; using copier label or transparency media in a laser printer can result in damage to the printer due to melted label adhesive, labels coming off in the copier, or melted transparency media.

In larger offices, you might find that a networked copier/printer, such as the Xerox DocuCentre, has replaced traditional photocopiers and printers. The printing method used by these devices is similar to a laser printer, but these machines often use separate toner bottles and a long-life drum, rather than the toner/drum combination used in most desktop and smaller network laser printers.

Even though laser printers share many characteristics with photocopiers, they need special media to avoid damage.

The Laser Printing Process

Understanding the sequence of events in the laser printing process is essential to successfully passing the A+ Core Hardware exam. About 70% of A+ printer questions concern laser printers, and about 10% of the entire exam is printer related. To master this section, make sure you

- Memorize the six steps involved in laser printer imaging.
- Master the details of each step.
- Be prepared to answer troubleshooting questions based on these steps.

The process often is referred to as the electrophotographic (EP) process.

Before the six-step laser printing process can take place, the following events must first take place:

- Laser printers are page-based; they must receive the entire page before they can start printing.
- After the page has been received, the printer pulls a sheet of paper into the printer with its feed rollers.

After the paper has been fed into the print mechanism, a series of six steps takes place, which results in a printed page:

1. Cleaning the excess toner from the drum and discharging the drum's electrical charge to prepare it for the next page
2. Conditioning the imaging drum
3. Writing the page to the drum
4. Developing the image on the drum with toner
5. Transferring the toner image of the page to the paper
6. Fusing the toner image of the page permanently to the paper

See Figure 9.11 to learn where each of these steps takes place in the printer.

Step 1: Cleaning

To prepare the drum for a new page, the image of the preceding page placed on the drum by the laser (see step 3) is removed by a discharge lamp.

Toner that is not adhering to the surface of the drum is scraped from the drum's surface for reuse.

Step 1 prepares the drum for the conditioning step (step 2).

Step 2: Conditioning

The cylinder-shaped imaging drum receives an electrostatic charge of -600Vdc from a primary corona wire or conditioning roller. The smooth surface of the drum retains this charge uniformly over all its surface. The drum is photosensitive and will retain this charge only while kept in darkness.

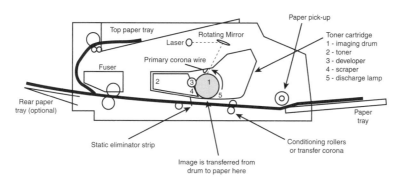

Figure 9.11

A typical laser printer's components. The heavy line indicates the paper path; paper enters the printer at the right and is pulled through the printer to either the left-hand side output tray or the top output tray.

Step 3: Writing

A moving mirror moves the laser beam across the surface of the drum. As it moves, the laser beam temporarily records the image of the page to be printed on the surface of the drum by reducing the voltage of the charge applied by the charger corona to -100Vdc.

Step 4: Developing

The drum has toner applied to it from the developer; because the toner is electrostatic and is also at -600Vdc, the toner stays on only the portions of the drum that have been reduced in voltage to create the image. It is not attracted to the rest of the drum because both the toner and the drum are at the same voltage, and like charges repel each other. This "like charges repel" phenomenon is the same reason two magnets repel each other.

Step 5: Transferring

While the sheet is being fed into the printer, it receives an electrostatic charge of +600Vdc from a corona wire or roller; this enables it to attract toner from the drum, which is negatively charged (see step 3). As the drum's surface moves close to the charged paper, the toner adhering to the drum is attracted to the electrostatically charged paper to create the printed page.

As the paper continues to move through the printer, its charge is canceled by a static eliminator strip, so the paper itself isn't attracted to the drum.

Step 6: Fusing

The printed sheet of paper is pulled through fuser rollers, using high temperatures (about 350F degrees) to heat the toner and press it into the paper. The printed image is slightly raised above the surface of the paper.

The paper is ejected into the paper tray, and the drum must be prepared for another page.

Memory and Laser Printers

Because a laser printer is a page printer and the graphics, text, and fonts on the page all use memory, the amount of memory in the laser printer determines the types of pages it can print successfully—and on some models, how quickly the pages are printed.

All laser printers are shipped with enough memory to print with built-in typefaces, and most printers sold since the mid-1990s have enough memory for documents containing several scalable TrueType typefaces used by Windows. However, graphics, especially photographs, require a great deal more printer memory.

If a page is sent to a laser printer that requires more memory than the laser printer contains, the laser printer tries to print the page but stops after the printer's memory is full. The printer then displays an error message or blinks error status lights, at which point you must manually eject the page. Only a portion of the page is printed.

If the page requires an amount of memory close to the maximum in the laser printer, most recent laser printers have techniques for compressing the data going to the printer. Although this technique means that more pages can be printed successfully, compressing the data can slow down the print process.

Three options can be used if the pages you need to print require too much memory:

- Reduce the resolution of the print job. Most laser printers today have a standard resolution of 600dpi or 1,200dpi. Reducing the graphics resolution to the next lower figure (from 1,200 to 600dpi or from 600 to 300dpi) will reduce the memory requirement for printing the page by a factor of four. The laser printer's graphics properties sheet (see Figure 9.12) enables this factor to be adjusted as needed.

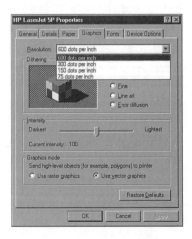

Figure 9.12
The Graphics properties sheet for a typical laser printer in Windows 95 enables you to adjust the graphics resolution from the default of 600dpi to 300dpi, 150dpi, or 75dpi; text quality is not affected by this option.

- Eliminate or reduce the size of graphics on the page.

- Convert color photos to black-and-white photos in the original document. This can actually enhance the output quality from a monochrome laser printer as well as reduce the memory requirement for pages with photos.

These options are temporary workarounds that are satisfactory for permanent use. The best solution to "out-of-memory" problems with a printer, as with the computer, is to add more RAM.

Printers generally use memory modules that are somewhat different from computer memory modules, although they might look similar. The memory modules might be in the form of a SIMM (shown in Figure 9.13), a credit-card module, or a slide-in board that is populated with memory chips.

After the memory is installed in the printer, the printer is ready to use it immediately. However, some Windows printer drivers might not automatically detect the additional RAM. Because many Windows printer drivers try to compress data to fit into the amount of printer RAM known, an inaccurate RAM value will cause slower printing; Windows will ignore printer RAM it doesn't know about. After installing the RAM in the laser printer, open the printer properties sheet in Windows and reset the total value for printer RAM to the correct value; a typical location for this option is Device Options.

To avoid memory problems, specify at least 4MB or more RAM for PCL laser printers and at least 16MB or more RAM for PostScript laser printers using 600dpi maximum resolution; add more RAM for higher resolutions.

Toner Cartridges

Most laser printers use *toner cartridges*, which combine the imaging drum and the developer with toner. This provides you with an efficient and easy way to replace the laser printer items with the greatest potential to wear out.

Depending on the model, a new toner cartridge might also require that you change a wiper used on some models to remove excess toner during the fusing cycle. This is normally packaged with the toner cartridge.

Recycled toner cartridges are controversial in some circles, but I've used a mixture of new and rebuilt toner cartridges for several years without a problem. Major manufacturers, such as Apple, HP, and Canon, encourage you to recycle your toner cartridges by enclosing a postage-paid return label in the box.

Reputable toner cartridge rebuilders can save you as much as 30% off the price of a new toner cartridge.

When you install the toner cartridge, be sure to follow the directions for cleaning near the toner cartridge. Depending on the model of laser printer, this can involve cleaning the mirror that reflects the laser beam or cleaning the charging corona wire on the toner cartridge itself. If you need to clean the charging corona wire (also called the primary corona wire on some models, the laser printer will contain a special tool for this purpose. The printer instruction manual will show you how to clean the item.

Figure 9.13

A typical laser printer's memory sockets with a 4MB SIMM module installed.

Keep the cartridge closed; it is sensitive to light, and leaving it out of the printer in room light can damage the enclosed imaging drum's surface. Figure 9.14 shows a typical laser printer toner cartridge and cleaning tool. The tool to the left of the toner cartridge is used to clean the printer's mirror. This printer features a drop-down tray for label and envelope stock at right, with its main paper feed beneath the printer.

Mirror-cleaning tool

Toner cartridge

Folding paper tray for labels, envelopes, letterhead

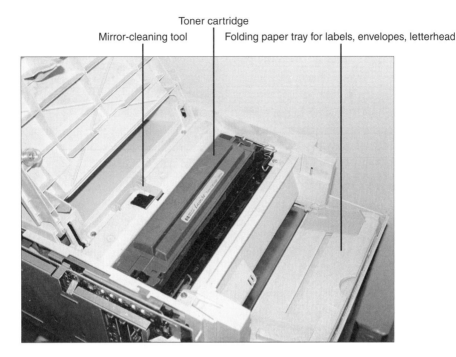

Figure 9.14
A typical laser printer toner cartridge after installation.

Paper, Labels, and Transparency Stock

Because the laser printer bonds the print to the paper during the fusing process, it can handle a wider range of paper stocks than inkjet printers. However, the same heat that produces an embossed feel to printing can also cause problems if the wrong types of labels or transparencies are used. For best results, follow these guidelines:

- Use paper made for laser or photocopier use. Extremely rough-surfaced specialty papers might not allow the toner to fuse correctly to the paper.

- Use envelopes made for laser printing, especially if the printer doesn't offer a straight-through paper path option. Standard envelopes can lose some of their flap adhesive or have the flap stick to the back of the envelope when used in a laser printer.

- Use only labels made for laser printers; these labels have no exposed backing, requiring you to separate the labels from the backing after printing. Labels made for copiers have exposed backing, and the labels can come off inside the printer, leading to expensive repairs.

- Use only laser-compatible transparency stock; it can resist the high heat of the fuser rollers better than other types, which can melt and damage the printer.

■ Avoid using paper with damaged edges or damp paper; this can cause paper jams and lead to poor-quality printing.

■ Load paper carefully into the paper tray; fan the paper and make sure the edges are aligned before inserting it.

Troubleshooting the Laser Printer

Common causes of laser printer problems and their solutions are provided in this section. Use this information to prepare for laser printer troubleshooting questions on the A+ Certification exam and your day-to-day work with laser printers.

The following are typical problems:

■ Black marks on the page

■ Print lighter than normal

■ Slow printing

■ No page printed after data received by printer

■ Line-draw characters printed as foreign-language characters

■ Envelopes curl after printing

■ Parts of two documents on the same printed page

■ Printer can't feed paper

■ Printer runs but page output is blank

■ Toner not fused to paper

■ Printer can't accept print job

■ Printer smells of ozone when turned on

■ Large amounts of loose toner inside the printer

■ Error or status lights blinking or error messages displayed

Black Marks on the Page

These usually are caused by debris stuck to or surface damage to the imaging drum or dirty components in the printer (fuser, paper rollers, charging rollers, and so on). To determine which component is the cause, compare the distance between marks on the paper with the circumference of each component. The printer's manual will provide this information. Replace the imaging drum (part of the toner cartridge on many printer models) if the drum is at fault. Clean other components if they're at fault, and retest.

Print Lighter than Normal

If printing is uneven or there are blank spots on page, the toner is running low. Remove the toner cartridge and gently shake it to redistribute the toner. Install a new toner cartridge as quickly as possible. If the printing is even, the printer might be set for Economode or a similar mode that uses less toner. Adjust the printer properties to use normal print modes for final drafts.

Slow Printing

When a printer slows down in printing certain pages, this usually means that the page contains too much data to fit into the printer's memory unless the printer driver compresses the data (which takes more time). Add memory to the printer and adjust the printer properties if necessary to reflect the printer's additional memory.

No Page Printed After Data Is Received by Printer

If the printer displays an error indicating a data overflow, or if only part of the page printed when the page was ejected, the printer's memory was not sufficient to accept all the data on the page. Add memory to the printer and adjust the printer properties if necessary to reflect the printer's additional memory.

If the printer displays no error message, the print job didn't send a page-eject command; this happens most often when the Print-Screen key is used at an MS-DOS (command) prompt to print the current screen's contents. Take the printer offline and press the page eject or form-feed button to eject the page.

Line-Draw Characters Printed as Foreign-Language Characters

Line-draw characters sometimes are used in plain-text documents to highlight information or to add visual interest to batch-file menus. Most laser printers are set by default to use a character set that has foreign-language characters in place of the line-draw characters. Use the printer's setup software or menu to select a character set that supports line-draw printing, such as PC-8 or PC-850.

Envelopes Curl After Printing

The fuser mechanism uses heat to bond laser output to paper, and this high heat causes some envelopes to curl. Using the default curved paper path increases the likelihood of curled envelopes. Use laser-compatible envelopes to reduce curl, and adjust the printer's paper path to a straight-through path.

Parts of Two Documents on the Same Printed Page

If the printer doesn't receive a form-feed command after printing the first document, the second document will start right after the first document. Make sure the proper printer driver is used by your operating system, and be sure to eject print-screen output immediately.

Printer Can't Feed Paper

Paper-feed problems can be caused by running out of paper, incorrect insertion of the paper tray, blockage of the paper path by stuck labels or paper jams, and mechanical problems with the paper feed rollers.

If the printer indicates that the paper is out, check the paper tray; if there is paper in the paper tray, make sure it is properly inserted into the printer. Copier labels should never be used in a laser printer; their lack of backing around the labels makes it very easy to leave a label stuck inside the printer. Check the paper path carefully with the printer turned off if the printer tries to feed paper but has a paper jam. If the paper feed mechanism makes an unusual sound or doesn't operate at all, check the gears; they might be jammed or damaged.

Printer Runs but Page Output Is Blank

If the printer produces a blank page immediately after the toner cartridge has been changed, remove the toner cartridge and make sure the tape that holds the toner in place has been removed; without toner, the printer can't print.

If the printer produces a blank page after printing thousands of pages, the toner probably is exhausted. Replace the toner cartridge.

Toner Not Fused to Paper

If the printed output can be wiped or blown off the paper after the printout emerges from the laser printer, the fuser needs to be repaired or replaced. The fuser is supposed to heat the paper to fuse the toner to the paper; if it fails, the toner won't stick to the paper.

Printer Can't Accept Print Job

If the printer has both a serial and parallel port, or both a parallel and USB port, make sure the correct port is selected in the printer's setup and that the computer is using the correct port for the printer. Some older laser printers with both serial and parallel ports use the serial port as the default.

Printer Smells of Ozone When Turned On

Some printers use corona wires to produce the electrostatic charges used in EP printing. Printers that use corona wires typically have ozone filters that must be changed periodically to protect the health of nearby users. Run the printer's self-test to determine the number of pages the printer has produced; compare this number to the number of pages the ozone filter is designed to handle, and replace the filter when the rated life has been reached.

Large Amounts of Loose Toner Inside the Printer

Large amounts of loose toner inside the printer normally indicate a defect in the toner cartridge. Remove the cartridge, turn off and unplug the printer, and wipe away the spilled toner. Don't use a vacuum cleaner to pick up loose toner unless the vacuum cleaner is rated specifically for laser printer toner.

Return the toner cartridge for exchange or refund; if the cartridge was rebuilt, consider switching to another source.

Error or Status Lights Blinking or Error Messages Displayed

Many of the problems listed will be detected by the printer and reported by either alphanumeric error codes and messages or blinking lights. Consult the printer's documentation to see the meaning of the error codes or blinking light patterns.

Laser printers have multiple points of failure; fortunately, the widespread use of toner cartridges enables you to replace a defective drum or developer simply by replacing the toner cartridge, which contains both. However, failures of the paper feed or fuser mechanism are not affected by a toner cartridge change. Failures of these portions of the laser printer will need to be repaired individually.

If your laser printer uses toner cartridges, have a spare or two available at all times. Replacing the toner cartridge can fix many imaging problems with laser printers.

Using the Self-Test for Laser Printers

The laser printer self-test is far more important for diagnosing problems than are the self-test options for other printers. The procedure varies with the printer. Some printers must be turned on while you hold down a key to start the printing process, while others can be self-tested after they are started.

Regardless, the self-test for laser printers typically tells you the following:

- The firmware date or revision
- The number of pages printed
- The amount of RAM onboard
- The emulations or "personalities" (PCL, PostScript, and so on)
- The current default font and symbol set
- The resolution and special settings (if any) available to help print quality

Note the information produced by the self-test to help you answer troubleshooting questions on the A+ Certification exams.

In the event of printing problems (see the section "Troubleshooting the Laser Printer," earlier in this chapter), the information supplied by the self-test can be very valuable.

Periodic Maintenance for Laser Printers

Because laser printers use fine-grain powdered toner, keeping the inside of a laser printer clean is important in periodic maintenance. Turn off the laser printer before using a damp cloth to clean up any toner spills.

To keep the paper path and rollers clean, use cleaning sheets made for laser printers. To use the sheets, do the following:

1. Insert the sheet into the manual feed tray on the laser printer.
2. Create a short document with Notepad, WordPad, or some other text editor and print it on the sheet.

As the sheet passes through the printer, it cleans the rollers.

Change the toner cartridge as needed, and the ozone filter on models that use one as required.

Software and Printers

Like any other device, a printer requires software to drive it. MS-DOS can print plain-text output to all printers except PostScript printers. Windows can also output plain text but must use the Generic/Text-only printer driver for this. To use the printer's special fonts, graphics, or other features, printer drivers made for the printer model or for its emulation must be used.

Printer drivers are selected in either applications or the operating system. MS-DOS software uses its own printer drivers; Windows applications use the printer drivers installed in Windows.

Windows printer drivers can be installed from

- The Windows installation disks or CD-ROM
- Installation disks or CD-ROMs supplied with the printer
- Driver files downloaded from the manufacturer's Web site

The most recent printer drivers are found on the manufacturer's Web site, followed by the driver disks or CD-ROM included with the printer. These often have enhanced features not found in the standard printer drivers supplied with Windows and are usually much newer, too.

A new printer can be installed at any time; with Windows, any programs that use printers should be closed to enable common files used by all printers to be updated.

If you are installing a printer without a printer driver made especially for it, use the following options to configure the printer:

- Download a new driver from the manufacturer's Web site.
- Check the manual for recommended emulations.
- For inkjet printers used with an MS-DOS program, choose the most similar inkjet printer made by the same maker, or a dot-matrix printer that the inkjet printer emulates.

Always use the Windows test print feature or create and print an MS-DOS document to see how well the substitute printer driver performs. Acquire and install the correct printer driver as soon as possible.

Summary

Dot-matrix printers provide the lowest cost per page of all major print technologies, but their relatively low print quality, difficulties with single-sheet paper, and high noise level have relegated them to utility tasks.

Many inkjet printers can print laser-like text as well as stunning photograph-quality images, but their need for special paper and short ink cartridge life makes them the highest cost-per-page printer. They are used in office and home environments but should not be the only printer where high volumes of pages are produced.

Laser printers provide low cost per page, high output quality, and high print speed, and are found in most offices today.

With any printer, high-quality paper and media appropriate to the printer are needed for best print quality.

QUESTIONS AND ANSWERS:

1. Which current printer technology is impact-based? What part of this type of printer might break if not set correctly?
   A: Dot-matrix printers are impact printers; the pins in the printhead can break if the head gap isn't set correctly.

2. Why do inkjet printers need smooth paper for best results?
   A: Inkjet printers use neither impact nor a heat process to make the image; the ink needs a smooth, fast drying surface to look good.

3. Which printer type produces warm printouts? Why?
   A: Laser printers produce literally "hot off the press" printouts because the fuser rollers melt the toner onto the paper.

4. Which printer technology is suitable for multipart forms? Why?
   A: Dot-matrix printers are suitable for multipart forms because they make an impact against a ribbon to print.

5. How does the laser in a laser printer help produce the image on the page?
   A: It reduces the charge on the imaging drum to correspond to the page image. These parts of the drum then attract toner, which is transferred to the paper.

6. Should you use the surge protector on/off switch to turn off an inkjet printer?
   A: No. The printer will not cap the printheads properly and the printheads will clog. This causes frequent service calls.

CH
9

10

Portables

1. Does PCMCIA correctly describe what these devices can be used for? What is a newer name for this technology?
2. What does a portable need in order to use a docking station or port replicator?
3. Can you use the same memory in both a portable and desktop computer? Why or why not?
4. Do portables use interchangeable batteries?

Introduction

As more and more businesses discover the usefulness of portable computers, allowing data processing to take place away from the desk and the network, the need to understand how to maintain and service these units is also increasing.

To successfully maintain portable computers, you must understand their unique features and the special challenges they present for repair and upgrades.

Portable computers have several distinctive features that separate them from desktop computers, even though portable and desktop computers increasingly perform the same types of tasks. Table 10.1 lists the major hardware differences between portable and desktop computers.

Table 10.1   Portable and Desktop Computers Comparison by Features

Feature	Desktop Computer	Portable Computer
Display	Separate CRT or LCD display connected to VGA port	Integrated LCD plus external VGA port
Keyboard	Standard 101- or 104-key with separate numerical keypad; full-size keys	Compact integrated keyboard with embedded numerical keypad; nonstandard layout of directional keys
Mouse or pointing device	Separate unit; wide choice of types	Integrated into keyboard; can be replaced with external units
Battery use	Battery used for CMOS maintenance only	Battery used to power computer and many peripherals attached to computer
Expansion bus	PCI, ISA, AGP slots allow interchange of many different components	Connector for docking station and/or port replicator is proprietary—PC Card is standard
PC Card card	Optional card reader	Standard on most systems
Floppy drive location	Internal	Can be internal or external, using hot-swappable proprietary interface
CD-ROM drive location	Internal	Can be internal or external
Memory expansion	Uses standard DIMM or SIMM modules	Can use proprietary modules or SODIMM
CPU upgrades	Common on virtually any model	Not available on most models due to special CPU types used for portable computers

Although portable and desktop computers have many differences, systems that use the same version of Microsoft Windows and have similar CPU types, CPU speeds, and memory sizes are capable of performing work in similar ways.

This is definitely not the case with the smallest and newest portable unit, the Portable Digital Assistant (PDA). PDAs, such as the popular Palm series and others, differ not only in their size but in their user interface (stylus-based with handwriting recognition or an optional keyboard on some models), their operating system (proprietary or a special version of Windows that is not fully compatible with standard 32-bit Windows versions), and their storage (flash memory). Whereas PDAs have a limited capability to synchronize address and email with regular computers, and units based on Windows CE can exchange data files, PDAs should be looked at as a supplement, rather than as a partial replacement, for larger computers.

In the following sections, you'll learn about the distinctive challenges of portable hardware.

LCD Display

One of the biggest differences between portable and desktop computers is the display. Desktop computers allow both the screen and graphics cards to be changed; in portable computers, both the screen and graphics cards are built into the system. Although most portables feature an external VGA port allowing a separate monitor to be plugged into the computer, that is the extent of the video expandability of most portable systems.

Two major types of LCD display screens are used on portables: dual scan and active matrix.

Dual Scan

A dual-scan display is an improved variation on the "passive matrix" displays used for many years on portable computers. These screens are controlled by an array of transistors along the horizontal and vertical edges of the display; a 1,024×768 resolution display features 1,024 transistors along the horizontal edge of the display and 768 along the vertical. The transistors send out a pulse of energy, and the individual LCDs polarize at varying angles to produce the picture. "Dual-scan" screens split the screen into a top half and bottom half for faster response.

Dual-scan LCD displays are dimmer, have slower response times, and feature a narrower viewing angle than active-matrix screens. The main advantage of dual-scan LCD displays is that they are far less expensive to replace when broken, and portable computers with dual-scan displays are less expensive to purchase.

Active Matrix

Active matrix refers to screens that use a transistor for every dot seen onscreen: a 1,024×768 active-matrix LCD screen has 786,432 transistors. Active-matrix LCD displays are nearly as bright as CRT displays, offer wide viewing angles for easier use by groups of people, and tend to display rapid movement and full-motion video with less blur then dual-scan displays.

Active-matrix LCD displays are very expensive to replace when broken, and computers with these screens are more expensive to buy initially.

Active-matrix LCD displays are also used by a small but increasing number of desktop computers. Unlike portable active-matrix displays, these displays are attached to the video card or built-in video port the same way that standard CRT-based monitors are.

Graphics Circuitry

The other built-in portion of the display system is the graphics circuitry; portable computers have built-in graphics that can't be interchanged or upgraded with more onboard RAM. This can limit the number of colors that can be displayed onscreen in resolutions above 640×480.

On portable systems that have external VGA, some VGA modes might work only with the external display because they have a higher resolution (more dots) than the built-in LCD display.

Troubleshooting LCD Displays and Graphics Circuits

As with desktop computers, portable computers rely on the display as the primary means of informing users about computer activity. The following problems and solutions are typical of those you might encounter in A+ Certification troubleshooting questions on LCD displays and in your day-to-day work with portable systems.

Display problems can result from two major causes:

- Configuration errors
- Component damage or failure

Configuration Errors

The quality of the screen display can be affected by configuration errors; these usually result from incorrect settings made by the user and do not indicate actual display failures.

- **Washed-out dual-scan LCD display**—This problem usually is caused by an incorrect brightness adjustment on the screen or by using the portable system in a brightly lit area or outdoors. You can adjust the brightness/contrast control on the display to resolve the first issue, and using an anti-glare screen or visor or switching to a high-contrast color palette in Windows can help you cope with the second issue. However, you should note that dual-scan displays are not designed for use in daylight or brightly lit interiors.

- **User cannot select desired color depth and resolution combination**—This is caused by a lack of available video RAM. Because the onboard video can't be upgraded, the user will need to stick with the choices available.

- **Image occupies only a portion of the LCD screen (see Figure 10.1)**—This is caused by selecting a lower display resolution than the LCD panel's native resolution; the resulting image uses only a portion of the screen's horizontal and vertical pixels. The user should select the resolution the panel is designed to use or attach the system to an external monitor.

- **User must scroll screen to see all the Windows desktop**—This is caused by selecting a higher display resolution than the LCD panel's native resolution. The user should select the resolution the panel is designed to use, or attach the system to an external monitor.

- **No display on built-in LCD screen**—If the system can work with an external monitor, check to see if the system has been toggled to display to the external monitor only. Many systems use a keyboard shortcut to switch between internal only, external only, or dual display functions. The user might have accidentally pressed the toggle keys or the BIOS might be configured to use external display only.

Figure 10.1
The user of a 1,024×768 resolution portable sees a wide dark border around the display area if the LCD resolution is set to 800×600.

Component Damage or Failure

LCD screens are vulnerable to damage, either to the transistors that change the LCD's colors or to the LCD itself.

- **Black lines or boxes onscreen at all times in the same location when display is turned on**—The liquid crystals in the display have leaked (usually due to impact damage); the screen must be repaired or replaced (see Figure 10.2).

- **One or more full-brightness or black "dots" are visible in the same location at all times when an active-matrix display is turned on**—The transistors for these pixels (dots) are stuck in the on or off position and are not responding to commands. Manufacturers of systems with active-matrix displays have differing standards for how many pixels must have failed before a screen replacement under warranty will be performed.

Neither of these problems will prevent the portable from being used with an external display.

- **No display on either the internal LCD screen or an external display**—This problem usually indicates the video circuit on the motherboard has failed; repair or replace the computer. To make sure that the system is not in a power-saving mode that blanks the screen, shut down the system and restart it. You should see a BIOS display, memory counter, or similar onscreen text if the video circuit is working correctly.

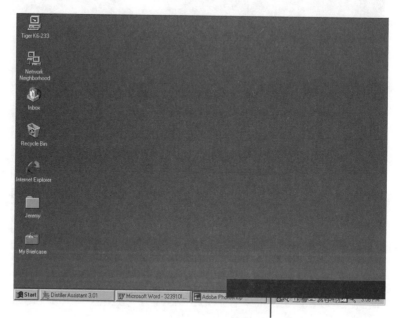

The broken area of the screen

Figure 10.2
A simulation of a broken LCD screen. The area where the liquid crystals have leaked cannot respond to signals and is black at all times. The glass cover might still be intact.

Installation and Removal of LCD Display Panels

LCD display panels built into portable computers are customized for each model of portable computer and require the disassembly of the computer for removal and replacement. Replacements should be obtained from either the vendor or an authorized repair parts depot. Many vendors require that you be an authorized technician before you remove or replace LCD display panels in portable computers. However, the process of replacing the entire LCD display assembly is simpler and might be possible for you to perform in the field.

The details of the process for removing an LCD display assembly from a portable computer will vary by model, but will follow these basic steps:

1. Remove the screws holding the display assembly in place.

2. Remove the cover over the monitor connector.

3. Unlatch the LCD panel from the base unit.

4. Rotate the display assembly to a 90-degree angle to the base unit.

5. Lift the display assembly free from the base unit.

6. Remove the cover over the FPC cable attachment on the system board; the FPC cable transmits power and data to the LCD display assembly.

7. Disconnect the assembly's FPC cable from the system board.

8. Be sure to save all screws, ground springs, and other hardware that you removed during the disassembly process.

Depending on the vendor, you might be able to purchase a replacement LCD display assembly that can be installed by following the previous steps in reverse order, or you might need to disassemble the display assembly to remove and install the LCD display panel itself. Replacing the LCD display panel (which requires the disassembly of the display assembly) should be performed at a repair depot.

Because of differences in chipsets, BIOS, and display circuitry between systems with dual-scan and active-matrix LCD panels, dual-scan and active-matrix LCD panels are generally not interchangeable.

CH
10

Portables' Keyboards

Portable systems feature keyboards that are designed to be compact in size and light in weight. Internally, the keyboard module attaches to the notebook's main portable computer circuitry with a relatively fragile ribbon cable. In many cases, the keyboard is also the primary pointing device (see Figure 10.3).

Portable keyboards also differ from desktop keyboards in their layout:

- An integrated numeric keypad typically occupies the right side of the keyboard; instead of a Num Lock key, the normal letter and number functions are switched to the number pad functions with a special key, often marked Fn (see Figure 10.4).

- The classic "inverted T" layout for directional arrows is sometimes not used because of space limitations.

Because of the portable keyboard's design, it is vulnerable to a heavy touch while typing, abuse of the pointing device, and spills, dirt, and dust.

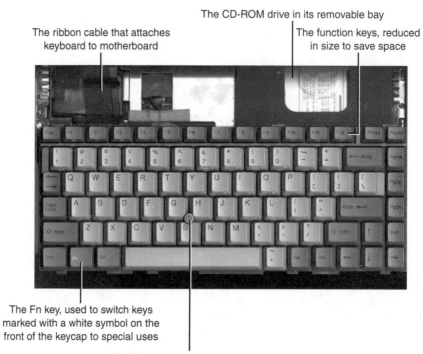

The CD-ROM drive in its removable bay

The ribbon cable that attaches keyboard to motherboard

The function keys, reduced in size to save space

The Fn key, used to switch keys marked with a white symbol on the front of the keycap to special uses

The IBM TrackPoint pointing device

Figure 10.3
A typical notebook computer with an integrated pointing device (the IBM-designed TrackPoint), reduced-size function keys, and the special Fn key that switches the normal function keys to special uses, such as power management.

Portable Keyboard Replacement

Replacing a portable keyboard requires the unit to be partially disassembled. Details vary from unit to unit, but the following is the basic procedure:

1. Remove the display assembly if the vendor recommends this; some portable systems don't require this step.
2. Remove screws or bezels that hold the keyboard in place.
3. Lift up the keyboard to expose the keyboard cable.
4. Remove any hold-down devices used to hold the keyboard cable in place.
5. Disconnect the keyboard cable from the system board.
6. Remove the keyboard.

If the keyboard has an integrated pointing device, such as the IBM TrackPoint or similar devices, this procedure will remove the pointing device but might not replace the buttons. If the buttons are built into the palmrest, see "Replacing Portable Pointing Devices," page 299, for details.

The U key, which doubles as the 4 key when
the Fn key is pressed at the same time

The pointing device (its buttons are
below the keyboard's spacebar)

Figure 10.4

A closeup of the integrated pointing device and the right side of the keyboard. The keys with white arrow and number markings on the front of the keycaps work normally unless the Fn key is held down at the same time (refer to Figure 10.3). Then, the key switches to its alternative use; these keys become a numeric keypad.

To install a replacement keyboard, reverse the steps. Note that because of differences in design, form factor, and system board interface, integrated portable keyboards are not usually interchangeable between brands and models.

Mouse and Mouse Alternatives on Portable Computers

Some very old portable computers you might still encounter used clip-on trackballs that plugged into standard PS/2 or serial mouse ports. Most recent portable computers use one of the following technologies as an alternative to a separate mouse, which can still be used.

IBM TrackPoint "Eraserhead" Pointing Stick

This mouse alternative (originally called the TrackPoint II by IBM) allows the user to keep his hands on the keyboard all times, pushing a small button shaped like a pencil eraser located in the middle of the keyboard to move the mouse pointer. Although this technology was developed by IBM for its portable computers, it has been licensed by several other vendors, including Toshiba and HP.

The mouse buttons for the TrackPoint are located beneath the spacebar; some systems use the conventional left and right buttons, but others use buttons arranged vertically, in which the top button corresponds to the left mouse button, while the bottom button corresponds to the right mouse button. Newer systems might feature an additional button used to scroll the screen.

Touchpad

This mouse alternative uses a square or rectangular touch-sensitive surface located beneath the spacebar. To move the mouse pointer, the user slides his or her finger on the surface. Clicking and double-clicking can be done by tapping on the trackpad surface with the finger or with the mouse buttons.

The mouse buttons for the touchpad are also located beneath the spacebar; if the buttons are arranged vertically, the top button corresponds to the left mouse button, whereas the bottom button corresponds the right mouse button. Newer systems might feature an additional button for scrolling the screen.

Trackball

This mouse alternative uses a ball similar in size to a mouse ball below the spacebar. The user rolls the trackball to guide the cursor. The mouse buttons for the trackball are also located beneath the spacebar—as with other pointing devices, the buttons can be arranged horizontally or vertically.

Troubleshooting Portable Keyboards and Pointing Devices

Portable keyboards and pointing devices can present unique problems, including

- The inability to use integrated pointing devices
- Interference between the pointing device and the keyboard
- Damage to the keyboard
- Power management issues

Use the problems and solutions in this section to prepare for troubleshooting questions regarding portable keyboards and pointing devices on the A+ Certification exam and in your day-to-day work regarding portable computers.

Can't Use Pointing Device

If the mouse pointer won't move when the user tries to use the integrated pointing device, check to see if an external pointing device has been plugged in. On some systems, plugging in a conventional mouse or similar pointing device can disable the integrated pointing device. To enable the integrated pointing device, turn off the system, disconnect the external pointing device, and restart the system. On other systems, the integrated pointing device can be disabled in the system BIOS. To enable the integrated pointing device, access the system BIOS setup program, enable the integrated pointing device, and restart the system.

Integrated Pointing Device Cursor Movement Problems

When using portable systems with integrated touchpads or trackballs below the spacebar, it's easy for users to accidentally bump the pointing device with their fingers while typing.

This causes cursor movement and can lead to typing errors. If a portable user with this type of pointing device prefers to use an external pointing device such as a conventional mouse, you might need to disable the integrated touchpad in the system BIOS to prevent additional typing errors.

A defective IBM TrackPoint or other pointing stick can lead to unwanted cursor movement. These pointing sticks respond to pressure on the head of the pointing stick; if the cap is sending impulses to the pointing stick, the cursor can move without the user touching the cap. Remove and replace the cap on the pointing stick. If the problem persists, repair or replace the keyboard containing the pointing stick.

Delayed Response from Keyboard After a Period of Idleness

If it takes several seconds for typed characters to appear after a portable system has been left idle for some time, this is a normal condition caused by the use of power management. Most portables use power management features, such as shutting down the hard drive to save power. If the user complains about too-frequent delays because of power management, adjust the drive suspend settings with the Windows Power icon or through the system BIOS setup program.

Some Keys Don't Respond when Pressed

The most common cause of this problem is debris wedged between keys; clean out the areas between and beneath keytops with compressed air or a computer-grade vacuum cleaner. If cleaning the keyboard doesn't help, replace the keyboard module.

"Phantom" Keystrokes Activate Special Functions or Put Extra Characters Onscreen

Keystrokes that appear to come from nowhere can actually come from a defective keyboard, a defective keyboard ribbon cable, or a loose keyboard ribbon cable. Carefully remove and reattach the ribbon cable that connects the keyboard to the portable system's main board. If this fails to solve the problem, replace the keyboard module.

Replacing Portable Pointing Devices

Pointing devices in portable computers are normally located in two places

- **The palm rest**—Used for touchpads and integrated trackballs and for the buttons on some pointing sticks

- **The keyboard**—Used for integrated pointing sticks, such as the IBM TrackPoint II and later versions

To replace defective pointing sticks, follow the steps listed in "Portable Keyboard Replacement," page 296, earlier in this chapter.

Replacing pointing devices built into the palmrest requires the unit to be partially disassembled. Details vary from unit to unit, but the following is the basic procedure.

To remove the palmrest

1. Remove the display panel assembly and keyboard.

2. Turn over the system.

3. Remove the screws holding the palmrest in place.

4. Turn the system right side up.

5. Remove the palmrest from the system.

To remove a pointing device, such as a touchpad or others, from the palmrest

1. Disconnect or unscrew the pointing device from the touchpad.

2. Remove the pointing device from the touchpad.

3. You might need to remove the pointing device cable from the pointing device or from the system board; check the specific instructions for the device.

To replace the pointing device, follow these steps in reverse order to install a new pointing device into the palmrest and to reinstall the palmrest into the portable computer.

Battery Technologies

Battery power is a vital feature for portable computers, which are used away from an AC power source. Battery life depends on several factors, including

- Battery type
- Power-management options
- Memory size
- CPU speed
- PC card type and use

Battery Types

Computers use rechargeable batteries, and the rechargeable battery type has a great deal to do with the amount of time you can use a computer between recharges (the "run time").

The most common battery types include

- Nickel Metal Hydride (NiMH)
- Lithium Ion (Li-Ion)
- Nickel-Cadmium (NiCad or NiCd)

The original rechargeable standard, NiCad, has fallen out of favor for use as a notebook computer's main power source because of a problem called the "memory effect." If NiCad batteries are not fully discharged before being recharged, the "memory effect" allows the battery to be recharged only to the level it was used. In other words, if you use a NiCad battery and recharge it when it's only 50 percent exhausted, the memory effect will allow you to use only 50 percent of the battery's actual capacity. You might be able to correct the memory effect if you'll allow your battery to fully discharge before recharging it; however, the memory effect can permanently affect your battery's condition.

Most low-cost notebook computers now use NiMH batteries instead of NiCad. NiMH batteries have fewer problems with the memory effect.

The most efficient battery technology is Li-Ion, which has little problem with memory effect, puts out the same power as NiMH, but is about 35% lighter.

NiCad batteries are still used today but as CMOS batteries or as "RAM" or "bridge" batteries, which store a system's configuration when the suspend mode is used.

Batteries for PDAs

PDAs, such as the Palm series, often use off-the-shelf alkaline or NiMh rechargeable batteries in AA or AAA sizes. These batteries usually can be purchased at local retail stores. Use non-alkaline rechargeable batteries only in systems that are designed for them. Rechargeable alkaline batteries made by RayOVac and others can be used in systems that were designed for standard alkaline batteries.

Battery and Charger Interchangeability

Both battery types and battery form factors prevent free interchange of batteries between different brands, and even different models, of portable computer systems. The Duracell standardized battery packs found in a few models of portable computers have never become widely adopted.

Rechargers, too, are matched to particular brands and models of portable computers.

AC Adapters and Battery Chargers

Many systems still use an external AC adapter and battery charging unit, sometimes referred to as a "brick." To make portable use easier, some systems build the AC adapter/battery charger into the portable computer and use a special polarized power cord for recharging.

Just as with desktop power supplies, notebook battery recharging systems must be compatible with the local electrical power source. Most portable computers use an automatically switching recharger, capable of handling either European and Asian 50-cycle, 230v power or North American 60-cycle, 115v power. However, a few systems are shipped with a single voltage recharger, requiring that you use a power converter or different recharger if you travel internationally.

If the portable computer doesn't appear to be receiving power from either an external or internal AC adapter/battery charger, check the following:

- Loose or defective line cord
- Battery failure

Check the line cord for damage or loose connections; reconnect or replace the line cord between the wall outlet and the computer or external AC adapter, and retest the system.

If the system still will not start and run correctly, remove the batteries from the portable computer and try to run it from wall current only, if the unit will work in this fashion. If the batteries are the problem, the unit should work properly on wall current only—replace the batteries.

If both of these tests fail, repair or replace the external AC adapter or computer with internal AC adapter. Use only manufacturer-approved parts for replacement. Because of differences in battery technology and system boards, internal units from different models of portable computer usually are not interchangeable. Make sure that you replace single-voltage AC adapters with the correct voltage for your country or region.

Battery Replacement

Most batteries in portable computers can be replaced by the user in the field. Generally, replacement batteries fall into two categories

- **Proprietary batteries that are customized for a particular portable computer model**—You can purchase these batteries from specialized battery stores as well as from the manufacturer of the computer.
- **Industry-standard models that fit into a wide variety of computer and other devices**—These batteries can be purchased at most retail stores. Most computers that use industry-standard AA and AAA-sized batteries are PDAs.

Follow this procedure to replace computer batteries:

1. Turn off the computer.
2. Unplug the AC adapter or line cord from the computer.
3. Locate the battery compartment in the unit; it might be secured by a sliding lock or by screws.
4. Remove the cover.
5. Slide or lift out the battery or batteries. If the battery is a flat assembly, it might be held in place by a clip; push the clip to one side to release the battery.
6. Check the battery contacts inside the computer for dirt or corrosion, and clean dirty contacts with a soft cloth.
7. Insert the replacement battery or batteries. Make sure you insert batteries so the positive and negative terminals are in the right directions.
8. Close the cover and secure it.
9. If the battery must be charged before use, plug in the line cord or AC adapter into both the computer and wall outlet. Check the computer's manual for the proper charge time for a new battery.
10. Unplug the system or AC adapter when the battery has been charged for the recommended time period.

Power Management

Power management originated with portable computers because of their heavy dependence upon battery power. Power management for notebook computers is usually simpler to configure than for desktop computers. There are two major hardware standards for power management. Windows 95 supports only Advanced Power Management (APM), and Windows 98/Me/2000 also support Advanced Configuration and Power Interface (ACPI).

Advanced Power Management (APM)

APM uses a combination of BIOS configuration options and matching configuration settings in Windows to control power usage by devices such as the display, the CPU, and disk drives. Frequently, Windows-based portable computers come with a special program that enables you to select timing options for power management, different power-management settings for battery and AC power, and options that enable the suspend and resume modes featured in many portable computers.

Systems that use APM power management normally control the power usage of the following parts of a portable system:

- **Screen brightness**—The brighter the screen, the faster the battery runs down.
- **Hard disk spin down**—Next to the screen, the biggest user of power in the notebook computer is the hard disk. Allowing the hard disk to spin down during a period of inactivity saves a lot of power.
- **Adjustable CPU speed**—Reducing the CPU speed, even by a modest amount in MHz, greatly improves battery life in two ways: Slower CPUs use less power, and slower CPUs run cooler, allowing the built-in fans on many portables to run slower or less often.
- **Suspend and resume**—For busy users, suspend and resume can be very useful. The suspend feature allows the user to shut down the computer without closing all the programs; the matching resume feature allows the theater restart in a few seconds where the user stopped, without having to restart all the programs. Suspend and resume functions depend on
  - Correct BIOS power-management settings
  - Correct settings in Windows-based power management
  - A working "RAM" or "bridge" battery and charged main battery

The best power-management settings won't interfere with normal work but will put the computer into power-saving modes during periods of inactivity (see Figure 10.5). A good starting place is to reduce screen brightness and CPU speed immediately and to set the hard disk spin down to take place after about 10 minutes of inactivity. Adjust as needed.

CH
10

Figure 10.5
A typical portable system's power-management screen, with options for screen brightness, hard disk auto-off timing, and other settings.

Advanced Configuration and Power Interface (ACPI)
ACPI power management goes far beyond APM to provide power management for all Plug-and-Play devices installed in a system, and it permits Windows to perform all power-management configurations rather than force the user to modify the BIOS setup to make some of the needed changes. ACPI requires the following:

- Windows 98/Me/2000
- An ACPI-compliant BIOS with ACPI features enabled

Because ACPI puts Windows in charge of power management, it's essential that an ACPI-compliant BIOS be installed in a system before a system is upgraded to Windows 98/Me/2000. Contact the portable system vendor for information on which systems can be upgraded to ACPI compliance and what the method is for performing the BIOS upgrade.

After an ACPI-compliant BIOS has been installed, the upgrade should then be performed. Performing the upgrade on a system without ACPI BIOS support will cause the Windows setup program to install only APM power management features.

Memory Size and Its Impact on Battery Life
Increasing the amount of RAM in the portable computer can also improve battery life on systems running any version of Microsoft Windows. Microsoft Windows makes heavy use of the hard disk as "virtual memory" when actual RAM is too small for all the programs and data that are in use. The hard disk, because it uses a motor, is a very power-hungry

component. Increasing the amount of RAM has these benefits: It delays the need to use the hard disk as virtual memory and increases the amount of memory available as a disk cache (memory used to hold a copy of data read from the disk drives).

PC Cards and Power Usage Issues

As you'll see later in this chapter, PC Cards provide many options for notebook computers. However, PC Cards can also decrease your battery's running time per charge. To avoid unnecessary loss of power

- Remove PC Cards from the computer when not needed.
- Use PC Cards that have power-management features.

Troubleshooting Power Systems on Portable Computers

Because portable computers frequently are used away from AC power sources, making sure that batteries, power management, and charging systems work properly is critical to their proper operation. Use the following problems and solutions to help you prepare for portable power-related troubleshooting questions on the A+ Certification exam and in your day-to-day work with portable computers.

Short Battery Life

A short battery life can be caused by any of the following:

- Improper discharge and recharge of NiCad batteries
- Incorrect power-management settings
- Use of power-hungry PC Cards and external peripherals that are powered by the portable system

To avoid "memory effect" problems with any systems that uses a NiCad battery, be sure to completely discharge the battery before recharging it. If the battery has gone through repeated partial discharge-recharge cycles, it might need to be replaced. Some systems can use NiMH batteries in place of NiCad.

Portable systems should have power management enabled whenever they are used on battery power. If the "always on" power management setting is used by mistake, the screen, CPU, and drives will use full power continuously until the battery is exhausted. Adjust power-management timers to meet user needs.

Some PC Cards support power-management features or have built-in power management. Remove any PC Cards from the system when not in use if they do not reduce their own power consumption when idle to avoid using up power prematurely.

Battery Overheats During Recharge

An overheated battery can be caused by any of the following problems:

- Poor connection between battery and external charger or the battery and the battery compartment on systems with an integrated charger
- Overcharged battery

To avoid overheating the battery, which will eventually ruin it, be sure that the connection between the battery and the charging contacts is tight. If the battery is charged inside the system, make sure the battery compartment cover is properly attached to hold the battery securely in place.

Some recharging systems monitor battery charge and stop charging the battery when it has achieved a full charge. If the portable system lacks this feature, note the recommended charge time and remove the battery from the charger (or unplug the system if the charger is integrated) after the full charging time has elapsed.

Resume Failure After Suspend Mode Used

The suspend/resume feature can save time for users who need to use their systems in different locations for just a few minutes. Suspend/resume depends on three factors:

- Adequate disk space to record the current system's configuration (open programs and documents, windows open, and so on)
- Adequate battery charge to maintain the suspend option
- Correct BIOS setup configuration

If the system can't resume after suspend mode has been selected, check all three issues. The system instruction manual should indicate how much free disk space is needed on the system for a successful suspend and how the BIOS must be configured for suspend/resume to work. Also, the battery must be fully charged for suspend to work.

If the battery appears to be fully charged, the system has adequate disk space for suspend/resume, and the BIOS is properly configured but resume doesn't work after suspend, check the system's bridge battery. This is a small NiCad battery that is normally built into the system; it is often used for suspend/restore. If it will no longer hold a charge, it must be replaced; this can require having the unit serviced by an authorized repair center.

Expansion Bus

To save weight and space, portable computers do not use standard expansion bus designs, such as the ISA or PCI expansion slots used on desktop computers. Instead, many, but not all portable computers have proprietary connectors (see Figure 10.6) on the rear or bottom of the system case that will connect with either a docking station or a port replicator.

Docking Stations

A docking station expands the capability of a portable computer by adding features such as

- One or more ISA and or PCI expansion slots
- Additional I/O ports, such as serial, parallel, PCMCIA, or VGA

- Additional drive bays
- Connectors for a standard keyboard and mouse

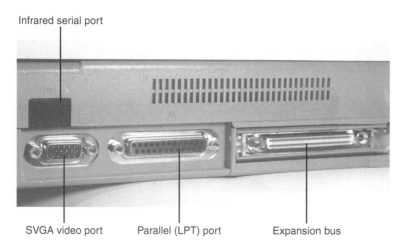

Infrared serial port

SVGA video port   Parallel (LPT) port   Expansion bus

Figure 10.6
A typical notebook computer with Infrared serial port, SVGA video port, parallel port, and expansion bus for use with a docking station or port replicator (not shown). Dual folding doors, retracted here, protect the expansion bus from damage.

Most docking stations are produced by the vendor of the notebook computer.

Docking stations are also used by PDAs, such as the Palm series and others. These computers use their docking stations primarily for data transfer or battery recharging.

Configuring Docking Stations and Devices

A docking station doesn't require any special hardware configuration, but the devices attached to it often do.

Windows 9x/Me/2000 use Plug and Play to support devices available to a portable computer when it is docked; the PnP devices are automatically detected and used.

If some devices or the computer are not PnP, you can create an alternative hardware profile from the System properties sheet, Hardware Profiles screen. Using this feature requires you to manually enable and disable hardware features in the "Docked" profile you will create by copying the original configuration.

Port Replicator

A port replicator usually connects to the same proprietary expansion bus that can be used by a docking station; many portable computers that do not have docking stations have optional port replicators.

Port replicators don't have expansion slots or drive bays; port replicators feature standard I/O ports (serial, parallel, VGA, USB), keyboard, and mouse connectors. They allow a portable computer user fast, easy connection to a full-sized keyboard, regular mouse or pointing device, desktop VGA monitor, modem, and printer without needing to attach or remove multiple cables. Because portable cable connectors can wear out, this extends the life of the system and makes desktop use faster and easier.

Some company systems use devices similar to conventional port replicators to provide access to the system's I/O ports; these systems provide just the expansion bus, without any normal ports, to save space and weight. This is true of systems such as the Toshiba Libretto series and others. In these cases, the port replicator is normally supplied with the system instead of being an optional extra.

Port replicators normally are built by the same company that makes the portable computer, but some third-party vendors produce both "dedicated" models (designed to attach to the proprietary expansion bus of a given model) and "universal" versions, which attach through the PC Card slot or USB port and can be freely moved among different brands and models of portable computers.

Software drivers are required for universal port replicators but not for standard port replicators.

Troubleshooting Docking Bays and Port Replicators

Use the following list of problems and solutions involving docking stations and port replicators to help you prepare for troubleshooting questions on the A+ Certification exam and for your day-to-day work with these devices.

Problems with docking bays and port replicators usually involve problems with devices in the docking station not being recognized or the ports in the docking station or port replicator not working.

Devices in Docking Station Aren't Recognized

If the devices in a docking station aren't being recognized by your computer, check the following possible causes:

- **Docking station is not firmly attached to your system**—Shut down the system and make sure the proprietary bus in your computer is firmly attached to the corresponding connection on the docking station.

- **Device drivers are not loaded for the devices in the docking station**—If the computer or devices in the docking station don't all support Plug and Play, you will need to use Windows' Hardware Profiles feature to set up a hardware profile called Docked that lists the devices in the docking station. You will need to select this hardware profile manually when you boot the system.

Ports in Port Replicator Don't Work

If the ports contained in a port replicator don't work, check the following possible causes:

- **Port replicator is not firmly attached to your system**—If the port replicator attaches to the proprietary bus in the computer, shut down the computer and make sure the connection is tight and locked into place. If the port replicator attaches through the PC Card slot or USB port, make sure the PC Card or USB cable is inserted tightly into the slot or port.

■ **Driver software for universal port replicator isn't loaded**—Port replicators that connect through the PC Card slot or USB port need software drivers to function. Reinstall the software drivers for the port replicator and version of Windows in use.

■ **USB port is disabled**—If the USB port has not previously been used for other devices, it might be disabled. Check the version of Windows (must be Windows 98/Me/2000) and the BIOS setup program (USB functions must be enabled) to assure that the USB port can be used. See "USB Ports," page 139, for details.

■ **PC Card support disabled**—If the PC Card port has not previously been used for other devices, the PC Card Card and Socket Services software might not be loaded. See "PC Cards (PCMCIA Cards)" later in this chapter for details. Load the software support for the PC Card slots before using any PC Card-based devices.

**CH
10**

Portable Storage

Portable storage devices use the same major internal technologies as desktop storage devices, but differ in matters such as bus connections, cost per MB, and form factor. Systems that have no internal provision for the type of drive desired can attach an external drive to any of the following:

■ PC Card slot interface

■ Parallel port interface

■ USB interface

Other drive interfaces, such as SCSI and IEEE-1394, require the portable user to install a port by means of a PC Card to use devices of these types. SCSI devices also can be connected by means of a parallel to SCSI adapter, although performance is slower than with a normal SCSI device.

Hard Drives

Both hard drive form factors and connectors are different on portable computers and on desktop computers. To save space and weight, portable computers use a 2.5-inch–wide hard drive with a single ribbon cable for both power and data. Although the technology is based on IDE, this is a different interface than standard desktop IDE hard drives use. Because of the smaller size and different connector style, portable hard drives are more expensive per gigabyte than desktop hard drives.

Normally, a special kit must be purchased to replace a failed or too-small portable hard drive. These kits come with data-transfer software and a data-transfer cable to "clone" the old hard drive's contents to the new hard drive.

Some portable computers have interchangeable drives built into a special drive bay. These drive bays are often able to accommodate the user's choice of

- Hard drive
- Standard or high-capacity removable media drive, such as ZIP or LS-120
- Optical drives, such as CD-ROM, CD-RW, or DVD-ROM
- Extra batteries

Some models with interchangeable drives allow "hot-swapping," which allows the user to exchange drives without shutting down the computer, whereas others require the user to shut down the system, change drives, and then restart the computer.

Portable computers with this capability are more expensive but are also more versatile.

Replacing a Portable Hard Drive

Portable hard drives that are not installed in interchangeable drive bays can be replaced by partly disassembling the computer. The details of the process varies from system to system, but will follow this basic procedure:

1. Turn off the system.
2. Unplug the AC adapter or power cord from the system.
3. Remove the battery pack.
4. Determine the location of the hard drive.

Follow the correct procedure, depending on the location of the drive

1. If the hard drive bay is accessible from the outside of the computer, remove the cover or screws that hold the drive in place.
2. Slide the drive out of the system.

OR

1. If the hard drive bay requires disassembly of the computer, remove the keyboard and other components to gain access to the drive.
2. Disconnect the drive from the power/data cable (a single assembly on portable computers).
3. Remove any bracket or hold-down device securing the drive in position.
4. Remove the drive from the system.

To install the new drive in place, reverse the sequence as required by the drive type.

After the new drive is installed, start the computer's setup program and make sure the drive is properly detected. Then, use either the operating system's partitioning and formatting utility (Fdisk and Format for Windows 98 or Setup for Windows 2000) or a drive or system manufacturer–provided setup program to prepare the drive for use.

Note that some manufacturers provide a data-transfer cable for use in transferring data between the old and new drives. Consult the drive's documentation to see when to perform this step.

Floppy and Removable-Media Drives

The traditional 1.44MB 3.5-inch floppy drive can be found in three forms on portable computers:

- Built-in
- Removable bay (see Figure 10.7)
- External proprietary bus

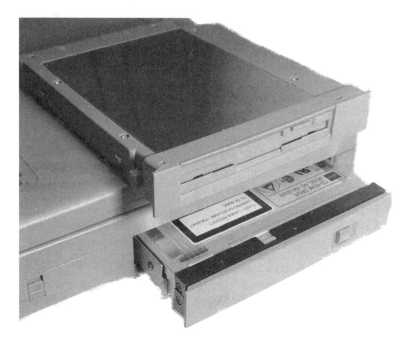

Figure 10.7
Interchangeable CD-ROM (in bay) and 3.5-inch 1.44MB floppy (on top of the computer).

Some portable computers have replaced the standard floppy disk drive with the LS-120 drive, which uses both proprietary 120MB media and standard 1.44MB media.

Optical Drives

Optical drives, such as CD-ROM, CD-RW, and DVD-ROM (see Figure 10.8), are found in three locations on portable computers:

- Built-in
- Removable bay
- Docking station

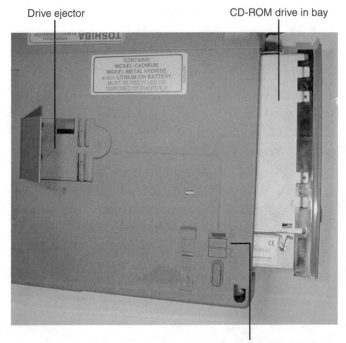

Drive ejector

CD-ROM drive in bay

Lock for interchangeable drive bay

Figure 10.8
A removable optical drive and its release mechanism (on bottom of computer); slide the lock open and flip the ejector open to release the drive. This drive interchanges with a 3.5-inch 1.44MB floppy disk drive, which can also be used in an external case.

Internal optical drives must be built specially for the portable system they're used with. Unlike hard drives, optical drives do not use a common interface that would allow them to be freely upgraded or replaced.

Flash Memory Storage

Some portable systems, primarily those in the PDA category, use flash memory instead of magnetic or optical storage for program and data storage. Some PDAs have fixed amounts of flash memory, while others use industry-standard devices, such as Compact Flash, Smart Media, or the Sony Memory Stick, to store information.

Card readers that attach to the serial, parallel, or USB ports can be used to move data between removable flash memory devices and conventional PC storage devices. Some PDA and other very compact systems use a docking station or special cable instead.

Troubleshooting Drives

Reliable storage is just as essential for portable devices as it is for desktop devices, and problems with portable device storage can differ significantly from those associated with desktop devices. This section deals with specific problems and solutions of portable storage, and is useful both for preparing for troubleshooting questions on the A+ Certification test and in your day-to-day work with portable systems.

Drives Not Recognized by the System

Drives might not be recognized by the system due to any of the following issues:

- Failure to insert drive properly into internal drive bay
- No drivers installed for drive
- Drive or computer failure

Some notebook computers have removable drives in bays that do not support hot swapping. If these drives are not recognized, shut down the system, remove and reinsert the drive, lock it into place with the system's locking mechanism, and restart the computer.

On systems with hot-swappable drives, use a similar procedure, but the power can be left on during the drive remove-and-reinsert process.

Verify that all drives installed in the system have the correct software drivers installed by using the Windows Device Manager to view the properties for listed drives. If a physically connected drive isn't listed, use the Add Hardware Wizard in Windows 98 or the Add/Remove Hardware Wizard in Windows 2000 to manually install drivers and configure the drive. If the drive is still not recognized, move the drive to an identical system to see if it can be recognized there. If a drive can be recognized by some systems but not others, the systems that cannot recognize the drive are defective and must be fixed or replaced. If the drive cannot be recognized in any system, the drive itself is defective.

Drives Installed in a Docking Bay Are Not Recognized

See "Troubleshooting Docking Bays and Port Replicators" earlier in this chapter for information on this problem.

Drive Slow to Respond After Period of Inactivity

It's normal for both hard drives and optical drives installed in portable computers to respond slowly after a period of inactivity due to power management. If power management is using settings that cause frequent delays, adjust the settings in either the BIOS (for systems with APM) or the Windows Control Panel Power icon (for systems with ACPI).

CH
10

PC Cards (PCMCIA Cards)

PC Cards (also referred to as PCMCIA cards) provide a wide range of options for portable computers with PC Card slots. Typical uses for PC Card slots include

- Memory
- Modem
- Network interface
- Removable media drive interfaces
- SCSI
- Data transfer cables for hard drive upgrades
- IEEE-1394

Most portable computers have a pair of Type II PC Card slots, as seen in Figure 10.9.

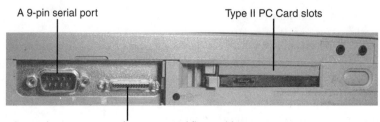

A 9-pin serial port   Type II PC Card slots

A proprietary connector for an external floppy drive

Figure 10.9
A typical notebook computer with two Type II PC Card/PCMCIA slots. The top one is empty and the bottom one contains a modem; note the dongle connector. Also visible is a 9-pin serial port and a proprietary connector for an external floppy drive.

PC Cards require special software known as *Card & Socket Services.* This software is built into Windows 95, 98, Me, and 2000. A special version must be installed for notebooks that use Windows NT 4.

Most Card & Socket Services software allows PC Cards to be hot-swapped; the card can be shut down, removed, and replaced with another without shutting down the system. Cards must be "stopped" before being removed or the system can become unstable and the cards or system can be damaged.

PCMCIA Hardware Resource Requirements

The Card & Socket Services software used for PC Card support reserves a large area of upper memory (empty space between 640KB and 1MB) for use by PCMCIA cards. I/O port address space and IRQ usage depends on the specific card(s) used.

PC Card Types

The Personal Computer Memory Card International Association gave PC Cards their original name of PCMCIA cards and is responsible for developing standards for these cards. There are three types of PC Card slots, each designed for particular types of devices:

- **Type I**—The original version of the PC Card standard. These cards are just 3.3mm thick and have one row of connectors.
- **Type II**—The most common PC Card type is 5.5mm thick and has two rows of connectors.
- **Type III**—Used primarily for PC Card-based hard drives, this type is 10.5mm thick with four rows of connectors.

Most systems with PC Card slots feature two stacked Type II slots that can handle all types of cards: a single Type III card, two Type II cards, or two Type I cards at a time.

CardBus and Zoomed Video (ZV)

Some newer portable systems use a special high-speed type of PC Card slot known as *CardBus*. CardBus slots are compatible with both ordinary (16-bit) PCMCIA cards and 32-bit CardBus cards, but CardBus cards *can't* be used in ordinary PCMCIA slots.

Another variation on standard PC Card slots is Zoomed Video (ZV) support. Portable systems that support ZV can use PCMCIA cards with a high-speed video connector for processes such as teleconferencing. As with CardBus, use ZV-compatible cards only in compatible systems.

Combo PC Cards

"Combo" PC Cards contain multiple functions on a single card. The most common combination includes a modem plus Ethernet network interfacing.

PC Card Dongles

Most PCMCIA cards aren't thick enough to use standard RJ-11 telephone (for modem), SCSI, or RJ-45 UTP network cables. Some PCMCIA cards use a pop-out connector for telephone or network cables; others require the use of a device called a *dongle*—a proprietary extension to the PCMCIA card that allows standard cables to be connected to the card. Lose or damage the dongle and your PCMCIA card is useless. Figure 10.10 shows a typical 56Kbps PC Card modem with its dongle cable.

Inserting and Removing PC Cards

Inserting PC Cards into a system is a simple process.

1. Hold the PC Card between your forefinger and thumb.
2. Turn the card so that the end with the pin connectors is facing toward the PC Card slot in the computer.

CH
IO

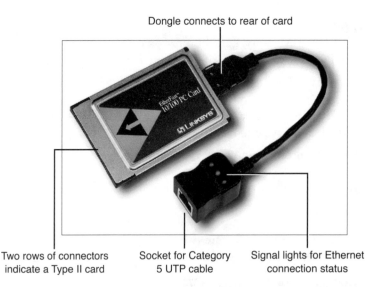

Dongle connects to rear of card

Two rows of connectors
indicate a Type II card

Socket for Category
5 UTP cable

Signal lights for Ethernet
connection status

Figure 10.10

A typical Type II PC Card 10/100 Ethernet card with the dongle used to attach the card to standard Category 5 UTP cable. Photo courtesy Linksys.

3. Make sure the top side of the PC Card is facing up; the front side normally has a decorative label listing the card model and manufacturer, as in Figure 10.10.

4. Slide the card straight into the PC Card slot in the portable computer until it interfaces with the connectors inside the slot.

5. The Windows taskbar will display a PC Card icon when the card is detected.

6. If this is the first time the PC Card was installed, insert the driver disk or CD-ROM as directed to complete the installation.

7. Attach any cables or dongles required to make the PC Card ready for use.

To remove the PC Card

1. Look for an ejector button next to the PC Card slot; you might need to rotate it 90 degrees.

2. Disconnect any cables or dongles from the card.

3. Right-click the Windows taskbar PC Card icon and select the card you want to remove from the list of cards.

4. Click Stop and wait for the system to acknowledge the card can be removed.

5. Click OK to close the message.

6. Push the ejector button in to eject the PC Card. Pull the PC Card the rest of the way out of the slot and store it in its original case or another antistatic bag.

PC Card Troubleshooting

This section is designed to prepare you for questions relating to PC Card troubleshooting on the A+ Certification exam and for the day-to-day challenges of working with PC Cards on portable systems. For troubleshooting issues related to the cards' features (modem, network, and so on), see the appropriate chapter.

Typical problems with PC Cards are caused by issues with Card & Socket Services software, improper card insertion and removal, and PC Card slot or device failure.

PC Card Not Recognized by System

If the Card & Socket Services (CSS) software is not installed on a portable system, no PC Cards will be recognized by the system. Windows 9x/Me/2000 place a PC Card icon in the Control Panel when CSS software has been installed. If the system has PC Card slots but no PC Card icon, check the system BIOS to verify that the PC Card slots are enabled, and then use the Add New Hardware or Add/Remove Hardware Wizard to install PC Card support.

If CSS has been installed but a PC Card is not recognized by the system, the card might not be inserted properly. Open the PC Card icon in the system tray to see if the card is listed as installed. If it is not listed, eject the card and reinsert it. The card should be detected. Make sure the card is properly aligned with the connectors in the slot; eject and reinsert it if the card is misaligned.

If the card is still not recognized, either the card or the slot is defective. To determine whether the card is defective, install it into another notebook computer. If the card is detected and works correctly, the original computer's PC Card slots are defective. If the card cannot be installed into any computer successfully, the card itself is defective.

PC Card Is Hot when Removed from System

PC Cards are normally warm to the touch when ejected from the system; however, a very hot card might have failed. After the card becomes cool to the touch, insert it and try using the card. If the card will not work or fails after a period of time in the system, replace the card.

Infrared Ports

Most portable computers feature an infrared (IR) port. This port usually follows the IrDA standard and can be used for the following tasks if the other device also follows the same standard:

- Networking using the Windows Direct Cable Connection program to connect to computers with compatible IR ports
- Printing to laser and other printers equipped with a compatible IR port

CH

10

Installing the Infrared Port

Windows will generally detect a built-in IR port and add it to the Device Manager. You can also install the port manually with the Add/Remove Hardware Wizard, but you will need to know the port brand and model or use the Have Disk option. In either case, have the operating system CD-ROM available to supply necessary hardware and software drivers for the port.

Infrared Port Hardware and Software Configuration

The IR port usually is considered a serial port by the system's setup program, and it will be assigned a serial port number, IRQ, and I/O port address (see "Serial Port," page 127, for details). It may be configured as COM 2, COM 3, or COM 4, depending on the system. However, Windows will assign it a simulated serial (COM) port number and a simulated parallel (LPT) port number to enable the port to be used for networking with Direct Cable Connection and for printing. The value assigned might not match the actual COM port usage in hardware. You can also select your own serial and parallel port numbers.

Printing with the Infrared Port

Printers you want to use with the IR port are configured like any other printers through the Windows Printer wizard. Simply specify the simulated parallel (LPT) port set aside for use by the IR port as the port to use for printing. Follow this procedure to print with the IR port:

1. Place your portable computer so that its IR port is aimed at the IR port on the printer.

2. Make sure the printer is turned on and is ready to receive a print job.

3. Select the printer in the printer properties sheet for your application, and start the print job.

4. The printer will receive data and print the document.

Because of the low transmission speed of IR ports, expect printing to take longer when you use the IR port than when you use parallel or USB connections.

Troubleshooting the Infrared Port

If you have problems with the IR port, check the following:

- Make sure you specify the correct simulated parallel (LPT) port when you use the IR port for printing.

- Make sure you specify the correct simulated serial (COM) port when you use the IR port for Direct Cable Connection.

- If the port stops working after you install another internal device, check for IRQ or I/O port conflicts with the Windows Device Manager.

- Remove dust, dirt, and other materials from the IR transceiver (a dark-red plastic rectangle) on the unit. If the transceiver's window is dirty, IR signals cannot be sent or received.

- Make sure you have a clear line of sight to the IR receiver on the target device.

- Don't move the portable computer around during printing or DCC connections; a broken connection could cause data loss.

Memory Upgrades

Portable systems need extra memory as much as desktop systems do, but portable memory is both far more expensive and far less versatile than memory for desktop systems.

Portable systems might have only a single proprietary connector for memory rather than the multiple standard memory slots found on desktop computers. Because of the considerations of weight, cost, heat, and bulk, many portable systems do not feature level 2 cache memory, and less level 1 cache is incorporated into the CPU. Some recent portable systems use SODIMMs (a reduced-size version of a DIMM module), but they are far from universal.

For these reasons, the best memory upgrade for a portable system is to add the largest memory module (in megabytes) that can be installed in the system. Because a future memory upgrade would require the removal of the original memory module on systems with a single memory upgrade socket, it's best to add all the memory a system can take from the beginning. Figure 10.11 shows how a typical proprietary module compares to standard SIMM modules.

CH
10

Connector for memory upgrade

Figure 10.11
Standard 30-pin and 72-pin SIMMs (left) compared to a proprietary notebook memory upgrade (right). The connector for the memory upgrade plugs into the memory module I/O connector in Figure 10.12.

Memory upgrades often can be performed without removing the keyboard, which covers most other internal components. Follow these steps to perform a typical memory upgrade:

1. Remove the cover over the memory upgrade socket on the bottom of the system.

2. Remove any screws or hold-down devices.

3. Remove the old memory upgrade if necessary.

4. Insert the new memory upgrade, making sure the contacts (on the back side or edge of the module) make a firm connection with the connector shown in Figure 10.12.

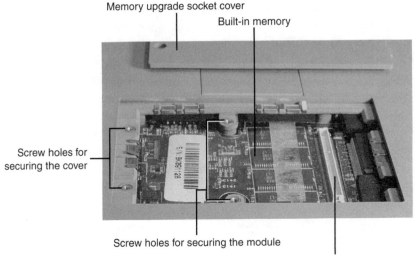

Memory upgrade socket cover

Built-in memory

Screw holes for securing the cover

Screw holes for securing the module

The memory module I/O connector

Figure 10.12
The memory upgrade socket on a typical notebook computer. Screw holes to secure the cover and the module are visible, as is the module I/O connector. The system's built-in memory is visible under a plastic protector. The cover for the socket is visible in the background.

5. Secure the memory in place with the screws removed in step 2.

6. Test the module by starting the system and observing the memory counter; use third-party diagnostics if possible.

7. Close the cover and secure it to complete the upgrade.

In addition to the standard memory troubleshooting steps listed in Chapter 4, "RAM," be sure that you have selected the correct proprietary memory module for the portable computer, and it is secured correctly.

Standard I/O Interfaces Used on Portable Computers

Most portable computers feature a wide range of standard I/O connectors that can be used in the same way as those on desktop computers:

- Serial (RS-232) ports (see Chapter 5, "Input/Output Devices and Cables")
- Parallel port (see Chapter 5)
- External VGA (see Chapter 6, "Video")
- PS/2 jack for keyboard/mouse (see Chapter 5)
- USB ports (see Chapter 5)

For details on using these options, see the chapters referenced for each port type.

CH
10

Summary

Portable systems have many different technologies from desktop systems. To share devices between portable and desktop systems, users should select devices that use the standard serial and parallel ports, or add the appropriate interface (such as SCSI) to the portable system.

Portable systems are highly proprietary and allow little if any interchange of components with other portables or with desktop systems. Thus, parts swapping is difficult to do with portable systems.

PDAs can interchange data with desktop or portable computers, but use different operating systems and use flash memory rather than magnetic or optical storage.

QUESTIONS AND ANSWERS:

1. Does PCMCIA correctly describe what these devices can be used for? What is a newer name for this technology?
   A: PCMCIA stands for "Portable Computer Memory Card International Association," but PCMCIA cards can be used for many different I/O and storage applications. PC Card is the newer name.

2. What does a portable need in order to use a docking station or port replicator?
   A: A proprietary external expansion bus is needed for the "dedicated" versions of these devices. Some port replicators can use the PCMCIA Type II slot instead.

3. Can you use the same memory in both a portable and desktop computer? Why or why not?

   A: No. Portable computers normally use proprietary memory modules, or SODIMMs, rather than the standard DIMM or SIMM modules used by desktop computers.

4. Do portables use interchangeable batteries?

   A: No, because the size and technologies have changed many times.

Safety and Recycling

1. What document tells you how to handle hazardous chemicals?
2. Name two ways to recycle toner cartridges
3. Should you throw away batteries?

Cleaning Equipment Safely

To clean equipment safely, use materials designed especially for electronics and computer use, or general-purpose cleaners proven to work well on electronics and computer equipment. Some useful cleaning materials include

- Endust for Electronics
- Glass and surface cleaners
- Isopropyl alcohol
- Specialized device cleaning kits for mice, tape backups, floppy disk drives, and inkjet and laser printers
- Compressed air
- Stabilant-22a

Use Endust for Electronics for monitor cases and glass surfaces, keyboards, LCD screens, and all types of plastic and metal cases for computers and peripherals. This product combines effective cleaning and antistatic properties, which protect your computer investment.

Glass and surface cleaners can be used on monitor glass and LCD screens and on other surfaces. They are second choices because they usually lack any antistatic properties.

With both of these products, always spray the product onto the cleaning cloth, and never on the product to be cleaned. Spraying any kind of cleaner directly onto a keyboard or monitor will damage or destroy the product.

Isopropyl alcohol can be used along with foam (not cotton!) cleaning swabs to clean tape drive heads, floppy disk drive heads, and some keyboards.

Specialized device cleaning kits, as I have recommended in other chapters, are good ways to clean the devices they are built for. Without them, I might have needed to repair or replace at least one floppy disk drive and one inkjet printer.

Compressed air is a powerful but "brainless" cleaner. Unlike liquid or cleaners mentioned previously, compressed air cannot trap dirt and dust. Instead, dirt, dust, grit, and assorted fuzz is expelled violently out of its hiding places. If you use compressed air, make sure you have plenty of old newspapers available to catch the gunk it expels from a computer or a drive.

Stabilant-22a (sold by D. W. Electrochemicals) is often recommended for use when assembling or reassembling a system for use in memory module sockets and expansion slots. It cleans the sockets and provides a more effective electrical connection.

Safely Using a Vacuum Cleaner

Because of its design and use of static-prone plastic parts, an ordinary office or home vacuum cleaner is actually a dangerous device to use around a computer. Instead, purchase a model especially suited for computer use.

Computer-compatible vacuum cleaners have features such as

- Small-sized tips and brushes perfect for cleaning out keyboards and working around motherboards and add-on cards
- Antistatic construction
- Hand-held with an adjustable neck for easy use inside a system

Use a vacuum cleaner as an alternative to compressed air whenever possible, especially when working at the client's site because it's neater—there's no flying gunk that can land in awkward places.

Recycling and Disposal Issues

Nothing lasts forever in the computer business. Whether it is a worn out real-time clock battery, an obsolete monitor, or an empty toner cartridge, there's a right way to get rid of it or to recycle it. Generally, the more "durable" a computer-related item is, the more likely it is that it should be recycled when it reaches the end of its useful life, instead of simply being discarded.

To prepare for the A+ Certification exam, you should know which items are suitable for disposal, which should be recycled, and the proper methods for handling each type of item.

Disposal of Batteries

Batteries no longer contain significant amounts of mercury, a highly toxic chemical responsible for the insanity of many real-life "Mad Hatters" in 19th-century England, but today's batteries still contain chemicals that should not go into landfills.

Depending on the type of battery that you have replaced, you might find more than one option for disposal of the old ones:

- Some stores have drop-off bins for watch and calculator batteries; the popular 3.0V lithium CR-2032 or equivalent battery used for RTC maintenance could be disposed of this way.
- Contact your local EPA for disposal instructions for Li-Ion, Ni-Cd, or Alkaline batteries found in portable computers.

How to Recycle Toner and Printer Cartridges

As you learned in Chapter 9, "Printers," many manufacturers of laser toner and even inkjet printer cartridges want you to recycle the empty cartridges; these companies provide postage-paid envelopes or mailing labels to help you return the empty product.

Otherwise, contact local rebuilders of laser toner or inkjet cartridges. Some of these companies will pay you a small fee per each empty toner cartridge.

CH
11

How to Dispose of Chemical Solvents and Cans

When you use up the contents of a cleaning product container, check the label for container-disposal instructions. Depending on the product, you might

- Be able to recycle the plastic container in household recycling; this is most often true for citrus-based and other mild cleaners.
- Be required to follow toxic material disposal procedures; check with your local EPA office for a "Tox-away Day" and store your empty containers for safe disposal at that time.

Disposing of Obsolete Monitors and Other Computer Equipment

If you send your obsolete PC, printer, or monitor to a landfill, it will have plenty of company. Millions of old units go there every year; it's legal, but it's also a waste of equipment that could teach somebody something or still be useful to someone. Here are some better ways to deal with obsolete computers and peripherals.

If possible, try to dispose of your working, cast-off computer equipment by giving it to a school or charity. These organizations might be able to wring an additional year or two of useful life out of the equipment, and are usually grateful for the opportunity.

Disposing of non-working equipment can be more difficult. In some cases, you might be able to arrange to have an electronics trade school take the equipment for classroom use. Some electronic and computer service facilities will allow you to drop off defective monitors with payment of a small disposal fee.

Use "computer" and "recycling" in a major search engine such as Northernlight.com to find options for constructive disposal of both working and non-working equipment.

How to Read an MSDS (Material Safety Data Sheet)

Many consumable products such as cleaners and printer cartridges have an MSDS, or Material Safety Data Sheet. In more and more cases today, this information is available from the manufacturer's Web site on the Internet.

The MSDS can be used to

- Determine safe storage practice
- Determine treatment if the product is accidentally swallowed or contacts the skin
- Determine safe disposal methods
- Determine how to deal with spills, fire, and other hazards

The MSDS is divided into sections 1 through 16. For example, to determine first-aid measures in case of ingestion or inhalation, you would view section 4; to view fire-fighting information, go to section 5 (see Figure 11.1).

For easy reading, many manufacturers use the Adobe Acrobat (.pdf) format; documents in this format can be read by anyone with the free Adobe Acrobat Reader program, obtainable from www.adobe.com.

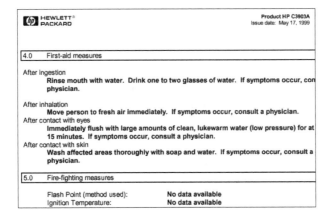

Figure 11.1
A portion of an MSDS for a typical laser printer toner cartridge, viewed with Adobe Acrobat Reader.

Electro Static Discharge (ESD)

ESD is the static-electricity discharge that happens when two differently charged objects (such as your body and a computer component) come in contact with each other. ESD is an invisible killer of memory modules, interface cards, hard disks, and other computer components, because ESD buildup and discharge happens long before you actually notice it.

You might dread shaking hands with a new acquaintance in the winter because you'll get a shock, but ESD discharges far below the 3,000-volt level that you can actually feel can still destroy chips. As little as 30 volts of ESD is enough to destroy the current generation of low-powered chips, and you can build up as much as 20,000 volts of ESD from walking across a carpeted room in the winter if you shuffle along.

ESD damage is "invisible" for another reason: It leaves in its wake equipment that has no visible damage but simply won't work reliably.

ESD damage is a major cause of intermittent failures, which are the bane of computer technicians everywhere. An intermittent failure is the classic "it wasn't working when I called you" kind of problem that "goes away" when you examine the system but recurs from time to time later.

Preventing ESD

You can prevent ESD by taking proper precautions when you do the following:

- Install or remove components
- Store and transport components
- Use computers

CH
II

One way to prevent ESD is to equalize the electric potential of your body and the components on which you're working.

Unequal electrical potential between you and the device on which you're working is the major cause of ESD. When your body has a higher electric potential than the device or component with which you're working, an ESD from your body to the device or component equalizes the potential—but at the cost of damage or destruction to the component.

Although the greatest danger of ESD occurs when you have the system open and are working with components, PC users can also cause ESD problems when working with closed-up systems. I once delivered such a big static shock to a keyboard after a coffee break that I couldn't save my document and had to power down and restart the computer to restore my keyboard to working order.

Protection Devices

You can best equalize the electrical potential of a computer or component that is being serviced by placing the computer or component on an antistatic work mat equipped with a wrist strap; attach your wrist strap to the mat. This will help place you and the component at the same level of electrical potential, and thus eliminate the "need" for ESD to occur to equalize the potential.

For additional safety, use the alligator clip on the antistatic mat to attach to the component or computer you are working on. This provides superior equalization for the mat, you, and the hardware on the mat.

Table mats connected to a grounded power supply are useful tools for preventing ESD on working computers, especially if users are reminded to touch the mat or grounded keyboard strip first. Endust for Electronics and antistatic carpet spray should be used in any carpeted office to reduce static, especially in the winter when dry heat causes buildup.

Correct Storage for Equipment

Correct equipment storage should have two goals:

- Eliminating the possibility of ESD
- Protecting equipment from impact damage

To protect equipment from ESD, store equipment in the "Faraday cage" antistatic bags originally supplied with the equipment; retain bags for installed equipment for reuse. Faraday cage antistatic bags feature a thin metallic layer on the outside of the bag, which is conductive and prevents ESD from penetrating to the components inside. Thus, metalized metallic bags should *never* be used for temporary mats for components; if you lay a component on the outside of the bag, you're laying it onto a conductive surface. Colored antistatic bubble wraps also work well for parts storage, and can also be used as a temporary mat, too. If you use bubble wrap, make sure it is antistatic (see Figure 11.2).

All work mats and wrist straps should have a 1-Megohm resistor, as shown in Figure 11.2, to stop high voltage coming through the ground line from injuring the user.

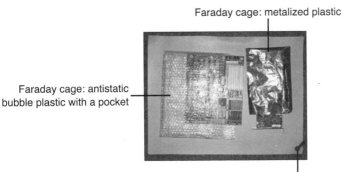

Faraday cage: metalized plastic

Faraday cage: antistatic
bubble plastic with a pocket

1-megohm resistor for protection
against high voltage

Figure 11.2
A grounded work mat, suitable for use on either a work area or under an office
computer in a high-static area, and antistatic Faraday bags.

Store components in appropriate boxes to avoid physical damage. If the original boxes
have been discarded, use cardboard boxes that have enough room for the component, the
Faraday cage bag around the component, and antistatic padding.

Hazards

Computer equipment poses several hazards for the technician:

- High-voltage sources, such as computers, and peripherals, such as printers and
  monitors
- Mechanical devices, such as printer mechanisms
- Laser-light sources, such as laser printers and optical drives

Computers and their peripherals can kill or injure you if you don't take reasonable precautions. This section discusses typical dangers of computer maintenance and the precautions you can take against these dangers.

High-Voltage Sources

The number one hazard created by computer equipment is high voltage that can be present while devices are turned on and plugged in and even when some devices are
unplugged and turned off. The major sources of potentially dangerous voltage include

- Printers
- Power supplies
- Monitors
- Systems in suspend mode

Printers also pose laser and mechanical hazards to technicians. All these risks are covered
in the following section.

Printers

Unlike computers, printers normally do not run on safe, low-voltage DC current. Although laser printers typically do use DC current, it is at a high voltage. Most dot-matrix and inkjet printers also use high-voltage AC.

Although normal operation is safe, defeating safety features that shut off the laser printer can put you at risk of a shock or a zap in the eyes from a laser beam. In addition to being potential shock sources if opened while running, dot-matrix and inkjet printers also can pinch or crush fingers in their gears and paper feeders if the cover is removed while the printer is in operation.

Any printer should be turned off and unplugged before being serviced. In the event of ink or toner spills, water should not be used to clean up the mess unless the printer is turned off and disconnected, due to the risk of a potentially fatal electric shock.

The Power Supply

The exterior of virtually every power supply is marked something like this:

> **CAUTION! Hazardous area! Severe shock hazards are present inside this case. Never remove the case under any circumstances.**

Believe it. You can see the danger if you understand what is in the "cage" at the back of the typical power supply. Past the cooling fan it contains, you'll see coils of heavy wire. These windings retain potentially lethal high-voltage levels for a long time.

Because any power supply you buy as a replacement is likely to have a higher wattage rating and can also have a quieter fan, don't go cheap and wind up dead. Heed the warnings and replace the power supply *without* opening it to find out why it is broken.

Monitors

As with the power supply, the outside of the monitor is safe. However, if you remove the cover of the monitor for servicing or adjustments, you expose the danger. The high-voltage anode (a metal prong covered with a red insulator, found on the wide top of the CRT) holds dangerously high voltage long after the power is turned off.

Disassembled monitors also pose the following hazards:

- X-rays coming from the unshielded neck of the CRT when the monitor is on
- Dropping the monitor and breaking the CRT

Replace the shielding around the neck of the CRT before using the monitor, and use padding and carefully balance CRTs and monitors during storage and transport to avoid damage.

Systems in Suspend Mode

Since the introduction of the ATX motherboards, a computer with only a case-mounted power switch might not really be off when it appears to be off. Today, many systems go into a deep suspend mode rather than a true "off" condition when shut down by

Microsoft Windows. Some ATX systems have power supplies with a separate on/off switch on the back of the unit, but most do not. For these reasons, you should disconnect the power cord from the system.

I learned about this feature of ATX systems the hard way: I reached down into a system that was supposedly "off" and received a nasty tingle from a modem.

As with other devices, the power can be on unless you disconnect it at the source.

Precautions

This section discusses the precautions you should take to avoid the hazards covered in previous sections.

To work with electricity safely, follow these simple precautions:

- Remove jewelry, including rings, bracelets, and necklaces. Metal jewelry provides an excellent path for current.

- Use rubber gloves for extra insulation—rubber gloves prevent your hands from touching metal parts; however, they do not provide sufficient insulation to allow you to work on a live system.

- Work with one hand out of the system if possible, to avoid electricity passing through your chest if your arms complete a circuit.

- Keep your hands and the rest of your body dry; your body's natural shock resistance drops to virtually nil when your skin is damp.

Disconnecting Equipment

Regardless of the level of service you will provide to a component, devices such as printers, computers, monitors, and so on should be disconnected from power as well as turned off before service. This will help prevent shock hazards as well as mechanical hazards.

Do *not* leave the computer plugged in while you work inside it. At one time, an acceptable practice was to leave the computer plugged in but shut down and to keep one hand on the power supply as a ground. This is no longer appropriate because ATX-based units aren't really "off"; they're in a suspend mode and power is still running through memory, expansion cards, and so on.

Discharging CRTs

If you must open a CRT-based monitor for service, discharge the high-voltage anode following this procedure:

1. Turn off and unplug the monitor.

2. Attach a large alligator clip and wire from a long, flat-bladed, insulated screwdriver to the metal frame surrounding the monitor.

3. Slide the flat blade of the screwdriver under the insulator until the tip touches the metal anode clip (see Figure 11.3).

CH

11

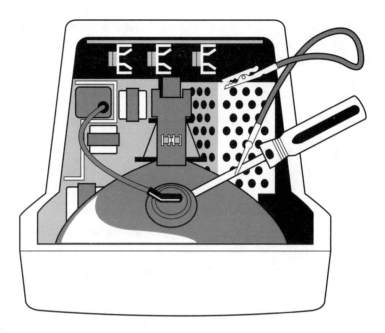

Figure 11.3
Discharging the high-voltage anode on a typical CRT. Note the ground wire clipped between the metal monitor frame and the screwdriver.

4. Be prepared for noise—anything from crackling to a loud pop—as the anode discharges its stored electricity. Keep the screwdriver in place for several seconds to fully discharge the anode.

5. Slide the screwdriver out without twisting it; you could damage the CRT.

This process must be repeated after each time the monitor is powered up until the housing is replaced.

Using a Commercial Wrist Strap

You should use a commercial wrist strap for most types of computer service, but there is one major exception: *Never* ground yourself when you are working with high-current devices, such as when you discharge a CRT. Grounding yourself to such devices could cause your body to receive a fatal high-current electrical charge.

Additional ESD Precautions

A grounded wrist strap can help prevent ESD, but you should also follow these additional precautions:

- If you must handle expansion cards and other devices with chips without suitable antistatic protection, *never touch the chips!* Most current products use a CMOS (Complimentary Metal Oxide Semiconductor) design, which has virtually no resistance to ESD; as little as 30 volts of ESD can damage CMOS-based devices.

- Hold expansion cards by the brackets, never by the motherboard connectors.
- Wear natural fibers, such as cotton and leather-soled shoes, instead of synthetics to avoid ESD buildup.
- Use an antistatic spray (commercial or antistatic fabric softener/water mixture) to treat carpeting to reduce ESD.
- Use products such as Endust for Electronics on keyboards, monitors, and computer cases to reduce static buildup. Turn off the power, and always spray the cloth, never the device!

Summary

Safely cleaning computer components requires the use of appropriate materials. Use the MSDS to determine what to do if a cleaner or computer consumable is spilled or improperly ingested.

Batteries are a major recycling issue; most batteries require special disposal methods. Similarly, obsolete computers should not be discarded, but should be disposed of by donation to nonprofit organizations or refurbishing facilities.

ESD is a major threat to computer components. The use of antistatic storage and grounding devices, such as wrist straps and mats, help prevent damage to components.

Many computer components represent potential hazards, including the high-voltage hazards caused by the interior of monitors and power supplies. Monitors can be discharged safely when disassembled, but power supplies should be replaced, never repaired.

Precautions against both ESD and hazards include using wrist straps during service, disconnecting the equipment being serviced, properly handling the components, and avoiding shock hazards through the use of one-hand repair techniques and removal of jewelry.

CH
II

QUESTIONS AND ANSWERS:

1. What document tells you how to handle hazardous chemicals?
   A: The Material Safety Data Sheet

2. Name two ways to recycle toner cartridges.
   A: Return to the manufacturer or to a local toner cartridge rebuilder

3. Should you throw away batteries?
   A: No. They contain toxic chemicals and should be disposed of through correct channels.

Preparing Hard Drives with Windows

── WHILE YOU READ ──

1. If you want to add a second hard drive to a system running Windows 9x or Me, what kind of partition should you use? Why?

2. If you are adding a hard disk to a system running Windows 2000, what program contains the disk-preparation tools you need to use?

3. If you are installing an 8GB hard disk on a Windows 2000 system that will also be dual-booting Windows 98, what file system should you use?

4. You have installed a 20GB hard disk on a system but the partitioning program reports only 7.88GB. What must be changed to allow the system to access the entire drive capacity?

5. What Format command option should be used to reuse a floppy disk in drive A: that has been stored for a long time?

Hard Disk Preparation Prerequisites

Before a hard disk can be prepared for use with Windows, the hard drive must be correctly configured by one of the following:

- The system BIOS setup program
- The hard disk host adapter's BIOS

As you learned in Chapter 7, "Storage," IDE hard disks are normally controlled by the system BIOS, whereas SCSI hard disks are controlled by a SCSI host adapter with an onboard BIOS. In either case, if the hard drive is not properly configured, the operating system preparation programs either will not function or will prepare only a portion of the hard disk.

Creating a Boot Disk Suitable for Hard-Disk Preparation

The method for preparing a boot disk suitable for hard-disk preparation on a new system varies with the operating system. Some operating system versions designed for installation on a new computer include a boot disk already designed to prepare a hard disk, but in many cases you will need to create one yourself.

Windows 9x

With Windows 9x, you can create a suitable hard-disk–preparation boot disk by creating an emergency startup disk (ESD—also called the emergency boot disk, or EBD) on a computer that already has the same release of Windows 9x installed. You will need to have one blank disk available. Windows 95 refers to this disk as the Startup disk.

Follow these steps to create the emergency startup disk:

1. Open the Control Panel and select Add/Remove Programs.
2. Select the Startup Disk tab.
3. Click Create Disk and insert a blank formatted floppy disk into drive A: as prompted.
4. Insert the Windows 9x CD-ROM if prompted; the ERD is created from operating system files that are stored on the CD-ROM (or, on some systems, in the \Windows\Options\Cabs folder).
5. Remove the disk when prompted and label it Windows 9x Emergency Startup Disk. Be sure to indicate what release of Windows was used to create the ERD—whether the disk was made with the original release of Windows 98 or with Windows 98 Second Edition (Windows 98SE).

The Windows 98 ESD contains the Fdisk and Format programs needed to prepare the hard disk, as well as CD-ROM drivers for popular IDE and SCSI hard disk drives. Therefore, when you boot a computer with the Windows 98 ERD, you can Fdisk and Format the hard disk and immediately install Windows 98 from CD.

Adding CD-ROM Drive Support to the Windows 95 Startup Disk

The Windows 95 Startup disk also contains the Fdisk and Format programs, but you must add the following files to the Startup disk if you want to use it to start the computer with CD-ROM support:

- **The MS-DOS CD-ROM device driver for your CD-ROM drive**—This was provided by the drive manufacturer on a disk (if you installed the drive in the field), or it might be on the system's hard disk. The filename will usually contain ATAPI or CD and will end in .sys.

- **Mscdex.exe from the \Windows\Command folder**—This file is used to assign your CD-ROM device a drive letter.

These files must be referred to by the Config.sys and Autoexec.bat startup files you need to create on the Windows 95 Startup disk. After you create the Startup disk and copy these files to it, follow this procedure to create the Config.sys and Autoexec.bat files:

1. Click Start, Programs, Accessories, Notepad.
2. Click New on the Notepad menu.
3. Type the following line into the text-editing window (use the actual name of your CD-ROM device driver in place of MYCDROM.SYS):

   ```
   DEVICE=MYCDROM.SYS /D:CDROM01
   ```

4. Click File, Save As.
5. Select A: drive from the Save In pull-down menu.
6. Type `config.sys` in the File Name window.
7. Click Save to save the file.
8. Click New to create a new file.
9. Type the following line into the text-editing window (add the /1:x switch and substitute the drive letter you want to specify for the CD-ROM drive for x; otherwise, the next available letter will be used):

   ```
   mscdex /d:cdrom01 /m:10
   ```

10. Click File, Save As.
11. Select A: drive from the Save In pull-down menu.
12. Type `autoexec.bat` in the File Name window.
13. Click Save to save the file.
14. Click File, Exit to leave Notepad.

Test the disk by leaving it in drive A: and clicking Start, Shut Down, Restart. The system should start from the floppy disk and display the CD-ROM drive letter.

CH
12

Windows 2000

The Windows 2000 CD-ROM contains the disk images of four startup disks that might be needed to prepare the hard disk and install Windows 2000. These disks are used only if you cannot boot from the Windows 2000 CD-ROM to start the setup process. Follow these steps to create the setup disks needed to install Windows 2000:

1. Insert the Windows 2000 CD-ROM into the CD-ROM drive on a computer running a 32-bit version of Windows (NT, 9x, 2000, or Me).

2. View the contents of the CD-ROM in the Windows Explorer, or use the Browse option on the Windows 2000 CD-ROM splash screen. Find and open the folder called Bootdisk.

3. If you are viewing the CD-ROM from a computer with Windows NT or Windows 2000, open the program file called Makebt32; if you are viewing the CD-ROM from a computer using Windows 9x or Me, open the program file called Makeboot.

4. A program window opens onscreen, prompting you to insert the first of four blank, formatted floppy disks into drive A:. Follow the prompts to create the floppy disks, labeling them Setup x (replace x with numbers 1–4) for Windows 2000.

5. Close the window and remove the last floppy disk from drive A: when you are finished.

Use Setup disk 1 to start the system if you cannot boot from the Windows 2000 CD-ROM when you want to install Windows 2000 on a new system. You'll be prompted to insert disks 2–4 and then the Windows 2000 CD-ROM to prepare the hard disk for Windows 2000 and install it.

Understanding File Systems and Partition Types

Regardless of whether you are preparing a drive for use by Windows 9x or Windows 2000, you must understand the implications of two major options you will exercise during this process:

- File system
- Partition type

This section discusses the file systems and partition types supported by Windows 98 and Windows 2000, including the guidelines for use, the benefits, and the limitations of each type.

File System Types Used by Windows 9x and Windows 2000

The choice of a file system affects the following system-configuration issues:

- Whether a single physical drive can be treated as a single logical drive or whether it must be partitioned into multiple logical drives
- How efficiently a system stores data
- How secure a system is against tampering
- Whether a system can be accessed by more than one operating system

Depending on the operating system, the choice of a file system is made either during the partitioning process, as with Windows 9x Fdisk, or during the unified partitioning/formatting process, as with Windows 2000.

Windows 95 OSR 2.x and Windows 98 can create the following file systems on a new drive:

- FAT16
- FAT32

Windows 2000 can create the following file systems on a new drive:

- FAT16
- FAT32
- NTFS 5.0

FAT16

FAT16 (also referred to as FAT) is the oldest and simplest file system used by modern versions of Windows, dating back to MS-DOS versions 3.3 and above. Windows 9x's version of FAT16 is similar to that of MS-DOS, but it permits the use of long filenames and enhanced file attributes, and storing the date a file was created, last modified, and last viewed.

The major characteristics of FAT16 include

- The 16-bit file allocation table, which allows for a maximum of 65,536 allocation units (2^{16}). An allocation unit (cluster) can be occupied by a folder (subdirectory) listing or by a portion of a file.
- A limit of 512 entries in the root directory. Because 32-bit versions of Windows, such as Windows 98, store both the actual long filename and its 8-character plus 3-character short filename (or DOS alias) as separate entries, the actual number of files and folders in the root directory cannot exceed 256 (512 divided by 2).
- A maximum logical drive size of 2048MB (2 GB); Fdisk must split larger physical drives into multiple logical volumes.
- File allocation unit sizes that range from 2,048 bytes (2KB) up to 32KB, depending on the size of the logical drive. See Table 12.1 for details.

CH
12

Table 12.1   FAT16 Drive and Allocation Unit Sizes

Drive Minimum Size	Drive Maximum Size	Allocation Unit Size (KB)	Allocation Unit Size (Bytes)
16MB*	127MB	2	2,048
128MB	255MB	4	4,096
256MB	511MB	8	8,192
512MB	1023MB	16	16,384
1024MB (1GB)	2047MB (2GB)	32**	32,768

*Drives smaller than 16MB use the FAT12 file system, which uses an 8KB allocation unit size.
**Windows NT 4.0 also supports a 64KB allocation unit size for drives up to 4095MB (4GB), but this is not supported by Windows 98 and is not recommended.

Because a file smaller than the allocation unit size still uses an entire allocation unit, you can see that a large hard disk prepared with FAT16 will waste space. For example, if you store an 8KB Word document on a hard disk with a 32KB allocation unit size, 24KB of that allocation unit is unavailable.

If you use hard disk drive sizes of 1024MB or above, the 32KB allocation unit size could cause as much as 30%–40% of your disk to be wasted.

The following are major limitations of FAT16:

- Large allocation unit sizes cause a lot of wasted disk capacity.
- Efficient allocation units (8KB or smaller) require multiple drive letters for drives more than 512MB in size.
- Preparing a hard drive more than 2,047MB in size with FAT16 requires that the drive be divided into multiple drive letters, which can interfere with network drives and CD-ROM drive letter assignments.

To overcome these limitations, FAT32 (Large Drive Support) is the default for preparing drives with the Windows 98 Fdisk program. Note that FAT16 is the only file system supported by the original version of Windows 95 and Windows 95a.

FAT32

FAT32 was introduced with late OEM versions of Windows 95 (Windows 95 OSR 2.0 and above; also referred to as Windows 95B or Windows 95C). FAT32 is also known as Large Disk Support. FAT32 has the following benefits when compared with FAT16:

- The 32-bit file allocation table, which allows for 268,435,456 entries (2^{32}) per drive. An entry can be a folder or an allocation unit used by a file.
- The root directory can be located anywhere on the drive and can have an unlimited number of entries.
- The allocation unit (cluster) size is much smaller on similarly sized drives than is possible with FAT16 (see Table 12.2). Smaller allocation unit sizes make FAT32 drives far more efficient, especially for the storage of small files. Note that FAT32

uses an 8KB allocation unit size for drives as large as 16GB; a FAT16 drive using the same 8KB allocation unit size is limited to 511MB as its maximum size.

■ The maximum logical drive size allowed is 2TB (more than 2 trillion bytes). Large drives no longer must be partitioned into multiple drive letters, although many users still prefer this option for safety.

Table 12.2   FAT16 and FAT32 Disk Usage Compared

Allocation Unit Size	FAT16 Drive Sizes	FAT32 Drive Sizes
4KB	128–255MB	260MB–8192MB (8GB)
8KB	256–511MB	8GB–16GB
16KB	512MB–1023MB	16–32GB
32KB	1024MB–2047MB	32GB–2TB

You can prepare a drive as a FAT32 drive if the following requirements are met:

■ **Enable FAT-32 support when you start Fdisk**—Windows 98's Fdisk calls this feature "large hard disk support," and when you Fdisk a drive with more than 512MB of capacity, you are offered the opportunity to use this feature.

■ **Have adequate BIOS support**—Fdisk can work with only as much of your drive as it can see. As you learned in Chapter 7, Logical Block Address (LBA) support is required for any drive more than 504MB used with Windows. To use a drive larger than 8GB, your system must also have an enhanced BIOS that supports extended Int13h functions; these functions are enabled automatically on compatible BIOSes when LBA mode is enabled.

Virtually all systems shipped with Windows 98 preinstalled will use FAT32 for their hard drives. Follow this procedure to determine what file system has been used on a hard drive in a system running Windows 98:

1. Open Windows Explorer.

2. Right-click the drive letter in the Explorer Window and select Properties.

3. The properties sheet for the drive will list FAT for a drive prepared with FAT16, and FAT32 for a drive prepared with FAT32 (see Figure 12.1).

Unless the system occasionally must be booted with MS-DOS or older versions of Windows, FAT32 is the recommended file system for use with Windows 98 because of its efficient use of disk capacity. If you must boot a Windows 98 system with older versions of Windows, or with MS-DOS, you will need to use the FAT16 file system for any drives you want to access with older versions of Windows or with MS-DOS. However, if a Windows 98 system is accessed over a network, any operating system used on the network can access the files on a FAT32 drive because Windows 98 reads the files before sending them to the other stations on the network.

CH

12

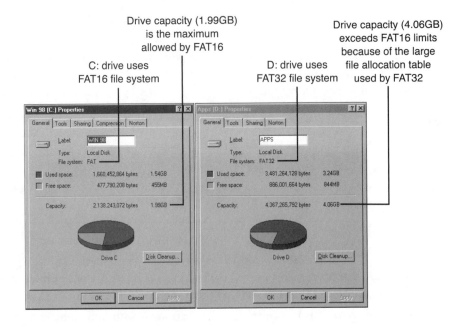

Drive capacity (1.99GB) is the maximum allowed by FAT16

Drive capacity (4.06GB) exceeds FAT16 limits because of the large file allocation table used by FAT32

C: drive uses FAT16 file system

D: drive uses FAT32 file system

Figure 12.1
Two drive partitions on a typical Windows 98 system; drive C: was prepared as a FAT16 partition; drive D: resides on a FAT32 partition.

NTFS

The New Technology File System (NTFS) is the native file system of Windows NT and Windows 2000. NTFS has the following differences from FAT16 and FAT32:

- Individual files and folders can be granted different levels of access by user or group
- Support for the compression of individual files or folders or an entire drive without the use of third-party compression programs, such as WinZip, or the use of add-on drivers, such as Windows 98's DriveSpace 3
- Filenames stored with upper- and lowercase letters intact, and treats filenames, such as letter.doc, LETTER.DOC, and Letter.doc, as three separate files
- A practical limit for drive sizes of 2TB (the same as with FAT32), although drives theoretically could reach a maximum size of 2 Exabytes (2 billion billion bytes)
- A recycle bin for each user

NTFS 5.0, the version of NTFS used by Windows 2000, supports these additional features:

- Support for the Encrypted File System (EFS). EFS allows data to be stored in an encrypted form

- Support for mounting a drive. Drive mounting enables you to address a removable-media drive's contents, for example, as if its contents are stored on your hard disk. The hard disk's drive letter is used to access data on both the hard disk and the removable media drive

- Disk quota support. The administrator of a system can enforce rules about how much disk space each user is allowed to use for storage

- Hot-swapping of removable-media drives that have been formatted with NTFS (such as Zip, Jaz, and others)

- Indexing service support, helping users locate information more quickly when Search is used

NTFS 5.0 is the version of the New Technology File System supported by Windows 2000; when a Windows NT 4.0 system using NTFS 4.0 is upgraded to Windows 2000, the NTFS 4.0 file system is upgraded to NTFS 5.0. If you plan to dual-boot Windows NT 4.0 and Windows 2000, you should make sure that Windows NT 4.0 has been upgraded to Service Pack 4 or above; older versions of Windows NT 4.0 cannot access an NTFS 5.0 partition. Windows 2000 drives can be prepared with FAT16 or FAT32 partitions, but this is recommended only if the drive will be used in a dual-boot configuration with Windows 98 or a similar operating system that does not support NTFS.

Follow these steps to determine what file system was used to prepare a Windows 2000 hard drive:

1. Open Windows Explorer.

2. Right-click the drive letter in the Explorer Window and select Properties.

3. The properties sheet for the drive will list FAT for a drive prepared with FAT16, FAT32 for a drive prepared with FAT32, and NTFS for a drive prepared with NTFS (see Figure 12.2).

HPFS

The OS/2 High Performance File System (HPFS) was supported by Windows NT 4.0 but is not supported by Windows 2000. HPFS partitions should be converted to NTFS before you upgrade a system running HPFS drives to Windows 2000.

Primary and Extended Partitions

Disk partitioning sets up disk structures called disk partitions, which are later assigned drive letters during the high-level format process. Two major types of disk partitions are supported by both Windows 9x and Windows 2000:

- **Primary**—The primary partition can contain only a single drive letter and can be made active (bootable). Although a single physical drive can hold up to four primary partitions, you need only one primary partition on a drive that contains a single operating system.

CH
I2

■ **Extended**—An extended partition differs from a primary partition in two important ways:

   ■ An extended partition doesn't become a drive letter itself but can contain one
   or more logical drives.

   ■ Neither an extended partition nor any drive it contains can be bootable.

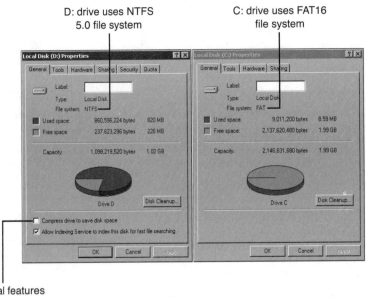

D: drive uses NTFS
5.0 file system

C: drive uses FAT16
file system

Additional features
supported by NTFS 5.0
(disk compression and
indexing service)

Figure 12.2
Two drive partitions on a typical Windows 2000 system; drive C: was prepared as a
FAT16 partition; drive D: resides on an NTFS partition.

Only one extended partition can be stored on each physical drive.

Typically, a drive will be partitioned in one of the following ways:

■ **Primary partition occupies 100% of the physical drive's capacity**—This is
typical for factory-installed drives, and is also the default for disk preparation with
Windows 98 and 2000. This is suitable for the only drive in a system or an additional drive that can be used to boot a system, but should not be used for additional drives in a system that will be used for data storage.

■ **Primary partition occupies a portion of the physical drive's capacity, and the
remainder of the drive is occupied by an extended partition**—This allows the
operating system, applications, and data to be stored on separate logical drives, but
requires the partitioning process be performed with different settings than the

defaults. This configuration is suitable for the only drive or first drive in a multiple-drive system.

■ **Extended partition occupies 100% of the physical drive's capacity**—The drive letters on the extended partition can be used to store applications or data, but not for the operating system. An extended partition cannot be made active (bootable). This configuration is suitable for any drive in a system except for the first drive; an extended partition can contain only one logical drive or multiple logical drives.

The operating system must format all drive letters created during partitioning. The format process creates the file allocation tables and root directory on the drive being formatted.

Drive Letters and Partition Types with Windows 9x

A common mistake many technicians make is to prepare a second Windows 9x hard disk the same way a first hard disk is prepared: with a primary partition and possibly one or more logical drives in an extended partition. The result is a mess if you have two or more drive letters on your original hard disk. Table 12.3 indicates how Fdisk assigns drive letters; study this for a moment and you'll understand why.

Table 12.3 Fdisk Drive Letter Assignments by Priority		
Physical Drive	*Partition Type*	*Order*
1st	Primary	1st
2nd	Primary	2nd
1st	Extended	3rd
2nd	Extended	4th

Assume that you have a single hard drive divided into C: and D: logical drives. C: is the primary partition; D: is a logical drive inside an extended partition. When you add a second hard drive to expand capacity, you want to use the next available drive letters, starting with E:. Figure 12.3 shows what happens if you place a primary partition and an extended partition (containing one logical drive) on the second hard disk.

This creates an almost unmanageable problem, because you will need to copy all the contents of the "old D:" (now E:) drive to the "new D:" drive, and so on. The chances of data loss are fairly high in such a case, and the primary partition on the second drive is virtually useless because you would need to use advanced BIOS options or a boot manager to use any drive other than C: as a bootable drive.

If you are adding a second (or third or fourth) hard drive to a system and you want its drive letters to follow the existing drive letters, prepare the new drive with an extended partition occupying 100% of the space on the drive. There's no need to use a primary partition for any drive other than the first hard drive in a system. If an additional drive is added as an extended partition, its logical drives will follow the existing drive letters, as seen in Figure 12.4.

CH

12

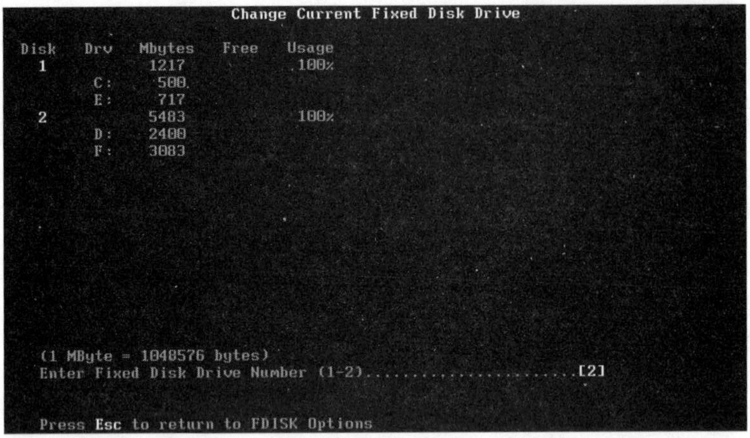

```
              Change Current Fixed Disk Drive
  Disk   Drv   Mbytes   Free    Usage
   1            1217             100%
         C:      500
         E:      717
   2            5483             100%
         D:     2400
         F:     3083




  (1 MByte = 1048576 bytes)
  Enter Fixed Disk Drive Number (1-2)......................[2]

  Press Esc to return to FDISK Options
```

Figure 12.3
Because primary partitions come before drive letters in extended partitions, the second
hard drive has "taken over" D: drive, forcing the old D: drive to E:.

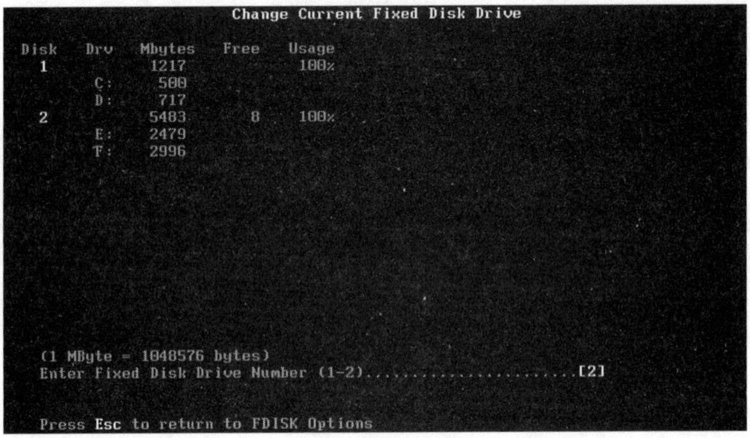

```
              Change Current Fixed Disk Drive
  Disk   Drv   Mbytes   Free    Usage
   1            1217             100%
         C:      500
         D:      717
   2            5483      8      100%
         E:     2479
         F:     2996




  (1 MByte = 1048576 bytes)
  Enter Fixed Disk Drive Number (1-2)......................[2]

  Press Esc to return to FDISK Options
```

Figure 12.4
All drive letters are in sequence if the second hard drive is prepared as a 100%
extended partition.

Comparing Windows 9x's Fdisk and Format

Windows 9x uses Fdisk and Format to prepare a hard disk in very much the same way
that the old MS-DOS versions of Fdisk and Format were used—all hard drives must have
disk partitions created by Fdisk and formatted by Format before the drive can be used.
Floppy disks usually are factory-formatted, but they can be reformatted with Format.
Fdisk is not used with floppy disks. Table 12.4 summarizes the differences between these
disk utilities, which are discussed in detail later in this chapter.

Table 12.4   Windows 9x Fdisk and Format Compared

Comparison Factors	Fdisk	Format
Order of use	First	Second
Destroys existing data	Yes	Yes*
Old data can be recovered after use	No	Yes*
Works on hard disk drives	Yes	Yes
Works on floppy disks	No	Yes
Menu-driven	Yes	No
Command-line driven	No	Yes
Works within Windows Explorer	No	Yes
Reboot required after use	Yes	No
Must work with single drive letter per use	No	Yes
Can create multiple drive letters per use	Yes	No

*The Safe Format option for floppy disks can be used to erase files on the disk. A third-party utility, such as Norton Utilities or Norton System Works, is required to unformat a drive prepared with Safe Format. This is not possible if the disk has been formatted with the Full or Unconditional option.

What Fdisk.exe Does

Fdisk is the hard-disk preparation utility that must be run before any hard disk receives its high-level format. Before a hard drive can be used with Fdisk, it must be made ready to accept data by having magnetic markings called sectors placed on the drive; these sectors are designed to hold 512 bytes of data and are arranged in concentric circles called tracks (see "Hard Drives," page 203, for more information). The process of placing sector and track information on a hard drive is referred to as *low-level formatting*. With IDE drives, this process takes place at the factory, so an IDE drive is ready for Fdisk as soon as it is installed and identified in the system BIOS. SCSI hard drives must be prepared by the BIOS on the SCSI host adapter before Fdisk can be used.

Fdisk is used to perform the following tasks during a new hard-disk installation:

- Set all or selected portions of a hard disk for use by the operating system by creating a "partition table."
- Create one or both types of partitions: primary (can be bootable) or extended (can be one or more nonbootable drive letters).
- Select which file system (FAT16 or FAT32) will be used by all or a portion of the drive.

Fdisk can also be used to

- Remove existing partitions or logical drive letters, which destroys any data on the drive.
- Verify system BIOS is set correctly to allow full capacity of the drive to be used.
- Make a primary partition active (bootable).

CH
12

What Format.com Does

Format works in very different ways, depending on whether it is used on a hard or floppy disk. When Format is used on a hard drive, it creates a master boot record, two file allocation tables, and a root directory (also referred to as the root folder). The rest of the drive is checked for disk surface errors—any defective areas are marked as bad to prevent their use by the operating system. Format appears to "destroy" the previous contents of a hard disk, but if you use Format on a hard disk by mistake, Norton Utilities and some other programs can be used to unformat the drive and allow you to recover most, or even all, your information because most of the disk surface is not changed by Format.

If a floppy disk is prepared with Format and the unconditional /U option is used from the command line, or the Windows Explorer Full Format option is used, sector markings (a sector equals 512 bytes) are created across the surface of the floppy disk before other disk structures are created, destroying any previous data on the disk. If the default Quick Format or Safe Format option is used, the contents of the disk are marked for deletion but can be retrieved with Norton Utilities or Norton System works. For more information about using Format with hard drives, see Table 12.5. For more information about using Format with floppy disks, see Table 12.6.

A floppy disk can be only a single drive letter, but a hard disk can be subdivided into one or more drive letters. Every drive letter created by Fdisk must be formatted.

The hard disk format process performed by the Format command is sometimes referred to as a *high-level format* to distinguish it from the low-level format used by hard drive manufacturers to set up magnetic structures on the hard drive. When floppy disks are formatted with the Full or Unconditional options, Format performs both a low-level and high-level format on the floppy disk surface.

Preparing a Hard Disk for Use with Windows 9x

The Windows 9x hard-disk preparation process varies according to whether you are

- Preparing a new hard disk for use with Windows 9x
- Adding a new hard disk to a system already running Windows 9x

Also, the process varies when partitioning according to whether you are

- Using the entire drive as a bootable (primary) partition
- Using a portion of the drive as a primary partition and the remainder of the drive as an extended partition containing logical drives
- Using the entire drive as an extended partition containing logical drives

Partitioning the Drive with Fdisk

Fdisk, the disk partitioning program supplied with Windows 98, cannot be run from Windows Explorer or from a command-prompt window if you need to create or delete partitions. You can open a command-prompt window to use Fdisk to view partitions.

Fdisk can be used with its default selections or by changing the default selections to suit the needs of the user. You can make default selections in Fdisk by pressing Enter at each screen. The default selections result in

- A single hard disk letter occupying the entire usable space of the hard disk. The amount of disk space available varies according to the size of the drive and whether large disk support (FAT32) was enabled when Fdisk was started.
- An active partition (bootable when formatted with the /S option).
- Automatic restart of the system.

The user selections allow the user to

- Divide a single physical hard disk into two or more logical drives by creating a primary and extended partition or an extended partition.
- Balance logical drive size and storage efficiency by creating logical drives that are sized to use the largest amount of space relative to the desired allocation unit size (refer to Table 12.2).
- Leave room for non-DOS operating systems to be added later.

Follow this procedure to start the partitioning process with Fdisk:

1. Start your system with your Windows 9x Emergency Boot Disk.
2. Start Fdisk from the command prompt; type Fdisk and press Enter.
3. Press Enter to accept the default (Yes) when prompted to enable Large Disk support if you want to create FAT32 partitions (see Figure 12.5). If you answer N(o), any partitions you create will be FAT16 and will be limited to a maximum size of 2047MB.

CH
12

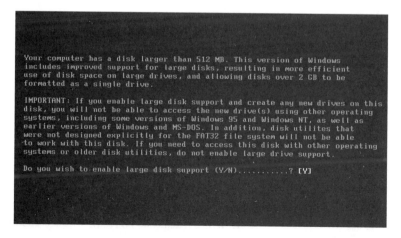

Figure 12.5
The FAT32 enable/disable screen is displayed when you run the Windows 9x Fdisk program with a "large" hard disk (512MB or larger). Note the information about compatibility limitations.

If you have one physical hard disk installed, the main Fdisk window resembles Figure 12.6.

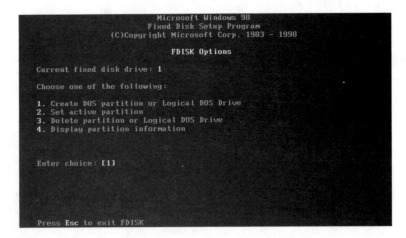

```
              Microsoft Windows 98
             Fixed Disk Setup Program
         (C)Copyright Microsoft Corp. 1983 - 1998

                   FDISK Options

Current fixed disk drive: 1

Choose one of the following:

1. Create DOS partition or Logical DOS Drive
2. Set active partition
3. Delete partition or Logical DOS Drive
4. Display partition information



Enter choice: [1]




Press Esc to exit FDISK
```

Figure 12.6
The Windows 9x Fdisk main menu screen for single-drive systems.

When two or more physical disks are installed, Fdisk lists a #5 option: Change Current Fixed Disk Drive.

There are three major ways to run Fdisk:

- Set up a physical hard drive as a 100% primary partition; the drive will be used as a single drive letter.
- Set up a physical hard drive with a primary and extended partition; the drive will contain two or more drive letters and can be bootable.
- Set up a physical hard drive as a 100% extended partition; the drive will contain two or more drive letters but will not be bootable.

Each of these Fdisk options is outlined in this section.

Creating a Single, Bootable Drive Letter with Fdisk
To use Fdisk to set up the only hard drive on a system as a single drive letter that's bootable, follow this procedure, which uses the Fdisk defaults:

1. Choose Enable Large Disk Support when prompted to make the entire physical drive available as a single drive letter.
2. Select #1, Create DOS Partition or Logical DOS Drive from the main menu.
3. From the Create DOS Partition or Logical DOS Drive menu, press Enter to select #1, Create a Primary DOS partition.

4. Press Enter again to select the entire usable capacity of the drive as a single primary partition and make it active.

5. After you press Enter again to accept these changes, you're prompted to shut down the system and reboot it.

This creates a single primary partition on the hard disk that must be formatted by the Format program using the system option before it can be used to boot the system.

Creating Primary and Extended Partitions with Fdisk

To use Fdisk to set up the only hard drive on a system as two or more drive letters with a bootable partition, follow this procedure:

1. Choose Enable Large Disk Support when prompted to allow partitions larger than 2GB in size. If you answer No to this question, following these instructions will prepare only the first 2GB of disk space on the drive.

2. Select #1, Create DOS Partition or Logical DOS Drive from the main menu.

3. From the Create DOS Partition or Logical DOS Drive menu, press Enter to select #1, Create a Primary DOS Partition.

4. Type N (no) when asked if you want to use the entire capacity of the drive.

5. Enter the amount of space you want to use for the primary partition in either MB or percentages (for example, to use 2GB, enter 2048; to use 50% of the drive, enter 50%) and press Enter (see Figure 12.7).

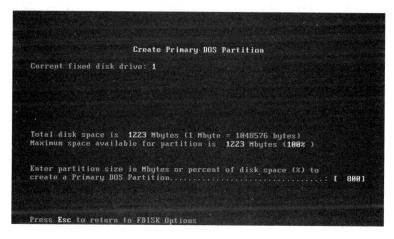

CH

12

Figure 12.7
The primary partition on this 1.2GB drive is being set as 800MB by Fdisk.

6. Press Esc to return to the main Fdisk menu.

7. Because you created a primary partition using only a portion of the disk space, a warning appears to remind you that the primary partition is not yet active; it must be marked active to be bootable.

8. To mark the primary partition as active, type 2 (Set Active Partition) and press Enter to display the Set Active Partition menu.

9. Type the number of the partition you want to make active (normally 1), and press Enter. The status line will display an A for active partition, as in Figure 12.8. Press Esc to return to the main Fdisk menu.

10. To prepare the rest of the drive for use by Windows 9x, select #1, Create DOS Partition or Logical DOS Drive.

11. From the Create DOS Partition menu, select #2, Create an Extended Partition.

12. Press Enter to accept the default (the remaining capacity of the drive); the logical drives will be stored in the extended partition.

13. Create one more or logical drives when prompted, specifying the size you want for each letter. The drive letter for each logical drive is listed; note the letters because you will need to format each logical drive after you finish using Fdisk and reboot.

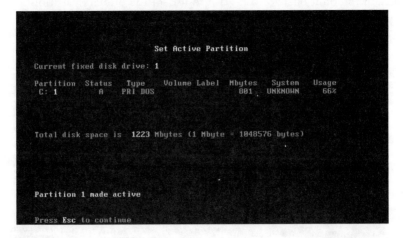

Figure 12.8
The 800MB primary partition after Fdisk sets it as Active. To be bootable, this partition must also be formatted with the /s (system) option.

14. When the entire capacity of the drive is used, the Fdisk display will resemble Figure 12.9. Press Y to view the logical drives stored in the extended partition.

15. After you press Enter again to accept these changes, you're prompted to shut down the system and reboot it.

The Volume Label remains blank until
the drive is formatted; both Format
and Label can apply a volume label, or the user
can choose not to use a volume label

The system is listed as
unknown on an
unformatted drive

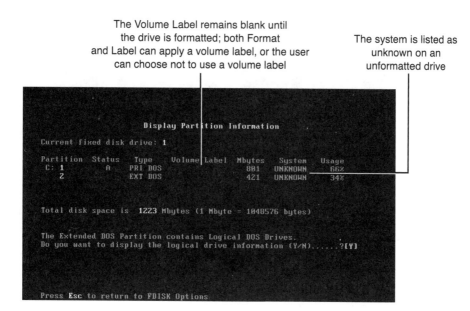

```
                    Display Partition Information
Current fixed disk drive: 1

Partition Status    Type    Volume Label   Mbytes   System   Usage
  C: 1        A     PRI DOS                  801    UNKNOWN    66%
     2              EXT DOS                  421    UNKNOWN    34%


Total disk space is  1223 Mbytes (1 Mbyte = 1048576 bytes)


The Extended DOS Partition contains Logical DOS Drives.
Do you want to display the logical drive information (Y/N)......?[Y]



Press Esc to return to FDISK Options
```

Figure 12.9
This drive contains both a primary and an extended partition; logical drives in the
extended partition make this entire drive available to Windows 9x.

Creating an Extended Partition with Fdisk

Follow these steps to install a fixed disk with an extended partition as an addition to a
system with one or more existing drives:

1. Select #5 from the main menu.

2. Select the drive you want to change from the drives listed. For this example, disk
   #2 would be selected, as in Figure 12.10.

3. From the main Fdisk menu, select #1, Create DOS Partition or Logical DOS
   Drive.

4. From the Create DOS Partition menu, select #2, Create an Extended Partition.

5. Press Enter to accept the default (the entire capacity of the drive); the logical drives
   will be stored in the extended partition.

6. Create one or more logical drives when prompted, specifying the size you want for
   each letter. Note the drive letters are listed that you will need to format later.

7. When the entire capacity of the drive is used, you will see a message similar to
   Figure 12.11.

8. Exit Fdisk and restart the computer.

Existing disk partitions on Disk #1

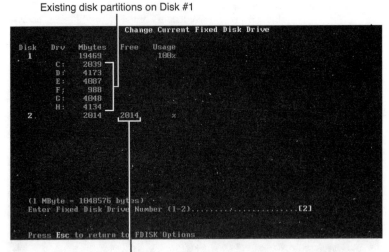

Free space (no disk partitions) on disk #2

Figure 12.10
Hard disk #2 (a 2014MB drive) has no disk partitions. Type 2 and press Enter to select it and continue.

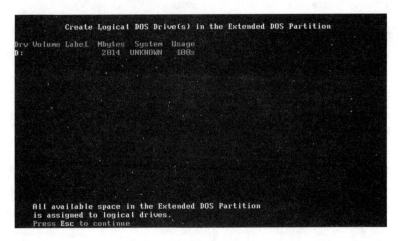

Figure 12.11
Hard disk #2 now has a single logical drive occupying 100% of its extended partition.

The examples in this section describe the use of Fdisk to prepare an entire drive for use by Windows 9x; however, you also can prepare only a portion of a drive with Fdisk. If you prepare only a portion of the drive, the rest of the drive can be prepared by Windows 2000 or another operating system in the future.

All drives created with Fdisk (whether in the primary or extended partition) must be prepared with Format. You can run Format from the command prompt or by opening the Windows Explorer, right-clicking the drive, and selecting Format.

After you reboot, you can use Fdisk's option 4 to see how the drive's partitions have changed. The display will resemble Figure 12.9, earlier in this chapter.

Windows 9x Format

The Format program is the last step required to make a hard drive or floppy disk ready for use with Windows 9x. Format uses different options depending on whether it's being used with a hard drive or floppy disk.

Using Format with Hard Drives

Each drive letter you create with Fdisk must be formatted; Fdisk is used first, followed by Format. The Windows 98 Format program offers two different options when used on hard drives. See Table 12.5 for details.

Table 12.5	Format Options for Hard Drives		
Format Command	Meaning	Used for...	Example
Format x:/s	Formats x: drive with system (boot) files	Any bootable drive (normally C:)	Format C:/s
Format x:	Formats x: without system files	Any non-bootable drive (D: or higher)	Format D:

To format the hard disk, follow these steps:

1. Start the format process with the correct command from Table 12.5. The system displays a warning of possible data loss and allows you to stop if you are about to format the wrong hard disk (see Figure 12.12).

   If you continue, a progress indicator is displayed. If your hard disk has any surface damage, a message `Trying to recover allocation unit number xxxxx` will appear as the system marks the damaged area as a "do not use" area.

2. At the end of the format process, you can add a volume label (up to 11 characters) and you'll see the disk statistics listed, including the drive's total size and the allocation unit size and number available.

Using Format with Floppy Drives

Format can also be used to prepare or recondition floppy disks for use. Although most floppy disks today are preformatted at the factory, Format is still useful as a means to

CH

12

- Erase the contents of a floppy disk quickly, especially if it contains many files or folders.
- Place new sector markings across the disk.
- Create a bootable disk more reliably than by using the Sys command with a preformatted disk.

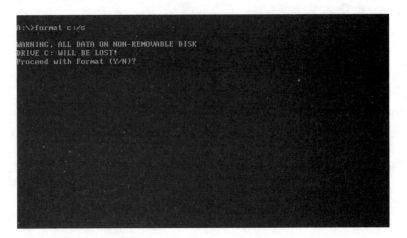

Figure 12.12
The warning message Format displays is the same regardless of whether you are reformatting a drive with contents or an empty drive that's just been Fdisked.

Table 12.6 covers the different Format options that apply to floppy disks.

Table 12.6 Format Options for Floppy Drives

Format Command	Meaning	Used for...	Example
Format x:/s	Formats x: drive with system (boot) files	Makes a bootable floppy disk; assumes floppy disk is same capacity as the drive	Format A:/s
Format x:	Formats x: without system files	Erases the contents of a floppy disk; used for a data floppy disk	Format A:

Table 12.6   continued

Format Command	Meaning	Used for...	Example
Format x:/u	Unconditionally formats the floppy disk; wipes out all previous data	Rewrites the sector markings on an old floppy disk which might have developed weak areas; /u can be added to any other option	Format A:/s/u
Format x:/v	Allows user to add a volume label to the drive	Label can describe floppy disk's contents or be arbitrary text; can be added to any Format command	Format A:/s/v
Format x: /f:720	Formats a 720KB (DSDD) 3.5-inch disk in a 1.44MB (DSHD) drive	Forces the drive to handle the 720KB floppy disk correctly; some IBM drives without media sensors will format 720KB media as 1.44MB media, but with poor reliability	Format A:/f:720
Format x: /f:360	Formats a 360KB (DSDD) 5.25-inch floppy disk in a 1.2MB (DSHD) drive	Allows 1.2MB hard drives to create a floppy disk usable on a 360KB XT-style floppy disk drive; works well for new floppy disks, but might not reliably overwrite tracks made by a 360KB drive	Format B:/f:360

Format x: *and* Format x:/s *allow any existing data on the disk to be unerased with a program such as Norton Unformat.*

Format x:/f:360 *and* Format x:/f:720 *are needed only when formatting disks that are not the default size of the drive, which is seldom.*

CH

12

To prepare for the A+ Certification exam, you will find it useful to take a few blank floppy disks and practice the appropriate commands listed in Table 12.6 to help you memorize the command-line switches used.

Using Format in Windows 9x Explorer

Windows 9x Explorer can be used to format both hard drives and floppy disks. Right-click the drive you want to format, select Format, and the Format options are displayed, as in Figure 12.13. Whether you are formatting a hard drive or a floppy disk, the same options are available—the only difference is that you can also choose the capacity of the floppy disk from the Capacity menu.

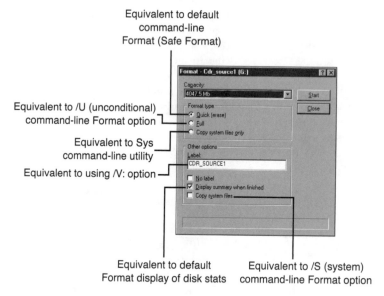

Figure 12.13
The Windows 9x Explorer Format menu allows the user to select the same options that can be used with the command-line Format program, as well as providing an alternative to the Sys command.

Preparing a Hard Disk for Use with Windows 2000

Unlike Windows 9x, Windows 2000 does not use the Fdisk and Format programs to prepare hard drives for use. Instead, Windows 2000 uses the following programs:

- The Windows 2000 setup program can partition and format unpartitioned drives or unpartitioned portions of drives encountered during the installation process.
- The Disk Management portion of the Microsoft Management Console (MMC) is used to prepare hard disks added to an operational Windows 2000 system.

Using the Windows 2000 Setup Program to Prepare a Hard Drive

To prepare an empty hard drive for use with the Windows 2000 Setup program, follow this procedure:

1. If the system can be booted from a CD-ROM drive, insert the Windows 2000 CD-ROM into the CD-ROM drive and start the system; the installation program starts automatically.

   If the system does not support booting from a CD-ROM drive, insert the Windows 2000 CD-ROM into the CD-ROM drive and insert the first of the four Windows 2000 setup disks you created on another system (see "Creating a Boot Disk Suitable for Hard-Disk Preparation" earlier in this chapter for details).

   Change disks as prompted until the Windows 2000 Setup program starts.

2. Press Enter when prompted to start the Windows 2000 installation process.

3. Press F8 to accept the end user license agreement.

4. Select the unpartitioned space on the empty hard drive for the installation. Press C to continue.

5. Specify the partition size. You can press Enter to accept the default (the entire capacity of the drive), or type a smaller size and press Enter.

6. Select the partition into which to install Windows 2000—specify the partition you created in step 4.

7. Select NTFS or FAT for the partition, and press Enter.

8. Windows 2000 formats the partition with the file system you specify and continues the installation process. See Chapter 13, "Operating System Installation and Upgrades," for details.

Using MMC's Disk Management to Prepare a Hard Drive

After Windows 2000 is installed on a system, additional hard disks you install are prepared with the Disk Management portion of the Microsoft Management Console. Disk Management is an extension of the Computer Management subset of tools and is a visual, mouse-driven environment.

To prepare a hard disk with Disk Management

1. Right-click My Computer and select Manage to open Computer Management. Disk Management will be expanded under Storage.

2. Click Disk Management. Your current drives appear in the right window, color-coded for easier identification (see Figure 12.14):

   - ▪ **Dark blue**—Primary partition
   - ▪ **Light blue**—Logical drive
   - ▪ **Dark green**—Extended partition

CH
12

- **Light green**—Free space
- **Black**—Unpartitioned space

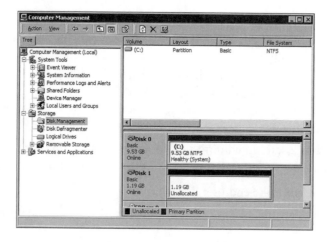

Figure 12.14
This system has one drive prepared as a primary partition and one drive that has no partition.

3. Right-click the new drive and select Create Logical Drive to continue.
4. The Create Partition Wizard starts. Click Next to continue.
5. Select Primary Partition or Extended Partition—Select Primary Partition if you want to make the partition bootable, or select Extended Partition if you are installing the drive for program or data storage (see Figure 12.15). Click Next.

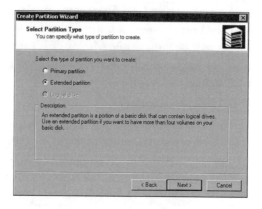

Figure 12.15
Logical Drive is not available as a choice until you have created an extended partition.

If you select Extended Partition

1. Specify the amount of space (the default is all available space)—Do not select the amount of space for a logical drive because that must be done after the extended partition is created. Click Next.

2. Click Finish to close the wizard; your drive is now marked as Free Space.

To create logical drives

1. Right-click Free Space and select Create Logical Drives to restart the Create Partition Wizard.

2. The logical drive option is already selected. Click Next to continue.

3. Click Next to accept the full capacity of the partition as a logical drive, or enter the size you want the drive to be. Click Next.

4. On the next screen, choose from specifying a drive letter (next available or higher), mounting the drive as a folder on an existing drive, or not assigning the drive a letter or folder. Make your selection (see Figure 12.16) and click Next.

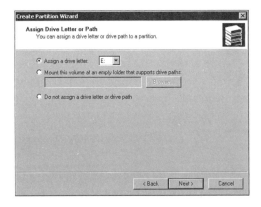

Figure 12.16
Unlike Windows 9x, which cannot map hard drive letters around an existing CD-ROM drive letter, Windows 2000 enables you to leave the CD-ROM drive at its existing letter (D: on this computer) and choose the next available drive letter (E: or higher) for the new hard disk.

5. Specify the file system (NTFS, FAT, or FAT32), the allocation unit size, and whether you want to use options such as Quick format (doesn't verify the media) or compression. You also can elect to skip formatting the drive (see Figure 12.17). Click Next to continue.

6. On the final screen, scroll through the listed settings and verify they're correct. You can use the Back button to return and make changes, or click Finish to set up and format the drives as listed (see Figure 12.18).

CH
12

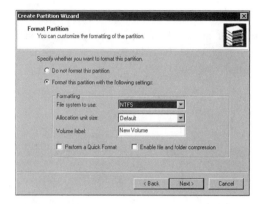

Figure 12.17
This drive will be prepared as an NTFS drive.

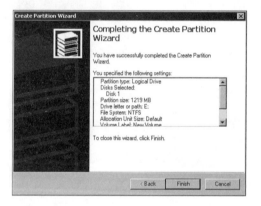

Figure 12.18
Review the complete configuration details for the drive, and use the Back button to make any changes you need.

Troubleshooting Drive-Preparation Problems

Hard drive preparation is one of the major upgrade tasks of a computer technician. Review this section to prepare yourself for troubleshooting questions on the A+ Certification exams and to improve your skill in day-to-day troubleshooting.

Troubleshooting Drive-Preparation Problems with Fdisk

Fdisk can be used to troubleshoot BIOS configuration and compatibility options with IDE drives. Because some of these options work only on a drive that's already been Fdisked, if you are concerned about BIOS issues, use the Fdisk defaults to prepare the drive; you can always delete the primary partition and start over again if you have problems. See Figure 12.19; this section shows you how to compare the Fdisk values marked

A and B with each other and with the rated capacity of a hard drive to find configuration problems with your system.

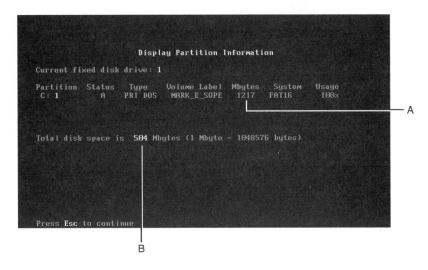

Figure 12.19
If the values listed for (A) and (B) don't match each other, as in this example, or don't match the drive capacity, you have a problem with BIOS configuration.

You can use Fdisk to determine problems with either the LBA configuration of the system BIOS or with support for enhanced Int13h functions.

LBA Mode Troubleshooting
If the value for A on your system lists the full capacity of the drive (greater than 504MB), but the value for B lists the drive capacity as only 504MB, the drive was prepared with LBA mode enabled in the BIOS but LBA has been disabled since the drive was prepared. The drive cannot be used at full capacity until LBA mode is enabled, and it will not be bootable if it is the primary or sole drive on the system.

If both A and B indicate the drive is only 504MB, but the actual capacity of the drive is larger, LBA must be enabled in the system BIOS before the drive is prepared.

To restore proper operation in either case, restart the computer, activate the system BIOS setup program, and enable LBA mode. Save the setup changes and restart the computer. Both A and B should display correct values for the drive. For more information about LBA mode, see "Overcoming Hard Disk Capacity Limitations with LBA Mode," p. 211.

Enhanced Int13h Troubleshooting
If A and B both indicate your hard drive's capacity is 8,064MB (7.88GB) but the drive has a larger rated capacity, this indicates the system BIOS supports LBA mode, but not

CH
12

the enhanced Int13h functions needed to support drives beyond 7.88GB. Choose one of the following options for a solution, in order of desirability, best to worst:

- System BIOS upgrade if the upgrade supports Enhanced Int13h
- Add-on IDE host adapter card with its own BIOS that supports Enhanced Int13h
- Hard disk BIOS replacement software that supports Enhanced Int13h (supplied by the drive maker)

Troubleshooting Hard Disks That Can't Boot After Format

If you can't boot from drive C: after format, check the following:

- Did you use Format C:/s?

  The /s, as you saw previously, transfers the system files used to boot the system. Use C:\>DIR /AH to see whether the system files listed previously are present on the drive. If not, reboot with a floppy disk and run A:\>SYS to transfer boot files to the hard disk. Reboot the system without the floppy disk and see whether it starts.

- Did you make the primary partition (C: drive) active with Fdisk?

  If you used Fdisk to create two or more drive letters, you must make the primary partition active. Boot from a floppy disk and rerun Fdisk; select option 2 and make the primary partition active.

- Hard Disk not listed in boot options in BIOS.

  Some BIOSes allow you to skip the hard disk as a bootable drive; make sure the hard disk is listed as a bootable device.

- Floppy disk in drive A: prevents booting system if it is listed before the hard disk in the boot order.

  A floppy disk that is not formatted with the /S option cannot be used to start a system. Remove the floppy disk and restart the computer to allow Windows to start normally with full features.

- LBA mode disabled after using it to prepare the hard drive.

  Any drive using Windows 9x can't boot if LBA mode has been disabled after it was originally used to prepare the drive. This is because LBA mode changes the logical layout of the drive, and thus the location of the boot files.

Using setup defaults or BIOS defaults with some AMI BIOS versions will disable LBA mode; restart your system and re-enable LBA mode in the BIOS setup program.

Repairing the Master Boot Record

Boot sector viruses and magnetic errors can corrupt the master boot record (MBR), which is used by the BIOS's bootstrap program to locate a bootable drive. A damaged

MBR will prevent your system from starting from a bootable hard disk. To repair a damaged or corrupted MBR, you can use one of the following options:

- Windows 9x users can use an undocumented Fdisk switch called Fdisk/mbr.
- Windows 2000 users can use the Recovery Console command Fixmbr.

Because damaged MBRs can be caused by a computer virus, systems should be tested with an up-to-date antivirus program before either of these commands is used. If a boot-sector virus is located by an antivirus program, the program's own disk-repair options should be used first.

If this is unsuccessful, you can use the appropriate repair tool to attempt to fix the MBR. Fdisk/mbr or Fixmbr should not be used if a third-party disk utility, such as DiscWizard, Disk Manager, EZ-Drive or other programs packaged with hard drives, was used to partition the drive; some of these programs create a non-standard MBR that cannot be restored by Windows' own MBR repair programs.

To run Fdisk/MBR, boot from the Windows 9x EBD and type `Fdisk/mbr` at the command prompt; press Enter.

To run Fixmbr, start the Windows 2000 Setup process, select Repair, Recovery Console, and type `Fixmbr` at the Recovery Console prompt. Press Enter.

Summary

A hard drive isn't ready for use until its surface has been partitioned and formatted. Windows 9x uses separate Fdisk and Format programs to perform these tasks, but Windows 2000 uses its Setup program (on new installations) or the Disk Management portion of the MMC to perform both tasks at the same time.

FAT32 is the recommended file system for use with Windows 9x, unless the drives will be accessed by MS-DOS or older versions of Windows, which support only FAT16. NTFS 5.0 is the recommended file system for use with Windows 2000. A Windows 9x/Windows 2000 dual-boot system must use FAT32 or FAT16 because Windows 9x can't use any version of NTFS.

Primary partitions are intended for use in starting a system, and extended partitions contain one or more logical drives that cannot be used to boot the system, although they can hold programs and data. The default operation of Fdisk in Windows 9x creates primary partitions only; the Fdisk menu must be used to create extended partitions.

The Format program uses different command-line options for use with floppy disks and hard drives, but it uses the same menu in the Windows Explorer for both types of drives.

For maximum utility and data safety, consider creating at least two partitions on your hard drives; one for programs and operating system; one for data.

CH
12

QUESTIONS AND ANSWERS:

1. If you want to add a second hard drive to a system running Windows 9x or Me, what kind of partition should you use? Why?

A: The entire second drive should be configured as an extended partition because its logical drive letters will follow the existing drive letters.

2. If you are adding a hard disk to a system running Windows 2000, what program contains the disk-preparation tools you need to use?

A: The Microsoft Management Console (MMC)'s Disk Management utility is used to prepare a hard drive.

3. If you are installing an 8GB hard disk on a Windows 2000 system that will also be dual-booting Windows 98, what file system should you use?

A: Use FAT32 because it is recognized by both Windows 98 and Windows 2000.

4. You have installed a 20GB hard disk on a system but the partitioning program reports only 7.88GB. What must be changed to allow the system to access the entire drive capacity?

A: The system BIOS must be upgraded, or a new IDE host adapter card with enhanced Int13h support must be installed. The current system BIOS supports LBA mode but not enhanced Int13h, which is needed to use larger drives.

5. What Format command option should be used to reuse a floppy disk in drive A: that has been stored for a long time?

A: `Format A:/u`**. The** `/u` **option rewrites the entire disk structure, repairing or marking bad sectors and making any previous disk contents very difficult to recover. The magnetic signals on floppy disks tend to deteriorate over time, making the Safe Format default unsatisfactory because Safe Format doesn't fix magnetic signal problems on the media surface.**

Operating System Installation and Upgrades

1. Under what circumstances can you not dual-boot to MS-DOS after installing Windows 98?

2. What must you provide to "prove" you can use the Windows 98 Upgrade?

3. How can you determine whether your system is compatible with Windows 2000 if you don't have a working Internet connection?

4. Why does Windows 98 disable some MS-DOS 6.x utilities when you install Windows 98 in a dual-boot configuration?

5. Can you convert a FAT drive to another type of file system during a Windows 2000 upgrade? What other type of file system can you choose?

6. Do you need to create disk partitions before installing Windows 2000 on a new drive? Why or why not?

Installing Versus Upgrading an Operating System

The processes of installing a brand-new operating system and upgrading an old operating system to a new one are quite similar in many ways. In both cases, you must verify that the computer is powerful enough for the operating system you want to install in terms of CPU type, CPU speed, and RAM; that it has compatible hardware installed; and that it has enough disk space for the operating system.

The following are the major differences:

- New operating system installations usually are performed to empty hard drives. Windows 9x requires the user to run Fdisk and Format on a drive before Windows 9x can be installed on a hard drive, whereas Windows 2000 incorporates partitioning and formatting into its setup program.

- New operating system installations often are performed using original equipment manufacturer (OEM) versions supplied for a particular type of computer. OEM versions often come with a bootable disk used to start the system and require no proof of a previous version. Upgrades require the user to install the operating system to a drive containing the previous version or to provide the previous version during installation to qualify the system for the upgrade installation.

Preparing to Upgrade Your Operating System

Virtually every computer in a business of any size (and many home-based computers as well) is likely to undergo at least one operating-system upgrade during its operational life. A major part of the A+ Certification exam concerns the process of installing operating system upgrades. The process of preparing for an operating system upgrade includes

- Verifying that your system has sufficient performance and free disk space for the upgrade

- Selecting the proper version of the operating system to use for the upgrade

- Determining whether you want to replace the previous operating system or set up a dual-boot configuration that will allow you to run either the old or new operating systems

Verifying Your System Is Ready for Windows 98

Generally, the system requirements for Windows 98 are similar to those for Windows 95:

- **486DX/66 or faster processor**—Any Pentium-class processor or faster will thus qualify.

- **16 to 24MB RAM**—Systems with more RAM will run Windows 98 faster; 16MB was required for Windows 98's original version, but Windows 98 Second Edition requires 24MB.

- **145MB to 315MB of free hard disk space**—This depends on installation options, but 205MB or more is recommended.

- **CD-ROM or DVD-ROM drive**—CD-R or CD-RW drives are considered CD-ROM drives.
- **VGA or higher-resolution display**—For best results with multimedia display, the video card and monitor should be able to display at least 16-bit (65,536) color at 800×600 or higher resolutions.
- **Microsoft Mouse**—A compatible pointing device can also be used.

If you install the upgrade version of Windows 98 on a system containing Windows 95 or Windows 3.1, Windows 98 will use your current Windows installation to verify your system's eligibility for the upgrade. If you plan to install the upgrade version onto a bare hard disk as discussed in Chapter 12, "Preparing Hard Drives with Windows," you must have your original Windows CD-ROM or floppy disks available during the upgrade; the Windows 98 setup program will request your CD-ROM and might check several of your Windows floppy disks to verify that you qualify to use the upgrade version.

You should also

- Download any Windows 98-specific drivers for your hardware. Windows 95 drivers sometimes work, but Windows 98 drivers work better with Windows 98. Windows 3.1 drivers will not work with Windows 98; although Windows 98 comes with most drivers needed for common hardware, older hardware might require you to obtain drivers yourself.
- Remove any uninstall backup files created when the previous version of Windows was installed.
- Use Scandisk to verify that the hard drive(s) is working properly.
- Remove outdated files from the \Windows\Temp folder to free up space.
- Remove *.chk files from the root folder of each drive to free up space.

If you need to add RAM to your system to meet or exceed system requirements, do so before the upgrade; the upgrade process will run faster if you do.

Windows 98 cannot be installed in a dual-boot configuration with Windows 95 without the use of third-party software. However, Windows 98 can be installed to perform a dual-boot configuration with MS-DOS (with or without Windows 3.1). Table 13.1 summarizes the steps you should take before starting the upgrade to Windows 98.

Follow these procedures to prepare for installing Windows 98 to an empty drive or upgrading your existing operating system to Windows 98:

- Upgrade RAM to 24MB or more to improve performance.
- Download Windows 98-specific hardware drivers; copy them to floppy disks or other media for use during installation.

CH 13

- Disable antivirus settings in system BIOS; sometimes this is referred to as "write-protect boot sector."

- Scan Windows 98 CD-ROM and boot floppy media for viruses. Remove any viruses found.

- Scan computer for viruses and remove any viruses found.

- Disable antivirus scanning programs that run in Autoexec.bat or run within Windows; these can interfere with software installation.

- Disable delete-tracking programs, such as Undelete, found in the Autoexec.bat; these can interfere with software installation.

- Check BIOS for Plug-and-Play (PnP) compatibility if you are upgrading from MS-DOS/Windows 3.1. Check with the system vendor for a BIOS upgrade.

- Locate your previous version of Windows media if you are installing an upgrade version to an empty drive. The installation program will ask for media to verify you are eligible for the upgrade.

If you are upgrading from MS-DOS/Windows 3.1 or Windows 95, also follow these procedures:

- Back up hard drives. If a full hard drive backup isn't possible, back up data files to avoid data loss in case of a problem with the upgrade. For maximum safety, use the byte-by-byte verify option during backup if available, and test the backup by restoring some files to an empty hard drive or empty folder.

- Disable EMM386.EXE or other memory managers in Config.sys that provide access to UMBs; these can interfere with software installation. Keep Device=Himem.sys and DOS=High options in Config.sys.

- Disable Load= and Run= statements in the Win.ini file used by Windows 3.1; verify that drivers in the System.ini file used by Windows 3.1 refer to installed hardware only.

- If Windows 98-specific drivers are not available for your video card, set your Windows video type to VGA before the installation because all SVGA cards will also run as VGA.

If you are upgrading from Windows 3.1 to Windows 98, you should also back up the following .GRP files to a floppy disk:

- Startup.grp
- Oldstart.grp

Then, delete all icons listed in your Startup folder; many of these programs will not run properly under Windows 98 and might not be needed.

Editing System Configuration Files

The Windows Notepad or DOS Edit program can be used to edit files such as

- Config.sys
- Autoexec.bat
- Win.ini
- System.ini

A faster way to open these files for editing is to use the Sysedit program available in some versions of Windows. Do not use a word-processing program to edit the files unless it can save the files as plain-text (ASCII or ANSI) files with no word wrap.

Follow these tips to make needed changes referred to in the previous section:

- To disable a device driver in Config.sys or a command in Autoexec.bat, place the word REM at the beginning of the line containing the command or driver. For example,

  ```
  device=c:\windows\emm386.exe RAM
  ```

  can be commented out by editing the line like this:

  ```
  REM device= c:\windows\emm386.exe RAM
  ```

  A line preceded by REM in Config.sys or Autoexec.bat is not processed by the system.

- To disable a statement in Win.ini or System.ini, use a semicolon instead of the word REM. For example,

  ```
  load=printspl.exe
  ```

  can be commented out by editing the line like this:

  ```
  ; load=printspl.exe
  ```

  Be sure to save any files you edit.

Verifying Your System Is Ready for Windows 2000 Professional

The hardware requirements for Windows 2000 Professional (which is based on Windows NT technology) are much more stringent than those for Windows 98; many systems that can run Windows 98 comfortably will not be fast enough to install Windows 2000 Professional. Windows 2000, unlike Windows 98, will test systems for minimum RAM and CPU speed requirements, and will not install on systems that do not meet those requirements.

The following list summarizes the minimum requirements for a computer capable of running Windows 2000 Professional:

- 133MHz or higher Pentium-compatible CPU—Windows 2000 Professional supports both single and dual CPU systems.

CH

13

- 64MB of RAM recommended minimum; add more memory to improve performance.
- 2GB hard disk or larger with a minimum of 650MB of free space.
- CD-ROM or DVD drive.
- VGA or higher-resolution monitor.
- Keyboard and Microsoft Mouse or compatible pointing device.

You should also verify that your computer, devices, and software are compatible with Windows 2000 Professional. There are several ways to accomplish this:

- Before the installation, you can inventory your system and then use the Microsoft Compatibility search tool available at the Windows 2000 Web site. Some devices that are compatible with Windows 98 will not be compatible with Windows 2000, and devices that are compatible with both Windows 98 and Windows 2000 require different drivers for Windows 2000.
- If you install Windows 2000 as an upgrade to Windows 98 (but not as a new installation), Windows 2000 will automatically check your system for problem hardware. A report details the hardware that the installation CD does not have drivers for.
- You can run the Windows 2000 setup program in a report-only mode to check compatibility. Open a command-prompt session under Windows 95, Windows 98, or Windows NT 4.0. Insert the Windows 2000 CD-ROM, change to the \i386 folder on the Windows 2000 CD-ROM, and give the following command:

```
winnt32 /checkupgradeonly
```

This displays a report of any problems. If you save the report, it creates a file called Upgrade.txt in the \Windows folder if run from Windows 95/98, or a file called Winnt32.log in the \WinNT folder on Windows NT 4.0.

Windows 2000 can be used to upgrade systems running Windows 95 and Windows 98 or Windows NT 3.51 or NT 4.0, but Windows 3.1 or earlier versions cannot be upgraded. In such cases, a new installation is necessary.

Windows 2000 can be installed in a dual-boot configuration with Windows 95 or Windows 98.

Windows 2000 Professional is available in the following versions; choose the version that is correct for your requirements:

- **Version or product upgrade**—Upgrades Windows NT Workstation 3.51 or 4.0 or Windows 95/98; proof of previous version is required.
- **Standard product**—Requires no previous version of Windows.

When Bootable Disks Are Necessary

In Chapter 12 you learned how to prepare the bootable floppy disks that might be needed to install your operating system. Depending on the type of operating system upgrade you perform, you might not need to prepare bootable disks.

If you want to install Windows 98 onto a bare drive, you will need either an OEM-supplied Windows 98 boot disk or a Windows 98 ESD created on a system running the same release of Windows 98. If you want to install Windows 2000 and your system can boot from a CD-ROM drive, you will not need to make Windows 2000 Setup disks. If you are installing the operating system onto a drive that already is running an operating system, you normally will not need to prepare bootable disks.

Upgrading to Windows 98—Overview

The process of starting the Windows 98 upgrade differs depending on which version of Windows is being upgraded or whether the old version of Windows or MS-DOS is being retained for dual-boot purposes. If you install Windows 98 to a bare (empty) drive, the hard drive must have been Fdisked and Formatted before you start the installation. However, after the upgrade process has begun, the basic steps are similar with any Windows 98 upgrade. The installation process for the Windows 98 upgrade is listed here:

1. Start SETUP.EXE from the CD-ROM.

2. If you agree to the *End-User License Agreement* (EULA), click OK, and the installation continues.

3. If you install to a system with only MS-DOS or to an empty drive, provide the CD-ROM or floppy disks for your previous version of Windows. If you provide floppy disks, Windows 98 will check several before continuing.

4. Select a path; to set up a dual-boot with Windows 3.1/MS-DOS, change the default path from C:\Windows to another folder.

5. Select the installation type. Choose from

   ■ Typical

   ■ Portable

   ■ Compact

   ■ Custom

   To save disk space and time, choose Compact. For maximum control over optional features, choose Custom. Typical installs options most useful for desktop users; Portable installs options most useful for notebook users.

6. Enter your name and company name.

7. Choose the default options for the selected installation type, or view the list of options and change them as desired.

CH

13

8. If you have a network card detected by Windows 98 setup, enter your computer name, workgroup name, and a short description—see your network administrator for details.

9. Choose your location (country or region).

10. Choose to create a startup disk. Skip this step only if you already have made a Windows 98 Emergency System Disk (ESD) from the same Windows release.

11. The file-installation process starts. A status bar indicates system progress.

12. The system reboots automatically after completing the file-installation process.

13. The setup program continues after the reboot, detecting hardware and Plug and Play devices.

14. A status bar appears while the system checks for non-PnP hardware in the system.

15. The system restarts after non-PnP hardware is detected and installed.

16. The system loads drivers for hardware after the second reboot.

17. Select the Time Zone when prompted. The US English version of Windows 98 defaults to the Pacific time zone.

18. Windows sets up the following for you:
    - Control Panel
    - Programs on Start menu
    - Windows Help
    - MS-DOS program settings
    - Tuning up application startup
    - System configuration

19. Windows reboots for a third time.

20. After restarting, Windows prompts you for a username and password.

21. Your monitor, printer, and other external devices are detected and configured if turned on.

22. Windows sets up Internet Explorer and other software.

23. Windows displays the Welcome screen.

From MS-DOS

Windows 98 enables you to dual-boot with MS-DOS automatically if only MS-DOS is installed on the system before you start the installation process.

If MS-DOS has CD-ROM support already installed:

1. Boot the computer to an MS-DOS prompt.

2. Insert the Windows 98 CD-ROM.

3. Change to the drive letter for the CD-ROM drive.

4. Proceed as listed previously in the Overview section.

To boot back to MS-DOS after installing Windows 98, do one of the following when the system restarts:

- Press the F4 function key.
- Press the Ctrl key and choose Start Previous Version of MS-DOS from the list of options.

Most MS-DOS programs stored in the \DOS folder will work as they normally do, but the following programs are removed or disabled because they won't work with long file-names:

- Drvspace (MS-DOS 6.22)
- Dblspace (MS-DOS 6.0, 6.2)
- Defrag (MS-DOS 6.x)
- Scandisk (MS-DOS 6.x)

When you try to run any of these programs, a message appears onscreen informing you of the steps you need to follow to run the Windows 98 equivalent.

From Windows 3.1

Installing Windows 98 on a machine that has Windows 3.1 running on it requires that you first decide whether you want to replace Windows 3.1 or create a dual-boot environment that will allow you to run your choice of Windows 3.1 or Windows 98.

If you use the default installation location for Windows 98 (C:\Windows), you will replace your Windows 3.1 installation with Windows 98 and prevent dual-booting with your old version of Windows. If you choose a different installation location (for example, C:\Win98), you can dual-boot Windows 3.1 as well as MS-DOS as discussed earlier. However, you will need to reinstall Windows 3.1 applications you want to use with Windows 98.

The easiest way to start the upgrade to Windows 98 is to follow these steps:

1. Start Windows 3.1.

2. Open the File Manager.

3. Insert the Windows 98 CD-ROM.

4. Open the Setup.exe file on the CD-ROM and continue as described in "Upgrading to Windows 98—Overview" earlier in this chapter.

You can choose to upgrade Windows 3.1 or install Windows 98 in its own folder when you start the Windows 98 upgrade from within Windows 3.1. You can specify any name for Windows 98's own folder, but I recommend using the name Win98.

CH
13

Upgrading the Windows 3.1 Installation to Windows 98

If you install Windows 98 into the same folder as Windows 3.1, the Windows 3.1 program groups (.grp files) and .ini files, such as Win.ini, System.ini, and others, will be used to set up the Windows 98 desktop and Registry. Each .grp will become a folder of shortcuts visible when you click Start, and then Programs. The .ini entries will be transferred to the Windows Registry.

From Windows 95

As with Windows 3.1, the easiest way to start the upgrade process to Windows 98 is to

1. Start Windows 95.
2. Open the Windows Explorer.
3. Insert the Windows 98 CD-ROM—this starts the Autorun.exe program in the root folder of the CD-ROM, which displays several options onscreen.
4. To start the upgrade process, answer Yes when the computer asks "Do you want to upgrade your computer to this new version of Windows 98 now?"
5. Answering Yes starts the Setup program for you and carries over your existing Windows 95 program groups and preferences to Windows 98. Close the Autorun menu after the setup program starts so you can make the user entries needed.

According to Microsoft, Windows 95 and 98 cannot be used in a dual-boot configuration, although third-party boot managers, third-party partition managers, and unofficial hacks on the World Wide Web all provide unauthorized methods for bypassing this limitation.

Installing Windows 2000—Overview

Windows 2000 can be installed in several different ways, including

- As a brand-new installation on an unpartitioned drive
- As an upgrade to Windows 9x
- As a dual-boot option on a system that is running (and will continue to run) Windows 9x
- As an upgrade to Windows NT 4.0

Installing Windows 2000 on an Unpartitioned Drive

Follow this procedure to install Windows 2000 on an unpartitioned (empty) drive.

1. If the system can be booted from a CD-ROM drive, insert the Windows 2000 CD-ROM into the CD-ROM drive and start the system; the installation program starts automatically. Unlike other Windows 2000 installation options, installing Windows 2000 this way starts by using a text-mode display. Use the keyboard rather than a mouse to make menu choices.

If the system does not support booting from a CD-ROM drive, insert the Windows 2000 CD-ROM into the CD-ROM drive and insert the first of the four Windows 2000 setup disks you created on another system (see "Creating a Boot Disk Suitable for Hard Disk Preparation," page 336, for details). Change disks as prompted until the Windows 2000 Setup program starts.

2. Press Enter when prompted to start the Windows 2000 installation process.

3. Press F8 to accept the end-user license agreement.

4. Select the unpartitioned space on the empty hard drive for the installation; press Enter to install Windows 2000 on the unpartitioned space, and skip to step 7. To specify a partition size, press C to continue.

5. Specify the partition size; you can press Enter to accept the default (the entire capacity of the drive) or type a smaller size and press Enter.

6. Select the partition into which to install Windows 2000; specify the partition you created in step 5.

7. Select NTFS or FAT for the partition, and press Enter. If you specify FAT, the partition will be FAT16 if it is under 2GB in size and FAT32 if it is 2GB or larger.

8. Windows 2000 formats the partition with the file system you specify and continues the installation process.

9. After copying files, the system reboots.

10. The Windows 2000 graphics-mode Setup Wizard starts after the reboot; click Next.

11. After hardware is detected, the Regional Settings screen appears. To change languages from the default, click the Customize button in the Locales portion of the screen. To change the default keyboard layout, click the Customize button in the Keyboard portion of the screen. The current defaults for both are displayed. Click Next.

12. On the Personalize Your Software screen, enter the user name and company name. Click Next.

13. On the Product Key screen, enter the 25-character product key found on the back of the CD-ROM case or sleeve.

14. Enter the computer name and Administrator password; ask the network administrator for this information. Click Next.

15. On the Date & Time Settings screen, select the date, time, time zone, and whether to use daylight savings time adjustments. Click Next.

16. On the Networking settings screen, choose whether to use typical or custom network settings after network components are copied. If you choose custom settings, specify the protocols and other settings desired and click OK. Click Next.

CH

13

17. Enter workgroup or domain information—consult the network administrator for this information—and click Next. If you enter a domain name, enter the name of a user and password that can be used to connect to the specified domain. Click Next.

18. After components are installed, the Final Tasks screen appears. Click Next.

19. Click Finish on the Completing the Windows 2000 Setup display, and the system reboots.

20. After the reboot, click Next and complete the Users of This Computer dialog box. Specify either Users Must Enter a Username and Password or Windows Always Assumes a Particular User. Enter the username and password to use for the default user and click Next.

21. Click Finish. Windows 2000 logs on the default user (if any) or prompts you for a username and password.

Upgrading Windows 9x to Windows 2000

You can upgrade Windows 9x to Windows 2000 by following these steps:

1. Start Windows 9x.

2. Insert the Windows 2000 CD-ROM.

3. To start the upgrade process, click Yes when the computer asks "Would you like to upgrade to Windows 2000 now?"

 Note

If Autorun has been disabled on your system, you can open the SETUP program on the Windows 2000 CD-ROM from Windows Explorer to start.

4. On the Welcome to the Windows 2000 Setup Wizard, select Upgrade to Windows 2000 (the default). Click Next (see Figure 13.1).

5. Accept the Windows 2000 end-user license agreement (EULA), and click Next to continue.

6. Enter your 25-character product key from the back of the CD case or sleeve that contained your Windows 2000 CD-ROM. Click Next to continue.

7. Click Next on the Preparing to Upgrade screen.

8. Select whether to install upgrade packs provided by software vendors to make their software work with Windows 2000, and click Next. If you selected the option to install upgrade packs, specify their location.

Figure 13.1
Select the default Upgrade to Windows 2000 to replace Windows 9x with Windows 2000.

9. Select whether to use the NTFS file system on your drive. If you want to dual-boot, choose the default of No, but to enjoy the additional benefits of the NTFS file system, choose Yes. If you are unsure, skip this option and convert the drive after installation. Drives other than C: will not be converted.

10. You can run the Upgrade Analyzer to check hardware and software compatibility and view or print a report; skip this step if you already checked compatibility. If some of your hardware needs new drivers, you can provide updated Plug and Play driver files now (recommended), or click Next if you want to provide file updates later.

11. After you review the Upgrade Analyzer report, you can continue or quit the installation.

12. The system reboots for the first time.

13. After rebooting, the setup program examines your hardware and begins to load driver files, checks your C: drive for errors, and begins to copy files. After your system is configured, Windows 2000 reboots your computer for a second time.

14. After the reboot, a fully graphical desktop appears during the setup process, and your input devices are recognized and set up.

15. Networking components are installed if your system is connected to a local area network (LAN). You might be asked whether the computer is part of a domain or workgroup; specify the domain or workgroup.

16. Additional components are installed and configured, including advanced network features, such as COM+.

17. After final tasks are performed, the system is rebooted a third time.

18. Press F8 for special startup options, or allow the system to boot normally.

CH
13

19. After the startup process is completed, you'll be asked to provide a password for the administrator and the last logged-in user. Because the passwords for these two accounts will be identical (a single password is used for both), you'll want to assign a new password to the regular user as soon as possible to maintain security.

20. The Getting Started screen is displayed; you can register your copy of Windows 2000, set up your Internet connection, and tour Windows 2000. Uncheck this option to prevent it from running on each reboot. Do not use the Set Up the Internet option if you already have a working Internet connection.

Dual-Boot Installation Overview

You can select whether to install Windows 2000 as an upgrade to Windows 9x (replacing it) or whether to install Windows 2000 in a separate folder or separate disk partition, allowing you to dual-boot Windows 9x and Windows 2000. Selecting dual-boot is the preferable option for systems that have hardware or software that can function with Windows 9x but not Windows 2000.

If possible, install Windows 2000 in its own disk partition on the system; installing it on the same disk partition as Windows 95 or Windows 98 might prevent these versions of Windows from running correctly.

If you select the dual-boot option, make sure you do not change the file system on the boot drive from the default (FAT16 or FAT32) to NTFS when prompted during installation. Although NTFS has many advantages as described in Chapter 12, NTFS is not compatible with Windows 9x. Thus, you must keep the drive's current file system if you want to use the same disk partition for both Windows 2000 and Windows 9x. If you install Windows 2000 to its own disk partition, you can convert the partition to NTFS during installation.

You will make the following user inputs if you choose to install Windows 2000 for dual-booting with Windows 9x:

1. Start Windows 9x.

2. Insert the Windows 2000 CD-ROM.

3. To start the upgrade process, click Yes when the computer asks "Would you like to upgrade to Windows 2000 now?"

 Note

If Autorun has been disabled on your system, you can open the SETUP program on the Windows 2000 CD-ROM from Windows Explorer to start.

4. On the Welcome to the Windows 2000 Setup Wizard, select Install a New Copy of Windows 2000; click Next (refer to Figure 13.1).

5. Agree to the end-user license agreement, and enter the CD-ROM key when prompted.

6. Use the Special Options menu to adjust defaults for location (language), Advanced options (source and destination folders), and Accessibility settings if desired (see Figure 13.2).

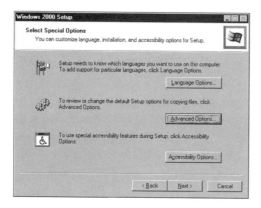

Figure 13.2
Use the Windows 2000 Special Options menu to customize Language, Setup, and Accessibility options. Click each button to display a menu.

7. Use the Advanced button to specify the disk partition to use for Windows 2000, choose the location of the Windows 2000 files, choose the installation folder name, or copy the setup files to the hard disk for extra speed (see Figure 13.3). Click OK when you're finished.

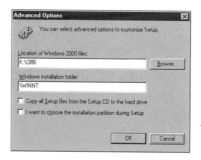

CH
13

Figure 13.3
The Advanced Options menu allows you to control file and folder names and locations for the Windows 2000 installation.

8. The file-copying process starts. The computer reboots after setup files are copied.

9. After the system reboots, select Setup from the list of options (which also includes Repair or Exit installation).

10. If the drive has more than one partition, select an empty partition for installation; you can install into the same partition as Windows 9x or choose a different partition or free space if available (recommended).

11. When asked to keep the partition as the current file system or to convert the partition to NTFS, keep the current file system unless you have selected a different partition for Windows 2000 than for Windows 9x.

12. Adjust Regional settings if needed; these include location settings (language and country/region), numbers, currency, time, date, and input languages.

13. Adjust the keyboard layout if needed—QWERTY is standard for U.S. locations.

14. Enter your name and organization.

15. If the computer has a network card, you'll be prompted to enter the computer name and administrator password (consult the network manager for this information).

16. Confirm the date and time.

17. Choose the default network components (TCP/IP with automatic IP address, Client for Microsoft Networks, and File and Print Sharing) or select options and settings as needed (consult the network manager for this information). See Chapter 17, "Networking," for details about network protocols and configuration.

18. Enter the domain name or workgroup.

19. Click Finish when the configuration tasks are completed. The system reboots.

20. Complete the Network Identification Wizard. Default assumes that a single user will log on to the system; change this option to require a name and password if a domain controller (specified in step 14) will be used to verify users.

When you install Windows 2000 with the dual-boot option, a startup menu always appears. The system will start Windows 2000 in 30 seconds unless you select Microsoft Windows, which runs your previous version of Windows (95/98).

Upgrading Windows NT 4.0 to Windows 2000

You can upgrade Windows NT 4.0 to Windows 2000 by following these steps:

1. Start Windows NT 4.0

2. Insert the Windows 2000 CD-ROM.

3. To start the upgrade process, click Yes when the computer asks "Would you like to upgrade to Windows 2000 now?"

Note

If Autorun has been disabled on your system, you can open the SETUP program on the Windows 2000 CD-ROM from Windows Explorer to start.

4. On the Welcome to the Windows 2000 Setup Wizard, select Upgrade to Windows 2000 (the default); click Next.

5. Accept the Windows 2000 end-user license agreement (EULA); click Next to continue.

6. On the Your Product Key screen, enter your 25-character product key from the back of the CD case or sleeve that contained your Windows 2000 CD-ROM. Click Next to continue.

7. If the Windows NT 4.0 hard disk is not using NTFS, the Upgrading to the Windows 2000 NTFS File System screen appears. Choose Yes to upgrade your drive to NTFS, or choose No to keep its current file system.

8. Windows 2000 runs the Upgrade Analyzer to check hardware and software compatibility—it allows you to display or print a report. If some of your hardware needs new drivers, you can provide updated Plug and Play driver files now (recommended) with Have Disk, or click Next if you want to provide file updates later.

9. After you review the Upgrade Analyzer report, you can continue or quit the installation.

10. The system reboots for the first time after copying files.

11. After rebooting, you are prompted to press F6 to load third-party SCSI or RAID drivers. The setup program examines your hardware and begins to load driver files, checks your C: drive for errors, and begins to copy files. After your system is configured, Windows 2000 reboots your computer for a second time.

12. After the reboot, your drive is converted to NTFS if you selected this option earlier in the setup process. The system is rebooted again.

13. The setup program detects hardware devices and installs network components.

14. Additional components are installed and configured, including advanced network features, such as COM+.

15. After Final tasks are performed, the system is rebooted a third time.

16. Log on to the system when prompted to start your upgraded Windows 2000 Professional installation.

Verifying System Compatibility During Windows 2000 Installation

Windows 2000 provides three options you can use to help make sure your system is compatible with Windows 2000. Depending on the installation type, you might not see all these options during the same installation.

■ **Link to the Microsoft Compatibility Web Site**—You can go straight to the Microsoft Compatibility Web site from the Windows 2000 installation if you have a working Internet connection.

CH
13

- **Upgrade packs for software**—If your software vendors provide software packs to provide compatibility with Windows 2000, you can install them on the screen after the option to go to the Microsoft Compatibility Web site.

- **The Upgrade Analyzer**—After selecting whether to upgrade to NTFS, the system will run this option to analyze the hardware in your system. This is the same analyzer you can run separately before starting the Windows 2000 installation.

After you review the results of the upgrade analyzer (which can be saved or printed), you can immediately provide a replacement driver for any hardware listed, or provide a replacement driver later. Any hardware listed on the report will not work correctly until a Windows 2000-compatible driver is installed; drivers from earlier versions of Windows will not work.

Troubleshooting Installation

Windows 9x and Windows 2000 both provide troubleshooting tools you can use to determine why an installation isn't working properly. This section discusses the files that are created during installation and what can be learned from each type of file.

Troubleshooting the Windows 9x Installation

The four files that provide valuable clues to why a Windows 9x installation or initial startup has failed are

- Detlog.txt
- Netlog.txt
- Setuplog.txt
- Bootlog.txt

All these files are hidden files stored in the root folder of the Windows installation drive (normally C:\). Change the default settings in the Windows Explorer to Show All Files to display these files. For more information about displaying all files in the Windows Explorer, see "Changing Viewing Options in Windows Explorer," page 436. You can examine the contents of these files with either Notepad or WordPad.

If Windows 9x fails to complete its installation, a very long file called Detlog.txt can be used to figure out what happened. Detlog.txt lists the hardware devices that Windows 9x is looking for. If the Windows 9x upgrade process stops, the last entries in Detlog.txt indicate what was being checked at the time of the lockup, allowing you to remove or reconfigure the hardware that caused the installation to fail.

The Netlog.txt file records the network configuration of Windows 9x during initial installation. If network devices do not work, examine this file to see if the end of any lines indicate error messages or error numbers.

Setuplog.txt is a file that records every event of the installation process. If the Windows 9x installation process doesn't finish, check the end of the file to see at what point the installation failed.

An installation might appear to succeed, but it isn't really finished until the system restarts successfully. The Bootlog.txt file records every event during the startup process. Bootlog.txt is generated automatically the first time Windows 9x is started; whenever a new Bootlog.txt is generated, the previous version is renamed Bootlog.prv (replacing any existing Bootlog.prv). As with the other files discussed here, the end of the file is the critical location to look at if Windows 9x can't start. Unlike other files, which are very complex to read, Bootlog.txt is relatively simple: Virtually every START event will have either a matching SUCCESS event, a FAILED event, or no match (if the system locks up after STARTing an event). If Windows 9x locks up, check the end of the file to determine the last driver or process that was STARTed without a matching SUCCESS or FAILED; that is the usual cause of the problem.

Troubleshooting the Windows 2000 Installation

Unlike Windows 9x, a Windows 2000 installation doesn't offer an automatic uninstall option. Therefore, it's important to make sure that installation works correctly.

The following problems can prevent you from upgrading a system to Windows 2000 (or installing it on a system already running Windows 95 or Windows 98):

- **Hardware conflicts**—Change the hardware resource settings on legacy (non-PnP) hardware to values that don't interfere with PnP devices, or remove them for reinstallation later.

- **Not enough disk space**—To assure that you can complete the installation, make sure the partition you will use for installing Windows 2000 has at least 1GB of free space. Converting the partition to NTFS during the installation will make it more efficient.

- **Can't start the installation automatically**—If you cannot start the installation automatically (the Autorun feature of the Windows 2000 CD doesn't work), you can start the installation by opening one of these files instead:

  - For upgrades from Windows 95 or 98, open the Winnt32.exe file stored in the \i386 folder on the CD-ROM with the Windows Explorer.

  - For new installations, open the Winnt.exe file stored in the \i386 folder from an MS-DOS prompt.

  - Use the setup disks described in Chapter 12.

CH
13

QUESTIONS AND ANSWERS:

1. Under what circumstances can you not dual-boot to MS-DOS after installing Windows 98?

   A: You must install Windows 98 to a folder other than the default C:\Windows to allow dual-booting with MS-DOS.

2. What must you provide to "prove" you can use the Windows 98 Upgrade?

   A: The Windows 98 upgrade checks your system for a qualifying version of Windows; it will ask for media if it can't find a qualifying version.

3. How can you determine whether your system is compatible with Windows 2000 if you don't have a working Internet connection?

   A: Run the Windows 2000 Setup program in a report-only mode to generate a compatibility report before you start the installation process, or run the Upgrade Analyzer during installation.

4. Why does Windows 98 disable some MS-DOS 6.x utilities when you install Windows 98 in a dual-boot configuration?

   A: Some MS-DOS 6.x utilities, such as Scandisk, are not compatible with the long filenames Windows 98 uses on the hard disk. Such utilities are disabled to prevent data corruption or loss.

5. Can you convert a FAT drive to another type of file system during a Windows 2000 upgrade? What other type of file system can you choose?

   A: You can convert a FAT drive to NTFS during a Windows 2000 upgrade; do this only if the drive will not be used in a dual-boot configuration.

6. Do you need to create disk partitions before installing Windows 2000 on a new drive? Why or why not?

   A: Disk partitions can be created, formatted, and used for installation by the Windows 2000 Setup program.

Using and Optimizing Windows 9x and Windows 2000

WHILE YOU READ

1. What is the procedure for locating a file containing specified text between a range of dates?
2. What is the Windows Registry and where is it stored in Windows 9x? In Windows 2000?
3. What are two ways to access the System properties sheet?
4. What command-prompt command displays Windows 9x release info?
5. What Control Panel properties sheet and tabs are used to adjust system performance in Windows 9x? In Windows 2000?
6. What Windows 2000 program can be run to set up a command-prompt session within the Windows GUI? Which Windows 2000 feature allows command-prompt operations at boot time to repair errors?

Differences Between Windows 9x and Windows 2000

Windows 9x (used in this book to refer to Windows 95 and Windows 98) and Windows 2000 have similar user interfaces but are profoundly different operating systems beneath the surface. The following are some of the major differences:

- **MS-DOS legacy support**—Windows 9x is preferred.
- **Windows 3.1 legacy support**—Windows 9x is preferred.
- **Security**—Windows 2000 is preferred.
- **File System Support**—Windows 2000 is preferred.
- **Networking**—Window 9x is preferred for simple networks, and Windows 2000 is preferred for corporate networks.
- **Hardware compatibility**—Windows 9x supports more hardware types, especially older products, multimedia, and entertainment.
- **Hardware requirements**—Windows 9x is preferred if you must use slower computers, but Windows 2000 supports multiple CPUs for faster performance.
- **Stability**—Windows 2000 is preferred.

MS-DOS Legacy Support

Windows 9x supports dual-booting to MS-DOS and uses the Autoexec.bat and Config.sys files to support older hardware that requires real-mode (MS-DOS–type) device drivers. Each MS-DOS program run under Windows 9x can use its own Autoexec.bat and Config.sys file if needed when run in MS-DOS mode. Windows 2000 can run some MS-DOS programs, but it does not support features such as upper memory blocks, EMS memory, direct access to hardware, real-mode device drivers, or data compression with DriveSpace or DoubleSpace. If you need MS-DOS legacy support, use Windows 9x.

Windows 3.1 Legacy Support

Windows 9x supports Windows 3.1 applications better than Windows 2000 does because of Windows 9x's better support of MS-DOS functions and features, such as direct access to hardware and support for 16-bit device drivers.

Security

Because Windows 2000 is an improved version of Windows NT, Windows 2000 offers better security features than Windows 9x, including user-level security and encryption when NTFS is used to prepare the hard drives.

File System Support

Windows 9x supports only the FAT file systems (FAT16 and FAT32). Although FAT32 is much more efficient in terms of disk storage, it does not support the advanced features of NTFS. Windows 2000 supports FAT for backward compatibility with Windows 9x and MS-DOS, but its native file system is NTFS. NTFS provides advanced user-level security that can be applied to individual files and folders, compression for individual files, and encryption for individual files. When advanced file management and security are major requirements, Windows 2000 is recommended.

Networking

Both Windows 98 and Windows 2000 can be integrated easily into existing small-office and large networks; however, Windows 2000 is a better choice because of its improved security and stability. Even on a simple peer network, Windows 2000 Professional's user-level security can prevent unauthorized users from accessing shared resources.

Hardware Compatibility

Windows 9x, particularly Windows 98, is supported by a much wider range of hardware than is Windows 2000. For example, Windows 98 can use legacy MS-DOS drivers for some storage devices, Windows 95/98 drivers for most types of devices, and new Windows Driver Model (WDM) drivers for certain types of devices. Windows 2000 is designed to use the new Windows Driver Model (WDM) style of device driver and can sometimes use Windows NT 4.0 device drivers. Although both Windows 98 and Windows 2000 are designed to use WDM drivers, differences in the operating system still require separate Windows 98 and Windows 2000 drivers for video cards and many other types of devices.

Device driver support for Windows 2000 is weaker than for Windows 9x in areas such as multimedia, imaging, and gaming. However, Windows 2000 is better than Windows 9x at using IRQ steering and will install a wider range of devices without requiring you to reboot the computer. Windows 2000 requires faster CPUs, more RAM, and more disk space than Windows 9x; Windows 2000 will not install on systems that do not meet the minimum requirements. Windows 2000 will work on multiple-CPU systems, unlike Windows 9x, which is designed for single-CPU systems only.

Stability

Windows 2000 is much more stable than Windows 9x because of its superior internal design for multitasking and because it uses a memory-protected virtual machine to run Windows 3.1 and MS-DOS programs.

Use Windows 9x, particularly Windows 98, when compatibility with MS-DOS, Windows 3.1, and multimedia applications and hardware is important. Windows 2000 is

CH
14

the preferred choice for business applications, for heavy multitasking, and for secure networking.

Windows 9x Startup Files and Their Uses

During the startup process of Windows 9x, several files are used and processed by the operating system. Understanding how these files work is important to troubleshooting startup problems and to modifying how Windows 9x operates.

These files include

- **Io.sys**—Binary startup file
- **Msdos.sys**—Editable text startup configuration file
- **Config.sys**—Editable text startup device driver and configuration file
- **Autoexec.bat**—Editable text startup configuration file

These files are loaded and processed in the order listed during the initial startup of your system. All these files are located in the root directory of your default startup drive (normally C:\).

Tasks Performed by Io.sys

The Io.sys file is loaded into memory by the bootstrap loader built into the system BIOS. After it's in memory, Io.sys performs the following tasks:

- Reads the configuration stored in the Msdos.sys configuration file and starts the computer accordingly.
- Checks for multiple hardware configurations (created by the Hardware Profiles feature in the System properties sheet) and prompts the user to select one.
- Loads the following files into memory:
    - **Logo.sys**—Displays the standard or optional Windows splash screen.
    - **Drvspace.ini or Dblspace.ini (Microsoft disk compression setup files) if present**—These will be present only if the hard drive has been previously compressed.
    - **Himem.sys**—XMS memory manager.
    - **Ifshlp.sys**—Installable file system driver.
    - **Setver.exe**—Handles compatibility issues for some older programs that might not work correctly otherwise.
- Checks User.dat and System.dat (the Windows Registry) for valid data and opens System.dat. If System.dat is not available, System.da0 (the backup) is opened instead and is renamed System.dat.

Io.sys then loads the hardware profile you selected and checks the Registry for any drivers located in the following Registry key:

```
\Hkey_Local_Machine\System\CurrentControlSet
```

The drivers and parameters referenced there are loaded before the Config.sys file is processed.

Note that Io.sys is a binary file, not a text file. If you want to override its default settings, change the appropriate options in Msdos.sys or Config.sys. See "Msdos.sys—Configuring Your Boot Options," page 392, and "Config.sys in Windows 98," page 395, for details.

Default Settings and Values Stored in Io.sys

In Windows 9x, the Io.sys file replaces much of the functionality of Config.sys. The following statements, formerly found in Config.sys, are now integrated into Io.sys:

- **Dos=high**—Loads MS-DOS into the High Memory Area (HMA—the first 64KB of extended memory); if Emm386.exe is loaded from Config.sys, DOS=UMB is also used to allow TSR programs to load into unused upper memory blocks.
- **Himem.sys**—XMS memory manager needed for Windows.
- **Ifshlp.sys**—32-bit file system manager; enables Windows to work with network and real-mode file system APIs.
- **Setver.exe**—Provides MS-DOS version information to programs that need to be told that they are running under a particular version of MS-DOS.
- **files=**—Specifies 60 file handles by default; used only by MS-DOS apps running under Windows 9x.
- **lastdrive=**—Default is Z; used only by MS-DOS apps; value is stored in the Registry.
- **buffers=**—Specifies 30 disk buffers by default; used only by MS-DOS apps that make calls directly to Io.sys.
- **stacks=**—Specifies a value of 9,256 (9 stack frames, 256 bytes each); used for compatibility with older programs that need stack frames to properly handle hardware interrupts.
- **shell=command.com**—Indicates command processor to use; /p is included by default to make Command.com permanent in memory.
- **fcbs=**—Specifies a value of 4; needed only for very old applications running under Windows 9x.

Because these values are designed to be appropriate for older applications running under Windows 9x, there is seldom a need to override them in the Config.sys file.

CH

14

Msdos.sys—Configuring Your Boot Options

The first configuration file processed by Io.sys is the Msdos.sys file. In Windows 9x, the Msdos.sys file is not a binary file (as it was with MS-DOS), but is instead a specially formatted text file that controls the boot process. Msdos.sys is a hidden file; to view its contents most easily, open an MS-DOS prompt window and enter the following commands:

```
C: [changes to C: drive]
CD\ [changes to the root folder of C: drive]
EDIT MSDOS.SYS [opens Msdos.sys with the text editor]
```

The contents of a typical Msdos.sys file are displayed in Figure 14.1.

Figure 14.1
A typical Msdos.sys file; it is located in the root directory of the default Windows 9x boot drive (normally C:).

The Msdos.sys file can contain many different configuration options; in most cases, only a few of them are needed, as shown in Figure 14.1. In special cases, additional configuration options might need to be added. Table 14.1 lists all the possible configuration options for Msdos.sys and their uses. When 1 is used as a value, it enables the option; when 0 is used as a value, it disables the option.

The Msdos.sys file is divided into two sections:

- **Paths**—This section indicates where Windows 9x is installed and what drive is used to start Windows 9x (see Table 14.1).
- **Options**—This section sets the startup options that will be used when booting Windows 9x (see Table 14.2).

When you make changes to add or adjust configuration settings, be sure you do not remove the lines that begin with a semicolon. These lines make the file over 1KB (1,024 bytes), which is required for proper operation of the system.

Table 14.1 Configuration Settings for the [Paths] Section of Msdos.sys

Setting	Typical or Default	Use
HostWinBootDrive=	C	Drive letter used to boot Windows
WinBootDir=	C:\Windows	Folder where Windows 98 is installed
WinDir=	C:\Windows	Usually same as `WinBootDir`
UninstallDir=	C:\	Where uninstall information is stored

Table 14.2 Configuration Settings for the [Options] Section of Msdos.sys

Setting	Typical or Default	Use
AutoScan=	1	Runs ScanDisk automatically after 1 minute delay if Windows 9x wasn't shut down correctly; set to 0 to disable; set to 2 to run ScanDisk immediately if Windows 9x wasn't shut down correctly.
BootDelay=	2	Delays Windows startup the number of seconds listed; adjust to allow user to press Ctrl or F8 to bring up menu; use 0 to disable.
BootFailSafe=	0	Set to 1 to run Windows 9x in Safe mode.
BootGUI=	1	Set to 0 to boot Windows 9x to a command prompt.
BootMenu=	0	Set to 1 to display the Windows 9x startup menu.
BootMenuDefault=	1	Selects default boot option if startup menu is displayed.
BootMenuDelay=	30	Selects how long (seconds) to wait after Windows startup menu is displayed to boot.
BootMulti=	0	If set to 1, enables dual-booting with MS-DOS or Windows NT.
BootWarn=	1	If set to 0, disables Safe Mode warning message.

CH

14

Table 14.2 continued		
Setting	Typical or Default	Use
BootWin=	1	Set to 0 to make MS-DOS 5.x or 6.x the default operating system (if installed).
DblSpace=	1	Loads DoubleSpace driver (if installed); set to 0 if DoubleSpace compression hasn't been installed.
DblBuffer=	0	Set to 1 if a SCSI host adapter on the system requires double buffering.
DrvSpace=	1	Loads DriveSpace driver (if installed); set to 0 if DriveSpace compression hasn't been installed.
LoadTop=	1	Loads Command.com and Drvspace.bin at top of conventional memory for compatibility with 16-bit (real mode) network drivers, such as some older NetWare drivers.
Logo=	1	Set to 0 to disable the Windows splash screen; set to 0 also avoids conflicts with some third-party memory managers.
Network=	0	Left over from Windows 95; Windows 98 doesn't support Safe Mode with Networking, so leave this set to 0 or omit option.
WinVer	Varies	Indicates Windows version.

Changing the Contents of Msdos.sys

To change the contents of Msdos.sys, which will modify how your system starts, follow this procedure:

1. Click Start, Find, Files or Folders.
2. Enter Msdos.sys.
3. Select the C: drive from the Look in menu.
4. Click Find Now.
5. Msdos.sys should be displayed in the list of files; use the copy on C:\ if more than one is displayed.
6. Right-click the File and select Properties.
7. Uncheck the Read-only and Hidden attributes and click Apply. Click Close.
8. Double-click Msdos.sys to open it.
9. Because the .sys extension is not associated with a program, the Open With window appears. Scroll down and select Notepad from the programs listed. Do not check the Always Use This Program box.

10. Click OK to open Msdos.sys with Notepad.

11. Add the commands from Tables 14.1 or 14.2 to Msdos.sys with the Notepad text editor, or modify existing commands. Do not remove any of the lines beginning with a semicolon that have a long line of x's; these lines are needed to make sure Msdos.sys is large enough (in bytes) to work properly.

12. Save the changes with Notepad: use File, Save.

13. Close Notepad.

14. Right-click Msdos.sys, recheck Hidden and Read-only attributes, and click Apply. Click Close; the changes made to Msdos.sys will take effect on the next reboot.

Config.sys in Windows 9x

The Config.sys file in Windows 9x is needed primarily for installing real-mode device drivers for devices that are not supported by Windows 9x's 32-bit device drivers. As you saw earlier, Io.sys contains most of the values formerly found in Config.sys. If you need to override values in Io.sys with Config.sys statements, add the statement you want to change to the Config.sys file with the value you want to change. You also can add a reference to a memory manager to Config.sys. Config.sys is a plain-text file that can be edited with Notepad.

Follow these steps to open the Config.sys file with the Windows Notepad program:

1. Click Start, Find, Files or Folders.

2. Enter Config.sys.

3. Select the C: drive from the Look In menu.

4. Click Find Now.

5. All copies of Config.sys on C: drive are displayed. The only one that needs to be edited is the one located in the root folder of the C: drive (C:\). Double-click this Config.sys file.

6. Because .sys is not associated with a program, the Open With window appears. Scroll down and select Notepad from the programs listed. Do not check the Always Use This Program box.

7. Click OK to open Config.sys with Notepad.

The Config.sys file on many Windows 9x systems will be empty and waiting for any changes you might need to make. For example, to change the default setting for `Files=` from the Windows 9x Io.sys default of 60 to a value of 80, follow these steps:

1. Use a text editor such as Notepad to open the Config.sys file.

2. Add the following line:

```
Files=80.
```

CH

14

   3. Save Config.sys and exit Notepad.

   4. Restart the computer to put the new value into operation.

To add support for a device that is not supported by Windows 9x's protected-mode device drivers (such as an older CD-ROM drive, for example), add a reference to the device driver to the Config.sys file. The following command will install the Cddriver.sys file found in C:\CDROM folder into memory and assign it a device name:

```
Device=C:\CDROM\cddriver.sys /D:MSCD001
```

To enable upper memory block usage for DOS-based device drivers and TSRs under Windows 9x, add the following to Config.sys:

```
Device=C:\Windows\Emm386.exe NOEMS
```

As you learned earlier in this chapter, Io.sys will add the DOS=UMB reference during its startup process to allow you to use Devicehigh= statements in Config.sys and Loadhigh statements in Autoexec.bat.

Autoexec.bat in Windows 9x

Like Config.sys, most of the functionality of Autoexec.bat is now provided by Io.sys. The major reasons to add commands to Autoexec.bat will be to perform tasks (such as virus scanning) that should take place before the Windows 9x GUI loads or to change the defaults loaded by Io.sys.

If you need to override values in Io.sys with Autoexec.bat statements, add the statement you want to change to the Autoexec.bat file with the value you want to change. For example, to change the default setting for SET TEMP= from the Windows 9x Io.sys default of C:\Windows\Temp to a different folder such as D:\Temp, follow these steps:

   1. Use a text editor such as Notepad to open the Autoexec.bat file.

   2. Add the following lines:

```
SET TEMP=D:\TEMP

SET TMP=D:\TEMP
```

   3. Save the changes to Autoexec.bat and exit.

   4. Use the Windows Explorer to create a folder on D: called \TEMP.

   5. Restart the computer to put the new settings into operation.

Win.com in Windows 9x

Win.com is used to start Windows 9x. Normally, there is no need to run Win.com manually; it is loaded automatically during the Windows 9x startup operation. However, if Windows 9x cannot start correctly, it might be necessary to start Windows by using Win.com's special startup switches.

The startup switches discussed in this section can be used in place of making changes to the System.ini file. If Windows 9x will start when one or more of these switches is used, the equivalent System.ini statement should be added until the underlying problem has been solved.

To use any of the following startup switches with Windows 9x

1. Start the computer.

2. Press the Ctrl key (or F8 on some systems) after the POST (power-on self test) has been completed to display the Windows 9x Startup menu.

3. Select the Command Prompt Only startup option (not safe mode command prompt). This option processes the Registry, Config.sys, and Autoexec.bat and boots the system to a command prompt.

4. Enter this command at the prompt and add the desired switches at the end of the command. For example, this command uses four of the possible six switches:

```
win/d:fsvx
```

Win.com Startup Switches and Their Meanings

You can combine the startup switches that can be used with Windows 9x's Win.com. They include

- **:F**—Turns off 32-bit disk access. The equivalent to adding this statement to SYSTEM.INI is `32BitDiskAccess=FALSE`.

- **:M**—Enables Safe mode. This is automatically enabled during Safe start (function key F5).

- **:N**—Enables Safe mode with networking. This is automatically enabled during Safe start (function key F6).

- **:S**—Specifies that Windows should not use the ROM address space between F000:0000 and 1MB for a break point. The equivalent to adding this statement to SYSTEM.INI is `SystemROMBreakPoint=FALSE`.

- **:V**—Specifies that the ROM routine will handle interrupts from the hard disk controller. The equivalent to adding this statement to SYSTEM.INI is `VirtualHDIRQ=FALSE`.

- **:X**—Excludes all the adapter area from the range of memory that Windows scans to find unused space. The equivalent to adding this statement to SYSTEM.INI is `EMMExclude=A000-FFFF`.

The :M (safe mode) and :N (safe mode with networking) options might seem redundant because these commands can also be run from the Windows 9x startup menu, but they can be very useful if you need CD-ROM support while you're in Safe mode. Add the

CH

14

correct CD-ROM device driver to the Config.sys and the matching MSCDEX.EXE command to Autoexec.bat, and boot the computer to the command prompt to load the CD-ROM driver into memory. Then, use the :M or :N switch to start Windows 9x. You'll be able to use the CD-ROM drive to install drivers or to repair a damaged installation.

Windows 2000 Startup Files and Their Uses

The Windows 2000 startup process is substantially different than that used by Windows 9x. The following files are required to start Windows 2000:

- **NTLDR**—The Windows 2000 loader program.
- **Boot.ini**—Options in this file affect how Windows 2000 starts up.
- **Bootsec.dos**—This contains the boot sectors for another operating system if you are multi-booting.
- **Ntdetect.com**—This detects the hardware installed on your system.
- **Ntbootdd.sys**—This device driver is used only if Windows 2000 is being started from a SCSI drive whose host adapter does not have an onboard SCSI BIOS enabled.
- **Ntoskrnl.exe**—The Windows 2000 Kernel, which completes the boot process after being initialized by NTLDR.
- **Hal.dll**—The Hardware Abstraction Layer; software that translates hardware.
- **SYSTEM key in the Registry**—This is read to determine the system configuration.
- **Device drivers**—These are loaded according to the information stored in the Registry.

NTLDR and Starting Windows 2000

After the computer completes the POST and the system BIOS's bootstrap loader locates the NTLDR, NTLDR performs the following tasks:

- Enables the user to select an operating system to start (if more than one is installed). NTLDR examines the contents of Boot.ini to find out which operating systems are installed.
- Loads the Windows 2000 startup files.
- NTLDR uses the Ntdetect.com program to determine what hardware is installed and places a list of the detected hardware into the Windows 2000 Registry.
- Loads Ntoskrnl.exe (the Windows 2000 Kernel) and the Hardware Abstraction Layer (Hal.dll) into memory and hands over control to Ntoskrnl.exe after loading device drivers appropriate for the system configuration.

Memory Management in Windows 9x

Windows can use two types of memory:

- Physical memory (RAM)
- Virtual memory (swapfile on disk)

Because Windows 9x is built on an MS-DOS foundation, it supports the different types of physical memory specifications that result from the design of the original IBM PC and its many descendants:

- **Conventional memory**—Memory addresses between 0 and 640KB. MS-DOS programs normally run in this area.

- **Upper memory**—Memory addresses between 640KB and 1MB, some of which are already in use for the system BIOS, Plug and Play BIOS, video BIOS, and video RAM. Depending on the system, between 96KB and 160KB of this space is not in use by hardware, but these addresses are not available unless additional memory managers (such as Emm386.exe) are installed during the startup process.

- **Extended memory**—Memory over 1MB. This is the primary memory area used by Windows 9x. Windows 9x loads the XMS (Extended Memory Specification) driver Himem.sys to make this memory available to Windows and compatible MS-DOS programs during Windows startup.

- **High memory**—The first 64KB of extended memory after an XMS driver is loaded. The Io.sys file installs Himem.sys and activates the DOS=HIGH option to copy the MS-DOS kernel used by Windows 9x into the High Memory Area (HMA).

- **Expanded memory**—Memory that can be accessed through a 64KB page frame that can be established in unused upper memory blocks. Expanded Memory Specification (EMS) memory originally required special memory boards, but can now be created from XMS memory through the use of Emm386.exe in the Config.sys. This type of memory is useful only for older MS-DOS programs.

Adjusting Default Memory Configurations in Windows 9x

Memory management takes place during the startup process of Windows 9x. By default, the following memory configuration is installed by Io.sys:

- Memory starting at 1MB (extended memory) is converted into XMS memory by the loading of Himem.sys.

- The DOS=HIGH option is used to move the MS-DOS kernel into the HMA portion of XMS memory.

CH
14

If you have MS-DOS TSR (terminate and stay resident) utilities that you want to install into upper memory blocks (UMBs), you will need to add the following statement to the Config.sys file:

```
Device=C:\Windows\Emm386.exe NOEMS
```

The DOS=UMB statement will be added to the memory configuration by Io.sys to make the UMBs available to MS-DOS TSRs.

If you have MS-DOS applications that need access to EMS memory, you need to add the following statement to the Config.sys file:

```
Device=C:\Windows\Emm386.exe RAM
```

This converts XMS memory into a common pool of XMS/EMS memory that can be used by both Windows and DOS applications. The DOS=UMB statement will be added to the memory configuration by Io.sys to make any UMBs not used by the EMS page frame available to MS-DOS TSRs.

Managing Virtual Memory in Windows 9x

Windows 9x uses disk space called virtual memory as a supplement to physical memory. Windows 9x configures virtual memory through the System properties sheet of the Control Panel. You can access the System properties sheet in one of the following ways:

- Right-click My Computer and select Properties from the right-click menu.
- Click Start, Settings, Control Panel, and open the System icon.

Follow this procedure to view or set virtual memory options in Windows 9x:

1. Click Start, Settings, Control Panel.
2. Click the System icon in Control Panel.
3. Click the Performance tab.
4. Click Virtual Memory (see Figure 14.2).

By default, Windows uses a variable-sized swapfile that can grow to the available disk space on the C: drive. You can make the following adjustments:

- Set the minimum and maximum sizes of the swapfile (including making the swapfile a fixed size).
- Set the swapfile to another drive.
- Disable the swapfile (not recommended).

If you have two or more logical hard drive letters or two physical drives, you might want to set the swapfile to a drive letter other than the default. This can improve performance (especially if you have two physical drives), and will prevent C: drive from running out of space needed for additional program installations or temporary Internet files.

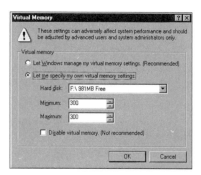

Figure 14.2
The Virtual Memory dialog box in Windows 9x shows that this system has been set to use a fixed-size swapfile on F: drive (the default is an adjustable-size swapfile on C: drive).

To avoid disk thrashing (which slows down the system) caused by resizing the swapfile, you can set the swapfile to a fixed size. The swapfile should be set to about three times your system's available RAM; if your system has 64MB of RAM, set your swapfile to 192MB. Use a larger swapfile size if you routinely edit large database or graphics files.

If you make any changes to the swapfile, you need to restart your computer for the changes to take effect.

Managing the Windows 9x File System Properties

You should also view and adjust the File System settings (also located on the Performance tab) to achieve maximum performance for the Windows 9x system.

There are five tabs on the File System properties sheet:

- Hard disk
- Floppy disk
- CD-ROM
- Removable disk
- Troubleshooting

Click the Hard Disk tab to adjust the disk caching settings for the computer. There are three possible settings for the Typical Role of This Computer setting, which control settings for Windows 9x's VFAT disk caching as shown in Table 14.3.

CH
14

Table 14.3 Typical Role of This Computer—Windows 9x			
Setting	# of Most Recently Accessed Folders Stored in RAM	# of Most Recently Accessed Files Stored in RAM	RAM Required
Desktop Computer	32	677	10KB
Mobile or Docking System	16	337	5KB
Network Server	64	2,729	40KB

As you can see, selecting Network Server uses a relatively small amount of RAM but provides much better disk caching because it stores much more recently read data in RAM than the other settings.

For maximum performance, set the Typical Role of the Computer to Network Server and the Read-Ahead Optimization to Full (see Figure 14.3); full read-ahead optimization uses up to 64KB of RAM to cache sequential disk reads. If your system is short of RAM, you can drag the slider to the left; each click reduces the RAM requirements by half. The leftmost click on the slider eliminates read-ahead caching completely.

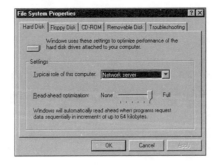

Figure 14.3
The Hard Disk portion of the File System dialog box is shown here.

Click the Floppy Disk tab to select whether to search for new floppy disk drives whenever you start the computer. Generally, searching for new floppy disk drives should be disabled on desktop computers; you might want to enable it on notebook computers with removable or hot-swap drives.

Click the CD-ROM tab to adjust caching for the CD-ROM. Generally, you should optimize for a quad-speed or higher access pattern and maximize the cache size.

Click the Removable Disk tab to select whether you want to enable write-behind caching for removable-media drives such as Zip, Jaz, Orb, and others. If you enable write-behind caching you increase performance, but you must also verify that all data has been sent to the media before you remove it from your system.

Click Troubleshooting to selectively disable normal file-system features, such as write-behind caching, protected-mode hard disk interrupt handling, and 32-bit disk drivers. The options on the Troubleshooting tab should be used only when systems are not functioning correctly using default settings; using these options will degrade performance significantly.

If you make any changes to the File System settings, you must reboot your computer for the changes to take effect.

Memory Management in Windows 2000

Windows \2000 automatically manages physical memory, unlike Windows 9x. Virtual memory, on the other hand, can be managed by the user. Virtual memory (also referred to as the paging file) is not used unless there is not enough physical memory to perform a task.

When additional RAM is added to a computer running Windows 2000, it is automatically used in place of the paging file.

The Windows 2000 System Monitor can be used to determine whether more RAM should be added to a computer. Follow these steps to monitor performance with the System Monitor:

1. Click the Start button.
2. Click Run.
3. Type `perfmon.msc` and press Enter.

Many different types of performance factors can be measured with the Windows 2000 Performance Monitor. To see if additional RAM is needed in a system, set up the Paging File % Usage and Pages/Sec counters:

1. Right-click in the blank area beneath the graph and select Add Counters.
2. Choose Paging File as the Performance Object, and then choose Paging File % Usage.
3. Choose Memory as the Performance Object, and then choose Pages/Sec.
4. Click Add.
5. Click Close, and then open the normal program load for this computer.

If the System Monitor indicates that the Paging File % Usage is consistently near 100% or the Memory Pages/Sec counter is consistently above 5, add RAM to improve performance (see Figure 14.4).

CH
14

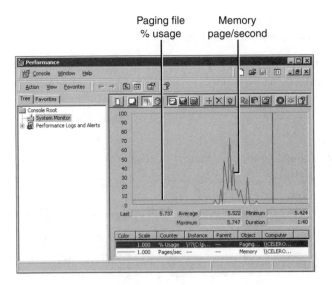

Figure 14.4
This system has adequate memory at this time, as indicated by the low levels of usage of the Paging File % Usage and Memory Pages/Sec counters.

The performance of the paging file can be improved by

- Setting its minimum and maximum sizes to the same amount
- Moving the paging file to a physical disk (or disk partition) that is not used as much as others
- Using a striped volume for the paging file. A striped volume is identical areas of disk space stored on two or more dynamic disks that are referred to as a single drive letter. A striped volume is created with the Windows 2000 Disk Management tool.
- Creating multiple paging files on multiple physical disks in the system
- Moving the paging file away from the boot drive

To adjust the location and size of the paging file:

1. Right-click My Computer on the Windows desktop and select Properties or open the Control Panel and open the System icon.
2. Click the Advanced tab.
3. Click the Performance Options button.
4. Click the Change button.

5. Choose the minimum and maximum sizes you want to use for the paging file and its location (see Figure 14.5). Click Set, and then click OK to finish.

6. If you make any changes to size or location, you must restart the computer for the changes to take effect.

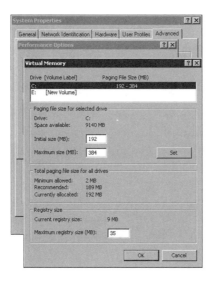

Figure 14.5
The Virtual Memory dialog box of Windows 2000 enables you to set the size and location of virtual memory.

Core Files and Commands of Windows 9x and Windows 2000

Windows files covered on the A+ Operating Systems exam fall into these categories:

- System configuration
- System maintenance and reporting
- Command-prompt utilities

Windows 9x System Configuration Files

The primary files used to store the system configuration are

- **System.dat**—Stores computer-specific configuration information
- **User.dat**—Stores user-specific configuration information

These files are found in the default \Windows folder.

The Regedit program (see Figure 14.6) is used to view and change the contents of the Registry. To start Regedit:

1. Click Start.
2. Click Run.
3. Type regedit and press Enter.

Changes made in Regedit are automatically saved when you exit.

Under most normal circumstances, the Registry will not need to be edited or viewed. However, Registry editing might be necessary under the following circumstances:

- To add, modify (by changing values or data), or remove a Registry key that cannot be changed through normal Windows menus or application settings. This might be necessary to remove traces of a program or hardware device that was not uninstalled properly, or to allow a new device or program to be installed.
- To back up the Registry to a file.

The Registry should *never* be edited unless a backup copy has been made first, because there is no undo option for individual edits and no way to discard all changes when exiting Regedit.

Microsoft's online Knowledge Base provides numerous examples of using Regedit to make manual changes. For example, if you need to install a Microsoft pointing device that supports Plug-and-Play and the system cannot detect it, you will need to remove Registry keys that refer to the previous pointing device (article # Q142405).

Figure 14.6 shows a typical Windows 9x Registry, as viewed in Regedit. The left window displays keys, which are displayed as folders. Click a key to open it in the right window. A key can contain multiple values and data, as shown here.

You should edit the Registry only with careful instructions from a software or hardware vendor and only if other alternatives for solving a problem do not exist.

Follow these steps to back up the Registry to a text file:

1. Start Regedit.
2. Click Registry.
3. Click Export Registry.
4. Select a folder for the Registry backup.
5. Enter a name for the backup.
6. Select All to back up the entire Registry.
7. Click Save.

Registry key

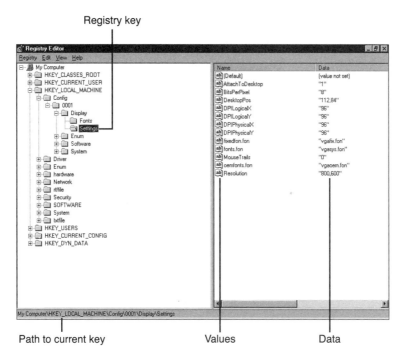

Path to current key   Values   Data

Figure 14.6
Regedit is being used to view the display settings for the current configuration.

Using Scanreg

To keep the Windows 98 Registry in working order, Windows 98 includes the Scanreg program. Scanreg automatically runs whenever you restart your computer to check your Registry for problems; if any problems are detected, the backup copy of your Registry is used instead of the primary copy. However, you can also run Scanreg yourself. To run Scanreg within Windows 98, follow this procedure:

1. Click Start.
2. Click Run.
3. Type Scanreg (or Scanregw) and press Enter.

If you run Scanreg from within the Windows 98 GUI, it calls the Windows 98 GUI version, Scanregw, to perform the Registry check. A status message appears onscreen after a few seconds. If no errors are found, you can select Yes to back up the Registry again (the default is No if you've rebooted the system already this day).

Scanreg will replace a defective Registry with a backup copy if errors are detected, but it will not remove Registry entries for programs that are no longer on the system.

CH
14

Win.ini and System.ini in Windows 9x

A limited amount of Windows 9x configuration information is stored in the Win.ini and System.ini files familiar to users of Windows 3.x. Although most 32-bit applications and utilities will change the Registry when installed, some older applications and utilities might need to make changes to the Win.ini and System.ini files. The System.ini file might also need to be changed to allow Windows to run as you learned earlier in this chapter; see "Win.com Startup Switches and Their Meanings," page 397, for details.

Both Win.ini and System.ini files can be changed through the use of a text editor such as Notepad, or by running the Sysedit program (see Figure 14.7), which opens both of the preceding files, plus Protocol.ini, Msmail.ini, Config.sys, and Autoexec.bat.

All four .ini files are stored in the default \Windows folder, whereas Config.sys and Autoexec.bat are stored in the root directory of the boot drive.

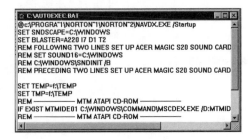

Figure 14.7
Sysedit enables you to edit Autoexec.bat, Config.sys, and the four major .ini files, such as Win.ini and others, are used by Windows 9x primarily for backward compatibility with older applications.

System Configuration Maintenance in Windows 98

As discussed previously, Regedit and Sysedit can be used to view and change the startup configuration for Windows 98. However, these tools (carried over from Windows 95) are difficult to use and can easily damage a configuration if used incorrectly.

If you need to start the computer and load only some of the normal startup programs and commands, use the MSConfig utility provided with Windows 98 (see Figure 14.8). MSConfig works with Config.sys, Autoexec.bat, Win.ini, and System.ini (just like Sysedit), but also provides control of startup programs and tasks.

MSConfig enables you to

- Create a backup copy of your Autoexec.bat, Config.sys, Win.ini, and System.ini files before you use the integrated editor.
- Disable programs in the Startup group and Registry Run and Run Services keys.

- Provide your choice of normal, interactive, or selective booting (allows you to choose which files and processes to run or skip over).
- Select various advanced diagnostic settings, such as 16-color VGA mode, excluding the upper memory area (A000-FFFF), and others.

Figure 14.8
The Startup tab of MSConfig allows you to selectively disable startup events and programs.

You can restart Windows after changing its configuration with MSConfig to see whether the changes you made solve the startup problem. To run MSConfig, use the Run dialog on the Start button, type MSConfig, and click OK.

The Windows 2000 Registry

Windows 2000 Professional uses its own Registry editors, Regedt32, or its own version of Regedit to view and change its Registry, which is stored in the files found in the \WinNT\System32\Config folder. Regedt32 is the primary Registry editor; however, Regedt32 does not enable you to search for particular Registry values or data, but only for Registry keys. If you need to search for Registry values or data, use the Windows 2000 version of Regedit instead, which has the same look and feel as the Windows 9x version of Regedit.

The Windows 2000 Regedt32 Registry editor uses five separate editing windows, which can be resized and repositioned for viewing the Registry, as in Figure 14.9.

Regedt32 also enables you to view the Registry in read-only form, making it the preferred Windows 2000 Registry tool for viewing the Registry's contents.

**CH
14**

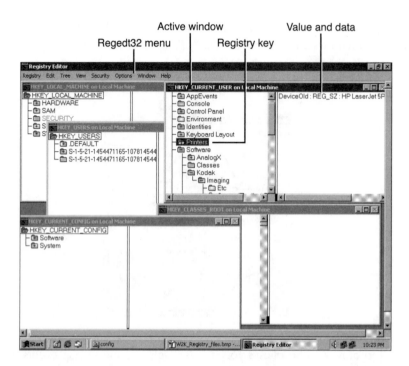

Figure 14.9
The Windows 2000 Regedt32 program is Windows 2000's primary Registry editor.
Note the use of overlapping Windows for each of the Registry's major sections and
additional menu options compared to the Windows 9x Regedit program.

As with the Registry in other versions of Windows, the Windows 2000 Registry should
not be edited by hand unless there is no alternative to solving a particular problem and
unless the Registry has been backed up first.

To back up the Windows 2000 Registry, use the Windows 2000 backup program. From
the opening menu, select Emergency Repair Disk, and select the option to back up the
Registry on the next screen; insert a blank, formatted disk when prompted to complete
the process.

Because the Windows 2000 Registry can occupy as much as 20MB of disk space on some
systems, the Emergency Repair Disk (ERD) does not contain a copy of the Registry itself
but includes other information necessary to help restore the system in case of a crash. The
Registry is stored in a folder called RegBack, which is contained in the \WinNT\Repair
folder. In the event of a serious system problem, both the Windows 2000 Emergency
Repair Disk and the Registry backup in the RegBack folder would be used to restore the
system. You should re-create the ERD and Registry backup whenever you install new
hardware or software to keep a record of the latest system configuration. For more

information about creating the ERD and backing up the Windows 2000 Registry, see "Backup/Restore," page 442.

Using Command-Prompt Commands and Utilities

Windows 9x and Windows 2000 both allow the user to perform certain operations from a command prompt. Most Windows tasks can be performed from the Windows Desktop or by launching a program. However, Windows 9x includes most of the commands and programs familiar to users of MS-DOS 6.x. Several of these commands and programs are included on the Windows 9x Emergency Startup Disk. Windows 2000 includes some of these commands. A list of the major command-prompt commands used by Windows 9x and Windows 2000 is provided in Table 14.4.

If you need to use command-prompt commands and utilities after the Windows desktop has been started, you can use either of the following methods:

- Click Start, Programs, MS-DOS prompt (Windows 9x) or Start, Programs, Accessories, Command Prompt (Windows 2000).
- Click Start, Run, type Command (Windows 9x) or Cmd (Windows 2000), and press Enter.

Either option starts the command interpreter (Command.com in Windows 9x or Cmd.exe in Windows 2000) and opens a command-prompt session. By default, Windows opens the command-prompt session in a window onscreen, but you can toggle between a windowed and full-screen view by pressing the Alt+Tab keys.

Internal Commands Overview

Command.com (Windows 9x) and Cmd (Windows 2000) contain the following internal commands (see Table 14.4). Commands marked with an asterisk (*) can also be used by the Windows 2000 Recovery Console.

Table 14.4   Major Internal Commands

Internal DOS Command	Category	Use	Example
DATE	System management	Views system current date and allows it to be changed	DATE
TIME	System management	Views system current time and allows it to be changed	TIME
COPY*	Disk management	Copies one or more files to another folder, drive, or filename	COPY *.* A:\

CH
14

Table 14.4   continued

Internal DOS Command	Category	Use	Example
DEL* (DELETE)	Disk management	Deletes one or more files on current or specified folder or drive	DEL *.TMP
ERASE*	Disk management	Same as DEL	ERASE *.TMP
DIR*	Disk management	Lists files on current or specified folder or drive	DIR *.EXE
MD (MKDIR)*	Disk management	Makes a new folder (subdirectory)	MD TEMP
CD (CHDIR)*	Disk management	Changes your current location to the specified folder (subdirectory)	CD TEMP
RD (RMDIR)*	Disk management	Removes an empty folder	RD TEMP
RENAME (REN)*	Disk management	Renames a file	REN joe.txt jerry.txt
VER	System management	Lists the version of operating system in use	VER
VOL	Disk management	Lists the current volume label and serial number for the default drive	VOL
SET	System management	Used to set options for a device or program; SET without options displays all current SET variables	SET TEMP=C:\TEMP
PROMPT	System management	Sets display options for the command prompt	PROMPT=$P $G (displays drive letter followed by greater-than sign)
PATH	System management	Sets folders or drives that can be searched for programs to be run	PATH=C:\ DOS;C:\WINDOWS
ECHO	Batch files	Turns on or off the echo (display) of commands to the screen	ECHO OFF

Table 14.4 continued			
Internal DOS Command	Category	Use	Example
CLS*	Batch files, system management	Clears the screen of old commands and program output	CLS
LH (LOADHIGH)	Memory management (Windows 98 only)	Loads TSR programs above 640KB (see memory management discussion previously)	LH C:\MOUSE\ MOUSE.COM
TYPE*	System Management	Views text files onscreen	TYPE AUTOEXEC.BAT

Because these commands are built into Command.com (Windows 9x) or Cmd (Windows 2000), they can also be used from the command prompt if you boot the computer with the Windows 9x Emergency Boot Disk. All but LH (Loadhigh) can also be run from the Windows 2000 command prompt.

Using DIR

The DIR command, which lists files and folders in either the current or any other specified drive or folder, has many options, as shown here:

```
A:/>DIR/?

Displays a list of files and subdirectories in a directory.

DIR [drive:][path][filename] [/P] [/W] [/A[[:]attributes]]
  [/O[[:]sortorder]] [/S] [/B] [/L] [/V] [/4]

  [drive:][path][filename]
              Specifies drive, directory, and/or files to list.
              (Could be enhanced file specification or multiple filespecs.)
  /P          Pauses after each screenful of information.
  /W          Uses wide list format.
  /A          Displays files with specified attributes.
  attributes   D  Directories           R  Read-only files
               H  Hidden files          A  Files ready for archiving
               S  System files          -  Prefix meaning not
  /O          List by files in sorted order.
  sortorder    N  By name (alphabetic)   S  By size (smallest first)
               E  By extension (alphabetic)  D  By date & time (earliest first)
               G  Group directories first  -  Prefix to reverse order
               A  By Last Access Date (earliest first)
  /S          Displays files in specified directory and all subdirectories.
```

```
/B            Uses bare format (no heading information or summary).
/L            Uses lowercase.
/V            Verbose mode.
/4            Displays year with 4 digits (ignored if /V also given).
```

```
Switches may be preset in the DIRCMD environment variable.  Override
preset switches by prefixing any switch with - (hyphen)--for example, /-W.
```

To use the DIR command

1. Open a command prompt window or boot the system to a command prompt.

2. Type DIR, followed by any optional switches you want to use.

3. Press Enter to view the results.

4. To pause the output from DIR, add /P (Pause) to the command.

By default, DIR run under Windows 9x displays the following information about a file or folder, as shown in Figure 14.10:

- The current drive and folder
- MS-DOS alias filename
- File extension
- File size in bytes (not applicable to folders)
- Date file last changed
- Time file last changed
- Long File Name (LFN)—displayed only when DIR is used within the Windows 9x GUI
- Prompt to continue—displayed only when /P (pause after each screen) is added to the DIR command

When the last screen of DIR information is displayed, the number of files and file space used by displayed files will also be listed onscreen.

If DIR/W is used, only the MS-DOS alias filenames are displayed across the screen in up to five columns.

If DIR/B is used, only the MS-DOS alias filenames are displayed in a single column down the left side of the screen.

When the DIR command is used with Windows 2000, the default order of information is different but the options used for DIR are similar to those for Windows 9x. Windows 2000's DIR command lists the file date, time, folder information, file size, and filename in that order from left to right.

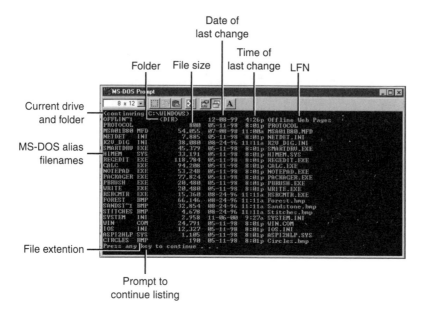

Figure 14.10
Typical output from Windows 98's DIR/P.

The options listed for DIR can be combined with each other, allowing you to use DIR to learn many different types of information about files and folders.

The following are some examples:

- **DIR/AH**—Displays files with the hidden attribute (see the discussion of ATTRIB later in this chapter) in the current folder.

- **DIR/S command.com**—Displays all instances of Command.com in the current folder and all folders beneath the current folder.

- **DIR/O-S C:\WINDOWS**—Displays all files in the folder C:\Windows in order by size, largest first.

Using VER

The VER (Version) command can be used to determine the exact version of Windows in use. Unlike DIR, VER has no optional switches (see Figure 14.11).

To use the VER command:

1. Open a command-prompt window.
2. Type VER and press Enter.
3. The version number information will be displayed.

CH

14

Figure 14.11
VER for Windows 98; the information in brackets indicates this is the original version of Windows 98 [4.10.1998].

Windows 98 Second Edition or Second Edition Step-Up (a system that has been upgraded from the original version of Windows 98 to Second Edition with a separate CD-ROM) will report a version number of [4.10.2222 A].

Using COPY

The COPY command copies files from one drive and folder to another folder and drive. The folder specified by COPY must already exist on the target drive. COPY will not work with files that have the system or hidden file attributes; to copy these files, use XCOPY32 instead.

The options for COPY are

```
A:\>COPY/?

Copies one or more files to another location.

COPY [/A | /B] source [/A | /B] [+ source [/A | /B] [+ ...]] [destination
    [/A | /B]] [/V] [/Y | /-Y]

    source       Specifies the file or files to be copied.
    /A           Indicates an ASCII text file.
    /B           Indicates a binary file.
    destination  Specifies the directory and/or filename for the new file(s).
    /V           Verifies that new files are written correctly.
    /Y           Suppresses prompting to confirm you want to overwrite an
                 existing destination file.
```

```
/-Y                Causes prompting to confirm you want to overwrite an
                   existing destination file.
```

```
The switch /Y may be preset in the COPYCMD environment variable.
This may be overridden with /-Y on the command line
```

```
To append files, specify a single file for destination, but multiple files
for source (using wildcards or file1+file2+file3 format).
```

To use the COPY command:

1. Open an MS-DOS command prompt window or boot the system to a command prompt.
2. Type COPY, followed by the filename or names and destination drive or folder.
3. Press Enter.

Here are some examples:

- **COPY *.* A:**—Copies all files in the current folder to the current folder on the A: drive.
- **COPY *.TXT C:\Mydocu~1**—Copies all .txt files in the current folder to the Mydocu~1 folder on the C: drive.
- **COPY C:\WINDOWS\TEMP*.BAK**—Copies all *.bak files in the \Windows\Temp folder on drive C: to the current folder.
- **COPY C:\WINDOWS*.BMP D:**—Copies all .bmp files in the \Windows folder on drive C: to the current folder on drive D:.

Windows Command-Prompt Utilities

Command-prompt utility programs are found in these locations in Windows 9x:

- C:\Windows\Command
- The Windows 9x Emergency Startup Disk (also called the emergency boot disk, EBD, or Startup disk)

For more information about the Windows 9x Emergency Startup Disk, see "Creating a Boot Disk Suitable for Hard Disk Preparation," page 336.

Most of these commands can also be run from the Windows 2000 command prompt or from the Recovery Console, which can be started from the Windows 2000 CD-ROM or can be installed to the hard disk for troubleshooting startup problems.

These utilities are also referred to as external commands because, unlike the built-in commands stored in Command.com or Cmd, each of these are separate programs.

CH

14

Table 14.5 lists the major command-prompt utilities supplied with Windows, how each is used, and whether it is part of the Windows 98 Emergency Boot Disk, Windows 95 Startup disk, or the Windows 2000 Recovery Console.

Table 14.5   Major Windows Command-Prompt Utilities

Utility	How Used	Windows 98 EBD	Windows 2000 Recovery Console
Attrib.exe	Changes file attributes (read)	Yes*	Yes
Chkdsk.exe	Simple disk repair and statistics reporting tool (replaced by Scandisk in Windows 9x)	No	Yes
Cvt.exe (Win98 only)	Converts FAT16 drive to FAT32 file system	No	N/A
Debug.exe	Debugging utility	Yes*	No
Deltree.exe (Win9x only)	Deletes folders and files contained in folders	No	N/A
Extract.exe (Win9x only)	Used to manually uncompress files from Windows .cab compressed archives	Yes	N/A
Expand.exe (Win2000 only)	Used to manually extract files from Windows 2000 .cab archive files	N/A	Yes
Fdisk.exe (Win9x only)	Partitions hard disks	Yes	N/A
Mem.exe	Displays overall memory usage and programs in conventional memory	No	No
Move.exe	Moves files from one location to another	No	No
Mscdex.exe (Win9x only)	Provides access to CD-ROM drives after CD-ROM device drive is loaded in Config.sys	Yes*	N/A
Scandisk.exe (Win9x only)	Disk repair and disk statistics tool (replaces CHKDSK)	Yes*	N/A
Scanreg.exe (Win98 only)	Registry repair tool	No	N/A
Uninstal.exe (Win98 only)	Uninstalls Windows 98	Yes*	N/A

Table 14.5   continued

Utility	How Used	Windows 98 EBD	Windows 2000 Recovery Console
Xcopy.exe	Faster version of COPY that can create folders and copy files based on many different criteria	No	No
Xcopy32.exe (Win9x only)	Used in place of standard Xcopy when run from a DOS Window while the Windows 9x GUI is active; supports long filenames and additional options	No	N/A
Diskcopy.com	Makes a bit-by-bit exact copy of a floppy disk	No	No
Doskey.com (Windows 9x only)Windows 2000 includes this function in CMD	Allows user to cycle through previous command-prompt commands for reuse	No	N/A
Edit.com	Text editor	Yes*	Yes
Format.com	High-level formatter for hard disk and floppy disk drives	Yes*	Yes
Sys.com (Win9x only)	Transfers system files to formatted hard disk or floppy disk drives	Yes*	N/A

Extracted from the EBD.CAB file to RAMDISK created when Windows 98 EBD is used to start computer.

Windows 95's Startup disk contains all the Windows 98 EBD files listed in the table except for Debug and Mscdex. You can copy these files manually from the \Windows\System folder to the Startup disk if needed.

For more information about the Windows 2000 Recovery Console, see "Windows 2000 Recovery Console," page 498.

The command-prompt utilities listed in Table 14.6 are part of Windows 2000 only. For a more complete list, type HELP from the Windows 2000 command prompt. To see command options, type /? after each command.

CH

14

Table 14.6   Windows 2000-Only Command-Prompt Utilities

Utility	How Used
Assoc	Displays or changes file extension associations
At	Schedules the running of commands or programs
Cacls	Displays or changes access control lists (ACLs) of files
Chkntfs	Displays or changes the operation of Chkdsk at startup time
Compact	Displays or changes the current compression status of files on NTFS partitions only
Convert	Converts FAT partitions other than the current drive to NTFS
Ftype	Displays or changes file types used in file extension associations
Title	Sets window title for a command-prompt (CMD.EXE) session

Using ATTRIB

The ATTRIB program is important to understand because the correct setting of file and folder attributes is vital to the correct operation of Windows. ATTRIB is used to view and set basic file attributes, which include

- **Archive**—Files with the archive attribute have not yet been backed up. The COPY command does not change the archive attribute for files it copies to another drive or folder, but XCOPY and all backup programs do. Change a file's attribute to archive to force a backup program to back it up if "changed files only" are being backed up.

- **Read-only**—Files with the read-only attribute cannot be deleted or overwritten at an MS-DOS prompt, and cannot be overwritten within a 32-bit Windows application. A read-only file can be deleted within Windows Explorer, but only after the user elects to override the read-only attribute. Change a file's attributes to read-only to provide protection against accidental deletion or changes.

- **System**—Files with the system attribute are used by the operating system, and often have the hidden attribute as well.

- **Hidden**—Files with the hidden attribute cannot be copied with COPY or with XCOPY and cannot be viewed with the normal Windows Explorer settings. Some log files created by Windows (such as Bootlog.txt) are stored with the hidden attribute.

Folders can also have these attributes; for example, the folder C:\Windows\Fonts has the system attribute. A file or folder can have multiple attributes; for example, the Msdos.sys file has system, hidden, and read-only attributes. If you need to edit Msdos.sys, you must use ATTRIB to remove these attributes before changing the file, and reapply these attributes after changing the file.

The following are the options for ATTRIB:

```
C:\>attrib /?
Displays or changes file attributes.

ATTRIB [+R | -R] [+A | -A] [+S | -S] [+H | -H] [[drive:][path]filename] [/S]

    +    Sets an attribute.
    -    Clears an attribute.
    R    Read-only file attribute.
    A    Archive file attribute.
    S    System file attribute.
    H    Hidden file attribute.
    /S   Processes files in all directories in the specified path.
```

When the ATTRIB command is run within the Windows 2000 GUI, an additional option, /D, is also available to process folders as well as files.

When the ATTRIB command is run from the Windows 2000 Recovery Console, the /S and /D options are not available, but +C can be used to compress a file and -C can be used to uncompress a file.

Here are some examples:

- **ATTRIB**—Displays all files in the current folder with attributes (A for archive; R for read-only; S for system; H for hidden).

- **ATTRIB +R Command.com**—Sets the file Command.com to have the read-only attribute.

- **ATTRIB -H -R -S C:\MSDOS.SYS**—Removes the hidden, read-only, and system attributes from the Msdos.sys file in the root folder of drive C:.

- **ATTRIB +H +R +S C:\MSDOS.SYS**—Restores the hidden, read-only, and system attributes to the Msdos.sys file in the root folder of drive C:.

- **ATTRIB +C *.doc**—Compresses all .doc files in the current folder (valid for Windows 2000 Recovery Console only).

Using MEM

The MEM command can be used to determine details about the physical and managed memory in a system. The following are MEM options for Windows 9x:

```
C:\WINDOWS\Desktop>mem/?
Displays the amount of used and free memory in your system.

MEM [/CLASSIFY | /DEBUG | /FREE | /MODULE modulename] [/PAGE]
```

CH

14

```
/CLASSIFY or /C  Classifies programs by memory usage. Lists the size of
                 programs, provides a summary of memory in use, and lists
                 largest memory block available.
/DEBUG or /D     Displays status of all modules in memory, internal drivers,
                 and other information.
/FREE or /F      Displays information about the amount of free memory left
                 in both conventional and upper memory.
/MODULE or /M    Displays a detailed listing of a module's memory use.
                 This option must be followed by the name of a module,
                 optionally separated from /M by a colon.
/PAGE or /P      Pauses after each screenful of information.
```

Windows 2000's MEM uses the /C and /D options the same way as in Windows 9x, but the /P option displays program detail. The /F and /M options are not valid for MEM under Windows 2000. MEM does not display total XMS memory, but only the XMS memory available for a command-prompt session under Windows 2000. Here are some examples:

- MEM—Displays total memory and free memory in the system (Windows 9x); displays total conventional memory and free XMS memory available for the current command-prompt session (Windows 2000).

- MEM/C/P—Displays overall memory information as well as listing programs and devices running in conventional and upper memory blocks (Windows 9x).

- MEM/P|MORE—Displays program details and overall memory information; |MORE redirects the output to the MORE program, which breaks the output into screen pages (Windows 2000).

If MEM indicates that no extended (XMS) memory is free, there is no XMS memory manager (Himem.sys or equivalent) loaded, and Windows will not be able to run.

Windows 9x ScanDisk

ScanDisk performs the following tasks:

- Checks the disk surface of the specified drive for read errors
- Repairs problems with the logical disk structure
- Provides disk usage statistics at the end of its operation

If ScanDisk is run from the command prompt while the Windows 9x GUI is active, the Windows version of ScanDisk will be run. If ScanDisk is run from the command prompt without the Windows GUI being active, a text-mode version of ScanDisk will be run.

When ScanDisk is run from the EBD or from the command prompt when the Windows GUI is not active, the following options (which can be combined) are available:

```
A:\>SCANDISK/?

Runs the ScanDisk disk-repair program.

To check and repair a drive, use the following syntax:
    SCANDISK [drive: | /ALL] [/CHECKONLY | /AUTOFIX [/NOSAVE]] [/SURFACE]
To check and repair an unmounted DriveSpace compressed volume file, use:
    SCANDISK drive:\DRVSPACE.nnn [/CHECKONLY | /AUTOFIX[/NOSAVE]]
To examine a file for fragmentation, use the following syntax:
    SCANDISK /FRAGMENT [drive:][path]filename
To undo repairs you made previously, use the following syntax:
    SCANDISK /UNDO [drive:]
For [drive:], specify the drive containing your Undo disk.


/ALL          Checks and repairs all local drives.
/AUTOFIX      Fixes damage without prompting.
/CHECKONLY    Checks a drive, but does not repair any damage.
/CUSTOM       Configures and runs ScanDisk according to SCANDISK.INI settings.
/NOSAVE       With /AUTOFIX, deletes lost clusters rather than saving as files.
/NOSUMMARY    With /CHECKONLY or /AUTOFIX, prevents ScanDisk from stopping at
                summary screens.
/SURFACE      Performs a surface scan after other checks.
/MONO         Configures ScanDisk for use with a monochrome display.

To check and repair the current drive, type SCANDISK without parameters.
```

The Scandisk.ini file can be used to customize the operations of ScanDisk. Scandisk.ini can be opened with any text editor and contains complete notes on how to adjust the default configuration settings for Scandisk.exe.

If ScanDisk is run from the Windows Startup group, the previous options do not apply. Instead, the following options (which can be combined) are used, because the Windows GUI version of ScanDisk will be run instead of the text-mode version:

■ `Scandisk X:`—Runs ScanDisk on drive specified.

■ `Scandisk /a`—Runs ScanDisk on all local hard drives.

■ `Scandisk /n`—Runs ScanDisk on current drive and quits automatically when finished.

■ `Scandisk /p`—Runs ScanDisk in read-only mode; no errors will be fixed.

Using Windows 2000 CHKDSK

Windows 2000 uses the CHKDSK program to perform disk repair tasks from the command prompt. Examples of Windows 2000 CHKDSK options (which can be combined) include

■ `CHKDSK volume`—Tests specified volume name, mount point, or drive letter (C:).

■ `CHKDSK filename`—Valid for FAT16/FAT32 drives only; checks specified file for fragmentation.

CH
14

- **CHKDSK D:/F**—Tests drive D: and fixes errors.

- **CHKDSK /V**—Displays full pathname for all files on current drive for FAT16/FAT32 drives only; displays cleanup messages if any for NTFS drives only.

- **CHKDSK /R**—Locates bad sectors and recovers readable information.

- **CHKDSK /L**—Displays current log file size (KB); CHKDSK /L:64 changes log file size to 64KB.

- **CHKDSK /X**—Dismounts volume before checking.

- **CHKDSK /I**—Faster, less thorough check of index entries (NTFS drives only).

- **CHKDSK /C**—Speeds up testing by skipping checks of cycles in folder structure (NTFS drives only).

By default, CHKDSK runs automatically at boot time if a drive is dirty (has errors); to adjust this behavior, run CHKNTFS with appropriate options from the command prompt. Use CHKNTFS/? to see the options you can use.

Using EDIT

The EDIT program can be used to view and change the contents of text-based .sys (boot configuration) files, .ini (program configuration) files, .bat (batch) files, and .txt (text) files in Windows 9x, and text, log, and other files in Windows 2000.

The options shown here apply to both versions of EDIT:

```
C:\WINDOWS\Desktop>edit /?
MS-DOS Editor    Version 2.0.026    Copyright (c) Microsoft Corp 1995.

EDIT [/B] [/H] [/R] [/S] [/<nnn>] [/?] [file(s)]

   /B      - Forces monochrome mode.
   /H      - Displays the maximum number of lines possible for your hardware.
   /R      - Load file(s) in read-only mode.
   /S      - Forces the use of short filenames.
   /<nnn>  - Load binary file(s), wrapping lines to <nnn> characters wide.
   /?      - Displays this help screen.
   [file]  - Specifies initial files(s) to load.  Wildcards and multiple
             filespecs can be given.
```

Here are some examples:

- **EDIT C:\MSDOS.SYS**—Opens the Msdos.sys file in the root folder of drive C: for editing; user must change file attributes of Msdos.sys with ATTRIB first to allow changes to file.

- **EDIT**—Opens editor; user must open File menu within Edit to select file(s) to open.

Using XCOPY

The XCOPY command can be used in place of COPY in most cases and has the following advantages:

- **Faster operation on a group of files**—XCOPY reads the specified files into conventional RAM before copying them to their destination.

- **Can create folders as needed**—Specify the destination folder name in the XCOPY command line, and the destination folder will be created if needed.

- **Operates as backup utility**—Can be used to change the archive bit from on to off on XCOPied files if desired to allow XCOPY to be used in place of commercial backup programs.

- **Copies files changed or created on or after a specified date**—Also useful when using XCOPY as a substitute for commercial backup programs.

The following XCOPY options apply when the Windows 9x GUI is not active:

```
A:\XCOPY.EXE/?

Copies files (except hidden and system files) and directory trees.

XCOPY source [destination] [/A | /M] [/D:date] [/P] [/S [/E]] [/V] [/W]

    source       Specifies the file(s) to copy.
    destination  Specifies the location and/or name of new files.
    /A           Copies files with the archive attribute set,
                 doesn't change the attribute.
    /M           Copies files with the archive attribute set,
                 turns off the archive attribute.
    /D:date      Copies files changed on or after the specified date.
    /P           Prompts you before creating each destination file.
    /S           Copies directories and subdirectories except empty ones.
    /E           Copies any subdirectories, even if empty.
    /V           Verifies each new file.
    /W           Prompts you to press a key before copying.
```

Here are some examples:

- XCOPY *.txt A:\TEXT\—Copies all .txt files in the current folder to the \TEXT folder on drive A:; creates folder if needed.

- XCOPY *.txt /d:01-01-01 \TEXT\—Copies all .txt files in the current folder that were created on or after 01-01-01 to the \TEXT folder on the current drive; creates folder if needed.

- XCOPY *.DOC /S/E F:\—Copies all .doc files in the current folder and folders below the current one to the root folder of drive F: and duplicates the folder structure below the current folder on F:.

CH
14

If XCOPY is run with the Windows 9x GUI active, many additional options are available because XCOPY will launch Xcopy32.exe. The following are Xcopy32.exe's options:

```
C:\Windows\Desktop>XCOPY32/?

Copies files and directory trees.

XCOPY source [destination] [/A | /M] [/D[:date]] [/P] [/S [/E]] [/W]
                            [/C] [/I] [/Q] [/F] [/L] [/H] [/R] [/T] [/U]
                            [/K] [/N]

  source       Specifies the file(s) to copy.
  destination  Specifies the location and/or name of new files.
  /A           Copies files with the archive attribute set,
               doesn't change the attribute.
  /M           Copies files with the archive attribute set,
               turns off the archive attribute.
  /D:date      Copies files changed on or after the specified date.
               If no date is given, copies only those files whose
               source time is newer than the destination time.
  /P           Prompts you before creating each destination file.
  /S           Copies directories and subdirectories except empty ones.
  /E           Copies directories and subdirectories, including empty ones.
               Same as /S /E. May be used to modify /T.
  /W           Prompts you to press a key before copying.
  /C           Continues copying even if errors occur.
  /I           If destination does not exist and copying more than one file,
               assumes that destination must be a directory.
  /Q           Does not display filenames while copying.
  /F           Displays full source and destination filenames while copying.
  /L           Displays files that would be copied.
  /H           Copies hidden and system files also.
  /R           Overwrites read-only files.
  /T           Creates directory structure, but does not copy files. Does not
               include empty directories or subdirectories. /T /E includes
               empty directories and subdirectories.
  /U           Updates the files that already exist in destination.
  /K           Copies attributes. Normal XCOPY will reset read-only attributes.
  /Y           Overwrites existing files without prompting.
  /-Y          Prompts you before overwriting existing files.
  /N           Copy using the generated short names.
```

The options for Windows 2000's XCOPY are identical to those used for Windows 9x's XCOPY32, and the following options also apply:

- /O—Copies file ownership and ACL information
- /X—Copies file audit settings
- /Z—Copies network files in restartable mode

In Windows 9x, XCOPY32 has the following advantages over XCOPY:

- Copies file attributes without resetting them
- Can copy system and hidden files
- Automatically creates a destination folder when copying multiple files to a specified location
- Optional file overwrite protection

XCOPY32 can be used to "clone" an entire drive's contents to another drive. For example, the following copies the entire contents of C: drive to D: drive:

```
XCOPY32 C:\. D:\ /H /S /E /K /C /R
```

Using MSCDEX (Windows 9x)

The MSCDEX program provides the CD-ROM extensions needed to allow CD-ROM drives to run in a command-line environment when the Windows 9x GUI has not been started; MSCDEX is not used by Windows 2000.

MSCDEX is loaded automatically by the Windows 98 EBD if you select Start Computer with CD-ROM Support from the Windows 98 Startup menu. The Windows 95 Startup disk must be modified manually as described in "Adding CD-ROM Drive Support to the Windows 95 Startup Disk," page 337.

MSCDEX will not load unless a valid CD-ROM device driver (loaded by Config.sys) is already in memory.

You can edit the Autoexec.bat provided on the Windows 98 EBD if you need to use any of the optional switches listed in this section.

At a minimum, the MSCDEX command line must include the /D:devicename option (which must match the device name provided by the CD-ROM device driver in Config.sys). Other options are shown here.

The following are some MSCDEX examples:

- **MSCDEX /D:MSCD001 /L:K**—Loads MSCDEX, specifying drive letter K: (/L:K).
- **MSCDEX /D:MSCD001 /V**—Loads MSCDEX and displays memory usage after loading the program.
- **MSCDEX /D:MSCD001 /M:10 /S**—Loads MSCDEX, specifies 10 sector buffers (/M:10), and allows the drive to be shared over MS-NET based networks (/S).
- **MSCDEX /D:MSCD001 /E**—Loads MSCDEX into EMS expanded memory (/E) if present to reduce conventional memory usage. It requires the use of Emm386.exe with RAM option in Config.sys

CH
14

Using SETVER (Windows 9x)

You use the SETVER program to report a particular MS-DOS version number to enable device drivers or programs written for an older version of MS-DOS (or Windows 9x command line) to run with Windows 9x. Use SETVER if a device driver or program reports an "incorrect DOS version" when you attempt to load it.

SETVER is used in two ways:

- When run from the command line, as in the following output, SETVER can display the version information stored in the program and let you add or remove programs from its version-table entries.
- When added to Config.sys, SETVER's version-table entries are loaded into memory. Any program listed in SETVER's version table that queries for the version of MS-DOS in use will receive that information from SETVER.

The following options are used with SETVER when it is run from the command prompt:

```
C:\WINDOWS\Desktop>setver /?
Sets the MS-DOS version number that Windows reports to a program.

Display current version table:  SETVER [drive:path]
Add entry:                      SETVER [drive:path] filename n.nn
Delete entry:                   SETVER [drive:path] filename /DELETE [/QUIET]

  [drive:path]    Specifies location of the SETVER.EXE file.
  filename        Specifies the filename of the program.
  n.nn            Specifies the MS-DOS version to be reported to the program.
  /DELETE or /D   Deletes the version-table entry for the specified program.
  /QUIET or /Q    Hides the message typically displayed during deletion of
                  version-table entry.
```

To install SETVER in memory, add the following line to Config.sys:

```
C:\Windows\Command\setver.exe
```

Using EXTRACT

Windows 9x uses EXTRACT to work with the compressed .CAB files that store the major programs and support files used by Windows 9x. EXTRACT is used during the Windows 9x installation process to create working files from .CAB file archives, but it can also be used to

- View the contents of compressed .CAB file archives
- Determine which .CAB file contains a specified Windows program or support file
- Create a working version of a specified Windows program or support file stored in a .CAB file and copy it to the correct location

The following options are used with EXTRACT:

```
C:\WINDOWS\Desktop>extract /?
Microsoft (R) Cabinet Extraction Tool - Version (16) 1.00.603.0 (08/14/97)
Copyright (c) Microsoft Corp 1994-1997. All rights reserved.

EXTRACT [/Y] [/A] [/D | /E] [/L dir] cabinet [filename ...]
EXTRACT [/Y] source [newname]
EXTRACT [/Y] /C source destination

  cabinet  - Cabinet file (contains two or more files).
  filename - Name of the file to extract from the cabinet.
             Wild cards and multiple filenames (separated by
             blanks) may be used.

  source   - Compressed file (a cabinet with only one file).
  newname  - New filename to give the extracted file.
             If not supplied, the original name is used.

  /A         Process ALL cabinets.  Follows cabinet chain
             starting in first cabinet mentioned.
  /C         Copy source file to destination (to copy from DMF disks).
  /D         Display cabinet directory (use with filename to avoid extract).
  /E         Extract (use instead of *.* to extract all files).
  /L dir     Location to place extracted files (default is current directory).
  /Y         Do not prompt before overwriting an existing file.
```

.CAB files can be stored on floppy disks, on a CD-ROM, or in a folder called \Windows\Options\CABS.

The following are some examples of how to use EXTRACT.

```
C:\WINDOWS\Desktop>extract /a /d K:\win98\win98_22.cab esdi_506.pdr|more
```

This command searches Windows 98 .CAB files on the CD-ROM to find which file contains the ESDI_506.PDR hard disk miniport driver. | MORE will stop the display after each screen is filled, prompting the user to press a key to continue.

```
C:\WINDOWS\Desktop>extract K:\win98\win98_46.cab esdi_506.pdr /l
c:\windows\system\iosubsys
```

This command extracts the ESDI_506.PDR file from the WIN98_46.CAB file and copies it to the C:\Windows\System\Iosubsys folder.

Getting Help with a Particular Command

As you have seen in the previous sections, most command-line utilities provide you with concise help for options; type the command name followed by /? to see options for that command.

CH
14

Most Windows 9x command-prompt commands and utilities have similar options to those used by MS-DOS 6.x. The MS-DOS 6.x Help file (which contains more detailed help and examples than those provided by /? help) is stored on the Windows 9x CD-ROM in the OldMSDOS folder. To view the help file, switch to that folder and open Help.com.

Disk Management

Both Windows 9x and Windows 2000 use the Windows Explorer as their primary means of disk management, although some operations can also be conducted from the command prompt.

Major disk management topics you need to understand include

- How to use My Computer and Windows Explorer to view the contents of a drive or folder
- How to set file and folder attributes
- The rules for naming files and how MS-DOS aliases are derived from long filenames
- How Windows 2000 performs compression and encryption
- How to use ScanDisk and Defrag to maintain drives
- How to back up and restore data
- How to locate files and folders by name, date, size, and contents

My Computer

The My Computer icon on the Windows desktop might be the single most-important icon for maintaining and working with Windows. My Computer provides access to the following features and utilities:

- Open My Computer to view the local drives on your system, available network drives, and the Control Panel folder. My Computer in Windows 9x also displays the Printers folder, Dial-Up Networking folder, and other options, which can vary by system.
- Right-click My Computer to choose options such as Properties (which opens the System properties sheet), the Windows Explorer, Search/Find, drive mapping, and creating shortcuts.

My Computer can open a separate window for each object you open, or you can change the contents of the My Computer window to display the contents for each object. You can change this option by clicking View, Folder Options, and selecting Custom from the Folder tab.

In Windows 95, opening My Computer does not start the Windows Explorer unless Internet Explorer 4.0 or above is installed. When Internet 4.0 or above is installed, Windows 95 will work like Windows 98 and Windows 2000, which open Windows Explorer when My Computer is opened.

The Windows Explorer

The Windows Explorer is the file-management utility used by Windows. Windows 98 and Windows 2000 can use Explorer to view both local drive/network and Internet content; Windows 95 can view only local or network drives with Explorer unless Internet Explorer 4.0 or above is installed. Windows Explorer uses a split-screen display; the left window displays a list of objects that can be browsed, such as My Computer, local and network drives, My Network Places or Network Neighborhood, the Recycle Bin, Internet Explorer, and other folders. The right window displays the contents of the currently selected object. Click the plus sign next to an object to expand the object to view folders inside the object; click the minus sign next to an object to shrink the object and conceal folders inside the object (see Figure 14.12).

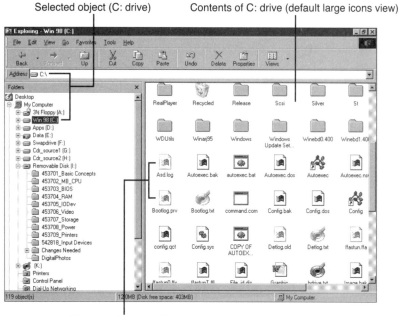

Figure 14.12
The Windows Explorer in Windows 98 (classic view); the selected object's name appears in the Address bar.

By default, Windows Explorer doesn't display hidden and system files unless the View options are changed; see "Changing Viewing Options in Windows Explorer," p.436, for details.

Starting Windows Explorer

Windows Explorer can be started in any of the following ways:

- From the Start menu, click Start, Programs, Windows Explorer (Windows 9x) or Start, Programs, Accessories, Windows Explorer (Windows 2000).
- From the command line, type `Explorer` and press Enter.
- Open My Computer in Windows 98 and 2000 to start Explorer automatically.

To start Windows Explorer from My Computer in Windows 95 if Internet Explorer 4.0 or above is not installed, use either of the following options:

- **Right-click My Computer and select Explore**—Use this option to display the contents of My Computer in the right-hand Explorer window.
- **Right-click any object in My Computer and select Explore**—Use this option to display the contents of the object in the right-hand Explorer window.

Classic and Web View

Windows Explorer can be set to display objects in either Classic or Web view. Classic view is similar to the original Windows Explorer in Windows 95; Web view requires that Internet Explorer 4.0 or above be installed on Windows 95. It's a standard option with Windows 98 and Windows 2000.

Figure 14.12 shows Explorer's Classic view, which uses the entire Explorer window for viewing object and folder information. Some users prefer the Web view, which treats a Web-view folder like a Web page—the user can add background wallpaper to each folder, view properties for the selected object in the middle of the screen, and single-click an object to open it. Figure 14.13 shows the Web view of the C: drive in the Windows 2000 Explorer (Windows 9x's Web view is almost identical).

Setting and Displaying File Attributes in Windows 9x Explorer

As discussed earlier in this chapter, the ATTRIB command can be used to set and display basic file attributes (read-only, system, hidden, and archive). The Windows 9x Explorer can also display advanced file attributes.

Contents of selected object (Details view)

Selector for large icons (default),
small icons, list, details views

Selected object (C: drive)

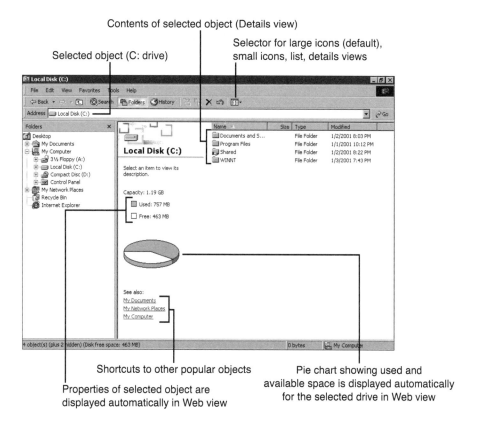

Shortcuts to other popular objects

Properties of selected object are
displayed automatically in Web view

Pie chart showing used and
available space is displayed automatically
for the selected drive in Web view

Figure 14.13
Windows Explorer in Windows 2000 (Web view) is being used to display the contents
of the C: drive

To view the attributes for a file or folder with Windows Explorer:

1. Start Windows Explorer.
2. Right-click a file or folder.
3. Select Properties.
4. The General tab indicates attributes for the file or folder. In addition to the basic
   attributes listed previously, Windows can also display the creation date of the file,
   the date the file was last accessed, and the date the file was last changed (see
   Figure 14.14).

CH
14

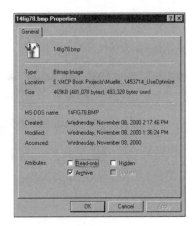

Figure 14.14
This file has the archive attribute set, which can be used by a backup program to detect which files are not yet backed up (archived).

Setting and Displaying File Attributes in Windows 2000 Explorer

Windows 2000 uses only three of the basic file attributes used by Windows 9x:

- Read-only
- Hidden
- Archive

These attributes can be viewed or changed through the Windows 2000 Explorer:

1. Start Windows Explorer.
2. Right-click a file or folder.
3. Select Properties.
4. The General tab indicates read-only or hidden attributes for the file or folder. In addition to the basic attributes listed previously, Windows 2000 can also display the creation date of the file, the date the file was last accessed, and the date the file was last changed.

To select or deselect the archive attribute, or to set encryption and compression options, click the Advanced button (see Figure 14.15).

Windows 2000 Compression/Encryption

Encryption and compression are available only on Windows 2000 drives formatted with the NTFS file system. To set these options for a file or folder in Windows 2000, you can use the Windows Explorer or the command-line programs Compact (to compress a file) or Cipher (to encrypt a file). To use the Windows Explorer, follow these steps:

1. Start Windows Explorer.

2. Right-click a file or folder.

3. Select Properties.

4. Click Advanced.

5. Select Compression to reduce the disk space used by the file, or Encryption to restrict access to only the system's administrator or the user who encrypted the file.

6. Click OK to apply either option (see Figure 14.16). Files can be compressed or encrypted, but not both.

7. If you are encrypting the file, Windows 2000 recommends that you encrypt the folder containing the file (which will also encrypt the file).

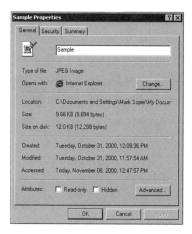

Figure 14.15
You can view the file properties for a bitmap file in Windows 2000.

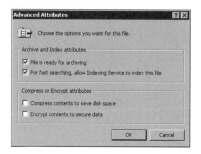

Figure 14.16
The Advanced Attributes dialog box in Windows 2000.

CH
14

Only the user who originally encrypted the file (or the system's Administrator) can open an encrypted file and view its contents. Only the Administrator can apply compression to a file or folder.

Changing Viewing Options in Windows Explorer

By default, Windows Explorer in Windows 9x and Windows 2000 prevents users from seeing information such as

- File extensions for registered file types; for example, a file called LETTER.DOC will be displayed as LETTER because WordPad (or Microsoft Word) is associated with .DOC files.
- The full path to the current folder.
- Files with hidden or system attributes, such as Bootlog.txt and Msdos.sys.
- Folders with hidden or system attributes, such as INF (used for hardware installation).

Concealing this information is intended to make it harder for users to "break" Windows, but it makes management and troubleshooting more difficult.

To change these and other viewing options, follow this procedure:

1. Start Windows Explorer.
2. Click View.
3. Click Folder Options.
4. Click the View tab.
5. Select the options you want. I recommend the following:
   - Display the Full Path in the Title Bar—enable
   - Hidden files—Show All Files
   - Hide File Extensions for Known File Types—disable

   To enable an option, make sure the selection box is checked; to disable an option, make sure the selection box is cleared (see Figure 14.17).
6. To apply these settings to all folders, click Like Current Folder.
7. Click OK to apply and close the Folder Options menu.
8. Click File, Close to close Windows Explorer.

Objects such as files and folders can be displayed in four ways within Windows Explorer:

- **Large icons**—The default (refer to Figure 14.12)
- **Small icons**—Displays more objects onscreen without scrolling vertically; might require the user to scroll horizontally to view multiple columns

- **List**—Displays more objects onscreen than large icons in a single column
- **Details**—The same size of icons used by Small or List, plus size and last-modified date details (refer to Figure 14.13)

To change the view for the current folder, use the Views button in Figure 14.13 or the View pull-down menu.

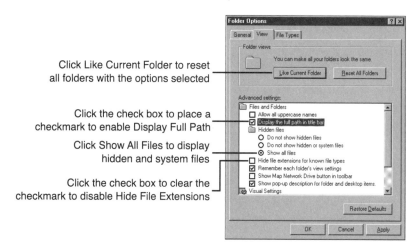

Click Like Current Folder to reset all folders with the options selected

Click the check box to place a checkmark to enable Display Full Path

Click Show All Files to display hidden and system files

Click the check box to clear the checkmark to disable Hide File Extensions

Figure 14.17
The Windows Explorer Folder Options, View menu in Windows 98 after selecting recommended options. The Windows 2000 menu is similar, but also includes an option to hide or display operating system files. Windows 95 uses a simplified version of this list.

Naming Files

Both Windows 9x and Windows 2000 support the use of long file and folder names (LFN). LFNs can be up to 255 characters and can contain spaces and most other alphanumeric characters, but cannot contain any of the following characters (which are used by the operating system):

\ / : * ? " < > |

A file can contain more than one period, but only the characters after the last period are considered the extension. In the following example, .doc is the extension:

mydocument.ltr.doc

By default, the Windows Explorer doesn't show file extensions for registered file types. You can adjust the settings in Windows Explorer to show all file extensions, or use the DIR command from a command prompt to view the extension for a specified file.

Most Common File Extensions

Table 14.7 is a list of the most common file extensions and their meanings. For more file extensions, I recommend the WhatIs? Web site's "Every File Format in the World" section, which lists more than 3,100 file formats at www.whatis.com.

Table 14.7   Common File Extensions and Uses

File Extension	Most Common Use
ADM	Windows NT/2000 Policy template
AFM	Adobe font metrics
AI	Adobe Illustrator graphics
ANI	Microsoft Windows animated cursor
ARJ	ARJ-type archive (compressed)
ASF	Microsoft Advanced Streaming Format
ATM	Adobe Type Manager
BAK	Backup
BAT	Batch file
BFC	Windows 9x Briefcase
BIN	Binary file
BMP	Windows or OS/2 Bitmap graphics
CAB	Microsoft Cabinet archive
CCM	Lotus CC:Mail "box" file
CDR	CorelDRAW vector drawing
CGI	Common Gateway Interface script
CGM	Computer Graphics Metafile
CHK	Recovered file fragments created by CHKDSK or ScanDisk
COM	Executable file (program)
CSV	Comma-separated–value file; plain-text file used for database import/export
DA0	Backup of Windows 9x Registry
DAT	Data file; also used for Windows 9x Registry files
DBF	dBase (xBase) data file
DLL	Dynamic link library (Windows program) file
DOC	Microsoft Word document (also used by WordStar, WordPerfect, DisplayWrite, and others for different formats)
DRV	Windows driver file
DWG	AutoCAD drawing

Table 14.7 continued	
File Extension	Most Common Use
DXF	Drawing Exchange Format used for import/export with AutoCAD
EMF	Enhanced Windows Metafile
EML	Microsoft Outlook Express email message
EPS	Encapsulated PostScript graphics
EXE	Executable file (program)
FAQ	Frequently Asked Questions file
FLT	Document or graphics file filter
FOT	Installed TrueType Font
GIF	CompuServer Graphics Interchange File
HTM or HTML	Hypertext Markup Language file (Web page)
INF	Information file; used to install Windows software and hardware; stored in \Windows\INF folder
INI	Initialization file; used to configure Windows and some applications
JAR	Java Archive
JPG	JPEG graphics file
LGO	Microsoft Windows startup logo file
LOG	Log file
LZH	LHArc compressed file
MAC	MacPaint image file
MMF	Microsoft Mail message file
MME	Multi-part file stored in Multipurpose Internet Mail Extensions (MIME) format; open with WinZip
MOV	QuickTime or other movie file
MP3	MPEG music file
MPG	MPEG animation file
NDX	dBase (xBase) index file
NT	Microsoft NT/2000 startup file
OBJ	Object file
OLE	Object Linking and Embedding control file or object
OVR	Overlay (program) file
PBK	Microsoft Phonebook
PCL	Printer Control Language (HP LaserJet) bitmap

CH

14

Table 14.7 continued	
File Extension	*Most Common Use*
PCX	PC Paintbrush graphics file
PDF	Portable Document File read by Adobe Acrobat
PIF	Program Information File; used by Windows 9x to set up DOS apps to run under Windows
PLT	Plotter file from AutoCAD and other CAD programs
PNG	Portable Network Graphics file
PPT	Microsoft PowerPoint presentation file
PRN	Print-to-disk file from various programs
PS	PostScript printer-ready file
PUB	Microsoft Publisher or Ventura Publisher file
ROM	Disk image of various video game cartridges for use with an emulator
RTF	Rich Text Format document; used by WordPad and most word-processing programs
SCR	Windows 9x screensaver
SIT	StuffIt (Mac) archive
SYS	System file; can be binary or text
TIF	Tagged Image File Format graphics file
TMP	Microsoft Windows temporary file
TTF	TrueType font
TXT	ASCII (plain-text) document file
URL	Universal Resource Locator (Internet Web site document name)
UU	File encoded with Uuencode
VBA	Visual Basic file
VIR	File identified as containing a virus by Norton Antivirus
VXD	Windows Virtual Device Driver file
WAB	Microsoft Windows Outlook and Outlook Express file
WAV	Digitized audio file
WK1, WK3, WK4	Lotus 1-2-3 worksheet files
WKQ	Quattro Pro worksheet files
WKS	Lotus 1-2-3 or Microsoft Works worksheet file
WMF	Windows Metafile graphics file
WPD	WordPerfect document file

Table 14.7 continued

File Extension	Most Common Use
WPG	WordPerfect graphics file
WPS	Microsoft Works document
XLS	Microsoft Excel worksheet
XML	Extensible Markup Language file
ZIP	PKZIP-compatible archive file, also compatible with WinZip and others
123	Lotus 1-2-3 worksheet file
386	Driver file used by Windows 3.x

MS-DOS Alias and LFN

If you use only 32-bit Windows applications, files are referenced with the LFN (Long Filename). However, if you use the Windows 9x EBD or the Windows 2000 Recovery Console, you will need to understand how the MS-DOS alias name is created from the LFN.

In Windows, the MS-DOS alias is created from the first six characters of the LFN, followed by the tilde (~) and a number. The first file uses 1 with the same initial six letters saved to a given folder, the second file uses 2, and so forth. If more than nine files with the same initial letters are saved to a given folder, the first five letters are used for files numbered ~10 and up, and so forth.

Using Windows Error Checking

Both Windows 9x and Windows 2000 provide integrated error-checking programs for fixing disk problems. The Windows error-checking program for Windows 9x is ScanDisk, and the error-checking program used by Windows 2000 is CHKDSK; in Windows Explorer both are referred to as error checking. To run error checking from the Windows GUI

1. Open the Windows Explorer.
2. Right-click a drive.
3. Select Properties.
4. Select Tools.
5. In Windows 9x, the Error-Checking Status section of the Tools menu indicates how long it has been since you checked the drive (see Figure 14.18); Windows 2000 does not indicate this information.
6. Click Check Now to start the process.

CH

14

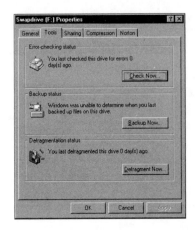

Figure 14.18
The Windows 9x Tools menu lets you launch error-checking, backup, and defragmentation utilities.

You can also start Windows 9x's ScanDisk by choosing Start, Programs, Accessories, System Tools, ScanDisk.

With Windows 9x, after the process starts, you can select either Standard or Thorough testing. Thorough testing takes longer but checks the disk surface for errors as well as checking files and folders. Use the Options button to select whether to check the entire drive, to perform write testing, and to fix bad sectors in system and hidden files. Check the Automatically Fix Errors box to have ScanDisk fix disk and file errors it detects without user intervention. Click Advanced to specify how to handle cross-linked files, lost file fragments, and other problems.

With Windows 2000, you select whether to automatically fix errors and attempt the recovery of bad sectors as soon as you start the process.

Click Start to begin the test process. A progress bar indicates the progress of testing.

Backup/Restore

Windows 9x and Windows 2000 provide backup and restore programs you can use to safeguard information on a system. Backup and restore programs differ from conventional file copy routines in these ways:

- Backups are typically compressed; file copies performed with COPY or XCOPY/XCOPY32 generally are not.
- Backups can span a large file onto two or more separate pieces of media; COPY and XCOPY/XCOPY32 cannot subdivide a large file.

■ Backups must be restored by the same or compatible program; files copied by COPY or XCOPY/XCOPY32 can be retrieved by Windows Explorer and standard Windows programs.

■ Backups can be stored to tape, floppy disk, or other types of removable storage; COPY and XCOPY/XCOPY32 can work only with drives that can be accessed through a drive letter or a UNC (Universal Naming Convention) network path.

To run the Windows backup program

1. Open the Windows Explorer.

2. Right-click a drive.

3. Select Properties.

4. Select Tools.

5. On Windows 98, the Backup Status section of the Tools menu indicates how long it has been since you backed up the drive.

6. Click Backup Now to start Backup.

You can also start Backup by clicking Start, Programs, Accessories, System Tools, Backup.

The Windows Backup program supports backups to a wide variety of drive types, including tape drives, floppy disk drives, and removable-media drives, but not CD-RW or CD-R drives. Windows 95 uses a simpler backup program than Windows 98.

During the backup process, you can specify the following:

■ Which drive(s) to back up

■ Which files to back up, selecting all files or new and changed files only

■ Where to back them up—to tape drive, floppy disk, or removable-media drive

■ How to back them up—use the Option button (Windows 98) or Tools, Options menu (Windows 2000) to set compression, passwords, backup types, files to exclude, report settings, and whether to back up the Windows Registry (Windows 98 only)

Windows 98 launches a Backup Wizard to guide you through the backup process, or you can cancel the wizard and select the options you want.

Windows Backup will prompt you for additional tape or disk media as needed throughout the backup process. Figure 14.19 illustrates the Windows 98 Backup program.

The Windows 2000 backup program is also used to create the Windows 2000 Emergency Repair Disk (see Figure 14.20), and can also optionally back up the Registry. The Windows 2000 backup program also features an integrated scheduler.

CH

14

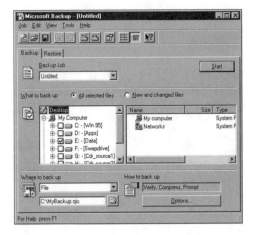

Figure 14.19
Set up a backup job with the Windows 98 Backup program.

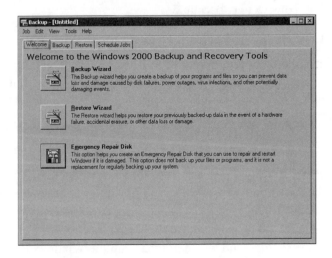

Figure 14.20
The Windows 2000 Backup program's main screen.

Using Defragment

Over time, the empty space available on a hard disk becomes fragmented as temporary files are created and deleted. When a file can no longer be stored in a contiguous group of allocation units, Windows stores the files in as many groups of allocation units as necessary and reassembles the file when it is next accessed. The extra time needed to save and read the file reduces system performance.

Both Windows 9x and Windows 2000 offer defragmentation utilities that can be used to reassemble files into contiguous allocation units and create a single large block of empty disk space.

To run the Windows Defragmentation utility

1. Open the Windows Explorer.
2. Right-click a drive.
3. Select Properties.
4. Select Tools.
5. In Windows 9x, the Defragmentation Status section of the Tools menu indicates how long it has been since you checked the drive.
6. Click Defragment Now to start the Defragmentation process.

You can also start Disk Defragmenter by clicking Start, Programs, Accessories, System Tools, Disk Defragmenter.

There are no configuration options for Windows 9x Defragment. However, you can switch to a full-screen view and display a legend during the operation.

The Windows 2000 defragmenter features an Analyze button that determines whether defragmentation is necessary (see Figure 14.21).

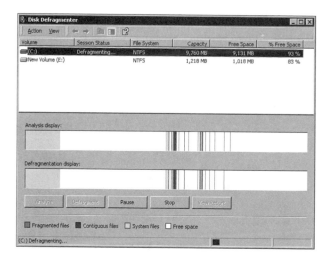

Figure 14.21
The Windows 2000 Defragmentation program can analyze the drive before beginning the defragmentation process.

CH
14

Locating Files and Folders

Windows 9x uses the Find command to locate files and folders, whereas Windows 2000 calls this option Search. Both Find and Search can be used to locate computers on a network, people, Internet content, or other options that vary according to the software installed on a particular system. To start the process of locating a file or folder

1. Click Start.
2. Click Find (Windows 9x) or Search (Windows 2000).
3. Click Files or Folders.

Windows 9x uses a small multitabbed window for its Find command; Windows 2000 uses the Windows Explorer for its Search command. Each are discussed separately.

Using Windows 9x Find

To find a file or folder with Windows 9x after the Find menu is displayed

1. Enter the file or folder name (or a portion of the name) in the Named field on the Name & Location tab; you can use wildcards such as the following:
   - NOTE*—Finds all files or folders starting with NOTE.
   - *NOTE—Finds all files or folders ending with NOTE.
   - *NOTE*—Finds all files or folders containing NOTE anywhere in the name.

   You also can click the down arrow to reuse a previous search.
2. Select the drives or other locations to search with the Look In menu.
3. Click Find Now to begin the search (see Figure 14.22).

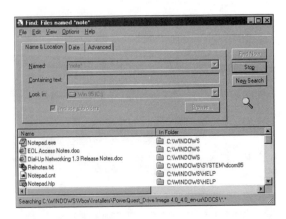

Figure 14.22
All files containing NOTE in the name on the C: drive are located by a search specifying *NOTE* and the C: drive.

To customize the search, specify any or all of the following options:

On the Name & Location tab

- **Containing text**—Enter text contained in the file.
- **Include subfolders**—Clear this checkbox to search only the location specified in Look in.
- **Browse**—Specify a starting folder with this option.

On the Date tab

- Select Find all Files and one of the following options:
    - **Modified (default)**—Finds all files last changed in the date range specified
    - **Created**—Finds all files originally created in the date range specified
    - **Accessed**—Finds all files accessed in the date range specified
    - **Between**—Specify starting date (first field) and ending date (second field)
    - **During the previous ___ month(s)**—Select 1 to 999
    - **During the previous ___ day(s)**—Select 1 to 999

On the Advanced tab

- **Of Type**—Choose the file type to search for, or use All Files and Folders (default)
- **Size is**—Leave blank or select At Least or At Most to specify file size limits; specify 0–999999KB for size

4. Click Find Now to start the search with the specified options. Click New Search to create a new search.

Using Windows 2000 Search

The Windows 2000 Search tool offers similar options to the Windows 98 Find tool, although it uses the Windows 2000 Explorer. The following are some differences:

- Search options are not displayed unless you click the Search Options box.
- To specify values for each search option, click the check mark box next to the search option.
- Advanced options also include
    - **Case sensitive**—This option enables you to specify capital or small letters in your search.
    - **Search slow files**—This option will temporarily copy files on removable media to your system's hard disk to speed up searches.

Figure 14.23 shows the Windows 2000 Search tool with Advanced options specified.

CH

14

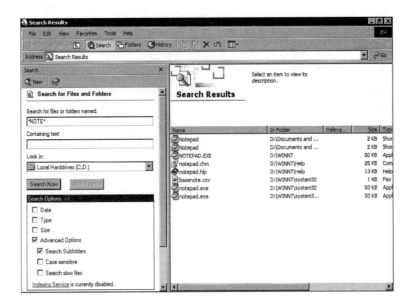

Figure 14.23
All files containing NOTE in the name on C: and D: drives are located by a search specifying *NOTE* and Local hard drives C: and D:.

Installing Windows Software

Most Windows software is installed through the use of a setup program, usually called Setup.exe. Sometimes an .inf file is used instead.

To install a program

1. Open the Add/Remove Programs icon in Control Panel.
2. Click the Install/Uninstall tab and click the Install button.
3. Insert the installation disk or CD-ROM and use the Browse button to highlight the setup program (usually called Setup.exe).

If you are installing an addition to Windows, use the Windows Setup tab instead. If the Windows program is not listed among the details for the Components listed, you might need to use the Have Disk button to install it. Have Disk uses the .inf file provided with some software to guide its installation.

After the setup program starts, typical steps include

- Selecting a destination drive and folder for the software
- Selecting a typical or other type of installation

A typical installation uses default settings for program components to install, and might even use a default setting for the program location.

If you want to choose where to install the program and what portions of the program to install, choose the Custom option instead.

Making Program Menu and Desktop Shortcuts

Most installation programs will install a shortcut (a .lnk file) on either the Windows desktop or on the Start button or folder of the Start button. Some installation programs do not, but you can add your own.

To add a shortcut to the Windows desktop

1. Right-click the Windows desktop (not on an existing icon).
2. Select New, and then Shortcut.
3. You can enter the path to the program (such as C:\Windows\Pbrush.exe) or click the Browse button to locate the program you are making a shortcut for. Click Next.
4. You can keep the program name as the shortcut name, or enter the name you prefer.
5. Click Finish. The shortcut appears on your desktop.

To add a shortcut to the Program menu:

1. Right-click the Start button.
2. Select Explore.
3. The Windows Explorer opens; shortcuts and folders for shortcuts appear in the right window.
4. If you want your shortcut to be displayed as soon as you click the Start button, right-click below the last shortcut and select New, Shortcut. Follow the directions given earlier for making a shortcut on the desktop.
5. If you want your shortcut to be stored in an existing folder, open the Programs shortcut in the right window. Open a folder and right-click below the last shortcut and select New, Shortcut. Follow the directions given earlier for making a shortcut on the desktop.
6. If you want your shortcut to be stored in a new folder, open the Programs shortcut in the right window. Right-click in the open space in the right-hand window and select New, Folder. Enter the folder name. Open the new folder and right-click in the right window and select New, Shortcut. Follow the directions given earlier for making a shortcut on the desktop.

CH
14

Starting Windows Software

Windows software can be started in any of the following ways:

- Open the executable file in Windows Explorer.
- Open the shortcut in Windows Explorer.
- Open the shortcut on the desktop or from the Start button.
- Search for the executable file or shortcut with the Find button; select Files or Folders and open the correct file.

Installing Non-Windows Software

Non-Windows (MS-DOS) software usually requires several manual steps for installation. Typical steps include

- Creating a folder for installation with Windows Explorer
- Copying the files to the folder
- Extracting files from a compressed archive to the folder
- Running an installation program (Install.exe or similar)

After the program is installed, desktop and Start button shortcuts should be created for the program, as described earlier.

Starting Non-Windows Software

The default settings for non-Windows software can be adjusted by setting the program properties for the executable file. The program properties file is called a .pif file; it performs a task similar to the Program Information Files of the same name that were used by Windows 3.x for MS-DOS programs.

To adjust the default settings for a non-Windows program

1. Open the Windows Explorer.
2. Right-click the executable file.
3. Select Properties.
4. The General tab lists file attributes; adjust the program's operation with the Program, Font, Memory, Screen, and Misc tabs. Each tab is described in the following sections.

Adjusting the Environment with the Program Tab

The Program tab allows you to adjust the command line, working folder, starting folder, and batch file to use to start the program, the shortcut key used to start the program, and whether to start the program in a normal, maximized (full-screen), or minimized window. Click the Change Icon button to choose a custom icon for the shortcut.

Click the Advanced button to specify MS-DOS mode (which restarts the computer before running the program); you can also specify contents of the Config.sys and Autoexec.bat files to use in running the program. If you elect to use a new Autoexec.bat and Config.sys, you can manually adjust the suggested configuration or use the Configuration button to choose the most common settings from a list.

Adjusting the Appearance of the Program Window with the Font Tab

A non-Windows program running in a desktop window can use any of a variety of different sizes of TrueType (TT) and bitmap fonts. Windows will choose a default based on your current screen's size and resolution. You can override the choice with the Font tab. Select the font you want from the right-hand list and see a preview of how the font will look. Generally, bitmap fonts are easier to read than TrueType fonts when used for non-Windows programs.

Adjusting Memory Usage with the Memory Tab

You can adjust how the non-Windows program uses the amount and types of memory available through adjusting settings on the Memory tab.

Adjustments include

- How much conventional memory to use
- Whether to place the program in a protected section of memory
- Whether to use XMS or EMS memory and how much
- Whether to use DPMI memory and how much

Screen, Keyboard, and Other Adjustments

Adjust screen handling, including whether to run the program in a window or full-screen, and how to handle video with the Screen tab.

Use the Misc tab to control various additional settings, including whether to use the Windows screensaver with the program, which Windows shortcut keys to be overridden by program usage, and adjustments for running the program in the background and when multitasking.

All changes are saved to a .pif file, which is stored in the same folder as the non-Windows program and is referred to when the program is started.

QUESTIONS AND ANSWERS:

1. What is the procedure for locating a file containing specified text between a range of dates?
    A: Click Start, Find (Windows 9x) or Search (Windows 2000), Files or Folders. Click Date and enter the date ranges to search (Windows 9x); click Search options, date, and enter the date ranges to search (Windows 2000).

2. What is the Windows Registry and where is it stored in Windows 9x? In Windows 2000?
    A: The Windows Registry stores hardware and software settings for Windows. Windows 9x uses the User.dat and System.dat files in the \Windows folder to store the Registry; Windows 2000 stores the Registry in the \WinNT\System32\Config folder.

3. What are two ways to access the System properties sheet?
    A: Right-click My Computer and select Properties or open the System icon in the Control Panel.

4. What command-prompt command displays Windows 9x release info?
    A: The VER command displays release information.

5. What Control Panel properties sheet and tabs are used to adjust system performance in Windows 9x? In Windows 2000?
    A: Windows 9x uses the System properties sheet, Performance tab, File System option. Windows 2000 uses the System properties sheet, Advanced tab, Performance Options button.

6. What Windows 2000 program can be run to set up a command-prompt session within the Windows GUI? Which Windows 2000 feature allows command-prompt operations at boot time to repair errors?
    A: Cmd.exe starts a command-prompt session while the Windows 2000 GUI is in use. The Recovery Console enables you to repair a Windows 2000 installation with command-line commands and utilities.

Installing and Configuring Hardware in Windows

WHILE YOU READ

1. Are print jobs in Windows sent straight to the printer? If not, in what folder are they stored?
2. Which tab on the Printers properties sheet is used to test a printer?
3. When a network printer is not available, the print spooler is set to what mode? How will the user release stored print jobs after the printer becomes available?
4. What is required for PnP hardware installation besides Windows 9x or Windows 2000?
5. Besides the Windows Device Manager, what other Windows utility can be used to determine IRQ, DMA, I/O port, and memory usage for devices?
6. If a Windows 2000 user needs to free up disk space, which tool can be used to perform this task?

This chapter discusses how different types of hardware, including add-on cards and printers, are configured and used by Windows. The chapter also provides troubleshooting information for the hardware types covered in this chapter.

Using the Control Panel

The Control Panel is the major starting point for adjusting the hardware and user interface settings in Windows. It contains the following hardware-related icons; open the icon to see and adjust the current settings:

- **Add New Hardware (Windows 9x)/Add/Remove Hardware (Windows 2000)**—Installs new PnP and legacy hardware. The Windows 2000 wizard also troubleshoots and removes hardware.

- **Display**—Adjusts monitor, video adapter, and Windows desktop settings.

- **Game Controllers**—Adjusts settings for joysticks, steering wheels, and other game controllers.

- **Internet Options**—Adjusts Internet settings used by Internet Explorer and other Microsoft products.

- **Keyboard**—Adjusts keyboard repeat rate and language.

- **Modems**—Adjusts, installs, and tests modems and serial ports.

- **Mouse**—Adjusts and installs mice and similar pointing devices.

- **Multimedia**—Adjusts multimedia device settings.

- **Network**—Installs and configures network hardware and software.

- **Power Management**—Enables, disables, and adjusts power management settings.

- **Printers**—Installs and removes printers and adjusts printer settings.

- **Sounds**—Configures sound playback during specified system events.

- **System**—Displays and configures Device Manager and other hardware settings including Performance, and general Windows information, performance, and hardware profiles.

- **Telephony**—Configures telephony device drivers and dialing settings used by modems and similar devices.

Other Control Panel icons are primarily software-related; some user-installed software and devices also add icons to the Control Panel (see Figure 15.1).

Opening the Control Panel and Its Icons

You can open the Control Panel folder from the Start button, My Computer, or the Windows Explorer.

- **Click Start, Settings, Control Panel**—The Control Panel will open a new window onscreen.

- **Open My Computer and select the Control Panel**—The Control Panel's contents will be displayed in the right-hand window or in a new window, depending on the settings you use for My Computer.

- **Open the Windows Explorer and select the Control Panel**—The Control Panel's contents will be displayed in the right-hand Explorer window.

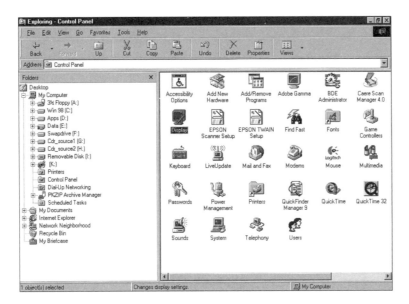

Figure 15.1
The Windows 98 Control Panel as viewed in Windows Explorer.

Open any Control Panel icon to see current settings and make adjustments for the devices it controls. If the Classic view is used for the Control Panel folder, double-click an icon to open it. If Web view is used, a single click will open an icon.

Shortcuts to Control Panel Icons

Some Control Panel icons can be accessed through properties sheets. If you right-click any of the items in Table 15.1, you will open the Control Panel icon listed.

Table 15.1 Popular Shortcuts to Control Panel Icons

Properties Sheet	Control Panel Icon Opened
My Computer	System
Display	Display
Network Neighborhood or My Network Places	Network

Printing and Printer Configuration

Windows provides extensive control over printer installation and configuration. Although printers vary widely in resolutions, print technologies, and features, most printers use the standard Windows Add Printer Wizard and Printer Properties sheets for installation and setup.

Installing the Printer

To install a printer in Windows:

1. Click Start, Settings, Printer.

2. Open the Add Printer Wizard.

3. Specify whether the new printer is connected through a local port or through a network—Windows 2000 will automatically detect a Plug and Play printer by default.

4. For Windows 2000, select the port, then the brand and model of your printer; for Windows 9x, select the brand and model followed by the port.

   If you have an installation disk or CD-ROM provided by the vendor, click Have Disk and browse to the installation disk or CD-ROM for the printer (see Figure 15.2).

5. Choose the port (for local printers) or network share (for network printers). If the printer is a network printer, specify whether you want to send MS-DOS print jobs to the printer.

6. Specify whether the printer will be the default printer (if you are installing an additional printer).

7. Specify whether you want to share the printer if prompted.

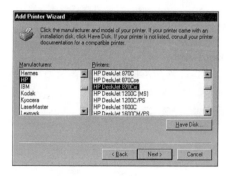

Figure 15.2
Choose the brand and model of the printer, or use Have Disk to install a vendor-supplied driver for your printer.

8. Specify whether you want to print a test page. This is the default and is recommended to make sure your printer is working properly.

9. Windows 2000 displays the printer selections. Click Finish if you are done or click the Back button to make changes.

After you click Finish, the printer will be installed into the Printers folder, and it will be available to all Windows applications.

Setting the Default Printer

If you have more than one printer installed, you can choose which printer will be the default at any time. The printer indicated with a check mark in the Printers folder is the current default printer. To change to a different default printer

1. Right-click the printer you want to set as the default printer.

2. Select Set as Default from the menu.

Using the Print Spooler

Windows automatically uses the default TEMP folder for print jobs, spooling them to disk for printing on the printer selected by the user.

Most printers use the standard Windows print spooler, although some inkjet printers use their own spooler software instead. To view the print spooler, you can

- Double-click the Printer icon shown in the Windows toolbar; this icon appears whenever one or more print jobs are waiting to print.
- Double-click the Printer icon in the Printers folder.

The spooler (see Figure 15.3) displays the following information:

- The name of the printer
- The print jobs waiting to print in order
  - Document name
  - Status
  - Owner (user who sent the job)
  - Progress (number of pages or size of document)
  - Time and date the job began printing
  - The number of print jobs waiting to print

Printing to a Network Printer

The requirements for network printing vary between Windows 9x and Windows 2000 because of the difference in security features of these versions of Windows.

Printer name

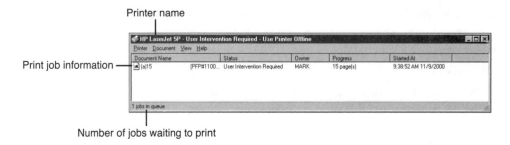

Print job information

Number of jobs waiting to print

Figure 15.3
The Windows 9x print spooler.

For network printing to take place with Windows 9x, the printer must be set as a shared resource on a computer that has Windows File and Print Sharing enabled. If share-level security is used on the network, password protection is optional (see Figure 15.4). A remote user needs to know only the password (if any) to use the printer. If the computer hosting a shared printer is connected to a Windows NT, Windows 2000, or Novell NetWare server, the server's list of users and groups can be used to restrict access; anyone who wants to use the printer must be on the list of users or groups that have been granted access. The password or server containing the user list is specified in the properties for the shared printer.

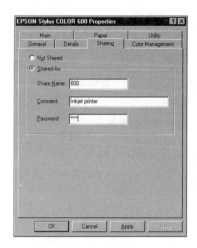

Figure 15.4
Sharing a printer with Windows 9x; the Sharing tab is used to specify the name and description that the shared printer will display over the network, and the password is used to restrict access to the printer.

Windows 2000 also requires that the printer be set as a shared resource. Security for Windows 2000 printing is controlled by user lists and permissions; only users on the list of authorized users who have been granted permission to use the printer can use the printer. Windows 2000 is designed to provide drivers to users of most current and older versions of Windows, so that after the remote user selects the printer, Windows 2000 will download the correct drivers to the remote user's computer.

To enable Windows 2000 to provide drivers for users of other versions of Windows, click Additional Drivers after you set the printer as a shared device, and select the driver versions you want to make available (see Figure 15.5).

Printer Troubleshooting

Windows provides a variety of means for dealing with common printing problems, including

- Printer properties sheet
- Printer test
- Spooler options
- Troubleshooters in the Help system

Figure 15.5
A Windows 2000 computer with a shared printer can provide drivers for remote users of Windows NT 3.1 through 4.0, Windows 2000, and Windows 95 and 98.

To view the printer properties sheet, right-click the Printer icon in the Printers folder and select Properties.

All printers have the following tabs in the properties sheet:

- **General**—Features the Print Test Page button, which prints a test page of graphics and text, listing the driver files.
- **Details (Windows 9x)**—Lists the printer port (or network print queue), driver, and print-capture settings. Windows 2000 lists local printer ports on the Ports tab and network settings on the Advanced tab, instead of using a Details tab.

- **Sharing**—Available only if File and Print Sharing is enabled on the system; this lets the user enable or disable printing. Windows 9x users can also set up a password to restrict access.
- **Security**—Available only on Windows 2000, this tab allows you to select which users can print and manage print jobs and documents.

Other tabs vary by printer brand, model, and type. Some typical optional tabs include

- **Graphics**—Printer's graphics resolution and mode (called Main on some models) settings.
- **Utility**—Alignment and cleaning options for inkjet printers.
- **Fonts**—Laser printer font cartridges and TrueType font handling settings.
- **Device Options**—Varies by printer and Windows version; check here for options not found on other tabs. This tab can include memory sizing and options, paper type, fonts, print quality, and other options.
- **Paper**—Paper size and orientation settings.

Many print problems can be solved using the printer properties sheets.

Inability to Print

If you can't print to a local printer, follow this procedure:

1. Check cables to make sure they are tight and in good working order.
2. Check the printer port in the Windows Device Manager and make sure the port is working properly. See "Using the Windows Device Manager," page 469, for details.
3. Try a test print with the printer General properties sheet (see Figure 15.6).
4. If you can't get the printer to print a test page, check the Details properties sheet to verify that the correct port and printer driver have been selected; change settings as necessary, and retry the test print.
5. Check the print spooler; if the printer is a network printer, you might need to set the printer to online mode if the network printer was unavailable the last time you tried to print to it.
6. If the paper goes through the inkjet printer and the printhead is moving, but there is no ink on the paper, the printheads might be clogged. Check the Utility tab on the printer driver to locate the head cleaning utility. Retry printing after cleaning the printhead.
7. If you still can't print, use the Windows print troubleshooters.

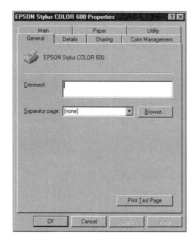

CH
15

Figure 15.6
Use the Print Test Page button on the General properties sheet to test the printer; if the printer will not print, no Windows applications will be able to use the printer until the problem is isolated and solved.

To access the Windows 98 print troubleshooter:

1. Click Start.
2. Click Help.
3. Click the Contents tab (open by default).
4. Click Troubleshooting.
5. Click Windows 98 Troubleshooters.
6. Select Print Troubleshooter.

To access the Windows 2000 print troubleshooter:

1. Click Start.
2. Click Help.
3. Click the Contents tab (open by default).
4. Click Troubleshooting and Maintenance.
5. Click Windows 2000 Troubleshooters.
6. Select Print Troubleshooter.

Follow the prompts to a possible solution (see Figure 15.7).

To troubleshoot problems printing to a network printer

1. Make sure you are logged in to the network; no network resources will work if you are not logged in.

Figure 15.7
Select the best response to each question and the print troubleshooter will try to find the solution to your printing problem.

2. If the printer uses share-level security, try to log in to the printer; make sure you provide the correct password.

3. If the printer uses user-level security, make sure you are on the list of authorized users; check with the administrator of the computer or network.

4. Verify that the share name is correct on the Details tab of the printer (see Figure 15.8).

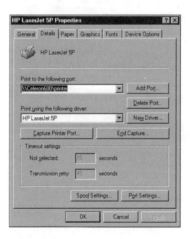

Figure 15.8
Check the server name (\\server) and print queue name (\printer) with the network administrator if you are unable to print; you also might need to obtain a password or make sure you are on the list of approved users for the printer.

5. Make sure that your print spooler isn't set to offline mode; if the network printer isn't available, offline mode is set by default. A red icon over the Printer icon in the system tray indicates the print spooler is in offline mode.

Working with the Print Spooler

Normally, the print spooler is transparent to the user, sending print jobs to the printer as they are received and as the printer is available. However, special circumstances, such as a network printer going offline or the need to discard a print job, might require the user to open the print spooler.

To release print jobs stored in the spooler in offline mode after the network printer is available

1. Open the print spooler.

2. Click Printer.

3. Uncheck Use Printer Offline and the print jobs will go to the printer.

To discard a print job in the spooler

1. Open the print spooler.

2. Right-click the print job you want to discard.

3. Select Cancel Print and the print job will be discarded.

To discard all print jobs in the spooler

1. Open the print spooler.

2. Click Printer.

3. For Windows 9x, click Purge Print Documents; for Windows 2000, click Cancel all documents. All print jobs are discarded.

Garbage Output and Its Causes

Garbage output from the printer is frequently caused by using the wrong printer driver to communicate with the printer; if the printer is sent commands it cannot understand, it tries to print them anyway.

Some common causes for this problem include

- Failing to select a new printer, connected to the same port as the previous printer, as the default printer
- Forgetting to move the lever on a two-printer to one-computer switchbox

Other causes for garbage output might include

- Selecting a printer driver that would work if the printer were set to the correct emulation mode. For example, if a printer is both LaserJet- and Postscript-compatible, you might need to manually select which mode to use for printing.

■ Turning on the printer after the start of the print job. If the first portion of the print job isn't received, the printer will produce garbage because the printer setup data wasn't received.

Installing Hardware

Most hardware, whether installed in an expansion slot, a drive bay, or through an external port, is now Plug and Play (PnP) compatible. Plug and Play installation means that Windows will detect the device during startup, install the correct software drivers, and configure the device for correct operation. On systems that don't have a PnP BIOS, or when installing devices that are added after the system has started, use one of the following options:

■ Windows 9x uses the Add New Hardware Wizard in the Control Panel.

■ Windows 2000 uses the Add/Remove Hardware Wizard in the Control Panel.

Plug and Play Requirements

Both Windows 9x and Windows 2000 support Plug and Play, but how Plug and Play actually works varies between these versions of Windows.

For Plug and Play to function correctly, the following must be true:

■ The device must support Plug and Play. Some legacy devices can be switched into Plug and Play mode.

■ The operating system must support Plug and Play (true of both Windows 98 and Windows 2000).

■ The system BIOS must support Plug and Play. Depending on the system, you might also need to set the BIOS to indicate that a PnP-compatible operating system is in use.

PnP spells the end of fixed hardware resource settings; whenever a new PnP device is installed, existing device settings can change to allow the new device to be properly installed.

Most current devices are designed strictly as PnP devices; no manual configuration is possible. Some ISA cards can be set to PnP mode by moving a jumper block, flipping a DIP switch, or running a configuration program.

Installing a PnP Device

The following is the basic procedure for installing a PnP device:

1. Install or connect the device to the system.

2. Turn on the system. As soon as the Windows desktop begins to appear, Windows detects the device.

If Windows already has a suitable driver, the device will be installed and configured.

The remainder of the steps vary, depending on whether you are installing the device under Windows 98 or Windows 2000.

Follow these steps for Windows 98 (Windows 95 is similar):

1. If a suitable driver is not available, Windows 98 will start the Add New Hardware Wizard.

2. Choose from Search for the Best Driver (default) or Display a List of All the Drivers. Then click Next.

3. You can edit the default search options (see Figure 15.9) or specify a location for the driver if you downloaded it. After you have selected the best places to search, click Next to continue.

Figure 15.9
By default, the Windows 98 Add New Hardware Wizard searches the floppy disk drives and CD-ROM drive for hardware drivers (.INF files); select different locations as needed to find the drivers for your device.

4. If Search is unable to locate a driver, click Back and select Specify a Location. Click Browse to search the CD-ROM or floppy disk for the correct files.

5. Confirm the device name and the driver file location, and click Next to continue. You might need to exchange the driver CD for the Windows CD during installation.

6. Click Finish when prompted. After the device is installed, you might be prompted to reboot the system.

Follow these steps for Windows 2000:

1. If a suitable driver is not available, Windows 2000 will start the Add/Remove Hardware Wizard.

2. Choose either Search for a Suitable Driver (default) or Display a List of the Known Drivers.

3. You can edit the default search options or specify a location for the driver if you downloaded it. After you have selected the best places to search, click Next to continue.

4. If Search is unable to locate a driver, click Back and select Specify a Location. Click Browse to search the CD-ROM or floppy disk for the correct files. Windows 2000 will allow you to disable the device if no suitable driver can be located.

5. You might be able to choose either the recommended driver or an alternative driver from the list of drivers found by Search. Select Install One of the Other Drivers to see alternatives. Select the driver you prefer from the list to continue.

6. The driver will be checked for a digital signature, which indicates the driver has been tested by Microsoft for proper operation. If no digital signature is found on the driver, a warning message will be displayed, and you can choose a different driver if you prefer (see Figure 15.10). Click Yes to continue or No to return and choose another driver.

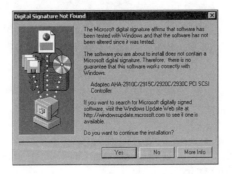

Figure 15.10
Drivers supplied by the device vendor may not have the Microsoft Digital Signature. In most cases, they can be used, but Windows 2000 will warn you about such drivers, as seen here.

7. Click Finish after installing the device. You will not need to reboot the system.

Installing a Legacy Device

If a legacy (non-PnP) device must be installed, the procedure is somewhat different. The Add New Hardware (Windows 9x) or Add/Remove Hardware Wizard (Windows 2000) must be run, and the default settings the wizard assumes might need to be altered to match the actual settings used by the device.

Follow this procedure to install a legacy device under Windows:

1. Use the Device Manager tab of the System Properties sheet to view the current hardware resource usage for the system.

2. Compare available resources to those that can be used by the card, and record the available settings.

3. Shut down the system.

4. If the card uses jumper blocks or DIP switches to select IRQ, DMA, I/O port, or memory addresses, set the resources to match available resources in the system before you install it.

5. If the card uses a software configuration program, you will need to set the card with its own software before you install it.

6. Restart the system, and access the BIOS setup program by pressing the correct key(s).

7. Go to the PnP configuration screen and see if you can set the IRQ you will use for the card to ISA instead of PnP/PCI. This will prevent Windows from trying to use the IRQ for existing cards. Save any changes and exit.

8. If the card uses software configuration, boot the computer to a command prompt. Run the card's setup program and set the card to the available hardware resource settings you noted earlier.

9. Restart the computer.

10. After the computer has completed the boot process, open the Control Panel and start the Add New Hardware Wizard (Windows 98) or Add/Remove Hardware Wizard (Windows 2000). Click Next to continue.

11. For Windows 2000, select Add/Troubleshoot a Device and click Next to continue.

In Windows 98, the Add New Hardware Wizard searches for PnP devices first and lists any new ones it finds. Select Yes to install newly found devices, or No to install a legacy device. Click Next to continue.

In Windows 2000, the Add/Remove New Hardware Wizard searches for PnP devices and lists all existing devices (this allows the wizard to be used to trouble-shoot existing devices). Click Add a New Device and Next to continue.

12. If the device is already installed, Windows can search for it. If you know the brand name and model of the device or if you have a driver disk, skip the search process and choose the device type (see Figure 15.11). Click Next to continue.

13. On the next screen, you can select the brand and model, or choose Have Disk and supply the driver disk or CD-ROM.

14. If you chose to search for the device, verify that the correct device has been located, and click Next.

15. In Windows 9x, the system will select default values for the device (which might not work), as shown in Figure 15.12. You can either adjust the device to use those settings or use the Device Manager to choose other settings for the device.

CH
15

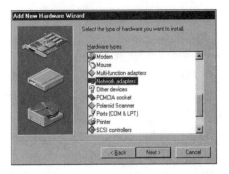

Figure 15.11
If your hardware isn't already installed, or if you prefer to specify it yourself, start by
selecting the hardware type (Windows 98 shown here).

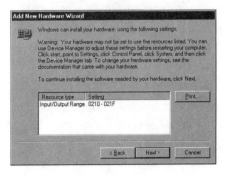

Figure 15.12
The default values listed for the device won't work unless the device is already set to
use these values. Either change the device or change the settings in Device Manager.

Windows 2000 can normally detect the device's actual settings; if the device isn't
installed yet, click the Change Setting button and select the correct Interrupt
Request (IRQ) and other hardware resources when prompted.

16. In Windows 9x, if the device is set to different values, open the Device Manager
tab of the System Properties sheet and change any hardware resource settings that
are incorrect to match the actual settings you used.

17. After the software for the device is installed, you might be prompted to shut down
and restart the system.

18. After you restart the system, the device will be ready to work.

Troubleshooting Hardware
Windows provides the following tools for troubleshooting hardware:

■ **Device Manager**—Lists basic information about devices, including driver and
hardware configurations.

- **Microsoft System Information**—Lists advanced information about devices, including .INF files, Registry keys, driver files, hardware configurations, and problems.

- **Troubleshooters**—Windows 98 includes Networking, Modem, Display, DirectX, Sound, and Hardware Conflict troubleshooters.

- **Add/Remove Hardware Wizard (Windows 2000)**—Can be used to unplug hot-swap devices, troubleshoot devices, and remove devices.

Some of the typical hardware problems that can be isolated with these tools include

- Incorrect parameters for hardware
- Bad or missing drivers
- Conflicts between devices
- Hardware options that don't work

Using the Windows Device Manager

To use the Device Manager:

1. Open the System Properties sheet in the Control Panel, or right-click My Computer and select Properties.

   To continue with Windows 9x:

2. Click the Device Manager tab; any devices with problems are displayed immediately (see Figure 15.13).

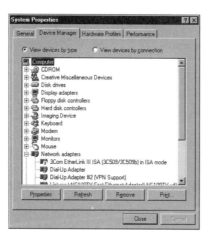

Figure 15.13
The exclamation mark next to the entry for the 3Com Etherlink III indicates it is not working properly; all problem devices are displayed when you open the Device Manager (Windows 9x version shown).

3. To see the overall hardware resources in use, double-click the Computer icon at the top of the list of devices.

4. By default, IRQ usage is displayed; click the DMA, I/O port, and memory buttons to see usage for each of these resources. Conflicts between devices are indicated with a yellow ! sign next to the conflicting settings.

5. To continue with Windows 2000, click the Hardware tab and select from the following:

- **Hardware Wizard**—Runs the Add/Remove Hardware Wizard.

- **Driver Signing**—Allows you to permit, block, or ignore digital signatures for driver files; helps you determine whether legitimate driver files for Windows 2000 are being used.

- **Device Manager**—Allows you to view and change hardware properties.

Click Device Manager to continue. Any devices with problems are highlighted immediately, as with Windows 9x.

6. To see the overall hardware resources in use, click View and select Resources by type. Click the plus sign next to each resource type listed to see its usage. In Figure 15.14, IRQ and DMA resource usage are displayed in detail. The user could view I/O resource usage by clicking the plus sign, and could view memory resource usage by scrolling down to Memory and clicking its plus sign.

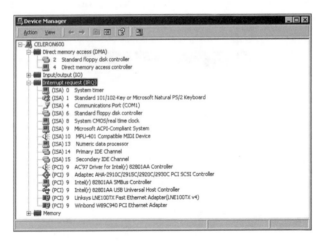

Figure 15.14
IRQ and DMA usage on a typical Windows 2000 system. Because this computer uses PCI slots and an advanced chipset that supports IRQ steering, multiple devices share IRQ9 without any problems.

To see the resource and driver information for a particular device:

1. Click the plus (+) sign next to the device category containing the device.
2. Click the device.
3. Click Properties.
4. Click the General tab to see if the device is working properly; a device with a problem will display an error message on this tab (see Figures 15.15 and 15.16).

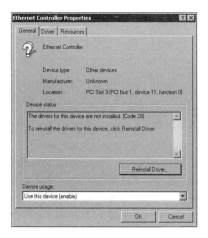

Figure 15.15
Windows 2000 reports missing driver errors with very specific messages in the Device Manager. Click the Driver tab to start the process of installing new drivers.

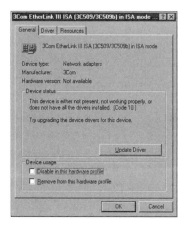

Figure 15.16
How Windows 98 reports a network card error in the Device Manager; use the Update Driver button to install new drivers for the device.

5. Click the Driver tab for driver file details; use Update Driver to install new drivers.

6. Click the Resources tab to see which hardware resources the device is using and to see whether there are any conflicts.

If the device has a conflict with another device, you might be able to change the settings in Control Panel. If the device is a legacy (non-PnP) device, you might need to shut down the system and reconfigure the card manually before you can use the Device Manager to reset its configuration in Windows.

You can also use the Device Manager to disable a device that is conflicting with another device. To disable a device

1. Click the plus (+) sign next to the device category containing the device.

2. Click the device.

3. Click Properties.

4. Click the General tab.

5. Look for the Device Usage display at the bottom of the window. With Windows 9x, click the box next to Disable in This Hardware Profile. You might need to restart the computer. With Windows 2000, click the menu and select Do Not Use This Device (disable). If you prefer to solve the problem with the device, click the Troubleshooter button to launch the appropriate Windows 2000 troubleshooter.

Depending on the device, you might need to physically remove it from the system to resolve a conflict. To use the Device Manager to remove a device

1. Click the plus (+) sign next to the device category containing the device.

2. Click the device.

3. Click Remove.

4. Confirm that you want to remove the device—the Registry entries for the device are removed, but the drivers remain on the system.

5. Shut down the system when prompted, and remove the device. Windows 2000 might not prompt you to shut down the system, but you will need to do so to remove an internal device.

Using Microsoft System Information (Windows 98/2000 Only)

Compared to the Device Manager, Microsoft System Information provides more information about your hardware. And, unlike Device Manager, System Information is strictly a reporting tool, so users cannot accidentally change their system configuration by using it.

To use Microsoft System Information for more information about your system's devices, select Start, Programs, Accessories, System Tools, and then click System Information to start the program.

Click the plus (+) sign next to Hardware Resources to select from the following options:

- **Conflicts/Sharing**—Lists IRQs that are shared among devices.
- **DMA**—Lists DMA channels in use by device.
- **Forced hardware**—Lists PnP hardware that has been set manually (see Figure 15.17). Any hardware resources used by forced hardware cannot be reassigned by the PnP features of Windows; try to avoid setting PnP hardware manually unless compatibility issues force you to do so.
- **I/O**—Lists I/O port addresses in use by device.
- **Memory**—Lists memory addresses in use by device.

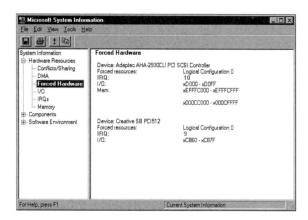

Figure 15.17
Microsoft System Information displays devices with forced hardware settings (PnP devices that are set manually by the user); Windows 98 version shown here.

For information about components (video, audio, ports, and so on), click the plus (+) sign next to Components, and click a component category for more information.

In addition to current hardware resource information, Components also lists drivers, Registry keys, and alternative hardware configurations (see Figure 15.18). Devices with problems are flagged. You can toggle between Basic Information and Advanced Information at the top of the screen as needed.

The System Information tool used by Windows 2000 has different cosmetics but similar features (see Figure 15.19). With most devices, you can switch between basic and advanced information. Figure 15.19 shows the Advanced view of display information.

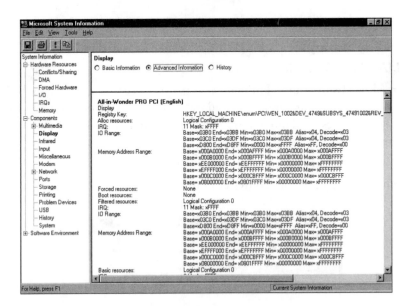

Figure 15.18
Use the Advanced Information option (seen here) to view the Registry key for a particular hardware device (Windows 98).

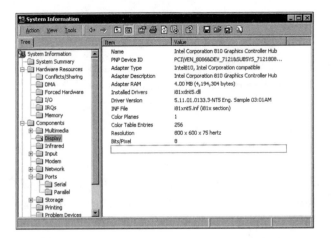

Figure 15.19
The Windows 2000 version of the Microsoft System Information utility provides detailed information about installed hardware. Note the details about video memory size, screen resolution, and refresh rates listed for the display.

Using System Information Tools

Click the Tools menu to choose from the following utilities (those marked with an asterisk * can also be run outside of System Information):

- **Windows Report Tool***—Complete this when requested by Microsoft support engineers.
- **Update Wizard Uninstall***—Uninstalls updates to Windows performed by the online Update Wizard.
- **System File Checker***—Verifies system files and replaces corrupt or damaged files from the originals stored in CAB files (Windows 98 only).
- **Signature Verification Tool***—Checks driver and other files for digital signatures (used to verify their authenticity). (Windows 98 and Windows 2000 use the File Signature Verification Utility.)
- **Registry Checker***—Replaces a corrupt Registry with a backup copy (Windows 98 only).
- **Automatic Skip Driver (ASD) Agent***—Lists devices that are not working and are skipped by Windows 98 at startup, and allows user to re-enable the device (Windows 98 only).
- **Dr. Watson***—When loaded into memory, captures details about the system's configuration when a system fault occurs. It can also be loaded from the Startup group.
- **System Configuration Utility (MSConfig)***—Can be used to troubleshoot startup problems (Windows 98 only).
- **ScanDisk***—Checks for disk errors (Windows 98 only).
- **Version Conflict Manager***—Lists system files that have been replaced with newer versions, and allows backups of those files to be restored (Windows 98 only).
- **Internet Explorer Repair Tool**—Replaces missing or corrupt Internet Explorer files (Windows 98 only).

Windows 2000's version of Microsoft System Information features the following additional tools:

- **Disk Cleanup**—Can remove temporary files, index files, and (optionally) Windows components and applications to free up disk space.
- **DirectX Diagnostic Tool**—Verifies, tests, and reports on the system's DirectX configuration.
- **Hardware Wizard**—Runs the Add/Remove Hardware Wizard.
- **Network Connections**—Opens the Network Properties sheet.
- **Backup**—Runs the Windows 2000 backup program.

Using Windows Hardware Troubleshooters

Windows supplies hardware troubleshooters as part of the Windows help system. Some troubleshooters require you to open the Device Manager to resolve the problem.

To resolve hardware conflicts, you might need to

- Change the settings of one of the devices.
- Remove one device and reinstall it.
- Disable one device to allow the other one to function.

QUESTIONS AND ANSWERS:

1. Are print jobs in Windows sent straight to the printer? If not, in what folder are they stored?
   A: Print jobs are stored in a print queue, which uses the default TEMP folder as its location.

2. Which tab on the Printers properties sheet is used to test a printer?
   A: The General tab has the Print test button.

3. When a network printer is not available, the print spooler is set to what mode? How will the user release stored print jobs after the printer becomes available?
   A: Offline mode is used to store print jobs when a network printer is not available. To release jobs, open the print queue, click Printer from the menu, and deselect Use Printer Offline.

4. What is required for PnP hardware installation besides Windows 9x or Windows 2000?
   A: PnP hardware installation also requires PnP hardware, PnP-compatible hardware drivers made for your operating system, and a PnP system BIOS.

5. Besides the Windows Device Manager, what other Windows utility can be used to determine IRQ, DMA, I/O port, and memory usage for devices?
   A: Windows System Information provides this information along with a lot of additional details about hardware.

6. If a Windows 2000 user needs to free up disk space, which tool in System Information can be used to perform this task?
   A: The Disk Cleanup program can be run from the Tools menu.

Troubleshooting Windows Software

1. If you want to start a Windows 2000 system without loading the normal video drivers, but don't want to lose other features, which startup mode should you select?

2. Which startup mode records the events that take place during startup?

3. There are three ways to start a system with minimal drivers for troubleshooting. What are they called and how do they differ from each other (briefly)?

4. What Windows 2000 feature minimizes the chances of having the Himem.sys file being replaced or deleted?

5. What Windows 98 disk is a very useful troubleshooting tool?

6. What happens to performance if you use the File System Troubleshooting options for Windows 98?

7. List two causes for SCSI error messages.

8. What is another name for a Windows Stop error? List two sources for troubleshooting Stop errors.

9. What Windows 98 utility can be used to capture system information during a GPF or other error? Which Windows 2000 feature captures system information?

10. What are two symptoms of a virus infection spreading from one computer to another?

Windows software problems can occur both during the startup (boot) process and during normal operation. Both the A+ Operating System examination and day-to-day maintenance of Windows-based PCs demand that you understand both the causes of errors and typical solutions for errors.

Startup Error Messages and Solutions

Startup errors can come from a variety of causes:

- Problems with Windows configuration, including Registry, Config.sys, and Autoexec.bat files
- Failure to load vital device drivers, such as Himem.sys
- Problems with drives, including virtual memory (swapfile), IDE, and SCSI configuration
- Problems specific to Windows 2000 (which is a Windows NT-based technology)

The following sections describe in greater detail typical error messages that usually result from Windows configuration problems as well as the causes and solutions to these problems.

Safe Mode

Windows uses Safe Mode to recover from startup problems. There are three different Safe Mode startup options:

- Safe Mode
- Safe Mode with Network Support (Windows 9x)/Safe Mode with Networking (Windows 2000)
- Safe Mode Command Prompt (Windows 9x)/Safe Mode with Command Prompt (Windows 2000)

Safe Mode

In Safe Mode, the system uses a standard VGA display driver, doesn't process the Config.sys or Autoexec.bat files present on a Windows 9x system, and doesn't load most 32-bit device drivers, including those used for hard disk and CD-ROM access and for networking. This mode loads the Windows GUI and allows the user to access the Windows Explorer and Windows Device Manager, although Windows 9x cannot display hardware resources used when the system is in Safe Mode.

Safe Mode with Network Support/Networking

You also can select Safe Mode with Network Support (Windows 9x) or Safe Mode with Networking (Windows 2000) to add bare-bones network support to Safe Mode. This mode also uses the Windows GUI and allows network connections so you can access drivers or needed support items through the network.

Safe Mode (with) Command Prompt

When this mode is selected, the computer does not boot to the Windows GUI, but boots to a command prompt, allowing the use of special Windows startup options with Windows 9x or special command-line options with either version of Windows.

Starting Windows in Safe Mode

Windows 9x automatically starts in Safe Mode if the system didn't start successfully on the previous startup. To run Safe Mode or other startup options, you can display the Windows 9x startup menu by pressing the Ctrl key on a Windows 9x system (or F8 on some systems) as soon as the system's power-on self test (POST) is complete. To see other startup options for Windows 2000, press the F8 key as soon as the POST is complete. With either version of Windows, select the Safe Mode option you want to use from the options listed.

CH
16

Using Safe Mode

Safe Mode can be used to start the system if normal startups fail, because Safe Mode uses a minimal set of drivers (for example, VGA instead of chipset-specific SuperVGA drivers) and services. By using only the minimum drivers and services to start the system, potential conflicts that can prevent the system from starting are bypassed.

You can use the Windows Device Manager to remove devices in Safe Mode, but Safe Mode in Windows 9x cannot show you configuration details.

You can access troubleshooters in either version of Windows, and if you start Windows in Safe Mode with Network Support, you might still have access to the Internet for additional help.

Other Startup Options for Windows 9x

Windows 9x offers additional startup options, which include the following:

- **Step-by-Step Confirmation**—Select this option to selectively run or skip commands in Config.sys, Autoexec.bat, and the Windows Registry.
- **Logged**—Select this option to create a hidden text file called Bootlog.txt, which is stored in the root folder of the default Windows drive. Bootlog.txt records startup events and is useful for finding problems that prevent Windows from starting.
- **Command Prompt Only**—Select this option to start the system at a command prompt after processing Config.sys, Autoexec.bat, and the Windows Registry. This provides a DOS-like environment suitable for running legacy programs that cannot run with Windows in memory.
- **Previous version of MS-DOS**—Loads the previous version of MS-DOS (if still present on the system).

Some of these options are discussed later in this chapter.

Other Startup Options for Windows 2000

Windows 2000 offers additional startup options, which include the following:

- **Enable boot logging**—Creates a bootlog.txt file.

- **Enable VGA mode**—Uses a VGA driver in place of a normal display driver, but uses all other drivers as normal. Useful for solving display problems without the slowdown of Safe Mode.

- **Last Known Good Configuration**—Starts the system with the last configuration known to work; useful for solving problems caused by newly installed hardware or software.

- **Directory Services Restore Mode**—Enables restoration of the Active Directory on Windows 2000 Server and Advanced Server computers used as Windows 2000 domain controllers.

- **Debugging Mode**—Enables the use of a debug program to examine the system kernel for troubleshooting.

Some of these options are discussed later in this chapter.

Error in Config.sys line xx (Windows 9x Only)

As you learned in Chapter 14, "Using and Optimizing Windows 9x and Windows 2000," most of the tasks previously performed by Config.sys in Windows 9x are now performed by the Io.sys file. The Config.sys file in Windows 9x can be used to load CD-ROM drivers for older drives not fully supported by Windows 9x, Emm386.exe for upper memory block, and/or EMS support for MS-DOS applications run under Windows 9x or other legacy uses.

An `error in Config.sys line xx` error message usually can be traced to one of the following causes:

- A reference to a driver file or folder that isn't present or might be misspelled

- A misspelling of the command in the Config.sys file; for example,
  `Device=C:\Windows\Emm386.exe RAM` is correct, whereas `Devise=C:\Windows\Emm386.exe RAM` is not a recognized command because Devise is not a recognized word

Because the Config.sys file provides primarily legacy support, the contents of Config.sys might not be necessary for your system anymore, particularly if your system has been upgraded from earlier versions of Windows to Windows 9x. You can use the Step by Step startup from the Windows 9x boot menu referred to earlier to bypass all or selective lines in Config.sys to see if your system performs normally. With Windows 98, but not Windows 95, you can also use the MSConfig utility (see "System Configuration Maintenance in Windows 98," page 408, to disable the loading of Config.sys or edit its contents).

Bad/missing Command.com (Windows 9x Only)

This error message could indicate one of the following problems:

- **The Command.com file has been deleted from the root folder of the Windows drive (normally C:\)**—Restart the system with the Windows 9x EBD and run Sys C: to restore Command.com and other boot files.

- **The Command.com file has been replaced with a Command.com file from a different version of Windows or MS-DOS**—Restart the system with the Windows EBD and run Sys C: to restore Command.com and other boot files.

- **The wrong Command.com file was reloaded into memory after a command-prompt program such as Xcopy (which overwrites Command.com in memory) was run**—If you are not using a multi-boot feature to allow you to run MS-DOS on the same system, delete all MS-DOS versions of Command.com on your system (such as in the \DOS folder).

- **A computer virus is present on the system**—Boot with the Windows 9x EBD and run an antivirus program to repair the problem.

The Windows 9x EBD should be created during installation of Windows 9x and stored for future use, because it is needed for many types of repairs to a Windows 9x system.

Himem.sys not loaded

Himem.sys, as you learned in Chapter 14, converts extended memory (memory over 1MB) into XMS memory, and it must be loaded to allow most Windows modes to function. You will see this message if you attempt to load the Windows GUI or run any other program that requires XMS memory.

If you start Windows 9x in Safe Mode command prompt or Windows 2000 in Safe Mode with Command Prompt, neither the Windows Registry nor the Config.sys files (either of which can run Himem.sys) is processed, so Himem.sys will not be loaded. Restart the computer normally and Himem.sys will be loaded into memory.

Missing or corrupt Himem.sys

If you are starting either version of Windows normally and see a message indicating that Himem.sys is missing or corrupt, the file might be damaged or deleted. On Windows 9x, Himem.sys is normally found in the \Windows folder, whereas Windows 2000 stores Himem.sys in the \Windows\System32 folder. If Himem.sys is accidentally deleted from the Windows 2000 folder, Windows 2000 can normally restore it automatically with its built-in System File Protection feature. If this doesn't work, however, you can restore it yourself.

To fix a missing or corrupted Himem.sys in Windows 98, you can restore Himem.sys from the Windows 98 EDB. With Windows 95, you must copy Himem.sys from the Windows 95 installation CD-ROM or disks. To restore a missing or corrupted Himem.sys in Windows 2000, you can restore it from the Windows 2000 CD-ROM.

Make sure you use the correct media for your version of Windows; mixing up Himem.sys could cause a system crash.

You can boot Windows 2000 from the CD-ROM and use the Repair Windows 2000 option to restore missing files; select the Recovery Console option. You can also use the Windows 2000 Emergency Repair disk to restore Himem.sys or other missing files. Unlike Windows 98's EBD, the Emergency Repair disk must be made after Windows 2000 is installed; start the Backup program and select Emergency Repair Disk from the menu of choices.

With Windows 98, you can boot with the Windows 98 EBD and copy Himem.sys from the floppy disk, or from the \Win98 folder on the CD-ROM back to the \Windows folder.

If you restart the system after restoring Himem.sys and get the missing or corrupt Himem.sys message again, there might be a problem with your memory modules or with a computer virus on the system.

Device referred to in System.ini/Win.ini/Registry not found

The Windows Registry is the primary location of hardware and software configuration information for both Windows 9x and Windows 2000; Windows 9x also uses the System.ini and Win.ini files for a few configuration settings.

These configuration files refer to driver files that must be accessed during the boot process. If you see an error message such as `Device xxx referred to in System.ini/Win.ini/Registry not found`, the most likely cause is that the file being referred to has been removed from the system.

If correct uninstall procedures are not followed, references to driver files for third-party hardware and software might remain in these files after the files themselves have been removed from the system.

To solve these problems, use the following appropriate option:

- For hardware, use the Remove button in the Device Manager before you physically remove the hardware from the system. Using Remove removes Registry and .ini file entries for the device so it will not be referred to when the system is restarted.

- Open the Add/Remove Programs icon in the Windows Control Panel, select the program you want to remove and select Add/Remove (Windows 9x) or Change/Remove (Windows 2000). This starts the uninstall program for applications and utilities listed on the menu.

- Use the program's own uninstall option. Some programs might place an uninstall shortcut in the shortcut folder for the program on the Start button.

- Use a third-party uninstall program.

Any of these options should remove both the program and references to it in the Registry and other locations, such as System.ini or Win.ini.

If the program is removed by deleting its folder, leaving references in the Registry, System.ini, or Win.ini, use the error message to determine which file contains the reference.

For Windows 98, the easiest way to remove a reference in System.ini, Win.ini, or any startup routine (including the Registry) is to use the Msconfig program. Click Start, Run, type Msconfig, and press Enter to start it. Uncheck the Win.ini, System.ini, or Startup line that contains the device and restart the computer to bypass it. You can also manually edit the Win.ini and System.ini files with Msconfig. Start the computer in Safe Mode if you cannot start the computer in normal mode. See "System Configuration Maintenance in Windows 98," page 408, for details about Msconfig.

Alternatively, you can use a text editor such as Notepad or Edit to remove references to a missing program or device in Windows 9x's System.ini or Win.ini. Start the computer in Safe Mode or Safe Mode Command Prompt if you cannot start the computer normally.

It is also possible to manually edit the Windows Registry to remove references to a missing device. Start the computer in Safe Mode and run Regedit (Windows 9x) or Regedt32 (Windows 2000) to start the Registry Editor. Because editing the Registry can be dangerous if done improperly, try all other options first before directly editing the Registry to remove references to missing program or hardware drivers.

Swapfile and Disk Access Problems

The swapfile (paging file on Windows 2000) is an area of disk space on a local hard disk that is used as a supplement to memory. A swapfile must be stored on a local hard disk; Windows 2000 can use multiple hard disks or partitions for its paging file.

Problems with the swapfile can result from

- **Disk surface problems with the partition used for the swapfile**—These problems can cause the system to halt with various types of errors including page faults, general protection faults, and others. Use ScanDisk in Windows 9x or Chkdsk in Windows 2000 to check the drive for errors and repair them, and then retry the operation. Check for program-specific causes if the errors occur again.

- **Lack of space for the swapfile**—By default, Windows uses remaining space on the current Windows drive (normally C:) for the swapfile. If the remaining space on the C: drive drops below 100MB, some disk operations will become very slow or might cause page faults or general protection faults. Free up space on the default swapfile drive or change to a different drive for the swapfile; Windows 2000 can use multiple drives for its paging file. For Windows 9x, see "Managing Virtual Memory in Windows 9x," page 400, for details. For Windows 2000, see "Memory Management in Windows 2000," page 403, for details.

- **Serious hardware problems with the hard disk subsystem (Windows 9x)**—If incorrect 32-bit busmastering drivers are installed for the IDE hard disk interface, data loss could result from disk accesses to save data or swap data to and from the swapfile.

To disable some or all advanced disk-access features

1. Open the Windows 9x System properties sheet.
2. Click the Performance tab.
3. Click File System.
4. Click the Troubleshooting tab.
5. Click the check box for one or more of the entries shown in Figure 16.1 and restart the system.

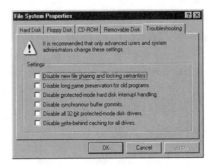

Figure 16.1
The File System Properties Troubleshooting menu in Windows 9x enables you to disable disk-access features that might be malfunctioning.

Disabling the options shown in Figure 16.1 might enable you to run the system until correct drivers can be obtained or hardware conflicts are resolved.

Using the Troubleshooting Options for Disk Access

Disable options based on the specific problems you are having with Windows. If data is not being written properly to the drives, you could try one of the following options:

- Disable Write-Behind Caching will send data directly to the drives instead of storing it temporarily in RAM before saving it to disk.
- Disable Synchronous Buffer Commits will force Windows to verify that data written to the drive was written properly.

If disk input/output errors are happening, you could try one of the following options:

- Disable 32-Bit Protected Mode Drivers will return control of the drives to BIOS routines or to 16-bit legacy drivers in Config.sys. Drives that depend solely upon 32-bit drivers will not work, but hard and floppy drives will continue to work.
- Disable Protected-Mode Interrupt Handling will return interrupt handling to the system ROM BIOS.

If you have compatibility problems with 16-bit applications that don't support long filenames, use Disable Long Name Preservation. If you have problems with file locking on a network, use Disable New File Sharing and Locking Semantics. These options will slow down your system and should be used only as workarounds until updated device drivers and applications can be installed.

Missing Operating System Files

An error message such as `Missing Command interpreter` (Windows 9x) or `Missing NTLDR` (Windows 2000) indicates that boot files in the root folder of the drive have been removed.

With Windows 9x, start the computer with the EBD and run the Sys command to restore system files to the computer:

```
Sys C:
```

Remove the floppy disk and reboot the computer to return to normal operation.

With Windows 2000, boot the computer from the Windows 2000 CD-ROM (or setup disks) and select Repair from the boot menu. Supply the Emergency Repair disk (if available) when prompted, and Windows 2000 will replace the missing files on your system with the originals on the CD-ROM. After the files are restored, the computer will reboot from the hard disk; remove the floppy disk and CD-ROM.

Hardware Configuration Problems

Improperly configured hardware can cause your computer to fail to boot at all. This section discusses typical causes and solutions for hardware configuration problems, including problems caused by incorrect drive configurations, damage to disk data structures, boot sector viruses, and SCSI configuration problems.

Missing operating system **Error**

A `Missing operating system` or similar error is generated by the system BIOS's boot loader if it is unable to locate the operating system. This can take place for any of the following reasons:

- **Incorrect BIOS configuration of the hard disk's geometry (cylinder, head, sectors per track) or LBA mode**—This information is used by programs such as Fdisk and Format to place boot sectors and operating system files on the drive. If the BIOS values for these settings are altered after the drive is installed, the operating system files can't be located.

- **Damage to the drive's master boot record**—This section of the drive points to the location of boot files if present.

- **No active partition set for the drive**—When Windows 9x Fdisk is used to create multiple partitions (primary plus secondary), the primary partition must be set as active by the user.

- **Boot sector virus**—A boot sector virus can prevent the system from booting from the hard disk, even if the other settings listed here are correct.

CH
16

To fix the problems in the previous list, follow these steps:

- To fix incorrect BIOS configuration, restart the computer and enter the BIOS setup program. Reset the drive type to Auto and enable LBA mode if listed separately for any drive above 504MB in size. Restart the computer.

- To fix damage to the drive' master boot record, restart the computer with the EBD and run FDISK/MBR to restore a normal MBR (for Windows 9x systems). For Windows 2000, restart the computer with the CD-ROM or boot disks, select Repair, and select the Recovery Console option. Use the FIXMBR command to restore a normal MBR. Remove the disk or CD-ROM and restart the computer.

- If there is no active partition set for the drive, restart the computer with the EBD and run FDISK (for Windows 9x systems). Select #4 (view partitions) to see the current partition setting. If the primary partition on disk #1 is not Active, make it active. Exit Fdisk, remove the floppy disk and restart the computer.

   For Windows 2000, the partition containing the Windows 2000 system startup files is automatically set as active during preparation.

- If a boot sector virus is preventing the system from booting from the hard disk, use the FDISK/MBR or FIXMBR commands listed previously for your version of Windows.

SCSI Error Messages

If Windows 9x or Windows 2000 is started from a SCSI hard disk instead of from an IDE hard disk, the configuration of the drive is set by the SCSI host adapter, which must support bootable drives. SCSI error messages can be caused by a variety of problems with how devices (including hard disks and other types of devices) are configured on the SCSI bus. SCSI errors are covered in detail because they differ widely from standard drive configuration errors. The following are some typical SCSI error messages and their causes:

- **Device connected but not ready**—No answer was received from a connected SCSI device.

   Solutions:

   - Make sure the device is turned on before the system boots.
   - Set the SCSI host adapter to Send Start Unit Command to the device.
   - Make sure that there are no duplicate SCSI ID #s.

- **Start unit request failed**—Device didn't respond to Start Unit Request command.

   Solution:

   - Disable Send Start Unit command option for that device.

- **Time-out failure during...**—A device attached to the SCSI host adapter caused a time-out.

  Solutions:

  - Check termination on the SCSI bus. Both ends of the SCSI daisy-chain of devices must be terminated.
  - Check cables. Loose or damaged cables can cause this problem; retighten cables and restart devices, and then restart the system.
  - Disconnect all SCSI devices and restart the system; if the SCSI card without devices runs okay, one or more of the devices is defective.

- **Driver software error messages**—old `DLL` or `ASPI` `not loaded`.

  Solution:

  - Download and install new software for the host adapter and ASPI (Adaptec SCSI Programming Interface) or equivalent services for your host adapter.

- **Can't access data on a SCSI hard disk after attaching it to a new SCSI host adapter**—Each brand of host adapter uses its own translation schemes to communicate with a drive.

  Solution:

  1. Reattach the drive to the original SCSI host adapter (if possible) and back up data.

  2. Attach the drive to the new host adapter and perform a low-level format with the new SCSI host adapter's utility program. This deletes all data on the drive but will allow the drive to communicate with the new host adapter.

- **A disk read error occurred after creating a boot partition more than 7.8GB in size**—This can take place on a Windows 2000 system if the SCSI BIOS doesn't support INT13 extensions for support of larger drives, or if the INT13 extension support has been disabled in the SCSI BIOS. Enable this option, or install a SCSI host adapter that supports INT13 extensions.

To avoid the potential loss of data, use the same brand (and model if possible) of host adapter if a host adapter must be replaced on a system whose SCSI drive already contains data.

Can't Start Windows 2000 GUI Errors

Systems that cannot start the Windows 2000 GUI will normally display a Stop error when the user attempts to start the system. This is also referred to as the Blue Screen of Death (BSOD) because the background is normally blue (or sometimes black) with the error message in white text (Windows 9x can also have BSOD errors).

**CH
16**

BSOD errors can be caused by any of the following:

- Incompatible hardware or software
- Registry problems
- Viruses
- Miscellaneous causes

This section provides methods for finding the cause of a particular error and solutions for typical errors.

Incompatible Hardware or Software

If the BSOD error takes place after installing new hardware or software, start the system in Safe Mode if possible and remove the hardware and uninstall the software. Get new drivers or software versions before reinstalling.

Registry Problems

Press the F8 key during the Windows 2000 initial boot process to display the Windows 2000 Advanced Options boot menu. Select Last Known Good Configuration from the menu and see if the system will start.

Viruses

Viruses can cause all types of system errors. Test the system for boot sector or other types of viruses. Because Windows 2000 does not include antivirus software, third-party antivirus software should be installed and kept up to date.

Miscellaneous Problems

To research BSOD problems that don't appear to be caused by the previous factors, use the following information sources for help:

- **Windows 2000 Event Log**—Start the system in Safe Mode and open the Event Log to see if the log has information about the failure.
- **Microsoft Knowledge Base**—Research the BSOD error with the Microsoft Knowledge Base by searching for the error number or error message at Microsoft's Web site.

System/Application/Security/Directory/DNS log is full Error

When the user logs into a Windows 2000 computer, the ...log is full error might be displayed if any of the logs listed in the heading for this section are full. The logging feature in Windows 2000 records both routine events and problems involving these services, so the log files should be emptied periodically.

To save and clear the logs:

1. Open the Administrative Tools icon in Control Panel.
2. Open Event Viewer (see Figure 16.2).

3. Click the log file reported in the error message.

4. Click Action and select Save File As (if you want to save its current contents); provide a filename.

5. Click Action and select Clear All Events.

You must be the administrator of the system or have been granted permission to use this tool.

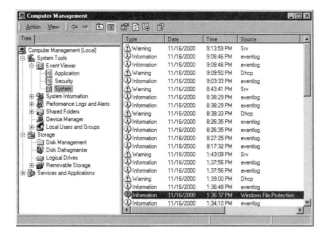

Figure 16.2
Because Windows 2000 logs all types of events, it won't take long for log files such as the System Log shown here to fill up.

Operating Error Messages and Solutions

After a system running Windows has started successfully, problems can still take place. This section covers typical problems and solutions you need to know about both for the A+ Operating Systems exam and for day-to-day troubleshooting and maintenance.

General Protection Fault and Illegal Operation Errors

An illegal operation can be defined as any software problem that requires Windows 9x to shut down the program to recover from it, including General Protection Faults (GPFs), Page Faults, and other problems. An illegal operation is hardly ever caused by the user of the program, but is caused by the interaction of programs with each other or with Windows itself. One of the most common types of illegal operation errors is the General Protection Fault.

General Protection Fault errors are caused by two Windows programs attempting to use the same area of memory at the same time; they are more likely to occur with Windows 9x than with Windows 2000 because of differences in how these versions of Windows allocate memory for multiple applications.

To determine the cause of a GPF:

- Note which programs were in memory when the GPF happened; generally, an interaction between the last program loaded into memory and programs already in memory is the cause.

- Consider getting updates to older programs on your system; mismatches between .dll support files used by new and older programs is a frequent cause of GPFs and other software problems.

Using Dr. Watson to Capture System Information

If you add the Dr. Watson utility supplied with Windows 98 to your startup group, the task of isolating problems such as GPFs and other types of illegal operations will be much easier. Drwatson.exe is located in the \Windows folder. When you run it, it is installed into the system tray.

Dr. Watson captures a large amount of information about your system when a GPF or other illegal operations error takes place; you can also use it to generate a snapshot of your system whenever you want. To see complete information about the system, as in Figure 16.3, select the Advanced View.

Figure 16.3
Dr. Watson traps system information when an illegal operation takes place or whenever you ask for a system snapshot.

Illegal operations, such as GPFs and others, have many possible causes; the Microsoft Windows online Knowledge Base has specific information covering illegal operations and GPF errors for many popular software titles used with Windows 9x.

Invalid working directory Error

This error message can refer to where a program is stored or to the folder that will be used for temporary files generated by a program. Generally, Windows programs use the default temporary folder (typically \Windows\Temp) for storage of temporary files. However, some sophisticated Windows programs can be set to use additional temporary folders.

MS-DOS programs run under Windows can be set to use any folder available on the system by adjusting the Working (folder) setting on the program's Program properties sheet.

If either a Windows or MS-DOS program is set to use a folder that isn't available, the Invalid working directory error might be displayed.

The following are solutions to this error:

- Adjust the program's operation to use a folder that is available using the program's properties sheet.
- If the working folder is on a network drive, make sure the user is logged on the network.
- If the working folder is a removable-media drive, the user must insert the correct disk or CD-ROM before starting the program.

System Lockups

System lockups can result from any of the following causes:

- Programs that stop responding
- Hardware that stops responding or has conflicts
- Exhaustion of Windows' user heap or GDI resources

A program that has stopped responding can normally be shut down by Windows. To view the status of programs in memory, press Ctrl+Alt+Del to display the Close Program dialog box (see Figure 16.4).

Figure 16.4
Press Ctrl+Alt+Del to bring up the Windows 9x Close Program dialog box, which allows you to close programs that are malfunctioning or are not needed.

Programs and background tasks in memory are displayed. Programs or tasks with [not responding] at the end of the listing have stopped working; select them and click Close

Program to shut them down. In some cases, other programs that are running will continue to work properly. In other cases, you will need to restart the system to restore normal operations.

Can't Log On to Network

A user must be on the list of authorized users to log on to a network managed by a Windows 2000, Windows NT, or Novell NetWare server. To access shared resources on a peer-to-peer Windows 9x network, the user must log on to the network and provide passwords for password-protected resources.

If the user has not logged on to the network, the user should click Start, Shutdown, and Logoff the System. All open programs will be closed, and a new logon screen will be displayed. The user should make sure to enter the correct username and password. Pressing the Escape key or clicking Cancel does not log the user onto the network, although the logon screen is removed from the desktop.

After the correct username and password are entered, the user will have access to any Windows NT/2000/NetWare-managed resources that the user is authorized to use. However, the user will need to provide a password the first time a peer-shared resource on a Windows 9x network is used; if the password is stored in the user's password cache, it will not need to be entered again unless the password for the resource is changed.

TSR Program Error

TSR (Terminate-and-Stay-Resident) programs, such as mouse drivers, CD-ROM drivers, and others, were common when MS-DOS was the predominant operating system. However, Windows 9x is primarily a 32-bit operating system and Windows 2000 is completely 32-bit, and both provide 32-bit drivers for hardware.

The only reason for most users to load a 16-bit MS-DOS–type TSR or device driver is for operations that take place outside the Windows GUI. Loading these drivers before Windows 9x boots could cause interference with 32-bit drivers.

You can set a particular MS-DOS application that must run from the MS-DOS mode to use TSRs or device drivers by editing the Advanced features of its Program properties sheet (see Figure 16.5). Add or remove drivers, TSRs, or other commands from the default settings listed for Config.sys or Autoexec.bat. The options set here will be run when the program is started and removed from memory when the user returns to the Windows GUI.

Can't Install Applications

There are several reasons why an application might not be installable on a particular computer:

- **Not enough disk space on C: drive**—Use the Custom installation option, if available, to choose another drive, delete old files in the default Temp folder, or delete .chk files created by ScanDisk or Chkdsk in the root folder to free up space.

This can be a problem even when the program will be installed to another drive because of the shared files that are installed to the Windows\System folder (which is normally on the C: drive).

■ **Computer doesn't meet minimum requirements for RAM or CPU speed—** Check for installation program switches to turn off speed and RAM checks, or upgrade system to meet or exceed minimums.

■ **No more space available in root folder—**A FAT16 drive with 256 folders and files in the root folder cannot create any more folders or files in the root. Install to another folder, or convert the drive to FAT32 or NTFS to eliminate this limitation.

Figure 16.5
If you are running an MS-DOS program that needs particular device drivers or TSRs to work in MS-DOS mode, specify the MS-DOS configuration you need.

Can't Start or Load Application Errors

Errors encountered when you try to start or load an application can be caused by a variety of issues, including the following:

■ The application has been removed from the system

■ The application has been moved to another folder

■ The application is installed on removable media that must be inserted

■ The application is installed on a network drive

All these issues stem from a single cause: Most Windows applications are launched from the Start menu or the Desktop, both of which contain shortcuts (.LNK files) that point to the actual location of the program. If a program is removed from the system or moved to another drive or folder and the shortcut is not removed or updated, the removable media containing the program is not inserted into the correct drive. If the user has not logged on to the network, the system will display a Problem with Shortcut error message similar to that shown in Figure 16.6. Follow the instructions listed in the error message to correct the problem.

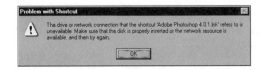

Figure 16.6
The Problem with Shortcut error message lists the actual .LNK filename and the most likely solutions for the problem.

Fixing Problems with Shortcuts
If the program is no longer installed on the system, the shortcut should be deleted. If the program has been moved to a different drive or folder, the shortcut should be edited. If the shortcut is located on the Windows Desktop, right-click the shortcut, select Properties, and click the Shortcut tab to view the current settings. The Target field contains the command line to start the program; change the folder, drive, or application name as needed and be sure that the command line has double quote marks at both the beginning and the end of the line. In most cases, the Start In field should be set to use the same folder and drive used in the Target field (see Figure 16.7).

Figure 16.7
Edit the shortcut (.LNK) file properties to indicate the correct path to the program (Target field) and startup folder (Start in field).

If the shortcut is located on the Start menu, right-click the Start button and select Explore. This will open the \Windows\Start Menu folder. Navigate the folder and subfolders to locate the shortcut. Select it to delete it or edit it as discussed earlier in this section.

If the shortcut points to a removable-media drive, consider modifying the name of the shortcut to indicate to the user that the removable media must be inserted first. If the user needs to log in first, remind the user that no network resources are available until he or she logs in.

Windows Version Issues

Some programs will not run on certain versions of Windows because of compatibility issues. To see which version of Windows you are using, you can use VER or open the System properties sheet and click the General tab. The Windows version number will be listed. In some cases, the version of Internet Explorer installed will also be listed. If the Windows or IE version listed is not suitable for the program, you cannot use the program until you upgrade to a supported version of Windows or IE. The program should be uninstalled.

CH
16

Hardware Performance Issues

If the program won't start because of hardware considerations, check the minimum program requirements for the system against the RAM, free disk space, CPU type/speed, display color depth, display resolution, and other requirements installed in your system. Programs that perform compliance checking will not start if any of these values are less than the minimum requirements for the program.

To check the amount of RAM or the CPU type, open the System properties sheet and click the General tab; the amount of RAM and the CPU type are listed.

To check the CPU speed, watch the system configuration screen at startup. Many systems will display the CPU speed then. Alternatively, use Norton Utilities, Norton System Works, or other programs that report CPU type and speed to determine this information.

To check free disk space on a drive partition, right-click the drive in the Windows Explorer, select Properties, and click the General tab. The total space and free space are listed in text form and displayed graphically. To free up space, delete .TMP files in the \Windows\Temp or other Temp folder, delete .CHK files created by ScanDisk from lost allocation units, and clear temporary Internet files from the browser's temporary folder.

To check the screen resolution and color depth, open the Display properties sheet and click the Settings tab. Some applications will not work with less than 256 colors, or they might prompt you to increase colors to 16-bit or higher for better results.

Using Windows Utilities for Troubleshooting

Both Windows 9x and Windows 2000 provide many utilities that can be used for troubleshooting disk and system problems. This section provides an overview of major utilities covered on the A+ Operating Systems exam and a brief description of how each is used.

ScanDisk and CHKDSK

Use ScanDisk to check hard drives, floppy disk drives, and removable-media drives for errors on systems running Windows 9x. You can run ScanDisk (called Error-Checking) from the Tools tab of the properties sheet for any drive in the Windows Explorer, or from the command-prompt modes of Windows. ScanDisk also provides statistics about drive usage.

Windows 2000 initiates error-checking in the same manner, but uses the Chkdsk utility to perform the tasks. Chkdsk can also be run from a Windows 2000 command prompt.

Device Manager

The Device Manager allows you to view the hardware installed in both Windows 9x and Windows 2000 by type or connection. You can see the overall IRQ, DMA, I/O port, and memory usage for the system, or details of hardware resource, configurations, and drivers for each device installed.

Device Manager can also be used to produce reports about onboard devices, and it can be used to enable, disable, and remove devices from the system. To access Device Manager with Windows 9x, open the System properties sheet and click the Device Manager tab. With Windows 2000, open the System Properties sheet, click the Hardware tab, and click the Device Manager button.

Computer Manager

The Windows 2000 Computer Manager is a comprehensive management tool that allows the administrator of a Windows 2000 system to have one-stop access to

- Events
- System information
- Performance logs
- Device management
- Shared folders
- Local users and groups
- Storage tools and management
- Service and application management

Start system management by right-clicking My Computer and selecting Manage from the menu (see Figure 16.8).

To view details about a managed resource, click the resource in the left-hand window and the information will appear in the right-hand window.

Msconfig.exe (Windows 98)

The Microsoft System Configuration tool allows you to selectively disable and enable portions of the startup process for Windows 98. It is easier and more foolproof than manually editing Win.ini, System.ini, Autoexec.bat, Config.sys, or the Windows Registry. To start Msconfig, click Start, Run, and enter Msconfig. See "System Configuration Maintenancein Windows 98," page 408 for details.

Figure 16.8
The Windows 2000 Computer Management tool can also be used to manage remote systems.

Registry Editors

Both Windows 9x and Windows 2000 feature Registry editors, which allow you to view, search, and change Registry values:

- **Regedit.exe**—This is the name of the Windows 9x Registry Editor and a limited-feature command-prompt version of the Windows 2000 Registry Editor. To make changes to Windows 9x individual Registry values, Regedit should be run within the Windows 9x GUI. Regedit also can be run from a command prompt outside Windows to export all or portions of the Registry (for backup) or to import all or portions of the Registry (to change its contents). Windows 2000 also features its own version of Regedit for use at a command prompt. It allows the Registry to be searched, but for full Registry editing capabilities, use Regedt32 instead.

- **Regedt32**—This is the Windows 2000 Registry Editor. It provides a multipane interface that is easier to use than the Windows 9x Registry editor, but performs the same tasks within the Windows 2000 GUI.

Remember, editing the Registry of any version of Windows should be performed as a last resort if other methods of modifying it are not possible. The Registry should always be backed up before editing, especially because there is no undo command or other method for discarding changes made to the Registry.

Command-Prompt Troubleshooting Utilities

The following command-prompt utilities are covered in detail in previous chapters:

- **Attrib**—Views and changes file attributes.

- **Extract**—Extracts files from Windows 9x .cab archives; useful for replacing damaged, missing, or corrupted Windows 9x files.

- **Edit.com**—Views and edits text files, such as Autoexec.bat, Config.sys, .ini files, and others.
- **Fdisk.exe**—Partitions disks in Windows 9x.
- **Scanreg.exe**—Repairs, backs up, restores, and optimizes the Windows 98 Registry.

Windows 2000 Recovery Console

The Windows 2000 Recovery Console can be started from the Windows 2000 CD-ROM or can be installed to your system to become a boot option. It provides access to many command-line utilities that can be used to fix problems with a Windows 2000 installation.

Table 16.1 lists the major recovery console commands and their uses. Use the Help command to see the syntax of these commands; some commands work similarly to MS-DOS and Windows 9x command-line programs, and others have different options.

Table 16.1   Windows 2000 Recovery Console Commands and Uses

Command	Use
Attrib	Changes the attributes (such as read-only, system, hidden, archive, compressed, encrypted) of a file or folder (directory).
Batch	Executes the commands specified in the text file following the command.
ChDir (Cd)	Displays the name of the current folder (directory) or changes the current folder (directory) to the one specified in the command.
Chkdsk	Checks a disk for errors and displays a status report.
Cls	Clears the screen.
Copy	Copies a specified file to another location.
Delete (Del)	Deletes one or more specified files.
Dir	Displays a list of files and subdirectories in a directory.
Disable	Disables a system service or a device driver.
Diskpart	Manages partitions on your hard drives.
Enable	Starts or enables a system service or a device driver; use Listserv to see services.
Exit	Exits the Recovery Console and restarts your computer.
Expand	Extracts a file from a compressed file; useful for repairing damaged or deleted files.
Fixboot	Writes a new partition boot sector onto the system partition.
Fixmbr	Repairs the master boot record of the partition boot sector.
Format	Formats a disk.
Help	Displays a list of the commands you can use in the Recovery Console and their uses.
Listsvc	Lists the services and drivers available on the computer; use Enable or Disable to start or stop a given service.
Logon	Logs on to a Windows 2000 installation.
Map	Displays the current drive letter mappings.
Mkdir (Md)	Creates a specified folder (directory).
More	Displays a specified text file.
Rename (Ren)	Renames a single specified file.
Rmdir (Rd)	Deletes a specified folder (directory).

Table 16.1	continued
Command	Use
Set	Displays and sets environment variables.
Systemroot	Sets the current folder (directory) to the systemroot folder (directory) of the system you are currently logged on to.
Type	Displays a specified text file.

Windows Troubleshooting Utilities

The following utilities are available with Windows 98; some also work with Windows 2000 or Windows 95, as listed. Use them to solve the specified problems with the system.

■ **Scanregw**—The Windows GUI version of Scanreg.exe can back up the Windows 98 Registry. Adjust its operation by editing Scanreg.ini (stored in the \Windows folder) to allow it to back up system boot files and other important files to .cab files in the hidden Sysbkup folder beneath the default \Windows folder.

■ **Defrag.exe**—Realigns file fragments on Windows 9x and Windows 2000 drives and places all empty space on a drive into contiguous allocation units; must be run from the Windows GUI to preserve long filenames.

■ **Sysedit.exe**—Crude Windows 9x editor for Autoexec.bat, Config.sys, and important .ini files; Msconfig.exe is a better choice.

■ **Wscript.exe**—The Windows 98 and Windows 2000 Scripting host program; use it to create logon scripts for online services that require a logon script.

■ **Hwinfo.exe**—The Windows 98 Hardware Information program; this program is run by the Microsoft System Information program to gather detailed hardware information, including resource, driver, and Registry information. Open MS System Information, click Components, and select a component to view the information retrieved by Hwinfo.

■ **Asd.exe**—The Automatic Skip Driver program can be used to disable Windows 98's attempt to locate a device that is not present on your system.

To start ASD

1. Open a command-prompt session in Windows 98.

2. Type ASD and press Enter.

3. Any devices that do not respond will be listed; check the device(s) you want Windows to skip (see Figure 16.9).

To see the Registry key for the device, select the device and click Details. Click OK when you have selected the device(s) you want Windows to skip.

■ **Cvt1.exe**—The Drive Converter (FAT-32) for Windows 98 allows you to convert drives from the inefficient FAT16 file system to the more efficient FAT-32 file system using a Windows wizard interface (see Figure 16.10). The command-line version of the program is Cvt.exe.

Figure 16.9
Use ASD to keep Windows 98 from trying to install drivers for devices you don't use on your system, such as the tape backup listed here.

Figure 16.10
The Windows 98 Drive Converter displays the file system in use on drives. Drives that can be converted from FAT-16 to FAT-32 (C: and F: on this system) are highlighted.

Computer Viruses

Because computer troubleshooting and computer technicians have traditionally worked more with hardware than with software, computer viruses are an often-overlooked cause for computer failures. Any attempt to diagnose a system crash or computer failure, with or without data loss, should include virus detection. The user should also be encouraged to take steps to prevent the acquisition and spread of computer viruses. The A+ Certification exam covers important issues concerning viruses, reflecting their importance to proper system troubleshooting and maintenance.

What Is a Computer Virus?

A computer virus is a program that attaches itself without the user's knowledge to another program or a part of the computer's storage system. A computer virus also carries a "payload," which might be as harmless as an onscreen message or as harmful as the complete destruction of all data on the hard disk. These two characteristics can also be referred to as a "Trojan horse" program.

The essential difference between a Trojan horse and a computer virus program is that the computer virus program is also able to spread itself from one computer to another; after a single computer in an office has acquired a computer virus, it can easily spread to other computers. In practice, there is little practical difference between viruses and Trojans; both can be detected by up-to-date antivirus software and both pose significant threats to data and systems. For the rest of this section, "virus" will be used to describe both actual computer viruses and Trojan horse programs.

Clues Pointing to Computer Virus Infections

Several clues point to the likelihood that one or more computers and offices are infected with the computer virus:

- The same or similar problems spread from one computer to another.
- The computers with the same or similar problems are connected through a network, by email systems, or share data by physical transfer of floppy disk or other media.
- Unexpected system slowdown.
- Onscreen messages such as `your computer is now stoned`.
- Loss of system configuration in the CMOS.

Types of Computer Viruses

Computer viruses come in different types, each with its preferred method of transmission and infection:

- **Executable file virus**—This type of virus attaches itself to program files, such as .com, .exe, or .dll. This is the oldest type of computer virus, but is the type of virus also spread by Web-based or email-based file attachments.
- **Boot-sector virus**—This type of virus attaches itself to the boot sector of media, such as hard drives and floppy disk drives. Computer technicians who use floppy disk drives for diagnostic software can unwittingly spread boot sector viruses from one computer to another!

- **Macro virus**—This type of virus works by adding unauthorized commands to the macros stored as part of data files created with programs such as Microsoft Word and Microsoft Excel. Because the macro language used by Microsoft is so powerful, a macro virus can control the computer's operation: Transferring address books and passwords to unauthorized parties and wiping out hard drives are two known behaviors of this type of virus.

- **VB script virus**—This is the latest type of virus, responsible for the ILOVEYOU outbreak and many other recent virus attacks. This type of virus is spread through corporate and personal email systems and is carried by a Visual Basic script attached to an email message. These usually target Microsoft Outlook and Outlook Express email clients in particular.

To detect and defeat all these viruses, antivirus software with the following characteristics is needed:

- Can detect both known viruses (by an updated database of virus signatures) and unknown viruses (by watching for suspicious behaviors by programs)

- Can scan compressed files, programs, data files, and storage devices for viruses

- Can block infection by viruses carried by Internet file downloads and email systems

- Can remove widest assortment possible of detected viruses and allow file deletion when infections cannot be removed

Detecting Viruses on Client Computers

In an ideal world, every computer in use would have up-to-date antivirus software that was used on a regular and frequent basis. In the real world, you can't expect clients to achieve this level of protection. Windows 9x and Windows 2000 do not include any type of antivirus protection.

Because computer viruses target antivirus software on PCs, the best way to check a computer that might contain a computer virus is to start the system with a known "clean" bootable floppy disk or bootable CD-ROM. Then, a known "clean" antivirus program should be run on the system.

You can create a clean virus detection system by following as many of these steps as possible:

- Set aside an older computer strictly for antivirus software.

- Test all new virus programs and virus signatures before installation on a computer.

- Keep the antivirus computer off the network and off the Internet (if possible).

- Arrange to receive antivirus updates by mail subscription or by BBS download, rather than through the Internet to download.

- Use recordable CDs (CD-R or CD-RW) to store antivirus programs and signature files.

It is good practice to maintain more than one antivirus program, because antivirus programs differ in their capability to detect, eliminate, and protect against different types of viruses. The leaders in the field include Trend Micro, Symantec, and McAfee.

If you are working at the client location and no up-to-date antivirus software is available but the system has an Internet connection, Trend Micro (www.trendmicro.com) offers free online virus scanning.

What to Do when a Virus Is Located on a Client Computer

Because of the nature of computer viruses, you should assume that if one computer in an office has a computer virus, that virus has either spread to other systems or can be found on media that might be used on other systems. To prevent re-infection of the computer, take the following steps:

- Disinfect the infected computer by using an up-to-date antivirus program. If the virus can't be removed from the infected file, try a different antivirus program. Delete the infected file only as a last resort.

- Check all other computers that are connected to the infected computer through networks or have shared information through media exchange or email with the infected computer.

- Check all media, including floppy disks, removable media, tape, and CD-R/CD-RW that have been used on the infected computer. Frequently, you'll find more copies of the virus on this media as well. If the virus is not removed from the media, it will re-infect the same computer or infect other computers.

- If the infected computer shares files with a computer at home, encourage the client to check the home computer for viruses or bring it in for a checkup if permitted. Home computers will frequently re-infect office computers if not checked for viruses.

CH
16

QUESTIONS AND ANSWERS:

1. If you want to start a Windows 2000 system without loading the normal video drivers, but don't want to lose other features, which startup mode should you select?
    A: Enable VGA Mode will use a plain VGA driver instead of normal video, but will not affect other system features the way that Safe Mode will.

2. Which startup mode records the events that take place during startup?
    A: Logged mode (Windows 98) or Enable Boot Logging (Windows 2000).

3. There are three ways to start a system with minimal drivers for troubleshooting. What are they called and how do they differ from each other (briefly)?
   A: Safe Mode uses standard VGA and disables most drivers; Safe Mode with Network Support/Networking adds network support, and both use the Windows GUI. Safe Mode (with) Command Prompt disables all drivers and starts the system at a command prompt.

4. What Windows 2000 feature minimizes the chances of having the Himem.sys file being replaced or deleted?
   A: System File Protection.

5. What Windows 98 disk is a very useful troubleshooting tool?
   A: The Windows 98 EBD (Emergency Boot Disk—also called the Emergency System Disk)

6. What happens to performance if you use the File System Troubleshooting options for Windows 98?
   A: Performance drops because you are disabling features that run drives faster.

7. List two causes for SCSI error messages.
   A: SCSI termination problems, cabling problems, duplicate device IDs, device not powered on, mismatch between drive and host adapter.

8. What is another name for a Windows Stop error? List two sources for troubleshooting Stop errors.
   A: Stop errors are often called Blue Screen of Death (BSOD) errors. You can search the Windows Knowledge Base by error message or number, and the Error Log can also be useful.

9. What Windows 98 utility can be used to capture system information during a GPF or other error? Which Windows 2000 feature captures system information?
   A: Windows 98 uses the optional Dr Watson utility; Windows 2000 maintains several logs such as the System, Application, Security, Directory, and DNS logs.

10. What is a typical symptom of a virus infection spreading from one computer to another?
    A: Similar problems occur between computers that are on the same network, exchange email, or share media.

Networking

WHILE YOU READ

1. What is the difference between a client and a server?
2. Can you share just a folder rather than an entire drive?
3. What is the least expensive way to connect two computers for temporary networking?
4. Where do you adjust the TCP/IP properties for a dial-up connection?
5. Which type of cable is used by 10BaseT Ethernet networking? Can faster versions use it?

What Is a Network?

A network is a group of computers, peripherals, and software that are connected to each other and can be used together.

Networks come in many sizes and types. Several computers connected together in the same office are considered a LAN (Local Area Network). LANs in different cities can be connected to each other by a WAN (Wide Area Network). The Internet represents the world's largest network, connecting both standalone computers and computers on LAN and WAN networks all over the world.

Networks require both special software and special hardware to work.

Network Operating Systems

As you learned in previous chapters, an operating system is the software that allows you to work with hardware and application programs. Windows 9x and Windows 2000 are the major operating systems covered by the 2001 revisions to the A+ Certification test.

A *network operating system (NOS)* is a special type of operating system that allows your computer to communicate with other computers over a LAN, over a WAN, or through the Internet.

Although both Windows 9x and Windows 2000 Professional are designed primarily as desktop operating systems, they also include NOS features, such as network client options; support for multiple network protocols, such as TCP/IP and others; and file and print sharing for simple networking. They also can be used with networking hardware to build networks without purchasing additional network software.

If you want to create a network with user-based or group-based security, you must set up one or more dedicated servers (computers used only to share resources with other computers) that run full-featured NOSes, such as Novell NetWare, Windows NT Server, or Windows 2000 Server.

Servers

A *server* is a computer on the network that provides other computers (called clients or workstations) with access to resources, such as

- Disk drives
- Folders on a disk drive
- Optical drives
- Printers
- Modems

Because these resources can be used by different computers over the network, they are called *shared resources*.

Servers can also be used for different types of software and tasks:

- Application servers run tasks for clients.
- File servers store data and program files for clients.
- Mail servers store and distribute email to clients.

Clients

A *client* is a computer that uses the resources on a server. Depending on the network operating system in use, clients and servers can be separate machines or a client can act as a server and a server can act as a client. Figure 17.1 illustrates a client/server network, such as Novell NetWare or Windows NT/2000 Server.

Clients can refer to servers either by assigning drive letters to shared folders (see "Drive Mapping" later in this chapter) or by using a universal naming convention (UNC) path name to refer to the server, as in Figure 17.1 (see "The Universal Naming Convention (UNC)" later in this chapter).

CH
17

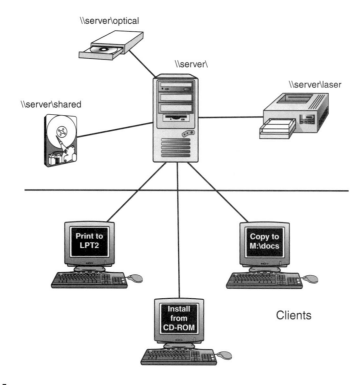

Figure 17.1
A server with three workstations, each of which is using a different shared resource:
One is using the server's CD-ROM drive, one is printing to the server's printer, and one is copying a file to the server's hard disk.

Built-In Networking Features in Windows

Both Windows 9x and Windows 2000 Professional have the following NOS features built in, enabling these operating systems to be used either as network clients or as peer network servers:

- **Client software**—Enables systems to connect with Windows and Novell NetWare networks, among others

- **Network protocols**—IPX/SPX, NetBEUI, and TCP/IP are all included

- **File and print sharing**—Enables Windows systems to act as peer servers for Windows and Novell NetWare networks

- **Services**—Enables specialized network services, such as shared HP laser printers, network backup, and more

The network features built into Windows 9x and Windows 2000 Professional allow for peer servers: Computers can share resources with each other, and machines that share resources can also be used as client workstations.

As Figure 17.2 shows, if mapped drive letters and printer ports are used in a peer-to-peer network, the same resource will have a different name, depending on whether it's being accessed from the peer server (acting as a workstation) itself or over the network. In Figure 17.2, the system on the left shares its CD-ROM drive with the system on the right, which refers to the shared CD-ROM drive as F:\. The system on the right shares its printer with the system on the left, which has mapped the shared printer to LPT2.

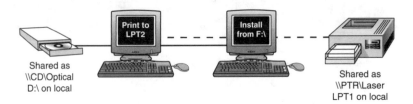

Figure 17.2
A simple two-station peer-to-peer network, in which each computer acts as a peer server to the other.

Protocols

All networks depend on protocols; a *protocol* is a common language used for interchanging data between different types of computers.

Protocols are essential to network computing because not every computer on a given network uses the same operating system; a typical corporate network can have clients running Windows 95, Windows for Workgroups 3.11, Macintosh OS, Windows NT, IBM OS/2, Windows 98, Windows 2000, Unix, and Linux. By using network client software with the same protocol, all these computers can interchange data with each other, as shown in Figure 17.3.

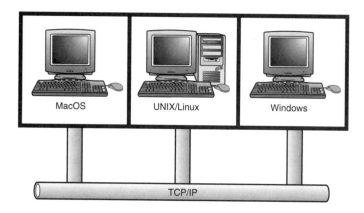

Figure 17.3
By using TCP/IP, computers running different, incompatible operating systems (MacOS, Unix, Linux, or Windows) can exchange information with each other. TCP/IP is the Internet's native network protocol and is becoming the leading network protocol for LANs as well.

The A+ Certification exams cover several different types of protocols, including

- Protocols that describe how computers are physically connected to each other, such as Ethernet and token-ring. These types of protocols are sometimes referred to as data-link protocols (see "Cabling Types and Network Topologies," page 512).

- Protocols that describe how data is transported between computers and how computers are identified on a network, such as TCP/IP, IPX/SPX, and NetBEUI. These types of protocols are sometimes referred to as network or transport protocols.

- Protocols that are used by applications running under the TCP/IP network protocol, such as HTTP, SMTP, and others. These are often referred to as application protocols.

Common Network Protocols: TCP/IP, NetBEUI, IPX/SPX

The most common network protocols you'll encounter include

- TCP/IP
- NetBEUI
- IPX/SPX

TCP/IP (Transmission Control Protocol/Internet Protocol) was originally designed for use with the Internet, but Novell NetWare 5.x, Windows NT 4.0, and Windows 2000 have adopted this protocol as their standard protocol for LAN use, replacing NetBEUI (used on Microsoft networks) and IPX/SPX (used on Novell Networks). Using TCP/IP as a network's only protocol makes network configuration easier because users need to configure only one protocol to communicate with other network clients, servers, or with the Internet

NetBEUI (NetBIOS Extended User Interface), the simplest major protocol in use today, is an enhanced version of a network protocol called NetBIOS (NetBIOS itself is no longer used for this purpose). NetBEUI is used primarily on peer networks using Windows and by some small networks that use Windows NT Servers. NetBEUI lacks features that allow it to be used on larger networks; it cannot be routed or used to access the Internet. NetBEUI is useful for creating a connection between two PCs with direct cable connection or for small networks that do not need Internet access.

IPX/SPX (Internetwork Packet Exchange/Sequenced Packet Exchange) is a suite of protocols created by Novell for use on older versions of Novell NetWare. Unlike NetBEUI and NetBIOS, IPX/SPX is designed for large corporate networks; it can be routed but cannot be used to access the Internet. IPX/SPX is the standard protocol suite used by NetWare 4.x and earlier versions, but NetWare 5.x uses this protocol for specialized operations only. Many networks use two or all three of these protocols, which makes configuration and troubleshooting more difficult.

Application Protocols Requiring TCP/IP

TCP/IP actually is a suite of protocols used on the Internet for routing and transporting information. The following application protocols used for different tasks on the Internet run under TCP/IP; it must be present to allow these protocols to work:

- **HTTP:// (Hypertext Transfer Protocol)**—Used by Web browsers, such as Internet Explorer and Netscape Navigator, to access Web sites and content
- **FTP:// (File Transfer Protocol)**—Used by both Web browsers and specialized FTP programs to access dedicated file transfer servers for file downloads and uploads
- **SMTP (Simple Mail Transfer Protocol)**—Allows the transfer of email
- **SNMP (Simple Network Management Protocol)**—Allows management and monitoring of network devices

Networking Configuration

A peer-to-peer network can be created using the software included with Windows 9x or Windows 2000 Professional. Although a peer-to-peer network has less security and lower performance than a dedicated network, the same hardware can be used with either type of network. This means that a small peer-to-peer network today can become part of a larger network using dedicated servers in the future. Windows 9x and Windows 2000 Professional also include client software enabling computers running these versions of Windows to connect with dedicated servers running Windows NT Server, Windows 2000 Server, or Novell NetWare.

The process of configuring a network can be divided into the following phases:

- **Selecting a network type**—This task must be performed before hardware can be specified and installed.

- **Installing and configuring network interface cards (NICs) and cables**—The NICs and cables chosen must support the network type being installed.

- **Setting up the server**—Server software must be installed before shared resources can be selected and configured.

- **Setting up clients**—Client software must be installed and configured before the network is fully operational.

Network Types

Most major networks are outgrowths of various networking standards created by the IEEE, the Institute of Electrical and Electronics Engineers, Inc., which sets electrical, electronic, and computer standards. The IEEE 802 family of networking standards provides the foundation for Ethernet, Token Ring, wireless, and other major types of networks. Table 17.1 lists the major IEEE 802 standards by their common names.

CH
17

Table 17.1 IEEE 802 Network Standards

IEEE Standard	Official Name	Popular Name and Notes
802.1	Internetworking	
802.2	Logic Link Control	
802.3	CSMA/CD Access method	Ethernet LAN, including Fast and Gigabit standards
802.4	Token Bus Access method	
802.5	Token Ring Access method	IBM Token Ring LAN
802.6	DQDB Access method	Metropolitan Area Network (MAN)
802.7	Broadband LAN	Broadband LAN can carry different types of signals over the same cable
802.8	Fiber Optic standards	Draft standard
802.9	Integrated services	Voice/Data networks
802.10	LAN/MAN security	Network security
802.11	Wireless	
802.12	Demand Priority Access Method	

Ethernet Types

Of the major network standards, you'll probably use some version of IEEE 802.3, commonly known as Ethernet. Ethernet networking is by far the most common type of networking. Ethernet varieties include

- Standard Ethernet 10Mbps (10BaseT, 10Base5, 10Base2)
- Fast Ethernet 100Mbps (100BaseTX)
- Gigabit Ethernet 1,000Mbps

Standard Ethernet uses a transmission method called Carrier Sense Multiple Access/Collision Detection (CSMA/CD). This allows any workstation to send data at any time; however, if data from two workstations collide (is transmitted at the same time), both workstations wait a random amount of time before retransmitting. This is similar to allowing cars to drive in any lane and in any direction, and backing up and waiting if they hit each other. This is actually quite efficient on a small network; large Ethernet networks (more than 100 PCs) should be broken into several separate networks to avoid excessive collisions.

For new network installations, I recommend Fast Ethernet. Its performance is 10 times faster than standard Ethernet, and the cost of network components is not much higher. Fast Ethernet can be connected to standard Ethernet networks by using dual-speed hubs or switches. Switches set up a dedicated connection between any two PCs that are exchanging information, allowing faster data transfer rates.

Most Fast Ethernet network cards support both 10BaseT and Fast Ethernet standards; these cards are normally referred to as 10/100 Ethernet cards.

Other Choices
The one-time low-cost favorite, ArcNet, is obsolete today because of its low speed (2.5Mbps); there was never an IEEE standard for ArcNet. Token Ring (IEEE 802.5) is still popular in companies that use IBM mainframe or midrange computers, such as the AS/400, but the hardware is much more expensive than Ethernet.

Cabling Types and Network Topologies
The network that you build will affect the type of network cables you install. The arrangement of cabling and access devices is referred to as a *network topology*. There are three different types of network topologies:

- **Bus**—All computers share a common cable.
- **Star**—All computers connect to a central hub.
- **Ring**—All computers connect in a ring.

There are four major types of network cables:

- Unshielded Twisted Pair (UTP)
- Shielded Twisted Pair (STP)
- Fiber-optic
- Coaxial

Network cards are designed to use one or more types of network cables.

Two other cable types can be used with direct cable connection, which is a special type of two-station network that uses standard network protocols but does not use network cards.

- Serial (RS-232) null modem
- Parallel (LPT) crossover

Figure 17.4 compares typical UTP and coaxial network cables.

The cabling type your network uses helps create the network topology your network uses.

UTP Cabling, Hubs, and Switches

UTP cabling is the most common of the three cabling types, especially for small networks. It comes in various grades, of which Category 5 is the most common and highest grade of the standard cabling grades. Category 5 cabling is suitable for use with both standard 10BaseT and Fast Ethernet networking, and can also be used for Gigabit Ethernet networks if tested for compliance.

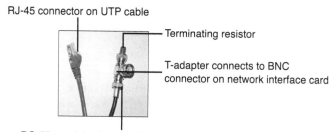

RJ-45 connector on UTP cable

Terminating resistor

T-adapter connects to BNC connector on network interface card

RG-58 coaxial cable with bayonet connector

Figure 17.4
An unshielded twisted-pair (UTP) cable (left) and an RG-58 coaxial cable with T-adapter and terminating resistor (right). The UTP cable connects directly with a hub, whereas the coaxial cable/adapter/resistor is ready to use at one end of a bus network.

The name refers to its physical construction: four twisted pairs of wire surrounded by a flexible jacket. The connector used by UTP is called an RJ-45 connector, and it resembles a larger version of the RJ-11 connector used for telephone cabling.

UTP cabling runs between a computer on the network and the hub, which routes signals to other computers (servers or workstations) on the network. It can be purchased in prebuilt form or as bulk cable with connectors, so you can build the cable to the length you need.

If electrical interference is a problem, some parts of the network can be wired with STP (shielded twisted-pair) instead. This uses wire mesh for electrical insulation between the wire pairs and the outer jacket. It's more expensive and harder to loop through tight spaces than UTP, however.

Hubs connect different computers with each other on the network. A hub has several connectors for RJ-45 cabling, a power source, and signal lights to indicate network activity. Most hubs are stackable, meaning that if you need more ports than the hub contains, you can connect it to another hub to expand its capabilities. A switch resembles a hub but permits full-duplex operation (sending and receiving data at the same time) and creates a dedicated full-speed connection between the two computers that are communicating with each other, instead of subdividing the full bandwidth (rated speed) of the network among all the ports as hubs do (see "Switches," page 526).

The combination of a hub or switch with cables reaching out to different workstations is called a *star* topology from its logical shape. Star topologies are popular because a failure of a single station on the network does not affect the other stations on the network.

To attach UTP cable to a network card or other device, plug it into the connector so that the plastic locking clip snaps into place; the cable and connector will fit together only one way. Squeeze the locking clip toward the RJ45 connector and pull the connector out of the RJ45 jack if you need to remove the cable. Some cables use a snagless connector; squeeze the guard over the locking clip to open the clip to remove the cable.

UTP cable can be purchased in prebuilt assemblies or can be built from bulk cable and connectors. See *Upgrading and Repairing PCs, 12th Edition,* Chapter 19, "Build Your Own Twisted-Pair Cables," for details.

STP and Token-Ring Networking

Shielded twisted-pair cabling is designed for use on IBM Token-Ring networks. Token-ring network stations are connected through a multistation access unit (MAU or MSAU), a device that resembles a hub externally but actually features a ring topology internally.

Token-ring networking refers to the passing of a "token" around the "ring" of network stations. The station with the token can "talk" to another station (send data), and then it releases the token to the next station. This approach eliminates the collision problem of Ethernet but is expensive and has limited performance. Because token-ring networking was developed by IBM, it is popular in corporations using IBM midrange and mainframe computers. Token ring runs at 4Mbps and 16Mbps speeds.

Fiber-Optic

Fiber-optic cabling transmits signals with light rather than with electrical signals, which makes it immune to electrical interference. It is used primarily as a backbone between networks. Fiber-optic cable comes in different types for different types of networks. It can be purchased prebuilt, but if you need a custom length, it should be built and installed by experienced cable installers because of the expense and risk of damage. Media converters are used to interconnect fiber-optic to conventional cables on networks.

Coaxial

Coaxial cabling is the oldest type of network cabling; its data wires are surrounded by a wire mesh for insulation. Coaxial cables, which resemble cable TV connections, are not popular today because they must be run from one station directly to another rather than to or from a hub.

Coaxial cabling creates a "bus" topology; each end of the bus must be terminated, and if any part of the bus fails, the entire network fails.

The oldest Ethernet standard, 10Base5, uses a very thick coaxial cable that is attached to a NIC through a transceiver that uses a so-called "vampire tap" to connect the transceiver to the cable. This type of coaxial cable is also referred to as Thick Ethernet or Thicknet.

Before UTP cabling became common, a less-expensive type of coaxial cable became popular for Ethernet networks: Thin Ethernet, also referred to as Thinnet, Cheapernet, or 10Base2 Ethernet. The coaxial cable used with 10Base2 is referred to as RG-58. This type of coaxial cable connects to network cards through a T-connector that bayonet-mounts to the rear of the network card using a BNC connector. The arms of the T are used to connect two cables, each running to another computer in the network (see Figure 17.5).

CH
17

Figure 17.5
A network card using Thin Ethernet cabling; this station is between the ends of the network because cabling is running through both sides of the T-adapter. Compare this with Figure 17.4.

If the workstation is at the end of a network, a terminating resistor is connected to one arm of the T to indicate the end of the network (refer to Figure 17.4). If a resistor is removed, the network fails; if a station on the network fails, the network fails.

Figure 17.6 compares bus, star, and ring topologies.

Ethernet Cable Length Standards
To keep your network running reliably, make sure that the cables do not exceed the maximum lengths recommended for the network card type you have installed. Table 17.2 lists the distance limitations for different types of Ethernet networks and cables.

Table 17.2   Ethernet Network Cabling Distance Limitations

Network Adapter	Cable Type	Maximum Length	Minimum Length
10Base2	Thin coax	607 ft	20 inches
10BaseT	UTP	994 ft	8 ft
100Base TX (Fast Ethernet)	UTP	328 ft	8 ft

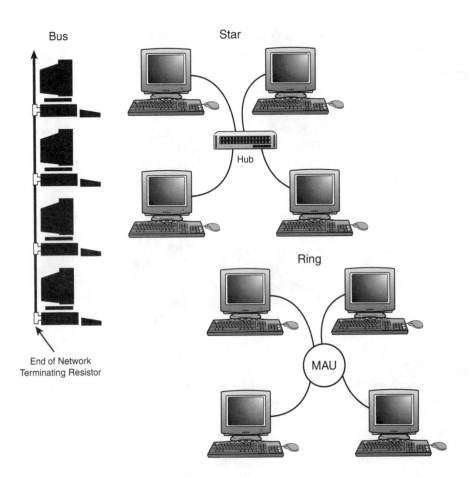

Bus

Star

Hub

Ring

MAU

End of Network
Terminating Resistor

Figure 17.6
A bus topology Thin Ethernet network (left) compared with a UTP-based star topology UTP Ethernet network (upper right) and a Token Ring network (lower right).

If you install dual-speed (10/100) network cards and use 10/100 hubs and switches, be sure to adhere to the 100Base TX (Fast Ethernet) maximum distance to ensure reliable operation. You can use repeaters to extend the maximum distances listed above.

Direct Cable Connection

Direct cable connection (DCC) is a special form of networking in which two computers are connected together through their serial (RS-232) or parallel (LPT) ports with special cables; infrared ports can also be used. Direct cable connection uses standard network protocols, such as NetBEUI, IPX/SPX, or TCP/IP, but Windows 9x also uses a special direct cable connection program to set up the connection; one computer is configured as host, and the other as guest. Both computers must use the same port type—serial, parallel, or infrared—and both computers must use the same network protocol.

DCC cables cross over the standard transmit and receive lines at one end of the cable, enabling two computers to connect with each other without needing a modem, hub, or switch. Serial cables in particular, which are made for use with DCC or similar services, are referred to as *null modem* cables, because the cable itself replaces the need for modems at the sending and receiving ends of the connection. Cables can be built especially for use with DCC, but cables made for the old MS-DOS Interlink program, as well as cables made for LapLink and other file-transfer programs, can also be used.

If infrared connections are used, use the simulated serial port address Windows creates for the port to refer to the port. Infrared is the slowest of the three DCC connection types, and should be used only if serial or parallel cable connections are not possible.

Network Interface Card Installation and Configuration

Very few computers have built-in network interfacing; you will almost always need to install a network interface card (NIC) into a computer you want to add to the network.

NICs come in either ISA or PCI bus types. As you learned in Chapter 5, PCI is much faster and is preferred. PCI cards must be used if you plan to network with Fast Ethernet.

Typical network interface card hardware settings include

- IRQ
- I/O port address range

If the workstation is a diskless workstation, a free upper memory address must also be supplied for the boot ROM on the card. A few older network cards also use upper memory blocks for RAM buffers; check the card's documentation.

To install a Plug and Play PCI-based network card, follow this procedure:

1. Turn off the computer and remove the case cover.
2. Locate an available PCI expansion slot.
3. Remove the slot cover and insert the card into the slot. Secure the card in the slot.
4. Restart the system and provide the driver disk or CD-ROM when requested by the system.
5. Insert the operating system CD-ROM when requested to install network drivers and clients; you might need to swap the network card driver CD-ROM back into the drive to finish the installation.
6. The IRQ, I/O port address, and memory address required by the card will be assigned automatically.

If you need to install a non-PnP (legacy) network card, see "Installing a Legacy Device," page 466, for the general process. You will need to use the operating system CD-ROM to install network drivers and clients when you install any type of network card.

Configuring Network Interface Cards

Network interface cards also have configuration issues that are specific to networks:

- Media/cabling type
- Full or half-duplex

The *media for cabling type* is a setting that you might need to make when installing a network card that supports more than one type of network cable. When you install this type of card, you might need to select the type of network cable (media type) that you'll use with the card; some cards can detect the media type automatically, but some cannot. The selection of media type might require that you adjust the network card configuration with a DOS-based network card setup utility or with the network card property.

Full-duplex or *half-duplex* refers to how the network card will communicate with other stations on the network. Full-duplex means that the network card can receive and send data at the same time; half-duplex means the network card can receive or send data and must stop one activity to perform the other. If full-duplex operation is supported on your network, select it because it's faster. Full-duplex operation usually requires the use of a switch rather than a hub.

After the network card is physically installed and properly configured, use the diagnostics software included with the card to test it.

Setting Up the Server

On a peer network using Windows 9x or Me, setting up a server includes the following tasks:

- Installing the protocols that will be used on the network
- Installing Windows File and Print Sharing
- Naming the workgroup
- Selecting which resources (folders, drives, printers) to share
- Setting up passwords and full or read/only access for each shared resource

With Windows 9x, for example, the Network icon in the Control Panel is used to perform the first three tasks. After the network protocols and file and print sharing software have been installed and the workgroup is named by way of the Network icon, the Windows Explorer is used to identify shared resources, select the access level, and set up passwords if desired (see Figure 17.7).

On networks using Windows NT 4.0 or Windows 2000 Server, setting up a server includes the following tasks:

- Naming the workgroup or domain
- Selecting which resources (folders, drives, printers) to share

- Creating lists of users or groups of users who will be granted access to shared resources

- Setting permissions for access to each shared resource by level of access and by which users or groups will have access

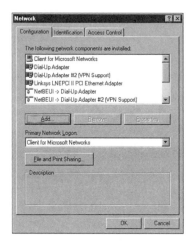

Figure 17.7
Use the Add button in the Network dialog box of Windows 9x to add protocols and services. Use the Identification properties sheet to identify the workstation and network. Use the File and Print Sharing button to install file and print sharing software for peer servers.

Installing Windows Networking Components: Windows 9x

The process of installing Windows network components is similar for both clients and servers. Some network components are installed by default when a network interface card is installed, but this checklist shows you how to install or remove any network components.

To see the currently installed network components, right-click Network Neighborhood and select Properties, or open the Network icon in Control Panel. The list of components will resemble Figure 17.7. Make sure your network card has been installed and is listed as a component.

To install the network components you need, follow this procedure:

1. Decide which protocols your network needs. See "Common Network Protocols: TCP/IP, NetBEUI, IPX/SPX" earlier in this chapter for details. If the protocol you want isn't installed, click Add, Protocol, Microsoft, and choose the protocol you need from the list. Click OK. Ask your network supervisor for help in configuring the IPX/SPX or TCP/IP protocols; NetBEUI uses the workgroup and computer

names you will assign in step 2. See "TCP/IP Configuration," later in this chapter, for details on configuring TCP/IP.

2. Click the Identification tab and enter a workgroup name (which must be used by all computers on the network) and a computer name (which must be unique). Enter a short description.

3. If the Client for Microsoft Networks isn't installed, click Add, Client, Microsoft, and select it from the list of clients. Click OK. Omit steps 4 and 5 if the computer will be a client.

4. If this computer will be used as a server, see whether File and Printer Sharing for Microsoft Networks is listed as a network component. If not, click Add, Services, Microsoft, and select it from the list of services. Click OK.

5. If this computer will be used as a server, also click the File and Print Sharing button and check the I Want to Share My Files and I Want to Let Others Use My Printer boxes.

6. Make sure the TCP/IP or IPX/SPX configurations (if needed) have been done correctly, and check the list of components. Click OK on the main Networks screen and supply the Windows 9x CD-ROM as needed to install the needed software. Reboot the computer when prompted after saving any open documents.

Differences in Windows 2000 Network Configuration

Windows 2000 installs network protocols through its Network and Dial-Up Connections folder. Open the Local Area Connections icon and use Select Network Component Type to install protocols, clients, and services.

Shared Folders and Drives

A shared folder or drive can be accessed by other computers on the network. On a peer network, each shared folder or drive can be password protected with a different password for each share. Separate passwords can be used to provide full access or read-only access for each resource—to control access levels, you would give some users the read-only password, other users the full-access password, and some users might not receive either password. To use a shared resource, users must log on to the network, and then provide the appropriate password for each shared resource they want to use.

On a server-based network, shares are protected by lists of users or groups. Only members who belong to a specific group or are listed separately on the access list for a particular share can access that share. After users log on to the network, they have access to all shares they've been authorized to use without the need to provide additional passwords. Access levels include full and read-only and, on NTFS drives, other access levels, such as write, create, and delete.

Shared Printers

Access control for shared printers on both peer and server-based networks is similar to access control for drives and folders. The following are the differences:

- Only a single level of access (and a single password) are supported on peer networks.
- Windows NT and Windows 2000 servers can distribute printer drivers for other versions of Windows when clients log on to the server and want to use its shared printers.

Setting Up the Client

The client in both peer-to-peer networks and dedicated server networks is a computer that uses shared resources. To access shared resources, a client computer needs

- Network client software
- The name of the network and server(s) with shared resources
- The correct password or passwords to access shared resources that use passwords
- The printer drivers for the network printers

With Windows 9x/Me/2000, the Network icon in the Control Panel is used to install network client software and to indicate the name of the network.

Network Neighborhood (Windows 9x) or My Network Places (Windows 2000) is used to locate shared resources and to provide passwords. The Printers icon is used to set up access to a network printer. See "Installing Windows Networking Components: Windows 9x" earlier in this chapter for the step-by-step procedure for setting up a client.

Using Shared Resources

With any type of network, the user must log on with a correct username and password to use any network resources. With a dedicated server, such as Novell or Windows NT/2000 Server, a single username and password is needed for any network resource the user has permission to use.

On a peer-to-peer network, such as a Windows 9x network, additional passwords might be required for each of your resources. On a dedicated server network, such as Novell NetWare, Windows NT, or Windows 2000, a single password provides a specified user with access to all the shared resources that user is permitted to use. This is called *user-level security*. A Windows 9x peer server connected to a dedicated server can also use the dedicated server's list of users to control access.

User-level security controls a wider range of activities on a system than does share-level security.

CH

17

A peer server used on Windows 9x uses a username and password for initial access, and can also use a separate password for each shared resource. This is called *share-level security* and is harder to maintain. A peer server has three security levels:

- No access if password is unknown
- Read-only access (can be password-protected or left open to all)
- Full access (can be password-protected or left open to all)

Information can be copied from a shared drive or folder if the user has read-only access; to add, change, or delete information on the shared drive or folder, the user needs full access.

Network printing is performed the same way as local printing after the network printer driver software has been set up on the workstation.

You can identify shared resources with Windows 9x/Me/2000 by using Explorer. On a system that is sharing resources with other users, a shared drive, folder, or printer will use a modified icon with a hand, indicating that it is being shared (see Figure 17.8).

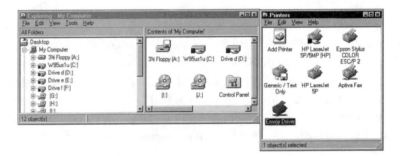

Figure 17.8
The Windows 9x Explorer (left) and Printers folder (right) display shared and nonshared resources. The hand icon indicates which drives and printers are shared with other computers.

To use a shared resource on a peer server that uses share-level security, the user must provide the correct password for any password-protected share. To use a shared resource on a network that uses dedicated servers with user-level security, the user must log on to the network. The administrator of the server or network has already assigned access levels and permissions to each user or group, so the user can immediately begin using shared resources as permitted.

Shared drives and folders can be referred to in one of the following ways:

- A mapped drive letter
- A universal naming convention (UNC) name
- A fully qualified domain name (FQDN)

Each of these is explained in the following sections.

Mapped Drives

Windows 9x/Me/2000 allow shared folders and shared drives to be mapped to drive letters on clients. In the Windows Explorer, these mapped drive letters will show up in the list along with the local drive letters. A shared resource can be accessed either through Network Neighborhood (using the share name) or through a mapped drive letter.

Drive mapping has the following benefits:

- A shared folder mapped as a drive can be referred to by the drive name instead of a long universal naming convention path (see "The Universal Naming Convention (UNC)" later in this chapter for details).
- Shared folders can be accessed by MS-DOS programs only if drive mappings are used.

To map a shared folder to a drive with Windows Explorer, follow this procedure:

1. Right-click the shared folder in the Windows Explorer.
2. Select Map Network Drive.
3. Select a drive letter from the list of available drive letters; only drive letters not used by local drives are listed. Drive letters already in use for other shared folders display the UNC name of the shared folder (see Figure 17.9).

Figure 17.9
The Map Network Drive menu lists already mapped folders and drive letters that are still available.

4. Click the Reconnect at Login box (not shown) if you want to use the mapped drive every time you connect to the network. This option should be used only if the server will be available at all times; otherwise, the client will receive error messages when it tries to access the shared resource.

CH
17

Shared folders can be accessed by either their mapped drive letters or by their folder names in Windows Explorer, as seen in Figure 17.10.

The Universal Naming Convention (UNC)

The Universal Naming Convention is designed to allow users to access network resources without mapping drive letters to network drives or specifying the type of device that stores the file or hosts the printer. A UNC name has the following structure in Windows:

    \\servername\sharename\path\filename

A typical UNC path to a document would resemble

    \\Aopen\O\NetDocuments\this_doc.doc

The following UNC elements are in use:

- ■ \\Aopen is the server.
- ■ \O is the sharename.
- ■ \NetDocuments is the path.
- ■ \this_doc.doc is the document.

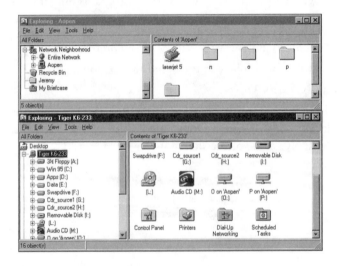

Figure 17.10
Windows Explorer shows the Network Neighborhood view of shared folders O and P (top); the same shares have been mapped to drives O: and P: in the Windows Explorer view of My Computer (bottom).

UNC allows files and printers to be accessed by the user with Windows 9x/Me/2000 applications. Windows 3.x and MS-DOS users must map drive letters to shared folders to access files and must map printer ports to shared printers to print. Because only 23 drive letters (maximum) can be mapped, UNC allows network resources beyond the D–Z limits to still be accessed.

Some Windows applications will display the UNC path to a file even if the file was accessed through a mapped drive letter, and other Windows applications will refer to the UNC path or mapped drive letter path to the file, depending on how the file was retrieved (see Figure 17.11).

Fully Qualified Domain Names (FQDN)

TCP/IP networks that contain DNS servers often use FQDNs to refer to servers along with, or in place of, UNC names. The structure of a FQDN is

```
Name-of-server.name-of-domain.root-domain
```

For example, a server called "charley" in the selectsystems.com domain would have an FQDN of

```
charley.selectsystems.com
```

UNC path to file and filename   Mapped drive path to file and filename

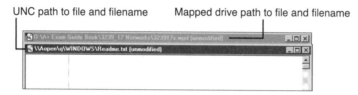

Figure 17.11

Two documents were opened from shared network resources in a word-processing program. The top document was retrieved using a mapped drive; the bottom document was retrieved using Network Neighborhood.

If you want to access the shared Docs folder on charley.selectsystems.com, you would refer to it as

```
\\charley.selectsystems.com\Docs
```

You can also use the IP address of the server in place of the server name. If 192.10.8.22 is the IP address of charley.selectsystems.com, you can access the Docs folder with the following statement:

```
\\192.10.8.22\Docs
```

You can use either UNCs or FQDN along with the Net command-line utility to view or map drive letters to shared folders.

The *Net* Command

Both Windows 9x and Windows 2000 offer the Net command for use in displaying and using network resources from the command line. Some of the Net commands you can use include

- **Net Help**—Displays help for a Net option; for example, use Net Help View for help with the Net View command

CH
17

- **Net Use**—Maps a network drive to a shared resource on the network; for example,
  Net Use Q: \\Celeron600\shared
- **Net View**—Displays network servers

To display a complete list of Net commands, type **Net /?** |**More** from the command prompt.

Beyond LANs—Repeaters, Switches, and Routers

An Ethernet network that grows beyond the capabilities of a hub might require additional connectivity hardware, such as the following:

- Repeaters
- Switches
- Routers

Repeaters

Repeaters boost signal strength to allow longer cable runs than those permitted by the "official" cabling limits of Ethernet.

Switches

While dual-speed switches are used to connect different speeds of Ethernet to each other, their primary benefit is to boost performance of high-speed networks when compared to hubs. Dual-speed hubs and dual-speed switches have replaced bridges because they can interconnect different speeds of Ethernet networks, allowing them to function as one. However, switches are much better to use than hubs because switches transport data faster between computers.

A switch is faster than a hub because of the type of connection it makes between two computers. A hub splits the bandwidth of the connection among all the computers connected to it. For example, a five-port 10BaseT Ethernet hub divides the 10Mbps speed of Ethernet among the five ports, providing only 2Mbps of bandwidth to each port. A five-port 10/100 switch, on the other hand, provides the full 10Mbps bandwidth to each port connected to a 10BaseT card and a full 100Mbps bandwidth to each port connected to a Fast Ethernet or 10/100 card. Most switches also provide support for full-duplex operation, which allows networking devices to send and receive data at the same time. When a switch is used with network cards that support this feature, the effective bandwidth is doubled—200Mbps when two 10/100 or Fast Ethernet cards are connected.

The name *switch* implies the device's similarity to a railroad switchyard, which moves cars from one track to another to create a dedicated train of "data" bound for a single destination at high speed. Hubs, on the other hand, broadcast data to all computers connected to the hub, even though the data is intended for just one of those computers.

Switches can be daisy-chained in a manner similar to stackable hubs, and there is no limit to the number of switches possible in a network.

Routers

Routers are used to interconnect LANs to other networks; the name suggests the device's similarity to an efficient travel agent, who helps a group reach its destination as quickly as possible. Routers can connect different types of networks and protocols to each other (Ethernet, Token-Ring, TCP/IP, and so on) and are a vital part of the Internet.

Router features and prices vary according to the network types and protocols supported.

Internet Concepts

Internet connections can be made in several different ways:

- By using Dial-Up Networking with a modem
- By using the local area network that is connected to the Internet
- By using special connection types, such as cable modems, xDSL telephone lines, or DirecPC satellite dishes

Dial-Up Networking Through an ISP

For small-business users, Dial-Up Networking is still the most common way of accessing the Internet.

An Internet service provider (ISP) provides a connection between the user with a modem and the Internet. An ISP can be selected from many different sources:

- National companies, such as Earthlink or UUNet
- Filtered services, such as Mayberry USA or Integrity Online
- Local or regional providers

Choose an ISP based on its rates, its reliability, or special services (such as filtration or custom contents) that are appropriate to your needs.

All ISPs must provide the following information to allow you to connect to the Internet:

- Client software, including the preferred Web browser, dial-up information, and TCP/IP configuration information
- Dial-up access telephone numbers
- Modem types supported (33.6Kbps, 56Kbps, X2, K56flex, v.90)
- The username and initial password (which should be changed immediately after first login)

Normally, the client software provided by the ISP automatically configures the system to use the Internet through that ISP's connection. However, the following information should be recorded in case it is needed to manually configure the connection:

- The dial-up access telephone number; this might be different for different modem speeds. Users with a 56Kbps modem should know both the standard and high-speed access numbers if different numbers are used.

- The username and password; Windows will often save this during the setup of a Dial-Up Networking connection, but it should be recorded in case the system must be reconfigured or replaced.
- The TCP/IP configuration; this is not set through the Networking icon in Windows, but is set individually for each Dial-Up Networking connection through its properties sheet.

TCP/IP Configuration

For a computer to connect to the Internet, its TCP/IP configuration must be correct. Any computer that needs to connect to the Internet must have an IP address. The TCP/IP protocol is also very popular for networking computers because it enables network administrators to set up a single protocol for both Internet use and networking between computers. Your computer's IP address might come from various sources:

- If you connect to the Internet through a LAN, you might use a static IP address, or DHCP (see the last item in this list) can be used to generate a new IP address each time you connect to the Internet.
- If you connect to the Internet with Dial-Up Networking, the ISP might assign you a dynamic address that is different every time you connect.
- The IP address might be assigned by a special server called a DHCP (Dynamic Host Configuration Protocol) server.

If you access the Internet through a LAN, you might also need to set the IP address for the gateway through which you reach the Internet.

If the IP address is incorrect, your computer will not be able to access the Internet.

Where you set the IP address varies with the connection type. If you are using a modem with Dial-Up Networking, you adjust the IP address on the properties sheet for the connection, as shown in Figure 17.12.

For a connection made on a LAN, you change the IP address and other settings with the Networks icon in the Windows Control Panel using the properties sheet for the network card, as shown in Figure 17.13.

You might need to change items, such as IP address, WINS Configuration, Gateway, and DNS Configuration, from their default values to set up your Internet connection. The network administrator will tell you what settings need to be changed.

The following sections explain the major settings used by Windows' TCP/IP configuration.

IP Address

The IP address might be provided by the network administrator as in Figure 17.12, or it might be set to obtain an IP address automatically. If automatic IP addressing is used, a DHCP server is used to provide the IP address.

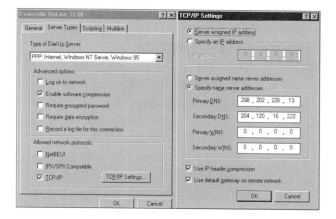

Figure 17.12
Click the Server Types tab, and select TCP/IP Configuration in the properties sheet for your Dial-Up Networking connection (left) to view or change the IP address (right).

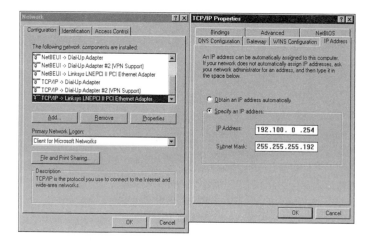

Figure 17.13
Select the TCP/IP -> (network card) icon in the Windows Network components list to view or change TCP/IP settings used for your LAN-based Internet connection.

IP addresses use four groups of numbers that range from 0 to 255. The subnet mask is used along with the IP address for routing. Both computers and other networked devices, such as routers and network printers, can have IP addresses, and some devices can have more than one IP address. For example, a router can have two IP addresses—one to connect the router to a LAN, and the other that connects it to the Internet, enabling it to route traffic from the LAN to the Internet and back.

WINS Configuration

If the IP address is provided by a DHCP server, or if a WINS server is used, you will need to make changes to this tab (see Figure 17.14).

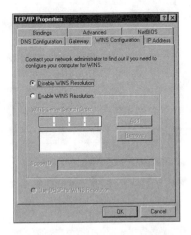

Figure 17.14
The WINS Configuration tab is used to enable both WINS and DHCP services.

Windows Internet Naming Service (WINS) matches the NetBIOS name of a particular computer to an IP address on the network; this process is also called resolving or translating the NetBIOS name to IP address. WINS requires the use of a Window NT or Windows 2000 Server that has been set up to provide the resolving service. If WINS is enabled, the IP addresses of the WINS servers must be entered.

Dynamic Host Configuration Protocol (DHCP) is used to receive an automatically assigned IP address from a DHCP server on the network. This allows a limited number of IP addresses to serve a larger number of computers.

The network administrator will inform you of the correct settings to use on this tab.

Gateway

A gateway provides a connection between a LAN and a wide area network (WAN) or the Internet. Computers that use a LAN connection to connect to the Internet might need to enter the IP address or addresses of the gateways on this tab (see Figure 17.15).

DNS Configuration

The Internet uses the Domain Name System (DNS) to map domain names, such as www.microsoft.com, to their corresponding IP address or addresses. A computer using the Internet must use at least one DNS server to provide this translation service. Use the DNS Configuration tab to set up the computer's host name, domain name, and DNS servers (see Figure 17.16).

After you have configured these settings, click OK and reboot the computer if directed to do so.

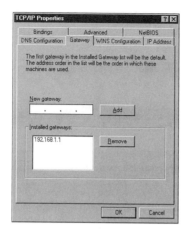

Figure 17.15
This computer uses a single gateway for Internet access; multiple gateways can be listed here in order of preference.

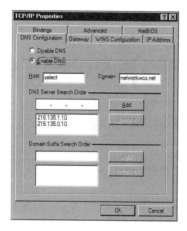

Figure 17.16
This computer can receive DNS information from two different DNS servers. DNS servers enable users to refer to an Internet site by name rather than by IP address.

Viewing the TCP/IP Configuration

Windows 9x users can see their system's TCP/IP configuration without using the Network icon by running the Winipcfg utility. To run Winipcfg, click Start, Run, type **Winipcfg**, and click OK.

Winipcfg displays TCP/IP configuration information for all physical and logical TCP/IP-capable adapters installed in a system. To determine the IP address and other information for your network card, select the network card from the Winipcfg main menu. Winipcfg's opening screen appears in Figure 17.17.

Figure 17.17
Use Winipcfg to display the IP address, subnet mask, and default gateway for your network card.

To obtain more information about your TCP/IP configuration, click the More Info button. This information will be displayed, as seen in Figure 17.18.

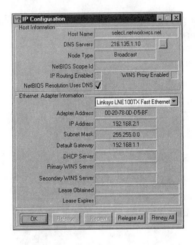

Figure 17.18
Click the More Info button on the Winipcfg opening screen to see the DNS servers, WINS or DHCP servers, and host name used by your computer.

Windows 2000 uses the Ipconfig command-line utility in place of Winipcfg. Ipconfig will display the computer's current IP address, subnet mask, and default gateway.

Using *Ping*

Windows 9x and Windows 2000 can use the Ping command to test TCP/IP and Internet connections for proper operation. Ping is a more reliable way to check an Internet connection than opening your browser, because a misconfigured browser could cause you to think that your TCP/IP configuration is incorrect.

To use Ping to check your connection, follow this procedure:

1. Start your Internet connection. If you use a local area network (LAN) to connect to the Internet, you might have an always-on connection.

2. Open a command-prompt window.

3. Type `Ping IP address` or `Ping servername` and press Enter. For example, to ping a Web server called www.selectsystems.com, type `Ping www.selectsystems.com`.

By default, `Ping` sends four data packets from your computer to any IP address or server name you specify. If your TCP/IP connection is working properly, you should see a reply from each ping you sent out, as in Figure 17.19.

IP address of URL specified by Ping

URL specified by Ping

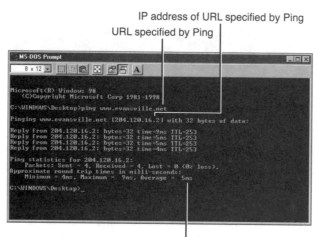

Average round-trip speed (ping rate)

Figure 17.19
Pinging the URL of a Web site checks the speed at which you can access the Web site and also displays its IP address.

The lower the time in milliseconds (ms), the faster your connection. Connection speeds vary a great deal due to various factors, such as Internet network congestion, server speed, and the number of relays needed to transfer your request from your computer to the specified server. To check this factor, use the `Tracert` command.

Tracert

The `Tracert` command is used by Windows 9x and Windows 2000 to trace the route taken by data traveling from your computer to an IP address or Web site you specify. By default, `Tracert` will check up to 30 hops between your computer and the specified Web site or IP address. To use `Tracert` to check the routing, follow this procedure:

1. Start your Internet connection. If you use a local area network (LAN) to connect to the Internet, you might have an always-on connection.

2. Open a command-prompt window.

CH
17

3. Type `Tracert` *IP address* or `Tracert` *servername* and press Enter. For example, to trace the route to a Web server called www.selectsystems.com, type **Tracert www.selectsystems.com**. `Tracert` will produce a report similar to the one shown in Figure 17.20.

To see help for the `Tracert` command, type `Tracert` without any options and press the Enter key.

Figure 17.20

Use `Tracert` to see how many hops it takes to reach the Web site or IP address you specify. Even Web sites in the same city might require many hops if you and the server use different ISPs, as in this example.

Troubleshooting with `Ping` **and** `Tracert`

If `Ping` and `Tracert` don't display any output or display error messages, check the following:

- Make sure you have a working Internet connection. Start your dial-up connection and check your modem or network cables.
- Make sure you logged on to the network.

HTML

Hypertext Markup Language (HTML) is the language used by Web pages. An HTML page is a specially formatted text page that uses tags (commands contained in angle brackets) to change text appearance, insert links to other pages, display pictures, incorporate scripting languages, and provide other features. Web browsers, such as Microsoft Internet Explorer and Netscape Navigator, are used to view and interpret the contents of Web pages, which can have the following typical file extensions:

- `.HTM`
- `.HTML`
- `.ASP` (Active Server pages generated by a database)

You can see the HTML code used to create the Web page in a browser by using the View Source or View Page Source menu option provided by your browser. Figure 17.21 compares what you see in a typical Web page (top window) with the HTML tags used to set text features and the underlined hyperlink (bottom window). The figure uses different text size and shading to distinguish tags from text, and so do most commercial Web editing programs used to make Web pages.

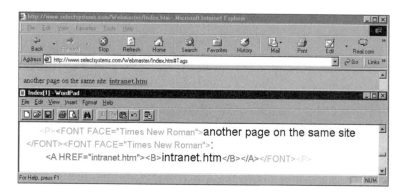

Figure 17.21
A section of an HTML document as seen by a typical browser (top window) uses the HTML tags shown in the bottom window for paragraph breaks (<P> tags), font settings (<FONT> tags), and hyperlinks (<A HREF> tags).

Tags such as <P> are used by themselves, and other tags are used in pairs. For example, <A HREF...> is used to indicate the start of a hyperlink (which will display another page or site in your browser window), and </A> indicates the end of a hyperlink.

The World Wide Web Consortium (http://www.w3c.org) sets the official standards for HTML tags and syntax, but major browser vendors, such as Microsoft and Netscape, often modify or extend official HTML standards with their own tags and syntax.

Browser Configuration

Web browsers, such as Microsoft Internet Explorer and Netscape Navigator, are the main interface through which you navigate the Internet. Depending on how you connect with the Internet, you might need to adjust the browser configuration.

Typical options you might need to change include

- **Proxies for use with LAN-based or filtered access**—Users who access the Internet through a local area network might be doing so through a proxy server. Proxy servers receive a copy of the Web site or content the user wants to look at and checks it for viruses or unapproved content before passing it on. The proxy server information is set through the browser's configuration menu.

- **Automatic dial up for convenience**—Some browsers can also be set to dial up the Internet automatically whenever you start the browser to make Internet access easier. This option is very useful for dial-up connections but should not be used for connections made through a LAN.

- **Default colors and fonts**—Visually impaired users might prefer to select default fonts and colors that can override the document defaults.

- **Default start page**—Users who prefer a different Web site as the startup site can change the default opening page.

- **Email configuration**—Most browsers include an email client; the settings for the email server and other options must be made to allow email to be seen and replied to within the browser.

- **Disable graphics**—Users with extremely slow connections who view primarily text-based pages can disable graphics for extra speed.

- **Security settings for Java**—Advanced features, such as Java and ActiveX, make sites more interactive, but might also pose a security risk; these features can be limited or disabled through the Security menu.

Generally, you should use all the features possible of the browser unless you have speed or security concerns that lead you to disable some features.

Setting Up Your Browser to Use Your Internet Connection

A Web browser can be used to view both online Web pages (pages on Web servers) and offline pages (Web pages stored on your hard disk). In most cases, users will want the Internet to be available as soon as they open their Web browser. Because some users have dial-up connections and some networks use proxy servers to provide firewall protection or content filtering, you might need to adjust the browser configuration to permit Internet access.

To view or adjust the browser configuration for Internet Explorer, follow this procedure:

1. Open Internet Explorer.

2. Click Tools.

3. Click Internet Options.

4. Click Connections.

5. If the Internet connection uses a dial-up modem, select the correct dial-up connection from those listed and choose Always Dial (to start the connection when the browser is opened) or Dial Whenever a Network Connection Is Not Present. Click Set Default to make the selected connection the default (see Figure 17.22).

6. If the Internet connection uses a network, click Never Dial a Connection, and click LAN Settings to check network configuration.

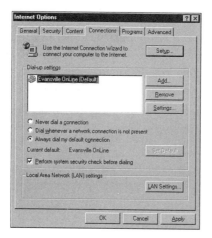

Figure 17.22
To enable your browser to start your dial-up Internet connection automatically, set the
Connections tab to dial your preferred connection for you.

7. Ask the network administrator if you should use Automatically Detect Settings or
whether you should specify a particular automatic configuration script.

8. If a proxy server is used for Internet access, it must be specified by server name
and port number. If different servers and port numbers are used for different
TCP/IP protocols, such as HTTP, FTP, and others, click Advanced and specify
the correct server and port number to use (see Figure 17.23).

9. Click OK to save changes at each menu level until you return to the browser
display.

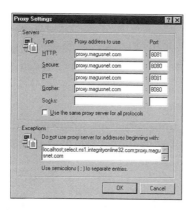

Figure 17.23
You can specify different proxy servers, ports, and which servers can be accessed
directly by using the Advanced option for proxy server settings.

FTP

The File Transfer Protocol is another popular Internet protocol that you often use without really noticing. When you visit a major commercial Web site for a printer or other hardware driver and click a link, you are often directed to an FTP server. If you watch the address in your browser you'll see the HTTP:// change to FTP:// in such a case.

FTP sites are divided up into folders resembling the folders on a hard disk, and might control access in several different ways.

Controlling Access to FTP Sites

Public FTP sites allow anonymous logins and will use the email address in your browser for identification if necessary. Other FTP sites are password-protected, requiring a username and password for access. Some sites that allow you to buy software for electronic download work this way.

Browser Versus FTP Client

Although a browser can download files through FTP, it isn't as fast as a dedicated FTP client, and a browser can't upload files to an FTP server or a Web server hosting your Web site.

To update files on your Web site or to download files faster, use a dedicated FTP program, such as CuteFTP, WS_FTP LE, or WS_FTP Pro. These programs allow you to create a customized setup for each FTP site you visit, and will store passwords, server types, and other necessary information. They also allow faster downloads than typical Web browsers running in FTP:// mode.

Both Windows 9x and Windows 2000 have command-line FTP clients, but the commercial products mentioned in the previous paragraph are easier to use and more powerful.

Email

Email can be used in a variety of ways over the Internet:

- Web browsers contain email clients.
- Standalone email clients, such as Eudora Light, can be installed and used freely.
- More powerful standalone email clients, such as Eudora Pro, offer additional features but must be purchased.
- Users who travel away from corporate networks might prefer to use a Web-based email account, such as Hotmail, that can be checked from any system with a properly configured Web browser.

All email systems provide transfer of text messages, and most have provision for file attachments, allowing you to send documents, graphics, video clips, and other types of computer data files to receivers for work or play.

To configure any email client, you need

- The name of the email server for incoming mail
- The name of the email server for outgoing mail
- The username and password for the email user

To access Web-based email, you need

- The Web site for the email service
- The username and password

Domain Names

Domain names have replaced the once-ubiquitous toll-free numbers in advertising for more and more companies. The Internet's DNS (Domain Name System) is what translates domain names, such as www.selectsystems.com (the author's Web site), into the IP address used by the actual host computer.

The following are some common errors in domain name use:

- **Assuming that all domain names end in** .com—Other popular domain name extensions include .net, .org, .gov, .us, .cc, and various national domains such as .uk (United Kingdom), .ca (Canada), and many others.
- **Forgetting to use the entire domain name in the browser**—Some browsers will add the www. prefix used on most domain names, but others will not. For best results, spell out the complete domain name.

If you want a unique domain name for either a Web site or email, the ISP that you will use to provide your email or Web hosting service often provides a registration wizard you can use to access the domain name registration services provided by companies such as Network Solutions.

Some Web sites have a folder under a domain hosted by an ISP:

www.anisp.com/~asmallsite

A domain name has three major sections, from the end of the name to the start:

- The top-level domain (.com, .org, .net, and so on)
- The name of the site
- The server type; www indicates a Web server, ftp indicates an FTP server, mail indicates a mail server, and search indicates a search server

CH
17

For example, Microsoft.com is located in the .com domain, typically used for commercial companies. Microsoft is the domain name. The Microsoft.com domain has the following servers:

- www.microsoft.com hosts Web content, such as product information.
- search.microsoft.com hosts the Microsoft.com search features, enabling users to search all or selected parts of the Microsoft.com domain.
- ftp.microsoft.com hosts the File Transfer Protocol server of Microsoft.com; this portion of the Microsoft.com domain can be accessed by either a Web browser or an FTP client.

Many companies have only WWW servers, or only WWW and FTP servers.

Many small Web sites don't have unique domain names. For example, www.safelink.net is the Web site of an Idaho-based ISP that also hosts small Web sites, such as www.safelink.net/danrose, the home of Dan Rose's Abandonware Web site, which features the history of still-useful DOS and Windows 3.1 application programs, and www.safe-link.net/cquilts, the online home of Carole's Quilts.

Troubleshooting

Use this section to prepare you for troubleshooting questions involving network hardware and software on the A+ Certification test and in your day-to-day work as a computer technician.

The following are some of the typical network problems you might encounter:

- Can't access network resources
- Drops in network speed
- Unattended PC drops its network connection
- All users lose network connection
- Users can access some shared resources but not others
- Can't print to a network printer
- Ping and Tracert work, but user can't display Web pages with browser

Can't Access Network Resources

Users who don't log in to the network can't access network resources. To restart the login process, use the following steps in Windows 9x:

1. Click Start.
2. Click Log Off *(user)*.
3. Re-enter the correct username and password.

Windows 2000 systems require a login with a valid username and password before the system can be started.

If an error message such as Duplicate Computer Name or Duplicate IP Address is displayed during system startup, open the Network icon and change the name of the computer or the system's IP address. Contact the network administrator for the correct name or IP address settings to use.

Significant Drops in Network Performance

Significant drops in network performance can be traced to a variety of causes, including

- Damage to cables, connectors, network cards, hubs, and switches
- Expanding network capacity with hubs in place of switches
- Connecting high-speed NICs to low-speed hubs or switches

If network usage patterns remain constant but some users report lower performance, check cables, connectors, and other network hardware for physical damage. Dry, brittle, and cracked cables and connectors can generate interference, which forces network stations to retransmit data because it wasn't received correctly. Replace damaged cables and connectors.

To isolate networking problems between Windows 9x computers, run the Net Diag command (click Start and select Run or use the DOS prompt) on all Windows 9x computers on the network, setting one of them as a diagnostics server. If some computers run Windows NT 4.0 or Windows 2000, use diagnostic programs supplied with the network card if the same card is used by multiple computers. These diagnostics programs send and receive data and provide reports of problems.

If all the users connected to a single hub or switch report slowdowns, check the hub or switch. Replace a hub with a switch to see an immediate boost in performance. Continue to use switches to add capacity.

Make sure that 10/100 cards are connected to dual-speed hubs or switches to get the benefits of 100Mbps performance. 10/100 cards will work at 10Mbps only if connected to 10Mbps hubs or switches.

An Unattended PC Drops Its Network Connection

Incorrect settings for power management can cause stations to lose their network connections when power management features, such as standby mode, are activated. Check the properties for the network card to see if the card can be set to wake up the computer when network activity is detected. If APM power management, which is controlled in the system BIOS, is enabled, use the Device Manager to determine which IRQ is used by the network card and set up this IRQ in the APM power management screen for monitoring.

All Users Lose Network Connection

If the network uses a bus topology, a failure of any station on the network or of termination at either end of the network will cause the entire network to fail. Check the terminators first, and then the T-connectors and cables between computers. If you suspect that a

CH
17

particular computer is the cause of the failure, move the terminator to the computer preceding it in the bus topology. Repeat as needed to isolate the problem. Replace cables, connectors, or network cards as needed to solve the problem.

If the network uses a star topology, check the power supply going to the hub or switch, or replace the hub or switch. Hub or switch failures will cause all users connected to the hub or switch to lose the network connection.

If only the users connected to a new hub or switch that is connected to an existing hub or switch lose their network connection, check the connection between the existing hub or switch and the new one. Most hubs and switches have an uplink port that is used to connect an additional hub or switch. You can either use the regular port next to the uplink port or the uplink port, but not both. Connect the computer using the port next to the uplink port to another port to make the uplink port available for connecting the new hub or switch.

If the uplink port appears to be connected properly, check the cable. Uplink ports perform the crossover for the user, enabling you to use an ordinary network cable to add a hub or switch. If you use a crossover cable, you must connect the new hub or switch through a regular port, not the uplink port.

Users Can Access Some Shared Resources but Not Others

Users who need to access shared resources on a peer network must provide the correct password for any password-protected resources. Passwords can be saved automatically the first time the resource is used, but if the password is changed, the user must provide the new password for access. Check with the peer server's user for the correct passwords to use for a shared resource.

Users who need to access shared resources on a server-based network using user-based security must be granted permission to access resources; different users are typically allowed different access levels to network resources. Contact the network administrator for help if a user is prevented from using a resource; the network administrator will need to permit or deny access to the user.

Can't Print to a Network Printer

Just as with shared folders, network printers can use either share-level or user-level security (see the previous section). Problems with network printing can also come from incorrect print queue settings and incorrect printer drivers.

When you configure a network printer connection, you must correctly specify the UNC path to the printer. For example, if the printer is shared as LaserJ5 on the server Celeron600, the correct UNC path to specify in the printer properties sheet would be

```
\\Celeron600\LaserJ5
```

If the share name or server name is changed, the network printer will not be accessible until the properties are changed on the clients that want to use this printer. You must also use the correct printer driver for the printer and the operating system. If the network printer is connected to a Windows NT 4.0 or Windows 2000 system and your clients use Windows 9x, configure the server to provide the correct printer drivers, or make sure each client already has the correct driver installed before attempting to use the network printer.

See "Printing to a Network Printer," page 457, for more details.

Ping and *Tracert* Work, but User Can't Display Web Pages with Browser

If Ping and Tracert receive output from the specified Web sites but the Web browser cannot display Web pages on those or other sites, the browser configuration might be incorrect.

If the browser doesn't use the correct configuration for the connection type, no pages will be displayed. With dial-up Internet connections, either the user must manually open the connection or the browser should be set to dial the connection. If a proxy server or special network configuration is needed, this must be configured in the browser. See "Setting Up Your Browser to Use Your Internet Connection," earlier in this chapter, for details.

CH 17

Summary

A network is a group of computers that can share resources, such as disk drives, printers, and services, with each other. Many networks are also configured to access the Internet.

Both Windows 9x and Windows 2000 provide the necessary features to create a simple peer network. Windows 9x uses share-level security, which can assign a separate password to each shared resource. Windows 2000 uses user-level security, which enables the network administrator to create lists of users who have different levels of permissions to use shared resources.

A client uses network resources located on other computers on the network, while a server provides shared resources for use by clients. In a peer network, computers can act as both clients and servers.

Windows NT Server, Windows 2000 Server, and Novell NetWare servers are used on server-based networks to provide security and services to clients and are not used as clients themselves.

Protocols such as Ethernet and token-ring describe how computers physically connect to each other. Ethernet is the overwhelming favorite today.

Protocols such as TCP/IP, IPX/SPX, and NetBEUI describe how computers communicate with each other. TCP/IP is used in all but the smallest networks today because it also allows Internet access.

TCP/IP must be present for application protocols, such as HTTP, SMTP, FTP, and others, to work.

Basic network configuration requires that network cards must be installed; network cables, hubs, and switches must be used to connect computers; and server and client software must be installed and configured.

The most popular network type, Ethernet, normally uses UTP cables for 10BaseT, Fast Ethernet, and Gigabit Ethernet, although older 10Base2 and 10Base5 versions used coaxial cable. STP cable is typically used by token-ring networks. Both Ethernet and token-ring networks can also use fiber-optic cable.

Direct cable connection allows two computers to connect through serial or parallel ports.

Network cards (NICs) typically use an IRQ and I/O port address range. PCI versions are preferred over ISA versions.

Both servers and clients must use the same network protocol (such as TCP/IP) and use compatible network card and cable types to communicate with each other.

When a client tries to access a shared resource on a server, it must provide a password if the server uses share-level security and has set a password for the resource. If the server uses user-level security, each network user is already assigned to a group with a defined level of network access; as soon as users log in to the network, authorized resources are available.

Clients can map frequently used shared folders to drive letters (mapped drives) or can refer to a shared resource by its universal naming convention (UNC) path or its fully qualified domain name (FQDN) path.

The Windows Explorer and command-line Net commands can be used to view network servers and shared resources.

To expand a network and boost performance, users can add repeaters to allow longer cable runs, replace hubs with switches, and use routers to connect local area networks (LANs) with wide area networks (WANs) or the Internet.

TCP/IP configurations for dial-up and LAN-based Internet connections vary in details, but all TCP/IP configurations require that the proper settings for IP address, gateway, DNS server, and WINS or DHCP servers be configured in the Network properties sheet.

Windows 9x users can use Winipcfg and Windows 2000 users can use Ipconfig to view important TCP/IP configuration information, such as IP address and default gateway.

Ping can be used to test a TCP/IP configuration; a working connection will return the IP address and round-trip speed of the site that was Pinged.

Tracert (the Windows version of Traceroute) can be used to check the number of hops between your computer and a Web site.

HTML is the language used on Web pages; special tags format the page and text appearance and specify hyperlinks and graphics content, among other features.

The Web browser can be configured to allow the user to override default page colors, provide protection against Java and script dangers, and specify the desired home page. The Web browser can also be configured to automatically set up an Internet connection when the browser is started.

FTP (File Transfer Protocol) can be performed with both Web browsers and FTP clients, although FTP clients can usually download files faster and also provide the capability to upload files to FTP servers.

Email is among the most popular uses of the Internet. Some email services, such as Hotmail, can be accessed through Web servers, but others require that you use an email client. Email clients are supplied with popular browsers or can be purchased separately. Most email services allow you to transfer binary files, such as picture or program files, as well as text messages.

Domain names have three parts, including the top-level domain (.com, .edu, .gov, .net, and country-specific domains, such as .ca and .uk), the site name, and the server type. For example, www.microsoft.com is the www server at the microsoft.com domain.

Problems with network configuration, cabling, and other hardware can all lead to network slowdowns and failures.

CH
17

QUESTIONS AND ANSWERS:

1. What is the difference between a client and a server?
    A: A client uses shared resources, whereas a server shares resources with clients.

2. Can you share just a folder rather than an entire drive?
    A: Yes, you can. Either type of shared resource is used the same way by clients.

3. What is the least expensive way to connect two computers for temporary networking?
    A: Direct Cable Connection. It requires only a special cable.

4. Where do you adjust the TCP/IP properties for a dial-up connection?
    A: In the Dial-Up Networking connection's properties sheet.

5. Which type of cable is used by 10BaseT Ethernet networking? Can faster versions use it?
    A: UTP cable is used by 10BaseT. If it is Category 5, it can be used by Fast Ethernet, and possibly by Gigabit Ethernet.

Troubleshooting Principles

1. What is the most important question you can ask when a system fails?
2. Are new parts working parts?
3. Name two sources for known-working parts.
4. What Windows features allow you to record system settings before making changes?
5. What can you attach to a serial or parallel port for more accurate testing?

Introduction

Two factors make for successful troubleshooting: extensive computer knowledge and an understanding of human psychology. You must understand how hardware and software work to troubleshoot them. That's what the preceding chapters of this book were all about. You also must treat customers with respect. By combining these two factors, you can quickly detect and solve computer problems.

Because computer failures happen to the customer (who usually is less technically aware than you of the possible causes for the problem), you must work with the customer to create as complete a list of symptoms as possible so you can find the right solution quickly and accurately. To do this, you need to

- Carefully observe the customer's environment to look for potential causes of computer problems, such as interference sources, power problems, and user error.
- Ask the customer detailed questions about the symptoms, including unusual system behavior, such as noises or beeps, office events taking place around the same time, onscreen error messages, and so on.

Because some types of computer problems aren't easy to replicate away from the customer site, your customer might see system problems you never will, even if you attempt to reproduce the problem.

Remember, troubleshooting is the art and science of quickly and accurately determining what is wrong with a customer's system. Troubleshooting is an art because every technician will bring his or her own experience and personality to the task. Troubleshooting is also a science because you can apply a definite method that will bring you a great degree of success.

Troubleshooting Methods Overview

To become a successful troubleshooter, you need to

- Learn as much as possible during the client interview.
- Evaluate the client's environment.
- Use testing and reporting software to gather information about the system.
- Form a hypothesis (a theory you will try to prove or disprove).
- Use the troubleshooting cycle to isolate and solve the problem.

The First Step—The Client Interview

The client interview is the all-important first step in solving any computer troubleshooting situation. During this interview, you need to determine the following facts:

- The software in use at the time of the problem
- The hardware in use at the time of the problem

- The task the customer was trying to perform at the time of the problem
- The environment in the office or work area at the time of the problem

The number one question you're trying to answer is, "What changed since the last time it worked?" I learned this question years ago from the writings of long-time *Byte* magazine columnist Jerry Pournelle, and it's been endlessly helpful over the years.

During the client interview, you need to ask questions to determine the following information:

- **What hardware or software appears to have a problem?**—The user might have an opinion about this, but don't be unduly swayed by a statement such as "the printer's broken"; the device or software the user believes to be at fault might simply reflect a problem coming from another source.

- **What other hardware or software was in use at the time of the problem?**—The user probably will answer these types of questions in terms of open applications, but you will also want to look at the taskbar and system tray in Windows for other programs or routines that are running. Pressing Ctrl+Alt+Del will bring up a task list in Windows that has the most complete information about programs and subroutines in memory.

- **What task was the user trying to perform at the time of the problem?**—Ask the questions needed to find out the specific issues involved. For example, "Printing" isn't a sufficient answer. "Printing a five-page brochure from PageMaker to a laser printer" is better, but you'll probably want the user to re-create the situation in an attempt to get all the information you need.

- **Is the hardware or software on the user's machine or accessed over the network?**—If the network was involved, check with the network administrator to see if the network is currently working properly. If the hardware and software are not networked, your scope for troubleshooting is simpler.

- **What were the specific symptoms of the problem?**—Some users are very observant, but others might not be able to give you much help. Ask about the approximate time of the failure and about error messages, beeps, and unusual noises.

- **Can the problem be reproduced?**—Reproducible problems are easier to find than those that mysteriously "heal" themselves when you show up. Because power and environmental issues at the customer's site can cause computer problems, try to reproduce the problem at the customer's site before you move the computer to your test bench, where conditions are different.

- **Does the problem repeat itself with a different combination of hardware and software, or does the problem go away when another combination of hardware and software is used?**—For example, if the user can print from Microsoft Word but not from PageMaker, this means that the printer is working, but there might be a problem with configuration or data types used by different applications. If the user can't print anything, there might be a general problem with the printer hardware or drivers.

Sometimes, the client interview alone will reveal the answer. More often, however, you'll need to go to the client's work area and evaluate the hardware and software that are involved.

How to Evaluate the Client's Environment

Depending on the clues you receive in the initial interview, you should go to the client's work area prepared to perform a variety of tests. You must look for three major issues when evaluating the customer's environment:

- Power issues
- Interference sources
- Symptoms and error codes—this might require that you try to reproduce the error

You can select from the tests listed in Table 18.1 based on your evaluation of the most likely sources of problems. You might need to perform several tests to rule out certain problems.

Table 18.1   Troubleshooting Tests and Requirements

Test	Requires
Power	Multimeter, circuit tester
BIOS beep and	List of BIOS codes, POST card error codes
Printer self-test	Printer and paper
Windows bootlog	Start Windows with bootlog option enabled
I/O Port	Connect Loopback plugs and run third-party
Loopback tests	diagnostics
Video tests	Run third-party diagnostics (see "Useful Hardware and Software Tools," later in this chapter)
Hardware resources (IRQ, and so on)	Use third-party diagnostics, IRQ/DMA card, Windows Device Manager
Device Drivers	Windows Device Manager, Autoexec.bat, Config.sys (Windows 9x)

For more information about the requirements listed in Table 18.1, see "Useful Hardware and Software Tools" later in this chapter.

Testing Power

Systems that won't start or that have lockups or shutdowns with no error messages could be the victims of power problems. To determine whether power problems are located inside the computer or are coming from outside the system, use the tests described in Chapter 8, "Power Supplies and Circuit Testing." If a system malfunctions at a customer site but works properly at your test bench, power problems due to improper wiring might be to blame.

Looking for Sources of Interference

Power problems also can be caused by interference from other devices, such as copiers, vacuum cleaners, and elevators. If a system performs properly when moved away from its normal work area, but malfunctions when it is returned to its normal location, interference might be to blame. See "Power Conditioning Devices," page 253, for suggestions on dealing with sources of interference.

Recording Symptoms and Error Codes

If your tests rule out power and interference, you must proceed to tests that focus on the hardware or software that appears the most likely cause of the problem.

Which test or diagnostic routine is the best one to start with? Before you perform any specific tests, review the clues you gathered from the client. In our example, Microsoft Word for Windows would print, but PageMaker would not. If these were MS-DOS–based programs, you might suspect a problem with the PageMaker printer driver because MS-DOS programs control the printer directly.

However, all Windows-based programs use the same Windows printer driver. Printer hardware or driver failures would prevent all software programs from printing; however, in this case printing works from some programs but not others when the same printer and printer drivers are in use. Before you can solve this problem, you need more information about the printer. It's time to use the printer's self-test, listed in Table 18.1, for more information about the printer.

A laser printer's self-test usually indicates the amount of RAM on board, the emulation (HP or PostScript), and firmware revisions. The amount of RAM on board is critical, because as you learned in Chapter 9, "Printers," laser printers are page printers: The whole page must fit into the laser printer's RAM to be printed.

Thus, there are two variables to this printing problem: the size of the RAM in the printer and the size of the documents the user is trying to print. The self-test reveals the printer has only the standard amount of RAM (2MB) on board. This amount of RAM is adequate for text, but an elaborate page can overload it. A look at the PageMaker document reveals that it has a large amount of graphic content, while the Microsoft Word document is standard-sized text only with a minimal use of bold and italic formatting.

Your theory is to add RAM to the printer, and it can print the brochure. If you don't have a suitable RAM module, how can you prove it?

Because Microsoft Word printed a text-only document flawlessly, you might be able to convince your client from that fact alone that the printer isn't "broken" but needs a RAM upgrade—or a workaround.

Devising a workaround that will help the printer work is good for client satisfaction and will prove that your theory is correct. Have the client adjust the graphics resolution of the printer from its default of 600 dpi to a lower amount, such as 300 dpi, and print the brochure again. By reducing the brochure's dots per inch, the brochure will print. The client will look at the lower print quality and at that point you can recommend the RAM upgrade. Point out the provision for RAM upgrades in the printer manual if necessary. Remember, you're not selling anything, but solving problems.

If the printer would not print at all, other tests from Table 18.1 would have been appropriate, such as the I/O port loopback test or hardware resources check.

Determining Whether a Problem Is Caused by Hardware or by Software

The oldest dilemma for any computer technician is determining whether a problem is caused by hardware or software. The widespread use of Windows operating systems makes this problem even more acute than it was when MS-DOS was the predominant standard, because all hardware in a Windows system is controlled by Windows device drivers.

The troubleshooting cycle is a method that you can use to determine exactly what part of a complex system, such as a computer, is causing the problem.

The first step is to determine the most likely source of the problem. The client interview will help you determine which subsystem is the best place to start solving the problem. In the previous example, the printing subsystem was the most likely place to start.

A *subsystem* is the combination of components designed to do a particular task, and it can include both hardware and software components. Use Table 18.2 to better understand the nature of the subsystems found in any computer.

Table 18.2   Computer and Peripheral Subsystems and Their Components

		Components	
Subsystem	*Hardware*	*Software*	*Firmware*
Printing	Printer, cable, parallel or serial port	Printer driver and application	BIOS configuration of port
Display	Graphics card, monitor, cables	Video drivers	Video BIOS, BIOS configuration of video type
Mouse and pointing device	Mouse or pointing device, serial or mouse port	Mouse driver	BIOS port configuration
Keyboard	Keyboard	Keyboard driver	BIOS keyboard configuration
Storage	Drives, data cables, power connectors	Startup files and drivers	BIOS drive configuration

Table 18.2   continued

| Subsystem | Components | | |
	Hardware	Software	Firmware
Power	Power supply, splitters, fans	Power-management software	BIOS power-management configuration
CPU	CPU, motherboard	System device drivers	BIOS cache and CPU configuration
RAM	RAM, motherboard	(none)	BIOS RAM configuration
Network	NIC, motherboard	Network configuration files and drivers	BIOS PnP and power management
Modem	Modem, motherboard or serial port	Modem drivers, application	BIOS PnP, power management, port configuration

You can see from Table 18.2 that virtually every subsystem in the computer has hardware, software, and firmware components. A thorough troubleshooting process will take into account both the subsystem and all its components.

The following steps are involved in the troubleshooting cycle:

1. Record the current configuration of the system or component.

2. Change one hardware component or hardware/software/firmware setting at a time; if you replace hardware, use a known-working replacement.

3. Retest after a single change and evaluate the results.

4. If you have no changes, return to the original component or settings and continue with the next item.

5. Repeat steps 2–4 until the subsystem performs normally. The last item changed is the problem; repair, replace, or reload it as appropriate to solve the problem.

Recording the Current Configuration

Before you change anything, record the current configuration. Depending on the item, this might include one or more of the following steps:

- Recording jumper or DIP switch settings
- Printing the complete report from the Windows Device Manager
- Printing a complete report from a third-party diagnostic program, such as AMIDiag or WinCheckit
- Recording BIOS configurations
- Backing up the Windows Registry

If you don't record the current configuration of the system's hardware and software before you start the troubleshooting cycle, you will not be able to reset the system to its previous condition if your first change doesn't solve the problem.

Changing One Component or Configuration Setting at a Time

After you have recorded the configuration of the system, it's time to change one component in the subsystem you suspect is at the root of the problem. No matter how concerned your client is and no matter how heavy your workload, change only one before you retest the system. The following are examples of changing a single component or configuration setting:

- Removing the device from the Windows Device Manager
- Changing a device's IRQ or other hardware resource setting
- Reinstalling a device's driver software
- Reinstalling an application

Performing two or more of these types of tasks before you retest the system can make matters worse, and if you fix the problem you won't know which change was the correct change to make.

"Known-Working" Doesn't Mean "New"—Best Sources for Replacement Parts

To perform parts exchanges for troubleshooting, you need replacement parts. If you don't have spare parts, it's very tempting to go to the computer store and buy some new components. Instead, take a spare system that's similar to the "sick" computer, make sure that it works, and then use it for parts. Why? Just because it's new doesn't mean it works.

I once replaced an alternator on my van with a brand-new, lifetime-warranty alternator that failed in less than a week. Whether it's a cable, a video card, a monitor, or some other component, try using a known-working item as a temporary replacement rather than brand-new.

Use a spare system if possible rather than knocking another working system (and user) out of action by "borrowing" parts from an operational system. Use the same brand and model of system for known-working spares if possible, because the components inside are more likely to be identical to the "sick" system you are diagnosing.

Where to Start? What Components to Check First

As the previous subsystem list indicated, there's no shortage of places to start in virtually any subsystem. What's the best way to decide whether a hardware, software, or firmware problem is the most likely cause? Typically, hardware problems come and go, whereas software and firmware problems are consistent. Why? A hardware problem is often the result of a damaged or loose wire or connection; when the connection is closed, the component works, but when the connection opens, the component fails.

On the other hand, a software or firmware problem will cause a failure under the same circumstances every time.

Another rule of thumb that's useful is to consider the least expensive, easiest-to-replace item first. In most cases, the cable connected to a subsystem is the first place to look for problems. Whether the cable is internal or external, it is almost always the least-expensive part of the subsystem, can easily come loose, and can easily be damaged.

If a cable is loose, has bent pins, has a dry, brittle, or cracked exterior, replace it. Good cables usually look good, and bad cables often look bad.

When new software or new hardware has been introduced to the system and a problem results immediately afterward, that change is often the most likely cause of the problem.

Hardware conflicts such as IRQ, I/O port address, DMA channel, and memory address, or conflicts between the software drivers in the operating system, are typical causes of failure when new hardware is introduced. New software can also cause problems with hardware, because of incompatibilities between software and hardware or because new software has replaced drivers required by the hardware.

Where to Go for More Information

After you've gathered as much information as possible, you might find that you still need more help. User manuals for components often are discarded, software drivers need to be updated, and some conflicts don't have easy answers. Use the following resources for more help:

- **Manufacturers' Web sites**—Most system and component manufacturers provide extensive technical information via the World Wide Web. You'll want to have the Adobe Acrobat Reader program in its latest version available to be able to read the technical manuals you can download (Acrobat Reader itself is a free download from www.adobe.com). These sites often contain expert systems, surgical newsgroups, download will driver updates, and other helps for problems.

- **Help for "orphan" systems and components**—It's frustrating to need information about a system whose manufacturer is no longer around. Sites such as www.windrivers.com and www.winfiles.com provide information and drivers for orphan systems and components.

- **Online computer magazines**—If your back-issue collection of major computer magazines is missing some issues, or even if you've never subscribed to the print versions, you can find a lot of technical content from the major magazine publishers online. One-time print stalwarts, such as *Byte* and *Windows Magazine*, no longer publish paper copies but have excellent Web sites with both current and archive information.

Keeping Track of Your Solutions

Make a practice of keeping detailed notes about the problems you solve. If your company has a help-desk system with tracking capabilities, use it. Even if the best you can do is write up your findings, you can use desktop search tools to find the answers to the same problems that might arise later.

Be sure to note symptoms, underlying problems, workarounds, and final resolutions.

Useful Hardware and Software Tools

The A+ Certification test's troubleshooting content expects you to know the use of basic diagnostic devices, so a review of this section will be useful before your exam. The following list of items also provides you with a handy reference for what you should bring on service calls.

Tools:

- **Hex drivers**—Use for opening and closing cases and securing and removing cards and motherboards; non-magnetic preferred

- **Phillips and straight-blade screwdrivers**—Use if hex drivers are not compatible; non-magnetic preferred

- **Torx drivers**—Required for some Compaq models; non-magnetic preferred

- **Three-claw parts retrieval tool**—Retrieves loose parts from computer interior; prevents lost parts, which can lead to dead shorts if not located

- **Hemostat clamps**—Superior replacement for tweezers for insertion and removal of jumper blocks and cables

- **Needle-nose pliers**—Straightens bent pins

- **Eyebrow tweezers**—Replaces normal tweezers in toolkit for removing and replacing jumpers

- **Penlight and magnifier**—Illuminates dark cases and makes small parts and marking easier to read

Power diagnostics and safety:

- **AC/DC multimeter with Ohm and Continuity options**—Tests power inside system and at wall outlets

- **Grounded AC circuit tester**—Fast testing for wall outlets; many offices and homes are incorrectly wired, and the tester will help you determine whether this is the problem

- **Antistatic mat and wrist strap**—Prevents ESD, which can damage parts and systems

Hardware diagnostics:

- **Testing software, such as WinCheckit or AMIDiag**
  - RAM testing, hardware configuration, and motherboard tests
  - Serial- and parallel-port testing
- **Serial and parallel loopback plugs designed for hardware diagnostics software**—These "loop back" transmit lines to receive lines during diagnostic testing
- **POST card (can also have IRQ/DMA signals)**—Displays hex POST codes during system startup to find boot errors that don't have matching beep codes
- **IRQ/DMA card**—Lights on card display IRQ and DMA channels in use; especially helpful for systems that don't support PnP devices

Cleaning and maintenance tools:

- **Compressed air**—Cleans gunk out of cases, fans, and power supplies
- **Keyboard key puller**—Safely removes keys to allow effective keyboard cleaning
- **Computer-rated mini-vacuum cleaner**—Cleans gunk out of cases, fans, power supplies, and keyboards and dust off motherboards and add-on cards
- **Wire cutter and stripper**—Used to build network cable
- **Extra case, card, and drive screws (salvage or new)**—Used as spares to replace missing or defective screws
- **Extra card slot covers (salvage or new)**—Used to replace missing covers to maintain proper system cooling
- **Extra hard disk and motherboard/card jumper blocks (salvage or new)**—Used as needed to replace missing or defective jumper blocks when needed to configure devices

Operating systems:

- Bootable Windows 9x Emergency System (boot) Disk
- Bootable Windows 2000 setup disks
- Other bootable OS disks as required for your clients' needs
- Windows 9x, 2000, others on CD-ROM as required for your clients' needs

Use these tools to help you perform the steps you need to follow during the troubleshooting process.

Summary

Troubleshooting systems requires careful attention to symptoms, an understanding of the computer's subsystems, and changing one component or setting at a time until the problem is solved.

CH
18

The client interview is a vital step for discovering the causes of computer problems. Building trust with good customer relations is important, as is learning the software, hardware, and tasks involved in the problem.

Gather information with reports and tests at the client's site to learn more about the underlying problem.

Use your diagnostics toolkit to test power, open systems, tighten cables, start computers, and check for viruses as part of the information-gathering process.

Evaluate the clues you gather in terms of subsystems. Each subsystem in the computer has a hardware, software, or firmware component. Choose a subsystem based on your evaluation to start the troubleshooting cycle.

Record configurations, change one item at a time, review the results, restore the original item, and repeat until the problem is solved. Use known-working spares for replacements.

For consistent problems, start with software or firmware settings; for occasional problems, start with hardware.

Use manufacturer and third-party resources for more technical information and drivers if needed.

To be well equipped for dealing with problems in the field, a well-stocked hardware and software toolkit is essential.

QUESTIONS AND ANSWERS:

1. What is the most important question you can ask when a system fails?
    A: What has changed since the last time it worked?

2. Are new parts working parts?
    A: Not necessarily. New parts can and do fail.

3. Name two sources for known-working parts.
    A: Spares already removed from systems (also called "pulls") and spares taken from a working system.

4. What Windows features allow you to record system settings before making changes?
    A: Printing out the Device Manager (complete report) will record this information.

5. What can you attach to a serial or parallel port for more accurate testing?
    A: A loopback plug made for use with the diagnostic program.

Glossary

24-pin A dot-matrix printhead type that creates good near-letter–quality (NLQ) printing.

286 The first CPU used in MS-DOS systems to allow more than 1MB of RAM.

32-bit disk access Windows disk access that bypasses the ROM BIOS for speed. It's optional in Windows 3.x and standard in Windows 9x/Me/2000.

32-bit file access The Windows for Workgroups 3.11 disk cache that replaces Smartdrv.exe; standard in Windows 9x/Me/2000.

386 The first CPU to allow upper-memory blocks and EMS memory with EMM386 memory manager. It's available in 32-bit (DX) and 16-bit (SX) versions.

486 The first CPU with a built-in math coprocessor (DX versions) and cache RAM (all versions).

586 CPUs roughly equal to Pentium-class. They're also used by AMD and Cyrix for CPUs that could be used to upgrade 486 systems to Pentium 75MHz performance.

6x86 A Cyrix Pentium-class CPU (also known as MII).

8086 A 16-bit sibling of the 8088; it's used by some compatible systems, such as Compaq.

8088 The original chip used in IBM PC and PC/XT. It has an 8-bit data bus and 1MB RAM limit.

9-pin A dot-matrix printhead type with high durability and good multipart form printing but poor CQ printing.

AC (alternating current) Lethal at household voltage levels. It must be converted to DC for use in computers.

ACPI (Advanced Configuration and Power Interface) Controls how peripherals, BIOS, and computers manage power. It's supported by Windows 98/Me/2000 and replaces APM.

active-matrix An LCD screen using a transistor for every pixel. It has a bright, wide viewing angle.

active partition A hard-disk partition that can be used to boot the computer. It must be formatted with the /S option to be bootable, and only the primary partitions can be active.

ActiveX Microsoft technology for interactive Web pages; used with Internet Explorer.

address bus The bus used by the CPU to access memory by its hexadecimal address.

Administrator The Windows NT and Windows 2000 term for the manager of a given computer or network; only users in the Administrators group can perform some management tasks.

AGP (Accelerated Graphics Port) A high-speed, dedicated video slot or circuit that can use system memory for 3D textures.

allocation unit size The minimum amount of disk space a file actually uses. It varies with FAT type and disk size. It also is known as the "cluster size."

AMD (Advanced Micro Devices)   The one-time second source for Intel 286-486 CPUs now makes advanced Pentium-class CPUs in the K6, Athlon, and Duron series.

analog   Infinitely variable; the opposite of digital. VGA is an analog display technology.

APM (Advanced Power Management)   Supported by most recent BIOS and Windows 3.1/9x/Me/2000; MS-DOS uses Power.exe to activate.

application program   A program used to create, modify, and store information you create. Microsoft Word 2000, Adobe Photoshop, and CorelDRAW are all application programs.

archive attribute   Indicates that a file has not yet been backed up. It's automatically set when a file is created or modified.

ARCNet (Attached Resource Connection Network)   An early coaxial-cable network used to replace IBM 3270 terminals that used the same RG-59 cable. It now is obsolete.

AT (Advanced Technology)   IBM's first 286-based PC.

AT command   A command used to control a modem. It's sent by telecommunications programs, such as Windows' HyperTerminal. ATDT 555-1212 (uses tone dialing to call 555-1212) is an example of an AT command.

ATA (AT Attachment)   A series of standards for IDE drives and devices.

ATAPI (AT Attachment Packet Interface)   CD-ROM and removable-media drives that can connect to an IDE interface.

Athlon   AMD's newest CPU, with top speeds exceeding 700MHz. It uses a slot rather than a socket.

ATX   Advanced motherboard and power supply design. The motherboard is wide, with two rows of I/O ports on the rear of the system. The power supply uses a 20-pin connector.

AUI (Attachment Unit Interface)   A 15-pin connection on 10Base5 Ethernet cards.

auto-detection   An IDE hard-disk setup procedure that allows the system to query drives for geometry at startup. It also can be used with some BIOS setup routines.

auto-ranging   A multimeter option that allows the meter to select the correct voltage range.

B-size paper   11×17-inch paper; it's the next size up from A-size paper used in Europe (similar to 8.5×11-inch U.S. letter size).

Baby-AT   A motherboard that uses same mounting holes but is physically smaller than the IBM AT motherboard.

backup   Making a copy of a file for safekeeping, especially with a special program that must be used to restore the backup when needed.

base memory   Also known as conventional memory; memory from 0–640KB used by MS-DOS.

bayonet   A mounting method used to attach ARCNet and Thin Ethernet cables to cards or T-adapters.

beep code   POST audio error messages.

binary   A numbering system used to store computer data: 0 and 1 are the only digits.

binding   Configuring network hardware with protocols it will use.

BIOS (Basic Input Output System)   Controls and tests basic computer hardware and the beginning of the boot procedure.

bit   1/8 of a byte; 8 bits = 1 byte. Many devices send and receive data in bits.

block mode   An IDE disk access method that reads multiple sectors before an IRQ is issued.

BNC (Bayonet Neil-Concelman)   A barrel-shaped connector used for Thin Ethernet and ARCNet Coaxial cable and T-adapters.

boot   Starting the computer. A *warm boot* is restarting the computer without a reset or shutdown. A *cold boot* is shutting down or resetting before startup.

boot disk   A disk (usually a floppy disk) with operating system files needed to start the computer.

boot sector   The starting location of operating system files on a floppy disk or hard disk.

boot sequence   A procedure followed by the system during the startup process; it's also called bootstrapping.

bootlog.txt   A hidden file created by Windows 9x in the root directory of the boot drive, it stores all startup events and can be used to troubleshoot startup problems.

browser A program that interprets HTML documents and allows hyperlinking to Web sites.

BSOD (Blue Screen of Death) A fatal system error in Windows 2000 that stops the system from starting; also called a stop error. It's named after the blue background for the white text error message.

bus mouse A mouse that plugs into a 6-pin port on an add-on card; obsolete.

bus speed Also called front-side-bus or FSB speed. This is the speed at which the CPU addresses the memory and motherboard components. Common bus speeds on current systems are 66MHz (Celeron CPUs), 100MHz (newer Pentium II, Pentium III, and Athlon CPUs), and 133MHz (very fast Pentium III and Athlon CPUs).

bus topology A network topology in which all systems share a common cable.

bus-mastering High-speed data transfer used by advanced IDE interfaces and some add-on cards.

byte One character; it's the basic building block of data storage.

C-shaped paper path A cross-section of the paper path used by many inkjet and some laser printers. The paper is pulled through the printer and returns to an output tray on the same side of the printer as the input tray.

cable select A method of IDE configuration in which a special cable indicates which drive is master and which is slave. It's used by UDMA/66 and UDMA/100 drives but is rarely used otherwise.

cache A holding place for information to allow faster access than normal. It's used for drives (disk cache) and memory (Level 1, Level 2 caches).

cache hit Data in cache.

cache miss Data not in cache. It must be retrieved from the next cache level, normal storage, or RAM location.

Card and Socket Services See *CSS*.

CardBus A 32-bit version of PC Card/PCMCIA slot used for fast network interfacing.

carpal-tunnel syndrome A common type of RSI affecting the wrists. See *RSI*.

CD-R (Recordable CD) The contents of CD-R can be added to but not changed.

CD-ROM A standard optical drive. Most can read CD-R, but they require MultiRead capability to read CD-RW.

CD-RW (Rewritable CD) The contents can be changed. It can also use CD-R media.

Celeron The "economy" version of Pentium II; available in slot or socket formats.

Centronics A double-sided edge connector originally made popular by the early Centronics parallel printers. Currently used for parallel ports in printers (36-pin version) and for older, narrow, SCSI external devices (50-pin version).

CGA (Color Graphics Adapter) The early digital video standard with 320×200 4-color or 640×200 2-color modes.

channel The pathway between two devices, as in DMA channel.

character printer See *line printer*.

chip A ceramic shell containing miniaturized computer circuits and connectors.

CHS (Cylinder-Head-Sector) Standard hard-disk geometry.

clean boot Booting the system without device drivers. Also refers to starting the system with an uninfected floppy disk for virus detection.

client A computer that uses shared resources on a network.

client/server network A network using dedicated servers, such as Novell Netware, Windows NT Server, or Windows 2000 Professional.

cluster size See *allocation unit size*.

CMOS (Complimentary Metal-Oxide Semiconductor) Refers to low-power chip design. It also is the common term for Real-Time-Clock/non-Volatile RAM chip (RTC/NVRAM).

COAST (Cache on a Stick) The standard pipeline-burst cache module. It resembles a SIMM but uses a different type of connector.

coast The time period that a computer's power supply can continue to run without AC power flowing to it. The coast time for typical PC power supplies is longer than the switchover time from AC to battery backup power.

coaxial Cable with a solid inner conductor and metal mesh shielding.

cold boot Starting a system from power-down or with the reset button. Memory count and other hardware tests are performed.

collating The process of holding a page in the memory of a laser or LED printer and printing multiple copies before receiving and printing the next page. Activated by the print options in the application being used to print the document.

COM port Serial port.

Combo card A PC Card (PCMCIA card) combining two functions, usually network and modem.

Compact A Windows setup option that does not load optional accessories to save disk space.

Compact Flash A popular flash-memory storage standard used by digital cameras. It can be attached to desktop and portable PCs by means of a card reader or PC Card adapter.

Config.sys A text-based configuration file used by MS-DOS and Windows 9x to load 16-bit device drivers and set up the system.

continuous-tone Original photographs contain tones from blacks to white; laser printers convert these to digital form for printing.

Control Panel A Windows 3.1x, 9x, Me, and 2000 feature that sets Windows hardware options.

cool-switching The Windows' use of Alt+Tab keys to move from one active program to another.

copy-protection Methods of preventing software from being duplicated or used without the developer's permission; old methods included

■ Using the original floppy disk at all times to run the program

■ Using an install program that rendered the original floppy disk useless after installation

Current methods include the use of a *dongle* that must be attached to the serial or parallel port of a computer before the program can be run.

CPU (Central Processing Unit) The computational "brains" of the computer, such as Pentium, K6, Celeron, and so on.

CQ (Correspondence Quality) The best print option on some 9-pin printers.

CRT (Cathode Ray Tube) A monitor's picture tube, a large vacuum tube that displays information.

CSS (Card and Socket Services) Software that allows computers to interchange PC Card (PCMCIA) devices.

Custom The Windows setup option that provides maximum control over the setup process.

Cycle Refers to alternating current sine wave; 50Hz (cycles per second) is the European/Asian standard; 60Hz is North American.

cylinder Part of hard disk geometry; all the tracks in a vertical row.

CYMK (Cyan Yellow Magenta Black) Refers to a four-color model for graphics and printing. These are the ink colors used by most inkjet printers. Sometimes referred to as CMYK.

daisy-chaining Connecting multiple devices through a single port. Used by EPP and ECP parallel-port modes, SCSI, and USB ports.

daisywheel Obsolete typewriter-style, fully formed character printing.

data bus Carries data between devices on the motherboard.

DB-9 A 9-pin D-shaped external cable connector used primarily for serial ports (DB9M) and for old video standards, such as EGA, CGA, and monochrome (DB9F).

DB-25 A 25-pin D-shaped external cable connector used for parallel port (DB25F) and some serial ports (DB25M) (F stands for a female connector [with holes] and M stands for a male connector [with pins]).

DC (Direct Current) Low voltage is used by the motherboard, and high voltage is used in some printers. It must be converted from AC.

DCC (Direct Cable Connection) A temporary "mini-network" used by Windows 9x to connect to computers through server or parallel ports for data transfer. It also can be used with IR ports that emulate serial ports.

Debug startup options /d: startup options used by Windows for troubleshooting.

decimal The base-10 numbering system used for ordinary calculations.

dedicated server A computer used strictly to provide shared resources, such as Novell NetWare, Windows NT Server, or Windows 2000 Server.

defragment   Reorganizing the files on a drive to occupy contiguous sectors to improve retrieval speed; an integral part of Windows 9x/Me/2000.

desktop   Windows 9x/Me/NT/2000 location for shortcuts, and a Windows 3.1 location for program groups.

device driver   A program used to modify an operating system to support new devices.

device ID#   A method of indicating different devices attached to a SCSI host adapter. Each device must use a unique device ID#, which is set on each device.

Device Manager   The Windows 9x/Me/2000 portion of a system properties sheet used to view and control device configuration—IRQ, DMA, I/O port address, memory address, drivers, and other configuration options.

DFP (Digital Flat Panel)   An early standard for LCD display panels for desktop PCs; superseded by DVI standards.

DHCP (Dynamic Host Configuration Protocol) Provides IP addresses as required. Allows a limited number of IP addresses to service many devices that are not connected at the same time.

disk cache   A section of RAM that holds data passing to and from a hard or floppy drive to speed up disk operation. Windows 9x/Me/2000 all feature integrated disk cache.

DIMM (Dual Inline Memory Module)   A high-speed, 168-pin memory module used in Pentium II, Pentium III, Celeron, and similar systems.

DIP (Dual Inline Pin)   A rectangular chip with legs on its long sides only.

directory entry   A directory (folder) or file allocation unit in use by a file or folder. All file systems have limits on the maximum number of directory entries per drive, and FAT16 has a limit of 512 entries in the root directory.

DMA (Direct Memory Access)   A high-speed device-to-RAM transfer that bypasses the CPU.

DNS (Domain Name System)   Translates domain names into IP addresses.

docking station   Allows notebook computers to use devices not built-in, such as standard PCI or ISA cards, external CD-ROM drives, and others. Requires a proprietary, dedicated, external bus connector.

domain   Windows NT and Windows 2000 Server term for a group of computers that share resources and use a common user account. A server called the domain controller stores the Active Directory data used to manage the domain.

domain name   The unique alphanumeric identifier for Web sites.

dongle   A removable connector that allows a PC Card (PCMCIA device) to use cables too thick to plug directly into a card. Also refers to copy-protection devices attached to serial ports or parallel ports to allow software to run.

dot-matrix   A printing method using a printhead with one or more columns or print elements to create the image; usually impact, using an inked ribbon.

DRAM (Dynamic RAM)   The slowest type of RAM, it requires frequent electrical refreshes to keep contents valid.

driver   See *device driver.*

DSDD (Double-Sided Double Density)   A type of floppy disk media.

DSHD (Double-Sided High Density)   A type of floppy disk media holding more than DSDD due to a different magnetic coating.

dual-boot   An operating system installation that enables you to run the previous operating system as an option. Both Windows 98 and Windows 2000 can be installed in a dual-boot configuration.

dual-scan   An advanced type of passive-matrix LCD screen that splits the screen into two sections. It's better than passive-matrix but has a slower and narrower viewing angle than active-matrix.

DUN (Dial-Up Networking)   A Windows 9x term for using a modem to connect with other computers.

duplex   A communication method that allows data flow in both directions. *Full-duplex* allows simultaneous send and receive at the same speed. *Half-duplex* allows alternating send and receive.

DVD (Digital Versatile Disk)   A high-capacity replacement for CD-ROM.

DVI (Digital Video Interface)   Replaces DFP as the standard for support of LCD displays on desktop computers. DVI-D is for digital displays only, and DVI-I supports digital and analog displays.

APP
A

ECC (Error Correcting Code)   Advanced memory that can correct errors. It requires special chipsets and is used primarily in servers.

ECP (Enhanced Capabilities Port)   A high-speed IEEE-1284 parallel port option that uses IRQ, DMA, and I/O port address settings. Good for daisy-chaining different devices.

EDO (Enhanced Data Out)   A faster version of DRAM used on some older Pentium systems and video cards.

EEMS (Enhanced Expanded Memory Specification) A nonstandard version of EMS memory used by some AST memory boards; obsolete.

EGA (Enhanced Graphics Adapter)   640×350 16-color digital graphics; obsolete.

EIDE (Enhanced IDE)   A marketing term for major features of ATA-2 version of IDE.

EISA (Enhanced Industry Standard Architecture) A 32-bit version of ISA slots. It's obsolete but might be found in older servers.

email   Electronic mail.

EMS (Enhanced Memory Specification)   Paged memory used by some MS-DOS programs. It can be created with the Emm386.exe with RAM option or by specifying the amount of EMS memory to create.

enhanced Int13h support   A BIOS feature required to support drives over 7.8GB (over 16,384 cylinders by 16 heads by 63 sectors per track).

EP (electrophotographic)   The process by which a laser printer creates a page.

EPA (Environmental Protection Agency)   The federal, state, and local organizations that set standards for the safe disposal of products.

EPP (Enhanced Parallel Port)   A high-speed IEEE-1284 standard that uses an IRQ and an I/O port address.

Epson ESC/P2   An enhanced version of the escape-sequence–based printer language used for dot-matrix and inkjet printers by Epson and other vendors.

ergonomics   The study of the usability of hardware and software products with an eye to comfort and efficiency.

ESD (Electro-Static Discharge)   Static electricity.

ESDI (Enhanced Small Device Interface)   An obsolete hard disk interface standard using two cables. Primarily used for drives over 100MB.

Ethernet   A network that uses the IEEE 802.3 access method.

executable file   A .exe file. A machine-readable program file that can be run in any area of memory or any type of program file, including .com and .bat files.

expansion board   Also known as "add-on card" or "add-on board."

expansion slot   A motherboard connection used for add-on cards; ISA, PCI, and AGP are typical types.

extended partition   A nonbootable hard disk partition that can contain one or more logical DOS drives.

external command   A command-prompt command that is actually a separate program.

Faraday cage   Describes antistatic equipment bags that have a metalized outside surface.

Fast SCSI   A version of SCSI with double the transfer rate of SCSI-2, up to 20MB per second.

FastDisk   Also known as 32-bit disk access.

FAT (File Allocation Table)   The part of the hard disk or floppy disk that contains pointers to the actual location of files on the disk.

FAT16   A FAT method used by MS-DOS and Windows 95; also supported by Windows 98/Me/NT/2000. It allows 65,535 (2^{16}) files maximum per drive and drive sizes up to 2GB.

FAT32   A FAT method optionally available with Windows 95 OSR2.x, Windows 98/Me/2000. It allows 2^{32} files maximum per drive and drive sizes up to 2TB.

fatal error   An error detected during POST that prevents the system from starting. Phoenix, AMI, IBM, and MR BIOS use beep codes to indicate most fatal errors.

FDISK   An MS-DOS and Windows 9x hard disk preparation program.

fiber-optic   Network cabling using photons rather than electrical signals to transfer information.

file attachment   Text or binary data, such as pictures, music files, and other types of data files, that is sent along with an email message.

file attributes   Controls how files are used and viewed; they can be reset by the user. Typical attributes include hidden, system, read-only, and archive. Windows 2000 also uses compressed and encrypted attributes.

file extension Up to three-character alphanumeric after the .; indicates file types such as .bat, .exe, .doc, and so on.

file system How files are organized on a drive. FAT16, FAT32, and NTFS are popular file systems supported by various versions of Windows.

FireWire Apple's name for IEEE-1394 high-speed serial connection (also known as *i.Link*).

firmware "Software on a chip," such as BIOS.

FlashROM A memory device that uses electricity to change its contents but does not require power to maintain its contents. Widely used for BIOS chips and for digital camera storage.

floppy disk Low-capacity removable media used by 3.5- and 5.25-inch floppy disk drives.

FM synthesis A low-cost, low-fidelity method used on some sound cards to play MIDI files by simulating the sound of different instruments.

font The characters in a particular size, shape, and weight of a typeface. 12-point Times Roman Italic is a font; Times Roman is the typeface.

forced hardware Hardware that is normally PnP (allowing changes to the hardware configuration as needed) that has been manually set to use fixed resources. Not recommended in most cases but might be necessary for compatibility with older programs.

form feed command Ejects the current page from the printer. It can be software-driven or you can use a button on the printer.

format Can refer to document layout or the process of preparing a floppy disk drive or hard disk drive for use.

FORMAT An MS-DOS and Windows 9x program to prepare a drive for use. Hard disks must be FDISKed first.

FPM (Fast-Page-Mode) The type of DRAM used on most SIMMs.

FQDN (Fully Qualified Domain Name) Similar to UNC naming but uses the domain name or IP address of the server rather than its network name.

FSR (Free System Resources) A Windows measurement of the lowest of system, user, or GDI heaps.

FTP:// (File Transfer Protocol) File transfer to or from a special server site on the World Wide Web

fuser A hot roller assembly in a laser printer that melts toner to paper.

gateway An access point that allows a network (such as a LAN) to access another network (such as the Internet).

GB Gigabyte. 1 Billion bytes (decimal) or slightly more (binary).

General Protection Fault A frequent type of illegal operation in Windows 9x; often caused by programs running incorrect DLL driver files.

generic driver A device driver that provides minimal functions for a hardware device. A generic/text-only printer driver in Windows that prints text but no fonts or graphics.

geometry The term for the arrangement of sectors per track, cylinders, and heads on BIOS-controlled hard disks, such as IDE/ATA. The manufacturer's recommended geometry typically appears on a label attached to the drive.

GPF (General Protection Fault) A Windows 3.1x/9x memory error caused by the clash between two programs wanting the same memory space. Common due to cooperative multitasking's weak memory barriers.

GRP file A file that stores icons for a program group in Windows 3.1x. .GRP files are converted into shortcuts stored in the \Windows\Start Menu\Programs\ folder when a Windows 3.1x system is upgraded to Windows 9x/Me/2000.

GUI (Graphical User Interface) A user interface with features such as icons, fonts, and point-and-click commands. Windows and MacOS are popular GUIs.

hard drive A storage device with rigid, nonremovable platters inside a case. Also called hard disk or rigid disk.

hardware Physical computing devices.

hardware profile Windows 9x/Me/2000 feature that enables the user to store multiple hardware configurations and select the desired configuration at boot time.

head Reads and writes data in a drive.

header The beginning of a document, an email message, or a file.

header cable A cable used on Baby-AT motherboards to route PS/2 mouse, USB, parallel, and serial port signals from the rear of the computer to the actual port connections on the motherboard. The header cables often are attached to brackets that can be used in place of empty expansion slots.

APP A

heatsink   A metal or plastic series of fins on a CPU or dot-matrix printhead used to dissipate heat quickly. CPUs normally use a heatsink equipped with a fan.

Hercules   The maker of the once-popular HCG monochrome graphics standard.

hexadecimal   The base-16 counting system used in computers for memory addresses and I/O port addresses.

hidden attribute   A file attribute that makes a file not visible to the default Windows Explorer view or Dir command.

high-level format   The type of format performed by the Windows Format program on hard drives. It rewrites file allocation tables and the root directory but doesn't overwrite existing data on the rest of the disk surface.

host adapter   SCSI or IDE drive interface. May be incorporated into the motherboard or located on a card.

host-based   Printers that use the Windows GDI to control printing rather than a printer language.

HTML (Hypertext Markup Language)   A standard for markup symbols that allow hyperlinking, fonts, special text attributes, graphics, and other enhancements to be added to text files for display with Web browsers, such as Microsoft Internet Explorer and Netscape Navigator. The "official" source for HTML standards is the World Wide Web Consortium (W3C), but both Microsoft and Netscape have added proprietary features to the HTML dialects they understand.

HTTP:// (Hypertext Transfer Protocol)   The basis for hyperlinking and the Internet; interpreted by a Web browser program.

hub   The central connecting point for UTP-based forms of Ethernet.

icon   The onscreen symbol used in Windows to link you to a program or routine.

IDE (Integrated Drive Electronics)   A popular 40-pin hard disk interface.

IEEE (Institute of Electrical and Electronics Engineers)   Sets standards for computer, electrical, and electronics devices.

IEEE 587A   The standard for surge protection devices.

IEEE 802.x   A series of IEEE networking standards used as the basis for Ethernet, Token Ring, and others.

IEEE-1284   The standard for parallel printer interfaces.

IEEE-1394   The standard for high-speed serial interface, also known as *FireWire* or *i.Link*.

i.Link   Another name for IEEE-1394.

illegal operation   The Windows 9x term for a wide variety of problems that cause programs to stop running prematurely. Use Dr. Watson to record the system condition to troubleshoot these problems.

in the wild   The term for viruses found outside virus labs.

INF file   A Windows 9x hardware installation file type.

INI file   A Windows configuration file type, used more often with Windows 3.1 but still used with Windows 9x/Me.

initialization string   A series of commands sent to a modem by a telecommunications program to configure the modem; sent before the modem is dialed to make a connection.

inkjet printer   A popular non-impact printer type.

install   The process of making a computer program usable on a system, including expanding and copying program files to the correct locations, changing Windows configuration files, and registering file extensions used by the program.

integrated port   Ports, such as serial, parallel, USB, floppy, IDE, keyboard, and PS/2 mouse, that are built into most recent motherboards. Some motherboards also integrate sound and video to reduce costs. Integrated ports make systems less expensive but require motherboard replacement when ports fail.

Intel   The leading manufacturer of CPUs.

interface   The connection between two devices.

Interlink   The MS-DOS file transfer program using serial or parallel ports with LapLink-style cables.

internal command   The command-prompt command that can be used as soon as a system is booted without other files. Stored in Windows 9x's Command.com or Windows 2000's Cmd program.

Internet   The worldwide "network of networks" that can be accessed through the World Wide Web and by Telnet, Archie, and other utilities.

I/O   Input/output.

I/O port address   The hardware resource used to transfer data between devices. The major resource used by Windows 9x to detect hardware during installation.

IPX/SPX (Internetwork Packet Exchange/Sequenced Packet Exchange)   The standard network protocols used by Novell NetWare versions 4.x and earlier.

IR (infrared)   The type of port common on portable computers and found on some desktop computers. Used for short-distance file transfer via DCC or for printing to IR-equipped printers. Normally configured as a serial port.

IRQ (Interrupt Request Line)   0–15; used by the CPU to receive and send signals to hardware devices needing or requesting attention.

ISA (Industry Standard Architecture)   A 16-bit version of the expansion slot originally created for the IBM PC. It's becoming obsolete in current and forthcoming systems.

isopropyl alcohol   A type of alcohol used as the principal solvent in many specialized computer cleaning kits.

ISP (Internet service provider)   A company that provides individuals and businesses with access to the Internet through dial-up, DSL, cable modem, wireless, or LAN connections.

Java   A programming language developed by Sun Microsystems for use on a wide variety of computers. It is widely used in Web browsers for animations and interactive features. It requires special files called Class Libraries to be added to the Web server.

JavaScript   A programming language that can be embedded in HTML files for simple, nongraphic calculations and interactive features.

K5   An early AMD Pentium-class CPU; replaced by the K6 family.

K6   AMD's highly successful Pentium-class chip. Current members include K6-2, K6-III, and others.

Kb   Kilobit (1,024 bits).

KB   Kilobyte (1,024 bytes).

known-working   A computer or component that has been tested and is known to work correctly; not the same as "new."

LAN (Local Area Network)   A network in which the components are connected through network cables. If a router is used, the network is a WAN.

landscape mode   A print mode that prints across the wider side of the paper—from the usual proportions of a landscape painting. This mode is usually slower than the default portrait mode because the fonts and graphics must be rotated. This mode is controlled by the application performing the print job.

LapLink   A popular MS-DOS and Windows file transfer program and cable standard. Windows Direct Cable Connection and old MS-DOS Interlink programs can use LapLink cables.

LARGE   Award BIOS disk option for translating drives over 504MB; not the same as LBA mode.

large disk support   A Windows 9x Fdisk option that, when enabled, allows you to create FAT32 drives. Also called large drive support.

laser printer   A type of nonimpact page printer.

LBA (Logical Block Addressing)   A popular method for translating hard drive geometry to allow drives over 504MB to be used by MS-DOS and Windows.

LCC (Leaded Chip Carrier)   An early method for packaging 286 CPUs. The chip was held in place by a hinged cover and wire retainer.

LCD (Liquid Crystal Display)   A type of screen used on portable computers. It can be monochrome or color.

Legacy USB support   A BIOS option that allows USB keyboards to work outside Windows in command-prompt and BIOS setup modes.

Level 1 cache   Memory cache located in the CPU core.

Level 2 cache   Memory cache located outside the CPU core. It can be on CPU assembly (Pentium II, Celeron 300A and above, Pentium Pro, Athlon, Duron) or motherboard (Pentium, K6 family, and so on).

line-draw graphics   Also known as box-draw characters. Used with many MS-DOS batch files and programs to create shapes onscreen. It's inserted with Alt+number pad entries if the PC-850 or IBM character set is in use.

line feed   Advances paper to next line; a button appears on many dot-matrix printers.

APP
A

line printer Refers to printers, such as inkjet and dot-matrix, that output documents one line at a time; also called *character printers*.

Lithium-Ion battery Abbreviated as Li-Ion. Advanced battery technology used by many notebook computers. It provides long battery life without any memory effect, so a partly discharged battery can be recharged completely.

local drive Not a network drive. A mapped network drive appears as a local drive in the My Computer view of the system in Windows 9x.

logging Recording events during a process, such as in Windows' Bootlog.txt file, used to record Windows startup events.

logical drive Drive letters that reside within a disk partition, especially within an extended partition. A single physical drive can contain two or more logical drives.

loopback plug A device that attaches to a parallel or serial port for diagnostic testing. It routes output lines to input lines. It's a common option for third-party diagnostic programs, such as Norton Utilities and AMIDiag.

low-level format A type of format performed by the FORMAT command on floppy disks if the /U option is used. It rewrites disk sector markings and deletes all prior disk information. It's performed at the factory on IDE/ATA hard drives but must be performed on SCSI hard drives during initial configuration.

LPT (LinePrinTer) A parallel port.

LPX A low-profile version of power supplies using the 12-pin motherboard connector or a nonstandard type of motherboard with a riser card.

macro A series of commands that can be stored inside a spreadsheet or word-processing file to automate certain operations. Many recent viruses exploit the macro feature of Microsoft Word or Excel.

macro virus A virus that uses Microsoft WordBasic or VBA commands to infect Microsoft Word or Excel documents. It can be used to damage or destroy files or drive contents.

mapped drive Using a drive letter as a shortcut to a network resource. This is optional with UNC-aware operating systems, such as Windows 9x/Me/2000, but necessary for MS-DOS programs to use network drives.

master The first drive in the logical sequence on IDE cable, determined by master/slave jumpers on each drive.

math co-processor Also known as FPU. Used for floating-point math computations performed by spreadsheet and CAD programs; now part of 486DX and all Pentium-class CPUs.

matrix Describes the arrangement of the pins in the printhead of a dot-matrix printer or the nozzles in the printhead of an inkjet printer. The smaller the pins or nozzles and the more closely they are positioned to each other, the better the print quality.

MAU (Media Attachment Unit) Connects 15-pin port (AUI) on 10Base5 Ethernet cards to Thick Ethernet cable; obsolete.

Mb Megabit.

MB Megabyte.

MBR (Master Boot Record) A pointer in the first sector of a drive indicating where operating system files can be found. It can be attacked by viruses.

MCGA (MultiColor Graphics Array) 320×200 256-color or 640×480 2-color subset of VGA used on low-end IBM PS/2 computers.

MDA (Monochrome Display Adapter) Nongraphics digital "green-screen" monochrome display standard.

media Anything used to carry information, such as network cables, paper, floppy disks, and so on.

memory address A hardware resource used by some add-on cards for RAM or ROM chips.

memory bank Memory bits equal to the data bus of the CPU. Might be one or more memory modules.

memory module Memory chips on a small board, such as COAST, SIMM, DIMM.

MIDI (Musical Instrument Digital Interface) A standard for recording musical scores used by electronic keyboards and most sound cards.

milliseconds (ms) One thousandth of a second. Used to rate storage or Internet access times—smaller is faster.

MMC (Microsoft Management Console) The Windows 2000 utility used to view and control the computer and its components.

modem   Short for Modulate-Demodulate; a device that converts digital computer information into analog form and transmits it via telephone system to another computer.

Molex   A type of rectangular power connector used on hard drives and optical drives. It features two clipped corners for positive keying.

monitor   A TV-like device that uses either a CRT or an LCD screen to display activity inside the computer. Attaches to the video card or video port on the system.

motherboard   Also known as system board or planar board. The circuit board that has expansion slots or a riser card, CPU, memory, and chipset that fits across the bottom of a desktop PC or along one side of a tower PC.

mouse   A pointing device that is moved across a flat surface. Most have a removable ball to track movement; some use optical sensors.

mouse elbow   Similar to tennis elbow; RSI (Repetitive Strain Injury) due to excessive mouse usage.

MPEG (Motion Picture Expert Group)   Creates standards for compression of video (such as MPEG 2) and audio (such as the popular MP3 file format).

ms   See *milliseconds*.

MSAU (Multistation Access Unit)   A hub-like device used on Token Ring networks to connect computers. The "Ring" refers to the token passing inside the MSAU between stations. Also known as MAU, although this term is not really correct.

MS-DOS alias   An 8.3-type filename created from a long filename in Windows 9x for use at an MS-DOS prompt or for older systems.

MS-DOS prompt   An onscreen location where commands can be typed. A normal prompt lists the current drive and folder (directory).

MSDS (Material Safety Data Sheet)   An information sheet for consumable products listing safety information.

MSDOS.SYS   In Windows 9x, a text-based configuration file that sets up options for boot management and system startup.

multimeter   A device used for multiple electrical tests, including AC and DC voltage, continuity, Ohms, and others.

multiplier   Also called clock multiplier, this is the number of times faster the CPU's internal speed is when compared to its bus speed. For example, a 450MHz Pentium II has a bus speed of 100MHz and a multiplier of 4.5 (100×4.5 equals 450MHz).

nanoseconds (ns)   One billionth (one thousand millions) of a second. The common measurement for DRAM chips and modules; a smaller ns rating equals faster RAM.

NetBEUI   Microsoft version of Net BIOS; a simple, nonroutable network protocol used for Windows 3.1x/Windows 95 networking.

network   A collection of computers and peripherals that can be accessed remotely.

network drive   A drive or folder available through a network. Usually refers to a network resource that has been mapped to a local drive letter.

nibble   4 bits.

NIC   Network interface card.

NiCD   Nickel-Cadmium. A rechargeable battery technology once popular for portable computers.

NiMH   Nickel Metal Hydrite. A battery technology used primarily today on low-cost notebook computers. It can be used to replace NiCD batteries for longer battery life per charge.

NLQ (Near Letter Quality)   The best print quality available from 24-pin dot-matrix printers.

NLX   A compact motherboard standard that allows fast replacement of a defective motherboard, it uses a riser card mounted at the end of the motherboard nearest the power supply.

nonparity   Memory that has data bits only.

NOS (Network Operating System)   Software that allows a PC to access shared resources. It might be part of a regular OS or might be an add-on.

ns   See *nanoseconds*.

NTFS (New Technology File System)   The native file system used by Windows NT and Windows 2000. The Windows 2000 version is called NTFS 5.0. All NTFS versions feature smaller allocation unit sizes and superior security when compared to FAT16 or FAT32.

APP
A

null-modem   A serial cable that crosses send and receive lines to allow two PCs to communicate directly with each other without a modem. LapLink, Interlink, and DCC serial cables are null-modem cables.

NVRAM (Non-Volatile RAM)   A motherboard chip that stores BIOS configuration information, also known as CMOS chip.

objects   Items that can be viewed or configured with Windows 98 Explorer, including drives, folders, computers, and so on.

OEM (Original Equipment Manufacturer) Products sold to system builders, not at retail.

OEMSETUP   Automatic Windows 9x setup option included on the boot floppy disk supplied with OEM versions of Windows 9x on CD-ROM.

optical   Storage, such as CD-ROM, that uses a laser to read data.

OS (operating system)   Software that configures and manages hardware. It connects hardware and applications. Windows 98 is an OS.

OSR (OEM Service Release)   Updates to the original version of Windows 95. OSR1 can be downloaded; OSR2.x must be purchased with hardware.

overclocking   Speeding up a computer by increasing the multiplier and/or bus speed used by a CPU past its rated limits. It can create faster systems but can also cause system crashes.

overload   Using devices that draw more wattage than a power supply is rated to provide.

page printer   Laser and LED printers; they must receive the entire page before transferring it to paper.

paper bail   A spring-loaded arm with rollers running in parallel with the platen on dot-matrix printers to hold single-sheet paper in place.

paper path   The route paper takes through a printer; straight-through paths have fewer jams.

parallel   A data-transfer method used to send 8 bits or multiples of 8 in a single operation. Used by parallel port, IDE, floppy, SCSI, and memory devices.

parity   RAM error-checking method that compares checksum from 8 data bits to parity bit. The system stops if values don't match.

partition   The section of a hard disk set aside for use by an operating system.

partition table   An area near the beginning of the hard disk storing disk geometry used to prepare the drive, operating systems in use on the drive, and partition start/end positions.

passive-matrix   An early LCD display technology that uses one transistor for each row and each column of the display. Compared to active-matrix, passive-matrix displays have a slow screen response, are dimmer, and have a narrow viewing angle.

password   Matched to username or resource name to allow access to network resources or accounts.

path   A series of drives and folders (subdirectories) that are checked for executable programs when a DOS command is issued. Or, a drive or network server and folders used to access a given file.

PC Card   A newer name for PCMCIA technology; credit-card–sized devices inserted into a notebook computer for networking, modem, memory and I/O expansion.

PCI (Peripheral Component Interconnect)   A high-speed 32-bit or 64-bit expansion bus developed by Intel in 1993. It's standard on almost all Pentium-class and better systems and some 486-based systems.

PCL (Printer Control Language)   Hewlett-Packard's printer language used on most LaserJet printers and many Deskjet printers. It's widely emulated by other laser printer makers.

PCMCIA (Personal Computer Memory Card International Association)   The original name for PC Card technology; see *PC Card*.

PDA (Personal Digital Assistant)   A hand-sized computer that provides datebook, notepad, and limited application software features. The Palm III series and the palm-sized PCs running Windows are popular examples of PDAs.

peer server   A client PC that also shares drives or other resources on a Windows 3.1x or Windows 9x network.

peer-to-peer network   A Windows 3.1x or Windows 9x network in which some or all client PCs also act as peer servers.

Pentium   The first Intel CPU with a 64-bit data path.

PGA (Pin Grid Array) A chip connector widely used for CPUs. It uses rows of pins projecting from the bottom of the chip to attach to sockets. Variations are currently used for Celeron, Pentium III, and Pentium-class CPUs.

phantom directory A problem with floppy drives in which the drive fails to detect a disk change and keeps the FAT from the original disk in memory, resulting in data loss if the new disk is written to using the old disk's FAT. Problems with line 34 (changeline support) are the cause of phantom directories.

physical drive Same as hard drive or hard disk; all physical drives must be partitioned and high-level formatted before they can be used by Windows.

photon A light measurement corresponding to the electron—used by fiber-optic cables to transmit data.

piezo-electric An inkjet printing technique in which ink is forced through the printhead by the activation of a piezo-electric crystal.

PIF file (Program Information File) A file that provides special instructions to Windows on how to run a particular MS-DOS program. It's manually created with Windows 3.1 and automatically created when program is run in Windows 9x.

PIO (Programmed Input Output) A series of IDE interface transfer standards (modes 0–4) for data flow that runs through the CPU. It is being replaced by faster UDMA modes.

pinfeed A simplified version of a tractor feed that uses pins fixed to either end of a platen to pull paper past the printhead of a dot-matrix printer. Unlike a tractor feed, a pinfeed mechanism cannot be used with labels or other narrow paper stock.

pipeline-burst An advanced form of memory caching that sends a continuous stream of data (pipelining) in a single operation called a burst.

platen A rubber roller in a dot-matrix printer; used for paper feed of single sheets.

PLCC (Plastic Leaded Chip Carrier) The most common chip package used for 286 CPUs and some support chips. The square chip has metal leads on all four sides that make contact with flexible-metal leads in the socket.

PnP (Plug and Play) A Windows 9x/Me/2000 technology for using the operating system to detect and configure add-on cards and external devices, such as modems, monitors, scanners, and printers. PnP hardware can be moved to different resource settings as needed to make way for additional devices.

pointing stick A pointing device used as a mouse replacement. It is integrated into some portable and desktop keyboards and responds to finger pressure. The best-known version is the IBM TrackPoint.

Port replicator Provides a single connection for serial, parallel, I/O, and video cables for portable computers. The port replicator is connected to the external devices, and is then connected to the portable computer through an external expansion bus.

portable A computer you can carry around and use with battery power. The most popular type is the notebook computer.

portrait mode The default print option, which prints across the short side of the paper. Comes from the usual orientation of portrait paintings and photographs.

POST (power-on self test) BIOS test of basic hardware performed during cold boot.

POST diagnostic card An ISA or PCI card that displays hexadecimal POST codes. It's useful for finding POST errors that are not reported by beep codes or onscreen error messages.

PostScript Adobe's printer language optimized for elaborate graphics and text effects. Used on many laser and inkjet printers used in graphics arts.

POTS (Plain Old Telephone System) The regular copper-wire telephone system that uses modems to connect one computer with another; distinguished from ISDN or DSL telephone systems.

power management BIOS or OS techniques for reducing power use by dropping the CPU clock speed, turning off the monitor or hard disk, and so on, during periods of inactivity.

PPGA (Plastic Pin Grid Array) PGA variation used by Socket 370 Celeron CPUs.

PQFP (Plastic Quad Flat Package) A surface-mounted technology used by 386SX CPUs as standard package.

primary partition   A hard disk partition that will become the C: drive on a single-drive system. It can start the system when formatted with the /S option and made active with Fdisk or other disk-partitioning program.

print spooler   A program that stores and manages print jobs on disk and sends them to the printer; an integral part of Windows.

printer language   The rules for printer commands issued by the printer driver. Popular languages include PostScript and HP PCL.

printhead   A printer component that places the image on paper using pins and ribbon or inkjet nozzles.

program group   A Windows 3.1 collection of icon shortcuts. It can be created when a program is installed or by the user.

properties sheet   The Windows 9x method for modifying and viewing object properties.

proprietary   The opposite of standard; refers to technologies that are used by only a single vendor. For example, a particular proprietary memory module will fit only a few models of notebook computers made by a particular vendor.

protocol   The common language used by different types of computers to communicate over a network.

proxy server   The Web server that sits between the actual server and client PC and sends a copy of the actual content to the PC. Used for security and to filter content.

PS/2   The IBM series of computers introduced in 1987. Replaced the IBM PC and AT. Models 50 and up introduced this Micro Channel Architecture, an unsuccessful attempt to make PCs easier to maintain and service.

pull tractor   A tractor-feed mechanism located after the printhead in a dot-matrix printer. It pulls the paper past the printhead and requires the user to waste a sheet of paper to tear off a print job.

push tractor   A tractor-feed mechanism located before the printhead on a dot-matrix printer. It pushes the paper past the printhead and makes zero tear-off printing possible.

QWERTY   The standard arrangement of typewriter keys is also used by most English or Latin-alphabet computer keyboards. The name is derived from the first five letter keys under the left hand.

RAM (Random Access Memory)   Memory whose contents can be changed.

read caching   A method of disk caching that uses RAM to hold data being read from disk. Data being saved to disk goes straight to the disk instead of being held in RAM. Windows uses read caching for floppy and removable-media drives by default to avoid data loss from disk changes.

read-only   Storage that is protected from changes.

read-only attribute   A file attribute used to protect a file from unauthorized changes. It cannot be overridden or altered and can be deleted only by explicit user override.

read-write caching   A method of disk caching that uses RAM to hold data being saved to disk as well as data being read from disk for faster performance. Windows uses read-write caching for hard drives by default.

Recovery Console   A special Windows 2000 command-line mode used to restore damaged systems. It can be launched from the Windows 2000 CD-ROM or can be installed as a boot option.

Recycle Bin   The Windows holding area for deleted files, allowing them to be restored to their original locations. It can be overridden to free up disk space.

refresh rate   The rate at which electron guns in a monitor's CRT repaint the picture onscreen—also called vertical retrace rate. It is measured in Hertz (Hz); 72Hz = 72 times per second.

register size   The CPU's internal data pathway in bits.

registration   The Windows process of matching file extensions with compatible programs.

Registry   The Windows 9x/Me/2000/NT structure that stores information on programs and hardware installed on the system and user configuration settings. The Windows 9x/Me Registry is stored in two files: system.dat and user.dat; the Windows 2000 Registry is stored in the \WinNT\System32\Config folder.

REM   Remark. Used at the beginning of any statement in Config.sys or Autoexec.bat to prevent the statement from being processed during system startup. The semicolon (;) is used for the same purpose on .INI files used by Windows.

removable-media   Any drive whose media can be interchanged—floppy disk, CD-ROM, optical, and tape.

repeater   Amplifies a network signal to enable it to run over longer cable than normal.

replicate   To make a copy.

resistor   Used on networks and drives to indicate "end of bus."

ribbon cable   A flat cable used to connect drives to interfaces.

RIMM (Rambus Inline Memory Module)   A high-performance memory module that uses serial instead of parallel data transfers. Used primarily by some recent Intel-chipset motherboards.

Ring topology   The logical arrangement of computers in a circle. Permission to transmit it is passed from one computer to the other. Used by token-ring networking.

RJ-11   The standard telephone cable connection used by modems and fax units.

RJ-45   The UTP network cable connection used by 10BaseT and Fast Ethernet.

ROM (Read Only Memory)   Memory whose contents cannot be changed.

root directory   The top-level folder on a drive that stores all other directories (folders). The root directory of the C: drive is C:\.

router   A device that routes data from one network to another.

RS-232   The standard serial port for PCs.

RSI (Repetitive Strain Injury)   Injuries that occur because of repeating the same movement again and again.

RTC (Real Time Clock)   Keeps time in a PC. It is part of the so-called "CMOS" chip.

S-Video   A high-quality video standard used in many recent VCR and DVD products for input and output of video signals. Many recent video cards with TV output also feature S-Video jacks.

safe format   The default floppy disk format for MS-DOS; it allows floppy disk to be unformatted.

Safe mode   The Windows troubleshooting startup mode. It runs the system using BIOS routines only.

sampling rate   The frequency at which analog sound data is stored for digital conversion. A higher sampling rate produces better quality but also larger .wav files.

SCAM (SCSI Configured Auto Magically)   An auto-configuration technique supported by many SCSI hard drives and SCSI interface cards designed for use with hard disks.

Scanreg   A Windows 98 utility that checks the Registry for errors automatically at boot time or upon request. It replaces a damaged Registry with the backup copy.

SCSI (Small Computer System Interface)   A flexible interface used for hard and optical drives, scanners, and other devices. It allows daisy-chaining of seven devices or more to a single port.

SDRAM (Synchronous DRAM)   Fast RAM that is synchronized to the motherboard's clock speed. Current types include 66MHz, 100MHz, and 133MHz.

SECC (Single Edge Contact Connector)   A connector type used by Slot 1-type Intel Pentium II CPUs.

SECC2   Improved SECC connector used by Slot 1 type CPUs.

sector   A 512-byte structure that is the basic storage unit for drives. The sectors arranged in a concentric circle on the media's surface are called a track.

SEPP (Single Edge Processor Package)   A bare-card type CPU package for slot 1 used by Celeron CPUs.

serial   A data-transmission technique that sends a single bit at a time at various rates. Used by RS-232, USB, and IEEE-1394 interfaces.

server   A computer that shares drives and other resources over a network.

SETUP   The normal Windows 9x installation program for OS and applications.

SGRAM (Synchronous Graphics RAM)   A variation on SGRAM used by advanced video cards.

shadowing   A method for speeding up ROM access by copying ROMs in upper memory area to RAM, which "shadows" the same area.

share-level   The type of network access used by peer servers. A separate password would be required for each shared resource. No central list of users is maintained.

shared resource   A drive, printer, or other resource available to other PCs over a network.

shortcut A Windows 9x icon stored on the desktop or in the \Windows\Programs folder with an .lnk extension. Double-click the icon to run the program or open the file.

single sheets Individual sheets of paper such as copy, laser, inkjet paper—the most common form of printer paper used today.

SIMM (Single Inline Memory Module) A 30-pin or 72-pin memory module with edge contacts used on 386 through Pentium-based systems.

SIP (Single Inline Package) A SIMM-like memory module with 30 projecting pins rather than edge contacts.

slave The second drive to be accessed on IDE cable; set with master/slave jumpers.

slot cover A L-shaped metal cover attached to the rear of the system in place of card brackets when cards are not inserted into every expansion slot.

Smart Media A type of flash memory used by some digital cameras. It requires a card reader or PC Card adapter to be compatible with portable and desktop computers.

SODIMM A type of DIMM module used in certain portable computers.

software Instructions that create or modify information and control hardware. Must be read into RAM before use.

SPGA (Staggered Pin Grid Array) A PGA variation used on Pentium and pin-compatible CPUs.

SPS (Standby Power Supply) The correct term for so-called UPS battery backup systems that switch from AC power to DC power when the AC power fails.

SR (Service Release) A Microsoft term for updates to Microsoft Office, Internet Explorer, and so on.

SRAM (Static RAM) RAM based on transistors. It requires electricity far less often. It's too expensive and bulky to use as main RAM, but popular for use as Cache RAM.

ST-506 An improved variation of ST-412 hard disk interface. The original hard disk interface for IBM PC/XT and AT. Uses two cables for data and signals; obsolete.

standby The power-saving mode in which the CPU drops to a reduced clock speed and other components wait for activity.

standoff spacer A plastic or brass device that attaches between the motherboard and bottom or side of case for installation.

star topology A network topology in which a central hub is connected to individual workstations with separate cables.

start page The Web page that is first displayed when you open a Web browser. It can be customized to view any Web page available online or stored on your hard disk.

startup event File loading and other activities during the startup of Windows.

static electricity High-voltage but low-amperage electric discharges between items with different electric potential. Harmful to equipment but not to people.

storage Any device that holds programs or data for use, including hard disks, floppy disks, CD-ROM drives, and so on.

STP (Shielded Twisted Pair) A protected version of UTP used for Token Ring and sometimes Ethernet.

straight-through paper path Paper path available as an option with most laser printers to allow labels and heavier stock to go straight through the printer without being curved around rollers.

subsystem The portion of a computer that performs a particular task. The printer subsystem, for example, contains the printer, cable, port, printer driver, and BIOS configuration settings.

surge protector A device that absorbs high-voltage events to protect equipment from damage.

suspend A power-saving mode that shuts down the monitor and other devices; saves more power than standby.

SVGA (Super VGA) Can refer to 800×600 VGA resolution or to any VGA display setting that uses more than 16 colors or a higher resolution than 640×480.

swapfile The area of a hard disk used for virtual memory. Windows 9x/Me/2000 use a dynamic swapfile (called the paging file in Windows 2000) that can grow or shrink as required.

switch A network device that sets a direct path for data to run from one system to another. Simpler than a router or can be combined with a router. Faster than a hub.

switchbox   A device that hich allows several external components to share a single serial, parallel, or other type of port or might allow several computers to share one printer.

system attribute   A file attribute used to indicate the file or folder is part of the operating system. Boot files are normally set as system and hidden.

system bus   A motherboard wire that traces carrying data, power, control, and address signals to components and expansion slots.

System Monitor   The Windows 9x/Me/2000 feature that monitors the performance of different portions of the computer. Can be customized.

T-adapter   Connects to rear of a 10Base2 Ethernet card to allow the RG-58 cable to be attached in a bus configuration.

TAPI (Telephony Application Programming Interface)   The Windows 95 method for interfacing with modems and other telephony devices. It allows the system to interface with POTS, PBX, videophones, and others by interfacing with their TAPI drivers.

TCP/IP (Transmission Control Protocol/Internet Protocol)   The Internet's standard network protocol now becoming the standard for all networks.

temp file   Temporary file. A file created to store temporary information, such as a print job or an application work file. May be stored in the default TEMP folder (such as \Windows\Temp) or a folder designated by the application.

terminator   A device attached to the end of a daisy-chain of SCSI devices or the end of a bus-topology network, such as 10Base2 Ethernet. Removing the terminator will cause device or network failure.

Token Ring   IBM-designed network based on the IEEE 802.5 standard.

toner cartridge   A one-piece unit containing toner, developer, and imaging drum. Used in many laser printer models; sometimes referred to as an EP cartridge.

topology   The arrangement of cables in a network.

Tracert   The Windows version of the Traceroute command. Used to track the routing between your computer and a specified IP address or server.

tractor-fed paper   Paper with perforated edges. Used by printers with tractor-feed mechanisms.

tractor-feed   Paper feeders that push or pull paper with perforated edges past the printhead on dot-matrix printers. Uses tractor-fed paper.

TrackPoint   An IBM-designed pointing device that is integrated into the keyboards of portable computers made by IBM and is licensed by Toshiba and other firms. Also referred to as a pointing stick, it resembles a pencil eraser located between the G and H keys. The buttons are located beneath the spacebar.

Trojan horse   A program that attaches itself secretly to other programs and usually has a harmful action when triggered. Similar to a computer virus but cannot spread itself to other computers, although some Trojan horses can be used to install a remote control program that allows an unauthorized user to take over your computer.

TSR (Terminate and Stay Resident)   A program that stays in memory to provide system services or hardware support, such as Mouse.com. Usually found in Autoexec.bat on MS-DOS and Windows 3.1 systems. Windows 9x/Me usually have 32-bit drivers that replace TSRs.

touchpad   A pressure-sensitive pad that is used as a mouse replacement in some portable computers and keyboards. It can also be purchased as a separate unit.

Type I   The narrowest PC Card slot; seldom used for devices.

Type II   The medium-size PC Card slot. Two Type-II slots can be used as a single Type-III slot. Common Type-II devices include modems, network interface cards, combo cards, and SCSI and USB cards.

Type III   The widest PC Card slot. Common Type-III devices include ATA-compatible hard disk drives.

typeface   A set of fonts in different sizes (or a single scalable outline) and weights. Times New Roman Bold, Bold Italic, Regular, and Italic represent the Times New Roman scalable typeface.

Typical   The Windows and application software installation option that should install the features needed by most users.

UART (Universal Asynchronous Receive Transmit)   The hardware "heart" of a serial port or modem. Modems that lack a UART depend on the OS to operate.

APP
A

UDMA (Ultra DMA)   Fast data-transfer methods for IDE drives; bypasses the CPU.

UL-1449   Underwriter's Laboratory standard for surge protectors.

Ultra SCSI   The various types of faster SCSI with transfer rates of 20MB–40MB/second.

UMA (Unified Memory Architecture)   Memory is shared between the system and video circuit. Reduces video cost but reduces performance.

UNC (Universal Naming Convention)   Allows network clients to access shared resources without use of mapped drive letters or port redirection.

unconditional format   The floppy disk format option that rewrites sector markings and destroys existing data.

undelete   The MS-DOS utility program that can retrieve "deleted" files still on the system. It can be run as a TSR to improve chances of file retrieval.

underclocking   Reducing the motherboard speed and/or the clock multiplier below correct values to slow down the CPU. Usually a result of incorrect system configuration or to allow a newer component to be used with an older system.

unerase   See *undelete*. A Norton Utilities program that performs the same task as undelete.

unformat   Reverses the safe format of a floppy disk or hard disk; cannot be used if new data has been copied to the drive.

uninstall   The process to remove Windows programs from the system. Windows 3.1 programs usually require a separate utility; Windows 95 programs usually include this option.

upgrade   Replacing an old version of software or hardware with a new version.

upgrade version   A version of a program (such as Windows 98) that requires proof of ownership of a previous version before it can be installed.

upper memory   Also known as reserved memory. Memory addresses between 640KB and 1MB set aside for ROM and RAM used on some add-on cards. Empty spaces can be used as UMBs by Emm386.exe.

UPS (Uniterruptable Power Supply)   The term for battery backup that uses battery at all times to power the system. Sometimes referred to as true UPS to distinguish them from SPS units (also, the employer of a friendly driver in a brown outfit who delivers computer products).

USB (Universal Serial Bus)   A high-speed eventual replacement for older I/O ports; requires Windows 95 OSR 2.1 or above. Windows 98/Me/2000 are recommended for best results because many devices won't work with Windows 95's USB support.

user-level   The network security used by Novell NetWare or Microsoft Windows NT Server. The server keeps a list of users and rights/permissions. A single password provides access to all resources the user is allowed to access.

username   Used with a password to gain access to network resources.

utility program   A program that enhances day-to-day computer operations but doesn't create data. Windows 98 includes ScanDisk and Defrag utilities, among others.

UTP (Unshielded Twisted-Pair)   The most common type of network cable; uses RJ-45 connectors.

VA (Volt-Amps)   A common way to rate battery backup units.

VBA (Visual Basic for Applications)   Microsoft's application development language used with Microsoft Office.

VCACHE (Virtual Cache)   Windows for Workgroups 3.11 optional 32-bit disk cache driver. A standard feature of Windows 95.

VESA (Video Electronic Standards Association)   The trade group of monitor and video card makers that sets video standards.

VESA BIOS extension   A TSR program supplied with many VGA cards to allow standard video drivers for MS-DOS games to work with different brands of video cards. Some VGA cards have built-in BIOS extension.

VESA Local Bus   A 32-bit extension of ISA bus used on many 486 and a few early Pentium systems. Developed for video cards but also used for IDE and SCSI interfaces.

VFAT (Virtual File Allocation Table)   Windows for Workgroups 3.11 optional 32-bit file access driver. A standard feature of Windows 95.

VGA (Video Graphics Array)   The first popular analog video standard. The basis for all current video cards.

virtual domain   A portion of a physical Web server. It appears as a separate Web server to the user and is accessed with a unique domain name.

virtual memory   Hard disk space used as a supplement to RAM; also known as a *swapfile* or paging file.

virus   A computer program that resembles a Trojan horse that can also replicate itself to other computers.

VL-Bus   See *VESA Local Bus.*

VMM (Virtual Machine Manager)   Windows 9x/Me uses VMM to provide multitasked services known as virtual machines to each running program, making each program think it has the entire computer at its disposal.

volt   A measurement of AC or DC electrical power.

voltmeter   A device that measures AC or DC electrical power; often integrated into a digital multimeter (DMM).

VRAM (Video RAM)   RAM used on some older high-end video cards. It can read and write data at the same time.

WAN (Wide Area Network)   A network that spans multiple cities, countries, or continents. Network sections can be linked by leased line, Internet backbone, or satellite feed. Routers connect LANs to WANs and WAN segments to each other.

warm boot   Restarting computer with software—no memory or hardware testing.

watt   The measurement of heat used to rate power supplies.

wavetable   A method of playing back MIDI files with digitized samples of actual musical instruments.

Wide SCSI   The 16-bit version of the SCSI interface.

wide-carriage   A dot-matrix printer equipped to handle wide tractor-fed paper.

wildcard   A character used to replace one or more characters as a variable in MS-DOS DIR and Windows 3.1 File Manager. Enhanced in Windows 9x/Me/2000 Find/Search, Windows Explorer. * equals multiple characters and ? equals a single character.

Winmodem   US Robotics term for modems that lack a UART chip and use Windows for data handling.

WINS (Windows Internet Naming System)   Windows NT and Windows 2000 Server's method of dynamically matching NetBIOS computer names to their IP addresses (NetBIOS name resolution).

word length   The number of bits in characters sent through a serial port. 8-bit word length is used in PC-to-PC communications; 7-bit word length is used to communicate with mainframe computers.

WordBasic   Microsoft Word's macro language.

WRAM (Window RAM)   A modified version of VRAM used on a few video cards.

write-protect   Storage area that cannot be changed. Sliders on floppy disks are used to write-protect the contents, and motherboard options are used to write-protect many FlashROM BIOS chips to protect them from unauthorized upgrades.

XCOPY   MS-DOS and Windows command-line utility that copies groups of files into RAM and then to disk for faster transfers than COPY. Can also create folders during the copying process. It offers many additional features when run with the Windows GUI in memory.

XMS (Extended Memory Standard)   A standard for managing memory above 1MB. Himem.sys turns extended memory into XMS memory.

XVGA (Extended VGA)   Commonly refers to 1024×768 display resolution.

Y2K   Year 2000.

zero tear-off   A dot-matrix printer feature that allows the user to remove a printout without wasting a sheet of paper; requires a push tractor.

ZIF (Zero Insertion Force)   PGA-type sockets that have a lever and clamp mechanism to allow 486 and Pentium-type chips to be inserted and removed without tools. Sockets 3 and above are ZIF sockets.

ZV (Zoomed Video)   A special PC Card slot type equipped to support full-motion video with appropriate MPEG cards.

APP
A

The A+ Certification Process

Overview of the Process

The A+ Certification process consists of

- Learning more about the exams
- Choosing an exam center
- Registering for the exams
- Preparing for the exams
- Exam day
- Receiving your certification information
- Learning from your mistakes
- Becoming A+ certified—for life!

Learning More About the A+ Exams

Now that you're reading the best A+ Certification study guide on the market, it's time to learn more about the process. Start by going to the CompTIA Web site: www.comptia.com.

CompTIA is the organization responsible for the creation of A+ Certification and the development of the A+ Certification exams.

Follow the "Certification" link to continue. The Certification page provides a brief overview of the A+ and other certifications offered by CompTIA. Use the "A+" link at the top of the page to proceed to the A+ portion of the site.

After you reach the A+ Certification page on the CompTIA site, you can learn more about the test, read the objectives (which are also listed on the CD-ROM in Appendix E, "Lab Exercises"), and choose an exam center.

Test Details

The test codes for the 2001 revisions to the A+ Certification exams are 220-201 (A+ Core Hardware) and 220-202 (A+ Operating Systems). Be sure to specify the correct codes when you register for your exams because the 1998 revisions (220-121 and 220-122) might still be offered for some time. You cannot mix-and-match tests; you must take both of the 2001 revision tests to receive your A+ Certification.

CompTIA recommends that you take both tests at the same time, especially if you must travel any distance to take the exams. You must complete both exams successfully to receive your A+ Certification.

Selecting a Test Vendor

After you read all the FAQ questions and answers you need, click the Register link.

The A+ Certification tests are administered by NCS/VUE or Prometric. Choose either vendor from the vendors displayed to continue the registration process. If you choose Prometric, you will be forwarded to the Prometric Web site (www.2test.com) for registration. If you choose NCS/VUE, you will be forwarded to the Virtual University Web site (www.vue.com) for registration.

Which test vendor should you choose? I recommend that you choose your test vendor based on convenience because you'll take the same test and pay the same price per test regardless of whether you take it at a Prometric or an NCS/VUE site. To determine which is most convenient for you, you will want to see both vendors' lists of test center locations.

Viewing Test Center Locations

Follow the links on the vendors' Web sites to locate the testing centers near you. First, specify that you are looking for the CompTIA A+ Certification examination test sites. Next, choose your country and state (or province) to see a listing of test centers. Location name, address, and telephone number are provided, and in most cases directions or a map feature are also supplied to help make sure you arrive on time. Visit both sites to see which test centers are most convenient for you.

Before you register for the exam, call the first center you want to use and make sure the location and other information listed online is correct. When I took my Core Hardware exam, I scared myself pretty badly by forgetting to double-check the location. The address listed online was incorrect, and I arrived at a deserted office a half-hour before the exam was scheduled to start. Fortunately, the company had relocated less than a mile away, so I still arrived on time (you can lose your fee for being late—it's also counted as a "no-show!"). Save yourself a scare by calling first.

If you live near a state border, check neighboring states to see if their test centers are closer to you; you can take the CompTIA A+ Certification tests in any state you like.

After you decide which vendor's test locations are more convenient, you will need to register with the vendor before you can register for the tests. During registration, you provide contact information and a username and password. Use this information to log on to the registration process. There is usually a delay of 24 hours between the time that you register and the time that your registration is activated for use online; it's longer on weekends. If it's Friday and you want to take the test on Monday, call in your registration instead.

Registering for the Tests

After you have registered with either vendor, the process for registering for tests online is similar. You must do the following (the order might vary by vendor):

- Provide your username and password to log in to the registration system.
- Select the tests you want to take. CompTIA recommends that you take both 220-201 (Core Hardware) and 220-202 (Operating Systems) on the same day.
- Select the test center. You will select country, then state/province to see a list of centers. Note the number assigned to the test center; you might need to refer to it during registration.
- Select the testing language when this option is available. English is the only language available for the tests until the third quarter of 2001, when other languages will be offered; check the CompTIA Web site for details.
- Select the date and times of your tests. The testing centers have a limited number of test stations available for the exam. Choose alternative dates and times before you start the process in case your first choice isn't available.
- Complete the registration process by providing a credit card for payment; you can use VISA, MasterCard, or American Express. The 2001 tests cost $132 U.S. each in the United States and can vary for international testers; see the CompTIA Web site for details. To take both tests, therefore, you will spend $264 U.S. in the United States.

If you prefer, you can register by phone. To register with Prometric, call 800-77-MICRO (776-4276). To register with NCS/VUE, call 877-551-PLUS (551-7587).

Whether you register online or over the telephone, make sure you do the following:

- Double-check all information you provide, including dates, exam names, times, and contact information. The exam confirmation and A+ Certificate will be mailed to you, so make sure your address is correct.
- Record the confirmation number you're given. If you need to reschedule one of your exams, you'll need that confirmation number to select a different date.
- Mark your calendar with the exam date, time, and location. There are no refunds for no-shows.
- Watch your mail for the confirmation information, which will arrive in a few days. If you are on a tight deadline, ask the operator about expedited test taking.

APP
B

Preparing for the Exam

You have in your hands the best A+ Certification study aid on the market, so take advantage of it! We suggest the following methods to help you get the most out of your study time:

- Work "live" with as much of the hardware the exam covers as you can.

  Open up actual systems and look at the components. Check your "junk" closets for older hardware you can cannibalize. As you work with equipment, compare it to the relevant chapter in this book. Trace the components identified. Try to locate common motherboard components. Use the manuals that come with equipment to help you become acquainted with the many variations in motherboards and systems.

  If you have spare hard drives, use Windows to prepare them for use. Try different upgrade processes. Install boards that use manual settings and PnP configuration.

  Pop open the cover on laser printers and use the manual to locate the major components covered on the exam.

  Build a simple network.

- Use the companion CD-ROM's resources.

  A team of content and media experts built the CD-ROM to be a useful tool; its contents, which include detailed help files, Acrobat electronic-book content, and audio and video content are covered in detail in Appendix C.

  With the CD-ROM, you can "sneak in" some study time at any computer.

- Reinforce your knowledge with the chapter questions and test.

  Each chapter is based on one or more portions of the A+ objectives. Spend more time on the chapters you're weakest in; but don't neglect any chapter. Use the questions at the beginning of each chapter to dig into the chapter and apply what you've learned there. The chapter test will measure how well you've mastered the chapter's contents.

- Use the hands-on labs for practical application.

  Use Appendix E, on the CD-ROM to apply what you learn in each chapter to a real-life problem or situation.

  Remember, you won't have this book or any other reference with you when you take the test. You don't need to get every question right, but careful, systematic study will help you pass with plenty of room to spare.

Online and Other Training Resources

You'll find a wealth of additional resources online. Start with the Que Publishing Web site (www.quecorp.com): the home base on the Web for many more great books like this one.

The new InformIT link (`www.informit.com`) takes you straight to carefully selected excerpts from many popular Pearson Technology Group's books on hardware, operating systems, and networking. You can also personalize InformIT to provide customized content just for you.

My company's Web site is located at `www.selectsystems.com`. Highlights on this site include my online bookstore, featuring books I've written, co-authored, or contributed to, and a complete bibliography of technical articles I've written since 1990 and links to more than 125 that are available online. Learn more about networking, printing, hardware upgrades, and operating system issues here.

Most of my articles are published by the folks at Sandhills Publishing, who produce the *SmartComputing* monthly, as well as a continuing series of *PCNovice and SmartComputing Guide* and *Learning Series* titles on all kinds of hardware, software, networking, and Internet subjects. Many of my PC Troubleshooting students over the years have found these publications extremely useful. Check them out online at `www.smartcomputing.com`.

Other online sites of interest include

- `www.whatis.com`—Provides concise, accurate definitions of computer terms as well as many excerpts from computer texts.

- `www.zdnet.com`—The Ziff-Davis Web site, home of *PCMagazine*, *PCComputing*, *PCWeek*, and many other Ziff-Davis print and electronic publications and services. From computer news to tutorials, shareware to hardware, ZDNet has broad and useful coverage.

- `www.TechTV.com`—The companion Web site to the computer user's favorite cable TV channel, TechTV.

For information about a specific hardware item, use the manufacturer's own Web sites. Most offer Web-based or Adobe Acrobat-based versions of their manuals, allowing you to get the inside story on hardware you might not have seen "in the flesh."

Additional books that I recommend include

Upgrading and Repairing PCs (12th Edition), by Scott Mueller (Que, 2000). I was on the team that helped revise this masterpiece, and I co-authored *Upgrading and Repairing PCs: Technician's Portable Reference, 2nd Edition* (Que, 2000) with Scott. These books provide you with a complete history and teardown of PCs old and new, along with field-tested tips for keeping them working.

As a long-time user of Norton Utilities, I also appreciate the work of Peter Norton, including *Peter Norton's Inside the PC, Eighth Edition* (Sams, 1999). He covers both hardware and operating systems (DOS and Windows).

These online, magazine, and book resources will help you be extra well prepared for both the A+ exams and for the day-to-day challenges of A+ Certification.

**APP
B**

Exam Day

The night before, make it your primary goal to get a good night's sleep. Don't "cram," although a last swing through your weakest objective or two is okay.

Give yourself plenty of time to arrive at the testing center, especially if it's in an unfamiliar city. The zoomable maps and directions provided online are handy, but use them along with reliable directions and a "real" map. If you forgot to call ahead, take a moment and do it now to make sure there are no last-minute glitches.

Arrive a half-hour early to allow for restroom breaks, general relaxation, and to register with the test center. Have a driver's license and a second ID (such as a major credit card) with you: No "ringers" are allowed!

Where I took the exam, the exam center was a small room with a single aging PC. The test center provides a few sheets of paper (which you return at the end of the test) and some pencils for taking work notes. That, plus your brain, is all you have.

Practice with the Simulated Test First

You're offered the opportunity to take a brief simulated test before you take the real thing. Don't be cocky—take it. It will help you get accustomed to the testing format.

As the simulated exam on the CD-ROM has shown you, some questions have a single right answer (chosen from four listed); some have multiple correct answers; some ask you to display an "exhibit" (a picture with labeled components) that you can choose from. The simulated test has an example of each of these.

My Testing Strategy for the Conventional Exam

The 2001 revisions to the A+ Certification tests have reverted to the conventional format, in which you have a fixed number of questions to answer. The testing strategy I outline below is based on the conventional test.

After you start the real test, the timer starts. Here's the strategy I used (and I got a 93%!):

- Answer the questions you know "cold" right away.

- Use the "review" option to mark questions you want to think about; those you're not sure about.

- Remember that you can go back at any time to a question to change your answer until you finish the last question and continue from there; after that, you can only work with the "review" questions.

- If you're concerned about how you're doing, look at the unanswered questions (marked for review) and do a bit of calculating to see how important they are. After I answered the "sure bet" questions, I only needed to answer 50% of the questions I was unsure of to pass. Figure the percentages and relax a bit.

- Watch out for trick questions; if you're unfamiliar with the area covered in the question, don't lunge blindly at the "obvious" answer. By putting aside this type of question for further study, I answered nearly every one correctly. It became clear after reflection that the "obvious" answer on some questions was dead wrong.

- Don't be afraid to apply what you learned in real life to this test. My real-world experience with electricity was very helpful in the safety portion of the test. Common sense plus computer knowledge is the key to passing.

- Use any notepaper and pencils provided to make notes and doodles; sometimes a bit of scribbling will help you understand the best answers.

Testing Strategies for the Adaptive Exam

The 2001 revisions to the A+ Certification exams were released in the conventional format. However, at some point after the introduction of the 2001 revision to the A+ Certification exams, an adaptive format might again be used, as it was during the second half of 2000 with the 1998 revision. If the 2001 revisions to the A+ Certification exams are released in adaptive format, read these notes for tips on how to take and pass this type of test.

An adaptive exam is quite different from the conventional format. Instead of a fixed number of questions, different test takers might answer a different number of questions within a fixed minimum and maximum amount (for example, the adaptive version of the 1998 revision tests asked between 20 and 30 questions per test). The questions are rated for difficulty, the time allocated for the test is much shorter than for a conventional test, and you cannot go back and change answers or skip ahead; you see and answer one question at a time. Basically, you answer questions until one of three thresholds are met:

- You are asked and answer questions until you accumulate enough points to pass. When you pass, the test is over even if you were not asked all the possible questions.

- You are asked the maximum number of questions possible in an attempt to reach a passing score. The answer you give to the last question might put you over the top with a passing score or fail you.

- You run out of time without answering enough questions to pass.

As the test proceeds, the questions will become more difficult as the testing engine calculates the points you need to have versus the maximum number of test questions remaining for you to answer.

Your objective in an adaptive test is to pass the test with the fewest number of questions answered.

Getting the Test Results

At the end of the test, the exam scoring is done by computer, and you'll have a printout of your results in just a couple of minutes. Although you won't get a printout of the questions or answers, the printout you get to keep provides both your overall score and a breakdown by A+ Objectives for that exam. By using this study guide carefully and completely, you should have a comfortable passing grade. Congratulations!

Receiving the A+ Certification Materials

Keep your test score printout; after you've passed both tests, you should receive your A+ Certification documents in the mail. Make sure the name and address listed for you are correct.

If you've scheduled both exams on the same day, pat yourself on the back and continue to test #2. After you pass the other exam, you should receive the A+ Certification materials in about three to four weeks; if you've waited five weeks without receiving the packet, call your test vendor.

Learning from Your Mistakes

Because the test results are broken out by objective, you'll know where you need to improve. Make it a personal objective to study your weak areas, as well as to continue to improve your mastery of your best subjects.

Use Appendix D, "Objectives Index," to help you use this book as a guide to reviewing particular topics. The CD-ROM–based tests included with this book also allow you to test yourself on specific objectives.

A+ Certified for Life!

After you receive A+ Certification, nobody can take it away from you. However, we encourage you to see this achievement as a milestone, not a destination. The more you learn, the more valuable you'll be to your employer, and the more you'll enjoy working with computers in any capacity.

CD-ROM Instructions

Introduction

To help you prepare for the A+ Certification exams and to provide you with additional insights into the day-to-day challenges of computer service, we've provided a CD-ROM full of useful content, including

- Self-test software
- *Upgrading and Repairing PCs: Technician's Portable Reference, 2nd Edition* in Adobe Acrobat (.PDF) format
- The Upgrading Help file and General Reference .PDF file from the companion CD to *Upgrading and Repairing PCs, 12th Edition, Academic Edition*
- Three Scott Mueller videos from the companion CD to *Upgrading and Repairing PCs, 12th Edition*
- Actual recordings of sample beep codes from computers using the AMI, Award, Phoenix, and Microid Research BIOSes

The following sections discuss each portion of the companion CD-ROM in more detail.

Self-Test Software

The tests on this CD-ROM consist of performance-based questions. This means that rather than asking you what function an item would fulfill (knowledge-based question), you will be presented with a situation and asked for an answer that shows your capability to solve the problem.

The program consists of three main test structures:

- **Non-Randomized Test**—This is useful when you first begin studying and want to run through sections that you have read to make certain you understand them thoroughly before continuing.
- **Adaptive Test**—This emulates an adaptive exam and randomly pulls questions from the database. You are asked 15 questions of varying difficulty. If you successfully answer a question, the next question you are asked is of a higher difficulty

because the test engine adapts to your skill level. If you miss a question, the next one asked is easier because, again, the test engine attempts to adapt to your skill level. This tool is useful for getting accustomed to the adaptive format, but not for intense study, because the actual number of questions presented is low.

- **Random/Mastery Test**—This is the big one. This test is different from the two others in the sense that questions are pulled from all objective areas. You are asked 50 questions, simulating a non-adaptive exam. At the conclusion of the exam, you will get your overall score and the chance to view all wrong answers. You also will be able to print a report card featuring your test results. All test questions are the type currently used by CompTIA for the A+ exam. In some cases, the content of the questions consists solely of multiple-choice, offering four or more possible answers. In other cases, you might be asked to view an exhibit as part of the question.

Equipment Requirements

To run the self-test software, you must have at least the following equipment:

- IBM-compatible Pentium
- 16MB of RAM (32MB recommended)
- 256-color display, configured as 800×600 display or larger
- Double-speed CD-ROM drive
- Approximately 5MB free disk space
- Microsoft Windows 95, 98, Me, NT (Workstation or Server) or 2000 (Professional or Server)

Running the Self-Test Software

Access the Setup.exe file, and the self-test software installs on your hard drive from the CD-ROM and runs directly from there. After you have followed the simple installation steps, you will find the software very intuitive and self-explanatory.

CD-ROM Content for Study and Mastery

In addition to the self-test software, you'll find the following content on the companion CD-ROM:

- *Upgrading and Repairing PCs: Technician's Portable Reference, 2nd Edition* **in Adobe Acrobat (.PDF) format**—Also co-authored by Scott Mueller and Mark Edward Soper, this book provides a fast review of the major hardware components of the modern PC, with an emphasis on quick-reference tables, diagnostic tools and techniques, and lots of illustrations of connectors and concepts.

- **The Upgrading Help file and General Reference .PDF file from the companion CD to *Upgrading and Repairing PCs, 12th Edition, Academic Edition*—** Use the Upgrading Help file for quick definitions to popular terms; because the file is in the Windows Help format, you can display it onscreen while you perform research or use other CD-ROM content. The General Reference file provides you with a single document containing Award, Phoenix, Microid Research, and IBM BIOS beep, hex (POST card), and onscreen error codes, modem control codes, DOS commands for use with MS-DOS or Windows 9x, metric/English measurement conversions, keyboard codes, and much more.

- **The following Scott Mueller videos from the companion CD to *Upgrading and Repairing PCs, 12th Edition*:**

  - **Tools of the Trade**—See Scott describe and demonstrate the essential tools you need to add to a standard PC repair toolkit.

  - **Static Electricity**—Scott shows you how to use wrist straps and other tools and techniques to prevent ESD from damaging your computer.

  - **Motherboard Components**—Scott takes you on a live tour of a typical motherboard and describes the function of its major components, including the CPU socket, the chipset, and much more.

    Use the Windows Media Player supplied with Windows 98 and later, available from Microsoft's Web site, or another MPEG movie player of your choice, to view these videos.

- **Actual recordings of sample beep codes from computers using the AMI, Award, Phoenix, and Microid Research (MR) BIOSes**—The Award, AMI, and MR BIOS beep codes are those played when no video card (or a bad video card) is installed; this is one of the most common problems that will trigger beep codes, and it shows how different BIOS vendors use different types of beep codes to indicate the same problem. The AMI BIOS uses different numbers of short beeps to indicate 11 different problems, and Award uses beep codes sparingly; the video beep code heard here is the only beep code used by the Award BIOS. The MR BIOS beep code is an example of this BIOS's use of high- and low-pitched beep codes to report more than 30 different problems. The Phoenix BIOS doesn't use a beep code to indicate video problems, so I chose the beep code that plays when the RTC (real-time clock) on the motherboard is defective. The Phoenix BIOS uses short and long beeps to report dozens of different system problems.

  You will find listening to these samples especially useful if you look at the General Reference file that's also on the CD-ROM. As noted earlier in this appendix, it lists the beep codes from all of these vendors. After hearing these samples and looking over the lists of codes, you will be better able to interpret the beep codes used by each vendor.

APP
C

Objectives Index

Core Exam

Domain 1.0: Installation, Configuration, and Upgrading

This domain requires the knowledge and skills to identify, install, configure, and upgrade microcomputer modules and peripherals, following established basic procedures for system assembly and disassembly of field replaceable modules. Elements included are listed below with each test objective.

Section	Objective	Subobjective	Page Range
1.1	Identify basic terms, concepts, and functions of system modules, including how each module should work during normal operation.	System board	29–34
		Power supply	236
		Processor/CPU	38–50
		Memory	93
		Storage devices	191–219, 229–231
		Monitor	172
		Modem	143–151
		Firmware	7
		BIOS	66–72
		CMOS	66–67
		LCD (portable systems)	291
		Ports	115–170
		PDA	116

Section	Objective	Subobjective	Page Range
		DB-25	26, 117, 127–134
		RJ-11	143–151
		RJ-45	513
		BNC	514
		PS2/MINI-DIN	26, 127–134
		USB	26, 139–142
		IEEE-1394	164–167
1.5	Identify proper procedures for installing and configuring IDE/EIDE devices.	Master/slave	206
		Devices per channel	206
		Primary/Secondary	206
1.6	Identify proper procedures for installing and configuring SCSI devices.	Address/Termination conflicts	228
		Cabling Types	220–228
		Internal versus external	220
		Switch and jumper settings	221–228
1.7	Identify proper procedures for installing and configuring peripheral devices.	Monitor/Video Card	182–183
		Modem	144
		USB peripherals and hubs	141
		IEEE-1284	119–124
		IEEE-1394	165–167
		External storage	228
	Portable devices.	Docking station	307
		PC Cards	314–317
		Port Replicators	307–308
		Infrared Devices	318

APP

D

Section	Objective	Subobjective	Page Range
1.8	Identify hardware methods of upgrading system performance, procedures for replacing basic subsystem components, and unique components and when to use them.	Memory	99–101, 107
		Hard drives	212–216
		CPU	51–59
		Upgrading BIOS	83–85
		When to upgrade BIOS	83–85
	Portable systems.	Battery	300–302
		Hard drive	309
		Type I, II, III cards	315
		Memory	319–320

Domain 2.0: Diagnosing and Troubleshooting

This domain requires the ability to apply knowledge relating to diagnosing and trouble-shooting common module problems and system malfunctions. This includes knowledge of the symptoms relating to common problems.

Section	Objective	Subobjective	Page Range
2.1	Identify common symptoms and problems associated with each module and how to troubleshoot and isolate the problems.	Processor/Memory symptoms	60–62, 110–113
		Mouse	157
		Floppy drive	200–202
		Parallel ports	125–126
		Hard Drives	218–219, 228
		CD-ROM	231
		DVD-ROM	231
		Sound Card/Audio	162–164
		Monitor/Video	186–188
		Motherboards	60–62
		Modems	150–151
		BIOS	86
		CMOS	86
		Power supply	247
		Slot covers	239
		POST audible/visual error codes	69

Section	Objective	Subobjective	Page Range
		Troubleshooting tools; for example, multimeter	69, 245, 556
		Large LBA, LBA	211, 362
		Cables	218–219, 540–543, 554
		Keyboard	153
		Peripherals	125, 136, 141, 167
2.2	Identify basic troubleshooting procedures and good practices for eliciting problem symptoms from customers.	Troubleshooting/ isolation/problem determination procedures	548–551
		Determine whether it's a hardware or software problem	552–556
		Gather information from user regarding, for example:	556
		Customer Environment	550–551
		Symptoms/Error Codes	553
		Situation when the problem occurred	548

Domain 3.0: Preventive Maintenance

This domain requires the knowledge of safety and preventive maintenance. With regard to safety, it includes the potential hazards to personnel and equipment when working with lasers, high-voltage equipment, ESD, and items that require special disposal procedures that comply with environmental guidelines. With regard to preventive maintenance, this includes knowledge of preventive maintenance products, procedures, environmental hazards, and precautions when working on microcomputer systems.

Section	Objective	Subobjective	Page Range
3.1	Identify the purpose of various types of preventive maintenance products and procedures and when to use or perform them.	Liquid cleaning compounds	324
		Types of materials to clean contacts and connections	324

Domain 4.0: Motherboard/Processors/Memory

This domain requires knowledge of specific terminology, facts, ways, and means of dealing with classifications, categories, and principles of motherboards, processors, and memory in microcomputer systems.

Section	Objective	Subobjective	Page Range
4.1	Distinguish between the popular CPU chips in terms of their basic characteristics.	Popular CPU chips (Intel, AMD, Cyrix)	38-50
		Physical size	40
		Voltage	39
		Speeds	44–45
		Onboard cache or not	44–45
		Sockets	41, 57
		Number of pins	41, 57
		SEC (Single-Edge Contact)	41, 57
4.2	Identify the categories of RAM (Random Access Memory) terminology, their locations, and physical characteristics.	EDO RAM (Extended Data Output RAM)	94–95
		DRAM (Dynamic Random Access Memory)	94–95
		SRAM (Static RAM)	107–109
		RIMM (Rambus Inline Memory Module 184-pin)	94–95
		VRAM (Video RAM)	180
		WRAM (Windows Accelerator Card RAM)	180
		Locations and physical characteristics:	
		Memory bank	91, 99–101
		Memory chips (8-bit, 16-bit, and 32-bit)	96–98
		SIMMS (Single In-line Memory Module)	102
		DIMMS (Dual In-line Memory Module)	103
		Parity chips versus nonparity chips	92

Section	Objective	Subobjective	Page Range
4.3	Identify the most popular type of motherboards, their components, and their architecture (for example, bus structures and power supplies).	**Types of motherboards:**	
		AT (Full and Baby)	29–34
		ATX	29–34
		Components:	
		Communication ports	26–28, 127–134
		SIMM and DIMM	25, 93
		Processor sockets	25, 41–43
		External cache memory (Level 2)	25, 29–34, 105
		Bus Architecture:	
		ISA	24
		PCI	24
		AGP	24
		USB (Universal Serial Bus)	25, 29–34, 139–142
		VESA local bus (VL-Bus)	24
		Basic compatibility guidelines	62
		IDE (ATA, ATAPI, Ultra-DMA, EIDE	17–20, 209, 212–217
		SCSI (Wide, Fast, Ultra, LVD)	223–225
4.4	Identify the purpose of CMOS (Complementary Metal-Oxide Semiconductor), what it contains and how to change its basic parameters.	**Sample Basic CMOS Settings:**	
		Printer parallel port Uni-, bidirectional, disable/enable, ECP, EPP	121–122
		COM/serial port memory address, interrupt request, disable	131–132
		Floppy disk drive enable/disable drive or boot, speed, density	191–202

Section	Objective	Subobjective	Page Range
		Hard drive size and drive type	205–219
		Memory parity, nonparity	92
		Boot sequence	73–81
		Date/Time	66, 73–81
		Passwords	66
		Plug and Play BIOS	66–72

Domain 5.0: Printers

This domain requires knowledge of basic types of printers, basic concepts, printer components, how they work, how they print onto a page, paper path, care and service techniques, and common problems.

Section	Objective	Subobjective	Page Range
5.1	Identify basic concepts, printer operations, and printer components.	Paper feeder mechanisms	260–261
		Laser	276–277
		Inkjet	270–274
		Dot Matrix	265–269
	(Types of printer connections and configurations.)	Parallel	117–118
		Network	521
		USB	139–142
		Infrared	317–318
		Serial	127–134
5.2	Identify care and service techniques and common problems with primary printer types.	Feed and output	268–269, 273–274, 282–284
		Errors (printed or displayed)	268–269, 273–274, 282–284
		Paper jam	268–269, 273–274, 282–284
		Print quality	268–269, 273–274, 282–284
		Safety precautions	325
		Preventive maintenance	268, 272, 285

Domain 6.0: Basic Networking

This domain requires knowledge of basic network concepts and terminology, the ability to determine whether a computer is networked, knowledge of procedures for swapping and configuring network interface cards, and knowledge of the ramifications of repairs when a computer is networked.

Section	Objective	Subobjective	Page Range
6.1	Identify basic networking concepts, including how a network works and the ramifications of repairs on the network.	Installing and Configuring Network Cards	517–518
		Network access	521–525
		Full-duplex, half-duplex	518
		Cabling: twisted-pair, coaxial, fiber optic	512–516
		Ways to network a PC	512–516, 521, 527
		Physical Network topologies:	
		Increasing bandwidth	512–516
		Loss of data	526
		Network slowdown	540–543
		Infrared	540–543
		Hardware Protocols	516, 509

A+ Operating Systems Exam

Domain 1.0 Operating System Fundamentals

This domain requires knowledge of underlying DOS (command-prompt functions) in Windows 9x and Windows 2000 operating systems, in terms of its functions and structure, for managing files and directories and running programs. It also includes navigating through the operating system from command-line prompts and Windows procedures for accessing and retrieving information.

Section	Objective	Subobjective	Page Range
1.1	Identify the operating system's functions, structure, and major system files to navigate the operating system and how to get needed technical information.		
	(Major operating system functions.)	Create folders	411–416
		Checking OS version	388
	(Major operating system components.)	Explorer	431

Section	Objective	Subobjective	Page Range
		Scandisk	441, 495
		Edit	411–429
		Xcopy	411–429
		Copy	411–429
		Setver	411–429
		Scanreg	409
1.2	Identify basic concepts and procedures for creating, viewing, and managing files and directories, including procedures for changing file attributes and the ramifications of those changes (for example, security issues).	File attributes read-only, hidden, system, and archive attributes	432–436
		File naming conventions (most common extensions)	437–440
		Windows 2000 Compress, Encrypt	403–404
		IDE/SCSI	478–488
		Backup/Restore	442–443
	(Partitioning/ Formatting/File System.)	FAT	338–345
		FAT16	339, 348
		FAT32	339, 348
		NTFS4	358–359
		NTFS5	358–359
		HPFS	358–359
	(Windows-based utilities.)	ScanDisk	441
		Device Manager	469–471
		Computer Manager	496
		Msconfig.exe	408
		Regedit.exe (view information/back up Registry)	409–410
		Regedt32.exe	409–410
		Attrib.exe	441
		Extract.exe	441
		Defrag.exe	444
		Edit.com	441
		Fdisk.exe	348–354

Section	Objective	Subobjective	Page Range
		Sysedit.exe	405
		Scanreg	430–447
		Wscript.exe	495–499
		Hwinfo.exe	495–499
		Asd.exe (automatic skip driver)	495–499

Domain 2.0 Installation, Configuration, and Upgrading

This domain requires knowledge of installing, configuring, and upgrading Windows 9x and Windows 2000. This includes knowledge of system boot sequences and minimum hardware requirements.

Section	Objective	Subobjective	Page Range
2.1	Identify the procedures for installing Windows 9x and Windows 2000 and for bringing the software to a basic operational level.	Startup	390–397
		Partition	348–354, 359
		Format drive	355
		Loading drivers	464–467
		Run appropriate setup utility	373–383
2.2	Identify steps to perform an operating system upgrade.	Upgrading Windows 95 to Windows 98	376
		Upgrading Windows NT Workstation 4.0 to Windows 2000	382
		Replacing Windows 9x with Windows 2000	378
		Dual-boot Windows 9x/ Windows NT 4.0/ Windows 2000	380–381
2.3	Identify the basic system boot sequences and boot methods, including the steps to create an emergency boot disk with utilities installed for Windows 9x, Windows NT, and Windows 2000.	Startup disk	336

Section	Objective	Subobjective	Page Range
		Safe mode	478
		MS-DOS mode	450
		NTLDR (NT Loader), Boot.ini	398
		Files required to boot	390-397
		Creating emergency repair disk (ERD)	409
2.4	Identify procedures for loading/adding and configuring device drivers and the necessary software for certain devices.	Windows 9x Plug and Play and Windows 2000	464–465
		Identify the procedures for installing and launching typical Windows and non-Windows applications	448–452
	(Procedures for setting up and configuring Windows printing subsystem.)	Setting default printer	457
		Installing/spool setting	456
		Networking printing (with help of LAN administrator)	457–458

Domain 3.0 Diagnosing and Troubleshooting

This domain requires the ability to apply knowledge to diagnose and troubleshoot common problems relating to Windows 9x and Windows 2000. This includes understanding normal operation and symptoms relating to common problems.

Section	Objective	Subobjective	Page Range
3.1	Recognize and interpret the meaning of common error codes and startup messages from the boot sequence, and identify steps to correct the problems.	Safe mode	478–479

Section	Objective	Subobjective	Page Range
		Option (sound card, modem, input device) will not function	468–476
		Application will not start or load	493
		Cannot log on to network (option—NIC not functioning	492
		TSR (terminate-and-stay-resident) programs and virus	492, 500–504
		Applications don't install	492
		Network connection	540–542
	(Viruses and virus types.)	What they are	501
		Sources (floppy, email, and so on)	501
		How to determine presence	502

Domain 4.0 Networks

This domain requires knowledge of network capabilities, Windows, and how to connect to networks, including what the Internet is about, its capabilities, basic concepts relating to Internet access, and generic procedures for system setup. The scope of this topic is only what is needed on the desktop side to connect to a network.

Section	Objective	Subobjective	Page Range
4.1	Identify the networking capabilities of Windows, including procedures for connecting to the network.	Protocols	508–510
		Ipconfig.exe	528
		Winipcfg.exe	528
		Sharing disk drives	520, 521–525
		Sharing print and file services	518–521
		Network type and network card	511–512
		Installing and configuring browsers	535–537

APP
D

X-Y-Z

Other Related Titles

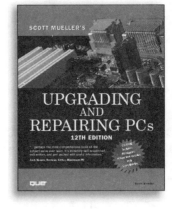
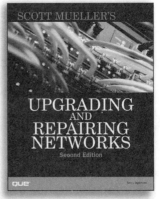

CD-ROM Installation

Windows 95 or Higher Installation Instructions

1. Insert the CD-ROM disc into your CD-ROM drive.
2. From the Windows desktop, double-click the My Computer icon.
3. Double-click the icon representing your CD-ROM drive.
4. Double-click the icon titled START.EXE to run the CD-ROM interface.

Note

If Windows 95 or higher is installed on your computer and you have the AutoPlay feature enabled, the START.EXE program starts automatically whenever you insert the disc into your CD-ROM drive.